ISBN 978-0-332-84869-3
PIBN 10824853

LOUIS XIV DELIVERING TO CHEVALIER DE CADILLAC THE ORDINANCE AND GRANT
FOR THE FOUNDATION OF THE CITY OF DETROIT. PRESENTED IN THE
NAME OF THE FRENCH REPUBLIC BY HIS EXCELLENCY,
M. JULES CAMBON, AMBASSADOR OF FRANCE
TO THE UNITED STATES.

F. LE QUESNE,

FROM THE ART MUSEUM OF DETROIT, NOVEMBER, 1902.

COLLECTIONS AND RESEARCHES

MADE BY THE

Michigan Pioneer and Historical Society

Vol. XXXIII

PREFACE.

It is with peculiar satisfaction that the Committee of Historians of the Michigan Pioneer and Historical Society invite attention to the present volume (33) of its Collections. It seems to us that these Cadillac papers comprise one of the most important series of documents, translated from the original preserved in the archives at Paris, France, that any State has ever issued, and that the knowledge of their being printed will be received by historical students with a great deal of pleasure. They furnish the best available data contemporary with the beginnings of civilization, about three centuries ago, in the vast territory whereof Michigan is now a conspicuous part, and it is eminently appropriate that they should first be made public by the Michigan Pioneer and Historical Society. They deal with a past which belongs largely to the realm of historical myth and tradition.

Indeed, the boundaries of New France of the seventeenth and eighteenth centuries are impossible clearly to define. It may be generally stated that the French government claimed, as their possessions, all of the lands forming the present Dominion of Canada, a large part of modern New York, the western portion of Pennsylvania, and all the region

In 1694, Antoine de la Mothe Cadillac was the military commandant at Michillimackinac. He remained at this post three years, studying the situation, and, by intercourse with the various Indian tribes that assembled there, preparing himself for accomplishing one of the most important events in the history of the Northwest—the establishment of a permanent colony in the wilds of America.

No name, in the annals of the West, stands out more prominent than that of Antoine de la Mothe Cadillac, the founder of Detroit, and the first colony builder in the West.

It is not necessary here to give a sketch of his life, as that information can be found elsewhere. He came to Detroit river in the summer of 1701, and there laid the foundation of a great city which now honors, and always will honor, his name as its founder.

Within a short time after the commencement of the settlement Cadillac sent an official report of his work to the Minister at Paris, after whom his place was named—Pontchatrain—and this report was followed by others of like nature, at intervals, during the period of Cadillac's command. These various reports were filed with other state papers and now remain in the archives at Paris. Along with those reports are various other papers and documents relative to Cadillac and to Detroit.

The state of New York, some years since, had all of these archives examined, and such of them as pertained to the history of that state were copied, translated, and printed in Documents Relative to the Colonial History of New York. In this series are a few that relate to Detroit. In this series, also, are a few that, in the original, relate to Detroit, but in which, in translating, the Detroit portions were omitted.

The state of Wisconsin has also, recently, republished some of those published by the state of New York, and has added a few from other sources.

When Governor Lewis Cass was Minister to France he obtained copies of some of these papers, and they were translated and put in the form of historical matter—not in the form of translations—and were printed by Mrs. Sheldon in her Early History of Michigan. A few, also, of these manuscripts were collected and printed in the original French by Pierre Margry, but his works have never been translated into English.

With the above exceptions the vast pile of manuscripts relative to Detroit and Michigan has laid in the archives at Paris, hidden, so far as American readers are concerned. The people of Michigan and the West are interested in these papers, and it is because they were of no special interest to the eastern states that they have remained so long unpublished.

Some ten years ago Mr. Clarence M. Burton, of Detroit, undertook, at his own expense, to have these records re-examined, and those that pertained to Michigan copied for his own use. The work of searching out and copying was a labor of some years and of considerable expense. After the copies were made Mr. Burton turned them over to a competent translator and obtained a careful, accurate and literal translation of them all. The manuscripts fill twenty-four volumes. They consist not merely of Cadillac's reports, but of everything to be found in the Paris archives relative to Detroit and Michigan, not heretofore printed.

Among the earliest of these documents is a series of letters from the Jesuit priests to Cadillac, with the notations of Cadillac and of the Minister on each letter. Several copies of these letters are in existence, but no complete translation has ever before been published. The letters from Cadillac to these priests have never been translated or published, but Mr. Burton has, through the kindness of Father Jones of Montreal, obtained copies of the originals, and these will appear in the series mentioned below.

During the period that Detroit was under the command of Cadillac— 1701 to 1710—there was a record kept of the transactions of the village. This record has but recently been discovered by Mr. P. Gagnon, archivist at Quebec. Mr. Burton has obtained a copy of this record, and it will be translated and printed with the other papers. There will also be attached an agreement for the support of Cadillac's daughter, Judith, with the Ursuline sisters at Quebec. This document has been recently found by Mr. Gagnon, and a copy was furnished by him to Mr. Burton. The importance of this paper consists in giving the name and age of one of Cadillac's children concerning whom but little is known.

All of the above translations have been given by Mr. Burton to the Michigan Pioneer and Historical Society for publication in its Collections, commencing in volume 33. Probably this will prove to be the most valuable contribution to western history ever published by any Society.

The cordial thanks of the committee of historians, and also of the Michigan Pioneer and Historical Society, in whose name and behalf they act, are tendered to Mr. Burton for his generous contribution to the earliest authentic annals of Michigan and Detroit. As the centuries pass these illuminating records will become more and more valuable.

L. D. WATKINS, *Manchester, Chairman.*
EDWARD W. BARBER, *Jackson.*
EDWARD CAHILL, *Lansing.*
PETER WHITE, *Marquette.*
GEORGE H. CANNON, *Washington.*
Committee of Historians.

LIST OF ILLUSTRATIONS.

CONTENTS.

OFFICERS.

OFFICERS, 1902.

Clarence M. Burton, Detroit, President.
Henry R. Pattengill, Lansing, Secretary.
Benjamin F. Davis, Lansing, Treasurer.

EXECUTIVE COMMITTEE.

*Robert C. Kedzie, LL. D., Lansing.
Hon. Daniel McCoy, Grand Rapids.
*H. B. Smith, Marengo.

COMMITTEE OF HISTORIANS.

Hon. L. D. Watkins, Manchester.
Judge Edward Cahill, Lansing.
Hon. E. W. Barber, Jackson.
Mrs. Mary C. Spencer, Lansing.
Hon. Peter White, Marquette.

OFFICERS, 1903.

Clarence M. Burton, Detroit, President.
Henry R. Pattengill Lansing, Secretary.
Benjamin F. Davis, Lansing, Treasurer.

EXECUTIVE COMMITTEE.

Daniel McCoy, Grand Rapids.
Mrs. Mary C. Spencer, Lansing.
George H. Cannon, Washington.

COMMITTEE OF HISTORIANS.

Barry, Mrs. Sarah E. Striker, Hastings.
Bay, George C. Cobb, Bay City.
Benzie, William A. Betts, Benzonia.
Berrien, Hon. Thomas Mars, Berrien Center.
Branch, Col. George A. Turner, Coldwater.
Calhoun, Hon. John C. Patterson, Marshall.
Cass, Hon. L. H. Glover, Cassopolis.
Charlevoix, E. H. Green, Charlevoix.
Cheboygan,
Chippewa, Hon. C. H. Chapman, Sault Ste. Marie.
Clare,
Clinton, Mrs. C. L. Pearse, DeWitt.
Crawford, Dr. Oscar Palmer, Grayling.
Delta, Hon. O. B. Fuller, Ford River.
Dickinson,
Eaton, Hon. Esek Pray, Dimondale.
Emmet,
Genesee, Mrs. H. C. Fairbanks, Flint.
Gladwin, Hon. Eugene Foster, Gladwin.
Gogebic, Judge Norman B. Haire, Ironwood.
Grand Traverse, Hon. Thomas T. Bates, Traverse City.
Gratiot,
Hillsdale, Joseph H. Edinger, Hillsdale.
Houghton, Hon. Orrin W. Robinson, Chassell.
Huron,
Ingham, John J. Bush, Lansing.
Ionia, Hon. P. H. Taylor, Ionia.
Iosco, John W. Waterbury, Tawas City.
Iron,
Isabella, Prof. C. S. Larzelere, Mt. Pleasant.
Jackson, Mrs. P. H. Loomis, Jackson.
Kalamazoo, Hon. E. W. De Yoe, Kalamazoo.
Kalkaska, Hon. A. E. Palmer, Kalkaska.
Kent, Hon. George W. Thayer, Grand Rapids.
Keweenaw,
Lake,
Lapeer,
Leelanau,
Lenawee, Hon. J. I. Knapp, Adrian.
Livingston, Hon. Albert Tooley, Howell.
Luce, Hon. Sanford N. Dutcher, Newberry.
Mackinac, Dr. J. R. Bailey, Mackinac Island.
Macomb, Hon. George H. Cannon, Washington.
Manistee,
Marquette, Hon. Peter White, Marquette.
Mason, Ralph H. Ellsworth, Ludington.
Mecosta, Judge C. C. Fuller, Big Rapids.
Menominee,
Midland, Hon. C. L. Jenny, Midland.
Missaukee, M. D. Richardson, Pioneer.
Monroe, John W. Davis, Monroe.
Montcalm, Hon. James W. Belknap, Greenville.
Montmorency,
Muskegon, Mrs. Mary E. Chamberlin, Muskegon.
Newaygo, Hon. Daniel E. Soper, Newaygo.
Oakland,
Oceana, Hon. C. A. Gurney, Hart.
Ogemaw, Dr. H. M. Ammond, Campbell's Corners.
Ontonagon,
Osceola,
Oscoda, Robert Kittle. Briggs.
Otsego, Charles F. Davis. Elmira.
Ottawa, Hon. G. T. Diekema, Holland.
Presque Isle, Henry Whiteley, Millersburg.

Saginaw, Mrs. Anna A. Palmer, Saginaw.
Sanilac,
Schoolcraft,
Shiawassee,
St. Clair, Mrs. Caroline F. Ballentine, Port Huron.
St. Joseph, Thomas G. Green, Centreville.
Tuscola, N. E. York, Millington.
Van Buren, Hon. C. J. Monroe, South Haven.
Washtenaw, J. Q. A. Sessions, Ann Arbor.
Wayne, Hon. Fred Carlisle, Detroit.
Wexford, Hon. Perry F. Powers, Cadillac.

.

MICHIGAN
PIONEER AND HISTORICAL SOCIETY.

ANNUAL MEETING, JUNE 3-5, 1903.

SENATE CHAMBER.

Wednesday, 2 p. m., the 29th annual meeting of the Michigan Pioneer and Historical Society was called to order in the Senate Chamber. Prayer was offered by Dr. William H. Haze. Music, "Song to Our Pioneers," by the audience preceded the regular part of the program, consisting of the reports of the various officers. The first paper, "The Boundaries of Michigan," by Prof. Claude S. Larzelere of Mt. Pleasant, Mich., was followed by a solo by Miss Maud Staley. "Evolution of Agriculture," by L. D. Watkins, was read by Mr. Arthur C. Bird, Lansing. Paper by Rev. F. A. Blades of Detroit, Mich., "Driving the First Stake for the Capitol at Lansing." "The Early Explorations of Dr. J. J. Bigsby," by Dr. A. C. Lane, Lansing. Music by Mrs. C. P. Black, Lansing. Miss Ella J. Ramsdell of Big Rapids, Mich., then read a paper on "Mecosta County and Its Hub." Solo by Mrs. Roy Moore, Lansing. Five minute speeches were given by Hon. Charles H. Dewey, a Lenawee county pioneer of 1829, Hon. James E. Scripps of Detroit, Hon. Isaac Bush of Howell, Rev. R. C. Crawford of Clinton county, Mr. Fitch of Shiawassee county, Morgan Hungerford of Lansing, Judge Fuller of Big Rapids, vice president for Mecosta county, and others. It was resolved that Judge Fuller be invited to prepare a paper for the next year.

ecutive committee, requested the different committees to meet June 4, at 9 a. m. The regular evening work was then commenced by a duet by Miss Maud Staley and Dr. D. Bokhof. Paper, "The Burnett Family," by Edward S. Kelley of St. Joseph. Music by the Episcopal Church Choir. A poem entitled "Pere Marquette and Petare Wite," was read by Miss Della Knight. Music by quintette consisting of Miss Staley, Messrs. Seevey, Walker, Willetts and Bates, students of the Michigan Agricultural College. Meeting closed with music by the Episcopal Church Choir. A reception in the Governor's parlors given by Governor and Mrs. Bliss to the members of this Society and to the Senators and Representatives followed. Beautiful flowers, suitable refreshments, and recitations by Miss Lothridge of Battle Creek were a pleasing feature of the evening.

THURSDAY, 9:45 A. M., Senate Chamber.

Meeting opened by music by the Industrial School Band, who responded to an encore. The paper prepared by Hon. Charles Moore of the "Soo," concerning the late Hon. Sullivan M. Cutcheon, was read by Mrs. Mary C. Spencer. Solo by Mrs. Roy Moore of Lansing. The committee appointed to make nominations for officers, through Mr. George W. Thayer, reported the following —

President—Clarence M. Burton, Detroit.

Secretary—Henry R. Pattengill, Lansing.

Corresponding Secretary—Mrs. Ellen B. Judson, Lansing.

Treasurer—Benjamin F. Davis, Lansing.

Executive Committee—Daniel McCoy, Grand Rapids; H. B. Smith, Marengo; Mrs. Mary C. Spencer, Lansing.

Committee of Historians—L. D. Watkins, Manchester; Edward H. Cahill, Lansing; Edward W. Barber, Jackson; Peter White, Marquette; George H. Cannon, Washington.

Moved that the report be accepted and adopted. Moved also that the corresponding secretary be authorized to employ an assistant. (Corresponding secretary absolutely declined to act.) Music by the Industrial School Band. Paper compiled by Prof. Frank S. Kedzie, regarding his father, Dr. Robert C. Kedzie, for so many years a member of the executive committee.

THURSDAY AFTERNOON, at the Congregational Church.

Preliminary to the meeting it was announced that Mr. E. Lockhart of Nashville, Mich., has a collection of curios which he has willed to the Society, and upon motion this was accepted and a vote of thanks tendered him for the ift. The o e · music was b the ils of the public

was extended to them for their kindness. Mr. John E. Day's paper, "The Moravians in Michigan," followed. Mr. Harold Jarvis of Detroit favored us with music entitled "Spring," and also responded to an encore. Mr. Lucius C. Storrs gave a paper on "Progress in Reformatory Work." Mr. Jarvis then sang again. Mr. Joseph H. Edinger related some of the trials of a relic hunter in gathering the specimens in his fine collection. After a song by Mr. Jarvis, Gen. B. M. Cutcheon's paper was read. Music by Mr. Jarvis. Upon motion the blind grandfather of Miss Ramsdell was voted an honorary member of this Society. Moved and carried that the thanks of this Society be extended to Mr. Jarvis for his enjoyable music, who then gave us "The Stein Song." with "Flow Gently, Sweet Afton" as an encore. Adjourned until evening.

. THURSDAY EVENING, 7:45, Senate Chamber.

Meeting opened by music by St. Mary's Church Choir, "Thou art so far and yet so near." An interesting paper, "A Basket of Fragments," by Mrs. Annie Bingham Gilbert of Grand Rapids was delivered. Mr. Harold Jarvis then sang a solo. By request he and Miss Staley sang a duet at this time. "The Seals of Michigan," by Mrs. M. B. Ferrey, followed, and Mr. Jarvis gave his final number. The Choir of St. Mary's Church favored us with a selection, and the program of the evening closed by the audience singing "America," and the benediction pronounced by the Rev. William Putnam, the Hon. L. D. Watkins occupying the chair.

PRESIDENT'S ADDRESS.

BY C. M. BURTON.

Ladies and Gentlemen of the Pioneer Society:

The thirty-second volume of the Collections of our Society has been printed, and is ready for delivery. Those interested in our work can tell, from that book, whether our labors during the past year have produced the proper result. The report of the various officers will give a statement of the condition of the Society. Our appropriation for the next two years is a trifle larger than we have had formerly, but the money can be well expended in the collection, transcription and publication of historical matter, and we could use a much larger amount if we had it.

We are grateful to the Legislature and to the Governor for listening to our requests, and we feel assured that if they will personally examine our rooms our collections and the works we are bl· h· the w'll a ree

There have been statements by various members and officers of our Society that pioneers are dying out. This is not a fact. The men who came to Michigan with La Salle, Tonti, Cadillac, Hennepin and L'Hontan were pioneers; so also were those who came with Robert Rogers, after the conquest of Canada. Those who came with General Wayne in 1796 were pioneers, as were also those who came with Hull and Cass and Woodbridge. Those men and women who penetrated the woods of Michigan, and cleared the farms, were pioneers; but the men who build new railroads, open new mines; erect new factories, are they not pioneers as well?

This Society was organized for the purpose of collecting memoirs relative to the pioneer life of our State, and for the purpose of publishing documents and papers relative to the history of our State.

The work is exhaustless, and the Society, if it fills its mission, will be as long lived as the State itself.

There are thousands of topics that seem to us now to be matters of no historical account, because we know, or think we know, all about them, but after the lapse of a few years they will be interesting subjects of study.

Let me instance a few: The copper and iron mines, the silk thread industry, the beet sugar industry, the making of alcohol, the salt wells and salt making, the telegraph, the telephone, the alkali works; all these and many others might be mentioned.

Papers on these topics might well be prepared now, and deposited in our Society's records, to be used in later years when pioneers in these various industries have passed away.

The collecting of material for our early history can only be done by those who have that subject at heart, and we may well leave that work to the enthusiasts in that line, but there is a work that ought to be attended to by the older members of our Society, those whom we look upon as the pioneers of the State—I mean the history of the early land clearers, the farmers, storekeepers, ministers, teachers, and others of fifty years since. We are able to read all about Cass and Mason, and Romeyn and

Indian relics—we wanted to purchase the collection for our Society, and asked for an appropriation for that purpose. We were not successful, but we hope to be at the next session of the Legislature. There have been presented to the Society, from time to time, articles in use in early days in pioneer households—we are anxious to have this collection increase, and we desire contributions of articles for that purpose—household utensils, china, and glassware, not necessarily such as the pioneers used in their daily life, but such as heirlooms and articles of a finer, rarer sort.

The proper and legitimate work of the Society is exhaustless, and every member is urged to do his best to see that it prospers along the lines that he may consider his own.

REPORT OF THE RECORDING AND CORRESPONDING SECRETARY.

To the Officers and Members of the Michigan Pioneer and Historical Society:

Soon after the close of the fiscal year 1902, an application was made to the Board of Auditors for additional room, which was kindly granted. It was expected to have this prepared for occupancy during vacation; but owing to the repairs to the building necessary before the meeting of the Legislature we were unable to move in until the last of October. The historic rostrum was given an honorable place, and not one improvement lately made in the building has been more approved and appreciated. At our next board meeting the committee voted to accept the loan for two years of the Indian collection owned by Joseph H. Edinger of Hillsdale, by paying cost of placing and cataloging, under contract to purchase it, if possible, at a given price. This, with a few other gifts, and judicious advertising, increased our visitors until our register shows from October 22 to May 22, 1,500 names and addresses recorded. It is fair to suppose that not more than two-thirds of the visitors responded to our request to register. This, however, gave us a fine mailing list. Nearly one-half of the members of the Legislature have visited us, and have been very interested and helpful in our work.

The Department of Public Instruction issued a fine special Pioneer Day exercise October 10th, reports of which were very satisfactory, and we noted with pride and pleasure that several states have followed Mich-

this line. Greater co-operation is necessary with these societies, and the local and county pioneer associations of the State.

Volume 32 was gotten out in time for the annual meeting. While unable to attend to the clerical work, your secretary in his travels around the State has sought to interest teachers and others in our historical work. Mrs. Ferrey, as clerk, has been indefatigable in her efforts to secure additions to the collection and interest visitors in the Society.

The correspondence has increased tenfold; the demand for the books is greater than ever before, and encouraging reports reach us regarding the use and value placed upon them. The principal of one of the best known schools in the State said that he relied upon our collection for the narrative and domestic side of Michigan history. Some volumes have been exhausted and it is greatly to be deplored that it necessitated sending out broken sets. We hope and expect that this will be remedied under the new appropriation.

While the Legislature allows us more means than for the preceding two years, it is a matter for great regret that we are so far behind our sister states in gathering and preserving the records and relics of what we regard as the best State in the Union. With double the scope and work of other years, the increased sum at our disposal will be very inadequate to serve the Society and the State as it deserves. It will be necessary to organize a branch in the Upper Peninsula. This can only be done by some personal labor performed by the secretary or some other interested person. Fine mineral exhibits have been promised and no time should be lost in securing and properly casing them.

It is high time that a curator should be added to gather up the records and relics soon impossible to obtain.

We have been sadly bereaved by the death of many active members, and of others who in the past have been greatly interested in and helpful to the Society. Dr. R. C. Kedzie, chairman of the executive committee, we shall miss greatly from his faithfulness to duty, his genial and winning way, and his readiness and ability to aid in our work, and his valuable suggestions. George S. Wheeler of Salem, a good friend and coworker; Rev. Mannasseh Hickey of Detroit, one of the oldest Methodists in the State, whose valuable paper is found in our collection; Harvey Haynes, a pioneer of Branch county, prominent in our circles but a few years since; Hon. J. H. Ramsdell of Traverse City; G. W. Bement of Lansing, a new member but a man greatly esteemed in his home, his city and his State; Dr. Fisk Day of this city, a scientist who had begun for us work of great value; Mrs. Mary Mayo of Ceresco and Mrs. Mary S. Hinds of Stanton, identified with charitable and Grange work.

Justice, pride and patriotism are not dead, sometimes a little dormant perhaps, and it needs but the opportunity to place before the people the

sponse. A few faithful followers have labored to effect this purpose, but more help and more money will sooner bring the fruition of our desires and of Michigan's deserts.

HENRY R. PATTENGILL,
Secretary.

TREASURER'S REPORT.

Report of Treasurer of the Michigan Pioneer and Historical Society from July 1st, 1902, to the close of business June 30th, 1903:

Cash on hand July 1st. 1902..................	$344.56
Received from State Treasurer................	2,000.00
Received for membership.....................	76.75

$2,421.31

Paid orders drawn by secretary...............	$2,276.44
Cash on hand July 1st, 1903.................	144.87

$2,421.31

$100 additional in special account.
(Checks, $10.50, and $4.60 outstanding.)

Respectfully submitted,
B. F. DAVIS,
Treasurer.

REGRETS.

The following regrets have been received:

Historical Society of Pennsylvania.
New York State Library.
Father O'Brien, Kalamazoo.
Bowen W. Schumacher, Chicago.
P. H. Taylor, Ionia.
Maj. J. C. F. Hollister, Orchard Lake.
Mrs. Fairbanks, Flint.
Miss Clara Avery, Detroit.
M. Adelaide Preston, Charlotte.
Frank Little, Kalamazoo.
William A. Betts, Benzonia.
S. D. Callender, Detroit.
E. W. De Yoe, Kalamazoo.
James Stoddard, secretary and librarian, Arizona.
Mrs. E. B. Minor, Traverse City.
G. K. Geer, Alden.
A. H. Owens, Lennon.
Mrs. A. A. Palmer, Saginaw.
Jennie Rauch, Ida.
N. B. Vivian, Calumet.
Mrs. S. G. Winpenny, Philadelphia.
Ex-Governor C. G. Luce.

Mortar, brought over in Mayflower, Mr. Overton, collected by L. M. Russell, Lansing.

Indian bird stone, Mr. Samuel Preston, Lansing.

Specimens from Bad Lands, Dakota, Miss Fanny Hoyt, Wayland.

Geography, printed in 1812, James Murray, Ludington, collected by Hon. C. I. Harley.

Emigrant's guide and book, used by Capt. Marsac and presented by his son, through Hon. C. L. Sheldon, Bay City.

Old pamphlet and stamps, Robert Smith Printing Co., Lansing.

Snuff box over 100 years old, Col. Geo. H. Turner, Coldwater.

Powder horn used in Revolutionary War, Geo. S. Wilson, Atlanta.

Wool rolls, Miss Brown.

Bullet moulds, owned by his grandfather, L. D. Baker, Lansing.

La Fayette plate, Mrs. Lenore O. Kimball, Detroit.

Michigan Manual, Hon. F. M. Warner, Farmington.

La Fayette badge, Mrs. Blosser, Lansing, collected by Mrs. F. Babbitt.

Log Cabin Paper, H. Greeley, editor; A. W. Nash, subscriber; presented by E. W. Nash, Paw Paw.

Manilla paper and stamps, Dr. R. J. Bailey, Mackinac Island.

Photographs, C. E. Walter, M. A. C., Lansing.

Wax figure, Hugh Lyons & Co., Lansing.

Judge Campbell's chair, John Brooks, Lansing.

Candlestick, N. E. York, Millington.

Hetchel for flax, Edwin A. Weston, Lapeer; collected by Mrs. A. R. Jones, Lapeer.

Chopping knife made in 1790, Mrs. Emily J. Phillips, Pere Cheney.

Sugar bowl over 100 years old, Mrs. W. C. Johnson, Pere Cheney.

Franklin Pierce, 1854; lieutenant's commission, 1847; Mrs. Sarah Merri-
field, Lansing.

Detroit Gazette, July, 1817; deed, 1824; pew in Presbyterian church
receipt, and assignment to Samuel Bidelman; lieutenant's commission
and discharge, 1834; Samuel Bidelman, Lansing.

Old dishes, flat-iron stands, wafers and receptacle, sand-box, snuffers,
tin trunk, uniform, trunk, and commissions, La Fayette handkerchief,
tea-kettle, skillets, fluter, pictures, from Mrs. Florence S. Babbitt, Ypsilanti.

French paper, Le Courrier—Canadien.

In addition Peter Mulvaney of Marengo gave us $5 for expenses of
annual meeting, collected by H. B. Smith, Marengo.

DRIVING THE FIRST STAKE FOR THE CAPITOL AT LANSING.

BY REV. F. A. BLADES.

I have been requested to furnish your society with some pioneer reminiscences of Michigan. I have never thought that any of my particular
early experiences were of sufficient consequence to call for recital, or be
of more than a passing incident that might be called up in connection
with something of modern times. One objection I have had and still have,
that one has in reminiscences to refer so often to his own personality that
it is "I," "I," until ego becomes "it" of modern times.

The incidents to which particular reference has been made, of my first
visit to Lansing, occurred, I would now think, in the early part of the
month of April, 1847. I think the bill for locating the capital where it
now stands was passed in March, 1847. Before referring to that particular event, I would say that my father immigrated from Western New
York to the State of Michigan, reaching Detroit in May, 1835. As I remember Detroit at that time, it seemed but a large village; I do not now

REV. F. C. BLADES.
CITY CONTROLLER OF DETROIT.

selves while on her premises. Seven miles was this day's progress, and it was a hard day's work, and we were all tired out. It took two and one-half days to go from this place to Grand Blanc. What is now known as Woodward avenue extended, was then known as the "Saginaw Turnpike," and was just being put through. Part of the way it had been plowed and scraped up in the center, but it was new and wet, and it was mud, "Michigan Mud." Michigan May rains furnished the water, and the immigrants' wagons churned and mixed up the mud. This trip was always fresh in the memory of the Blades family, consisting then of William and Charlotte, his wife, F. A. Blades, the writer, and J. H. C. Blades, a lawyer of Flint, who died in early manhood, and two daughters—one deceased in Grand Rapids, the other living in Chicago. On reaching Grand Blanc we found an old Indian trading house had been reserved for us by a friend of my father, Mr. C. D. W. Gibbson. At first this was thought to be almost a Godsend, as we did not know but that we would have to live in the wagon, until we could build something. As I said before, it was an old Indian trading house, and the Indians had come to think they had acquired some right there, at least they made themselves so familiar that they would come and go at their own sweet will, and the result was that we were very soon invaded by a lot of wild Indians; it was very embarrassing, and my mother was terror stricken with our new friends, as they afterwards proved themselves to be. I will relate a little incident that serves to encourage humanity to try and do right. The Indians came in great numbers soon after our arrival at Grand Blanc on their way to Saginaw, I think to receive their annual payment from the government. Chief Fisher had a beautiful daughter about sixteen years old, and when they camped near our house that night they came to solicit some advice from the "white squaw," as they called my mother, and she went over and tried to persuade the chief to let the girl go home with her, and she would take good care of her. The next morning, however, she was sick, and as the Indians must go to Saginaw and get their money, my mother took the girl and cared for her with all the tenderness she could bestow upon her own child. When the chief returned she was very much improved and gave evidence of a speedy recovery, but the human sympathy of the white squaw for the Indian girl was never forgotten by that tribe. I remember something over a year after that, when Fisher and some of his brave hunters were passing, they called at the house, and every member of the family was sick with ague, some shaking with chills, others burning with the fever, and I alone carrying on the work of relief. Provisions were scarce; there was not a pound of flour in the whole settlement, which consisted of four or five families within a radius of two miles, but we all expected some parties home with some flour almost any day or hour. Fisher inquired for something to eat, and when told the condition of things, he

before he returned with a saddle of venison, and for some time afterwards we had a call every few days from some of the Fisher Indians to know if we wanted anything.

The fact was that the malaria that was curing my consumption was seemingly killing the rest of the family with ague and bilious fever. My health improved very fast, and it was not long before I was racing through the woods with my rifle to supply the table with food, and for a time the family depended as much on my rifle for their meat as your households now depend upon the market. The friendliness of the Indians gave me the companionship of some of the Indian boys, and some of the older men of the tribe took me along with them and taught me their art in stalking or tracking deer or bear. These Indians were the soul of honor according to their standard. If I wounded the game, and the Indians pursued it to the finish and secured it, he was as sure to bring me the skin as he got the game. My mark or bullet hole made on it gave it to me. The carcass was his. Possibly a little incident of this Indian friendship may interest you for a moment. I was married in September, 1846, to Miss Helen Brown of Grand Blanc. We had been lovers from childhood. In the fall of 1847, I was returning with my wife for a short visit to the homes of both our parents at Flint and Grand Blanc, coming out of the woods on the then unopened road a part of the way between Shiawassee county, and Flint, Genesee county, Michigan, we came into what was known as the Miller settlement. I had not seen any of my Indian friends for several years; on coming into the settlement we noticed several Indian ponies picking grass by the side of the road, but thought nothing particular about them until we were right in the midst of their owners, who were lying in the shade of the trees and fences. All of a sudden a stalwart Indian arose and gave a whoop that brought every Indian man and woman to their feet, and rushing up to the buggy where we were sitting,— my wife shivering from fright and alarm of what might come next,—the Indian grasped my hand and arm, and I was on the ground beside him. "Boo-sheu, boo-sheu, ne-con-nis?" (I do not know if this is the right spelling for these Chippewa words.) "How are you, my friends?" It was

you think you are likely to meet any more of your personal friends, I wish you would tell me a little in advance, for I would like to be prepared for such a reception." That was the last I ever saw of my Indian friends; still I cherish the memory of their friendship. I remember their gratitude for a little service rendered that puts to shame the exhibition of more pretentious civilization and religion. I have never forgotten Shakespeare's words, "Ingratitude, thou marble-hearted fiend." If the recital of these incidents shall inspire gratitude in any heart, either toward God or man, then I am more than paid for the effort.

The events of early pioneer life are ordinarily very tame; they are only interesting as they magnify themselves when compared with the circumstances of modern civilized life. I think the friendships of the early pioneers were a little warmer and stronger than at the present time. I believe that the first settlers of Michigan lived and got as much out of life as any people or any civilization in any epoch of the world's history. In making this statement I am not unmindful of the privations, the coarse and sometimes scanty fare of the early pioneers; but then their life was simple, unpretentious; their fellowship in the family and neighborhood was hearty, whole-souled, overflowing with kindness, manifesting a desire to help rather than hinder. If a neighbor fell sick and ran behind in his work, the whole neighborhood would come together, sometimes men and women, the men to do the hard work on the farm like logging and clearing the land for sowing his fall wheat or gathering his harvest; the wife or daughter came along with some knic-knacs for the table, which was set in the yard for dinner and supper, and to help along with the work, and it became a gala day, and helped in soul and body the poor, sick man. When an invitation had been extended to several families to come together for a

of the fellowship. The old pioneers do not need your pity; no, not "a little bit." I believe that the young people in early pioneer days got as much out of life as do the young people of the present time. Fifteen or twenty boys and girls from sixteen to twenty years old would go six or eight miles on an ox sled to a party, and have a better evening's entertainment than could be had by a New York, London or Paris society party at $20 a plate. It was an ox sled and possibly two of them chained together, and straw thrown in; it was two or more feet deep, and every girl and every boy brought a blanket to protect them from the cold, and though the oxen moved slowly the party began as soon as the sled was full, and song and story and laughter made those old woods ring, and they ring yet as they echo back to-day the song and shout and laughter of those who have long since crossed the last river, I hope to mingle in eternal day. These parties were not pretentious. There was no latest fad in the gowns the girls wore; there was not a tailor-made suit in the crowd. Some of those gowns were spun and woven at home in the log cabin, and made by "mother's own hands." They were shapely, simple and beautiful, and they covered the forms of bright, beautiful girls, full of spirit and life. The boys were of like pattern, strong, courageous and manly, not a mean streak in them, ready to work or play or fight as the occasion demanded. These were the boys and girls who have since made Michigan what she is to-day. These boys and girls, or their like all over the State, were the fathers and mothers of the men who, from 1861 to 1865, said to the dark proud wave of slave civilization, "so far but no further," and they, with comrades from the other liberty loving States, put a million of human bodies with bayonets in their hands as the breastwork that that proud wave of death and dishonor never surmounted. These boys and girls, their children and children's children, produced the civilization and made the happy homes of this day in Michigan. The suppers that those boys and girls sat down to had no half-dozen different colored wine glasses at their plates. Oh, no! it was a plain, honest meal, produced by loving hands and eaten by innocent and happy humans, and when the supper was over the real fun began. Every flat iron or smooth flat stone that had been provided beforehand, and a hammer for each boy, was brought out, and every boy and girl separated in pairs, close in touch and reach with

the old song or new story, and shout and laughter lasted until we were all home. Next morning found the boys down in the woods with ax in hand, chopping to clear the land for next fall's wheat sowing.

Now, after this rambling prelude, let me say that in 1844, having rejected a very tempting offer of a place and an interest in a dry goods house to be established in Chicago, or what was then the place where Chicago now is, I accepted an appointment in the old Michigan conference of the Methodist Episcopal church with the privilege of traveling on horseback about three hundred miles, and preaching twenty-eight times every four weeks on an expected salary of $100 a year. The $100, however, did not materialize, only about $38. It was very seldom that I could sleep two nights consecutively in the same bed, but my wants were all supplied; I lived with the people and was one of them. My first appointment from the old Michigan conference, in 1844, was Shiawassee circuit—Rev. R. C. Crawford, preacher in charge; F. A. Blades, junior preacher; J. W. Donaldson, supply—a six weeks' circuit and three preachers, and if I remember, twenty-eight appointments and very nearly three hundred miles on horseback to get around to the several appointments with the necessary travel to get to our stopping places for the night. Wolverton's school house, within three miles of Fentonville, was the most easterly appointment; thence via Byron, Vernon, Shiawassee town, Corunna, Owosso, Dewey's, Bennington, Pitt's, Morrice, Perry, Shaft's, Fuller's in Ingham county; thence into Livingston via Rogers' school-house, Ramsdell's, Boutwell's and all the country within the circle.

This is from memory of fifty years ago, but it seems to me I could go over the road to-day if the old woods and blazed trees were as I left them. The people were poor, but their hospitality was unbounded. Although suffering all the privations incident to pioneer life, and living in cabins, on coarse fare, and sometimes short even at that, the pioneer minister was always welcome. Nor was this hospitality confined to the members of the church, but every house was open to him. In the fifty years now passed since I first went to old Shiawassee I have met courtly people in all the great cities of this country, and enjoyed the hospitality of many, but none of them while sitting at luxurious boards could out-do the old Shiawassee pioneers in cordiality and warm-hearted, home-making hospitality. My colleagues, Rev. R. C. Crawford and Rev. J. W. Donaldson, were most genial, courtly, Christian gentlemen and my year of hard work passed pleasantly. I could fill a whole paper with incidents, but will only mention one as illustrating some of the early experiences in pioneer work.

One day, I think some time in March, 1845, I was in a store in Corunna, and my attention was called to, and I was introduced to, a stranger and a new-comer in "these parts." On inquiry I learned that early in the fall before some five or six families had gone into the wilderness and had been

the brush and timber preparatory to their spring crop. He urged me to visit them, and for direction I was told to follow the road as far as it was cut north from Corunna, and then find a certain oak tree marked on four sides, and then follow marked trees north, when I would come to a large beech tree, also marked on four sides, there turn to the left and foliow a line of marked trees about two miles, when I would find an ironwood tree and certain witness trees near by, when I was again to turn north and keep on that line until I came to the settlement. I made an appointment to visit them, I think, the last Tuesday in April or the first Tuesday in May. The day appointed came around and about daylight I left my friend Kimberley's house and after, I think now, about three or four miles, I came to the end of the road as it was partly cleared out, and on looking carefully around found the oak tree, got my bearings and plunged into the woods, found all my tree marks, and about noon arrived at the settlement of five or six log shanties, as I remember them. I was most heartily welcomed, and arrangements had been made for worship, and some other parties from other settlements of four or five miles from them had come in. The people came together and I preached to them as well as I could and then had a class meeting. I remember the testimony of one woman who had walked four miles, carrying a child about two years old, to attend the meeting, who said she had come because she wanted once more to worship with somebody as she had not heard a sermon or a prayer in over three years. We sang, preached and prayed and had what I thought then and think now a "good time." But after meeting came the embarrassment. Two of the men of the settlement had gone to Saginaw for some flour and tea and were two days past due, and there was not a loaf of bread or a pound of flour in the settlement, but there was plenty of maple sugar, a few potatoes and plenty fresh fish from the river, and I was just as happy as I have since been when dining at Delmonico's, New York. It was getting late and two young men piloted me out of the woods. I noticed that each one had a large bundle of hickory bark on his

county, and over in Ingham just below Lansing, and an appointment or two in Eaton county.

In the winter of 1847 the legislature in Detroit resolved to change the location of the capital of the State of Michigan. The constitution adopted in 1835 fixed the seat of government at Detroit; it also provided that the legislature of 1847 should determine where the permanent capital should be located. Hence the preparation for the fight of 1847 over the place.

I see that Senator Scripps has been giving the public recently some interesting facts about the locating of the capital at and naming it Lansing; he deals with the records. In what I have to say I deal with the unrecorded legends of the times.

It was currently reported, and believed by many at that time, that the upheaving force to lift the capital from Detroit was a real estate deal in which a great many persons were involved, and it was believed by some that Detroit parties were largely interested. It was claimed by some that men having large land interests near Corunna were responsible for the move to get the capital from Detroit, and they thought they had the strength to locate it at Corunna, but there were other parties who kept very quiet as to where it should go, but were nevertheless active in the effort for its removal. The question once up, the struggle for its location became intense, and while nearly every village and town in central Michigan offered desirable places for it, the real struggle all the time in the deep water beneath the surface was between Corunna and what is now known as Lansing. The Corunna side claimed that the fight at first was between them and the Seymours (two brothers, one of whom was afterwards Governor of New York), who owned land adjoining the school section where the capitol now is, and some parties who were represented by Messrs. Bush, Thomas and Geo. Peck, who in those days were prominent men in Michigan. When these rival interests became reconciled on the plan of placing the capitol on the school section between them, they then became too strong for the Corunna crowd, and they were able to play the school interest for help, and hence it was located where it now is. The stories told of the masterful plays and manipulations of this fight were interesting and sometimes comical. I am only giving you the legends of the times immediately succeeding the events themselves, as they were told me by parties who were interested in the Corunna crowd and saw things from their standpoint. It was finally decided that the capitol should be built on this section of school land in the corner of Ingham county. News in those days did not travel as fast as it does now, but it got around that the capitol of the State was to be located in the wilderness, somewhere in Ingham county, so in the early days of April, 1847, when I went up to the eastern part of my circuit, I thought that I would go and see if I could find the ground that had been selected. I came up to a place that was afterwards known as "the lower town" of Lansing, but at that time known as

3

Page's saw mill. It was a saw mill on the property that belonged to the Seymours. I stopped there, near to the supposed location of the capitol, and went in and found an old gentleman by the name of Page, and a very pleasant family. I told him what my mission was, and he gave me certain directions following certain lines of marked trees by which I might find myself upon the school section indicated as the ground selected. At that time most of us were as ready to follow our way through the woods by the old marked trees and witness trees for the section corner or quarter section corner as we are now by the roads. After following the direction given by the old gentleman, I reached a spot that was clearly in my mind within the lines that were designated as the place upon which the capitol would be located. It was on a beautiful knoll in a dense wilderness. The outlook was grand and lovely beyond description; I never saw such a piece of timber before or since. I sat down on a log and was taking in the scenery, and remember well the thought that passed through my mind: "It is too bad to destroy such scenery as this; too bad to build a babbling town and break this silence and mar this scene so beautiful and so grand." While sitting there I heard a noise; it sounded as though it might be a bear or a deer, but a deer hardly made such a noise as that. I waited, and in a few minutes a man emerged from the shadow of the trees into the light; as I remember him he was about six feet high and well proportioned. He saw me nearly as quickly as I saw him, and he was the first to break the silence by saying, "I think this is probably a mutual surprise; it is on my part;" and I assured him that

told him that I left my horse down at the saw-mill, and he remarked that where there is a saw-mill there is always men, and usually there was something to eat. Following the lines back he went down with me, and we got there just before the horn blew for dinner. I introduced him to Mr. Page, and he was very cordially received. I remember we had pork and beans for dinner, and what else we had I don't know, but the "cheek" of Mr. Glen disclosed itself just as the dinner was over. He related to Mr. Page the incident of our meeting in the wilderness, and his proposition to "help me find a congregation;" he said we had already found what we thought to be a good place for the capitol, and he thought right here was a good place for a congregation, "and (addressing Mr. Page), with your approval, I move that Mr. Blades give us a sermon right here and now." The motion was carried unanimously, and as it was always a motto of my life to obey orders when it is possible, I arose, gave out a hymn, which was sung from memory, and after a short prayer, I proceeded to speak and preach to them the best I knew how for about twenty minutes, and this, so far as I know, was the first sermon preached in Lansing. Subsequently I was there in May. I had been invited to preach there Sunday morning, and a place had been selected over in the woods under a big beech tree in the vicinity of the place where the capitol now stands. The ground chosen was soon cleared, the woods disappeared as if by magic, and it was not long before streets were being laid out and buildings began to rise preparatory to the convening of the first legislature to meet in Lansing for the session of 1848. My father, William Blades, was the first Whig member ever elected from Genesee county to a seat in the State legislature, and he was a member of that session.

I took Lansing in as a regular appointment on my circuit and visited it periodically. I had some privileges in and about the houses that entire strangers could not have. At this time my intimate personal friend, William M. Fenton, was lieutenant governor, and Hon. Edwin H. Thompson of Flint was a senator; my relation with these gentlemen was as intimate and confidential as it was possible for men to be. To illustrate, I will tell a little story on Lieutenant Governor Fenton. My father was for a number of years justice of the peace in Grand Blanc, Genesee county, and had business with nearly every town in the county. Fenton came over from Fentonville to try the first case he ever had in court, which he lost. My father had an office built in his yard, and I persuaded him to let me have a bed in one corner. The day on which Fenton tried his case was rainy and cold, and I said to Fenton, "Bill, don't go home in the rain; you had better stay and sleep with me, and go home in the morning." He finally consented to do so. We went to bed, and after I had gone to sleep I was suddenly awakened, and was surprised to see Fenton standing in the middle of the floor, cussing himself. I said, "What is the

and so lost the case." "Well." I said, "come back to bed and don't make a fool of yourself the second time the same day."

I was in Lansing one day and went up to the Senate Chamber, and the first man I met was Senator Thompson, and he said to me: "Frank, Bill and I have put up a job on you; we are going to pass a resolution requesting you to preach before the State officers and Senate." The resolution was passed. I lay awake nights to prepare a sermon suitable for the occasion, but when the time came I sat there and looked down on that crowd of distinguished men—Governor Ransom and other men that I knew, and some who were strangers to me—and I laid my prepared sermon aside and turned to a passage in Romans, the first chapter and the sixteenth verse: "For I am not ashamed of the gospel of Christ; for it is the power of God unto salvation; to every one that believeth; to the Jew first and also to the Greek," and for my sermon I said what was in my heart and what I fully believed, without thought of oratory, or what anybody might say or think of me or my sermon. For the first time since my determination to be a minister, after preaching this sermon, I had the approval of Hon. E. H. Thompson. He felt that I ought to practice law, as I had read law under his direction for some time, and only after this sermon did he say to me, "Frank, it is all right; go ahead and do the best you can."

The legislature of 1848 was not a phenomenal but rather a typical one. From the amount of plank-road charters granted it might have been called the "plank-road legislature." And that we may have a little clue from the past to look and see if we can find anything that has a parallel in our present civilization and experiences with legislatures, I will call your attention to one thing that transpired during that session. I think the charter for some railway, I do not now remember the title, provided that the principal offices and shops should be either in the State of Michigan or in the city of Adrian, and whether there was any other question involved I do not remember, but I think there was something about

turned to the speaker, and in a very vehement manner said: "Mr. Speaker, I want something, this legislature wants something from the gentleman from Genesee beside rhetoric; I want facts, I want some tangible evidence in support of his position, and reason for his opposition to this measure." It was at this moment that the gentleman from Genesee arose in his place and said: "Mr. Speaker, will the gentleman permit me to interrupt him just for a moment? He demands some facts, some tangible evidence. Permit me to say in reply, sir, that there is no gold pen on my desk." And in less than one minute there was not a gold pen to be seen on any desk in either the upper or lower house, nor could you find anybody who had seen one! My recollection is that the measure did not prevail. In this I may be mistaken, as this was fifty-five years ago. Of course no such thing could possibly happen in a legislature in Michigan in this year of grace 1903.

I remember well some incidents of the last night of that legislature. The House was waiting to hear from the Senate and time was hanging heavily on their hands. A little incident of the evening may amuse you for a moment. I think it is quite common at the close of a legislature for the members to look about for some boxes in which to pack certain perquisites, the "aftermath" of the supplies for the session, in stationery, books, etc. Lansing was new and but few stores in the place. Empty boxes of the proper size were scarce, and one of the members, rather tardy, had to take what he could get, and this was three or four times as large as any of the rest, but even this was not large enough to pack a chair. It attracted attention, and finally a gentleman arose and made a motion that a certain, suspicious looking box then on the floor of the House be examined by a special committee appointed by the chair, which should make a prompt report to this House. The motion was carried, the gentleman making the motion was named chairman, and others selected to complete the committee. They sent for a hammer and opened the box, and scattered the contents about the floor, greatly exasperated the owner, who sat by in rage and disgust, but said nothing. In the box were found some soiled linen, some books and stationery, and a long piece of nice cord that had come around some packages during the winter, which he had saved for a cord for his boy's sled. When the committee had finished the examination, they made a report, recited the contents of the box and facetiously called attention to the cord and begged to be excused from further acquaintance with said cord. This was the opening for the owner of the box, who arose and protested against granting the request of the committee to be excused from further acquaintance with the said cord, claiming that the only proper use for it was to hang the chairman of that committee. And then such a discussion for over an hour! They fired off their oratory and raised their points of order and constitutional questions while they waited to hear from the Senate as to final adjournment. The owner of that box got even with his persecutors before it was over.

In the Senate Hon. N. G. Isabel of Livingston county was the only Whig member of that body. If my memory serves me, the legislature met Monday, January third, and on Saturday, New Year's day, there was a preliminary meeting of some kind of the members of the Senate who were in town to arrange for the organization of the Senate on Monday. As the story goes, Senator Balch gave notice that the Democratic members of the Senate would meet to select officers for that body, and expressed a hope that every Democratic member of the Senate would be present. As he sat down, Senator N. G. Isabel arose, and in a very grave and dignified manner, gave notice that the Whig members of the Senate would meet in his room at the hotel to caucus on the officers for the Senate and hoped every member would be present. As he sat down it dawned on the dazed majority that Isabel was the only Whig member of the Senate, and they saw his joke; they gathered around him, shook him by the hand, and from that hour he had a warm friend in every other member. On such little things often hangs the success or failure of public men.

THE JESUIT MISSIONARIES WHO LABORED IN THE LAKE SUPERIOR REGIONS DURING THE 17TH AND 18TH CENTURIES.

BY RICHARD R. ELLIOTT.

The northern extremity of the Lower Peninsula of Michigan is watered by the Straits of Mackinac, which contains the island of that name. It includes Cheboygan, Emmet and Presque Isle counties. Across the straits is St. Ignace, which may be said to divide the waters of Lakes Huron and Michigan. It is in the county of Michilimackinac, where commences the territory of the Upper Peninsula of Michigan. Lake Superior is reached by the River St. Mary. The approach to this stream, through which flow the surplus waters of the greatest fresh water sea in the world, is through the most charming water region in North America.

RICHARD R. ELLIOTT.
HISTORIOGRAPHER OF DETROIT.

traversed. This is the approach to the chilly and sterile region of Lake Superior, comprising the Upper Peninsula of the State of Michigan. It has memories of historic interest connected with the establishing of Christianity in this part of Michigan, 260 years ago.

In 1641 the Jesuit missionary fathers, Isaac Jogues and Charles Raymbaut, who had served in Huronia, zealous to propagate Christianity among the Indian nations of northwestern Michigan, as now constituted, crossed in their bark canoe the romantic Georgian bay and ascended the stream flowing from the north into its waters and leading to Lake Superior, which they named in honor of the mother of our Savior, St. Mary. The Sault Ste. Marie, "Leap of the St. Mary," as named by the Jesuits, Fathers Jogues and Raymbaut, is a historic locality in American Catholic annals. The standard of the Cross was raised here and the Chippewas were baptized by these Jesuit missionaries, before Eliot had begun to preach to the unfortunate Massachusetts tribes at Nonatum.

The river at the Sault is about a mile and a quarter wide, and the rapids or catract, whose bottom is formed by huge boulders, over which the overflow of the waters of the great fresh water sea, Lake Superior, leap and rush madly down to the level below, roaring and foaming for three-quarters of a mile, through a breadth of over 1,000 feet, creating an atmosphere of freshness which can be compared only to that of Niagara, where these same waters take their grandest leap on their way to the Atlantic. The scene is a wild one, while its natural features have changed but little, since the two missionary fathers gazed in wonder at the raging waters. But its surroundings at the present day are bewildering to the student of less than half a century ago. A system of lockage, the finest and most extensive in the world, with a double capacity, has been built by the American Government, under the supervision of General Orlando M. Poe and General Weitzel, United States Topographical Engineers, on the American side, which permits the passage from the lower lakes into Lake Superior, and vice versa, of the largest freight steamers known in modern times, with cargoes of coal, etc., going up, and cargoes of flour, cereals, ore, metals, etc., going down. A similar system of lockage has been built on the Canadian side; while the most gigantic water power system known on the American continent is in progress. An international bridge spans the rapids over which extensive trains run constantly. The arrivals and clearances and aggregate annual tonnage exceed that of any commercial port in the world, while the value of the product carried is enormous.

After an interval of nearly twenty years the veteran of the Iroquoian missions, René Menard, opened the first regular mission on the soil of Michigan at Keweenaw bay in 1660. There is something sublime and grand, writes Dr. Shea, in the heroism of these early missionaries. Menard was destitute and alone, broken with age and toil. His head was whitened with years, his face scarred with wounds received in the streets of Cayuga, for he had been one of the first to bear the faith into central New York. Thoroughly inured to Indian life, with a knowledge of many Huron and Algonquin dialects, René Menard sought to conclude his life's labors among the Ottawas of Michigan. His journey from Montreal with the fleet of returning Ottawa canoes to the waters of Lake Superior was a long drawn *Via Crucis,* while its narration is painful to read. The brutal Ottawa chiefs, who made the venerable man of God toil without food or rest, paid no regard to his silvered head or to his wasted frame. But he finally reached Keweenaw, which was his "first station" in missionary work on Michigan soil; where, like his brethren in other fields of apostolic work, he sought out, reaffirmed in the faith, encouraged and consoled such Christian families as were domiciled in the Keweenaw district. His own account of his apostolate is discouraging and sad to read. But where this venerable soldier of the cross rendered up his soul to God, whether he died by violence or by starvation, is one of the unsolved problems in the missionary history of Michigan.

Succeeding Father René Menard was the venerable Father Gabriel Druillettes, who labored at or near Sault Ste. Marie till 1699, when he returned to Quebec and died there in April, 1681, at the age of 88. He was, quotes Dr. Shea, a man of 50 when he came; he suffered more than most of his companions, while his extreme zeal for the conversion of souls and the great talent God had given him for languages made him one of our best missionaries. Charlevoix, after relating one of the miracles ascribed to him, says that God had rendered him powerful in word and work.

Another celebrated Jesuit missionary who labored on Michigan soil was Father Claude Dablon, who had accompanied Father Druillettes on an expedition overland to Hudson's bay, who was next with Father Marquette on Lake Superior in 1668, and who after founding the mission of Sault Ste. Marie, became superior of all the missions in 1670.

gun by Europeans in this State, Sault Ste. Marie, in 1668. He was the first white man that trod the soil of the Island of Mackinac or the territory which is now known as the State of Iowa. He erected the first cabin and said the first Mass in Chicago, and said the first Mass in what is now the State of Illinois. He discovered the tidal rise and fall in Lake Michigan 150 years before it was noticed by another, and last, and greatest of all in a historic sense, he discovered the Father of Waters, the Mississippi. The city of Laon, capital of Picardy, was the birthplace of James Marquette, in the year 1637. His family was among the first of the bourgeois class in his native city; while in the century succeeding, three of his name and kindred fought and bled for American independence under Lafayette. His mother, who was a La Salle, inculcated in his youthful mind that deep reverence for the Mother of God, which was always a feature in his religious life. At the age of 17 he joined the Society of Jesus; after the usual fourteen years' probation he was ordained to the priesthood. In 1666 he sailed for Canada and arrived at Quebec September 20 of the same year. His vocation was that of a missionary, awaiting the order of the superior of the Jesuits at Quebec. He was in the prime of life, 31 years old. After two years' study of the Indian dialects at the College of Quebec he was directed to prepare for the Ottawa mission in the far distant west. He had acquired a fair knowledge of the dialects of the Upper Lake Indian tribes. Father Marquette was sent to Sault Ste. Marie, where in 1668 he founded the first permanent European settlement in Michigan, which was located where the city of that name now stands. In the following year he was joined by Father Claude Dablon, Society of Jesus. There were, it is stated, about 2,000 Indians of the Algonquin tribes in the vicinity, but this number may have been an exaggerated estimate. They were well disposed towards Christianity, but the missionaries used extreme caution in administering the Sacrament of Baptism. The chapel erected was dedicated to the Blessed Virgin, as the rapids and the river had been given the name of the Mother of God by their brethren, Fathers Jogues and Raymbaut, the former of whom had, as stated, met a martyr's death at the hands of the Mohawks, while the latter had been called to his eternal reward. From Sault Ste. Marie Father Marquette was transferred to Chequamegon, subsequently known as La Pointe du St. Esprit, which he reached after a month's journey, attended by dangers and hardships. He arrived in 1669. War was provoked two years later between the Hurons and the Ottawas, and the powerful and warlike nation of the Sioux. As a result, the two former nations, accompanied by Father Marquette, were forced to leave Chequamegon. A settlement was made at Point St. Ignace, where a chapel was built. This locality was on the coast at a point subsequently known as Michilimackinac and was the centre of Catholic Indian missionary work as long as New France

Mackinac, peopled by some of the Ottawas, which, after the British conquest, was fortified and garrisoned. But St. Ignace, which, as Father
Marquette writes, was the central point between the three great lakes,
was a bleak and cold locality. In winter the cold was intense, while the
winds, now from Lake Huron, then from Lake Michigan, and worse than
all, from Lake Superior, made the climate at times intensely cold. The
cultivation of the soil was attended with poor results. But the finest
fresh water fish in the world abounded, while at certain seasons of the
year game was available. In 1672 Father Marquette reported to the
Father Superior at Quebec the prosperous state of his mission and expressed his readiness to leave and seek unknown nations to the South.
The assurance was brought him that he was to go as a missionary to explore the Mississippi. Joliet, the royal hydrographer, was sent by the
Intendant Talon as a scientific companion of the missionary. He arrived at St. Ignace on the Feast of the Immaculate Conception of the
Blessed Virgin, auspiciously, too, because Father Marquette had invoked
her aid to obtain from God the favor of being able to visit the nations on
the Mississippi. Preparations for the voyage were completed during the
winter. Toward the latter part of May, 1673, Father Marquette and M.
Joliet, with two bark canoes, five Indians and a supply of provisions, left
St. Ignace, and began their journey, according to their plans, which had
been outlined and mapped, to discover and explore the great river of the
South the missionary had set his heart upon reaching.

It does not fall within the purpose of this study to detail missionary
work outside the boundaries of Michigan. The history of the discovery
and exploration of the Mississippi, by Father Marquette, has been faithfully related by the accomplished and painstaking Mr. Weadock. For all
that he has proposed he quotes acknowledged historical gospel. We shall
therefore attempt to outline the melancholy ending of the career of
Father Marquette, which occurred on Michigan soil after his return from
his Mississippi voyage. He wished to die at Michilimackinac among his
brethren with the rites of the Holy Church, so he set out on his return

creed, to pay this tribute to Marquette, the late Bela Hubbard. So, also, another statue, by a celebrated artist, has been placed in the Capitol at Washington. It commemorates the memory of a priest, missionary and explorer, which the people of the States of the giant West decided to have placed there, but which the small souled pygmies whose narrow minds reject the freedom of religion, opposed under one pretext or another, until it happily fell to Mr. Weadock, to whose memoir we have been so much indebted for what we have written of Marquette, to have the wishes of the people of the West gratified. There is another monument to the young missionary and explorer, quite significantly placed in a locality equally suggestive; this is in the city of Marquette, queen city of Lake Superior, where a *replica* of Trentanova's statue at the Capitol at Washington has been erected in that city on the shores of Lake Superior, which perpetuates his name among the people of the State, where his young life was ended.

In 1676 Father Peter A. Bonneault and Henry A. Nouvel, Society of Jesus, labored at Sault Ste. Marie, while Father Philip Pierson, S. J., had succeeded Father Marquette in the care of the Christian Hurons at Michilimackinac.

Claude Jean Allouez, S. J., "the Apostle of the Ottawas and the builder of the first Indian missions in Wisconsin," as his most recent biographer, Rev. Joseph Stephen La Boule, Professor in the Provincial Seminary of St. Francis de Sales, Milwaukee, designates him, was among the early Jesuit missionary Fathers who traversed the soil of Michigan. His labors, however, were more identified with the neighboring State of Wisconsin, but more particularly with that portion whose soil is bordered by the waters of Lake Superior. Father La Boule writes: "I deem it a pleasure and a duty to my native State to survey the life of this remarkable man, and to trace, even though it be with unskilled eye, 'the footprints he has left behind him in the sands of time.'" Father Allouez was born in St. Didier near Lyons, apparently in June, 1622. His collegiate course is described by his biographer and his successful examination at Puy, after which he prepared himself to become a priest, a Jesuit and a missionary. At the age of 17 he was received a member of the Society of Jesus, and after the usual probationary term of fourteen years he was ordained to the priesthood and assigned to duty in the Jesuit church of Rhodez, France. But his soul moved him to a more heroic career, and he sought to develop it in missionary work in New France. Father Rocette, Society of Jesus, his superior at Toulouse, wrote him March 3, 1657, with permission to go to Canada and to join his brother Jesuits engaged in missionary work among the Indians. His qualities are thus noted: "He is possessed of a vigorous constitution, of a fine mind and disposition, of good judgment and great prudence. He is firm in purpose, proficient in literature and theology, and eminently fitted for missionary work." Here, then, writes his biographer. is a Frenchman of the mountainous Loire country type; a man of middle stature, of vigorous frame, yet graceful deportment; a man who is inured to exposure and toil, as he is trained in the science of spiritual perfection; capable of living contented in the huts of barbarians as well as moving with due tact in salons of refined French society. Such a man it is whom we presently see embarking on a project which, as Bancroft says, "has imperishably connected his name with the progress of discovery in the West," and which made him the apostle of the upper lake Indians. Father Allouez was invited to sail with M. D'Argenson, who had recently been appointed Governor of New France. Two lay brothers joined the party, and after a long and stormy voyage Quebec was reached July 11, 1658. He soon after commenced a preparatory course of the study of the Upper Lake Indian dialects. While awaiting at the College of Quebec a favorable opportunity to reach the Ottawa mission, intelligence was received of the death of two distinguished Indian missionaries; first of Father Leonard Garreau, who met a terrible fate; second of Father Menard, his dear friend, to whom he had bade farewell on his departure from Three Rivers for the Lake Superior country in 1660. In May, 1665, Father Allouez left the college to meet the Ottawa Indians, who annually came from the Upper Lakes to trade at Three Rivers. He was disappointed; he found them uncouth and brutal "beyond description." But this was not the worst, they were unfriendly. It was not without difficulty that he obtained an equivocal permission for himself and party, six in all, to accompany the Ottawas on their return journey to Michilimackinac, and then they were separated among 400 Indians. The route taken at that time for such parties was up the Ottawa river and by way of Lake Nipissing, with portages to the Georgian bay, and thence to Lake Huron. It was a journey of 500 or 600 miles from Three Rivers, with many portages, across which had to be carried the canoes and effects of the travelers. It is difficult to describe the cruel treatment experienced at the hands of these brutal Indians during this long and tedious journey lasting over two months, by this devoted missionary; starvation, over-work, and finally abandonment, after his canoe had been disabled, on a desolate shore. But Father Allouez had great faith in the Divine mercy; he survived the ordeal and won the admiration of the Ottawa chiefs.

found two Christian Huron women, whom he says shone like brilliant stars in this darkness of paganism. No doubt, adds his biographer, he also said Mass at this spot consecrated by his saintly brother missionary. On he went, still westward. He was now on what was to white men territory comparatively unexplored. His tone of correspondence becomes that of a keen observer. Game and fish are more abundant, and the quality, he tells us, is excellent. His attention is called to the presence of copper mines by the color of the water and the frequent discovery of copper in pieces of ten and twenty pounds on the shores.

The Indians, continues his biographer, seemed to have improved their treatment of Father Allouez, which was now much better. A box in which he had put a number of devotional and other articles and which his Indian companions had stolen from him, was now restored to him. Henceforth the missionary and his effects were regarded as "manitous," dangerous to touch. His mind became more cheerful and he continues to describe the scenes about him on "the lake that is so stormy and yet so beautiful and so rich in delicious fish and shining metal," that he did not wonder the Indians worshiped it as a divinity and offered it sacrifice. The Indian fleet had now traversed a distance which Father La Boule estimated at 1,250 miles from Three Rivers, in their bark canoes, and were approaching their destination. They were greatly elated when in the distance they perceived a tongue of land jutting out into the stormy bay at the southwestern end of the lake. It was the sandspit so familiar to the Lake Superior Indians famed in their early myths and later history as Chequamegon Point. Father Allouez, continues his biographer, landed with the flotilla at the head of Chequamegon bay October 1, 1665. Subsequently he located his mission, which he dedicated to the Holy Ghost, contiguous to the villages of the Huron and of the Ottawa nations; the location, in modern days, without wasting time in tracing its exact locality, may be said to be tributary to what is familiarly known as La Pointe, in the head waters of Lake Superior, or as described in the early annals, Fond du Lac. A chapel of bark and a "mission house" of the same material, of modest proportions, were soon constructed for Father Allouez. Then, after fervent appeals for heavenly assistance, he commenced his apostolic work. Like his saintly brethren in the cantons of the Iroquoian Confederacy, at a corresponding period, he found among the expatriated Hurons many Christian families, whose faith he revived; whose marriages he validated; and whose children he baptized. This experience was vouchsafed to the holy missionary, in consolation for the drastic and crucial incidents of the journey of over 1,200 miles, in which he had been made to endure more than an ordinary white man's share, between Three Rivers and the head waters of Lake Superior. Soon, his biographer

sweet tones the Pater and the Ave. From morning dawn to sunset the braves and the squaws, in great number, came to visit the "black robe" to be taught by him how to pray to the "Great Father." The example of the children soon had its effect upon the older Indians. The laxity of morals so common even among the children was now relieved by most edifying examples of purity; one of which Father Allouez mentions in his relations. Similar evidences of remarkable virtue in this connection is given in the diary of the missionary and are on record. Besides the little children baptized on New Year's day, 1666, whom the mothers brought to the missionary as "a gift to the little Jesus," he baptized more than 400 infants and adults of the Huron tribes, during his stay at the bay.

The Hurons were among the *elité* of the Indian nations of North America. They had been foremost during the seventeenth century in accepting Christianity. But their nation had been wiped out of existence in Huronia, by their hereditary foes, the warriors of the Iroquoian Confederacy; while their national autonomy for the time being was destroyed. Many prisoners, men, women and children, had been brought from Huronia to the Iroquoian cantons, where mothers mourned for sons, the flower of the youth of the Five Nations. The captives were adopted into the communities of the respective tribes. This new blood was much needed in the desolate families of the Iroquoian mothers. But this new blood was Christian, and thus was Christianity planted in the nations of the League, from the Mohawk to the shores of Lake Erie. We have here related another example of the tenacity of the faith planted in the hearts of the people of Huronia by the martyred brethren of Father Allouez. But this was mild work for this zealous apostle. Contiguous to the locality of the Hurons was the Pagan Ottawa canton, whose people Father Allouez determined to convert. He erected a birch bark chapel and mission house in the midst of their cabins. It was a bold, a heroic enterprise, inspired by confidence in the support of the Almighty Power. His biographer prefaces his experience by saying that the status of affairs found in the Ottawa village must have brought to his mind a picture of pandemonium. This he must have expected. But, in the description of no other Indian village, does Father Allouez employ terms so expressive of abhorrence as he does in describing the moral condition of the Ottawas at Che-

watamies, the Outagamies and the Illinois tribes who came during the
fishing season, he speaks more favorably: Great quantities of whitefish,
trout and herring are caught here. The season begins in November and
continues after the ice has been formed. Speaking of the Pottawatamies,
Father Allouez says "they are the most docile to our Frenchmen and
promising candidates for Christianity, their women are more modest
than those of other Indian nations, while the men are kindly mannered.
Father Allouez failed to make any progress among the Ottawas. Convinced that one missionary would be inadequate to combat so much opposition to Christianity, he turned his face homeward. But before commencing his return journey he courageously started for Lake Nepigon.
This involved a journey going and coming of more than 1,200 miles. But
this great labor was well rewarded. He was received by the Nipissings
with open arms. He revived their faith and restored the religious status
of their family life. He remarks: "The fervent devotion of this people
gave me sweet consolation and compensated abundantly for past hardships." The field, writes his biographer, had become too great for one
missionary. Help was needed. In 1667 Father Allouez returned to Quebec, where he arrived during the first days of August. The purpose of his
visit was to urge the establishment of permanent missions at Chequamegon and tributary territory; to get assistance and requisites for mission
chapels. He would take no rest after his long journey, and in a few days
was ready to return with the Indian flotilla.

Father Louis Nicolas, Society of Jesus, and one donné volunteered to
return with him, as also several French mechanics.* But the Indians refused to take the latter with the missionary party. All the equipments
for his chapels had to be left behind. Father Allouez returned to the
scene of his missionary labors, where his biographer states he remained
some years. Father Louis Nicolas, Society of Jesus, is described in the
relations as "a strong, practical, 'every-day' man and a tireless worker."
His progress was unsatisfactory and he became despondent. One day, it
is stated, he told the Ottawas he was going to Sault Ste. Marie. They
would not consent to this, admitted their past indifference and promised
to amend their lives, and in fact made a serious effort to abolish polygamy,
idolatry and superstition. In time many became fervent Christians.
Father Allouez returned to Sault Ste. Marie in 1669, and Father James
Marquette took his place at Chequamegon bay. Dr. Shea says: Father
Allouez was a fearless and devoted missionary; as a man of zeal and piety
he is not inferior to any of his day; and his name is imperishably connected with the progress of discovery in the West. This is a very high
tribute; for the days of Father Allouez were those of scholarly and scientific men; numbering saints, martyrs, explorers and heroes; such indeed

were his cotemporaries, his brethren of *l'ancien régime* of the Society of Jesus in North America. After thirteen years more of missionary work in Western fields the heroic career of this saintly man was ended.

Associated with him at times on Michigan soil was Father Louis André, Society of Jesus, of whom Father Arthur Jones, Society of Jesus, of St. Mary's College, Montreal, writes: Father Louis André was born in 1623, and previous to his coming to New France he had entered the Society of Jesus as a member of the Province of Toulouse. As a Canadian missionary he was within the jurisdiction of the Province of France. Father André reached Quebec on the 7th of June, 1669. But a short time elapsed before he was sent to the Western Missions, where Claude Allouez, James Marquette, Claude Dablon, together with the coadjutor Brother Louis Le Boesme, were already toiling in the Master's vineyard. André's year of apprenticeship to a missionary life was made probably in part at St. Ignace, Michilimackinac and at the *Baie des Puants*. The winter was probably passed at the former. Fathers André and Druillettes were at Sault Ste. Marie in the spring of 1670. To enable the reader, writes Father Jones, to form an adequate idea of the hardships endured by Father André, and to obtain a graphic account of his apostolic labors, the Jesuit Relations themselves should be consulted, as therein the facts are given, often in his own words. In 1671 Father André was again at Michilimackinac; from this year until 1681 he worked during all seasons for the conversion of the Western nations. In 1682 he rested from his continuous labors at Michilimackinac, but only for a year. The following year he was again on his missionary tours. He was a successful missionary wherever he worked. This was his last year's work in the Western Missions. He was now in his sixtieth year. The father superior at Quebec deemed it advisable to give him a permanent rest, and he was accordingly recalled to Quebec. He was named professor of philosophy in the Jesuits' College, and performed other literary work until 1690; in the meantime he had compiled his Algonquin and Ottawa dictionary, and had written other philological treatises. But this literary work did not satisfy the nature or the ambition of Father André. He was a passionate hunter for human souls. No sportsman in the pursuit of the wild game of the forest was so ardent as he was to convert from Paganism an Indian and to regenerate his soul with the Sacraments of the Church. He laid aside his literary labors and with the crucifix in hand labored among the Indian tribes in

Fathers Charles Albanel and Claude Aveneau. A few years later we find the names of Fathers Bailloquet and Nouvel. There were subsequently the names of Fathers James J. Marest, and the veteran Iroquoian Missionary, Father Stephen de Carheil, who at the close of the seventeenth century were in charge of the missions at Michilimackinac. This locality during the last decade of this same century had become a trading post of such importance that the government of New France maintained a small garrison under charge of a commandant and it was dignified with the name of post. Its locality was such that trading expeditions on the way to or from Montreal, Three Rivers or Quebec, going or coming by the route *via* the Ottawa river, etc., tarried at Michilimackinac. The Ottawas domiciled in the vicinity, particularly on the island of Mackinac, were successful hunters; they usually returned from their periodical expeditions to their hunting fields with valuable packs of furs, which, annually, earlier in the century, they had carried for sale and barter to Three Rivers; their flotillas of bark canoes were of considerable extent, the Indians numbering occasionally as many as 400. Gradually, however, the number of French traders annually coming to Michilimackinac had increased to such an extent that the Indians found it no longer necessary to make the long and toilsome journey to the St. Lawrence; they found a home market at Michilimackinac; this was before the garrisons and commandants were sent to this locality. Before the advent of the latter the missionaries controlled the Indians and had maintained stringent rules excluding the traffic in *eau de vie* among the Ottawas. Moreover, Christianity had been fairly well established, while morality and sobriety prevailed. There was peace and happiness in the Indian cabins. When, however, the commandants and soldiers came to the post from Canada, a great change succeeded; both officers and men became traders. Heretofore Michilimackinac had been the locality of missionary centres, over whose people the missionary fathers exercised a paternal control. Outside of the Indian population the commandants had properly controlled the soldiers and employés of the post. But the Commandant, his officers, his soldiers and his employés had become traders with the Indians; the principal article of their traffic was *eau de vie,* dealt in at first *sub rosa,* but later on openly and in cabarets. The protests of the missionaries were without result; for Governor General Frontenac's ear was closed to any Jesuit's appeal. Finally the Jesuits appealed to the Court of France, and with success. The traffic in *eau de vie* at Michilimackinac was suppressed.

rior of the missions centering at Michilimackinac; it was an exposé of affairs which was addressed to de Calliéres, Governor General of New France.

The original letter of the saintly Father de Carheil, is on file in the archives of St. Mary's College, Montreal.

Father Arthur E. Jones, archivist of the college, gave Clarence M. Burton, President of this Society, during the year 1903, a translation of this letter as well as of many other historical documents relating to the French history of Detroit and Michigan.

This letter and the other historical papers will be arranged for publication in volume 33 of the Historical publications by President Burton.

It is a sad story and contains a long detail of the gradual breaking up of the missionary work and the ruin of the bodies and souls of the Christian Indians at the mission.

Among other Jesuits who had been associated with Father de Carheil were Fathers Nicholas Potier and John B. Charndon; subsequently the depopulation had become so great at Michilimackinac and at the Island of Mackinac that Father de Carheil, in 1706, abandoned the mission, burned the chapels and mission houses and returned to Quebec. But the government induced Father James J. Marest, Society of Jesus, to restore the missions at Michilimackinac; the Ottawas who had been drawn to Detroit by Cadillac became dissatisfied to a considerable extent and many of them, with their families, returned to their former homes on the Island of Mackinac and to Michilimackinac. The Jesuit mission of St. Ignatius at this locality was reopened. In 1721 Father Charlevoix, Society of Jesus, as an envoy of the King of France, visited Detroit and the missions on Michigan soil in the West. These finally devolved to the care of the Jesuit Fathers, M. Louis Le Franc and Peter du Jaunay, with headquarters at Michilimackinac. One of the out missions occasionally visited by the latter was at Arbre Croche. We find his name as a visitor to Detroit at the Huron Mission in 1765. Both of these venerable missionaries passed to their eternal reward soon after the latter year.

The names of the Jesuit fathers who labored on the soil of Michigan between the years 1641 and 1781, with chronological approximation, may be stated as follows: Isaac Jogues, Charles Raymbaut, Gabriel X. Drouillettes, Henry Nouvel, Peter A. Bonneault, Anthony Silvy, René

spent some time while engaged in spiritual work in 1721 at Detroit, and later in western Michigan; as also that of Francis Vaillant de Gueslis, Society of Jesus, who came with Cadillac in 1701, but who was promptly recalled by the father superior of the Jesuits at Quebec. In the acknowledged high class histories of North America great praise has been written by non-Catholic writers on these saintly and scholarly priests for their missionary work among the Indian nations, and for their intrepid and extensive explorations of the Western, the Northwestern and the Southwestern regions, which they first explored and scientifically described.

1720905

CADILLAC PAPERS.

'PROCLAMATION OF FRANCE ON TAKING FORMAL POSSESSION OF THE WEST.

We here undersigned certify that we have seen the arms of the King of France set up on the lands of the Lake called Erie, at the foot of the cross with this inscription—

"The year of salvation 1669. Clement IX being seated in the chair of St. Peter, Louis XIV reigning in France, Monsieur de Courcelles being Governor of New France, and Monsieur Talon being Intendant for the King, two missionaries from the seminary of Montreal having arrived at this place accompanied by 7 other Frenchmen who, the first of all the European nations, have wintered on this lake, of which they have taken possession in the name of their King, as of an unoccupied land, by setting up his arms which they have affixed at the foot of this cross."

In witness whereof we have signed the present certificate.

  Francois Dollier, priest of the diocese of Nantes in Brittany.
  De Galinee, deacon of the diocese of Rennes in Brittany.

QUARREL BETWEEN CADILLAC AND SABREVOIS.

Sieur Desbergeres, the Sieur Desclavaux, sub-lieutenant of the company of the Sieur Desmeloises, and the Sieur de Troyes sub-lieutenant of the Compy. of the Sr. de Troyes, in order to state to us what they know about what passed at the quarrel which took place yesterday evening between the Sr. Chevalier de la Motte, Lieutenant of the Company of the Sr. de Vallerennes, and the Sr. de Sabrevoye, sub-lieutenant of the Compy. of the Sr. Desquerac, who, after oath by them taken, required in such a case, have separately stated to us; to wit, the said Sr. de la Perelle (saith) that yesterday at the end of supper, the said Sr. de la Motte came unexpectedly, and all requested him to take his place and drink a glass; on this the said Sr. de Sabrevoye asked the deponent whether he would not go up with him to the upper town, and on this he answered him, No. The said Sr. de la Motte replied that if he were in the place of the said Sr. de Sabrevoye's captain, and had a rival like him, he would very soon send him back to his quarters, and the said Sr. de la Motte added, regarding the said Sr. de Sabrevoye, the epithet of "sharper" by which he called him; to this speech the Sr. de Sabrevoye replied, smiling and without anger, that he would like to know why he told him to go to his quarters, to which the said Sr. de la Motte retorted. getting incensed— "Silence, my young friend; 's death! I am not supported here by my Lord the Marquis, as you are, but I will give you a thrashing." And he took the candlestick which was on the table, and threw it at the head of the said Sr. de Sabrevoye whereby he is grievously wounded, and by this blow the candle was extinguished, which compelled the deponent with the Sieur Declavaux to seize the said Sr. de la Motte and push him out of the house, [he] calling them all buggers of sharpers; during which time the deponent heard the said Sr de Sabrevoye crying—"Ah! I am a dead man!" which made him ask the said Sr. de la Motte whether he had struck him with his sword; on which he took the deponent by the hand saying these words, "My friend, I am lost; that will get to the ears of the Marquis; I struck him with the candlestick, and I beg you to assist me;" to which the deponent replied,—"You are very unfortunate, withdraw;" that is all he said. Witness that it was read over to him, he adhered to it and signed. Signed thus, La Perelle, Proust & Hubert.

· tain he would certainly send him to his quarters, seeing that he was his rival. And the said Sr. de Sabrevoye answered him smiling, that he had not wit enough to prevent him from kissing his mistress in front of him, if he had one. On this the said Sr. de la Motte spoke to him in these words—"Don't annoy me, you sharper, and never attempt to speak to me again." And the said Sr. de Sabrevoye answered him that when he would not think of him, he would not think of him either. And at the same time the said Sr. de la Motte said to him—"My little friend;" on which the said Sr. de Sabrevoye said to him,—"My little friend"—and the said Sr. de la Motte retorted—"Yes, my little friend, hold your tongue; I am not supported by My Lord the Marquis, as you are, for I would give you a thrashing;" and, rising, he took the candlestick and threw it at his head, by which he is grievously wounded. And the said Sr. de la Motte withdrew saying, "These buggers of sharpers." And (that) is all he said, to wit, read over to him [and he] adhered thereto and signed thus the Ch. de Troyes, Proust & Hubert.

And the said Sr. Desclavaux [saith] that yesterday evening, being at the end of supper, the said Sr. de la Motte arrived whom they requested to take a drink with them; and at this time the said Sr. de Sabrevoye asked the said Sr. de la Perelle whether he would go up to the upper town with him, to which the said Sr. de la Perelle replied, "No, you would not like it because I should wrong you." On this the said Sr. de la Motte joined in, and said to the said Sr. de Sabrevoye—"I should like to be your captain, as Desquerac (is), I would certainly send you to your quarters and would not have a rival like you;" on this the said Sr. de Perelle said to the Sr. de la Motte, that if he had a mistress the said Sr. de Sabrevoye would kiss her to his face. On this Sr. de la Motte rose and said to him "My little darling, I am not supported by My Lord the Marquis as you are, I will give you a thrashing;" and at the same time he took the candlestick which was on the table and threw it at the head of the said Sr. de Sabrevoye by which he is grievously wounded, after which he retired saying "These buggers of sharpers:" that is all he said to wit; read over to him, and adhered to and signed. Signed thus, the Chr. Claveaux, Proust & Hubert.

And on the fourth day of the month of May 1686, we, my aforesaid major, attended by the said Recorder of the marshal's court of this coun-

Sieurs de la Perelle, Desclavaux, de Troyes, and Sabrevoye, sub-lieutenants of the Companies of Srs. Desbergers, Desmeloises, des Troyes and Desquerac, being at supper together at the deponent's house, the Sr. de la Motte, Lieut. of the Company of the Sr. de Vallerennes arrived there, whom the said Sieurs named above begged to be seated and to drink a glass with them; and on the conversation which they had together, the said Sr. de Sabrevoye asked the said Sr. de la Perelle whether he would go up with him to the upper town, to which the said Sr. de la Perelle having replied that he would not go up there for fear of doing him an injury; the said Sr. de la Motte said to the said Sr. de Sabrevoye that if he were his captain he would certainly send him to his quarters; whereon the said Sr. de Sabrevoye having asked why he would certainly send him to his quarters, the said Sr. de la Motte answered him, "Because I would not have a rival like you." When he heard this, the said Sr. de Sabrevoye said to him, "If you had a mistress I should certainly be your rival;" hearing which the said Sr. de la Perelle said to Sr. de la Motte that the said Sr. de Sabrevoye would kiss her to his face, which things they said to each other smiling. And the said Sr. de Sabrevoye, following up what the said De la Perelle had said, speaking to the said De la Motte, "and without your having the wit to know it." To this the said Sr. de la Motte retorted several times, "the wit"! "the wit"! and said to the said Sr. de Sabrevoye—"Go, my little friend, I will not speak to you, and although I am not supported by My Lord the Marquis as you are, I will give you a thrashing." Hearing this, the said Sr. de Sabrevoye said, "What! a thrashing!" but put his hand on the hilt of his sword without, however, drawing it from its sheath, but only (raising) it a little from the sword belt. When the said Sr. de la Motte saw this he did the same, and the others threw themselves between them and prevented them from fighting, during which time the Sr. de la Motte caught up a copper candlestick which was on the table and threw it at the head of the said Sr. de Sabrevoye by which he is badly wounded; and this is all that he said, to wit, her deposition having been read over to her, she adhered to it and signed thus, Louise de Monsseaux St. Armand, Proust & Hubert.

Delivered as a copy to My Lord the Governor by me, Recorder of the Marshal's Court of this country, undersigned

Hubert

[1]LETTER TO MONSIEUR DU LHU.

At Ville Marie the 6th of June 1686.

Sir

Although I wrote you word this autumn to come to me for the purpose of conferring with us on many matters which cannot be written, as the Revd. Father Anjalran[2] has come here and will have to return to Michilimaquina as soon as the restoration of the prisoners has been made, your presence with the Outaoüax is much more necessary. Thereby I hereby send you word not to come down, but to join M. de la Durantaye who is to be at Michilimaquina to carry out the orders I am sending him for the safety of our allies and friends.

You will see from the letters which I am writing to M. De la Durantaye that my intention is that you should occupy a post at the strait* of Lake Erie with fifty men, that you should choose a post in an advantageous spot so as to secure this passage to us, to protect our savages who go hunting there, and to serve them as a refuge against the designs of their enemies and ours; you will do nothing and say nothing to the Iroquois, unless they venture on any attempt against you and against our allies.

You will also see from the letter I am writing to M. de la Durantaye that my intention is that you should go to this post, as soon as ever you can, with about twenty men only, whom you will station (there) under the command of whichever of your lieutenants you may choose as being the fittest for the command, and the one which suits you best.

After you have given all the orders you think necessary for the safety of this post, and have strictly commanded your lieutenant to be on his guard, and enjoined obedience on the others, you will repair to Michilimaquina to wait for the Revd. Father Anjalran there, and receive from him the information and instructions as to all I have communicated to him concerning what I wish from you. After [that] you will return to the said post with thirty more men, whom you will receive from M. de la Durantaye to take the said post. You will be careful to see that everyone provides himself with the provisions necessary for subsistence at the said post, where I have no doubt some trade in furs might be done; hence your men will not do badly to take some few goods there.

---

[1]For sketch of the life of Duluth, see Jesuit Relation and Allied Documents, Vol. 62, p. 274. See another translation of this letter in Wis. Hist. Col., XVI, 125.—C. M. B.

[2]For sketch of the life of Father Anjalran (or Enjalran), see Jesuit Rel. and Allied Doc., Vol. 60, p. 318.—C. M. B.

*[detroit.]

I cannot recommend you too strongly to keep up a good understanding with M. De la Durantaye, without which all our plans will come to nothing, and yet the service of the King and the public will suffer greatly from it.

The post[1] to which I am sending you is of all the more importance as I expect it will put us in connection with the Illinois, to whom you will make known the matters of which the Revd. Father will inform you. Depend upon it, nothing could be so important as to apply yourself to carrying out well all that I send you word of, and that I will inform you of through the Revd. Father on his return from Michilimaquina.

I send you the necessary commissions for the command of this post, and for your lieutenant.

I say nothing to you about your own interests, but you may count on my doing, with pleasure, all that may be necessary for your benefit after this; but I will repeat once more that you cannot be too diligent to succeed in all that I wish from you for the interests of the King's service.

I should be very glad if your affairs would permit of your brother being with you next spring, for as he is an intelligent fellow and would be of great assistance to you. he might also be of great use to us.

I beg you to say nothing about our plans, which you may catch a glimpse of, but to evade all that.

RETAKING POSSESSION OF DETROIT.

Endorsed—7th June 1687. [The] retaking possession of the lands in the neighborhood of the strait ("detroit") between Lakes Erie and Huron, by the Sieur de la Duranthais.

Ollivier Morel Esquire, Sieur de la Durantaye, Commandant for the King in the lands of the Outaoüax, Miamis, Poutouamis, Cioux [? Sioux], and other tribes, under the orders of the Marquis de Denonville, Governor-General of New France.

This seventh day of June, one thousand six hundred and eighty-seven, in the presence of the Rev. Father Angeliran, Superior of the missions to the Outaoüax at Missilimackinac de Ste. Marie du Sault, to the Miamis,

Lieutenant of the fort of St. Joseph at the strait between Lakes Huron and Eries, We declare to all whom it may concern that we came to the margin of the St. Denys River, situated three leagues from Lake Errier on the strait between the said Lakes Errier and Huron to the south of the said strait and lower down towards the entrance to Lake Errier on the north, on behalf of the King and in his name to repeat the taking possession of the said posts, which was done by M. de la Salle to facilitate the journeys he made, and had made by barge from Niagara to Missili-maquinac in the years .... at which said stations we should have had a post set up again with the arms of the King, in order to mark the said re-taking possession, and directed several dwellings to be built for the establishment of the French and savages, Chaouannous and Miamis, for a long time owners of the said lands of the strait and of Lake Errier, from which they withdrew for some time for their greater convenience. The present deed executed in our presence signed by our hand and by the Rev. Father Angeliran of the Company of Jesus, by M. M. de la Forest, De Lisle and de Beauvais. Thus signed in the original, Angeleran, Jesuit, De la Durantaye, Le Gardeur, de Beauvais and F. de la Forest. Compared with the original remaining in my hands by me Councillor, Secretary of the King and Registrar in chief to the Sovereign Council at Quebec, undersigned. Signed Penuset, with paraph. Compared at Quebec, this 1st Sept. 1712.   Vaudreuil.
                                               Bégon.[1]

THE NECESSITY OF A POST AT DETROIT.

The establishment of a post at the Detroit appears necessary in order to facilitate the trade of the inhabitants of Canada with the savages, and especially to prevent the English from seizing it.

The facility of this trade would be exceedingly great and advantageous to the Colony of Canada, if His Majesty permitted the inhabitants of this Colony to form a company which should have the exclusive privilege of

should be distributed among the public (generally). If the plans which the Sieur Charron proposes for conveying our goods to the savages and bringing back their skins should succeed, which it cannot fail to do so long as we have peace, this monopoly would not be necessary afterwards because it would be impossible for private persons to supply goods at those places at the same price as the Company.

These pla
are to ha
barges at
Frontena
navigatin
Lake Ont
and at th
that wou
establish
navigatin
lakes abo
the Fall o
Niagara.

This Company would very humbly beg His Majesty to approve of its being supplied with the necessary quantity of powder, lead, and arms, for trading with the savages at the same price as he gets them from the contractor, so that, by supplying them to the said savages cheaper than the English, we might take away from them, in this way, all inclination to take their furs to that nation.

It would be necessary for the establishment of this post that His Majesty should be pleased to keep up only about a hundred or a hundred and fifty men of [his] troops with a commandant and experienced officers, put forward by the Company and approved by the Court or by the Governor, to whom it should be most distinctly forbidden, to the officers under the penalty of being cashiered, and to the men of corporal punishment, to do any trade directly or indirectly. And, as regards their subsistence, since it would doubtless cost somewhat more than at Quebec or Montreal, the Company should be obliged to provide for it by supplying all they would require beyond the King's pay.

It would also be necessary not to grant any concessions [of land] at that place, for fear of weakening the Colony by extending it too much.

In this way we should make sure of Detroit which is a very advantageous post which the English are trying to seize upon in all sorts of ways. We should facilitate trade, especially in the skins of the ox, of which it is also claimed that the wool might be useful in France. To the savage, we should raise the value of his beaver-skins by lessening that of the goods we sell to him which is the only effective means of keeping those who are allied to us and also attracting those who are not. Finally we shall prevent this large number of traders travelling through the woods, which is the cause of all the worst irregularities which go on in that country; and being compelled to remain in the Colony, they would strengthen it by applying themselves to cultivating the land, to the cod fishery, or to setting up some manufacture.

And if it were hereafter absolutely indispensable to limit the quantity of beaver skins which could be received from the colony, the establishment of this Company would become absolutely necessary in order to avoid the difficulties which would inevitably arise constantly if the stock of beaver

This report was probably written in 1701 and before the resolution to establish Detroit was known to the writer. The treaty of peace with the Iroquois was signed Sept. 7, 1700. Kingsford's Hist. Can., II, 393. Two interesting letters showing the claims of the English on the western territory, and especially Detroit, are in the archives in the State Capitol at Albany. They are both printed in In the Footsteps of Cadillac.—C. M. B.

skins were divided [and] in the possession of several [different people] who would not fail to intrigue to the best of their ability, each for his own private interest, to get his part of the beaver skins taken in preference to other people's, which would greatly disturb the public peace of this colony; and in that case it would also be necessary to receive no skins except from the said Company.

OCCUPYING POSTS IN THE WEST.

M.M. de Frontenac and de Champigny at Quebec 15th Sept., 1692.

My Lord—

We have received the King's memorandum of the eleventh of April, with the letters and statements you sent us by the Sieur d'Hiberville commanding the "Poly" who arrived here a month ago with all the vessels which he convoyed, in which were a large part of the reinforcements which His Majesty had the goodness to order for this country: we are expecting to get the rest by the other vessels which are to arrive

As His Majesty proves to us, by sending us these, the special protection he continues to grant to the Colony, in order to aid it against its enemies, we are obliged, in order to act in accordance with his intentions, to represent to him that it is absolutely necessary for its preservation that it should be reinforced next year by a considerable number of soldiers, as indeed he was good enough to give us hope of in his memorandum; for it is impossible otherwise to protect it, and at the same time to enter on enterprises outside. Our letters and private memoranda will inform you, My Lord, of the plans we have as to the war, and will show you how important it is to send [us] a thousand soldiers.

The advantages which the King's arms have continued to carry off this year on different occasions, of which My Lord will be fully informed by the memoranda we are sending, should show that it has been necessary to use every endeavour, with the scanty forces we have, and that the other vessels should come as they are to bring us nearly four hundred thousandweight of flour out of that intended for this country, and about twenty-four thousandweight of bacon; otherwise we should have great difficulty in providing food for the troops. It is very necessary that His Majesty should have six hundred thousandweight of flour and a hundred and twenty thousandweight of bacon sent (here) next year, as he was good enough to do this year, together with one year's food for the troops which he sends over. We are sending you, My Lord, a statement of the stores which will also be necessary for us.

His Majesty may rest assured that he will be satisfied with the unity and the good understanding which he desires there should be between us, and that we shall agree to the utmost extent in all that is for the good of his service and to the advantage of the Colony. The express order which he gives us to maintain that unity cannot but be most agreeable to us, since we shall find therein, not the good of the service only, but also our own private pleasure.

The list of the troops annexed to the despatch of the Sr. de Champigny of the 12th Oct. 1691 was in conformity with the muster-roll which he drew up a short time before; and if there were only twenty men fewer than in the muster-roll drawn up at the end of 1690. and the loss of a greater number is shown, that arises from several cadets being incorporated in the companies, from the return of some prisoners, and because the number that has been lost consisted partly of inhabitants of the country. The said Sr. de Champigny sends My Lord the muster roll of the troops as he desires; no man will be accepted who is not fit to serve, nor cadets until they are sixteen years of age.

If, My Lord, you had received the plans which were sent to you at the end of 1691 by the ship "St. Francois Xavier," which is believed to have been lost at the mouth of the Gulf, you would have understood clearly how usefully the funds ordered by His Majesty for the fortifications have been used, and that all possible economy has been exercised in the expense which we have been obliged to go to. The lower town of Quebec has been fortified with two very large platforms; the upper town by two more and several covered redoubts; keeping the palisade in repair, and the one at Montreal, the re-construction of that at Three Rivers with redoubts and- other absolutely necessary repairs and works; this has caused all the expenses that have been incurred, and you may rest

of the citadel of Quebec, the circuit of which is too small as it does not enclose the powder magazine and the walls are falling in ruins and have no flanks, parapets or outworks. And, as it is no less needed for the purpose of sheltering us a little more from the attacks which Phipps continues to menace us with, we are also going to set men to work at once on a third platform at the lower town, the plans of which the engineer will bring you. This will not only use up the remainder of the twenty thousand livres sent for this year, but will also run to about fifteen thousand livres beyond without including indispensable repairs at Montreal, the enlargement of the enceinte of Three Rivers and repairing the stockade of Fort de Chambly, which is quite rotten, and keeping up several small forts. It is necessary therefore to send the fifteen thousand livres next year as you did this, and also the twenty thousand livres as usual, unless you will add a larger sum, in case you resolve according to the plans, to finish off the fortifications of this town—which, as you know, is the key and safety of the whole country—in stone. You will observe, if you please, that it is better to have all the works we have to undertake in future built of stone, in places where stone is met with, than to trifle with (the matter by) using stakes at which work has to be done every year, (thus) involving us in considerable repairs, as appears from the enceinte of Montreal.

We can assure you that the assistance we can obtain from the inhabitants must not be counted on for contributing to these works, as the merchants have sustained heavy losses in the "St. Francois Xavier" in which they had embarked a quantity of skins and ready money; the inhabitants [generally], on the other hand, are almost all ruined by the war which has compelled them to abandon the country, where their houses and dwellings were, to take refuge in the towns & forts where they are reduced with their families to huts.

It is one of the greatest benefits that His Majesty can confer (on us) during the war to send stores for distribution to the Savages, for it is an almost certain means of setting them in motion and keeping them so by sending a number of parties into the country against the enemy, as appeared this year. We shall employ those which His Majesty has sent as usefully as we possibly can, according to his intentions, which we will fulfil to the best of our ability by observing his orders in this respect so

We are seeing to it that the Savages do not dispose of their arms and stores under any pretext whatever; decrees have formerly been issued on this subject which are being exactly carried out.

What His Majesty wishes us to do concerning the distribution of the twenty-five licenses which he wants given for going to trade in the further districts shall be carried out as he directs us (to do) and in conformity with his decree of the 2nd of May 1681, and likewise his declaration of the 24th of May 1679, concerning intoxicating drinks.

The proposal of the Sieur Laporte de Louvigny to occupy the posts of the River of the Miamis, on condition of keeping up forty soldiers there at his own expense, cannot be accepted as that would only serve to exclude the inhabitants from the profits of the trade they might do and cause it to fall into his hands.

The (Religieuses Hospitallieres) of Montreal have had their six licenses which had been promised them by M de Denonville. They were greatly in need of them, this House being in great want. The Sieur Riverin, to whom His Majesty granted some, has had two this year in consideration of his fishery establishment which is becoming an important one.

Concerning what is owing for the advances made for constructing a fort for the Outaoüas and another on the strait of Lake Erie, and for other expenses in the said countries, it is right to inform His Majesty that, when M. de Denonville arrived in Canada, he gave his orders for the said forts to be built, and to send to all the tribes in order to get them to come in the spring of 1687 to the general meeting-place which he fixed for them on Lake Ontario, in order to join him and march against the Iroquois in their countries which was carried out by the diligence of the Sieur de La Durantaye who, for that purpose, borrowed from those who were trading in the said places at the time a part of their goods which he used for building the said forts and in the journeys which he had made by the French and savages in order to give notice to all the tribes. Each individual who supplied goods has put forward his bill certified both by the Sieur de La Durantays and by Father Angelleran, missionary at the said places, and it was afterwards decreed by M. de Denonville and the Sieur de Champigny that they should be reimbursed out of the first licenses which were issued and this was approved by His Majesty's

for making this repayment, so that the licenses may result in advantage to the poor inhabitants of this country; unless he orders additional licenses to be granted for this repayment.

The Sieurs Tonty and de Laforest, to whom His Majesty has granted the fort St. Louis of the Illinois, on condition of setting the savages in motion against the enemy, have begun to carry out that arrangement; several parties have laid waste the huts of the Iroquois who had withdrawn from their villages, and they are preparing to make them act more vigorously. It would be necessary to send us the Concession which was made of this fort to the Sieur de la Salles, so that the said Sieurs Tonty and de Laforest may be put in possession of it on the same conditions, as it has been granted to them to possess in conformity with his concession.

Whatever precautions may be taken of the preservation of Acadia, and for the assistance of the French inhabitants of that place, we could not succeed with such scanty forces if the English chose to take large forces there, which they can easily do. All that can be done is to send stores from time to time, as we do, to the inhabitants of the Mines, Beaubassin, and other places in order to prevent them from believing themselves to be abandoned, as they would do if we did not aid them, and being thus compelled to give themselves up to the English, which they have hitherto refused to do although they have been strongly urged to do so, and [that] with threats; and also to induce the Canibas and Abenaquis, by the

New England, will undertake that enterprise next year for all the reasons which we put before him in our letters of last year. We are awaiting his orders as to what is to be done at the same time on the Orange coast, where we cannot but think that we are not strong in troops now.

We have not been able to think of the re-establishment of Fort Frontenac; when the opportunity presents itself we will arrange the matter so well that it will be as successful as His Majesty can hope.

It was very gracious of him to deign to think of the rebuilding of the citadel of Quebec; it was assuredly not an unnecessary thing. We shall employ on it the three thousand livres which he sent; in the hope that he will give orders for the rest next year, for the work is pressing, considering the conspicuous danger in which the old building stands.

We shall send by the last vessels the roll of officers of the troops maintained in this country in which mention will be made of their services and of those who wish to enter the Navy; and we cannot sufficiently thank His Majesty for having regarded the entreaties which we made to him to bear in mind the promotion of the officers serving in this country, for nothing could contribute so largely to maintaining and increasing their zeal for his service. He has indeed done us the honor to send us word that he had granted posts to some; but, as the commissions were not addressed to us, we do not know their names nor the duties with which he has honored them. We have the same thanksgiving to render him for what he has done for Sieurs Provost Gallifet, Ramezey, and Grandpre, and for the gratuities he has granted to the Sieur de Monic, Repentigny, Jolliet and the Recollet Fathers. They could not be put to a better use; for the first does good service and has not the pay of a major; the second is a gentleman [who was one] of the first settlers in this country, who had twelve children, boys, seven of whom are now in the service, and two others were killed a year ago, the one burnt by the Iroquois and the other killed this [? last] summer by a musket-shot in the detachment of the Sieur de Vaudreuil; the third is one of the oldest inhabitants of the country, burdened with a numerous family, who has great talent for discoveries at which he continues to work still, and has a large establishment in the island of Anticosta on which he has spent the greater part of his property. And this compels us to beg him* graciously to continue them [i. e. the gratuities] to them as well as to the Recollet Fathers who, by their usefulness to all the tribes and their edification of them may hope that His Majesty will grant them yet other and larger charities to help them build their house, as he has done to certain communities in this country.

We have not received the letters of nobility granted by His Majesty last year to the Sieurs de St. Denys and Hertel as My Lord notifies to us by the memorandum of the King; we therefore beg him to send them to us next year. We will carry out what His Majesty directs regarding the Sieurs de La Durantys and Lamotte Cadillac.

The order which the King gives us, to grant concessions one after another as far as the Colony extends, cannot be carried out as there are no more lands along the river which have not been granted from the beginning of the dwellings up to the upper end of the Isle of Montreal. The places which are most exposed to enemies, which are above the Three Rivers, have been united in villages, and the inhabitants have withdrawn to them. This union is not so necessary for the place below the Three Rivers as they are less exposed; but we shall work at that as far as may be possible. We were pleased to learn that the disputes between the Bishop of Quebec and his seminary were terminated. His Majesty may rest assured that we shall forget nothing for keeping in harmony with him; he should be satisfied thus far since it has been preserved without any diminution. He has not yet formed regular curacies, for want of time since his arrival; we have spoken to him of it, and we hope he will form some at once. The continuance of the eight thousand livres, for part of the subsistence of the rectors will be very necessary, as a sufficient number cannot be maintained without this assistance. Also His Majesty should not doubt that we shall assist the Jesuits and the Recollets in every way we can.

As His Majesty, in his letters patent for the establishment of a general hospital at Quebec, has directed that the Governor and the Intendant conjointly with the Bishop are to be the heads of the governing body of the said hospital, it will be easier for them to remedy the abuses which might gain admittance into the said establishment, as His said Majesty very judiciously points out. And as, in the same letters, he permits us to grant others for Poor-houses in places where they might be useful when pious people come forward who have property and would like to contribute to the said establishment. Conjointly with the Bishop they have granted letters for setting one up at Montreal, people having been found who have property large enough for founding it; and this will not be a burden to His Majesty nor to the Colony, for their intention is not to afford an opportunity for laziness, nor to support it, but to try and prevent the idleness which prevails among most of the young people of this country by instructing children, making those who are poor learn trades, and, above all, occupying them in the cultivation of the land, so

have been put on board the ships, after those we are expecting have arrived, as there is a large part of them in them.

As the post of the Sieur Bosson has been filled up, and he is of a rather troublesome disposition, and very liable to get similar affairs on his hands on account of his constant drunkenness, we beg you My Lord not to permit him to come back to Canada.

The Comte de Frontenac did not fail, as soon as he received His Majesty's orders, to reinstate the Sieurs de Noyan and de Lorimier in the duties of their posts, being very glad for his part that His Majesty had been lenient toward them, because they are good officers.

No change has been made in values for ready money according to the private letter which the Comte de Frontenac has received about it. We will employ this year the same expedient we made use of last, by borrowing goods with which to provide for the expenses of next year until the ships arrive; but it is to be feared that it cannot be done in future years, as the merchants may have plans for using their money to advantage in other ways. It would be well, therefore. that there should always be funds for six months in advance which, being once provided, would remain afterwards.

And regarding the proposal you make to us, My Lord, to send us in future all the funds intended both for the troops and for other expenses in provisions and goods, we beg you to take into consideration that, unless a good part of them is sent in ready money, and the remainder is arranged according to the statements we send of the goods and provisions which we think necessary to us, which we are obliged to vary according to the condition of the affairs of the Colony, which is different almost every year, and especially according to the abundance or scarcity of the grains there, you would absolutely ruin the trade of this country and would take away from it the little ready money there is of which from the present time there is not much. The Sieur de Champigny will dwell on this point again in the private letter he is doing himself the honor to write to you.

It is certain that for many years the merchants have availed themselves of the pretexts which the war has given them to increase the price of goods, and that the inhabitants of the country have seized on the opportunity to raise prices to them, and to run up grains and other necessaries of life to exorbitant prices. Hence it arises that there is almost nobody here now who can live, the greater part of the provisions having gone up more than one-half.

It is true that the first cause of the increase in the prices of goods in this country proceeds from the merchants of La Rochelle who have raised, not only their price, but also their insurances, which now stand at twenty per cent. notwithstanding the convoys which His Majesty grants every year, and the freight, for which they have charged as much as 120#

text that they have now given a fourth of their ships to the King, whose intention could never have been that they should indemnify themselves out of the inhabitants of the country who send for goods, still less that they should make a profit thereby, as they are doing, for instead of the fourth which they give the King they have more than a half more for freight than they usually get. Therefore we beg you to remedy this abuse of which they are guilty at Rochelle, so that it may not continue in future.

We will take, on that, the opportunity of putting before you another [abuse] which has already been written about a long time ago, namely. that the same merchants of La Rochelle compel all who put goods on board their ships to pay them the freight in advance; this practice prevails in no other place in the world, and is very burdensome to the people of Canada for reasons which it is unnecessary to explain, as they are easily understood.

We believe those abuses would not go on if you thought fit to move the merchants of St. Malo and other towns to come & trade with this country, and would remove the fear, which they may have been made to feel, that they would be prevented from doing so. and that it would be allowed to the merchants of La Rochelle only.

We are doing all we possibly can to urge the merchants and inhabitants of this country to apply themselves to the cod fisheries, being the most profitable trade that can ever be done in this Colony. But it would have been impossible, this year, to carry on even the eel-fishery, which is the manna* of all the inhabitants, without the salt which His Majesty sent in his ships; for some of the other vessels did not bring any, and those which had some would not sell any, saying that they had intended it for carrying on the fishery on the great bank on their way back. The Sieur de Champigny had that which came in the King's ships distributed at a very reasonable price, which greatly pleased the inhabitants; and it is absolutely

dinary expenses which we have been compelled to incur these last (few) years.

We have had trouble enough hitherto in restraining the English prisoners, or (those) ransomed from the savages, and in preventing them from escaping and going back home; but, as the number of them has (now) become large and it is not easy, in a country as exposed as this is, to succeed in guarding them securely, and as they are a great burden, we have come to the conclusion that it would be advisable to distribute them among all the ships that return to France because, there, it will be easier to prevent them from going back to New England where it is very important that they should not return, especially the Sieur de Nelson who is a very turbulent spirit, capable of doing a great deal of harm if he goes back to Boston; therefore we beg you to give orders to M. Begon, to whom we are sending them, to have him carefully guarded, together with Colonel Stint and the son of a merchant called Aldain. They would have been useless here for exchanging since we have no French prisoners at Boston, as the Chev. d'Eau escaped from there a few days ago; and the soldiers of the garrison of Port Royal who are the only ones remaining there, according to your orders, cannot be reckoned as a set-off in any exchange.

The Sieur Demesnu, Recorder in Chief to the sovereign council, being a little broken down by age, would wish to see his remaining son succeed him in his appointment; and, as His Majesty had already granted him that favor on behalf of an elder son who died on his way back from the Islands, where he had been employed by M. de Gompy the Intendant who had made him his subdelegate, he (St. Demesnu) hopes that he [His Majesty] will not refuse it him for his younger son who has been serving under him as clerk in the office for five years.

We take the liberty of repeating the request which we made to you last year on behalf of the widow of the Sieur Desquairac, a captain who was killed at the engagement of the Prairie de la Magdeleine against the English in 1691, namely to grant her a pension to help her to bring up her children, as she is very poor.

We ask you, My Lord, for the honor of your protection, and that you will believe us (to be), with deep respect.

My Lord
Your humble, very obedient and most obliged Servants

Frontenac;
Champigny

THE ESTABLISHMENT OF THEATRES IN QUEBEC.

A LETTER FROM M. DE LA MOTHE CADILLAC.

Endorsed—M. M. Cadillac.   28th Oct.* 1694.

I cannot help reverting to the beginning of this year, in order to
inform you also of what has taken place up to the present. The successful in-gathering of beaver-skins and corn having diffused joy through the
hearts of all the people, we counted at first on seeing prosperity again
in a trade which had been on the verge of extinction and approaching,
so to speak, its last hour.

In this hope, the Colony began to forget its past misfortunes and made
up its mind to bear with more fortitude those which m$_i$gh$_t$ befall it in
the future; whereupon the Comte de Frontenac, delighted for his part to
see the people relieved by his care and vigilance, took a real pleasure in
giving everyone every advantage which could be looked for from him.

That afforded a prospect of passing the winter agreeably, especially to
the officers of the troops who lived in an exemplary (state of) harmony;
and, in order to contribute to their reasonable amusements, the Comte
consented to have two plays acted, "Nicomede" and "Mithridate." So far
all goes well, sir; but you are about to see other pieces besides those, in
which there will be no less poison poured out.

The clerics already began preparing for battle. Behold them armed
from head to foot, taking their bows and arrows. The Sieur G. Laudelet
began first and delivered two sermons, one on the 10th and the other on
the 24th of January, in which he labored to prove that it was impossible
to attend at plays without committing deadly sin. The Bishop, on his
part caused a charge to be read out at the mass sermon, on the 16th of
the same month, in which mention is made of certain plays (as) impious,
impure, and wrongful to one's neighbor, no doubt in order to suggest that
those which had actually been played were of that kind. The people,
being credulous, infatuated and led away by sermons and charges of this
kind, at once began to look upon the Comte as the corrupter of morals

As he was one of the actors in the play, they thought, and it was apparent, that he for his part, would be cowed by this clap of thunder, that the rest of the company would be disturbed by it, or at least that, having made him odious by a formidable pretext, the hatred of the play should become the lot of those who were prejudiced in its favor.

This officer complained of it and betook himself to the Bishop's house, but the Bishop would neither see nor hear him. He went a second and a third time; they took him by the shoulders and drove him away, telling him that they would have nothing to say to a man who was excommunicated. Such injurious proceedings compelled the Sieur de Mareuil to have recourse to the law and to apply to a notary in order to obtain a ruling against the Bishop to give him a copy of his charge. The notary refuses: Mareuil applies to the Intendant who orders the notary to do his duty. This order had no effect; Mareuil obtained a second; finally the notary obeyed. The Bishop perceived from this step that he was neither in Spain nor Portugal, and that means could be found to obtain redress for such a cruel wrong. It was this which made him bethink himself of a second expedient, worse than the first, entirely opposed to episcopal charity, to the principles of Christianity, and forming a very bad example. This prelate played a strange part; he went to the Supreme Council on the 1st of February* and stood forth as accuser against the Sieur de Mareuil, declaring him guilty of the crime of impiety against God, the Virgin, and the saints, and, to omit nothing which might advance this beautiful scheme, he delivered a fine speech to this court in the absence of the Comte, interrupted at times by the outbursts from a heart filled apparently with a deep and infinite charity, but driven to extremities by the rebellion—said he—of an intractable child whom he had often warned & caused to be warned by persons in authority; but all that was imaginary, not to say very untrue.

Here we have Mareuil changing his performance: from comedy, he is taken on to tragic things. The speech of this prelate was well contrived; that of the Procureur-Général in his decisions emanated from the same council chamber, as well as the hasty decree which was made on this matter.

I am determined to tell you what the Sieur de Mareuil's crime is, and

which they wish to put an end to, whatever it may cost, about which the ecclesiastical authority is determined not to be beaten.

It is indisputable, and cannot be denied without a blush, that since then Mareuil has sought penitence; he has confessed and communicated several times. He also fell into a dangerous illness, during which he received the Sacraments, and he has continued to do his duty as a Christian and an upright man. May that not be called*·refusing to let sleeping dogs lie? For even if it were true that the crime was as heinous as the Bishop pretends, should it not be sufficient that it had faded from men's memories and was buried in the grave of oblivion, instead of with calculated zeal bringing it to light again with all its surroundings. I leave the Sieur de Mareuil at the Supreme Council, appealing against the charge of the bishop as a grievance, to which he presents petition after petition, in vain, to demand justice; I leave him, I say, in the hands of M. de Villerai, his judge-delegate and his mortal enemy.

I cannot, however, so soon quit the Bishop who is setting out from Quebec; and I shall follow him along the line of his visitation and inform you that he began at the place called Batiscan to show his restlessness, and first allowed himself to be persuaded by the Sieur Frocantevré of the parish (an eccentric man if ever there was one) that the Sieur Desiourdy, a half-pay captain commanding the company of M. de Vaudreuil at that place, had a dishonorable intercourse with the wife of the Sieur Debrieux. You will, if you please, observe that this officer had changed his quarters and had been at Forelle for a month by M. de Vaudreuil's orders, on the request of the Bishop who had asked for this to free him from this suspicion & had promised on this condition, not to speak of the matter again. Yet, contrary to his promise, and always armed with the same weapons, he caused a charge to be read out in which the churches of Batiscan and Champlain were forbidden to the Sieur Desiourdy and to Mme. Debrieux. Having launched this thunderbolt he continues his journey to the Three Rivers, crosses Lake St. Pierre, and arrives at Forelle where the Sieur Desiourdy was, with several other officers. There he

nesses to be summoned, who deposed to having seen them at mass in the church of Forelle on the very day on which they were accused of having failed to do so, they carried their proof to the Comte, who was astonished at the Bishop's mistake.

I think it important to go down to Batiscan again, and refer once more to the charge which was read out there at the sermon in that parish and to bring to your notice that the Sieur de Desiourdy, not being able to believe in what had been told him about it, on his way down to Quebec repaired to the church of that place, to hear mass which he found begun, and a funeral service was proceeding over a corpse. When this priest perceived that the Sieur Desiourdy was present, he stopped the mass, went to the sacristy where he took off his sacerdotal vestments, and then returned to the church where he made known to the congregation that, as long as the Sieur Desiourdy was there, they would have no mass. This passionate declaration astonished these townsmen; and it is asserted that this priest's face, naturally swarthy, became as pale and as altered as that of the corpse which was there. The anger and passion shown and imprinted on his face affected everyone with seemly confusion, so that they all withdrew and he remained alone with his clerk; and, after having secured the door behind them, he went and finished the mass at which, (to judge) from the apparent temper of this rector, neither the Sieur Desiourdy nor the soul of the deceased could hope to be recommended at this august sacrifice.

However, the wife of the Sieur Debrieux, as well as the Sieur Desiourdy carried their complaint to the Supreme Council by petition and afterwards went (to it) appealing against the publication of the Bishop's charges as an abuse. I will not speak of the many extravagances of this rector, upheld by the authority of his prelate, even to preaching from the pulpit that no one but wretches and damned souls could depose to Madam Debrieux being a respectable woman; that if anyone were bold enough to do so, he would beat him to death, and that he would have them put into irons for six months on bread and water; that the Comte de Frontenac had not long to live, but the Bishop was young and would lead them a fine dance one of these days; that he laughed at the complaints made against him to the Supreme Council; that all that he did was by the orders of his Bishop, who recognized no one in this country as above himself, and that there was no judge of his actions except the Pope. Who would not think, at first sight, that this account is full of prejudice? Yet it is just as true as that there is a sun in the heavens.

It appears that there is no room for doubting that, when the Sieur Debrieux demanded satisfaction from the Supreme Council, for the wrong done to him and to his wife [who was] accused and condemned of adul-

preme Council when they saw the Church making a sudden invasion of the secular jurisdiction? They could not have been unaware that, in a case of adultery, no one is permitted to make an accusation except the husband; that this crime is a privileged matter, as to which the Church has no jurisdiction.

All this would have been well at another time, and on some other occasion. These judges were like that people of which the Scripture says, "I have sent a spirit of drowsiness upon their eyes that they might not see, and upon their ears that they might not hear." It was in vain to lay before them proof after proof, petition after petition. Their course was taken, and the alliance ratified; the Supreme Council generally, and the whole ecclesiastical calling except the recollet Fathers, had labored together and had intended that the Comte should infallibly fall into their snares, that he would not fail to be alarmed at the occurrence of so many outrages, and in order to stop their progress would no doubt employ violent measures either against the Bishop or the clergy or indeed, even against the Supreme Council. But this junto was greatly disconcerted; and bore the moderation, modesty and wise conduct, which the Comte showed on all occasions, with intelligible violence. See here more exactly how he treated the Bishop, in a letter which he wrote to him, of which I took a copy, word for word.

"Sir, I had requested the very reverend Commissary Father of the recollets to ask you for a copy of the charges which I have been told have been made public, and, as I found M. Trouné by chance yesterday at the hospital, I charged him to make the same request to you; but, as I have had no answer, I thought I ought to ask you for the same again by this note, for on all sides I hear these charges so differently spoken of that I know not what reply to make. Oblige me, Sir, by informing me definitely as to what they contain, so that, when I know what your intentions are in that matter I may be better able to conform thereto, and to contribute so far as I can to everyone doing likewise."

As to the remonstrance which the Comte addressed to the Supreme Council, which he demanded should be registered, on the 8th of March 1694, it is sufficient proof that he only wished that company to under-

by demanding that one or two commissioners should be 'appointed to investigate (as to) whether any one had played or caused to be played any scandalous plays, and whether any irregularity had taken place.

These decisions were required, as far as I can judge, for various ends. In the first place, to learn whether in fact some criminal play had not been acted, at which certain private individuals might have been present unknown to the Comte, whom they might have accused of having aided it and of having wanted in this way to introduce vice and bad habits, instead of restraining them. Or, again, it might indeed have been in order to discover whether, in the pieces which he himself had caused to be acted, there had not been concealed from him the knowledge of some indecent act which some person of rank might have committed, and he might thus have been accused of pernicious toleration. Lastly it was to show the resolve he had made to support the Bishop if anyone were found guilty of the crimes and impious acts referred to in his charge. I might add that the Comte wished to make the Supreme Council understand that he was experienced enough to foresee and to anticipate the snares of his irreconcilable enemies, or, rather, those of the governorship.

Could he indeed have been silent concerning a charge (which was) full of venom and poison under the apparent form of Christian truth? Would not his silence have passed for a confession? Everyone knows that those who have (any·) connection with, or·access to the Court have no other object than that of causing the King to lose the respect for the governors-general of this country which he has always shown; this constant attack will never ·be given up so long as the governmental authority is thus divided. ·

But let us return to the point. Would it not seem that the Procureur Général should have given his earnest attention to this remonstrance, and come to a conclusion at once as to the views which were there set forth? He ought to have hesitated far less on this occasion than he had done at the time of the odious and vindictive denunciation of the Bishop against the Sieur de Mareuil. The Intendant and the rest of the Council well knew that this same Mareuil had applied to them by a petition a week before to get the attorneys, notaries and bailiffs compelled to perform the duties of their offices. They knew very well that, in the end, a notary made up his mind, with large sums of money, to serve a summons on the Bishop who, in retaliation for this act, formed that fine resolution to ruin a man who was only the innocent cause of a premeditated spite. Finally by a decree of the same day, the eighth of March, it was ordered that the remonstrance should be communicated to the Procureur Général

concerning the Bishop. It is easy to see that the Procureur General in
his interim decisions of the 22nd of March as to the remonstrance of the
Comte, offered him a battle-ground, and sought to engage him in embarrassing discussions in order to furnish himself with pretences and proceedings, so as to come to no conclusion on the point in question, especially in the compliment he paid to the Comte, begging him to inform
[him] whether it is was not his intention to refrain from being present at
the voting which would take place as to his document and on his address,
as well as on the affair of Sieur de Mareuil, since he had declared—he
said—in the presence of all the Council that the latter was his servant
(which is a clear falsehood, since the Comte had never said a word of it),
and that therefore he ought in fact to refrain from voting on these two
matters.

The Procureur General had used different language on the demand and
information by the Bishop. He did not think of requesting that he
should refrain from being present at the voting, nor that the petition to
the Council against the Sieur de Mareuil should be referred to him.

The declaration which he sought to exact from the Comte was much
more odious and more daring. In claiming that a Governor Genl.
['s Vote] was liable to be challenged, as appears from the decree of the
29th of March, he was attempting an unheard of scheme. If that were
established neither he nor the Intendant would be able to give an opinion
on any matter concerning his government which, from its circumstances,
did not depend [solely] on the authority of one or the other of them.
Sometimes they would be objected to on the score of their patronage, or
their dislike; at others, they might be discovered to be creditors of some,

borne a hand in composing it. He says, without ceremony, in his first paragraph, that he sees nothing in the decree issued on the 1st of February as to the Bishop's declaration which either directly or indirectly concerns the carrying out of the King's orders and intentions. What inference does he wish to draw from this fine scheme. Has the Comte at any time opposed the prosecution of crimes, and particularly when they have been directed against the divine Majesty? Can he bring forward one instance? It is very clearly to be seen that M. de Frontenac's remonstrance was drawn up only with the purpose of making it known that the Bishop ought not, and could not publish charges enjoining the refusal of the sacraments or excommunication without the aid of justice and of the secular power; that this was an order which ought to be observed, being in conformity with the intentions of the King, who neither desires nor intends that the Church should usurp the royal power in any way, nor infringe upon his decrees. It was that unconquerable negligence to which the Procureur Général had given way, which the Comte had so ingeniously touched on in his remonstrance, which compelled him to employ all [possible] weapons in order to fight it so obstinately.

As to the second head of his address, the Procureur Général persists in saying that he sees nothing which offends against the authority of the Governor, who affects (as he pretends) to confuse the Sieur de Mareuil's affair with public interests.

It will be seen that this is a very superflous statement; for it is agreed

Général say as often as he likes that the affair of the Sieur de Mareuil is a private matter; he thereby proves sufficiently that he was unable to discern it, for [even] if the Bishop intended in his charge read out at sermon-time to condemn Mareuil of impiety, pure and simple, that was an outrage on the King's jurisdiction since this crime is not within the cognizance nor the jurisdiction of the Church. That was an occasion which ought to have roused the Procureur Général for two reasons; the first, not to allow the royal authority to be injured, and the second, to take cognizance [himself] of the crime and the criminal. But it is easy to see what diligence he used in this matter. Would he have made any move in it at all, if Mareuil had not taken action first, if he had not attacked the Bishop by legal documents and summonses, and if the Bishop himself, in order to shelter himself and justify his bad conduct, whatever the cost might be, had not gone to the Supreme Council to denounce him.

The public is not concerned, the Procureur Général pretends, in charges of this sort. What meaning, then, are we to give to the expressions contained in it, which only speak of plays [which are] impious, impure, and wrongful to one's neighbor. Either the Bishop intended thus to characterize those which had just been played, or else those which were to be played afterwards. Those just played were "Nicomede" and "Mithridate." If these two plays are impious, it was very wrong of the Procureur Général and the Supreme Council to have been present at them, and to set such a bad example. If they are lawful, what is the use of charges of this kind which serve only to upset [men's] consciences, [and] embarrass people, especially the common people who have not often much discernment, and conjure up scruples and prejudices, generally ill-founded, which by a rebound may reflect on a Governor personally.

Now if it refers to plays which are to be performed hereafter, even if the Bishop had been convinced that they would be impious or criminal, it would have been prudent on his part to have deferred the publication of his charge until such time as the impious play had been performed, or at least he should have had a certain and absolutely infallible knowledge that it would be played. Will he palliate his fault by saying that he

into his head that the Comte wished to have it acted, although he had never thought of it. He toiled & moiled and [all] to stem a torrent which existed only in his imagination; but when these hysterics had subsided, he saw that this was only a jest, and that he had been taken in by the report of some ill informed person. However, whether in order not to give way, or to dazzle the eyes of the public, he sought an opportunity of entering into conversation with the Comte near the Jesuit church, the Intendant being present, and took it into his head to offer him a hundred pistoles not to have "La Tartuffe" played. This proposal did not disconcert the Comte; he thought, as many others did, that this prelate, having trusted too easily to a rumor which had been spread through the town, without knowing the authority for it, had [now] regained his senses, and knowing his fault, had desired to avoid being confounded by it. Therefore the Comte, smiling, promised him that in consideration of that sum, he would satisfy him and would interpose his authority to prevent any such design being carried out. No sooner said than done; the Bishop gave his promissory note, and the Comte accepted it, which made all the onlookers laugh. That is what the Procureur Général meant in one of his paragraphs as well as what he said in another, that the Sr. de Mareuil was not made an officer until after the charge of the Bishop had been read out. You have only to compare the date of the one, the 17th of January, and the date of the commission of the other, the 1st of the same month, to see how well he understands evasions, and how he tries to turn matters to his advantage by giving them an opposite appearance, as he has done in his tenth paragraph in which he wishes to make it appear that the decree which was given as to the demand of M. Talon, then Intendant of this country, has never been carried out.

The matter did not take place as he tells it in this and the following paragraphs. Those who know the history of that time speak differently of it; and these are the facts. Mons. de Laval made various attempts, almost the same as those we see today, the object of which has always been to prevail over the authority of the governorship. Mons. de Tracy, then viceroy of this country, looked tranquilly on at the desire from that high position; and, as he was a pious man, he did not think it advisable to cope with that ecclesiastical cohort, the power of which was formidable. At this conjuncture, M. Talon showed greater resolution and risked the loss of his credit and his fortune for the King's interests. He saw

the consent of M. Talon, on the day of his reconciliation, to the decree in question being erased and struck out, not because it was disapproved of, or had been found contrary to true justice, as the Procureur Général wishes to persuade us, but in order that M. de Laval might not be liable to reproach for his errors and his unjust claims. It was a weakness on M. Talon's part, to allow himself to be defeated by such submissions. That is why the Comte made use of that decree in his remonstrance as a precedent which showed that the Bishop was only walking in the foot-steps of his predecessor. Finally, it is only necessary to study the decisions of the Procureur Général, and it will at once be seen that he has been well prompted and is very constant to his plot. He does not consider, he says, that any action should be taken against the Bishop, who has gone up to Montreal; that he asks that the decision on the documents as far as concerns the charges, should be delayed until his return; and so on.

I confess that it would not have been considered wrong of the Supreme Council to give the Bishop notice, out of deference to him, of the steps that were taken against him after his departure; but I maintain that it is a clear abuse that they would not give any decision regarding him after the decree of postponement of the 24th of March, whether before or after his return, although he had asked for this delay only, as appears from the answer he gave the Procureur Général on the 18th of April.

By the decree of the 28th of June we still see the Bishop's procedure carefully premeditated and arranged, not only with the Procureur Général but with all the Council, which trifled with the Comte de Frontenac, and the other parties; and this understanding is all the more clearly próved as, in the meanwhile, the Supreme Council took it into their heads to give two months vacation, a custom which had never before been intro-

would give reason for desiring this diligence. The first was that, supposing the said Mareuil was guilty of the heinous crime he was accused of, it was important to get his trial over and done with, and not to let it hang fire out of culpable lenity, since it is well known that in matters of this kind to gain time is everything, and long delays reduce the culpability of the crime. The [delay] is also contrary to the decrees, which require that criminals shall be proceeded against even during the vacation, all other affairs being set aside. It may also be said that the Sieur de Mareuil, who was an officer, kept urging the Comte to have his case tried, pointing out to him that he was told off¹ to go against the enemy and on account of conscientious scruples, felt very uncomfortable at laboring so long under the censure of the Church, although it was ill founded. In fact, either Mareuil was a criminal or an innocent man. If he was guilty, the inquiries concerning him ought to have been ready and duly arranged, in two months' time; for he was of opinion that the Bishop must have had in his hands genuine proofs of the impiety for which he had condemned him, and as to which he afterwards appeared as his accuser. We have seen enough of all the steps he took & caused to be taken by ecclesiastics of all sorts, to ruin an innocent man, exposed to his revengeful fury. The vehemence and passion with which the Procureur Général acted at the beginning of this affair ought to have promised a more prompt settlement of it; and if he was innocent, why not help him to throw off a yoke which could not be borne without extreme disquietude. That, then, was the ground taken up by the Comte, who, seeing the Procureur Général was hanging back in this matter, thought himself bound to tell him that he clearly saw whence these delays proceeded; and that, if he did not go on with it, he as head of the Supreme Council and Governor-General should order him to proceed and to do his duty.

It was exactly from this word "head" that the Supreme Council and the Procureur Général drew inferences so pleasing [to them]. The Comte knew very well the will of His Majesty and the decree of his Council of State of sixteen hundred and eighty, forbidding him to assume this rank in his titles. Where has he done so? Was it not sufficient for the Supreme Council that he explained his intention to them, and that he testified to them that nothing was further from his thoughts than to go beyond the decree of 1680, that he only claimed to enjoy the rights and prerogatives which the King has assigned to him. The Procureur Général had the good grace to show that the will of the King was that everyone in the Council should have complete freedom in giving his opinion without being forced in the matter by threats, commands, or instigation. Has the Comte used violence against anyone, that such language should be employed toward him? What is the good of so much talk? He should supply proofs, and not allegations. We are constrained, he says, in our votes because we have reason to fear the Governor's displeasure.

One might reply to the Procureur Général that with his own mouth he has judged himself. It is only necessary to see his writings, to weigh his words, and to examine his decisions, that will be amply sufficient to prove what precautions he has taken and the fear he has felt for his part of disobliging the Comte, who wished all his studied and crafty speeches to be inscribed on the registers, so that he may testify to his conduct on occasion.

The Procureur Général opposed it himself, and also the Intendant, with all the Supreme Council, under specious pretexts. For, what was the question in the first place? Only of having the Comte's remonstrance of the 8th of March registered, which was opposed with a blameworthy obstinacy. Finally, the Council shows itself in one aspect only, it protests that it abhors inscriptions of this kind and that they might bring with them dangerous troubles; that is all very well to tell to people who know nothing about it. The Council perceives that the mine is discovered, and knows that its alliance with the Bishop is found out; that the charges which he has had published were outbursts of angry temper; that the information he laid against Mareuil, without proof and without evidence, has become odious to the public and to private persons, and that, in consequence of this discovery, the Comte drew up a remonstrance upon it in order to leave as a precedent to posterity the efforts he has made to overthrow the usurpation and outrage by the ecclesiastical jurisdiction on the royal authority. However, after all these long debates and disputes, it was ordered that all these documents should remain in the recorder's office to be sent to His Majesty by despatches.

As the Comte saw that the Supreme Council only wished to gain time, and would give no definite decision either regarding his demands or those of the Sieurs Desiourdy, de Mareuil, or Debrieux, he thought it advisable, since it had already been decreed that all the writings on both sides should be sent to the Court, that their opinions should also be recorded in the register both as to the aims of his remonstrance and on proceedings concerning the Sr. de Mareuil and the others named. The Councillors saw from that that the Comte's intention was only to make their conduct known to the Court. Will it be said that this manner of voting con-

matters, instead of upholding [? the law] and counterbalancing the power of the Church, under which the weakness of private individuals is compelled to groan, seems to join it so as to make it more victorious. The Council ordered, on the 11th of June that this proposal should be communicated to the Procureur Général in order that, on his decisions, whatever was right should be decreed.

The Comte was not inclined to expect from the Procureur-General any decisions on his demand; therefore he spoke only through the mouth of the Council, which gave a decree of the 28th of June, by which it was ordered that the voting should be in the ordinary manner. The Comte on his part declared that he only wished his opinion to be registered in order that the King after having had it looked into, might be good enough to judge whether it was good or bad.

You will also see a document, presented to the Governor by the Sieurs Dupont, Depeiras, and de la Martiniere, deputed by the Council, of the 2nd of April, and the one which passed between the Comte and the Procureur Général. In addition, you will see the answer given to the words of the deputies, dated the 29th of April, and the resolution of the Council of the 29th of the same month, with another reply of the Procureur Général, of the 16th of May, to the memorandum of the Comte.

In order to see at once the intention which the Procureur Général had, of disgusting the Comte, it is only necessary to observe what was reported by the Council which, with much difficulty, makes up its mind to confess that it is true that the Comte has said that it was of no′ use to think of setting up a butcher's business, if several people go from one port to another to buy cattle.

Since the word "several" is a general term, why should the Procureur Général take it to himself. If that had in fact referred to him, it would have been prudent on his part to pretend to be unaware of it; if it did not, why commit himself with the Comte and the Intendant, by saying that when he saw their stewards going to buy calves he could do as much for his family. The continuation of this report shows the passion of the Procureur Général and the inclination he had to disoblige the Comte on all kinds of occasions.

It is well to consider all this dispassionately and to notice whether the Comte was not right in demanding that the Procureur Général should withdraw after having given his conclusion, before they passed to the voting; for besides interrupting them while they are deliberating,—as he pretends, with information and explanations on each point—it is clear that he disputes and contradicts the opinion of the judges. He is right to do so, and his interests require it. It only remains to find out whether there is a larger retail dealer than he; whether he does not re-sell butter, meat and bread after having traversed the coasts to buy them.

his servant, with his wife to receive the money for it? Take the trouble
to make inquiries about it, and you will find no one who does not give
this evidence. What opinion, then, can these gentlemen hold on the subject of meat in particular, since they are butchers themselves? Is there
(any) likelihood that they will decide against their own interests? And,
after that, a man of that stamp has no scruple in telling the Governor
that he looks upon him, in the Council as only an honorary councillor;
and the Intendant does not hesitate to tell the Comte, when he wishes to
speak, that he should only do so in his turn.

It is indeed very grievous to the Governor-General to find himself
treated in this manner by people who (except the Intendant) possess no
merit apart from the appointment which the King has done them the
honor to grant them. The annoyance which the Comte has put up with
in the course of these affairs, have compelled me, because of the share
I take in them, to set this faithful account before you. It would appear
indispensable for the Court to pay serious attention to the difficulties
and opposition which Mons. de Frontenac meets with wherever he goes.
Doubtless, the services he has rendered and is rendering to the King are
not recognized in all their distinction. His vigorous resistance, and his
opposition to the tyrants of the Colony cost him dear. This is a strange
country; from the [long] time you have been receiving information concerning it, you must know it well. They cannot bear either men of honor
or men of spirit; only fools, and the slaves of the ecclesiastical domination can live in it. It is a race, if I may venture to say so, which cares
neither for old friends nor old enemies. We breathe a pleasant and
comfortable atmosphere here because of the firmness of the Comte which
is altogether heroic. The Court has only to condemn it and it will see
the Colony at once overwhelmed by the flood, and it will be submerged
beyond all hope of rescue.

But let us return to Montreal, where we shall find the Bishop again,
in dispute with M. de Calliere and (arising from that) with the recollet
Fathers, to the great scandal of all the people. This is the origin of that
affair. A young postulant wishing to take the habit of the order, M. de
Calliere was invited to that ceremony. When he had entered the church
and knelt down at his praying desk, and the mass had begun, the Bishop
perceived it. He started off promptly at the same time, and went and
told him to change his place, or, otherwise, he would go out of the church,

The next day the Bishop sent word to Father Joseph, the Superior of the monastery, to have all the praying desks taken out of his church, particularly that of M. de Calliere; the Superior obeyed this order. M. de Calliere on his part attended mass and had his seat put back in its usual place. Father Joseph informed him of the prohibition which the Bishop had made against it. M. de Calliere declares that, if he will not do it, he will use his authority; and that, as regards the arrangement of the [various] ranks in church, he recognizes no one but the King and the Governor-General; that since the Bishop has taken his place, and no one has disputed it with him, he has his reasons for taking his place, and that no one could take it from him by his authority. Finally, on his wishing to hear mass, the Superior refused to say it so long as his praying desk was in the church. M. de Calliere thought that there had been enough of gentle means, and therefore he had it put back by soldiers. Father Joseph wrote to the Bishop, who was then at the mountain, and informed him of what had taken place in his absence. The Bishop, on his return, having passed in front of the door of the recollets' [church] and recognized M. de Calliere's seat in its place, stormed at Father Joseph, who gave him an account of all he had done, with which he ought to have been satisfied. However, next day the Bishop had notice served on them of the interdict of their church, which these poor priests obeyed blindly for two months setting in motion all sorts of means to persuade their Bishop, who was angry without any reasonable cause. But seeing at last that he was inflexible, and that he would not allow himself to be overcome either by the repeated solicitations of the Intendant or by the plans put forward on the part of the Comte, they resolved to open their church, claiming that the interdict was devoid of justification, contrary to due procedure, and against their privileges. As I am convinced that all the long account of this affair will be communicated to you, I leave it to those [most] interested. All I can say is that they are good priests, very zealous for their missions; who live irreproachable lives, doing their duty thoroughly well, loved, cherished and esteemed by everyone. It is that which makes them hated by all the other orders of priests.

If you received the letters which I had the honor to write to you last year you may have seen the opinions I held concerning the peace which the Abenakis had concluded with the English. What I had conjectured has happened. I informed you that, if the King continued to look after them and we reminded them a little of their dead, reproaching them that

lords of the coast to let their people know that peace had been concluded with the savages of Acadie, and that they had only to work and turn their places to account. As people ever love that which gives them pleasure, and reflect less on matters of joy than on those of sorrow, these ignorant men fell easily into this trap; so that, when they were no longer on their guard, two days after peace had been concluded, the savages fell upon the Pescadouet River and slew a hundred and thirty-five persons and took some prisoners. It may be said that the negotiations of the Sieur de Vilieu, his pains, his presence and his valor, greatly contributed, and did almost everything in this enterprise.

Nothing more remains for me to tell you except that the Colony is in very good condition; no such miseries as those of Europe are to be seen. Fortunately we have a happy, wise and most enlightened government, the protector of the liberty which the King grants to his subjects, the enemy of an odious, ecclesiastical and intolerable domination. One must be here to see the plots which go on every day to upset the design and the projects of a governor. A head as firm and level as that of the Comte is required to hold out against the snares laid for him everywhere. If he wishes for peace, that is enough to make them oppose it, and cry out that all is lost. If he wants to make war, they tell him the Colony will be ruined. He would not have so many troubles on hand if he had not abolished a Hiericho which was a house which the Seminary of Montreal had had built to shut up—they said—girls of bad life; if he had been willing to permit them to take soldiers, and to give them officers, for the purpose of going into houses at midnight to seize women, who had retired with their husbands, for having been at a ball or masked, and have them flogged in this Hiericho until they bled; if he had also said nothing against the curés who went the rounds with some soldiers and compelled the girls and women to shut themselves up at home at 9 o'clock [even] in summer; if he had been willing to forbid the wearing of lace; if he had said nothing about their refusing the sacrament to women of rank for having a "fontange;"* if he did not oppose the excommunications

had had prepared here by a skilful man, one for you, one for M. de la Touche, and the other for the Marquis de Cheury.

I begged the captain of the "Bretonne" to take care of it, but as I have received no news of all that, I am convinced they have been lost, and perhaps my letters intercepted. I have had no news from you this year, but I am much comforted at having learnt that you were in perfect health; I ask no more. I received a letter from Mons. Begon with my commission as captain and an appointment as second lieutenant of a ship of war.

I judged from that that you were not dead. Permit me to thank you very humbly for my promotion [and] to implore you not to leave me half way, and to consider that I am already rather too old for a naval second lieutenant.

I should fill the post of lieutenant much better. That costs the King nothing since we do not receive the pay. But if I were so fortunate, on my return from the Outavois, as to feel this further mark of your patronage I should make ready to go to France, and I might perhaps find opportunities of giving you no cause to repent your having made the fortunes of a man full of boundless gratitude, and of the most devoted follower you have, and [one] moulded by your hand. I beseech you to believe that I am with all my heart. Sir,

Your very humble and very obedient Servant.

La Mothe Cadillac.

Montreal, the 28th Sept. 1694.

I am setting out today to go to the Outavois.

They were received.

He was a naval 2nd tenant fro the 15th o April, 1694 a captain Canada fr the same 1691 he sei in Canada with the r of lieuten

---

The quarrels between Frontenac and Bishop Laval were very bitter. They are mentioned by nearly every writer of the history of Canada of this period.

The minutes of the Council show that a meeting was held August 30, 1694, and a vacation taken till October 11 following. A vacation of unusual length.

Cadillac was appointed to the command of Mackinac in 1694 and the postscript indicates the setting out for his new post.—C. M. B.

PROMOTION OF CADILLAC.

Endorsed—M. de Frontenac. 25th Oct. 1694.

My Lord
*   *   *

You could not imagine what a good impression has been made by the favor you have granted to Captain the Sieur de la Motte Cadillac by giving him a naval second lieutenancy. He is a man of rank, full of capability and valor; and I have just sent him to Missilimakina to command all those posts of the upper [country] and to fill the place of the Sieur de Louvigny de Laporte, who has applied to be relieved and is going to France to see his father who has been sending for him for two years, which you will approve of. He has performed his duty well while he has been in these distant parts for more than four years, and to the satisfaction of every one. I hope his successor will do no less well, since he has all the adroitness, firmness and tact which is required for managing the dispositions of all these savages, who are not easy to govern.

*   *   *

My Lord, Your very humble, &c

Frontenac.

At Quebec, the 25th of Oct. 1694.
P. S. of the 4th of Nov.   *   *   *

LICENSES TO TRADE ARE REVOKED.

Endorsed—Colonies. 13th Oct. 1697. M. de Champigny.

causing it to be published throughout all the Colony, with instructions
to issue a copy of it in the distant places where there have been any
Frenchmen up to the present time. You will see from the joint letter,
which Mons. de Frontenac and I are doing ourselves the honor of writing
to you, what arrangements we have made for putting a stop to this
trading in the distant countries altogether, and making all the French
return from them next year. But I feel obliged to tell you here that it
was not my fault that that was not done sooner. Last year, when we
were informed of your wishes, we could have sent our orders for the
French to come down this year. I spoke to M. de Frontenac about it,
and he replied that it was too late; I spoke to him of it again in the
Spring, but he told me that, independently of the order from the Court,
he had (before receiving it) sent word to the Sr. de la Motte Cadillac,
Commandant over the Outaouais, to make them come down, and he did
not wish me to send there before his return, which took place at the end
of the month of August, with only some of the French. I hope those who
are left, and those to whom we gave leave to go for their furs, will be
careful to come down next year.

21.

We held a meeting at the house of M. de Frontenac on the 11th of
Sept. to which he summoned MM. de Vaudreuil, Provost. the Marquis
de Crisafy, Galifet, Sabercase and La Motte Cadillac to consider what
it was most advisable to do regarding several officers belonging to the
upper countries; the measures which would be taken to bring the French
back, and to prevent them from trading there in future, were agreed
upon, which were committed to writing by me in a paper prepared at the
time, a copy of which is hereto annexed.

22.

M. de Frontenac, at the same meeting, having asked for our advice in
writing as to the preservation or abandonment of the forts we have at
Missillimakinac and in the other distant countries, I was of opinion that
they should be preserved, for the reasons which I state in the same paper
—Index letter H—But, as my chief aim is to carry out the orders of the
King, I pass by these said reasons to notify to you, My Lord, that, so
long as there are French garrisons not only at *Missillimakinac and
among the Miamis but also at Fort St. Louis of the Illinois, there will be
opportunities and pretexts for continuing to trade there, whatever precautions may be taken to prevent goods from being conveyed there, a
thing which it will always be easy* to do as this country is open on every
side for going there, or even by the trail of the savages, and this cannot
be stopped altogether until there is an end to Frenchmen going there or

*Forts of t
upper cou
will alway
supply pre
texts for
ing as lon
any of th
remain.*

10

being there; moreover these posts involve expenditure every year, *which we shall be freed from by abandoning them.*

You will see in the same paper, My Lord, my opinion as to Fort Fron-tenac.

t Fronte-
of no ser-
ɛ and of
at expense.

I have not discovered, thus far, that it has been of any service, but only a cause of expense and of dangerous risk to those who go in small parties to revictual it, if the enemy care ever so little to profit by their vantage. This my duty compels me to notify you again now; and that it is impossible to keep up this post with six times the cost of that of Chambly.

times as
ɔh expense
or Cham-

23.

Mention was made at the same meeting of the pretended settlement formed by the man named Le Sueur on the Mississipy river at a place where he says there are copper and lead mines. I believe the mines he is after in these parts are of beaver-skins only, and that when we put a stop to the trade in the other countries, he will well know how to profit by it, whether along the course of the Mississipy, where the savages in alliance with us are settled, or by attracting them to the same place. All my opinions on that matter are fully explained in my memorandum. Index letter H, to which I beg you, My Lord, to pay some attention.

24.

I was extremely surprised to learn from a letter which the Sr. de la Touche, Commissary, wrote me from Montreal at the beginning of the month of Sept. last, that the Sr. de Tonty, captain on half pay, had set out thence with five merchants of the same town to go to the country of Outaouais; and at the same time it was reported to me that several Frenchmen having appeared, on their example, to wish to do the same, had been prevented by authority. As soon as I received this news, I spoke to M. de Frontenac about it, being unaware for my part whether

or indirectly, for I have been informed that a quantity of goods left Montreal at the very time of their departure, and during the night.

25.

His Majesty has permitted the Sieurs de Tonty and de la Forest to keep Fort St. Louis of the Ilinois on condition that they do not trade in beaver-skins there. Fort St. of the Illi

I can assure you, My Lord, with absolute certainty, that they will not stay there, and in fact cannot stay there, except to trade in them; otherwise it will involve them in an expense which they will be unable to bear. Hence it must be expécted and taken as beyond doubt that, if they are allowed to go and to remain there with Frenchmen, they alone will carry on the trade with the savages in the distant countries with *immense profits.* It is well also to inform you, My Lord, *that they have* now a *warehouse at Chicagou in the country of the Miamis* and another at *Missillimakinac* and that they have sent boats to other places, two of which have been rifled by the Ilinois savages when they wished to take them to the savages called Scioux who are the enemies of the others. And to show you in what hand and under whose command all the distant countries are, it is right to inform you that the Sr. de la Forest *is in command at Missillimackinac; the Sr. de Tonty,* owner with him of Fort St. Louis of the Ilinois, has gone to the country of the Assinibouelles savages which is a very distant tribe to the north, where there are beavers in abundance: the Sr. de Tonty, half pay captain, his brother, is the one who left *Montreal unknown to me* at the beginning of September, to go and take *command in the place of the Sr. de la Forest at Missillimakinac;* and the Sr. de Liette, a subordinate ôfficer of the troops, cousin of the Sieurs de Tonty, commands at the post of Chicagou, in the country of the Miamis. All have but one and the same mind and but one interest, tending solely to trading.

26.

The aim of His Majesty, to bring the French together within the Colony, and put a stop to the journeys they used to make in the interior of the woods, is the surest means of succeeding in what he designs, namely to increase it for cultivating the land and the fishing industry,

King's ships which come to this country should be ballasted with it, the cost of which might be taken out of the funds which are ordered [for us], we should sell it at a price sufficiently profitable for the King, which nevertheless would be much less than that which our merchants sell it at, and it would be far easier and more profitable for the inhabitants to engage in that trade.

27.

His Majesty having resolved no longer to permit any Frenchmen to go to the distant countries, it will be important to make use of the missionaries to keep the savages who are allied to us, to our interests, and to divert them from the intentions they might have of attaching themselves to the English, making them understand that the King is withdrawing the French from them, only in order to give them the chance of trading themselves with the distant tribes, and that they will find a considerable profit in it, obtaining goods at Montreal much cheaper than in the places where they live, and thus profiting by the advantages which the French found in conveying them to their homes. And in order to strengthen their weakness of mind, it will be well to assure them of protection from His Majesty still more special than it has been; and that the Iroquois our common enemies, will be prevented by all means from making any attempts against them, so far as it is in our power.

28.

Besides the reasons which the King had for suppressing the licenses and ordering the French to be brought back from the back-woods, there is a very important one, namely that these said Frenchmen, by taking the side of one tribe against another, would infallibly have set all our allied savages at variance and at enmity [with us] which would afterwards have given rise to very great embarrassment. These Miami savages having made war this year on the Sioux, several Frenchmen who were on the spot sided with the latter against the others and killed some of them. It is to be hoped that that may not have further consequences for us, and that the Miamis will not take occasion from that to ally them-

of the savages to those who distributed to them His Majesty's presents, as it concerns chiefly the governors and officers commanding among the distant tribes, cannot be carried out without causing them some pain. The little I have said on this point pledges me to write thus to you of it; and, as it might be the occasion, especially as regards M. de Frontenac, of impairing the accord which you enjoin on me, allow me if you please, My Lord, to defer carrying out this order until I have learnt more fully your will.

*   *   *   *   *

Your very humble, very obedient and most obliged servant

Champigny.

Quebec, the 13th October 1697.

PLANS TO CAPTURE NEW YORK.

Endorsed—The Comte de Frontenac 15th Oct. 1697. Colonies.

My Lord

On the 28th of May I received through the Sieur Vincelotte, a Canadian whom M. de Gabaret had sent to me from Monts Dezerts, the first notification you gave me of the plans of His Majesty, and of the preparations he ordered me to make by your letter of the 6th of March last and, since, in the other dispatches which came to me by way of Plaisance on the same day, of the 9th of March and 21st of April.

After I had communicated it to M. de Champigny, we neither of us lost a moment in preparing Quebec to make a vigorous defence if we were attacked there, and in getting everything ready which would be necessary for going to join the squadron of the Marquis de Nesmond, on the notice which I was to receive from him concerning it.

They set to work forthwith on the fortifications which the Engineer, the Sr. Le Vasseur thought it advisable to construct; he has carried them out with great care and intelligence. I also arranged at the same time for the number of men you ordered, both of the troops and of the militia. I sent part of them down to Quebec. giving instructions that the rest should be prepared to go on the first word of command. The Intendant, on his part, got ready all the provisions and stores, with the boats which you wrote to me of; and hence all things were so well arranged that, a week after receiving news from the Marquis de Nesmond, I could have

·party; for, as to my good will, My Lord. I believe you would have no doubt.

But after having been nearly three months in this position and in a continual state of expectation, I saw with much regret from the letter which the Marquis de Nesmond wrote me, which I did not receive until the 8th of September, through the Sr. Desursins, with your dispatch of the 28th of April, that contrary winds had made him so long in crossing, that no room remained for hoping that the project committed to his charge could be carried out. He will not have failed, for his part, to give you a precise account of the obstacles he met with, and I will content myself with saying merely, that expeditions of this kind are always very uncertain, and that much more time ought to be taken for carrying them out than is thought likely to be required; these junctions, too, by sea and rivers as difficult as ours are always very doubtful; while the difficulty of conveying sufficient provisions in boats is almost insuperable.

Nevertheless we had resolved to take enough for a month which, whatever may be said and whatever memorandum may be presented [on the question], is very nearly the time which would have been required for a sufficiently large number of men and boats to go to the lower part of the St. John River. But I do not know how we should have had any left for the return unless the ships had had a sufficient supply to provide for our subsistence during the stay we should have made with them on these coasts, and to furnish what we should have been in want of for the return to this country.

If His Majesty still intends this scheme [to be carried out] it is absolutely necessary to reckon as I point out to you, My Lord, unless it be desired to make a mistake, and to put all those who set out from here in danger of perishing.

I will also take the liberty of saying that the capture of Manath would be much more advantageous for the safety of this Colony, and for delivering it from the Iroquois than that of Boston, by which it is in no

comes these little rivers and the lakes met with there are generally frozen.

I have no doubt My Lord that the manner in which you were good enough to give His Majesty an account of what I had done in the expedition of the last campaign, has largely contributed to his approving of what took place; and the satisfaction therewith, which you assure me he showed, is a new mark of the warmth with which you are good enough to make the most of the services which I endeavor to render him. I beg you to be pleased ever to continue to me the same support, for, without that, I should run the risk of being completely forgotten being at such a great distance as I am, and with such a number of people on the spot who are within easier reach of asking and obtaining the favors which may be proper for them.

I consider myself greatly honored by the one which the King has conferred on me by granting me a cross of St. Louis, since all the marks of his continued esteem which he gives must be exceedingly precious. Yet if His Majesty had been so gracious as to grant it me at the time of the establishment of that order, as I might have hoped with as much ground as many others, who had not been crippled for 50 years as I have and had not, like me, worked at its first institution, I should now be in a position to hope for the same distinction and advantages as they have derived from it, which at my age I probably cannot wait long for if His Majesty adheres to this, that I am [merely] to enter that order, and will not have some regard to the long standing of my service, of my wounds, and of my employment.

If I dared, My Lord, I would beg you to present to him my very humble and very respectful thanks, as I did not think I ought to take the liberty of offering them to him myself in a private letter.

You may think that, on account of the position I was placed in after receiving your dispatches, I could not make any important expeditions all this summer, nor carry out the plans I had formed for this campaign; and that I had to be contented with detaching very small parties to keep harrassing the enemy. This did not fail to have its effect for they have let us get through our sowing and our harvest very peacefully.

The Iroquois were so afraid that I should go and pay them another visit in their villages, and had also impressed it so deeply on the people of Orange, that the Governor of Manath passed part of the winter there and had strengthened the garrison by more than 500 men, savages and regular English troops. This he could not do without great expense,

use of the intervention of certain Onnejoust chiefs, (whom I had permitted to return to their country to bring back the rest of their families
which had not been able to come to our settlements last year,) to present
four belts to me and to ascertain from me whether I would consent to
their sending deputies to me to open entirely fresh negotations for peace.

Although I was convinced that this was only one of their usual arti-
fices for trifling with me, I would not quite shut the door against them,
and sent them word back by the same way that I gave them up to the end
of the month of September to come, not only with their principal chiefs
and their families, but with all the prisoners that they have left, after
which period I would not listen any more to any negotiation.   It has
expired; hence I do not think I was mistaken in telling you that there
was no great trust to be placed in anything they propose. The *Statement*
I am sending you will inform you of all particulars concerning everything most noteworthy which has taken place in this country since last
year.

His Majesty did me justice when he would not attribute to me the
abuses which it is stated there have been in the working of the licenses;
and if I have taken the liberty of representing to you the objections there
would be to suppressing them altogether, that was only because of the
fatal and ruinous consequences to the Colony which I foresaw would arise
from it.

As I have nothing to add to the reasons I sent you on the point last
year, I will not think of repeating them to you again; and I will content
myself with hoping that those of the persons who think they understand
this country so well may be found, from their success, better than mine.
We have, however, caused the decree of the King to be promulgated and
have begun to have it carried out with the utmost rigor; and orders have
been given for recalling generally, next year, not only all the Voyageurs
but also all the soldiers who are at the posts, and the commandants, not
excepting the Sr. de Tonty, captain on half-pay, to whom I had given
orders, in case the Sr. De la Mothe Cadillac should come down with the
convoy of the French and savages, which we were expecting to go back
again with these latter and five Frenchmen only in order to return speedily to Missilimakinac and take command there in the absence of the said
Sr. De la Mothe.

Although you left us at liberty to leave a few soldiers at Missilimakinac and with the Miamis, the difficulties or rather the impossibility of

and the other of Quebec, with the Sr. de la Mothe, Captain, who had recently returned from the post of Missilimakinac where he was Commandant, and consequently had more knowledge as to the disposition of the minds of the savages,—for the purpose of taking counsel with them as to what it would be most advisable to do.

They agreed, almost unanimously, that it would be impossible for any officers and soldiers who might be left there to live on their pay [*literally,* "their salary, and their pay"] ; and that the expense of sending it to them every year in the form of provisions or goods would be extremely heavy for, besides the fact that these consignments would often be very uncertain, strong escorts would always be required for taking them; also that that would give rise to sending up Canadians [*literally* "New Frenchmen"] among these tribes every year, which appeared to me to be contrary to the intention of His Majesty. Hence, I have resolved to order down not only all these Voyageurs but [also] the commandants and soldiers who are at the posts; and this the rather as I do not think the 28 or 30 soldiers whom we could have left in the posts of Missilimakinac and the Miamis would be sufficient to prevent the tribes of the upper country from insulting them if they once league themselves with the Iroquois and the English, as we foresee will very soon happen, seeing that they will no longer be supported by the Voyageurs who were in those countries, and that the Commandant of Missilimakinac used to call them together when he suspected mischief, which repressed their audacity and inspired them with fear.

The Intendant will no doubt send you long report, from which you will learn what we have decided without any difference of opinion with these gentlemen whom we called together, and that his [opinion] regarding the preservation or abandonment of these two posts was different from the decision I arrived at, his reasons not having appeared to me so strong as those of these other gentlemen and the special knowledge which I have of it, in which Mons. de Calliere to whom I had also written about it, has confirmed me too by the replies he made to me.

You will see, My Lord, from the same report, that it has not been forgotten to refer to Fort Frontenac there, which, as you know, has not had the good fortune to please him for a long time. But, as I find him almost alone in this country in his opinion, and as I am more and more convinced. of its utility, they have now set out to re-victual it; and I am sure you will find nothing excessive in the expense for, although he has sent you word that more than 700 men would be required for taking there what was necessary, that will be done with less than 150, who may also be able on their way back to strike some blow at the Iroquois if they are fortunate enough to find them.

The Sr. De la Mothe Cadillac, after having been in command at Missili-

the convoy safely, and, on the information which Mons. De Callieres found means of giving him, that we were threatened with an attack at Quebec, he of his own accord induced 300 of the most important [of the] savages to come down with him, which would have been a large reinforcement and a very necessary assistance.

He has given me a very precise account of the condition of his command. He put several parties in the field against the Iroquois, and our allies came back from them victorious, having killed or taken prisoners a hundred and two warriors of the tribe of the Sonnontouan. The last fight took place on the water, in Lake Erie, with equal numbers; and it was so fierce that, both sides having come to land with their canoes, they despatched each other with their knives. There remained on the field 40 Iroquois and there were 15 prisoners; our allies sustained a small loss.

I cannot forbear assuring you, My Lord, that it would be impossible to be more pleased than I am with the vigilance and good behavior of this officer, of which he has given us proofs on very important occasions; and that compels me to ask you, as I have done already, to grant him a commission as Lieutenant of a ship of war as a recompense for the fatigues and toils he has undergone.

I should have liked to have been able to induce him to return to Missilimakinac, where he has succeeded so well; but, as he has represented to me the quarrels and difficulties which the Missionaries there tried to raise against him, for having wanted to correct the abuses which they had introduced there, I yielded to his representations, all the more easily because the Sr. de Tonty had already set out to go and take his place, so as not to leave that post without a Commandant.

I feel myself also obliged to inform you that the said Sr. De la Mothe Cadillac furnished memorials to the late Mons. de Seignelay, and that he has since sent us plans of Baston, Manoth and the coasts from Acadie up to the latter place, with memorials concerning the schemes which might be carried out against our enemies. I have since examined them, and cannot but approve of them.

Up to the present time, the Intendant has given me but little informa-

that detachments of a hundred, or two hundred men at most, sent out repeatedly one after the other at suitable times, would produce a better result. That is also the course I should have taken this year, and in the direction you mention to me, if the orders from the Court had not, as I have already told you, kept me in a state of uncertainty. I still hold by the same plan, and I will seize the proper opportunity for carrying it out.

I have received the cipher which you sent me, and will not fail to make use of it when the opportunity offers.

No one can be more obliged to you than I can, for the promotion you have obtained for the Sr. de Bonnaventure. I hope he will never give you reason to be sorry for it.

Although you were not able this year to obtain for my Secretary, what he took the liberty to ask you for, he hopes,—as well as I—after the gracious terms in which you are good enough to write to me about him, that you will not forget him when the opportunity presents itself, and that you will not object to my wife and my friends reminding you of it.

It is true that the Sr. Sarrazin was, four years ago, surgeon-major of the troops; and that, having first withdrawn from this place for a year into a seminary with the intention of becoming a priest, and having notified us that he wished to give up his post, we were obliged to write for another to be sent to us, and he arrived here before the said Sr. Sarrazin left to proceed to France. He is a very skilful man, thoroughly accomplished in his profession, loved and respected here by everyone; and he has served in the armies for a very long time, both on land and sea.

I have since learnt that the said Sr. Sarrazin, having changed his plans, has applied himself to the study of medicine in Paris, in which it is said he has succeeded well, a thing which cannot but be very useful in this country. Therefore, My Lord, it will be good of you to consider granting him the means of subsistence there; but I ask you above all things that that may in no way, lessen the [value] which is placed on the Sr. Baudeau, Surgeon Major, who is a man who ought positively to be taken care of.

I am very glad His Majesty has deigned to confirm the arrangement I had made provisionally between the Sr. de Ramezay, and the Captains of the Marines, and that it is found to be in conformity with the one which had already been made for the islands of America, and with his intentions. He is a very good officer who has judgment, and can be employed

I have taken every possible pains to try and get the Sr. de Villieu out of prison, having several times charged the Sr. de Villebon to convey some very urgent letters which I wrote to the Commandant of Baston on his account. But, whether he has not found means of doing so, or whether, remembering the old quarrels they had together, he has neglected it, he does not appear to me to have put himself to much trouble in the matter, for, although I have received several of his letters, he has not even condescended to give me any answer regarding it, nor have I received any from the Commandant of Baston, so that I am unable to let you know, My Lord, what has become of him.

As to the Sr. de Beaucourt, I have learnt that he did not come over in the squadron of Mons. de Nesmond, not having, perhaps, proceeded to La Rochelle in time enough to embark there, and we have not heard word of him in this country.

They have sent me this year His Majesty's confirmation of the Captain's commission which I had given to the Sr. du Luth in the place of the Sr. Ohler de Crisaffy, who died at the beginning of last year. But they have forgotten to add thereto those of five or six different officers on whom I had bestowed at the same time, the posts which the promotion of the said Sr. du Luth to that of Captain, together with the absence of another Lieutenant on half-pay, who had gone to France the previous year, had left vacant. That was six months before I could know that it was the King's intention to abolish the captaincies and half-pay lieutenancies which might fall vacant, and that he did not wish me to grant any more commissions. However, they have been discharging the duties of their appointments since that time, and it would be a great agitation and a great mortification to them, and to me, if I may venture to say so, if it should now be necessary to deprive them of their rank. Therefore I take the liberty again *of sending you the statement* and begging you not to do this injury alike to them and to me, since I acted in good faith. Moreover they are very good men; and His Majesty may rest assured that these

tinction, to our securing to him his pay from the date of his commission. This is what we beg of you again this year.

For three months there has been a little dispute between the Intendant and me concerning a decree which he gave, together with certain Councillors of the Supreme Council, as to the adjudication of a prize which the Sr. Aubert, a merchant of this town, had taken under a warrant which he had from me to cruise against the enemy, of which [decree] I thought myself bound to suspend the execution, but only as regards the distribution of the moneys accruing from its sale, as I observed that Mons. de Champigny had had but little thought of preserving the rights of the King and of the Admiralty; and, in default of him [I thought] my duty compelled me to see to it and to secure their safety.

The Sr. de la Louisiere, in whom I beg you to have confidence, will hand you this dispatch. He is fully informed of all that has passed in this matter; and he will render a very precise account [of it] to you or to those whom you may wish to delegate for that purpose. I will content myself merely with telling you that Mons. de Champigny, who wants to convince everyone of his moderation, has been in terrible rages on this occasion having used abusive words and threats against people who had not deserved them, and could not help carrying out the orders I gave in the matter, especially the Sr. de Lotbiniere, Lieutenant General of the provost's district and admiralty of this town, who is a very honorable man and most upright, whom he threatened that he would get discharged from his post.

I myself have not escaped the manifestations of his temper, but mine has not been excited by it, and moreover, without being moved by it, I have simply pursued my own course and done what I believed to be my duty.

It only remains for me now, My Lord, to beg you ever to continue your goodness to me, and to procure for me the same favors as you have obtained for me every year, and I do not doubt that you will add new ones to them when the opportunity offers, for you must be quite assured that you will never interest yourself for anyone who is with more sincere and more respectful devotion

My Lord

Your very humble, very obedient and most obliged servant,

Frontenac.

Quebec, this 15th Oct. 1697.

You did me a great favor, My Lord, in obtaining a fund of 3000# for

The complaints made to me by the chief officers of the conduct of the Sr. Dupin, Lieutenant, induced me to compel him to make use, this year, of a permission you sent him the year before. He left here, with much difficulty, on a small vessel which was wrecked in our river. This officer is absolutely unfit to serve,—not to say more about it. Mons. de Vaudreuil may be able to give you still more information about it.

If you approve, My Lord, of the proposal which Mons. de Champigny and I make to you in our joint letter regarding Mons. de Valrenne, I should have to ask you to grant his company to the Sr. de la Valterie who is a captain on half-pay, a good officer, who has been married and settled in this country for a long time. He is the brother-in-law of the said Sr. de Valrenne who was in the regiment of Carignan when he came to this country, in which he had served with distinction, having been previously Lieutenant in the guard of Marshall Destrades.

F. F.

I am sending you, My Lord, a petition from the Sr. de Grandpré who has been the Major at Three Rivers for five years and is certainly worthy of the favor he asks of you, and what induces me to beg you to do so more urgently is that, as I am obliged sometimes to send Mons. de Ramezay out of his government on distant expeditions, it is necessary that some one should remain to fill his place on whom I can rely. The latter has all the [necessary] capability for it.

F. F.

A SUIT AGAINST CADILLAC.

Endorsed—Colonies. M. de Champigny 3d of July, 1698.

My Lord,

I find myself compelled to inform you of what has taken place during the preliminary consideration of an action which has been brought by two private individuals in this country called Moreau and Durand against the Sr. de la Mothe Cadillac, captain of a company of the detachment of

And on my warning him thereupon, in several letters, to put a stop to these causes of complaint, he assured me many times in his replies that there was no foundation for them, and that I should be satisfied of that when I had heard him on his return; which made me wait until the month of Sept. 1697 when he returned to the Colony.

He had no sooner arrived at Quebec than Moreau and Durand presented a long petition to me against him, in which I observed that he had in 1696 sent for boats fraudulently loaded with merchandise, of which Moreau and Durand had been in charge, and that he had done a large trade at Missilimakinac while he was in command there having sold to these two individuals goods to the amount of nearly 7000# in the year 1696, which he had had brought up in the spring of the same year, among which were included 198 pots of brandy at the rate of 25# a pot, French money, which only costs 3# at Montreal, ready money; and all that contrary to the express prohibitions of the King laid down in his dispatches written in common to Mons. de Frontenac and me in the years 1692, 1693 and 1694, and in two decrees issued by me in consequence, in the said years 1693 and 1694; which were published in the Colony before M. de la Mothe's departure for Missilimakinac.

As these acts of disobedience on his part were connected with the matters which formed the claims of Moreau and Durand against him, I thought myself bound to reserve the trial for my hearing and prepare it for hearing so that I might ascertain the truth concerning the complaints against the Sr. la Mothe.

As the incidents which have arisen in the prosecution of this suit are important, in that the Comte de Frontenac and the Supreme Council are mixed up in it, as well as myself in the duties of my office, it is indispensably necessary, My Lord, to inform you of all the circumstances. I will therefore begin by telling you that Moreau and Durand were hired by the wife of the Sr. la Mothe to take a boat to her husband at Missilimakinac in the month of April, 1696, according to the authority which Mons. de Frontenac had granted for it, for 100# wages each, with permission also to take goods to the value of 100# each which they were to trade in for their own profit.

Instead of adhering to that on both sides, the wife of the Sr. la Mothe made use of these two persons to take two boats loaded with goods for her husband, one of which was [taken] fraudulently; and these two guides, wishing to make the most of the opportunity loaded goods on their own account on these boats to the value of four or five hundred livres beyond what their agreement provided for.

The Sr. de la Touche, Commissary at Montreal, having gone to the upper part of the Colony in order to examine the boats which were going

in.it, for it was only partly loaded, and it was sold by auction, the proceeds of which after deducting expenses, were 675#, French money, which
were applied to the hospital at Montreal, to aid in rebuilding the wards.
for the poor which had been burnt down.   When the Sr. de la Touche notified me of this seizure, he informed me that, in the same boat, were
found about 40 pots of brandy, which were applied for by Moreau who
was taking the boat of the Sr. La Mothe for which there was a permit, to
whom he caused them to be given up on the evidence which was put before
him by the Sr. d'Argenteuil commanding the Voyageurs who were setting
out, and by other persons, that this brandy was for the use of the said
Moreau and his companions, at the rate of 13 pots each, as I had settled
in concert with Mons. de Frontenac.   This brandy,—the Sr. de la Touche
was assured—had been put, by mistake, on the boat taken fraudulently,
having been near to the goods which were intended for the cargo of that
boat.   Nevertheless, he might have paid no regard to this evidence.

Moreau and Durand as well as other persons whom I heard, informed
me that, notwithstanding this seizure, two and a half or three boat
[-loads] went up at the same time for the said Sr. la Mothe, which were
taken to him at Missilimakinac, where, a few days after their arrival,
goods to the value of nearly 7000# were sold to the said Moreau and Durand, of which I had the honor to speak to you at the beginning of this
letter.

About a month after this sale, the Sr. la Mothe having sent Durand to
prison for refusing to pay for the dog of a savage which he had wounded,
Durand sent word to the Sr. la Mothe that he would not keep the bargain
he had made about his goods; and Moreau his partner, having refused to
take it on himself alone was also put in prison. the Sr. La Mothe pretending that he had tried to get Durand out.   After that the Sr. la Mothe,
while they were prisoners, had taken out of their huts, not only the goods
they had bought from him, but also those which belonged to them, with
their arms, provisions, boats and clothing; and having opened their
chests, he found in Moreau's several promissory notes, a bond and other
papers which the Sr. de la Mothe also seized on the ground of the information he had, from the invoices which were there, of the goods.that Moreau

until about 18 months after. Their chief claims were that he must pay them 200# for their wages; [the price of] all the goods he had taken from them, at their value at the places of trade, and the sum total of their bills and bond, for having taken from them the means of obtaining payment for them from their debtors when they were at the said place, and for keeping them from them since, and not producing them, having also perhaps caused payment to be made to him for all expenses, damages, and interests under them; and that the Sr. la Mothe could not claim anything against them for having taken goods in excess of the 100# each for which they had permission, which had been taken on the boats fraudulently, in which they said they had the same right as he.

The Sr. La Mothe on his side, claimed that the profits arising from the goods brought by them beyond the 100# allowed them belonged to him; that they owed him for the goods that were wanting out of those he had sold them at Missillimakinac when he took them back; and that he ought not to be answerable for what was owing to Moreau and Durand under the bills and the bond he seized.

After these disputed points and others which proceeded from them had been argued before me and documents had been filed on both sides. I thought it advisable when the case was prepared to take it to the Supreme Council to decide upon it together with those who constitute it, as I had done in similar occurrences; and at this point the parties betook themselves to arbitration before two merchants of Quebec. to whom I referred the case, on condition that they should refer it back to me after judgment, as to the King's interests.

New disputes arose before these arbitrators which caused them to ask for an inquiry, which I commissioned the Sr. Dupuy, local* lieutenant of the provostship of Quebec, to make, on a petition which was presented to me by Moreau who was the only remaining suitor against the Sr. la Mothe on account of the withdrawal of Durand. It was a question of learning the price which the goods had been sold for both in the country of the Scioux savages, (where Moreau after he came out of prison at Missilimakinac had been to trade with goods he had borrowed in order to obtain a living), and at the place called the point of Chagonámigon and at Missillimackinac; and no explanation was given by these arbitrators of the reasons they had for asking for this inquiry. But the Sr. la Mothe, thinking it was for the purpose of valuing the goods which he had taken from Moreau and Durand at the rate at which similar articles had been disposed of to the Scioux in the journey which Moreau had made there,—which would have made them amount to large

orders were only not to go there through the country of the Renards; that the Sr. la Mothe had also sent trading [parties] there since, making his people go by way of the Illinois; and that many Voyageurs had likewise been there. On this incident, the Sr. Dupuy deferred holding the inquiry until the Sr. la Mothe should inform him of the intentions of M. de Frontenac on this matter. But as he did not comply with this within the period of the delay which he granted him, except by a declaration which he himself made in writing stating that my said Sr. de Frontenac did not think that anyone ought to have gone contrary to the orders given against going to the Scioux without having spoken to him about it, nor that anyone would be daring enough to show disrespect for it, which are the very words of which the Sr. la Mothe made use. the said Sr. Dupuy proceeded to the inquiry in question, thinking that he ought not to delay any longer merely on the report of an interested party who gave us evidence of what he put forward, moreover that his declaration was not in the least an order from M. de Frontenac not to do so, and that further the orders against going to the Scioux, if there had been any, might only have been given, as several witnesses deposed before me, against going through the country of the Renards. Nevertheless M. de Frontenac sent, next day, for the Sr. Dupuy and his clerk; and, after having had the inquiry they had made read to him, upon this judge telling him that he had proceeded with it, not in obedience to a judgment of the arbitrators, as he reproached him with doing, but in consequence of my decree having delegated him for that purpose, M. de Frontenac said to him—It is on that account that I send you to prison; which was done, and he remained there for two days. This all shows, My Lord, how far his violence has gone, against a man who was carrying out my order; who, on his part, being full of integrity and honor, did not deserve such bad treatment. And this should give you a good idea of the attitude of M. de Frontenac and should induce you, as I very humbly beg of you, to protect us from such outrages.

The arbitrators, being intimidated by this imprisonment and by the threats of M. de Frontenac of which I was a witness, and seeing his concern for the interests of the Sr. la Mothe, withdrew a few days after-

challenged on account of my mandate [as Intendant], and the other to the Council that he might be referred to the provostship of Quebec, the Lieutenant-General of which is the godfather of his wife. On this it was decreed at the said Council, after it knew how little ground there was for the suggestions of the two petitions of the Sr. La Mothe, that the case should be decided there and that I should remain one of the judges; which made him resolve to sue before the King and the gentlemen of his Council for an annulment of this decree, on the refusal of his request for the case to be referred to the provostship of Quebec for hearing; and M. de Frontenac, taking his side, came to the Council, to which he addressed a long remonstrance aiming at leaving the Sr. la Mothe at liberty to sue in France, and his speech ended by saying that if the members paid no regard to what he was putting before them, he would consider what he should have to do. On this, and after the Procureur-Général had stated his opinion, in which he cited the strong reasons there were for not trans-ferring poor suitors to France since they were unable to go to plead there, and also that it was not the will of the King, it was decided that the Council should be absolved from taking cognizance of this trial; that I should arrange for the suitors as I thought fit; and that the docu-ments referred to in the decree should be sent to you, My Lord, in order that you might be pleased to make known to the members the will of His Majesty as to this matter and others of a similar kind. And it having been declared by the same decree that I was to take up the case again and settle it, as Intendant, and under the powers of my appointment, M. de Frontenac who was present stated and caused it to be written down that, since I would take up the case again to try it, I should answer to His Majesty whether I had not exceeded the authority I claimed to have, and contravened his decrees.

I do not think, My Lord, that you would have approved of my conduct if, by weak compliance with the intention the Sr. la Mothe had of remov-ing the cognizance of this matter from all the judges in Canada, which is fully proved by the documents which he caused to be put in at the trial, I had assisted his purpose, which could not but be to prevent a decision on it, through Moreau, his adversary, being unable, as he knows he is, to go to France to sue regarding his claims. Moreover the parties had with-out raising any objection, pleaded, orally and in writing, and produced evidence before me, who may indeed be considered the natural judge of this matter, especially as it is a question of a trade carried on by the Sr. la Mothe contrary to the express prohibitions of the King, and as it is difficult for the nature of affairs of this kind to be understood in France. These reasons induced me to give judgment in this case, solely with the object of doing justice.

After I took up the case again, the Sr. la Mothe refused to appear at

the information that was possible as to the facts which were in question,
I gave my decision under which the Sr. la Mothe was ordered to pay
Moreau the sums of 1866# 0s 4d, 600# and 99# for the reasons therein
stated. I can assure you, My Lord, that I have taken all possible care
with this matter not only because it is my bounden duty to give decisions
full of justice and equity, but also to make it necessary for the Sr. la
Mothe to pay Moreau for what he is withholding from him. However, the
· day after the decision was reported to the Sr. la Mothe, he obtained from
M. de Frontenac an order prohibiting its being executed, on pain of disobedience, although M. de Frontenac had not taken cognizance of the case,
for which it would have been necessary to examine sixty-four documents,
which this trial consists of, which were in my possession; and he forgot
that he had said at the Supreme Council, namely, as I have before stated,
that since I was taking up this trial again to give judgment upon it, I
should give my reasons for doing so to His Majesty; to which, it seems
to me he ought to have adhered. Nevertheless this order has prevented
Moreau from obtaining payment. And as his only resource to succeed in
that was to attach the beaver and other skins of the Sr. la Mothe which
were to come down for him this year from the upper country, for the
rest of the trade he has done there; and as the said Sr. la Mothe had
taken the precaution last year—as I have since learnt at the Bureau des
Fermes—to send letters of exchange to France to the amount of 27596#
4s, which were handed to him for the beaver-skins he sent in; Moreau
presented a petition to me to beg M. de Frontenac to allow him to seize
the effects of the said Sr. la Mothe, or to give him responsible security.
But whatever request I have made to M. de Frontenac not to prevent
Moreau from obtaining payment, has had no effect, except many threats
and much ill-treatment to Moreau, and an increased assistance of the
Sr. la Mothe. And this I cannot understand, considering the bad conduct and the irregularities of that officer while he was in command at
Missillimakinac of which I shall have the honor of informing you, My
Lord, after I have completed the prosecutions which are going on against
him and others for contraventions of the orders of the King, which were
partly known to me through the law-suit he had with Moreau, in giving
judgment on which I reserved [my decision] on them, in order to obtain
more complete information before giving a decision on them.

you an account of it, you will be convinced of the justice of my decision. Permit me, in this spirit, to beg you to have justice done to Moreau. whom poverty renders unable to go to France to maintain his rights before the King's Council of State against the chicanery of the Sr. la Mothe; and to consider that, if the prohibitions issued by M. de Frontenac against executing my judgment take away from Moreau all hope of being paid (for the Sr. la Mothe will not fail to send all the rest of his property to France this year), it is entirely just to provide for that by your authority.

It is also necessary, and I beg you to approve, My Lord, of my informing you that on the very day on which the judgment was reported to the Sr. la Mothe, M. de Frontenac prohibited Moreau from leaving Quebec as he was just about to go fishing in the river, thus mortifying not only this poor settler, but also the Sr. Pachot, one of the arbitrators in this case, a just man, and one of the largest merchants of Quebec, to whom he had hired himself for that fishing; and that there is also reason to fear that the Procureur-General to the Supreme Council may experience what M. de Frontenac threatened him with in the presence of the King's Lieutenant of Quebec and of several of the Members of the Council, [namely] to make him go to France this year to account to His Majesty for the opinions he gave in this matter, which would indeed be most vexatious.

Moreover, as His Majesty has distinctly intimated to M. de Frontenac that he should take no cognizance of matters of law except to assist and support the Intendant with his authority in everything he may consider necessary and proper to do; and as you see, My Lord, that in place of carrying it out, he takes particular care to do the very opposite, even employing violence to that end by the imprisonment of the Sr. Dupuy for holding an inquiry in consequence of my warrant, by the threats addressed to the arbitrators of treating them in the same way when they were just about to give their judgment, which compelled them to withdraw from it; by threats of another kind offered to the Supreme Council assembled, which he also obliged to give up the cognizance of this affair; by prohibiting the execution of my decree, on pain of disobedience; and by threatening to send the Procureur-Général to France. All that, My Lord, will readily convince you that there is not a single man in Canada who can administer justice freely, without being exposed to very grievous consequences. And if I tell you also that persons who have claims against people protected by the Governor are reduced to the hard necessity of waiting for some other time to pursue them; and that others have been compelled to make secret protests against what they have been forced to do by his authority, although they concerned matters which may be done freely, without being dependent or subordinate, as it is becoming to the harsh authority of the Governor. I will await, My Lord, if you please, your orders on all this, assuring you that I desire nothing more earnestly than to see the King well served, and served as he wishes to be, feeling no distress from what happens save where it is contrary to His Majesty's will, to which I adhere absolutely, from the very sincere desire I feel to fulfill my duty and to deserve the continued honor of your patronage, which I beg you to grant me, being with very deep respect

My Lord

Your very humble, very obedient and most obliged servant

Champigny.

Quebec, this 3rd of July, 1698.

FRONTENAC PRAISES CADILLAC.

Endorsed—Colonies. The Comte de Frontenac 10th Oct. 1698.

My Lord,

*   *   *   *   *   *   *   *   *

8.

As to what concerns the Sr. de Tonty, there is nothing I desire more earnestly, than that the matters should be examined to the bottom, for when the truth is known it will be clearly seen that my intentions have ever been most upright; that the abuses which there has been such an outcry about have not been so great as they have been stated to be; and that, if there has been any, the persons who have made the greatest fuss about it have been those who contributed to it most through people who are intimates of theirs, with whom they have [common] interests; for it will not be found that I have any connection, direct or indirect with

pelled, of absolute necessity, to hire three Canadians to each of whom they give from four to five hundred livres wages a year. They are bound to buy a boat for their journey, which costs them 200#; and, besides that, their provisions and the stores required for going merely to Missilimakinac, to which place it is nearly three hundred leagues. These men whom they have in their pay serve them for drawing the wood from a distance of two leagues, which is necessary for fuel for them and for the officer; they are also busy every day in catching fish, which is their single and only food except that of Indian Corn. It is also well to inform you that, in times of the greatest abundance, every minot of Indian corn bought from the savages costs 30# there; that one minot is required for the food of each man per month; and that, when the harvest fails, either on account of the fogs or the frosts, which often happens, the minot of wheat is worth up to 80# there. If then, My Lord, you will give yourself the trouble of observing to what sum that may amount, even at the lowest price, how can it be possible for a captain, on his pay, and subalterns on their very moderate pay,—and more especially for soldiers, to live and defray their expenses without transacting any trade?

10.

Permit me to tell you, My Lord, that you have been misinformed if they have sent you word that during the time the [trading] licenses were issued we sent the commanding officers and the garrisons at these posts what they required for their subsistence. That has never been done and never could be done without putting His Majesty to enormous expense, and undertaking to send as large a number of men as used to go up in the boats allowed to the licensees. We contented ourselves with simply allowing them to load their boats with merchandise and all that they thought fit, in order to provide for the proper expenses both of their journey and of their stay [there]. It is quite true that some brandy has been taken there, for it is the only drink capable of aiding them to digest the fish and the bad food on which they are compelled to live, for they do not know what it is to use wine, bread or salt in those places; even the missionaries are obliged to use a little Spanish wine which is sent them for saying Mass.

11

It is then true and indisputable that if this officer wishes to get corn, whether for himself or his people, and the other things he requires. he cannot help but buy them from the savages with his merchandise; and if he, and the soldier likewise, do not do some trade, how can either of

true that they made some small profit there, it seems to me that they are
not to be envied the dangers' and the hardships they are obliged to undergo among these uncivilized tribes; and I also consider that if the Sr.
De lá Mothe Cadillac had luckily found some profit there, as well as
other people, that would be [but] a slight reward after the services he
has rendered there, with which I have already sent you word last year,
that I was well pleased.

* * *

29

It was very malicious of those who wanted to accuse M. de Calliere of
having aided the departure, last year, of certain men who are stated to
have gone up to the Outavouais, with the 'Sr. de Tonty; for it is certain
that he had issued all the orders required for carrying out those of His
Majesty, in conformity with which I had given mine.

* * *

The Sr. de la Mothe Cadillac, captain of the Marines, will give you my
letters, and will tell you more particularly all that relates to the condition of this country, of which he is fully informed. I am convinced you
will be pleased with the account he will give you of it if you will graciously permit him to speak with you about it. He has always done his
duty thoroughly well in all matters of the King's service, as I have
already informed you in several of my letters, and particularly in the
command of the Outaouais, where he was for three years. He is a man
who certainly deserves the honor of your patronage.

* * *

Your very humble, very obedient and most obliged servant

Frontenac.

Quebec, this 10th October, 1698
P. S.

M. de Pontchartrain having referred it this year to MM de Calliere and dè Champigny to press it on at once, provided there were no important objections, they both approved of it and retained me to carry out the establishment of this Strait which separates Lake Huron from Lake Erié.

It is greatly to be feared that the execution of this scheme has been delayed too long, from the news we have that the English have fortified themselves on a river which discharges itself into Lake Ontario, and that they will extend their posts toward Lake Erie.

If our Colony were not full of envy, disunion, cabal and intrigue, no opposition would have been offered to taking possession of a post [which is] so advantageous that, if it were separated from all those we [now] have, we should be compelled in a short time to abandon all; for it is that alone which will make the Colony and its commerce entirely safe, and cause the certain ruin of the English colonies. For that reason it is very important that it should not pass into other hands, which would be inevitable if we deferred taking it any longer.

The objections which have been raised also at the wrong time, in the belief that this post might cause us to be forever at war with the Iroquois, are now removed by the peace which has been concluded with them. That tribe was not in a position to keep up the war any longer, and will not be able to begin it again very soon; therefore there could not be a more suitable time for establishing Detroit, which will be fortified more quickly than the Iroquois can make up the loss of their numbers.

It is an incontestable fact, that the strength of the savages lies in the remoteness of the French, and that ours increases against them with our proximity. For it is certain that, with a little Indian corn, these people have no difficulty in traversing two hundred leagues to come and take some one's life by stealth; and when we want to get to their lands, we are obliged to provide ourselves with stores of all kinds and to make great preparations, which involves the King in extraordinary expenses, and always with very little effect since it is like beating drums to catch hares.

But, on the contrary, when we are the neighbors of that tribe and are within easy reach of them, they will be kept in awe and will find themselves forced to maintain peace since they will be unable to do otherwise unless they wish to ruin themselves irretrievably.

It would be in vain to establish this post if they would not comply with my memorandum; for if only a garrison pure and simple were kept up there, it would be liable to the revolutions which usually take place in the frontier posts, and it would make no impression on the minds of the Iroquois and of our allies, and much less still on those of the English. In order to succeed thoroughly, it would be well (in my opinion) to

1.

To go and station ourselves there with a hundred men, one half of
whom should be soldiers and the other Canadians. In order to carry out
this expedition with all necessary despatch, and to undeceive the Englishmen at once as to [their] having any claim there and to take from
them all hope of establishing any relations with our allies, this strength
is sufficient for the first year. For this number is absolutely necessary
to me for fortifying [the place] and for taking the proper steps for the
subsistence of those who wish to settle there subsequently.

2.

The year after, the fort being secure from insult, it is well to allow
twenty or thirty families to settle there, and to bring their cattle and
other necessary things which they will willingly do at their own cost and
expense; and this may be continued as it is permitted in all the other
settlements of the Colony.

3.

It is no less necessary that the King should send two hundred picked
men who should, as far as may be, be of different trades and also rather
young.

4.

It is not advisable that I, any more than the other officers, soldiers
and inhabitants, should do any trade with the savages, in order to take
away from the people of the other established posts their cause for complaint, as to which they are very active. But [it is advisable] to unite this
business to that of the general company which is formed; in which
[case] it will keep up a warehouse to supply all the goods needed by the
savages, our allies, and the Iroquois, while letting them have them at a

sions; they are laborers in the vineyard, and should be received without distinction to labor at the vine of the Lord, with orders in particular to teach the young savages the French ,anguage, [that] being the only means to civilize and humanize them, and to instil into their hearts and their minds the law of religion and of the monarch. We take wild beasts at their birth, birds in their nests, to tame them and set them free. But in order to succeed better in that. it would be necessary for the King to favor these same missionaries with his bounty and his alms, in proportion as they instruct the children of the Savages at their houses, on the evidence which the Commandant and other officers give of it.

6.

The third or fourth year we shall be able to set Ursulines there, or other nuns, to whom His Majesty could grant the same favors.

7.

It 'would be important that there should be a hospital for sick or infirm Savages, for there is nothing more urgent for gaining their friendship than the care taken of them in their illnesses. The hospitallers of Montreal seem to me well fitted for that, because they know beforehand the temper and the preferences of the Savages [from] often having them with them.

8.

It.would be absolutely necessary also to allow the soldiers and Canadians to marry the savage maidens when they have been instructed in religion and know the French language which they will learn all the more eagerly (provided we labor carefully to that end) because they always prefer a Frenchman for a husband to any savage whatever, though I know no other reason for it than the most ordinary one, namely that strangers are preferred, or, it were better to say, it is a secret of the Almighty Power.

9.

Marriages of this kind will strengthen the friendship of these tribes, as the alliances of the Romans perpetuated peace . with the Sabines through the intervention of the women whom the former had taken from the others.

We shall find, in the execution of this scheme, not only the glory of His

themselves to take away from me the honor of carrying out my scheme; and this appears not to have ceased. But MM. de Caliere and de Champigny have not opposed it; on the contrary they have retained me for that so as to begin it next spring. When it was seen that they had resolved on this, everything possible was done to persuade them that my memorandum is impracticable, and I have seen twenty parties formed to upset it. I venture to assure you there is nothing to fear and that everything will be favorable to this undertaking; I [will] answer for it with my life. Monsieur de Pontchartrain will no sooner have given his decision than the whole country will applaud it, according to the policy of all men, who are very glad to find difficulties in all that does not originate with them.

As I am taking my son with me to Detroit, I beg the Minister to be so good as to grant him an ensigncy or an order for the first vacancy; that of my company has been given to the son of M. de Ramezay, with which I am satisfied. I hope you will have the kindness to say a word in my favor to M. de Pontchartrain regarding it. As I was one of the ten who were chosen by the Colony to settle its concerns, we have approved the agreement made by Pascaud with M. de Roddes, but have rejected the one he made with M. Bourlay and his partners as being too burdensome and insupportable for the reasons which are noted on it, and to which you will no doubt give [your] attention as well as Monsieur Amelot who is very acute. The Colony sends two persons for the matters which concern it, and to manage the sale of the beaver skins; instructions have been given them, and there is reason to hope that they will conform to them, and that they will do their duty better than the first [men sent].

Permit me to assure you that I am, with deep respect

Monsieur

Your very humble and very obedient servant

Lamothe Cadillac.

at Quebec, this 18th Oct., 1700.

[On the back of this letter are the following two drafts of letters.]

which he is sending with him to be sold, sufficient to pay all his expenses, so that he may have his pay remaining at the end of the year; and as H. M. is preparing to transfer the trade of this post to the Company which has been formed in Canada for the beaver trade H. M. will induce that Company to grant him some additional pay while he remains at this post, for it is not his intention that his position in that place should be worse than it would otherwise be; and he will be very glad, on the contrary to give him marks of his satisfaction if he should succeed as he gives us hope of doing. In regard to his son, I shall have pleasure in taking advantage of the first opportunity I have of appointing him.

LETTERS TO CADILLAC FROM THE JESUIT FATHERS.[1]

Endorsed—Colonies.

Remarks made by M. de Lamothe on the letters which have been written to him by the revd. Jesuit Fathers.

By this 1st letter, Father de Carheil, missionary to the Hurons at Missilimakinack proves the necessity, in his opinion of the establishment of Detroit, for he admits having wished for it for so many years, and that he hears the news of it with pleasure.

Letters written to M. de la Mothe At Missilimakinac this 25th of July, 1701.

First

Sir,

After having indeed desired for so many years, as you say Sir, the establishment of Detroit, the letter you have done me the honor to write to me to inform me of the good news concerning it could not but give me much pleasure. I should be pleased to go there forthwith to render you what services I am capable of if the state of this mission would permit me. But you know that everyone has gone down from here to Montreal for the general assembly which is to be held there. It is necessary to await their return before being able to move at all; for no other steps ought to be taken than those they have taken themselves with the Governor as to the plan of their approaching migra-

In the 2nd letter, Father Maret, Missionary to the Outavois is only acting Pharisaically for he would not carry out the orders of the Governor-General nor even those he received (at least as it appeared) from his superior at Quebec.

Paragraph of the letter written by M. de Calliere to M. de La Mothe at Detroit dated the 24th of August, 1701.

I hope that the Hurons and the greater part of the Outavqis will go & join you at Detroit from this autumn, and I am writing to the reverend fathers Maret and De Carheil that I request them to go with them in order to arrange with you as to the place where it will be most convenient for them to settle.

These two missionaries, so far from conforming to the paragraph of this letter, employed every means to prevent the savages from coming there. That is seen in the councils held at the fort Pontchartrain on the 30th of October and the 4th Dec. 1701.

At Missilimakina this 28th of July, 1701.

Second

Sir

You do me justice in believing that I will contribute as far as I possiby can to the settlement at Detroit, and that if I can do so in no other way, I will at least do so with the feeble aid of my prayers to the Lord. Besides my natural inclination, and the will of our Superiors, your letter will be yet another inducement to me thereto. Since you entertain the opinions you notify [to me] there is no missionary but ought to take a pleasure in going there. You cannot do better than to carry out the intention of which you make mention concerning the brandy; that is the way to make this settlement a success—*nisi dominus aedificaveret domum, in vanum Laboraverent qui aedificant eam.* You cannot better aid the intentions of the king, who, in this kind of settlement which concerns the savages also, aims chiefly at the salvation of these poor souls, which the brandy traffic renders them incapable of. We are expecting the return of our savages immediately; it will be then we shall learn their real decision, and the intentions of M. de Calliere and of our superiors. As for me, I am quite ready to set out after this autumn if they wish it. Whether it is the autumn or whether the spring; or whether they even send me to another place (for you know we are obedient children) I shall ever be with much respect

Sr,

Your very humble and very obedient servant

Joseph J. Marest
of the Company of Jesus.

The 3rd letter has been incorrectly dated Aug. 7, 1702, hence appears in the wrong place.—C. M. B.

This fourth letter is from Father Germain, formerly an officer of the Society, a learned professor of theology, who is of great integrity and piety, as he is in fact a friend of M. de la Mothe's (which may indeed cause him to be transferred to another diocese) writes to him simply, at the end of his letter, what he knows, without reflecting that his Superior at Quebec had promised M. de la Mothe to grant him Father Vaillant to start his mission at Detroit, for it is evident from this letter that the return of this Father was expected, even before his departure from Quebec, and that this action has been taken only in order to entrap M. de Lamothe, and with the intention of making this settlement abortive.

This letter agrees with the 7th from Father Maret, in which he writes regarding the return of Father Vaillant, &c.

At Quebec, this 25th Augt. 1701.
Fourth

Sir

Although we have not yet had positive and certain news of your arrival at Detroit, we have nevertheless conjunctures strong enough for [us] to judge that you must have arrived there safely in the month of July. As you know, Sir, that I take great interest in whatever concerns you, allow me to congratulate you and to pray our Lord, as I do with all my heart, graciously to bless all your plans for the good of the missions and of the Colony. So long as you have these two things in view, you cannot fail to have good success in your undertakings not only as regards public matters but also in your private concerns. Everyone here admires the magnanimity of these two ladies who certainly have courage to undertake so laborious a journey to go and join their husbands, without fearing the great difficulties or the fatigue or other inconveniences which must be endured by roads so long and so rough for persons of their sex. Well! Sir: is it possible to show more sincere conjugal affection or a firmer attachment?

tell you by word of mouth better than I could in writing everything new we have learnt since your departure. Be assured, Sir, that I often recommend your two dear daughters to the Ursulines, and that I will try to contribute to their education as far as it may lie in my power. Young Cadillac promised me to embrace his brother once for me when he arrives at Detroit; if he forgets to do me this little service, reprimand him lightly. I am not writing to any of our Fathers because I have no doubt that Father Vaillant will have set out to return here before Madam de La Mothe arrives at Detroit, and I do not know whether any other will be allowed [to go there] in his place. Do me the favor to grant me some share in your good-will and the justice to believe that I shall ever be with all possible respect, Sir, your very humble and very obedient servant

. (Signed) Joseph Germain.

This 5th letter is from Father Anjalran; he still holds to his opinion, affirming that Detroit is the most important post. This Father had just passed through all the missions generally, and he admits that the whole of this further country is in need of reform. He is indeed right, but his upright conduct has made him hated by his fellows who have got rid of him, contrary to all justice. This letter also proves that M. de Calliere had cast eyes on this Father to take charge of all the missions; but doubtless it has been politic for the Governor-General to yield to the torrent, and sacrifice this good laborer, so necessary for the Lord's vineyard, to the envy of his colleagues. No one has ever understood the spirit of the Savages better than this Father, nor had so much influence over their minds; but his crime was having admitted that

At Three Rivers, the 30th August 1701.

Fifth

Sir .

I have met Madam de Lamothe on the way, quite resolved to come and see you at Detroit; I should have been very pleased if fate, which ought to have sent me up to your neighborhood, had permitted me to accompany her. No decision could be made regarding the mission of the post you are to establish, as one of the most important, until steps had been taken as to the other missions; for the whole of this upper country needs reforming. Our Governor-General, after having listened to me on this matter, thought I should be the most fit to serve in what concerns my ministry. When we have learnt all the intentions of the Court, if we learn them early enough, I should be able indeed to go and see you before the winter, and I should take peculiar pleas-

and to that end he writes to him that he will take pleasure in assisting him in his glorious undertakings. His letter refers to the words of M. de Calliere spoken in the general assembly held at Montreal on the 6th of August, 1701, 5th paragraph, in these terms: —The revd. Father Anjalran is quite ready to set out to go and live with you (as you have requested), you other four tribes of the Outavois, but he also asks that you should listen to his advice which tends to no other conclusion but [this] to take up our interests in all things.

This 6th letter is from Father Vaillant[1] and proves the respect with which M. de Lamothe treated him; the matter was publicly known and he could not deny it. No doubt this Father had his cue from his Superior at Quebec, & he is wishing to impose on M. de la Mothe when he writes him that one of the Fathers from Missilimakinak is to go down to Detroit, apparently to replace him there, which was not carried out.

His letter shows that he spoke to the Iroquois and that they testified to him that they were rejoiced at the establishment of Detroit: hence the apprehension that has been felt or pretended concerning this tribe is ill-founded.

---

[1]François Vaillant de Gueslis, Jesuit, born at Orleans, July 20, 1646. Went

undertakings, and to testify to you the feelings of esteem with which I am

Sir

Your very humble and very obedient servant

[Signed]

Enjalran. J.

At Fort Frontenac this 23rd Sept. 1701. Sixth.

Sir.

Our fortunate meeting at Fort Frontenac with Madame de la Mothe gives me a good opportunity of thanking you very humbly for all the courtesies with which you have overwhelmed me all the past summer both on our march and at Detroit. I beg you to be so good as to continue to grant them to me in the person of the one of our Fathers who is to come down from Missilimakinak to Detroit, for I have no doubt you will have one there very soon, for, on Lake Erie I met Quarante Solz, the Huron, who assured me that the Hurons were going to settle near you after this autumn, without fail. As regards the Iroquois whom we met on the way, we did not find them much opposed to your settlement; some even testified to me

CADILLAC STARTS FOR DETROIT.

Endorsed—Canada. The Chev. de Callieres, 4th Oct. 1701.

My Lord,

* * *

I have already had the honor of notifying to you, My Lord, in my first letter of the 6th of August, that I had sent the Srs. de la Motte, de Tonty, Duqué and Chacornacle on the 7th of June. with more than a hundred men, soldiers or Canadians, to establish the post of Detroit, with a recollet as almoner to the soldiers, and a Jesuit as missionary to the savages. You will see from the speeches of Teganisorens and of the other men of importance who accompanied him, which I have inclosed with this letter, under the index letter D, that he opposed it to me, telling me to wait until the chiefs who were to come to Montreal for the peace had arrived. But, as it appeared to me that he had not been commissioned to speak to me on this point, I still proceeded with that enterprise; for I feared lest, if those chiefs had requested me not to establish that post, and I had refused them, that might have given rise to some opposition to the peace, whereas, if they found the matter settled by the departure of the Sr. de la Motte. they would not speak of it; and that is what happened, I having made them approve of the reasons for [forming] that post, in spite of the distrust which the English inspired them with, although they had the intention of going there themselves, as I learnt in the winter, which was yet another reason for hastening the departure of the Sr. de la Motte and for making his detachment as strong as it is, for fear lest the English might anticipate me. I also made the Sonnontouans promise, when they returned to their villages, to take Indian corn there, on the news I had received that the Sr. de la Motte would not find any at Missilimakinac.

The Sr. de Chacornacle has just arrived now from the fort of Detroit, and has brought me letters from the Sr. de la Motte; but, as we are giving you an account, in our joint letter, of what we have learnt from them, I will not repeat it for you here.

You will see, My Lord, from what we have the honor to inform you of in the said joint letter. that when we handed over the trade of this fort to the Company, it pledged itself to pay the 6000# which you were good enough to have decided upon for the relief of the poor families of this country. You have thereby done a very charitable thing, because of the need they have of it; and they are greatly indebted to you for it.

* * *

DETROIT IN CHARGE OF THE COMPANY OF CANADA.

5th Oct. 1701.

Endorsed—Canada. The Chev. de Callieré and M. de Champigny.

My Lord,

* * * *

The licensed traders were suppressed owing to the fear that was entertained that too large a quantity of beaver-skins-would be traded for in the woods. Yet this country is chagrined to see that there are more traders than ever in the further districts, without any profit accruing to it therefrom since the whole trade is carried on simply by Le Sueur, the itinerant traders in the woods, and [agents] for the Srs. de la Forest and de Tonty, who, it is said, are not content to trade with the Ilinois only, but [do so] in all the other parts of these countries as well.

* * * *

We will do our best to reduce, as far as may be possible, the presents that will have to be made to the savages; but we cannot, at the present juncture, help making them large presents, as we had the honor of informing you before.

d, with 10my.

The savages do not make presents after presents have been made to them; moreover when anything is given them, it is generally as they are ready to depart, when they have transacted their trade and have none of their furs left. The Chev. de Calljerés has forbidden the officers in command at Fort Frontenac and Detroit to receive any.

* * * *

We are pleased to learn that he [? His Majesty] has granted to the Sr. de Louvigny the company he had; but we are in a difficulty, somewhat, on account of that company having been granted to the Sr. de Tonty by the promotion of the said Sr. de Louvigny to be Major at Three Rivers.

The Srs de la Motte and de Tonty,[1] Captains [and] Dugué and Chacornacle, Lieutenants on half pay, set out at the beginning of last June with
a hundred men, soldiers and settlers, in 25 boats loaded with provisions,
goods. stores, and necessary tools, to go and establish the post of Detroit.

We did not forget on behalf of His Majesty, to prohibit these officers,
soldiers and settlers from carrying on any trade, on pain of incurring
the extreme penalty of the decrees; and as it is necessary to trade with the
savages there, we have sent two upright men who will carry it on for the
profit of His Majesty with all possible fidelity; and we have taken Who?
the other precautions which were necessary in order to prevent any abuses
from creeping in, so as to be able to give you, My Lord, an exact account
of the consignments sent there which, up to the present time are very
large as you will see from the annexed statement which the Sr. de Champigny has had drawn up.   Index lett

Since the departure of the said Sr. de la Motte, we have sent him two
boats laden with provisions and goods, as we feared he might stand in
need of them; and at the same time we informed him of the conclusion of
the peace between us, our allied savages, and the Iroquois. We also sent
off two boats, at the beginning of September, to take the wives of the
Srs. de la Motte and de Tonty who have gone to join them, on the request
they made to us.

We will consider his memorandum which you have sent us, in which Pursue th
there are many things which are impracticable, especially in those coun- ject ener
tries.   ically and
                                                          carefully.

His Majesty having directed us to put the Company of the Colony in
possession of this post. to have the trade which may be done there to the
exclusion of everyone else, we have agreed, subject to his will and pleas- Good.
ure, to hand it over on condition that he is reimbursed for all the expenses he has incurred there, consisting not only of the goods which
have been sent there for trading but also of the provisions, stores, and
tools, boats bought for the journey, the construction of the fort which is
set up there, and the wages of those who are serving at that post, but on
condition of making it a reduction of the sum of 15000# which His Maj- Why?
esty granted for the construction of this fort.

This company binds itself also to provide food for the officers in com- Little.
mand there, so that they may have their pay clear, as His Majesty orders; to have the provisions and clothing of the soldiers conveyed there Much.
at the rate of 15# per cwt. which, otherwise would cost as much again.

They are also pledged to distribute to poor families of rank, from the
1st of January the sum of 6000#, in place and instead of of the licensed
traders, according to the orders of the Chev. de Callieres countersigned
by the Sr. de Champigny; and the statement of the distribution made of

---

[1]Henry Tonty was at Fort St. Louis and his younger brother, Alphonse, was at

this [sum] will be sent every year to the Court. And since this Company

does not at present possess the funds for making the repayment spoken
of above, it has appropriated for that purpose the returns which should
accrue next year from the goods which have been sent to this fort; and
if they are not sufficient, they will give letters of exchange for the remainder, payable in France the said year.

The Sr. de Chacornacle has just arrived now from Detroit with five
men, and has brought us letters from the Srs. de la Motte and de Tonty;
the former notifies us that he arrived at the mouth of that river on the
24th of July with all his detachment in good health, and that after having looked for the most suitable place to establish himself, he built a fort
with four bastions of good oak stakes 15 feet long, three of which are in
the earth, each curtain being thirty fathoms long; that he has placed this
fort three leagues from Lake Erie. and two from Lake St. Clair at the
narrowest part of the river towards the west south-west; that he began
by building a warehouse in order to put all his goods under shelter; that
he is setting them to work at the necessary dwellings, and that they are
not yet in a very forward state. which has obliged him to keep nearly
all his people trying to complete them before the winter.

We have no doubt that this post will attract the savages of Missillimakinac, and especially the Hurons, and that they will go and settle
there from this autumn, as they promised the Chev. de Callieres.

The Sr. de la Motte sends us a favorable description of the country
where he is; and although he says he is sending a copy of it to you, we
do not omit annexing a copy here.

We took the liberty of asking you last year for an annual gratuity for
the Srs. de la Motte and de Tonty, and we make the same request to you
again this year seeing the great hardships they have experienced in their
journey and in forming their settlement. The Sr. Dugue, lieutenant on

DESCRIPTION OF THE RIVER OF DETROIT BY M. DE LA MOTHE, THE COMMANDANT THERE.

Endorsed—f. [? *faite*=made, i. e. drawn up] 5th Oct., 1701.
Annexed to the letter from MM. de Callieres and de Champigny.

Since the trade of war is not that of a writer, I cannot without rashness draw the portrait of a country so worthy of a better pen than mine; but since you have ordered me to give you an account of it I will do so, telling you

That Detroit is, probably, only a canal or a river of moderate breadth, and twenty-five leagues in length according to my reckoning lying north-north-east, and south-south-west about the 41st degree [of latitude], through which the sparkling and pellucid waters of Lakes Superior, Michigan and Huron (which are so many seas of sweet water) flow and glide away gently and with a moderate current into Lake Erie, into the Ontario or Frontenac, and go at last to mingle in the river St. Lawrence with those of the ocean. The banks are so many vast meadows where the freshness of these beautiful streams keep the grass always green. These same meadows are fringed with long and broad avenues of fruit trees which have never felt the careful hand of the watchful gardener; and fruit trees, young and old, droop under the weight and multitude of their fruit, and bend their branches towards the fertile soil which has produced them. In this soil so fertile, the ambitious vine which has not yet wept under the knife of the industrious vine-dresser, forms a thick roof with its broad leaves and its heavy clusters over the head of whatever it twines round, which it often stifles by embracing it too closely. Under these vast avenues you may see assembling in hundreds the shy stag and the timid hind with the bounding roebuck, to pick up eagerly the apples and plums with which the ground is paved. It is there that the careful turkey hen calls back her numerous brood, and leads them to gather the grapes; it is there that their big cocks come to fill their broad and gluttonous crops. The golden pheasant, the quail, the partridge, the woodcock, the teeming turtle-dove, swarm in the woods and cover the open country intersected and broken by groves of full-grown forest trees which form a charming prospect which of itself might sweeten the melancholy tedium of solitude. There the hand of the pitiless mower has never shorn the juicy grass on which bisons of enormous height and size fatten.

The woods are of six kinds,—walnut trees, white oaks, red, bastard ash, ivy, white wood trees and cottonwood trees. But these same trees are as straight as arrows, without knots, and almost without branches except near the top, and of enormous size and height. It is from thence that the fearless eagle looks steadily at the sun, seeing beneath him enough to glut his formidable claws.

The fish there are fed and laved in sparkling and pellucid waters, and are none the less delicious for the bountiful supply [of them]. There are such large numbers of swans that the rushes among which they are massed might be taken for lilies. The gabbling goose, the duck, the teal and the bustard are so common there that, in order to satisfy you of it, I will only make use of the expression of one of the savages, of whom I asked before I got there whether there was much game there; "there is so much," he told me, "that it only moves aside [long enough] to allow the boat to pass."

Can it be thought that a land in which nature has distributed everything in so complete a manner could refuse to the hand of a careful husbandman who breaks into its fertile depths, the return which is expected of it?

In a word, the climate is temperate, the air very pure; during the day there is a gentle wind, and at night the sky, which is always placid, diffuses sweet and cool influences which cause us to enjoy the benignity of tranquil sleep.

If its position is pleasing, it is no less important, for it opens or closes the approach to the most distant tribes which surround these vast sweet water seas.

It is only the opponents of the truth who are the enemies of this settlement, so essential to the increase of the glory of the King, to the spread of religion, and to the destruction of the throne of Baal.

THE SEVENTH LETTER FROM THE JESUITS TO CADILLAC.

cision was come to in concert with M. de Calliere, which is not likely.

The Father is correct in writing that the Savages are not agreed as to the establishment of Detroit. The words they have uttered in open council show what the missionaries are, the ones who have divided them by the bad impressions they have given them, and by the threats they have offered them if they should come and settle at this post.

gratitude. As regards the return of Father Vaillant, it ought not to have surprised you, for I have been assured that that was in reality arranged from down there, and that M. de Calliere was expecting him, and that he expected him by way of Ktarok8i.[1] It is true, however, that this Father was much mortified that he was not able to pass this way, either going to Detroit or returning and so were we. It is true that the 8ta8as have brought us from down there news [that had] arrived from Europe, some of which is very consoling. M. de la Forest is only setting out from here; your boats for the Bay went off nearly 15 days ago. Father Chardon embarked with the latter to go also to the Bay to the assistance of Father Nouvelle laden with the weight of nearly 80 years, and with many infirmities. This Father brought us some letters for you from down there; there are two packets of them and one ordinary letter which I have charged Mikinak (who is not unknown to you) to deliver to you, he always behaves well towards the French. Your letters will no doubt tell you that most important news is expected by the last vessels; I don't know whether we shall be informed of it here this year.

I cannot tell you what the opinion of our 8ta8as is as to the establishment of Detroit, and I think they would be somewhat embarrassed to tell us themselves, for they are not agreed. Several of them fear that the Iroquois, not having returned them their slaves, which was the most essential article of the treaty, may be on the watch to deceive them; but if they are handed over to them this autumn, as they have been given to hope, that will calm them down a little. As for me I am expecting orders from our Revd. Father Superior every day, and I do not think any move could be made between now and the spring, nor could I be of serv-

ice to the savages who are quite determined to disperse in the woods, each
in his own direction and that as far as
ever they can. I recommend to you
those who go and visit you; and I am
with great respect, Sir, your very humble and very obedient servant.
[Signed]

                    Joseph J. Maret.[1]

This 8th letter is from Father Maret.
'It proves the contrary of what he wrote
to M. de Lamothe in the 2nd, dated 28th
July, 1701, in which he says he is quite
ready to set out from the autumn of
the same year, if it is desired; and he
appears to have been requested to do so
by M. de Calliere, as well as Father
de Carheil. But all this is practiced in
order to lull M. de Lamothe to sleep,
who was not disposed to be *   *   *

---

[1]Joseph Jacques Marest, Jesuit was in
Canada in 1687. He died July 17, 1738.
Repertoire General du Clergé Can-
adien, 70.
[2]Henry Nouvel, Jesuit, arrived at
Quebec August 4, 1662. Was Superior
to the Ottawas in 1673. Died at Quebec,
October 7, 1674. Rep. Gen. 52.—C. M. B.

At Missilimakinak, this 20th Oct.,
    1701.
Eighth,
Sir,
    The wife of Quarante Solz has re-
turned us the packet of letters of which
you speak in the one you have done me
the favor to write me. I was expecting
to find in it a letter from Father Chol-
lenu who, at the beginning of the one
he sent me by N. f. Louis de Boëme tells
me that he has already written to me
by way of Quarante Solz who had set
out before. I do not know what has
become of this 'letter; if it has been in-
advertently forgotten, I should be obliged by its being sent to me on the
first opportunity as I know not what it
may contain. I have already sent you
word by K8ta8ilib8a that I had charged
Mikinak with the letters Brother Louis

Amaise who arrived yesterday from down there with sundry letters not yet informing us of the arrival of the vessels which were expected. We have already taken to the Miamis what they had left here in our charge, everything shall be faithfully returned to them independently of [?=except] your ·note which I have not yet been able to send to Father Aveneau.[1] The fort which you have already finished and the fine building you tell me of will please our savages greatly, but what will please them more than all the rest is the cheapness of the goods which you will get for them especially if it is [?to last] for ever. I have already sent you word that I should apparently make no move this autumn; I have not even the authority to do so. I may indeed say the same of Father de Carheill, who has desired me to tell you that he is also, with respect, as I am and will ever be, Sir, your very humble and very obedient servant.

[Signed]

Joseph J. Marest.

[1] Claude Aveneau, Jesuit, came to Quebec June 4, 1683. Missionary to the Miamis on River St. Joseph after father Allouez. He was at this mission as late as 1708. Rep. Gen. 68.—C. M. B.

DETROIT GIVEN TO THE COMPANY OF THE COLONY.

Endorsed—Colonies. M. de Champigny. 30th Oct. 1701.

My Lord,

The great haste in which the King's store-ship "La Seine" left here, prevented me from sending you by that means all the documents referred to in my private letter, which has compelled me to annex to this one a statement of the quantities used up out of His Majesty's stores during the first eight months of the present year, which ought to have been under the Index Letter A in the former [letter.]

A detailed forecast of the disbursements to be made in this country next year, under·the letter C.

A statement with details of the expenditure incurred for masts dur- This paper cannot be

This latter store-ship arrived here on the 8th of this month, and brought us a hundred soldiers as reinforcements in sufficiently good condition. His Majesty's stores with which it was loaded have been found to be in a good state; but as it was unable to bring all the flour which ought to have been sent us, the cost of which has been reckoned in advance against the funds destined for this country for the present year, I am sending word to Mons. Begon, Intendant of Rochefort, to send it next year.

ex letter A,   I have had twenty masts and some planks put on board this store-ship, as you will see, My Lord, from the statement annexed hereto.

They could not make a large mast go in it, the port hole not being
ex letter B. large enough. I should very much have liked to put on board also thirty fine small masts which cost 20# each, French money, the bill for which I send you.

ter C, bis.   As the inhabitants of St. Paul's Bay have not carried out the arrangements I made with them for masts, I have made a considerable reduction against them in the price I was giving them for each mast; and I have made a fresh arrangement with the Sr. de la Chesnaye, a copy of which is attached, from which you will learn My Lord, that I am giving him 66# for each, which is an increase of 6#. But, as he relieves me of all the tackle I was obliged to supply under the former arrangement, I hope you will find this one more advantageous to His Majesty; moreover he is an upright man, and in a position to carry this out faithfully, to which he has pledged himself.

ex letter D,   I am very glad to annex to this, My Lord, a copy of the decision I have given between Guigne, farmer of the revenues of the western domain, and the Company of the Colony, regarding certain letters of exchange which were drawn on the former for the payment of what was contained in the

you on this point, to have a statement drawn up next year in which it should be explained from what day the salary or wages of each individual should commence.

As the parties in Paris formerly interested in the North Bay have not sent me any memorandum concerning the indemnification they demand from the New Company, and no one has come forward in their behalf, I have been unable to settle anything on this head. You will find at- Index lett tached, My Lord, a copy of a memorandum, concerning the establishment of Detroit.

You will see from the agreement I have made with the Company of the Colony, on putting it in possession of the forts of Frontenac and Detroit, that I have been obliged to advance large sums without being able to obtain payment until next year, in letters of exchange and furs which will have to be sent to France to be sold, and this will delay the repayment for two years. Therefore I most humbly beg you, My Lord, to take this into account to some extent, by granting us next year such increase of funds as you may think fit, having regard to the extraordinary disbursements we have been obliged to make this year both for the ratification of the peace with the Iroquois, and for the enterprise of Detroit, and for the fortifications of Quebec, as you know from the statements which have been sent to you.

I hope, My Lord, you will be good enough to send us a ship early next year, in order that the Intendant who relieves me may be able to be instructed sufficiently in the affairs of this country before I leave it.

Permit me, My Lord, to beg you to continue to honor me with your assistance in my desire to do all I can to retain it, being with the deepest respect

My Lord

Your very humble, very obedient, and most obliged servant,

Champigny.

Quebec, the 30th of October 1701.

NINTH LETTER FROM THE JESUITS TO CADILLAC.

At St. Joseph River the 19th of April, 1702

Ninth

Sir.

This 9th letter is from Father Mermet. From the first paragraph it contains it seems that this Father is very glad to make known to M. de Lamothe that he willingly gives him an opportunity to attain to glory if by his care and action he may avert the evils with which the colony and religion are threatened; and he claims by this action he is taking (although the thing is in itself greatly to be commended) to convince him that the Jesuits are more friendly to him than he thinks. This infers and means in good French [= in plain English] that, if the Jesuits had been enemies of M. de Lamothe, they would rather have let religion and the Colony perish than have informed him of the dangerous condition to which they were reduced or, it were better to say, according to his letters, of their imminent and almost certain ruin.

This father seems to be alarmed at the Miamis being more eager than usual for hunting, and pays no regard [to the fact] that it is evident that that is on account of the general peace that has been concluded, which invites them to hunt without fear. He asserts that Quarante Sous, Chief of the Hurons, is to settle 20 or 30 leagues from Detroit, and does not know that the same Quarante Sous is already settled with his village at Detroit in the place which M. de Lamothe has assigned to them;

Although I have not the honor of being known to you I cannot omit writing to you about an important matter which concerns the welfare of the Colony as well as of religion; and from that Sir you may see that the Jesuits are more friendly to you than you think unless you yourself will not honor them with your kind remembrance, and if I dare say so, with your friendship.

Five of our Miamis are betaking themselves to the English for goods which they will bring this summer. They have never been seen more eager in hunting the beaver than since they received fine belts from the English, brought by the Iroquois who have come here. That is in order to get permission from our Miamis to establish a post freely, three days from here near a river which is the source of the Oüabache, whence there is only one portage of half a league to get to this river here and another like [portage] to go to a river which runs down to Detroit. From thence the English would be able to go, or send from all sides the savages from our Lakes.

In this latter river which runs to Detroit M. Quarante Solz, who will not fail to inveigh against Father de Carheil, and is the moving spirit of every intrigue of our Miamis [?is going] to sent to M. de Lamothe to speak to him on behalf of the Hurons of Missilimakinak. Finally, after this Father has roundly abused the innocent Quarante Sous, he draws an inference for which there appears to be no grounds; these are his words,—judge from that, Sir, says he, how far we should trust to the report of the savages, and yet it is on their report that he informs M. de Lamothe of this important matter which concerns the welfare of the colony and even of religion. Finally in a postscript to his letter he returns to the charge; he urges me to send his letters filled with similar advice to the Governors and the Intendant, as well as to his Superiors. He writes through Missilimakinak, and there is reason for astonishment that he is not already in Quebec, and the English with the Miamis.

This is the Gordian knot of this important matter, on which M. de Lamothe was already informed. Two captains, namely MM. de la Forest and Tonty, arranged a meeting at Missilimakinak in the month of July, 1701, and they formed a scheme there with the Jesuits to form a post at the river where the Miamis are, with the intention of making the post of Detroit fail. That is why the missionaries of Missilimakinak invited the savages to go and settle there; and it was decided that this Father Mermet[1] should give this alarm to M de Lamothe with Father Davenant; the Jesuits undertook M. de Champigny and the two officers of M. de Calliere, the whole with the object of compelling the Governor-General to send a strong garrison to the Miamis in order to start that post under the pretext that the English would come there.

[1]Jacques Jean Mermet, Jesuit, arrived at Quebec June 24, 1700 and died in Sept. 1726. His remains were transported to the church at Kaskaskia Dec. 18, 1727 with those of Father Pierre Gabriel Marest. Rep. Gen. 82.—C. M. B.

ask permission to trade there on his own account [?saying] that if he does not go nearer to Detroit it is so as not to deprive the French of the advantage of the hunting, or from fear of incommoding the French who have sheep, cows or other domestic animals which their children could not help killing if they were nearer. But he ought not to disclose either the alliance he meditates with the English or the resentment which he will some day cause to break out against the 8ta8as; he has not even managed to keep himself from saying, to one of his confidants, that the French were preventing him from revenging himself on the 8ta8as, but that the English would assist him. Judge from that, Sir, how far we should trust to the report of the savages. You should, Sir, however, conceal [the fact] that the report I am making to you comes from us, especially as they might do us an ill turn; but I thought Sir, in writing this to you, to oblige you. You should not doubt that there will be no lack of denials of so infamous a case; but, if you think I am interested in this, so that you do not entirely credit it, inquire into it elsewhere and be on your guard against the Hurons. I take the liberty of addressing to you, on the same subject, letters to the Governor, and the Intendant and our Superior. I beg you to send them as soon as possible. If I have the opportunity you shall learn how far I am, Sir, your very humble and obedient servant.

[Signed]   Jean Mermet.[1]

In order to succeed, Sir, I beg you to use all possible diligence either in writing yourself or in forwarding our letters to the authorities. I think the matter so certain and so important that, if your man had not set out for Detroit I should have started specially to go down to Missilimakinak and thence perhaps to Quebec. Lest your man should be stopped by the Savages, I am writing the same matter by Missilimakinak,

This 10th letter is from Father Bonnart Superior of the Jesuits. He appears to wish that Fathers Maret[1] and Carheil should settle down near M. de Lamothe. This letter infers that he must have written about it to these two missionaries; or rather, it gives ground for thinking from the effects that they only wished to trifle with M. de Lamothe, in thanking him two years in advance for the courtesy he was to show to Fathers Maret and Carheil, who indeed resolved not to go to the missions of Detroit, and on the contrary contributed with all their power to ruin the settlement.

---

[1]There were two Jesuits named Marest, Joseph Jacques and Pierre Gabriel. It is probable that the one here mentioned as "senior" was the former as he came to Canada in 1687 while Pierre Gabriel Marest did not arrive until the following year. The name is sometimes spelled Maret, showing the elimination of the letter s, which was common at that time, as in Estienne, Etienne, Chesne, Chene and many other words and names.—C. M. B.

[2]François Dollier de Casson, a priest of the Sulpician order, came to Canada Sept. 7, 1666. He made a journey through the Detroit River at a very early period — years before Cadillac came, and made a very good map of the strait and of Lake Erie. He died

At Quebec this 20th of April 1702. f.
Tenth.

Sir.

It was with much joy that I learnt last autumn that Madame de la Mothe was very well during her journey. I congratulate you on it and her also, to whom with your permission I present my compliments, I hope your winter has been fortunate in all respects, and that some of our Fathers with their savages have settled down near you, namely Fathers de Carheil and Marest[1] senior. If so, I flatter myself I shall have as many thanks to give you on their account as I have already given you and as I give you again in regard to Father Vaillant[3] who prides himself most particularly on your friendship; I am therefore much obliged to you for it, Sir, and I feel I should be still more so if I could get any opportunity of serving you here. Meanwhile you must know, if you do not know it already, that the Quebec seminary was burnt on the 15th of Novr. 1701, and that the fort of Chambly was burnt somewhat in the month of March last; in the latter the Rev. Father Benjamin perished but no one perished in the former. We know nothing yet for certain as to the peace or the war between France, England and Holland. It is said that James II, the rightful king of Great Britain, is dead and that his son has been recognized successor under the name of James III. The ceremony took place at St. Germain without any religious ceremony.

ever be very respectfully and in all truth, Sir, your very humble and very obedient servant.

[Signed]   M. Bonnart.

At Missilimakinak this 30th May 1702. f.

Eleventh

Sir,

All that I have to answer at present, as to what you write to me of, by Miki-nick, is that what Father de Carheil and I have done has not been in order to hinder the settlement of your post but to act for the best; you will perhaps know that too well hereafter, condemn-ing your hasty accusations yourself. Things cannot be carried out as soon as you think, and wish. We will explain ourselves more at length to our superiors, sending them word what we have done for the best; and we hope that, judging well according to reason and justice, they will be satis-fied with it, for, in short, we are the servants both of God and of the King and have no other interest which could induce us to act contrary [to theirs.]

But here is another matter on which you should reflect. Our Fathers with the Miamis send us word that they wrote to you by one of your men who wintered at their mission, sent on purpose, that the Iroquois, the Loups and the Hurons who are near you, and par-ticularly the man who complains so loudly and whose complaints you lis-ten to,—who, apparently, only makes so much fuss in order the better to conceal his own designs [lit. to conceal him-self] by fixing your attention on us alone,—are acting in concert to estab-lish at 8abache an English post entirely opposed to that of Detroit, which if it once comes to be established will inevit-ably overthrow the trade of the Colony. As our Fathers who are on the spot in-form you of it, we have nothing to add on our part to what they have written to you, having no other knowledge of it than that which they give us; for a

This 11th letter is from Father Maret missionary at Missilimakinak. This style of writing to M de Lamothe, who is his Commandant, is too haughty, and it is clear that the expressions are those of a mind inflated with pride which cannot endure authority. But as M. de La-mothe has replied to this [letter], and sends me a copy, it is superfluous to give his observations on it.

The 2nd paragraph of his letter agrees with the 9th from Father Mermet and proves their scheme.

most profound silence is maintained
here towards us, which of itself serves
to inspire us with mistrust.

It is for you, on a warning of this
importance, not to fix your mind on
us so [exclusively] as not to take a
moment for turning it to the examination of the conduct of those near you in
order to find out the truth or falsity of
it. I could not understand how Mikinak, after so many obligations as he is
under to you, could resist the efforts you
have made to retain him at Detroit
without a reason as old and strong as
them [i. e. the obligations] but if people continue also to impute everything
to us as a crime, we shall be reduced,
even in matters in which we have some
credit, to the necessity of accusing no
one lest this accusation should be made
use of with the accused to make them
speak against us. For the rest, the savages of this place, having seen the
quality of the land at Detroit and having found, as they say, that there is no
fishing there or very little, and that the
hunting will not be long in falling off
there as people assemble more, near to
one another, are thereupon showing an
inclination, which it will not lie in our
power to change, and it will be unjust
to take offence at us for an impotence
opposed to our inclinations.

Mikinak told me yesterday and begged
me to write you that he has already

This 13th letter [is] from Father d'Avenaut, missionary to the Miamis. He acknowledges having received one from M. de Calliere, and [says] that he read it to the Miamis, having invited them to go and settle at Detroit. M. de Lamothe knows the contrary from the Frenchmen who were present there, having told the savages [before] them to remain steady in their village. And this agrees with what one of the chiefs of the Miamis told M. de Lamothe at the council of the 27th of June, 1702. On the last point, the Father relied on the speech which M. de Calliere had made to the Miamis at Montreal at the general assembly which was held there on the 6th of August, 1701, in which he begins in these terms at para. 6.

As regards what you ask me, Chichikatelo, that the other villages of the Miamis should form one only with us at the St. Joseph river, you may assure all those of your tribe that they will give me pleasure by joining you there, for I am convinced that as soon as peace is concluded they will live much better there than in all the other places where they [now] are.

It is agreed that this speech would have been a reason for dissuading the Miami savages from coming to settle at Detroit, if the letter which the Governor wrote to him to invite them to come there, had not been later.

From the St. Joseph River the 4th of June, 1702.

Thirteenth

Sir,

I no sooner received last summer the letter which the Governor did me the honor of writing to me as to the settlement of the French at Detroit, in which he invites the savages including the Miamis to come and settle near the French at the post of Detroit, than I read it to them in their tongue without concealing anything of the contents of the aforesaid letter from them. And now, when I remind them of it, they tell me that it is true that I read it to them, and that I added that, if they went and settled at Detroit I would not fail to go there also, not being willing to abandon them; they answered me that, amidst so great a number of people, they feared to be reduced in a short time to starvation, although the goods which they are encouraged to hope they will get cheap do not fail to shake their [resolution] greatly. The news of 100 or 200 Iroquois who were to come here this summer to speak to them, which St. Michel told me to tell them for you, has surprised them strangely and has given them occasion to doubt the truth of the peace, thinking they were not included, especially when they were told, also from you, that they were to stand upon their guard, which nevertheless did not prevent a few young men from setting out a few days ago on the warpath against the Si8s in spite of all that the old men and I could say to them to make them at least delay their march for some time till they should learn news of Onontio their father. You know still better than I the disposition of the savages, I mean their way of acting, they always pursue their own points, so that if they really wish to go to Detroit, they will go without fail; if not, they will remain just where they are, or at least they will make no great stir to change their dwelling place. I pray God that he will give us and them the grace to do ever and in all things his holy will. I greet your wife again and ask her for some share in her prayers; and am, Sir, with respect your very humble and very obedient servant.

Cl. Aveneau

As soon as the Father has returned here himself, I will hand him your letter and another from Detroit which St. Michel brought. He arrived yesterday and I gave him your letter with that from M. de Tonty to whom you will permit me to send greeting.

This 12th letter from Father Carheil was written to M. de Tonty who is the Captain at Detroit. He handed it over to M. de Lamothe to take it to M. de Calliere having made a sacrifice of it to him out of gratitude for M. de la Mothe having passed over a grave fault on his part.

In this letter the hand of providence may be seen; it is certain that M. de la Mothe had special confidence in M. de Tonty, who profited by it, like a good scholar of Naples, to betray him, working in concert with the missionaries to

At Missilimakinak, the 17th June 1702 f.

Twelfth.

Sir,

The good evidence which you have been good enough to give me of the diligence of Monique in constantly fulfilling, every Sunday and every saintsday, the requirements of Christianity could not but be very agreeable to me, not only because it assures me that for her part she desires her true welfare, but also because it assures me consequently for your part that what you value most in her is also what you most

that this defining of the intentions of the King is notified to them in all the letters they have received from the Governor-General, from M. de Champigny the Intendant, and from his Superiors and that this it is which will set everything right by removing the confusion which caused the uproar; that is to say, by getting M. de la Mothe recalled from his post and consequently by having M. de Tonty appointed there.

From all this we must draw an unanswerable conclusion, either what this Father writes is true, or it is false; if it is true the Governor-General, the Intendant and the Superiors of the Jesuits have worked together to ruin M de Lamothe and destroy the post of Detroit; if it is false it is an imposture of Father de Carheil, and he is calumniating these gentlemen and even his Superiors. All this was discovered by a voice from heaven which cast M. de Tonty and his horse to the ground, and by a light which blinded him on the road to Damascus.

The rage of this Father is also seen in that he boldly affirms that M. de Lamothe reduced Father Vaillant to the necessity of withdrawing from Detroit —so as to reduce him himself, he says, to not being able to come there.

Yet the contrary appears from the letters of the same Father Vaillant, of Father Bouvart[1] his Superior, of Father Germain,[2] and of Father Maret, the first two of these thanking M. de La Mothe for the good treatment and for the courtesies he showed him, and the two latter assuring him that the return of this Father was expected at Quebec.

Moreover you would say that this Father was suffering from a high fever, especially when he says that everything the Governor, the Intendant, or our Superiors, will set everything right by taking away the confusion which caused the uproar.

That I am not able to be at Missilimakinak with those who have remained there and at Detroit with those who have been attracted there, is not a matter which ought to cause an outcry against me, unless from a desire to compel me to do an impossibility by being in two places at the same time. Why were they divided without agreeing together as to such a settlement? And why was Father Vaillant brought back (whom they had sent to assist us) although they were not at all able to prepare us for it, except to reduce us also to being unable to go there at the same time that he was withdrawn from it, and when they began to raise an outcry there against us. However we have done nothing but for the best; a little delay to make one's arrangements is always necessary for prudence in one's enterprises, and chiefly in what relates to any fixed and permanent matter, such as a new settlement is. Moreover we are surprised that none of the letters which have come to us from Detroit tells us anything of an important new fort which our Fathers with the Miamis send us word that they have made known to M. de Lamothe by a messenger sent on this matter. As we have no other information of it here than that which they give us, we can for our part add nothing to it; and even if we could, and had learnt some private news which in itself should compel us to give warning of it, yet seeing what is going on regarding us, we know not whether it would not be better for our own safety to keep silent than to expose ourselves to the dangers of being accused again thereupon to the savages. For indeed everything is turned into an accusation and proceedings against our functions which there is a grudge against; but it will be in vain to bear

<hr />

[1]Samuel Bouvard, Jesuit, came to Canada in 1673. He sometimes signed his name Martin Bouvard. He left Canada Oct 10, 1710. Rep. Gen. 61.—C. M. B.

is turned into an accusation and proceedings against their functions, which
we have a grudge against. Where then
are these proceedings which have been
instituted? Assuredly they must be in
his own imagination.

As for you, Sir, I have no doubt you
condemn all these ———— so opposed
to reason, justice and truth. You have
not forgotten what we used to say here
in former times, in some of our con-
versations, that all our duties might be
reduced to these five heads; servant of
God for himself, servant of everyone for
God, servant of no one against God, servant of God against everyone, servant of
God against one's self. No one could
turn aside from his duty by following
these five rules and I wish with you that
they were followed at Detroit. I am,
with respect both for you and Madme,
to whom you will permit me to send
greeting, Sir, yr very humble and very
obedient servant.

[Signed]   Etienne de Carheil

Father Marest presents his compliments to you and begs you to permit
him to greet Madame.

This 14th letter is from Father Maret.
It will be seen that it is in answer to
one which M. de Lamothe wrote to him,
dated the 2nd of May, 1702, a copy of
which he is sending to the Court, which
relates to the councils held at Detroit
by the savages on the 30th Oct. and
4th Dec. 1701.

It is as well to know that all that this
Father writes does not originate with
him; that these letters are all in the
style of Father de Carheil who has indeed much intellect and is also very
learned; but he goes astray and it appears from all his conduct that it would
be well for him if his knowledge and
wit had a seasoning of good sense and
of a little more judgment. It is only
necessary to read the letter from M. de

At Missilimakinak this 23d of July, 1702.
              Fourteenth f.
Sir,
The first words of your letter inform
me that you wish me to answer it point
by point. I will do so, to content you.

It reduces itself to five or six points.
The first concerns our pretended correspondent; the 2nd, your conditional
judgment; the 3rd, the person of Quarante Solz; the 4th the place of your
settlement, its cause, its object and the
manner of it; the 5th the scheme of
Mikinak, and, finally, the sixth of promises.

On the first point which refers to our
pretended correspondent, I reply that
this faithful correspondent, but ill-in-
formed—you say—as to the memoranda
of which you have written to us, is you

[to·this] that the contents of his letter rests on an "If," whereby his judgment was conditional and is not decisive.

This Father also places himself in a difficulty in the 5th paragraph of his letter in which he says that he knows well that Quarante Sous could not have accused him, since he does not know him nor understand him; but that he knows that if he did not complain at Detroit, he complained very loudly to the Miamis.

There is a confession already. What! Quarante Sous only complained to the Miamis! Why then does this Father accuse M. de La Mothe, in the 2nd paragraph of his 11th letter, of listening to the complaints of him who complains so loudly, that is to say of the same Quarante Sous, since he admits that he knows this chief has not complained against them at Detroit.

M. de Lamothe has explained that they have confused matters, that they have taken one Quarante Sous for another man of the same name; he pointed this out to these fathers, but as they had taken the first step and claim to be infallible in all things, like the Pope in his council, they have censured this poor man in an unbridled manner, and also impute to him, without any consideration, that he had separated himself from his people in order to go and join the enemy. Where was his dwelling? They must either be asleep or dreaming, not to know that it was in the village of the Miamis; is this tribe hostile to us? He is accused of going with his story prepared, to Montreal to inveigh againt all the missionaries; but M. de Calliere knows that he was very silent and did not even open his mouth against them, and he was so pleased with his conduct that he proclaimed him chief of all his tribe, which approved him as such; but the missionaries, not having found this choice to their minds, have roused the malcontents against him.

In his 6th paragraph he replies to the 1st of M. de Lamothe's letter. He does

your opinions than by yourself, than by your own evidence?

As to the 2nd point on which you say there is no occurrence on your part, but a conditional judgment, I answer that the condition is lacking. In regard to the 3rd—where Quarante Solz is in question, I know that he could not accuse me since he does not know me nor understand me. But I also know that if he has not been at Detroit he has complained very loudly to the Miamis against the Revd. Father de Carheil, attributing to this Father what he ought to attribute to himself,—I mean the division in the tribe. He complained loudly that Father de Carheil had prevented his people from following him. But he ought not to call them his people since he separated himself from them to go and join the enemy; and he should have come and rejoined them as they had agreed last autumn before going down to Montreal, at a council held for that purpose in the presence of M. de Courtemanche, who committed it to writing in order to report upon it to M. de Calliere. It was at this council that Quarante Solz solemnly pledged himself to return here to put an end to the question of their settlement; but his failing [to keep] his word was the reason why all his tribe did not settle at Detroit. But although he had complained very loudly to the Miamis against Father de Carheil, we were informed also that he went down [the river] with* his story prepared against this Father. Ought we not to have believed that what he told the Miamis, and what he went declaiming on the way down to Montreal, was only expressing what he had said at Detroit? As to the accusation which has been made against him, if it is false, it is not we who have accused him, it is not we who should be blamed, but the Savages who reported it to our Fathers with the Miamis. We had expressly told you that we had no knowledge of it except what ·had been given us from the

Father de Carheil and Father Anjalran had good opinions of it; but he throws it on the savages. And yet it appears from the statements which all the tribes made to M. de Calliere by the mouth of Jean le Blanc, otherwise [called] Otoutagan, at the general assembly which was summoned at Montreal on the 6th of August, 1701, that they had resolved to come and settle there. Here are the very phrases of this chief in the 3rd paragraph of the replies.

"We ask you [that we may] set out tomorrow, and that we may return in good health because otherwise we should not be able to go to Detroit as you wish, and as we [also] desire" which proves that it is only the mischievous talk addressed to the savages when they arrived at Missilimakinak which made them change their intention.

This Father continues his letter by saying that M. De Lamothe dwells on the will of the king, that he says that the King wishes this settlement [formed], that he has no other aim but his service. But, to these words, this arrogant and bold Father answers him like a master and treats him as an inferior. We know, says he, what the real will of the King is; that is to say, in plain French, that M. de Lamothe does not know it, nor the Governor-Genl. either who, in his instructions, ordered him to invite all the tribes to come and settle at Detroit. This is the copy: M. de Lamothe will send to give notice to all the tribes of the upper countries who are our allies, of the post we have had formed at Detroit, in order to invite them to come there for goods which they will find reasonable in price, as well as to settle there, making them understand Miamis, where the Frenchmen could not help reproaching him about it in public; and it is this apparently, which caused his design to miscarry because he found he was discovered.

In your 4th paragraph you say that the land of Detroit has always been regarded as a land of promise. If that is so, and the savages make false statements as to the quality of the land at Detroit, as they are not willing to go and settle there, that should show you their disinclination for that place. This false reason which they bring forward, indicates true ones which they do not say, or at least a great opposition in their will. You dwell upon the will of the King; you say that the King wills it, that you have had no aim but his service. We know what the real will of the King is, we do not oppose anything that he wishes; when people will serve him only, there will be no dispute. Also do not think that we took the useless trouble of examining into the utility or the drawbacks of your settlement. It was the savages who examined it; we did nothing more than listen to them without coming to any conclusion in a matter of which we had no knowledge except from their report.

I wish you were speaking truly in your fifth paragraph, and that Mikinak were on the watch* to become indeed my hero; he would have to become a true Christian, that is the only way in which he could be so.

Finally, after having done us all the harm you could do on this present occasion, after having dealt us all the blows you could both at Detroit and with the Miamis, and at Montreal by sending there by your letters and your

This expression is insulting to their commandant, signifying that if there are disputes between them and M. de Lamothe it is because he does not serve the King. They set themselves up as judges and condemn him, while his Governor-Genl. does him the honor to approve of his proceedings in all the letters he has written him, and the consultations he has had with him. Finally he complains that M. de Lamothe, after having dealt all the blows he could against them, makes them fine promises, especially after having sent his letter and accusers to Montreal; as if he could have helped giving the Governor-General an account of what goes on at his post, and sending him a copy of the statements of the savages. If he acted otherwise he might be reprimanded for it; but he did not treat them in an underhand manner, for he gave them notice of it in his letter of the 2nd of May. The statement that he sent accusers against them to Montreal deserves a reprimand, he [?M. de Lamothe] refers that matter to MM de Calliere, de Champigny and de Vaudreuil. Finally, he concludes this beautiful letter by saying that they have laid their resentments at the foot of the crucifix. That may be true; but as they no doubt, often go to it, they can find them there again when they want them; and it would appear that he went there, to take up the postscript of this very letter.

In the 3rd letter Father Anjalran, who is one of the most able Jesuits, and the only one who has mastered the Outavois and Algonquine tongues, [who]

publish them everywhere you could, and in terms as outrageous as you have done? On what do you base the justice of your resentments? Do you base it on the accusation against us by the savages? There is no just foundation; you ought to have heard the defence and convicted it of falsehood. It is indeed for us to say, with much more reason, that we bury, or to speak in a more Christian spirit, that we lay at the foot of the crucifix—as indeed we do—all our just resentments; for I can assure you that I am, with all possible sincerity and profound respect, Sir, yr. very humble and very obedt. servant

[Signed]

J. J. Marest.

You will be good enough to permit me to present my compliments to Madame de Lamothe; I know that, as a Jesuit, I shall be neither unknown, nor indifferent to her.

---

¹Although this letter bears the date, on the endorsement, of 1702, it was probably written in 1701. Madam Cadillac went to Detroit in the fall of 1701 after the treaty of peace with the Iroquois. This alone would fix the date of the letter. Cadillac was in Quebec Sept. 25, 1702.—C. M. B.

At Montreal, the 7th August 1702¹
Third

Sir, I do not know what reply to make to the letter I have received from you, in which I have at the same time received an honor which I value greatly, in the confidence which you show you have in me. Everything here is in a state of such great uncertainty that I should not dare to give you any hope as to the proposal which you repeat that [I] should act as escort to Mme. de La Mothe and to Mme de Tonty to

was chosen to summon all the tribes to the general peace which has been concluded at Montreal as he had great influence over their minds, expresses himself clearly as to the importance of the settlement of Detroit, and proves in his letter of the 27th of August that it is important to unite all the missions and the other posts to this. He expresses it in these terms. As for me I have always held the same opinion, etc.

But because this Father stated his opinion about it in public, the Society of Canada made him go to France, and no doubt it afforded him some other pretext.

come and see you at Detroit although both of them are inclined for this journey with all their hearts. Madame de la Mothe does not make her appearance here yet, and someone told me that she was ill.

Our savages are thinking of going by Niagara and Detroit to Missilimakina; by all appearances they will go and pass the winter with you. The sickness of the greater part of them and the death of some has greatly disconcerted them; but for that, the conclusion of peace in that assembly, the finest that has ever been seen in this country, could not have been a greater success. I am looking forward to finding other opportunities which will give me more leisure to prove to you the sincere desire I have to please you and to show you that I am, with feelings of particular esteem, Sir, your very humble and very obedient servant, signed,

Anjalran, Jesuit, 27th August.

I had written this letter during the time of the perplexity in which I was thrown by the mad policy of the savages and by the various intrigues concerning the establishment of the post

ACCOUNT OF DETROIT.

Endorsed—Portfolio 127. Document 44. Description.

In order to give you an outline, My Lord, of what Detroit is [like], in case you may not have one, you must know that it is a River which is twenty-five leagues in length into which Lake Huron discharges [on its way] to empty itself into Lake Erie. Another is met with in this River, called Lake St. Claire, which is nearly ten leagues from the latter; it is ten leagues through and about fifteen broad, abundantly stocked with fish, as well as the River, which [? latter] is about the forty-first degree [of latitude] and runs from its exit to Lake Erie from the North-north-east to the South-south-west. The land to the north extends from the border of the Miamis, where there is a river by which the journey can be made in six days, whence it is easy to go up to the Mississippi; that to the south, as far as Toronto which is a [stretch of] dry land at the foot of Lake Huron ending at that of Ontario. Detroit is distant a hundred leagues from Missilimakinac, and a hundred also from the lower part at Niagara, which is distant from Montreal a hundred and fifty; and if a settlement is made of this post, it has been determined to build boats at Katarakoui to convey the necessary articles as far as Niagara where a fort will be constructed in order to keep carters there who will carry out the portage of them; they will be received by other boats which will convey them here, whence we shall be able to send them to the Miamis at Chikag8, and to the Bay to carry on the trade with the tribes which are in large numbers there.

Our fort is one arpent square without the bastions, very advantageously situated on an eminence, separated from the river by a gentle slope of about forty paces which forms a very desirable glacis. We took care to put it at the narrowest part of the River, which is one gunshot [across] being everywhere else a good half-quarter of a league; and if the post is [hereafter] inhabited, the ground is very good there for building eventually a large town.

more than three feet high; they are interrupted only by fruit trees, or by natural trees of very great height [and] of many kinds, as the walnut tree, soft and hard, oak red and white, ivy, whitewoods, elm, ash, and cotton trees. This variety extends into the distant parts of the lands, which we have taken the precaution of exploring and it turns out so good that it makes us hope that its fertility will not refuse to the hand of the careful husbandman what nature unaided has produced so abundantly. It is in these woods and on these vast prairies that an immense number of oxen, cows, stags, hinds, roebucks, bears and turkeys feed, which have been of very great assistance to us for providing food for our soldiers and voyageurs while occupied on the work for whom provisions would have failed from the time of their arrival. Four or five hunters have been sufficient up to the present time to keep them supplied, in spite of the great heat which has made them lose a part of their spoil; and this should enable [us] to judge of the number of animals which are to be seen in this continent. In the prairies, in Lake St. Clair, and the River, in which there are several islands, a great quantity of game is met with, consisting of pheasants, quails, rails, red-legged partridges, cranes, swans, wild geese, ducks of several species, teals and turtle doves.

If this settlement is continued it will be a means of preventing the English from coming and seizing on it in order to take from us the trade with the tribes of the further districts; of curbing the Iroquois; and of holding our allies to their duty; and it will be easier to frenchify them, and to proclaim the Gospel to them, on account of the proximity of the French and the number of missionaries there will be.

That Sir, is all I can tell you at present of the goodness of this country;

DESCRIPTION OF DETROIT; ADVANTAGES FOUND THERE.

THE NECESSITY AND THE MEANS OF PERFECTING THIS POST.

Endorsed—Portfolio 127. Document 45. M. La Motte Cadillàc, 25th. Sept. 1702.

My Lord,

It is my duty to give you an account of this country, I will begin with a short description, so that you may be more definitely informed about it.

Detroit is a river lying north-north-east towards Lake Huron and south-south-west to the entrance of Lake Erie. According to my reckoning it will be about 25 or 26 leagues in length and it is navigable throughout so that a vessel of 100 guns could pass through it safely.

Towards the middle there is a lake which has been called St. Claire, which is about 30 leagues in circumference and 10 leagues in length. This lake is scarcely noticed, on account of several large and fine islands which form various passages or channels which are no wider than the river. It is only for about four leagues that the channel is wider.

Through this passage, the waters of Lake Nemebigoün,* which is 300 leagues [? round], flow gently; those of Lake Superior, which is 550 leagues round; those of Lake Michigan or Illinois, 300 leagues; those of Lake Huron, 600 leagues. They go into Lake Erie 300 leagues, and afterwards, into Lake Ontario or Frontenac, 300 leagues; finally, they pass through the River St. Lawrence, or Quebec River, and mingle in the ocean.

All these lakes are of sweet water.

At the entrance to Lake Huron the lands are brown and well wooded; a vast and grand prairie is seen there which extends to the interior of the lands on both sides of the river up to Lake St. Claire, [where] there are fewer prairies than elsewhere.

All the surroundings of this lake are extensive pasture lands, and the grass on them is so high that a man can scarcely be seen in it.

This river or strait of the seas is scattered over, from one lake to the other, both on the mainland and on the islands there, in its plains and on its banks, with large clusters of trees surrounded by charming meadows; but these same trees are marvelously lofty, without nodes and almost without branches until near the top, except the great oak.

out that they might be taken for orchards planted by the hand of a gardener.

On all sides the vine is seen; there are some with bitter and rough grapes,—others whose berries are extremely large and plump. There are also white and red grapes, the skins of which are very thin, full of good juice. The latter are the best, and I have taken care to select some of these·plants and have them planted near the fort. I have no doubt that, by cultivating it as they do in France, this vine will produce good grapes and consequently good wine.

I have observed there nearly twenty different kinds of plums. There are three or four kinds which are very good; the others are very large and pleasant to look at, but they have rather tough skins and mealy flesh. The apples are of medium size, too acid. There is also a number of cherry-trees, [but] their fruit is not very good. In places there are mulberry trees which bear big black mulberries; this fruit is excellent and refreshing. There is also a very large quantity of hazel nuts and filberts. There are six kinds of walnuts; [the timber of] these trees is good for furniture and gun-stocks. There are also stretches of chestnuts, chiefly towards Lake Erie. All the fruit trees in general are loaded with their fruit; there is reason to believe that if these trees were grafted, pruned and well cultivated, their fruit would be much better, and that it might be made good fruit.

In places the woods are mixed, as white oak, red, walnut, elm, white wood trees, mulberry trees, cottonwood, chestnuts, ash; and in others they are not.

There is one tree which is unknown to me, and to all who have seen it; its leaves are a vivid green, and remain so until the month of January, it has been observed that it flowers in the spring, and towards the end of November; the flowers are white. This tree is a big one.

There is another tree which is well defended, the prickles of which are half a foot long and pierce the wood like a nail; it bears a fruit like kidney-beans. The leaf is like the capillary plant; neither man nor animal could climb it. That would be good for making fences, its grain is very hard; when it has arrived at maturity, the wood is so hard that it is very difficult to drive an axe into it.

There are also citron-trees which are the same in form and color as the

It is certain that, on both sides of the river of Detroit, the lands are very fertile and extend in the same manner and with the same pleasing character about ten leagues into the interior, after which few fruit trees are to be found and fewer prairies seen. But 15 leagues from Detroit, at the entrance to Lake Erie, inclining to the south-south-west, are boundless prairies which stretch away for about 100 leagues. It is there that these mighty oxen,* which are covered with wool, find food in abundance. Forty leagues from this lake, going straight towards the south, there is no winter; the French and the savages have reported that they have seen neither ice nor snow there.

I sent this spring to the Chevalier de Calliere some hides and wool of these animals, and he sent both to the directors of the Company of the colony to make trial of them, and it has been found that this discovery will prove a valuable one; that the hides may be very usefully employed, and this wool used for stockings and cloth-making. There is a number of stags and hinds, they are seen in hundreds, [with] roebuck, black bears, otters and other smaller fur-bearing animals [literally, "furs"]; the skins of these animals sell well. There are also numbers of beavers on this mainland and in the neighborhood.

Game is very common there, as wild geese and all kinds of wild ducks. There are swans everywhere; there are quails, woodcocks, pheasants, rabbits—it is the only place on the continent of America where any have been seen. There are so many turkeys that 20 or 30 could be killed at one shot every [time they are] met with. There are partridges, hazelhens, and a stupenduous number of turtle-doves.

As this place is well supplied with animals, the wolves, of which there are numbers, find abundant food there; but it often costs them their skins because they sell well also; and this aids in destroying them, because the savages hunt them.

There are wood rats which are as large as rabbits; most of them are grey, but there are some seen which are as white as snow. The female has a pouch under her belly which opens and shuts as she requires, so that, sometimes when her little ones are playing, if the mother finds herself pressed, she quickly shuts them up in her pouch and carries them all away with her at once and gains her retreat.

· I have seen a number of different [kinds of] birds of rare beauty. Some have plumage of a beautiful red fire color, the most vivid it were possible to see; they have a few spots of black in the tail and at the tips of their wings, but that is only noticed when they are seen flying. I have seen others all yellow, with tails bigger than their bodies, and they spread out their tails as peacocks do. I have seen others of a sky blue color with red breasts; there are some which are curiously marked like those great butterflies. I have observed that a pleasant warbling proceeds from all these birds, especially from the red ones with large beaks.

There are many cranes, grey and white; they stand higher than a man. The savages value these latter greatly, on account of their plumage, with which they adorn themselves.

In the river of Detroit there are neither stones nor rocks, but in Lake Huron there are fine quarries, and it is a country wooded like Canada, that is to say, with endless forests. Houses could be provided and buildings erected of bricks, for there is earth which is very suitable for that, and fortunately, [only] five leagues from the fort. There is an island which is very large, and is entirely composed of limestone.

We have fish in great abundance, and it could not be otherwise, for this river is inclosed and situated between two lakes, or rather between as many seas. A thing which is most convenient for navigation is that it does not wind at all; its two prevailing winds are the north-east and the south-west.

This country, so temperate, so fertile, and so beautiful that it may justly be called the earthly paradise of North America, deserves all the care of the King to keep it up and to attract inhabitants to it, so that a solid settlement may be formed there which shall not be liable to the usual vicissitudes of the other posts in which only a mere garrison is placed.

I could not send any of our oxen or calves to France until after barges have been built, on which I believe they are going to work at once. One of them will be on Lake Frontenac and the other at Detroit in order to facilitate the conveyance of hides and wool which could not be effected by canoe transport. These barges will serve also for the other large skins, for beaver skins, and other small furs which will be conveyed at less expense in this way. They will serve for everything in general that is included in trade; and, as they will be capable of sailing two thousand leagues in the surrounding districts, we shall not fail, in time, to make some discovery which perhaps will be no less lucrative than glorious to France.

It is necessary to have settlers, in order to develop the trade. We

of white oak, which is even and hard and as heavy as iron. This fort is in no danger provided there are enough people there to defend it.

Its position is delightful and very advantageous; it is [at] the narrowest part of the river, where no one can pass by day without being seen.

You know. that I set out from Montreal on the 2nd of June, 1701, with 100 men and three months' provisions; that I arrived at Detroit on the 24th of July, having gone by the ordinary route of the Utaüais, by which I made only 30 portages, in order to try it.

After the fort was built, and the dwellings, I had the land cleared there and some French wheat sown on the 7th of October, not having had time to prepare it well. This wheat. although sown. hastily, came up very fine and was cut on the 21st of July.

I also had some sown this spring, as is done in Canada; it came up well enough, but not like that of the autumn. The land having thus shown its quality, and taught me that the French tillage must be followed, I left orders with M. de Tonty to take care to begin the sowing about the 20th of Sept., and I left him 20 arpents of land prepared. I have no doubt he has increased it somewhat since my departure.

I also had twelve arpents or more sown this spring, in the month of May, with Indian corn which came up eight feet high; it will have been harvested about the 20th of the month of August, and I hope there will be a good deal of it. All the soldiers have their own gardens.

I believe we shall have 60 arpents of land sown this next spring, hence I count on having a large quantity of corn; and I will have a mill built on the spot, so as to be absolutely independent of Canada for provisions. I have also a fine garden in which I have put some vines, and some ungrafted fruit trees. It is one arpent square, and we shall enlarge it if necessary. In all this I have only complied with the orders of the Governor-General.

All that is no easy task, especially as everything has to be carried on the shoulders. for we have no oxen or horses yet to draw [loads] nor to plough; and to accomplish it, it is necessary to be very active.

I have also had a boat of ten tons burden built which will be useful for many purposes in the river.

On the right of the fort, at a good distance, there is a village of the Hurons to which I have granted lands in the name of His Majesty, according to my order. The chief of this tribe, with four of the most important men, in accepting them shouted "Long Live the King" three times with me; and I have myself set up the landmarks, and marked out the place where I wished them to build their fort and their village. By this means I have set all the tribes on the track of asking me for lands. and for permission to settle there. Having shown the others the way, this tribe has cleared up to the present about 200 arpents of land, and

There is also, on the left of the fort, a village of Oppenago, that is, of Wolves, to whom I have likewise granted lands, on condition, however, of giving them up to me if I want them afterwards, on granting them others further off; the spot where they are might be useful for a common land hereafter. These are the most tractable and most peaceable of the savages. I am convinced that, if only a little care is taken of them, they will very soon become Christians. They dress like the French, as far as they can; they are very caressing; they even make rough attempts at our language as far as they can. They have also made fine fields of wheat.

Above this village, half a league higher up, there is a village made up of four tribes of the Oütavois. to whom I have likewise granted lands; they have made some very fine fields of Indian corn there. Thus, within the space of one league, there are four forts and four hundred men bearing arms, with their families, besides the garrison.

Before I set out from the fort, eighteen Miamis came, on behalf of their tribe, to ask me for lands and to beg the savages who are there to approve of their coming to settle there and joining them. Thus the settlements could not promise better; these having prepared the way, the others will not be long before they come there, especially as, before I left, we learnt that the corn at Missilimakinak had been killed this year by the frost as it was the preceding [year], a thing which very often happens at that place.

Last year, my wife and Mme. Tonty set out on the 10th of Sept. with our families to come and join us there. Their resolution in undertaking so long and laborious a journey seemed very extraordinary. It is certain that nothing [ever] astonished the Iroquois so greatly as when they saw them. You could not believe how many caresses they offered them, and particularly the Iroquois who kissed their hands and wept for joy, saying that French women had never been seen coming willingly to their country. It was that which made the Iroquois also say that they well knew that the general peace which the Chev. de Calliere had just made

All that I have had the honor to state to you has been done in one year, without it having cost the King a sou, and without costing the Company a double; and in twelve months we have put ourselves in a position to do without provisions from Canada for ever; and all this undertaking was carried out with three months' provisions, which I took when I set out from Montreal, which were consumed in the course of the journey. This proves whether Detroit is a desirable or an undesirable country. Besides this, nearly six thousand mouths of different tribes wintered there, as every one knows. All these proofs, convincing as they are, cannot silence the enemies of my scheme; but they do begin to grow feebler and to diminish in violence. It may be said that nothing more remains to them, good or bad, but their tongues.

If the King had the kindness to look into this matter well, and to follow it up, numberless advantages would be obtained from it, to the profit of the state, the Colony and religion. It is very grievous that this matter, so successfully promoted, should be suddenly destroyed by the obstacles which as it seems to me are rising against it.

I shall ever maintain that, if this post is settled by Frenchmen and savages, it will be the safeguard of our trade with our allies, and the blow which will overpower the Iroquois, because in consequence of it he will not be in a position to begin or to maintain war, as I have proved in the memorandum which I had the honor to present to you in France.

I maintain also, and take the liberty of deciding definitely, that if the King keeps only a mere garrison there, it is a useless post which it would have been better never to have started, and it will without doubt produce troublesome consequences; for our allies, being disappointed in their expectations, and in the promises which were made to them that the French would settle there, may take some course which might make us repent of our instability. The Iroquois, seeing likewise that this post would be anything rather than what they have been led to expect, will infallibly fall into feelings of mistrust which might well upset the peace they have concluded.

Moreover it is not possible that our families could live in a place inhabited by savages only. Their distress would be extreme, for they would be without any relief; as happened to Mme. Tonty who saw her infant .die for want of milk, which she had not anticipated. I fear the same may happen to my wife who was just about to be confined when I left. That is not extraordinary because these ladies have wet nurses for their children. Hence there can be no hesitation in sending them down next year, unless a few families are permitted to go and settle there, so that they can find some assistance in these grievous conjunctures.

M. de Calliere having regard to that, has been good enough to permit six families to go and settle there next spring, and the Intendants who

of the Company about it, and they have made no objection to it, and have
agreed with me that these inhabitants of Detroit should be given goods
at one third cheaper than they are sold to the savages, so that they might
profit by this advantage through the trade they will do in them at the
fort, in consideration of which they will be obliged to hand over to the
agents of the Company the beaver and other skins, the proceeds of their
trade, for which they will be paid at the current price.

I take the liberty of sending you certain suggestions for contributing
to the progress of this post, while respecting the interests of the Company
to which the King has granted the trade.

As the subject of this post has been so often under consideration, and
as the King has recognized the importance of this settlement, the success of which has been so fortunate and so rapid up to the present time,
it would be superfluous to reply to the objections of an infinitude of
noisy fellows* who have no less an itching to speak of all the affairs of
this country than the newsmongers of the Palais Royal about the movements of all Europe.

You are convinced, My Lord, that I have never had in view anything
save the propagation of the Faith, the glory of the King, the care of his
interests, and the benefit of the colony.

How can these barbarians be made Christians, unless they are made
men first? How can they be made men unless they are humanized and
made docile? And how can they be tamed and humanized except by their
companionship with a civilized people? How bring them into subjection
and make them subjects of the King, if they have neither docility nor
religion nor social intercourse?

All that can be done easily by the means set forth in my memorandum;
and in perfecting the settlement of Detroit, I have done for my part all
that is necessary. It remains, on yours, to carry out what you have
promised me.

There are at Detroit a good fort, good dwellings, [and] the means of

Your Highness may rest assured that, in a little while you will see its progress. and you will have all the glory of it. If this affair does not advance with giant strides, see to it yourself. I have done my duty; [have provided] a good fort, dwellings, [and] corn, and have formed three villages of savages. All has been begun well; finish it, if it please you, My Lord. Give your orders; I answer for it that as far as I am concerned, I shall know how to have them carried out. Up to the present, I have succeeded in what I have undertaken. If I am not skilful, what matter?—I am fortunate. And when I succeed, they say it by a miracle. Again, what matters it, if I belong to a time when miracles are performed?

You know that in the same way that promises, contracts, bonds, agreements, &c. serve as security with civilized nations, so belts and presents, among the savages, confirm all the words we say to them and the steps we wish them to take; and without these they have no effect, and they let them fall to the ground. For as with us, when any dispute arises, we have recourse to the deeds, so the savages have recourse to the presents and belts which have been given them, as a pledge of the fidelity of the promises which are made to them, and a title which confers on them the right to possess or to abandon.

As no one can dispute the truth of this, it is the fact that it has been rendered morally impossible for me to succeed, and to induce the tribes to come and settle there; and this shows that those who are there, are so from liking for the place and because of the advantages they obtain from it.

If you wish the rest of the tribes to come there, it is necessary to order a few presents [to be made] for that purpose.

[I should be glad] if you would also look over the memorandum again which I had the honor of presenting to you in France, in favor of the former agents, in which I pledge myself to supply them with fresh beaver skins, and to prevent any quantity of dried ones from going down, as it is burdensome to them, for I intended to occupy the savages at Detroit in hunting the large skins of the elk, stags, hinds, black bears, and small furs. It is easy to see whether I have succeeded, since for two years, they have not received at the office the third part of the beaver skins of previous years; and, as the dried beaver skin is now in favor, that will be very convenient. I shall follow, in that matter, the advice of the directors of the company, the object I have at heart being to contribute with all my strength to the public good.

The unjust complaints which the town of Montreal makes are raised by the anger of five or six individuals who, having been accustomed to make the most of all the boats which went to the Outavois, maintain that they are deprived of that by the establishment of Detroit, and do not

had been accustomed to do by the consignment they sent to the Outavois. The Governor of Montreal thinks his governorship is at stake, and that all is lost. When it [?Montreal] was established, the inhabitants of Quebec told the same tales as they are now reciting at Montreal. But yet they cannot deny the utility of this post* for it has preserved, or rather, gained over [to us] some of the Iroquois, and has driven back the rest; it has very often supplied provisions to the town and neighbor-hood of Quebec which, without its assistance, would have perished of famine. Can it be shown that Rouen has destroyed Paris, or Paris, Rouen? Or that Bordeau has injured Tolose, or Tolose, Bordeaux? Quebec, Montreal and Detroit are in the same position as regards their respective trade, as these posts are to one another. What there is not in one country, is found in another; it is that which gives rise to trading, and it is that which maintains States. That is the policy of France, and not to unite all its resources in one place; the kingdom is strong enough. Discoveries must be made; and what is more, it is by this kind of post some new thing is always discovered, which would not be done without inhabitants.

So large a volume could be made of all that the missionaries have said, preached, and written, since they have been in the lands of the Utavais, against the trade in brandy and the [trading] expeditions in the woods that a man's [whole] life would not suffice to get through the reading of it.

The trade in that drink in the backwoods, and notably at Missili-makinak, has always given them occasion for inveighing against all the French who go to trade among the savages; and the [trading] expeditions in the woods have equally served as a pretext for accusing and decrying those who did not conform to their wishes. They have maintained that the brandy trade was an insuperable obstacle to the propagation of the Faith because it made the savages incapable of being taught; and the lewdness, which they stated the French were guilty of with the savage women, was the second head of their discourse, [they] maintaining that it was an obstacle to the success of religion by reason of the bad impression with which the minds of the savages were filled at the sight of such debauchery.

They complained next of the bad custom the Congés [licenses] or per-

They have accused the officers and commandants who were at these posts of being continually guilty of malversation and of obstructing the Voyageurs, in order to favor their own trade.

Lastly, they complained, with reason, that the excessive hunting by the French in the woods produced a burdensome influx of beaver skins for which there was no demand.

They persisted so obstinately in these complaints, whether well or ill founded, that the Court, having been disposed to listen to them, desired to put an end to them by the suppression of the licenses ["congés"] and permits, by prohibiting the brandy trade, by the evacuation of the posts which had been occupied there, and by the recall of the officers who were there for the purpose of keeping our allies united and attached to our interests.' The close connection which exists between the upper colony and the lower (which gives a framework to New France) did not allow of leaving it in this melancholy condition, to which the combined circumstances of the time had reduced it, with ruinous results.·

It was sedulously sought to repair this evil; and you found, My Lord, no better expedient than that of forming a substantial post, at a place which should be suitable on account of the fertility of the land, and the security of trade.

All Canada has agreed, at all times, that Detroit was the most suitable [place]; and you knew so well how useful and necessary it was that you resolved to have it established, and it has been begun with all the success that could be looked for.

What follows goes to prove that all difficulties have been remedied at a stroke, and that this was done by establishing Detroit where there is no longer any trade in drinks carried on with the savages, and if by chance they are sold any at times, that is done without them being intoxicated for, as the drinks are handed over to the charge of the warehouse guards, they are responsible for any bad use which may be made of them.

By means of this post the licentiousness of the French with the savage women is practically abolished; for your intentions were to send some families there, or at least to let the soldiers get married, who, having their wives, do not trifle with indecency. Nor will the Voyageurs, who are intended for conveying goods, cause any scandalous disorder; for, finding themselves included within the inclosure of a fort, and under the superintendence of missionaries, and of a commandant with the power of [inflicting] punishment, they will not dare to expose themselves to disgrace and to the confusion of being severely punished for it.

As the commandant and officers of this post are absolutely excluded from trading, or only trade for the interests of the Company, according to their agreements, they silence all the complaints which could be made against them; for, as they are assembled in one and the same fort, ex-

they would very soon be informed against if they contravened their orders.

By means of this post, the suspicions of trading, which have been entertained against the governors and others, stand completely effaced; and the accusations which have been made against their secretaries remain equally confounded.

The trade of the country is relieved and increased by it; for I have employed the savages at this post in hunting stags, hinds, elks, roebucks, black bears, otters, sables and other small furs, so that, as they have found the means of supplying their wants by the trade they do in the skins of these animals, they have at the same time given up hunting the beaver; and consequently the excessive stock of that article, of which there have been such loud complaints, is diminished by the purchases of it which have been made in France. Since it is a fact that the beaver trade which has been done at Detroit, has not exceeded ten thousand, as appears from the receipt of the warehouse keepers, the Company will only have to settle the quantity it will require in future, and I will try and satisfy it.

The post of Detroit is indisputably the most suitable as regards the security of the trade and the fertility of the land. If it remains the only one, with sufficient troops, there will be nothing now to be feared whether on the part of our allies or from the enemies of the State; for, if the French do not go about in the distant parts of the woods, and give up separating into small parties among the further tribes to transact their trade, they will no longer be exposed to the humiliations and insults which they have so often endured without being able to help it, such as being plundered and cruelly beaten, which has disgraced the name of France among these tribes. It is a very different matter when the savages come and trade under the bastion of a fort. There they take care to make no venture and offer no insult because they know well that they would be compelled to conduct themselves properly, and that a small number of Frenchmen united and inside a fort [lit. "shut up"] together are invincible to them.

It follows from all that has just been set forth, that, if there had been no other aim & no other motive but the conversion of the savages and

Missilimakinak. The revd. Father Bonnart, Superior of the Jesuits, at a conference which was held at M. de Calliere's house, at which M.M. de Champigny and de Beauharnois were [present], (and to which M.M. d'Auteuil and de Loftinieres were summoned), agreed to grant two missionaries for Detroit, one for the Outavois there and the other for the Hurons. But as he maintains that this action cannot be taken without expense, the Superior of the Jesuits proposed to defray it. These gentlemen wished to saddle the Company of the Colony with that expense, giving occasion to the two gentlemen who are directors, to reply thereto, making the following distinction.

If it is agreed to give up the mission at Missilimakinak entirely and to transfer it to Detroit, the Company will undertake to defray the expense; otherwise it must not be held liable for it. These are the reasons M. d'Auteuil gave for it. If all the savages at Missilimakinak come to Detroit, the Company may expect to have the greater part of the trade of that tribe, and this will serve to indemnify it for the expenses it is to bear; whereas, if that mission remains, as it is now the scene of all debauchery, serving as a retreat for all in rebellion against the orders of the King, and for the libertines who set out from Montreal every day, taking an enormous quantity of brandy there by the Grand river, which they sell to savages, it is impossible for the Company to keep up the post of Detroit. For, so far from the savages of Missilimakinak and the neighborhood coming there to trade, those of Detroit on the contrary will go to Missilimakinak on account of the attraction of finding brandy there, of which they are deprived. not only at Detroit by the good order that has been established there, but also at Montreal. And addressing himself to the Superior of the Jesuits, he told him that they had at all times complained of the abominations and the scandals which the French caused by liquors at Missilimakinak, and that they were right; but that he was surpised to see that, although the Governor-General had provided a remedy for it by the wise orders he had given regarding Detroit, and by the just measures the Company had taken with its agents, so that everybody could bear witness that nothing contrary to what had been ordered went on there, yet these same abominations and this same disorderly conduct were perpetuated at Missilimakinak by rebels and libertines, and nowadays they looked on without saying a word, and without complaining of them. This attack hit this revd. Father so hard that it took his breath away, and left him without a word to say and waiting for breath.

I added, My Lord, that it was indisputable that Missilimakinak was the emporium of all the tribes; that this place supplied provisions and boats to the Voyageurs to go from there into all the other countries; that the Voyageurs, on their return from trading, again obtained there what

were not in existence, there would be no need to watch deserters so care-fully at Montreal; for those who escape do so only with the object of the gain they hope to make by trading with Utauais, by taking a quantity of goods with them; that I begged these gentlemen to observe that if Missili-makinak were not in existence, and there were no more provisions there, it would be impossible for deserters to take goods there, for between Montreal and Missilimakinak there are 300 leagues of very bad road, and after that the Voyageurs are obliged to go 300 or 400 leagues further to carry on their trade, so that their boats would not be large enough to carry the provisions which they would need for subsistence, more espe-cially as those are sterile countries, where there are no animals; that on returning from trading they would necessarily die of hunger and want. And I concluded that, to break up this mission and take it to Detroit would be to complete a work worthy of the glory of the King, of religion, and for the welfare of the missions. And addressing myself to the Su-perior, M. the Governor-General, and M. de Champigny, I begged them to remember that I had informed them that the missionaries at Missili-makinak received into their houses the goods and beaver skins of fugitive rebels; that they had promised me, when I set out for Detroit, that they would write to them about it; that nevertheless I had proofs how they continued to do so, and that that was supporting a disgraceful brigand-age.

The Superior of the Jesuits replied to this statement, and opened his lips to say that his missionaries were unable to act otherwise for fear lest those people should murder them, as there was no one there to sup-port them; but that he requested the Governor to give him an order in writing on the King's behalf to forbid them to do it, and that that would protect them from insult.

I answered him that they had only to come to Detroit and they would be free from that difficulty.

M. de Champigny spoke and said that the King, when he gave orders for establishing Detroit, did not declare that Missilimakinak or the other posts should be broken up; that the orders were to take what they thought advisable from the memorandum of M. Charron and mine, and that he took Charron's memorandum; that a recollet was of no use there, and that Detroit would be established if there were none; that the recollets,

To all that I replied that it was apparent enough that the intention of the King was that the other posts should be broken up, for the Governor-General had included in the instructions he gave me [that I was] to invite all the tribes to come to Detroit; that the letters which you, My Lord, did me the honor to write me, enjoin it, as you wish me to make this post as successful, as I had given you to hope; that success depends on bringing the tribes together at this post, and especially those of Missilimakinak; that you expressed yourself pretty clearly about it, but that they would neither hear nor see; that as I met with so many hindrances, I should trouble myself no more about it; that I could not do the impossible.

The Governor said that he had spoken to them at the time he concluded the peace; that a part of the savages had told him they would go to Detroit, that the rest had replied that they must consider it; and that he had their answers, that he could not force them to settle there if they had no wish to do so; that to take their missionaries from them would be wanting to compel them to go there by force; that it would also be giving occasion to the rebels to go to the Mississippi for goods, and afterwards to come and trade with them outside Missilimakinak, for they would obtain meat in the direction of the Illinois, which they would dry, and that his opinion therefore was to let the mission of Missilimakinak alone, for they would go to Detroit of themselves if they thought fit to do so.

M. de Champigny also said that this mission would be useful in case the licensed traders were reinstated, and it was desired to send boats into Lake Superior and to the other posts.

Mm. d'Auteuil and de Lofbiniere, who spoke for each other, said that either the King wished to establish Detroit or not. M. De Beauharnois, who had said little and listened much, said that it was certain that the King wished it, and that he would answer for it. If that is so said M. d'Auteuil, what difficulty is there in the missionaries of Missilimakinak going there, since that would induce the savages to go there with them; that there were some of them who were faithful to them; that the others would let themselves [i. e. their decisions] be shaken when they saw the former departing; that some would follow them as a matter of honor, and the rest from the confidence they would be inspired with on seeing them settle at that place.

To this I added that to quit a mission or a post was not forcing the savages; that the missionaries are not their slaves; that this is very often done with them; that it is open to a missionary to tell them that he is going away to a desirable land to join his brethren, and to invite them to follow him; that the villages of the savages are always being removed, not only in the country of the Utavais, but in the neighborhood of Quebec and Montreal; that eo le do not o to seek savages axe in hand, that

Why, said M. de Beauharnois, does the King wish to make a great settlement of Detroit, since he makes no grant for that purpose. I told him that he had heard that, as regards the mission at Missilimakinak, the Company would bear the expense if the Governor thought fit to remove it. It was also said that, as the Jesuits do no trading, there were [their] expenses to be defrayed. I replied that I did not accuse them of it, but that many abuses went on among the people who brought them wine and wafers to say their masses, for their boats were laden with very heavy loads of goods; that a hundred men who were with me had seen them; that their hired men or servants had gone wherever they liked in the further parts of the woods to trade with them; that they had even had the impudence to come within one day's [journey] of Detroit; that I had informed the Governor and the Intendant of it; lastly, I pointed out to these gentlemen that it was more advisable to give these missionaries money to provide themselves with dwellings according to their own fancy, for, if I undertook to house them, they would perhaps ask me for more than I could do, and they would think that it was from ill-will; that I was very glad to have no disputes with them.

You know, My Lord, that you had promised me two hundred men to strengthen this post. If you continue of the same mind, it will be time to send them over next year; for it would be advisable to make them serve in Canada for a year, in order to give them a little elasticity and accustom them to the country before bringing them to Detroit. You had also given me hope of twelve companies, and I even had an order from Your Highness to go to the office of M. de la Touche to give him the names of the captains who would suit me best. So, if this settlement does not get on as well as it should do, it is not my fault. They will decry [it] enough to you; the machine with the great springs knows very well how to set everything going here; they will propose to you now a multiplicity of posts; they will even get the savages to ask M. de Calliere for it, although they have raised such an outcry against that, in order to cause the downfall of Detroit which stands in need of all your powerful protection. It seems that you wish that the Jesuits should be my friends. I wish it, too; but, as the quarrel dates from the time of the late Comte de Frontenac, and as they have very good memories, I must not think that they would forget the past, whatever I might do to attain that end, that that will not prevent me from having great regard for them, and much respect. All our quarrels have arisen only from the opposition they have offered to the orders of the King, which I know very well how to maintain, and

to beg you to grant me the appointment of major of the town of Quebec, and not of Montreal, if it is vacated by the promotion of the occupant of it, who is a very worthy man; that will not prevent me from remaining at fort Pontchartrain as long as you wish, and until this matter is completed. I shall assuredly continue to devote all my care to making it a success in the way that you wish, but you must aid me. I should be very glad merely to learn that I had received an appointment, since the opportunity presents itself in the Majority of Quebec, until you grant me the favors which, My Lord, you had the kindness to promise to me and M. de Tonty in the letters which you did me the honor to write to me. If however, you will grant me this governorship, or at least a commission as commandant of this post and all the others in the lands of the Utaüois (as I had in the time of the Comte de Frontenac, a copy of which I send you) I should prefer this favor to the majority of Quebec; and, if you attach a salary to it, that will mitigate the hardships which I am obliged to endure among these barbarians, and I will do my duty at this post so well that you will have every reason to be satisfied with the course I shall take to make it as great a success as you expect. The Chev. de Calliere promised me to write strongly to you on my behalf; he assured me that he was pleased with me, as I had complied very faithfully with his orders. No one can complain of me justly; there is no one [that does] except the envious and the malcontents, but they can fret and fume whenever they please.

You also promised me, My Lord, in the letter which you were good enough to write to me on the 31st of May 1701, that you would take advantage of the first opportunity which presented itself, to give my eldest son an appointment; but you have promoted four ensigns in this country [and] he has had the misfortune to escape your memory. I am therefore obliged to continue to ask you for an ensigncy of foot for him, and, if there are none vacant, to send him an order for the first that becomes vacant. I can assure you that he is a very fine lad, and a very good fellow and does his duty at Detroit, where he is serving, very well. As he is the first cadet who has come there, he would deserve this favor on behalf of this post and of the services he will render it, which I will take good care of.

As regards my memorials which you referred to MM. de Calliere and de Champigny to comply with them as far as they could, it will be very easy for me to carry out their orders, for they give me none (no doubt because they have no funds for that purpose) and they keep complete silence about it. For my part. I have done what I gave [you] to expect; do, on yours, what you wish. It seems to me they trouble themselves very little here about Detroit. The concession of the trade, which the King has granted exclusively to the Company of the Colony has paralysed all

pany makes no advance for it, and no one can live in a country where there is no trade. If it is only a question of bringing the savages together there, there will be some very soon, for there are three villages already. As to the rest, it is your business; a hundred pistols are required to begin the seminary [and] the Jesuits demand money for removing, forgetting that they are missionaries and that the King has given them five hundred pistols for their missions.

I am well satisfied with the reverend Father Constantine, the recollet who officiates at Detroit, that is to say for the garrison. Whatever may be said of it, it is very necessary that these reverend fathers should be there. The Jesuits are good for their missions, but if they make us beseech them too much, and continue to want money for coming there, this recollet in the meantime will be useful for the savages occasionally. Moreover there is nothing so sweet as liberty of conscience; for my part, I think that especially necessary in these distant places.

I am well pleased with M. Duguay, lieutenant on half pay; he has done his duty thoroughly well and has assisted me in every possible way. He is a very good officer and was very necessary to me; and M. de Calliere supported him through the obstacles and the hostile action of the company who would not accept the views of M. de Calliere regarding M. Duguay. He deserves your support both on account of his family and his services, and I am convinced, My Lord, that if you knew him well you would promote him on the first opportunity that offered.

I was one of those who were most surprised at the complaints made against M. Hauteville, M. de Calliere's secretary; I thought it necessary to see the Governor-General about it, so much the more as this difference was in a way referred to me, and I found him from the first with the best inclination in the world to settle it and to do justice to whomever it was due, although I had great difficuly in finding out the truth the matter being so involved that it could not be definitely cleared up. However, as M. de Chacornacle maintained that he had been struck first, I and all the officers then at Quebec thought that this confession was sufficient to have justice done to M. de Chacornacle; and, having informed the Chevalier de Calliere of it, he sent his secretary to prison, quite resolved to make him undergo the penalties provided in the decrees. But it happened that M.

M. de Chacornacle's pardon, which he instantly did, and when they had shaken hands and embraced, M. de Chacornacle promised him he would forget all that had passed, and M. Hauteville begged him to think no more of it. That, My Lord, is how the matter went, and those who have informed you of it otherwise are very wrong and are very dishonest. That is the first time M. Hauteville appears to have given anyone cause to complain of him, and indeed the matter was always very questionable to me, for M. de Chacornacle is a little too quick with his hand; moreover he is a worthy man who was strongly attached to the Comte de Frontenac and has never been suspected of any unfaithfulness, and I think that is why M. de Calliere employs him with confidence. We have need in this country for men of this kind, who are somewhat rare, for means are found of moving everyone.

I was very glad to be here when M. de Beauharnois arrived. He has such a fine face and such good manners that he gained the approval of everyone. I hope he may become favorable to the settlement of Detroit; there is ground for fearing that, if he follows the memorials of his predecessor, he may be against it.

I have had no one sick, and nobody has died, a thing which, moreover, has been rarely seen in distant posts such as this.

I have carried out submissively what you did me the honor to write to me concerning the revd. Jesuit Father Vaillant; that was done after my letter was written in the presence of his Superior and of the Revd. Father Germain, Father Vaillant having set out four hours after the arrival of the King's ship. This Father has gone to Senountoüan. Therefore, as this matter has just been arranged by the Chev. de Calliere, together with various things for the future which have been drawn up in clauses, we may trust you will receive no more complaints from them against me; and I do not think I shall be obliged to carry mine to you, because of the satisfactory arrangement concerning it which the Governor-General has made, and will make in case of dispute, as you will see, My Lord, from the agreement which has been made on the subject and signed in all due form, of which M. de Calliere is to send you a copy. If, therefore, anything is brought before you about it, directly, or indirectly, I beg you to pay no attention to it, for by the agreement which has just been made, it has all been put an end to.

Permit me, if it please you, to be with very deep respect, My Lord,
Your very humble and very obedient servant,

La Mothe Cadillac.

At Quebec, this 25th of Sept., 1702.

REMARKS MADE BY M. DE LA MOTTE CONCERNING THE BOARD OF DIRECTORS.

M. de la Motte says that when he was sent to Detroit by the Court to establish the post he did not think it would fall into the hands of a Company, and that if he had foreseen it he would not have undertaken it, because there is as much difference between the King and the Company as between a proprietor and his tenant. When a man manages his property himself, as he has an interest in not letting it run to ruin; he puts up with bad years hoping to recompense himself in others. But when this property is in the hands of a selfish farmer, he sucks the very marrow out of it while it is in his possession, not caring what may become of the land after that.

When M. de la Motte set out from Montreal on the 5th of June, 1701, he did so with the intention [shared] by the Governor-General, of making a success of the undertaking of the settlement of Detroit. In order to succeed in it, it was necessary not to apply himself to trading only, but far rather to laying the foundations of a post the ownership of which had not been decided upon between the Crowns of France and England: That is why it is thought advisable to choose good men and a sufficient number to drive the enemy out of it if they were posted there before him; or to be prepared to defend himself in case he should be attacked there. This is in conformity with his instructions; therefore his boats were loaded with quantities of provisions, iron and tools to enable them to house themselves conveniently, to fortify themselves, and finally to prepare themselves for repulsing the enemy, if they had come there.

It should be borne in mind that M. de la Motte, in going to Detroit, found himself in a district where there were no inhabitants; that he was obliged to provide food there for the garrison and the Voyageurs for a

They continued the following spring of 1702, to send him the same advice to confine himself to this business solely, and to exclude the trade in beaver-skins. He did so: and yet in the same year, in the month of October, it may be seen from the accounts that the directors made a reduction of more than one-half in the prices of these kinds of skins and furs, for which they ought to be censured; this question is left for consideration.

M. de la Motte says that the directors regulate their trade from Montreal to Detroit, as that from La Rochelle to Quebec is regulated, and that this should not be done. The whole expenditure incurred in 1701 should be shown, according to the time [occupied in sending] the consignments, as payable in 1702; of the following year, and so on. This is what the directors have not done in their account, having shown and mixed up sums belonging to the year 1702 in the return for 1701. They have also made a valuation of the goods remaining at Detroit which is outrageous, for they have only estimated them at 50 p. c. profit after having been conveyed to the place, so that there is no more than the cost returned. These goods are such as will produce two hundred per cent. profit at the least, there being 2015# of powder, which costs only 22s. to buy, one pound [of which] sells for a beaver-skin, [or] for a roebuck, otter, stag or bear's skin; four thousand two hundred and twenty pounds of lead, costing only six sols a pound, at 1½# to the beaver skin; eight hundred and twenty-three pounds of tobacco, costing only twenty-seven sols a pound, at three-quarters to the beaver-skin. This proves that two pounds of powder, costing forty-five sols [and] producing one stag skin at seven livres, two sols—even by the reckoning of the board of directors, gives more than two hundred per cent profit. If we take three pounds of lead at six sols, making eighteen sols, that works out to nearly seven hundred per cent. If we take three-quarters of tobacco, making twenty-one sols, that amounts to very nearly seven hundred per cent; if in bear skins or in otter skins, it ought to return three hundred per cent or more; if in roebuck skins and winter beaver-skins, thick and dry, on the average it should amount to very nearly the same. There is a reduction in [the price of] roebuck skins: but, in whatever way it may be reckoned, there is, or ought to be on the terms on which trade is transacted here, two hundred per cent profit on those goods, all expenses paid.

M. de la Motte says that the board of directors shows in its accounts that there were a number of skins spoilt, or of poor quality. If that is so they must have become wet in the boat, [going] from Montreal to Quebec, therefore it is for the directors to look to themselves for compensation for it. If they were of poor quality, that would arise from the ignorance of the agents, so that it is for the board of directors to choose

someone who is more experienced. Therefore this loss should not be
attributed to the post of Detroit.

M. de la Motte says that the goods which are sent to this post, especially
those which M. Radisson[1] has just brought, are exorbitant in price; there
is a part of them which is by no means suitable for the trade, and that
it appears that it is the directors themselves, who are merchants, that
are very glad to get rid of them, and to make for themselves alone the gain
which the public should draw from them. These goods are also of low
quality, and they will in part remain in the warehouse and no one will be
able to find a sale for them except at a loss; and to this M. Radisson, the
clerk, agrees himself, not being able to do otherwise. M. de la Motte says
that he is not surprised at the skins falling in price, for it is the directors,
as merchants who purchased them themselves or have them purchased in
an underhand manner by others, with whom they share the spoil; and this
sale is only a sham, for the understanding between the merchants concerning it is made beforehand; that the custom in Canada in these matters is sufficiently well known.

That that shows that the affairs of the Company are entirely ruined for
it has not [even] so small a capital as that [necessary] to bear for one
year the sending these skins to France although it would produce a
considerable profit; and it runs also into expense in paying for the food
and expenses of the Voyageurs engaged, who go down from Montreal to
Quebec in order to fetch their payment, whereas by remitting the money
to their principal clerk at Montreal, it could make these payments and
save its expenses.

M. de la Motte says that he does not consider that the Company has lost
on this first consignment, as it says it has, the sum of twelve thousand
two hundred and ninety seven livres, seventeen sols; and that. if he had
the honor to talk to the board of directors only two hours on this point
he is confident that they would agree to it and that he could make them
see it by pressing it well home.

He also says that the board of directors manages its trade in that
matter as a merchant does from the sale to the purchase, but that it ought
to have another object for it should be directed with reference to the
settlement and to the trade which will arise from it.

sailors; & to supply them with the provisions and the fittings necessary, as the expenses of the voyage; and this may amount to ten thousand millions; whence for this reason, or it were better to say for that of the directors, the owner of the vessel has lost twenty thousand livres. This is however, untrue; for the vessel remains and may continue to make a considerable profit every year, since the first outlay has been made. Hence, even if it were true, which M. de la Motte does not think, that the Company had lost twelve thousand livres on these first consignments, in [connection with] which it has been necessary to build many dwellings and to make large clearings for the lands, it counts them as nothing. Yet they will continue every year to give large profits to the advantage of its trade by the grain they have yielded and will yield, provided it has a mill built and sends cattle there, which they have been asked for.

THE COMPANY OF THE COLONY PROPOSES TO SURRENDER DETROIT TO CADILLAC.

Endorsed—Colonies. M. de Callieres, M. de Beauharnois, 3rd Nov. 1702.

My Lord,

*   *

The Directors of the Company have promised that, as soon as all their furs, which are the proceeds of the trade at the forts of Detroit and Frontenac, have come, they will carry out the obligations they entered into with the Srs. de Callieres and de Champigny. The Srs. de Callieres and de Beauharnois will take that in hand, and the Sr. de Champigny will give an account of what has taken place on that:

*   *   *

The Sr. de Callieres will give the Sr. de la Motte the necessary support; and he has already in anticipation [of your instructions] strongly urged the savages who came down to Montreal this summer to go and settle at Detroit.

The Directors of the Company of the Colony were right in informing you that the expense they were obliged to incur for conveying the articles necessary for the officers and the garrison is heavy, in regard to what has had to be taken for their settlement; but they have no ground for complaining of it, since we learn from those who have just come down from there that with the 15,000# which the King has granted them, the furs which have come down from those [posts] to Montreal, and the rest of the goods which still remain at that fort, they have now sufficient to reimburse themselves. And it appears to us that it will cost them, this year, only the refreshments they have taken for the officers, the wages of four hunters, and a few merchants for trading for Indian corn, in addition to what they have gathered on the spot, for the food of the garrison and their people. These expenses will decrease further in the future, as a greater harvest is made, and as they get a collection of animals on the spot.

As His Majesty wishes the soldiers to supply themselves with the wood necessary for their fuel, the Srs. de Callieres and de Beauharnois will issue the necessary orders on that point. The soldiers of Fort Frontenac will cut their wood, as they do elsewhere, and we will have it drawn for them by means of two horses which have been bought and are already there. And as regards those at Detroit, since there are neither oxen nor horses there yet, some gratuity—to be agreed upon—shall be granted them at the King's expense for the labor they will have in hauling it both for themselves and for the officers, who have not servants enough to cut their wood for them and carry it.

We do not think it is advisable that the Company of the Colony should be at liberty to carry on trade outside the forts of Detroit and Frontenac, because the savages who may be settled in the neighborhood will easily come there for what they need, in the same way as the savages of Le Sault and La Montagne come to Montreal; whereas, if it were permitted to this Company to take goods to them, it would do all the trade of Canada in the interior of the woods by itself under this pretext, and this would entirely ruin the trade of the settlers and merchants of Montreal who only subsist with difficulty [i. e. who only get a bare subsistence] on the little trade done there at present. Therefore the Chevalier de Callieres and the Sr. de Beauharnois will make the Directors of the Company understand that they should carry on trade only within the boundaries of their two forts.

We have no doubt that the Srs. de la Motte and de Tonty are devoting all their care and diligence to the benefit and advantage of the post of Detroit, with the intention of making themselves worthy of the favors of which His Majesty gives them hope, of which we have informed the Sr. de la Motte who has come to pay a visit here and will communicate to the Sr. de Tonty who has remained on the spot.

the Colony, it would have increased it, for some of the savages of Lake Superior carry their furs to the English of the Northern bay, and the rest on account of their great remoteness, and because they have not the use of boats, do not come either to Montreal or to Detroit.

    *   *   *

It has been reported to us that the agents of the Srs. de la Forest and de Tonty, contrary to the orders of His Majesty, which forbid them to trade for any beaver skins, even at Fort St. Louis of the Illinois, and only allow them to buy small furs at that place, are carrying on the trade with all sorts of tribes. When the Sr. de la Forest, whom we are expecting immediately, has returned, the Srs. de Callieres and de Beauharnois will inquire definitely what has been done on that point, and if it is shown that the orders of the King have been disobeyed, the Sr. de Callieres will suspend the exercise of their privileges, if they do not amend, until His Majesty shall signify to him his pleasure.

    *   *   *

The Sr. de la Motte has written from Detroit to the Sr. de Callieres that the savages had told him they had learnt that the Governor-General wished to have the orders against selling them brandy at Montreal kept up, and that they had requested him to send him word that, if that were so, they would be obliged to go elsewhere for it.

    *   *   *

The Directors of the Company, wishing to give the Sr. de la Motte an interest in the prosperity of their affairs at Detroit, have made an agreement with him under which they grant him 2000# a year, and two-thirds [of this] to the Sr. de Tonty[1]; the Srs. de Callieres and de Beauharnois have signed this agreement.

    *   *   *

Your humble, very obedient and most obliged Servants,

The Chev. de Callieres,
Beauharnois,
Rochart Champigny.

At Quebec this 3rd of November 1702.

P. S.

---

[1] Henry Tonty and Alphonse Tonty were brothers. Henry (bras de fer) was at Fort St. Louis with La Salle and with La Forest. Alphonse was at Detroit with Cadillac and, subsequently, as commandant. Henry died in 1704 and Alphonse died at Detroit and was buried November 10, 1727. The record of the families as given by Tanguay is somewhat in error.—C. M. B.

CADILLAC MAKES ARRANGEMENTS WITH THE JESUITS.

Endorsed—Colonies. M. de Callieres. 4th Nov. 1702.

My Lord,

       *   *   *

The Sr. de la Motte very conveniently happened to be here to settle the affair of the Revd. Father Vaillant in conformity with what you wrote to me; and an arrangement has been made in my presence between the exletterH. Sr. de la Motte and the Superior of the Jesuits, a copy of which I annex hereto, which I hope will prevent any new quarrels occurring in the future.

       *   -   -

The Sr. de Tonty also sends me word that certain savages, formerly settled at the Sault and now with the Hurons of Detroit, have been to trade at Orange*, with some of that tribe, and that they brought belts on behalf of the English to invite our Savages of the upper country to go and see them in order to make their acquaintance. On this the chiefs of those at Detroit went to the Sr. de Tonty to tell him that, if he did not cause the goods to be given them cheap, they could not prevent their young men from going to the English for them, who offer them to them at a low price, or from inviting the English to bring them some to some meeting-place; which makes me greatly fear that these intrigues may have disastrous consequences to the Colony.

       *   *   *

Your very humble, very obedient and most obliged Servant,

The Chev. de Callieres.

Quebec, the 4th of Nov. 1702.

---

*Albany.

THE FIFTEENTH LETTER OF THE JESUITS TO CADILLAC.

This 15th letter is from Father Maret, and M de Lamothe has replied to it; he contents himself, therefore, with sending a copy of it.

As to what refers to the savages of Missilimakinak, these are the suppositions of this Father; for the tribe of the Sinago Outavois sent a belt secretly to M. de Lamothe to tell him that, after they had gathered their Indian corn, they would come and settle at Detroit; and since the letter of Father Maret, a chief of the Hurons has come with 30 men to join those who are at Detroit, so that only about 25 of this tribe remain at Missilimakinak, where this poor Father de Carheil, as obstinate as Benedict VII at the time of the other two anti-popes remained in Aragon where he had himself buried in papal garments; and this one will die missionary to the Hurons at Missilimakinak, whatever it may cost, although there may be no one left for him any longer.

If M. de Lamothe were allowed to act according to the custom of the savages, viz. by presents and by belts, he would make them all come to Detroit.

Although this Father mentions in his letter his quitting Missilimakinak to go down to Quebec and come to Detroit, M de Lamothe well knows that they have done nothing but trifle with him for two years by similar promises.

At Missilimakinak this 12th of May 1703.

Fifteenth

Sir,

As I have strong reasons which make it indispensably necessary for me to go down to Quebec on leaving Missilimakinak, I find myself unable at present to avail myself of the boat and the man sent me in order that I might comply with the wish of those who invite me to go to Detroit. I am greatly obliged for the courtesy you show me in offering me your house until I can be provided with a habitation, and also for the comfort I have derived from your letter by the hope it makes me conceive and by the foretaste it gives me of the perfect harmony in which we shall dwell together.

You write me that you are sending me the letters from M. de Calliere. I have not received any of them, but only this decision which you know, and which you must not doubt has appeared to us the same as it has assuredly appeared to you and to us and to M. de Calliere, *intelligentes pauca;* why do you say that you have submitted to it willingly?

There is no submission in it for you but, on the contrary, submission which is entirely on our side without any sharing [of it]; and that in a matter wherein no other command from men is ever necessary but that of our State, which orders us in God's name to make all men observe the requirements of the King's service.

As soon as I knew from the letter of my Superior, that he summoned me to Detroit, I made it my business the next day to give notice to the savages of it, and that I was preparing to obey; that they knew well enough that the will of Onontio was that they should follow me there; that they were therefore to give me a precise and decided answer on that; that I was obliged to go first to Quebec, and that I would lay their words before Onontio. They asked me for three days to consider, which gave me occasion to think that they would assemble at Detroit, but I was much surprised when, on the third day, the leading men, having assembled with the Kiskakdus, all told me unanimously that they had resolved to die at Michilimakinac, and that even if they left it, it would never be to go to Detroit; that that was their final resolve; that I might assure Onontio of it from them, and that this was what they had themselves told him last year when they went down to Montreal. I have no doubt your astonishment at such a decision will be as great as mine.

As regards the Hurons, it will be for Quarente Solz to inform you of what he has arranged with them. Although Father de Carheil went to see him as soon as he arrived, he did not

REPORT OF DETROIT IN 1703.

Endorsed—31st August 1703. (Duplicate.[1]) Colonies. M. de la Mothe Cadillac.

My Lord,

I had the honor to write to you last year at great length the disposition of everything concerning the post of Detroit. I am writing to you again without knowing what decisions you have arrived at as to its settlement.

No doubt you have given your attention to the arrangement which was made by Chev. de Calliere[2] while I was at Quebec between the revd. Father Bouvart[3], Superior of the Jesuits, and me; and apparently you did not doubt, when you saw it, that everything contained in it had been carried out on both sides.

This arrangement obviously proves the resistance which the Jesuits of this country have offered in order to prevent the savages from settling at this post; and I had had reasons to hope that, fulfilling the promises which had been made to me, to which they had subscribed in so authentic an agreement[*]

You were good enough to write to me that the King wishes the missions of Detroit to be administered by the Jesuit fathers, and that their Superior at Quebec would grant me some who would be more in sympathy with me than Father Vaillant had been.

It would appear that your orders were sufficient to induce this Superior to provide for that mission promptly, especially after the special favor you have done him by approving of Father Vaillant remaining in this country after having opposed the will of His Majesty as he has done.

The arrangement made by M. de Calliere also seemed to compel him, absolutely, to have the mission provided for, as is clearly explained therein.

Yet you will see that up to the present, the Jesuits have done nothing to carry out His Majesty's intentions which you explained clearly both to M. de Calliere and to their Superior at Quebec, with which you were pleased to acquaint me.

I do not know whether they have sent you word that it was agreed, in consequence of the arrangement which had been made, that the Company of the Colony should pay to each missionary of Detroit the sum of eight hundred livres a year; that it would have the things they would want for their food, and the clothing necessary for their use, brought for them at its cost and expense; and that it would get dwellings for them in the villages of the savages until there was time to build them more conveniently.

I have carried out, for, my part, the arrangements which have been made; the Company has carried them out on its side, having this spring (in accordance with the agreement) sent a boat on purpose for Father Maret. Superior of Missilimakinak, who feigned [to have] important reasons for not coming here. So the Company has incurred that expense in vain, as it had already done regarding Father Vaillant.

You wish me to be friendly with the Jesuits, and not to pain them. Having thought it well over, I have only found three ways of succeeding in that. The first is to let them do as they like; the 2nd, to do everything they wish; the 3rd to say nothing about what they do. By letting them do as they like, the savages would not settle at Detroit and would not be settled there; to do what they wish, it is necessary to cause the downfall of this post; and to say nothing about what they do, it is necessary to do what I am doing; and [yet], in spite of this last essential point, I still cannot induce them to be my friends.

It is for you, My Lord, to consider whether you wish me to continue to get the savages to settle here, and for this post to be preserved and maintained in a flourishing state. If those are your opinions as I believe, I am perhaps fitted to have them carried out; but I venture to tell you that the intentions of the Jesuits of this country are entirely opposed to yours, at least on that point.

All that has not prevented the Sauteurs and Mississaguez from coming this year and forming another village on this river. These two tribes have united and incorporated [themselves] with one another, having followed my advice in that, and done my will. I thought this advisable, considering that their union will be an advantage to them, and to us if any rupture occurred with the enemies of the State and of the Colony.

Thirty Hurons from Missilimakinak arrived here on the 28th of June

with the Hurons and the others with the Outavois, and the Oppenago or Wolves.

The rest of the Sinago Outavois, who are still at Missilimakinak, have secretly sent me a belt to tell me they will come and join their brothers of Detroit after they have gathered their harvest. Six large households* of the Kiskakouns have sent to me to say the same thing. I replied to them by a belt that I was going to mark out the lands where they may make their fields.

This procedure on the part of the savages shows how they are restrained and that they are much intimidated by the fear which is insinuated into their minds that an ill turn will be done them here.

I take the liberty of sending you a copy of the letters which the Jesuits of this country have written to me since I have been at Detroit and, in part, the counsels which have been held within this fort. You will see my observations thereon in the margin. I also send you those I wrote in reply to them, or on business; and after you have considered them all you will know their design as to this post, and especially their good will towards me, from which you may judge whether it is easy for me to make them friends of mine.

When it pleases you that I should complete the mustering [of the savages] at this place, it will be a very easy matter for you. But, to succeed properly in it, a fund must be formed or an assignment out of the special war fund of Canada, of six thousand livres with orders to remit these sums to me to use in matters I think necessary to the success of this undertaking, but I will give an exact account of them to the Chev. de Calliere and M. de Beauharnois, the Intendant.

I have already had the honor to write to you that the presents and belts which are given to the savages, especially when it is a question of any migration, are pledges of the sincerity of the promises made to them, and a title which gives them the right of possessing or leaving, as contracts are among civilized nations.

You know also that. to this day, not a farthing has been sent me to help in inducing the savages to move. It is quite true that a considerable fund, in goods, has been put in my hands in order to form this post, without it having cost the King anything whatever for it. I believe they have had reason to be satisfied with my action in that matter, by the good order I have kept in this business; for it is certain that the Company has gained rather than lost, and that is a thing I am better informed about than anyone. However, if they come to complain of the expenses which it has been necessary, or is necessary to incur in order to keep up this post, I will agree to it. If this country has not fallen although trade has been excluded it would have grown strong if left alone [lit. "by itself"].

I think the shortest way would be to settle the matter with me. Be so good as to employ me in any undertaking; support me with the honor of your protection; and if, despite the malice and the wiles of my enemies, I do not succeed in it, never employ me again. The inclination of those who hate me is to kill time by constantly bringing forward arguments and insuperable difficulties in everything I wish to undertake, and mine is to take measures to get over them.

I do not know whether the trade in ox hides can be kept up, because of the low value set on them, for they will not reckon them as worth more than a hundred sous or six francs to the savages; and this does not suit them, for one skin weighs up to 250 and 300# which they are obliged to convoy three or four leagues by land. This they find too laborious, preferring to apply themselves to hunting the beaver and other animals because their skins are lighter and easier to convey. If the Company does not increase the price of them, I believe the savages will no longer bring themselves to hunt these except during the time when there are no other skins.

We have found a copper mine on Lake Huron, a sample from which I send you, which seems to me quite pure. I have sent some to M. de Calliere as well, and to the Directors of the Company, so that they could take steps to ascertain whether it is abundant enough to be worth taking in hand. The convenience of it would be great; for barges and even ships can go to the spot where it is and it is not very far from this post.

If you will give me permission to have search made for mines in the neighborhood of the lakes and rivers, I will devote to it all my care and all the information I can get hold of about it. I will go myself to the places if you wish it, by which means you will obtain more certain infor-

the King or to the public, and consequently there would be no good ground for complaining of it.

The Grand River, thus called in Lake Erie, near to the end of this lake about 15 leagues from here is supplied on its banks and in the interior with large numbers of mulberry trees, the ground also is perfectly suited for them. If you will have the goodness to grant me six leagues frontage on both sides and as much in depth, with the title of Marquis, and with higher, middle and lower jurisdiction, with hunting, fishing and trading rights, I will establish a silk industry by sending for suitable people from France for that purpose who will bring the necessary number of silk worms. If you grant me this favor I will take steps to bring them over by the first ships so that they may arrive here before winter. As regards the trade, I will do none until after the Company's lease is out.

You promised me, My Lord, last time you sent me back from France, that you would permit me to go back there as soon as Detroit was established; there it is now, on a sound footing, so I hope you will be so good as to send me a permit next year to go there, and to go and attend to my affairs for once in my life. For I have not been able to put them in order at all for twenty years, during which I have been in Canada or at Acadia; and by this means I shall be able to give you an exact account of this country, if you wish. I will not set out from here until I see everything beyond [all] risk.

As I do not know whether Your Highness has granted me the Governorship of this post and of all the other distant [posts], or at least the general command, as I had it in the lifetime of the Comte de Frontenac, and as the Chev. de Calliere granted it to me by his order of the 25th of Sept. 1703 (?) a copy of which I send you. I shall continue very humbly to beg you to grant me this favor, and to be good enough to attach to it suitable pay.

We have gathered in a very fine harvest, and I am able to provide food amply for a garrison of a hundred and fifty men; but I do not think I shall be put to that trouble, from the objections that are raised against giving me soldiers. I have contented myself with asking for only fifty effectives, for they had left me only twenty-five; and I do not know whether this number will be granted me. I beg that you will send word to M. de Calliere to grant me fifty more next year, so that this garrison may be composed of a hundred men and I may thus be able to answer for all emergencies, whether on the part of our enemies or of our allies, whom it is necessary to keep a little in awe. But it would be still better if you should think fit to send me some from France.

The Chief of the Hurons, who is very absolute over his tribe, has begged me to write to you that he would be very glad to proceed to France, to

lieutenant and an ensign, and that they are paid monthly, as well as their soldiers at the same rate as the officers and troops of the Navy are paid in this country. There is another chief of the same tribe who binds himself to do the same; they also beg you to have passages given them in the King's ships. I believe they intend to hunt for skins in order to present them to you, which is a token of their good will.

The principal chief of the Hurons, who is one of the best-informed men I have yet seen among all these tribes, and is Frenchified, has requested me to write to you regarding the same matter, but, as his age does not allow of his making so long a voyage, he will send his nephew to you at the same time with another of his friends, in order to offer the King his services.

If His Majesty will go to this expense, it would be the true means of bringing these two tribes gradually and entirely into subjection. I think it would be necessary to deal with them rather gently at the beginning by making them take arms only once a month when reviews might be held, and even by exempting them from it for three months in winter, because for that time they are busy in pursuing their hunting; but it is necessary to be very punctual in paying the companies every month. They ask to have flags. and to be permitted to make their clothes in their fashion, and that red stuffs may be given them; they hope that arms will be given them as we give them to the soldiers, and clothing the same, in which they are now instructed by the explanation I have given them. They have told me that they will obey me in everything that I order them for the time for the King's service, and every one else who may have his orders. I have explained to them perfectly well the bearing required by the military art and how necessary it is to catch the spirit of subordination, which they approved of.

We need not be surprised at it, for all men, in whatever condition they may be born, lack neither vanity nor ambition, and there are always some skilful enough to get credit. to make themselves esteemed and respected by others. The Huron chief is already so elated by this proposal that he has begged M. de Calliere to have a dwelling provided for him in French fashion; and I received orders for it when I was at Quebec, which I have complied with, having had a house built for him of oak timber-work of ten feet frontage by 24 in width. It is situated on rising ground on the edge of the river, overlooking the village of that tribe.

Following his example, the Outavois chief went. I think, to Montreal

peoples, they have made no progress, and that all the good resulting from it may be reduced to the baptism by them of infants who die after having received it.

Permit me to continue to persist in representing to you how necessary it is to set up a seminary here for instructing the children of the savages with those of the French in piety, and for teaching them our language by the same means.

The savages being naturally vain, seeing that their children were put amòngst ours and that they were dressed in the same way would esteem it a point of honor. It is true that it would be necessary at the beginning to leave them a little more liberty, and that it would be necessary for it to be reduced merely to the objects of civilizing them and making them capable of instruction, leaving the rest to the guidance of heaven and of Him who searches hearts.

This expense would not be very great. I believe, if His Majesty grants the seminary of Quebec a thousand crowns. it will begin this holy and pious undertaking. They are gentlemen so full of zeal for the service of God, and of charity towards all that concerns the King's subjects in this Colony, that one cannot tire of admiring them, and all the country owes them inexpressible obligations for the good education they have given all the young people, for their good example, and their doctrine, and it is that which has produced very good success in the service of the church in New France. I venture to tell you that you cannot begin this work too soon; if you fear its expense afterwards, I will supply you with devices for continuing this bounty to them by taking it on the spot, without its costing anything to the King.

For the rest, there is no fear that there will be any lack of savages to carry on the hunting, and to supply beaver and other skins; there are so many tribes round about the lakes and in the interior of the lands, who will perhaps never be reduced, that they are sufficient to kill off all these animals that are of use in trade.

The restraint of serving the King in the manner of which I have spoken to you will not prevent them from carrying on their hunting at the proper time; we shall only put them by that means in a position to Frenchify themselves. and to take up arms in the King's service when there is need of them.

I foresee that many objections will be made to you as to what I have the honor to write to you; that is a thing which I cannot prevent, the only assurance I can give you is that of succeeding, if you wish it. To attain that end it is necessary to send wise orders, very decided and precise; and to talk rather big. Be good enough to acquaint me with your

first drum-beat we should put under arms those who were disciplined,
and this would induce all the rest to follow them and to do as they did.
Thus, in the present war, those people in conjunction with us would make
incursions and terrible invasions [lit. "inundations"] into the English
colonies; whereas they are divided and content themselves with looking
on, and we are only too fortunate if we can keep them in that position.

If these memorials had been put forward by someone who had the
assistance of the Jesuits. they would have been found of excellent quality
and nothing could have seemed easier to put into practice. But because
I have not consulted them, or rather, because I have not been inclined to
allow myself to be treated like a slave, as some of my predecessors who
have commanded in this country have done, they make everything impossible that I put forward or propose. It seems to me, however, that
if the Court would pay attention to the plans. and to what I have had
the honor to put before it, on which M. de Latouche is well informed, it
could see clearly whether I have reasoned wisely or foolishly therein. In
what have I failed to succeed up to now?—whence [it appears] that the
matters I have put forward are not impossible.

There is no need to return, or go back to the various plans I have put
before the Court concerning many enterprises which His Majesty had pro-
jected. I confine myself merely to speaking of Detroit, and I leave it for
consideration whether what I have said about it is true or false.

Remember, if you please, what a difficulty we were in. at the time I had
the honor to present my memorial on it to you, concerning the too heavy
stock of beaver skins for which no demand was found in France. Those
were the complaints of the former tenants by which they state that they
are unable to keep up their lease. It was on this that I set forth, in a
paragraph of my memorial, that by means of the post of Detroit I
pledged myself to employ the savages in hunting the stag, hind, elk, roebuck, black bears, wolves, stag-wolves, otters, wild boars, and other small
skins, for the space of three years, without hunting the beaver, so that
in this way time might be found to sell a large part of the mass [of
beaver-skins] there was. It remains to be seen whether what I have promised up to the present has been carried out; for only about eight thousand
beaverskins have passed out of Detroit in three years, and the remainder

we can go in and out to trade with all our allies. That was a bad argument for forming such a post.

My third aim was to bring together several tribes there in order to strengthen it by this means and to keep the Iroquois in awe on account of [our] proximity, having on one side Montreal, and on the other Detroit which was their only place of retreat, where they found all their provisions when their fields and villages were burnt by [our] expeditions in force (which cost immense sums).

But [they say] there are various roads from Montreal to Detroit, that is, various ways in and out relative to one another, without even passing by the lakes. Therefore that is a post really very badly designed for keeping in check not only the English and the Iroquois, but even our allies.

I confess that, to secure for it full success, it is necessary to accomplish and effect what I have explained in my memorial, that is to say, to make it a substantial post, to keep a good garrison in it, to leave it free to settle there, to discontinue the licenses. [and] not to permit any other post in the upper country because it is only greed and avarice which gives rise to this sort of plan, and they cause endless disorder.

The other objects contained in my memorial are not essential to this post; they are only accessory to it and intended to make it complete. Yet this scheme has alarmed the whole Colony; has made all the bells ring and form a chime, and [has caused] a confused uproar in which nothing was understood. For my part, I well knew who the chimers were; I saw them before my eyes, but I had my reasons, however, for pretending to be blind. I had told you who they were in my first memorial; I have continued to bring them to your notice in all my letters; you may also see a little trace of them from this one. I do not fail to see that they have on their side the favor and the great influence (the great machine which moves the whole mass of the universe). and that.* revolving on this point, they continue to wish me to go down and be suffocated under the waters of vengeance and persecution. But, as long as I have for my protection Justice and Merit, I shall float, and swim over the waves like the nest of the ingenious King-fisher; I shall try to conduct myself better and better and to walk by the brightness and the light of these two illustrious patronesses. Without them. I should long ago have been unable to bear up against the torrent; it is true that sometimes, raising my eyes to heaven. I cry in the weakness of my faith *"Sancte Frontenac. ora pro me."* ["Pray for me, O Saint Frontenac."]

As several soldiers are desirous to settling here and are asking me for grants of land, be good enough to send me word whether you wish me to grant them some, of which they will obtain the confirmation from MM.

de Calliere and Beauharnois, and whether you also wish them to marry
when they are able to keep their wives; it will, I think, be advisable
to fix a certain number of them per year.   Be kind enough also, if you
please, to let me know whether you wish me to grant dwelling places to
the Canadians, there are several of them who importune me to obtain
them; it is for you to say positively as to that, for I cannot conceal from
you that they do not wish me to do so at all.   I believe they maintain that
this migration would reduce the strength of Quebec and Montreal.   For
my part I do not think that forty or fifty men, more or less, would seem
much in those places, nor prevent them from carrying out anything they
wished to do, while it would be a great help to this post, without which
nothing will ever be done here; and it is to be supposed that our allies
already settled there, and those who are about to come, will draw a bad
augury and unfortunate inferences from the non-fulfilment of our promises; for they were told that an important settlement would be established
here.

You may be aware that there is not a post in this country, especially
where there are French people, even as far as the dwelling of M. Juchereau, where there are no Jesuits; there is none but Detroit alone which is
without them, although they are so eager to conduct missions.   This
shows the good will they bear me; and, if people are very solicitous in
this country about what they do, for my part I am no longer at all eager
to see them there, for I am well aware that the living there is not so good
as elsewhere.   Nevertheless they ought to make their choice and speak
their minds, because we could [then] take means to bring other missionaries there.   Can they stretch their authority more than by not only
dispensing with conducting this mission themselves, as the King wishes,
but even preventing others from coming there.

It is right that you should be informed that, more than fifty years ago,

except to deluge and engulf those who have the temerity to wish to over-throw so lawful a design. The people has never known what it asked for; it broke the sceptre of its first king, who was God himself, and would have rejected and even stoned him who made it rain delicious meats for them on the most barren lands, and opened the rocks to quench their thirst. What does Montreal complain of concerning the post of Detroit since it was an abandoned country, the possession of which had remained with the Iroquois and the Loups. It was they who hunted there and in all the neighboring district, and brought its hides, beaverskins, and small furs to the English. This is an unanswerable fact, and anyone must be filled with obstinacy and injustice to deny it. Then I have chosen my time well for beginning this settlement; the Iroquois have entirely withdrawn or, if any remain, they are incorporated with our allies. All the hunting is done by our savages, and all the trade falls to us. It is therefore an ad-vantage to the kingdom, and a possession which we have withdrawn and snatched from England. Private individuals complain that the Company of the Colony profits by it; I do not deny it, I leave them free to complain. Only I wish they had eyes, to be able to see that that is not the fault of the post nor of him who originated the plan for it.

I also acknowledge that there was some hardihood in coming and set-ting up trading by a Company among uncivilized peoples, who are [just] beginning to have some glimmering of subordination; this might well extinguish it, seeing that they are all at once reduced to the necessity of taking what it is desired to give them, and of bearing the rough manners of the clerks of the Company, who treat them according to their caprice, or rather, according to the brutal disposition with which men of this sort are generally filled. I am willing to believe that the affairs of the Kingdom determined the Court to take that course for a time, with the intention of uniting this post, after its lease was up, to His Majesty's domain. It is in this same spirit that I have devoted myself to serving the King there by humoring our allies, making them understand that this second captivity, or rather this barbarity veneered* [with civiliza-tion], will very soon end. I do not know whether all my promises will be able to preserve their patience until that time; I am afraid that sort of servitude will make them determine to ally themselves. and trade with the English. I must not be blamed if that happens. Moses, when mur-murings arose, went up the mountain, there to consult Him who had sent him, with his rod or his stick only; and He replied to him in his oracles. I walk in his footsteps; I write to the Court, I give it an account of my conduct, [and] of the wranglings and the murmuring of a foolish people, but I receive no answer. The Clàmorers are allowed to clamor, they are even listened to; and I am left to pick this bone, no one being willing, as it seems, to concern himself about it although it would require only one clap of thunder to make all these grumblings tremble and to silence them. For, in a word, My Lord. I repeat what I had the honor of telling you myself, that this settlement is either good or bad. If good, it must be maintained without the matter being deliberated over any longer with the inhabitants of Canada, as you have already given orders to M. M. de Calliere and de Champigny about it. Why then permit further discussions on this same subject? You thundered by the orders you gave to start this post; it is a question now of your making the thunder roar, and of the lightening being mixed with it, in order to finish it and complete your work, and that their hearts may be inclined to pay attention to your orders thereupon without wishing to hear you speak further about it. For, in short, it is time these disputes were ended; I know well that, in order to succeed in it, it would be necessary that the Jesuits of this country should feel the thunder a little.

If this settlement is undesirable, it is well that the Court should settle [it] sooner than later. I have stated my opinion thereon, I have explained the circumstances. You were persuaded of the necessity there was for forming it, and of its usefulness for the glory of the King, the progress of religion, and the advantage of the Colony. What is there left for me to do now but to imitate that Governor of the Holy City, that is, to take water and wash my hands of it.

If you had wished to grant me the governorship of it, it would have been with this matter as in all others, the clamors and murmurs would have turned and changed to congratulations and compliments; for those who envy me and fear my promotion without cause, always find strength enough to misrepresent all I do in the hope of my dying in trouble. Whereas if they saw their hope disposed of and at an end, they would follow the usual course of the world which would be to praise the scheme against which they have inveighed so.

amongst these barbarians, where I have passed my good youthful days, being now forty-seven years of age.

If you would consent to decide yourself the matters which concern this post, without referring them to Canada, everything would go better; for, as I am not on the spot, that is, near the Governor General and Intendant, they have always some particular reason for not granting me the aid I ask from them; and all that is done to humor those who thwart me, and it is not in my power to prevent it whatever steps I may take. You may trust to what I tell you about it; so be good enough to express yourself decidedly about it. You should fear nothing as regards me; I will answer for the issue in the matters of which I write to you.

People are still sent to trade with all our allies under specious pretexts, and this is a continuation of the Congé [=license] system which causes endless irregularities by the bad conduct of the Frenchmen, who, finding themselves even more unrestrained than of old, give rise to all the scandals that debauchery is capable of devising; consequences even supervene which are shameful to the French nation; and enormities go on there which deserve correction. All that causes also such unusual disagreements with our allies that it will be difficult to manage to set them right.

Last year M. Boudor, merchant of Montreal, was sent into the country of the Sioux there to join Le Seur. He took advantage of this journey to such an extent that he brought goods there to the value of twenty-five or thirty thousand livres with the intention of trading with them in all the lands of the Outavois, which he did, though to no purpose, for he was plundered, partly by the Oütagaries. I think it necessary that you should be informed of that matter, so that you may yourself apply the proper remedy. I shall speak of it to you with a knowledge of the cause, for what I am about to tell you happened at the time I was at Missilimakinak. Here are the facts—

All our allies in general have at all times been at war with the Sioux. When I arrived at Missilimakinak in accordance with the instructions of the late M. de Frontenac, who was the most able man that ever came to Canada, I negotiated a truce between the Sioux and all our allies. I succeeded in that negotiation and made use of that opportunity, making them turn their arms against the Iroquois, on whom we had declared war, perhaps unjustly, on false statements which had been made to the Court. After that truce, I got peace concluded between our tribes and those of the Sioux. It lasted for two years; at the end of that time, the Sioux in large numbers, under the pretence of coming to confirm this peace and to ratify it properly with the Miamis, were thoroughly well received by them; and, after having passed some days in their villages, they left apparently well pleased, and they had in fact reason to be so from the good welcome which had been given them. The Miamis, think-

premeditated their attack, re-entered their village the same night, and, having surprised the Miamis, slaughtered three thousand souls, and put the rest to flight.

This treachery enraged all the tribes. They came to Missilimakinak to lay their complaints before me and to request me to join them in going to destroy the Sioux. But the war we had on our hands with the Iroquois and the English did not permit [me] to listen to that proposal. I had to adopt the course of haranguing them well and playing the orator to attain my ends. Finally the conclusion was to mourn their dead, to wrap them up and let them sleep warm until the day of vengeance should come, telling them that the way must first be cleared towards the Iroquois, the very memory of whom must be wiped out; and after that we could more easily avenge the atrocious deed which the Sioux had just committed against them. Finally I guided their minds so well that the matter was determined on as I had proposed. But, as the 25 Congés [licensed traders] existed at that time, and as avarice and the desire to trade for beaverskins urged the French to go to the Sioux in search of them, our allies complained strongly of it, and pointed out to me that it was unjust that at the very time when they had arms in their hands in our own quarrel against the Iroquois, the French were going to the Sioux taking munitions of war to have them killed. And they begged me to set that right, the more because the French passed over their lands and in front of their villages, which was violating the people's rights. I informed the late Comte de Frontenac and M. de Champigny of it; and they, having considered the reasons which I had put before them, had a decree promulgated at Montreal forbidding anyone to go among the Sioux to trade with them under the penalty of a fine of one thousand livres, of the confiscation of their goods, and other penalty at the judge's discretion, according to the advice I had given about it. This decree was sent to Missilimakinak with orders to have it published there and in all the other distant posts, which was done. I went down to Quebec the same year, having asked to be relieved; and from that time, in spite of this prohibition, Frenchmen have continued to go and trade with the Sioux, but not without having met with affronts and indignities even from our allies, which dishonor the French name.

Sioux, and taking arms and munitions of war there; and they declared that they were resolved to oppose it, all the more as a fight had just taken place in which were found two Frenchmen who had been killed among the Sioux with whom they had sided.

I have sent M. Calliere and M. de Beauharnois, my opinion on this matter, and I explain clearly to them that it is important not to break our promises in this manner, and that we cannot do so without making ourselves liable to lose the confidence which our allies have in us; and that I therefore think it advisable not to permit anyone to go to trade among the Sioux any more under any pretext whatever; more especially because M. Boudor has just been robbed by the tribe of the Renard and M. Junchereau has given a thousand crowns' worth of goods to get a free passage to go to his dwelling; for they claim that they have the right to do so, as they were carrying aid to their enemies. Altogether, I do not think they are far wrong.

They also represented to me that Le Sueür was going to the Sioux by way of the Mississippi, but that they were determined to oppose it; and, if he put himself in such a position as to force them to resist him, they would not answer for the issue. Hence this is a warning which you may give to Le Sueür through the Governor of the Mississippi.

All these disturbances arise only on account of the distant French dwelling places, which are all very useless, or to speak more correctly very injurious, for they only serve as pretexts for obtaining permits and licenses. And, instead of going about it straight forwardly, they carry on trade in beavers and all kinds of furs by the Grand river, on Lake Huron, on Lake Superior, in the Michigan district and in all the Country of the Oütavois in general. It is thus they were made use of, and that MM. de la Forest and Tonty even now make use of them. And now MM. Junchereau and Pascant, partners, are trading in all this country, even up to the neighborhood of Detroit. It is that which makes the public jealous, and causes all these escapades of licentious Canadians, who say bluntly that it is only the virtuous and the obedient who are victims to it. They are indeed, not altogether wrong in that; for it is grevious to them to see a few individuals skim the milk and take the pick of the wool of the coun-

and a few roebucks but they find enough of them everywhere else, having always had liberty to trade in all places without anyone saying a word about it to them.

It is not difficult to fathom why this may be. As for me, I am like St. Jean Bouche d'Or, for I say what I think. Thus I believe that all these too distant dwellings, where there is no order, do much harm and are of no use; those which are near a post are not the same. In a word it is certain that the statements which MM. de la Forest and Tonty have made, that they had advanced sums of money to M. de Lasalle, are delusions. They have never been in a position to advance any. Everyone knows their means and their inheritance; and they would have paid themselves for it well, since for nearly 20 years they have possessed, not this post only, but rather all those of the Outavois by that means.

It also happened that the Sauteurs, who as I have already told you are friendly with the Sioux, were willing to let M. Boudor[1] and others pass through their country to go and take arms and other munitions of war to that tribe; but the others having opposed it, disputes arose between them, whereupon there followed the pillage to which M. Boudor was subjected, which gave occasion to the Sauteurs to make an attack on the tribes of the Sakis and Malommisen of whom they have killed thirty or forty, so that there is war among these peoples.

I would have set all these disturbances right and put an end to all these quarrels, were I not here destitute of resources, without any fund of the King's to use on behalf of the savages to whom one never speaks on important matters with empty hands. Plenty of similar massacres have

object than to get together quantities of beaver-skins, and they even use the presents they are entrusted with for their own profit, as there is no one to supervise their action.

It would be much more natural for all that to be addressed direct to Detroit, and for everything to pass through my hands; for I should send word to the chiefs of the tribes to come here, and I should settle all their disputes with them; and as regards the distribution and the use I should make of these presents sent to me, or to anyone else at this post, I should give my certificates concerning them; the other officers there. the missionaries and even the agents of the Company could give theirs, so that no abuses would be committed. Moreover, who could be chosen, to send to settle the quarrels of the savages, who would know their ways, manners and inclinations better than I, and in whom would they have more confidence? But that is what the Jesuits will not agree to. They prefer certain hucksters, who have no weight with our allies, to me. That is why, My Lord, I think it would be expedient for you to be good enough to send me a commission as Commandant-General of this and the other distant posts, so as to spare me these acts of injustice.

Some savages have just told me that four boats are coming up, to go to the north of Lake Superior by the village of the Sauteurs. I do not know what this may be; no doubt it will be the usual thing. that is, specious pretexts.

I write many things to you which may perhaps make enemies for me. But, no matter, while I have truth and justice on my side, I am above [them] all. I think I owe that to the zeal I have in serving the King well.

Also, the Sioux are a tribe which should be indifferent to us, and too far off for [us] ever to obtain any service from them.

As the convoy which comes from Montreal generally stays here only two or three days, in order to spare their provisions, I had got this letter ready so as not to stop it. That is why I often mention M. de Calliere in it, for I did not know that he was dead. I learnt this with grief on account of the general loss sustained by the whole colony which needed a man of such experience. It is a great loss to me personally, for you may have seen from all the good reports he sent you of me that he honored me with his esteem, and his friendship. I hope you will be good enough to recommend my interests to the one you put in his place; I assure you I have great need of that protection, on account of the large number of those who bear me ill-will.

The Company having relied on my care for all its interests, I have undertaken them *con amore.* Hence it has arisen that I have caught its agents at fault, transacting trade at this point. I gave the Directors warning of it and they will proceed as seems good to them in that matter; it is for them to act according to their lights on the information which I

I have written to M. de Vaudreuil thinking I was writing to M. de Calliere. I have asked him to be good enough to raise this garrison to fifty
men so that I may be in a position to defend myself in case I am attacked,
as I cannot do with less, in a place where I should be cut off from all assistance. He answered me that he could not give up a single soldier because several of them had died since last year and some had deserted
him then. This also happens at this post, nine of them having deserted
who, however, ask to come back. Some say that they resolved on this only
because they had been promised, when they set out from Montreal, that
after three years' service at this post they would be granted their discharge; in fact the late M. de Calliere had publicly given his word for it.
Others say the reason of their desertion was because they were overwhelmed with work; that they were made to do duty besides that; and
that their annoyance was at seeing that the profits fell to a Company
which treated them in their times of need like Turks and Moors. Lastly
there were some who said that a promise had been made them to give
them lands, and to let them settle there; and that, seeing they had been
deceived, they resolved on this.

It is quite certain that, when I set out from Montreal, MM. de Calliere
and de Champigny did not give them hope of this; I am a witness to it. It
was that which made me refresh M. de Calliere's memory about it in my
letter. For this reason MM. de Vaudreuil and de Beauharnois, after con
sidering it, have permitted me to take them back, seeing that the new
decree against deserters had not been promulgated.

I had also applied for six families to come and settle here, which the
late M. de Calliere had granted me; but that was refused to me after his
death and I was told that none came forward, although I knew well, of
myself and in other directions, that as many would come as we wanted
if the liberty to do so had not been taken away from them.

I had also asked for some cattle. The Company was quite willing to
bear the expense; the directors sent me word that they have [tried to]
borrow two troop boats from M. de Vaudreuil to provide conveyances for
them and that he would not grant them.

You may believe that the Company has no other object but to make
money at this post, and not at all to contribute to its settlement. It has
no other aim but to have a warehouse and clerks, with no officers, troops,
nor settlers, caring little for what concerns the King's glory and his serv-

price as they were sold to them up to the present time. I have given them strong hopes; and that makes me think they will await your answer, by the vessels that will come next year.

The Company complains about the loss of its trade at this post. If that is so, it should not hesitate to give it up. Consent to it, My Lord, and I promise you that in two years your Detroit will be established of itself, provided you allow freedom of trading to those who are willing to settle there, without their being able to do any trade outside Detroit. I assure you, you shall have no complaint as to that. and that I will have very strict order observed on this point.

The Company appears to be disgusted with this post because, as it says, it loses by the trade it does there. I have replied to it on this head that, if it is willing to appoint me to its rights and to withdraw in my favor, I will accept them, pledging myself to indemnify it for the liabilities from the day on which it bore the expenses of this post up to that on which I enter into possession of it, and to pay it ready money for its advances provided it will honor the bills of exchange for the beaver-skins which I shall send it every year; and that, to that end, I will give it good and valid security. If it complains to you about that, take it at its word; and if you appoint me to its rights and make it withdraw in my favor, I offer you, My Lord. the sum of ten thousand livres a year which I will have remitted to the treasurers of the navy in this country on your order, or indeed in France if you wish it. That should be paid promptly as long as the Company of the Colony or another will honor the bills of exchange for the beaver-skins coming from it; it will only be necessary to retain in France a fund of a like sum, that is to say of 10,000#, and I will so humor the minds of the savages that they will have reason to be content. You see clearly, My Lord, that it is a good thing to have a man like me. I promise you that, if the Company accepts my proposal and you will approve of it, I will make your Detroit flourish; that nothing shall be lacking there. I fear I shall not be taken at my word; the machine with the great springs will know well how to prevent it, for they work diligently to overthrow this post, which can only happen by working it through the medium of a Company which takes every precaution to act so that no one may settle there. If I managed this matter. I should not follow their traces,—far from it, I should not prevent anyone from settling there. They set up for clever men, but I can assure you they understand nothing about it; they even sent me an account by which they showed a loss of 12297#, 17s., in which they are mistaken, or at least they pretend to be so; for I find in it, without saying where, for a reason, more than twenty thousand livres profit. I speak correctly, and my opinions

to make their fortunes in the first year they begin any enterprise; and the latter who behave more wisely, well know that in the first year one does nothing but distribute and sow; that in the second, one's enterprise is brought into shape; and that in the third, it is necessary to work effectively in order to reap in abundance what has been liberally scattered. Anyone who gets away from this point of view can never succeed when chance is not mixed up with it; also that only happens on passing occasions; and rarely when it is a question of forming any substantial post. One need not be surprised if the directorate of the Company of the Colony seem uneasy; that is due to the people who compose it. Two of them are lawyers. qualified for getting deeds drawn up; the others have been merchants for a little while but the business they do is only on commission and all their skill and knowledge consists in selling advantageously. There are even very few of them who have put their own private affairs in a good condition; that is an everyday experience in this country.

I do not know whether they have been careful to write [and tell] you that the board of directors made an agreement with me last year, [which was] approved by MM. de Calliere and de Beauharnois by which it pledged itself, in consideration of the pains and care I was to take for its interests at this post, in order to prevent frauds and malversations and trading by people other than their clerks, to pay me every year the sum of two thousand livres, and to supply food for me and my family during the term of its lease.

No one could have been more diligent, My Lord, than I have been in complying with the provisions inserted in this deed, executed before two notaries, signed by the seven directors, by the late M. de Calliere and by M. Beauharnois the Intendant. Yet I have learnt that they have written to you to get themselves released from [paying] this sum; but I do not believe you have listened to so unjust a proposal, which puts an end to plain dealing, for they themselves well know that I have thoroughly earned my money by the services I have rendered them, and continue to render them.

Moreover, as there is a valid deed executed, which is circumstantially stated with all the requisite formalities, I hope you will not annul it without giving me time to defend myself. This ingratitude on the part of that Company will not make me omit anything to aid in the preservation of its interests.

that you promised me in your letter to appoint him as soon as there was an opportunity; many have gone by since that time.

I annex hereto a copy of some observations regarding the directors of the Company, so that you may know how I have acted and whether it is very agreeable to me to answer for my actions to five or six merchants who, four days ago, were cleaning their masters' shoes but who wish to meddle with the concerns of the government. I except from it MM. d'Auteuil and de Lofbinieres as it seems to me from their private letters that they did not take part in a great memorial which they presented to MM. de Vaudreuil and de Beauharnois, which I think was not answered as a governor [should].

No one has died yet at this post. I will not weary you any more with such long letters. I thought I ought to do so this year in order to finish informing you, and to beg you very humbly to have a stop put to all these outcries in one way or another, for indeed all that will end in making our allies go to the English. I shall continue all my life to ask you only for the honor of your patronage being with very deep respect

My Lord

Your very humble and very obedient servant

Lamothe Cadillac

at fort Pontchartrain this 31st Augt. 1703.

M. de Tonty who is at Quebec writes me that MM. de Vaudreuil and de Beauharnois have forbidden him to write to you at length [on] matters concerning this post.

[The following is written on the last page, crossways at the end of the letter]

Canada

This is the original of the letter of La Motte Cadillac, all the documents are annexed to it; so I think all that must be sent to M. de Champigny to put with the rest to examine carefully, and to send his opinion in detail stating his reasons; for, as for me, I am in favor of keeping up the post and leaving La Motte Cadillac the master of it.

CADILLAC HAS TROUBLES WITH THE JESUITS.

Endorsed—31st August, 1703; apparently written to M. de la Touche — — M. de la Motte—I have replied to all that in answering the letter which M. de la Motte writes to Monseigneur.

Sir,

I am giving the Minister an exact account of all that concerns the post of Detroit; I should have informed you of it likewise had I not thought [it would be] falling into superflous repetitions, being quite assured that he refers to you all the affairs of this Colony.

You will see from the letter which I have the honor to write to him the condition of this settlement, the hindrances which are thrown in its way, and the means I am taking to overcome them.

It is very probable that the reverend Jesuit fathers have demanded from the Court the preference in officiating in the missions of this post, and no doubt there have been reasons for granting it to them. Yet, although the savages are settled here in number sufficient to require at least two Missionaries, we have been unable to succeed in getting any to come, although the matter has been decided upon as you will see from the order of the 25th Septr. 1702, which I am sending to M. de Pontchartrain.

The énvoys from the colony, who proceeded last year to France, will no doubt have told you the steps which the directors of the Company of

notified to them, but they have paid no regard to it and have treated it with contempt.

Can it be believed that I should have been willing without powerful reasons to thwart any Jesuits, or that I should have taken it into my head to attack that formidable Society? I have not lived so long without knowing full well how dangerous it is to cross its path. It is true that I have attacked, to no small degree but far rather as animated by zeal for the King's service, the whole society in this country only; and I have even been so well justified in all the contests I have had with it while I have had the honor of being in command at Missilimakinak (on which all the other distant posts depended at that time), and since I have been at Detroit, that I pledged myself to state all my reasons in writing, if it would do the same with its reasons, which it would never consent to, in order to avoid the decision thereon. Was I not right to lay down in my scheme that all sorts of laborers must be allowed to work in the Lord's vineyard? You would say that the souls of the savages are the private domain of the Jesuits; if that were true, they should at least cultivate it and not leave it as a prey to the ravishing wolf. Of what pretext can they avail themselves for refraining from coming to discharge their duties in the missions of this post? The service of God may be found there, as elsewhere; that of the King lies there, since he wishes it, and it is their duty to give these proofs of obedience to the authority of a Governor-Général. But this is the theory of the missionaries of the Society of this country; the will of the King, in the orders he gives, must coincide and be in conformity with the will of God. And they claim to have the right first to decide what the true will of the King is, with reference to the knowledge which they say they have of the true will of God. And this is the chief ground on which they have clamored and still clamor so against the brandy trade on which point they have been humored. Here is a specimen of it from Father de Carlier in his sermon of the 25th of March 1697— "There is" he says, "no power, divine or human, which could sanction the trade in this drink;" whence it follows that this Father passes boldly over all reasons of state, and that he would not even submit to the decision of the pope.

I am doing my utmost sufficiently to make them my friends, truly wishing to be theirs; but if I dare say so, all impiety apart, it would be better to sin against God, than against them. for on the one hand pardon is received for it, while, on the other, even a pretended offense is never forgiven in this world, and would perhaps never be so in the other if their influence there were as great as it is in this country. I think that if they are so slow to carry on the missions of this post, it is because they do not at all like the nearness of the French settlements. They put for-

oppose other missionaries taking possession of it? The delay they occasioned by making this move is founded on nothing but the useless and forlorn hope of inducing the savages to go back to where they were before, by punic fears which they try to instil into their minds. I will stake my life that that will not take place and I do not fear their influence in all this.

Permit me in concluding this letter, to beg you to be good enough to aid me with your intelligence by pointing out to me a way by which I may gain the friendship of the reverend Jesuit Fathers. I ask no better than to walk in this way, which now-a-days dazzles the eyes of the whole world; and (this)* is the stream by which it seems that all men allow themselves to be borne along, that will be easy to me as long as I have only my private interests to settle with them; but when it is a question of having the will of the King carried out and they oppose it, telling me that they know better than I, it is a matter of laying down for me what I must do in that case in order to remain in the path of their friendship. That is a thing that I have been unable to do up to the present; perhaps I shall do better in future on the ideas you suggest to me, if you will have this kindness. I beg you to be good enough to grant me the honor of your support with M. de Pontchartrain by speaking to him on my behalf concerning the favors I am asking him for. You have been pleased to assist me in the past, for which I shall be eternally grateful. I hope you will continue to [grant] me the same favor, since I am with very great respect, Sir,

Your very humble and very obedient Servant

Lamothe Cadillac

At Fort Pontchartrain this 31st of Augt. 1703.

---

*This word is in the text, but ought to have been omitted as the word "cella" further on is made the nominative of the sentence.—Ed. trans.

REFLECTIONS ON THE PRESENT STATE OF THE SETTLEMENT
OF DETROIT IN CANADA.

Endorsed—Canada. 29 April, 1704.

M. de Lamotte who originated the plan for this settlement maintains
two things which alike deserve that attention should be paid to them.

The first, that is for [the interests of] the King's service and for the
general good of the Colony, to keep up, to increase and to perfect this
settlement. The second, that the Colony in general, and almost all those
who compose it in particular, use all their endeavors to thwart him in
this undertaking.

Granting these two contentions, to avoid entering on endless discussions which would only serve to obscure the truth further, only one
means presents itself of conciliating matters. This would be to leave the
proprietorship and the management of this undertaking to the one who is
the originator of it.

The offers he makes to undertake it himself if the Colony finds it does
not suit it; the conditions on which he makes these offers, are also so
many favorable dispositions which point to putting this means into practice.

But since in the conditions he proposes there might be found points
prejudicial to the Colony, he ought not to object to their being examined
attentively.

He offers to reimburse the Colony for all its advances after deducting
what it has received. That ought to be done; but as, during the discussion of the expenses and receipts, disputes will infallibly arise, it appears
necessary that these accounts should be adjusted before the Governor-
General and the Intendant since there is no one in the country who has
not an interest in that matter.

He asks that the Colony may be bound to receive and to pay him for all
his beaverskins. That general proposal can never be accepted. All that
he could claim would be that as many beaverskins should be sold for him
each year as appears from the accounts of the Colony to have been received a year on the average. 10494#'s worth of them appears in these
accounts the first year, and 18239#'s worth in the second. That is
28733#'s worth in all in two years, and 14366#, 10s.'s worth per year on
the average. If 15000#'s worth are sold for him every year he would have
no cause to complain; and the Colony could not receive more without being considerably injured by it.

By the new agreement, which it has just made, it is restricted to supplying only 150000#'s worth of beaverskins to its agents every year. If they are compelled to receive 30000#'s worth of them from M. de la Motte, all the Colony together will be able to supply only 120000#'s worth. It would not be right that an entire country all settled and making a figure in the world should draw only four-fifths of 150000# while one settlement, in its infancy and with its success still doubtful, should draw by itself one-fifth of that sum.

Everyone is aware that the post of Detroit is in the midst of the savage tribes, and that, by means of the Lakes and the rivers, it can have intercourse with all the countries of the Outaouas. The Colony could never be reassured as to the reasonable apprehension it will feel that whoever remains its proprietor will have it in his power to transact alone the whole trade in beaver-skins. It only burdened itself with this post with the object of preventing this irregularity, and of reducing the [trade in] beaver-skins to the least that may be possible.

Whatever prohibitions may be laid on the proprietor of this post, at whatever quantity may be fixed the beaver-skins he may supply every year to the Colony, he will always find means of getting as many through as he likes, under borrowed names, and by the trail of the savages even. This point is of the utmost importance, and of itself may cause the ruin of the Colony.

Authority will be granted, it is said, to the Colony to establish an Inspector at Detroit in order to watch over the conduct of the proprietor. That is something; but what can private interest not effect? A small share which this proprietor will give this Inspector in the profits he will make by his trading will very soon corrupt him. However that may be, if it appears right and almost indispensable to leave this post in the hands of M. DelaMotte, granting the first points of which mention has been made, the Colony confirms itself to requesting

1st. To be reimbursed its advances after having rendered an account [of them] before the Governor and the Intendant; and that for this purpose M. de la Motte should be ordered to go down at once to Quebec.

2nd. Only to be bound to receive from M. DelaMotte annually at most 15000#'s worth of beaverskins coming from Detroit, for the reasons deducted above.

other property, which Inventory M. de LaMotte shall be bound to sign before going down to Quebec to adjust the accounts.

5th. That if M. De la Motte has changed his opinion in this matter, or if he does not adapt himself to the conditions it may please My Lord to lay down for him, the Colony shall be permitted to administer and govern this post for the benefit of the service of the King and for the general welfare of [the Colony], as it promises to do on the refusal of M. De la Motte, if My Lord allows it.

At Paris, the 29th of April, 1704

Riverin*

ENDORSED LETTER FROM THE COURT, OR ARRANGEMENT MADE BY THE KING AND M. D'LAMOTHE ON ACCOUNT OF DETROIT.

Versailles, 14th of June, 1704.

I have received the letters you wrote to me on the 30th & 31st of the month of August last, with the papers which were thereto annexed.

I received at the same time the complaints of the directors of the Company of the Colony as to the pretended losses it is making at Detroit; and, as you anticipate it by the offer you make to undertake this post at your own risk if that company will appoint you to its rights, I have proposed it to the King, His Majesty has agreed to it, and I am writing to these directors that he desires them to give it up to you on your paying them for the goods which they now have there, and reimbursing them for the useful erections they have put up there. For this purpose you must come to Quebec to make an agreement with them on this basis, and to take the orders of MM. de Vaudreuil and de Beauharnois thereon. The will of the King, then, is that you should have the management as well as the command of this post, and that you should transact its trade for your profit as the Company could have done. His Majesty indeed places a restriction on it which is (since the Colony will henceforward not be able to do more [trade] in beaver-skins than à hundred and fifty thousand [livres'] worth a year, the new commissioners with whom it has been necessary to come to terms not being obliged to pay for more than that sum with bills of exchange) that His Majesty has reduced the trade in beaverskins which you may do to fifteen, or at least twenty thousand livres a year, leaving you however at liberty to trade in other skins to whatever sum you think fit. But on the other hand His Majesty consents to release you from the sum of ten thousand livres, which you offer to pay him annually, until further orders.

His Majesty further forbids you to send boats to Missilimakinak and on the lakes, or agents into the more remote districts, desiring that you should transact your trade at Detroit; but it is open to you to attract the Savages there to bring the said skins. And, in order to avoid the complaints which the Company might unjustly make against you, His Majesty permits it to keep an Inspector [there] whom it is to pay at its own expense.

Moreover His Majesty is issuing orders to MM. de Vaudreuil and de Beauharnois to give you all the help and protection which may be in their power; he charges M. de Vaudreuil to give you as many soldiers as you ask for, and M. de Beauharnois to have their pay issued to them as usual, you of course bearing the cost of their transport.. He also orders them to permit all those who wish to go and settle there to do so; to stir up the Savages on whom you have counted to go and settle at Detroit; and also to see you are granted the missionaries required for that post.

With all this assistance, and any other just and reasonable request you may make, which His Majesty will grant you, he hopes you will succeed in realizing the outline you have given [us] of this post. From this success you may expect favors from His Majesty proportioned to the service you render; and you may count on my contributing on my part to procuring them for you as far as I can. I am explaining the intentions of H. M. on this subject definitely to MM. de Vaudreuil and de Beauharnois, and to the directors of the Company so that in the future you may find no more obstacles in this post. I am convinced that, on your side, you will act like a man of honor, and will give no ground for complaint against your conduct, especially as regards the beaver-skins the trade in

I have spoken to the directors of the Company who are in France about the ox hides, for which you say they do not pay enough; they contend that they could not pay more than six livres for them because they only sell them for ten in France, and if they gave more for them they would lose by it. As you are allowed to transmit trade on your own account without passing it through the hands of the Company, it will be for you to see whether you can give more for them.

His Majesty does not think it advisable for you to go in search of the copper mine of which you write to me; you will have enough business at Detroit without wasting your energy on an undertaking like that, which is always liable to many difficulties and to many incidental expenses which cannot be foreseen.

Nor can the concession you ask for, and the erection of it into a marquisate, be entertained at present; that would not be compatible with the establishment of Detroit. Work to compass the success of this settlement, and after that you shall not lack concessions nor even posts more important than that you [now] have.

I am very glad to learn that you had a good harvest at Detroit last year; the surest means of establishing that post firmly is for those who dwell there to have their livelihood assured there.

It is not expedient that the chief of the Hurons or his nephew should come to France, and still less to form companies of soldiers out of his savages to be paid by the King. I inform you above that M. de Vaudreuil will give you as many French soldiers as you wish.

His Majesty permits you to make grants of land at Detroit as you may think good and befitting the interests of the new colony; also that you leave the soldiers and Canadians who may wish to marry there [at] liberty to do so when the Fathers who discharge the duties of curés find no legitimate impediment thereto.

His Majesty believes he has anticipated by the orders he has given all the requests you might make, and remedied all the inconveniences of which complaint has been made. I may assure you again that if you succeed in firmly establishing this post, as you promise and as I hope, I shall take pleasure in doing you a service and in obtaining favors for you from His Majesty.

Signed Pontchartrain.

True copy Lamothe Cadillac. I have the original here.

On the 8th page, crossways:]

. Letter from M. de Pontchartrain to M. de la Motte, of the 14th June, 1704.

ex letter A.   While leaving you absolute master in all things at this place, I hope you
will find a means of attracting thither the savages on whom you have
counted, and that you will act in such a manner as to give no umbrage to
the Iroquois, nor [any] opportunity for a rupture with us. I must
acknowledge to you *that this was the only thing which caused His Majesty to hesitate as to your settlement of Detroit;* you cannot, therefore,
be too circumspect in order to avoid this misfortune which would recoil
on the rest of the Colony.

ex letter A.   His Majesty permits you to grant lands at Detroit as you think fit and
expedient for the interests of the new Colony; and to leave the soldiers
and Canadians who wish to marry there free to do so, as long as the
ecclesiastics discharging the functions of parish priests find no just impediment.

TALK BETWEEN THE DIFFERENT INDIAN TRIBES AT
DETROIT.

Speech of the Savages of Detroit,   Answers of the Sounôutonouans to

with the blood of your enemies. We want, today, to wipe them, that the pain which you feel for your dead may be forgotten, and that which your enemies, (now become your allies by the general peace which our father Onontio has given to all the tribes), might feel at seeing this blood thus marked on your calumets. We would also wipe away that which seems still to flow on your bodies.

. A Belt.

Long had we taken counsel in our village on coming to mourn with you; but how should we have been received if we had not possessed assured knowledge of those who had destroyed you.

You would perchance have accused us either of the act itself or of being in league with your enemies. · Now that we know who are guilty, we come to name them to you; it is the Agoiatanous. There are five dead on the spot, and five prisoners who are at peace on the mat in their villages.

A Robe of
Beaver-skin.

This robe is to cover the dead, that they may rouse secret impulses of vengeance in the hearts of the living.

A Belt.

We likewise are to be pitied, my brothers, for we have lost four persons who have been killed by the same Agoiatanouns.

China Beads.

If the whole tribe were contained in this village, we should be convinced that our course would be understood in all the huts. But we fear that, as you are so numerous and so distant, this message which we give you from the bottom of our hearts may tarry here and may not be able to spread to the end of your villages; and that someone, in ignorance of it, may disturb the peace and rest which we hope to enjoy under the general peace. Hence we invite you to have it spread throughout all your lands, and amongst all your allies.

news removes from us the doubt we felt, whether that could be the tribe which had attacked us. You know, my brothers, our customs· which are to avenge, or to perish in avenging our dead; but, to-day, when the heavens tell us that the sun is shining in favor upon us, you and we who have been murderously attacked, must wipe away our blood and our tears until we have spoken to our father Onoutio, who, in the general peace, reserved to himself the right of doing justice for us on whomsoever should not abide by his words. We have received your present to wipe the blood from our bodies and to wash our calumets. Receive ours for the same purpose. Believe not the false words which creep in secretly like serpents and inspire you with fear of us; they are always telling you that we are going to devour your village. Fear nothing; be assured that we wish to live in close alliance with you, and this I ratify with you by this belt.

You were misinformed when you were told that your message did not get past the Sounoutonouans. How could they tell you this falsehood? You have never said aught to us that has nct been faithfully reported to our brother L'Anglois; and to prove this my saying to you, you have now five boats which have come by the river of the Onontaguez. It is Amabauso, it is Ganatagonioun. Thus you see, my brothers, that it was without cause that they told you that your message was not in our village since the road has been open for you to go to Orange. And in order that you may have proofs of the sincerity of our hearts, we give you this powder to keep you here until we have answers from all the dwellings and also from Pitre Seul to whom we are sending your words. They shall set out tomorrow for that purpose.

our common father.

A Belt.

Remember, my brothers, it is to this you should give ear, remember the belts we have exchanged, one with another, in order to signify that if there should fall any tree between us we are to cast it out without looking at it. These are our thoughts; these are the words which proceed from the depth of the hearts of our old men and our warriors. We ask you to be of the same mind, and that this may be the will of the whole tribe of the Iroquois.

A Belt.

It is now with the Sounoutonouans that we, that we who come from afar, will light our council-fire.

A Belt.

Fear nothing, O ye Sounoutonouans; we will never think of doing any hostile act against you, nor against your allies.

A Robe of
Beaver-skin.

That you may be convinced of the sincere feelings of our hearts, we will leave our spirits with you, although they have been there for a long time. Unite them with yours, so that they may form but one heart, and one and the same will.

A Robe of

Speech of the Hurons of Detroit to the Governor-General on the 7th of August, 1704.

You have told me, my children that you came partly to testify to me of the joy you felt because the great Onontio had appointed me to be your father in this country; for this, I thank you.

You have also informed me, by a belt, that the Oyatauous had slain some of your men; but that remembering the promise you had given to your father at Montreal, you had not attempted to avenge yourselves until you should learn my counsel; and that you begged me to remember that, when the general peace was made, that it was ordered that any tribe which be attacked, should not avenge itself but should carry its complaints to its father; and that, if the one which had attacked it did not make reparation, all the tribes —should band themselves together to devour it.

Reply

I am obliged to you, my children, for having remembered the promise you gave to your father, and for coming here with your complaint of this instead of avenging yourselves. I had already learnt from M. de la Mothe that the Oyatauous had wrongfully slain three of your men, namely a Huron, an Outavois, and a Poutouatamy; and I have dispatched the Sr. de Vincenne, whom you must have met, to go and inform the Oyatauous that it is my will that they should give you satisfaction and should make amends for this wrongful act, or I will join with my other children to compel them. M. de Tonty sends me word that the Oyatauous have come to Detroit and that they have set matters right, and have given satisfaction to the Outavois and to you; that they have promised to do so also to the Poutouatamy. I rejoice, my children, to see that the land is united, and that tranquility reigns among you. I give you this belt to exhort you ever to be of the same mind; and I give you provisions and powder to make the way of your return easy to you and I enjoin you to take care of what I commit to your charge for M. de Tonty, to give to such of your elders as I name to him, because they have obeyed my voice.

RAMEZAY COMPLAINS OF THE TREATMENT OF CADILLAC.

Endorsed—Colonies. M. de Ramezay.' 14th of Novr. 1704.

My Lord,

＊   ＊   ＊   ＊

· The younger Rignolt and his brother Vaudry has permission to go and trade with the Outaouais under the pretext of going to the Illinois, for the Srs. de Tonty and de la Forest; this boat alone took two hundred pots of brandy, which they sold at Misilimakinac. The two Chauvins, Beamus and Richard, have also taken two boats under pretext of going to the Illinois for the Srs. de Tonty and de la Forest, and have traded with their goods at Missilimakinac, with the Miamis, and at other posts.

＊   ＊   ＊

I have thought it my duty, My Lord, in the position I hold, to inform you of the case they have got up against one of our officers, named M. de la Mothe Cadillac who commands at Detroit by the orders of the Court. He has the honor of being known to you, My Lord, and I feel obliged to say, on his behalf that he has always discharged his duty well, and has executed himself well in the work that has been intrusted to him for the King's service. So that, because he has acted most uprightly by denouncing the Sr. de Tonty and two agents of the Company at Detroit, who have, in effect, been convicted of malversation by his having seized a certain quantity of furs and having discovered a much greater quantity, a suit has been brought against him in order to render his evidence liable to be challenged. This affair is a scandal to the public generally, for it is very certain that the Srs. de Lobiniéres and de Linot, who are the chief of the board of directors, have only acted in this manner, as it would appear, in order to shelter the two agents; and the former is the father-in-law of the Sr. Arnolt while the latter is the brother-in-law of the Sr. de Linot, who have found a powerful protector in M. de Vaudreuil, the nephew of the Sr. de Lobiniere by his wife.

If the conduct of the Sr. de Linot were thoroughly looked into it would,

poisoned the Canadas with Hamburg gunpowder, which is good for nothing. This having been sold to the savages has wronged them, and this disgusts them.

The Srs. Arnold and Nollan, instead of being punished for their dishonesty, have been paid their wages, and the former has gone up to the Outauais with a boat laden with goods although M. de la Mothe had publicly declared that the said Arnold and Nolan had about six thousand livres' worth of beaverskins and furs at Michilimakinac, which had been stolen from the warehouse of the Company at Detroit.

*   *   *

Afterwards, when the country had extended and the King had taken over the rights of the Company, the Jesuits though no longer able to regulate the choice of the Governors and the Intendants, have never-the-less always tried to keep up the authority which they had acquired over the country, with a success which has varied according to the laxity or firmness of those who have governed the Canadas; and it has been found that those who have deferred to them too far, have not attained success in the King's service in this Colony. The Comte de Frontenac, whose birth and merits are known, when he arrived in Canada, governed it with so much wisdom that he was able to draw the love and respect of the whole people. It is hardly possible to imagine the intrigues, the plots and the calumnies which the Jesuits made use of at Court with the object of dislodging him from his first governorship, on which he would never communicate with them, any more than in their last reign. I can confidently assert that it would be very difficult to find one who would do so much good for the country, and would know so well how to govern it. The only fault he had was that of seeking too eagerly after honors.

*   *   *

But as regards the Jesuits, although at the bottom of their hearts they do not approve of it, there is no likelihood of them complaining of it because they are not triumphant.

Instead of distributing according to His Majesty's intentions the two thousand crowns which he is good enough to present to the best families in this country, a part of the sum is given at their urgent request, to peasants, dependants of theirs. They play the chief part in the government; nothing is considered without their councils, which are often held at their houses; moreover, that suits their private interests, as I shall have the honor of making known to you, My Lord.

The men named Despins and Desriusseaux, under the pretext of going up to take the four hundred livres' worth of goods which are required for the mission of the reverend jesuit fathers, have together with some savages, taken three boats, which were loaded with merchandise and brandy, and these they have sold to the rebels, which has tended to prevent them from taking advantage of the amnesty.

*   *   *

My Lord,

Your very humble, most obliged and very obedient servant,

De Ramezay.

Quebec this 14th of Nov. 1704.

LETTERS FROM VAUDREUIL AND DE BEAUHARNOIS COM-
PLAINING ABOUT CADILLAC.

Endorsed—MM. de Vaudreuil and de Beauharnois.

17th of Nov. 1704. Colonies.

My Lord,

*   *   *

The Sr. de Vaudreuil having learnt at Montreal, where we then were, that the Sr. de la Mothe, having been warned of the request which had been made to us at the general assembly last year to ask you that the post of Detroit might be abandoned, and fearing to lose that command, had incited the savages of that post, without it appearing to proceed from him, to demand of him that the agent whom the Board of Directors had sent by the first convoy to relieve the one of whom the said Sr. de la Mothe had complained should be dismissed, or else they would kill him, and to declare that they would not permit the furs which were in the Company's warehouses at Detroit to go down until the Board of Directors had sent a second large consignment of goods; which we learnt from some savages, who acquainted us that the said Sr. de la Mothe went down to Montreal and caused a request to be presented to himself in council, by the prin-cipal chiefs of those who were settled at Detroit, by two belts which they presented to him, (which they told us the said Sr. de la Mothe had sup-plied them with for that purpose), that as a pledge that he would return to command at the said post, and that the former Agent would also return there, they should leave their wives there. The said Sr. de Vaudreuil has

ests should do anything contrary to the welfare of the country (for he had, as it were, given them to understand from the demands he had got them to make to him that we feared them as if we dared not refuse them), though they could not find any person more capable of bringing them to their senses than the Sr. de Louvigny, major of Quebec, who was in command of them at Missillimakinac. He induced these savages to obey the orders of the said Sr. de Vaudreuil, and sent down a part of the furs which were at the said post; and they confessed to him that all that they had done before had been only through the advice of the said Sr. de la Mothe, whose wife he brought back. And the Srs. de Vaudreuil and de Beauharnois hope, My Lord, that you will perceive that it is only for the good of the country that they have labored in this matter, in which several persons, on account of private interests, have secretly interfered more than they ought to have done, angry at seeing us acting with a knowledge which has disconcerted them, after having tried in vain to alter it.

The Directors immediately after the arrival of the Sr. de la Mothe at Quebec, complained of the expenses he caused to the Company, and requested permission to lay an information against him, in a petition presented to the Sr. de Beauharnois, who replied to it and requested M. de Ramezay who commanded at Quebec, in conformity with the object of the said petition, to keep the said Sr. de la Mothe there until he had answered it. The latter declared, by a protest which he caused to be made known to the said directors that he recognized neither the Sr. de Beauharnois, nor even the said Sr. de Vaudreuil, as his judges; but this has not prevented the said Sr. de Beauharnois from proceeding with the preparation of that case, since, under the commission with which the King has honored him, he is not liable to challenge as to competency; and we believe that the said Sr. de la Mothe objected to us both only after he had been informed that we were aware of all that he had induced the savages of Detroit to do, contrary to the King's service and the welfare of the Colony.

*   *   *   *

MM. de Vaudreuil and de Beauharnois who, My Lord, have been lenient enough not to tell you who the persons are of whom they have reason to complain,—although these persons made use of many means for the purpose of setting them at variance, with one another, and even imposed upon the piety of a bishop under the pretext of keeping families at peace. —have just learnt that the Sr. de Ramezay, on advice of the Srs. de la Mothe, d'Auteuil, & Aubert and Mme. la Forest, and others, united by the hope of a future trade at Detroit, on the evening before he set out for Montreal notified the Directors of the annexed protest against the choice which the said MM. de Vaudreuil and de Beauharnois have made of the Sr. Pascault in preference to the Sr. Aubert.

It is also with these same objects that we take the liberty of representing to you that, if Detroit is made use of as the Sr. Riverin writes to the Board of Directors, the trade of Montreal which has already fallen away will be entirely ruined in less than four years. Of this, My Lord, the Sr. de la Valliere, major of that place, will be able to give you a faithful account.

*   *   *   *

Your very humble, very obedient and most obliged servants,

Vaudreuil.
Beauharnois.

Quebec, the 17th of Nov.

MEMORANDUM OF M. DE LA MOTHE CADILLAC CONCERNING THE ESTABLISHMENT OF DETROIT, FROM QUEBEC.

Endorsed—19th Nov. 1704.

Canada. La Mothe Cadillac gives an account of his conduct concerning the establishment of Detroit by questions and answers; it is Monseigneur who questions him and Lamothe replies. Q. signifies the question; A. the answer.

Q. Was it not in 1699 that you proposed to me the establishment of Detroit which divides Lake Erie from Lake Huron?

A. Yes, My Lord.

Q. What were the motives you had in wishing to fortify that place, and establish it?

A. I had several. The first was to make a strong post of it, which should not be liable to the revolutions of the other posts, by getting it inhabited by a good number of Frenchmen, and savages, in order to subdue the Iroquois who have always spoiled the Colony and have prevented its enlargement.

Q. That would be good if what you propose could be achieved without great difficulties; but it appears to me that instead of strengthening the Colony by this establishment, it would weaken it, since it would divide

expense; and often the result of the march is [merely] to kill four or five poor wretches, because large expeditions cannot be formed without bustle and without the savages getting to know of them, and this makes them take the course of retiring into the woods when their forces are inferior, by which means they make the raising of forces by the French useless, as well expensive.

Q. I see you are right, for the large expeditions that have been formed in Canada, and even the general marches of the whole Colony, have been unavailing, and have inflicted no loss on the Iroquois except laying waste their crops which they have done without by means of it prevented their hunting which they have carried on in the direction of Detroit, and this has sufficed for their sustenance, until the following years' harvest; and I see you are going to tell me that if Detroit were settled and strengthened with a good number of Frenchmen and savages, they could shut off the resource of hunting from the Iroquois; and that by constant incursions that would be made upon them, because of the nearness of the post, they would be reduced to the deepest misery and to perishing of famine.

A. Your acuteness, My Lord, is very great; I am sure that when you have heard the other grounds for [making] that settlement, you will remain still more convinced of the necessity for forming it. It is indisputable that all the waters of the lakes pass through that river at Detroit, and that it is the only practicable way by which the English can pass to convey their merchandise to all the savage tribes that have dealings with the French, and that they employ all [means they can] to obtain it. Hence if that post were fortified in due form, the English would give up their confidence in the undertaking of absolutely withdrawing from us this trade.

Q. I understand what you say; your argument is sound as regards taking away from the enemies of the state the means of going themselves to trade in that country. But how would you prevent the savages from going to them, if they wish, and if they are attracted there by the favorable price of goods?

A. I confess that this is a great attraction to them; but experience shows us that the savages who are round about Quebec, the Three Rivers, and Montreal, know perfectly well that their furs sell better with the English [and] that they give them goods cheaper, yet they do all their trade with us. Several reasons engage them to this; the first is that each savage, taking one with another, kills only fifty or sixty beavers a year, and as he is near the Frenchman he borrows from him, and is obliged to pay in proportion on his return from hunting, and [out of] the little which remains to him, he is compelled to make some purchase for his family, and in that way he finds himself unable to go to the English be-

reason is that in resorting to the French they receive many flattering attentions from them, especially when they are well off, making them drink and eat with them, and in fact they [the French] contrive matters so well that they never let their furs escape; hence the desire to go to the English always exists in them, but they are skilfully reduced to being unable to put it into execution. It is for this reason, if Detroit is not settled, you will see, My Lord, all the savages of that district go to the English or invite them to come and settle among them.

Q. Have you not also some other reason?

A. Excuse me, it cannot be disputed that our savages used to carry on their hunting only to the north of Lake St. Clair, but through this post they [now] carry it on as far as two hundred leagues to the south of Lake Erie inclining towards the sea; and consequently their furs, which used to form the greater part of the English trade, are [now] carried into the Colony by means of their savages and make an increase in its business which is very considerable.

Q. What skins are obtained in those places?

A. The skins of the deer, roe, elk,—roebuck, black bear, skins of bisons, wolves, otters, wild-cats, beaver, and other small skins.

Q. Are these kinds of skin worth money in trade, and is there found to be a demand for them; and could not some means be found of employing the savages in hunting for them, and making them give up hunting the beaver which has lost its reputation as merchandise and is so burdensome to France because there is no demand for it at all?

through that protection. Prepare, therefore, to return to Canada in order to begin the settlement of Detroit.

A. I will go since you order me to do so and because you wish it; but I shall find many hindrances in making that undertaking successful, for the Jesuits in that country are my personal enemies.

Q. Go, but do not trouble yourself, urge this matter on vigorously, and if it meets with obstacles which resist its being made to succeed you have only to return to give me an account of them. Lamothe dismissed these wor

Q. Whence comes it that you have returned, and that you have not carried out the settlement of Detroit? Lamothe i turns from Canada to Versailles

I am informed that you have neglected to insure the success of this scheme. I know you have sufficient ability to have succeeded in it, if you had so wished; but I shall punish you for your sloth, and I will teach you not to present plans to me which you have no desire to carry out. These are very word which the minister u to Lamot his return Canada.

A. You are not content, My Lord, with using bitter reproaches to me, you add threats also, which shows me that some one has done me an ill turn with your Highness. I can assure you that I have done my utmost to secure complete success for that scheme, and that I have supported my proposal with all imaginable ardor; but I was obliged to yield to the torrent. I will do myself the honor to present to you in writing all that I did and said on this matter in the Assembly, which will vindicate my conduct. Lamothe in writing Monsigne what he h said in the sembly in Canada.

Q. The King has again considered your scheme, and has ordered me to send you back to Canada at once to take possession of Detroit promptly, wishing you to command there until further orders. Go forth at once, and proceed to Rochefort to embark. Order and words of to La Mot

A. Those are two very laborious journeys, which have exhausted my money and that of my friends, without counting the expenditure I shall be obliged to make to perfect that settlement.

Q. I will take care of you; only act so as to succeed. Words of seigneur.

A. Provided I am supported by the honor of your protection I am confident of thoroughly completing this work.

Q. How were you received on your arrival in Canada?

A. Thoroughly well. The Jesuits, having had information by the first vessel that you had resolved to have Detroit settled, came to the water side and showed me much courtesy. I returned it as far as I could; and finally, when they learnt the confirmation of this settlement, they busied themselves effectively, in their usual manner, with the Governor-General and the Intendant in order to establish themselves there alone to the exclusion of all other ecclesiastics and monks, which was at first granted them, and they nominated Father Vaillant to go and take possession of it.

Q. At what time did you set out from Quebec to go to Detroit?

a change was made, the Franciscans having obtained [permission] for one of their fathers to accompany me and to remain at Detroit as Almoner of the troops, with the Jesuit as missionary. This outrage, as it were, against the Society in that country set it in commotion, for it was persuaded that I had done it this bad turn. It was in the interval that it settled on the task of opposing this settlement utterly. I set out from Achine' on the 5th of June with fifty soldiers, and fifty Canadians, MM. de Tonty, a captain, Dugué and Chacornacle, Lieutenants. I was ordered to go by the great river of the Outavois, in spite of the representations I made on the point. I arrived at Detroit on the 29th² of July; I fortified myself there at once, I had the necessary dwellings built, the lands cleared and prepared for sowing in the autumn.

Q. Apparently Father Vaillant contributed greatly by his exhortations to advancing the works.

s was for-
ded to
iseigneur
701 to-
her with
it is con-
ed in pages
d 7.
A. He exerted himself for this so well that if the soldiers and Canadians had believed him they would have set out after two days to return thence to Montreal on the promise which this Father made them that he would get their wages paid to them by the Intendant for a whole year, although they had been employed only six weeks.

Q. How did you manage to learn his ill-will, and to combat this intrigue?

A. I perceived it from the discouragement everyone showed as to the works, which gave me occasion to sound a few of the most worthy men in private about it; and these frankly confessed to me what this Jesuit had told them in order to persuade them to leave that post and to return with him.

Q. Did you not make known to this Father that you had seen through his bad conduct?

A. Excuse me, this is how the matter took place. We were still encamped; on leaving the [dinner-] table, I had the soldiers and Canadians assembled; Father Vaillant was present, but he did not know my intention, nor that I had discovered his. I asked the Canadians what reason they had for wishing to go back to Montreal, and I begged them to tell me who could have imbued them with sentiment so opposed to the service of the King; and addressing myself to an officer, I requested him to tell

so, one of them said he did not know what I had made Father Vaillant eat, that he was in a great hurry to get to the woods, and that, by the gait he was going we should apparently not see him again very soon. I knew from these remarks what the matter was; I contented myself with explaining to these people the King's intentions and the good of his service, after which they explained to me unreservedly the cause of their discouragement which arose from the instigation of this Father. I had reason, afterwards, to be more pleased with them.

Q. I see by all that you have just said that this Jesuit had had no other motive for going with you but that of making your scheme abortive. I suspect also that he resolved to return thence to Quebec, seeing that he could no longer conceal his design.

A. I have already had the honor to tell you that it was a conspiracy hatched with his superior before his departure; and this caused an expense of a hundred pistols to the King.

Q. But did you not point out to him his wrong-doing by some reprimand, or by some other means which would be disagreeable to him?

A. Not at all; I thought it was for the good of the service to keep silent. I showed him as much courtesy as I could have done to an Archbishop, contenting myself with informing the Governor-General, and with giving you an account of it.

Q. I remember you wrote to me about it. I was also informed of it from other sources; that is why his Superior at Quebec was ordered to make him go to France, and to send you another who would enter better into your spirit than the first had done.

A. This expedient would have been very good if it had been carried out. Examples of this kind are marvellous for keeping the service of the King in order. But there must surely have been a contrary [order], for this Jesuit remained in that country with more animus against me than ever, fanning his hatred with the members of the Society; and although that order did not have its effect, the Jesuits were so offended at it that I had no difficulty in understanding that they have sworn to ruin me in one way or another.

Q. It seems to me however that the late Chevr. de la Calliere had made an arrangement containing several paragraphs in order to enable you to dwell in perfect harmony and good understanding with the Jesuits of that country; and I expected that all the difficulties which could arise would be removed, and that the contents of this arrangement would be carried out on both sides.

A. It is quite true that this arrangement might have put an end to all disputes between us; but the fox sooner or later eats up the hen. The bad conduct of Father Vaillant being recognized; the King's orders to send him to France having come; and having on my part discovered a

the Jesuits of the country; also M. de Tonty, the captain who had been
given me to second me in that enterprise, having betrayed me; made it
necessary for that Superior to subscribe to that agreement with a view
to making peace only until the departure of the vessels, in order afterwards to proceed with the ruin of the post of Detroit.

Q. I see plainly that the King's orders lose their force as soon as they
have passed the Great Bank, and that the Governor-General and Intendant make others after their manner.

A. It is not they, who act as they understand; they are compelled to
yield to the authority of the Jesuits; it is indeed true that, by conforming to their will, and granting them all they [ask] with a blind acquies-
cence, they both fish in the same fishing place, while the rest of the people
groan and suffer, being yet forced to applaud the very things they condemn in their hearts and in secret.

Q. That is what you ought to have done. If you had kept silent, you
would not have so many enemies, and so many serious troubles would
not have been stirred up against you.

eats of-
d to
othe by
seigneur.

A. I should have treated them thus if you had not threatened, when
I was at Versailles, to chastise me for my indolence, and to send me to
the Bastile, if I failed in firmness for carrying out this scheme. You
spoke to me in so severe a tone, and you so set alarm in my flanks and
fear in my entrails, that I even preferred to expose myself to the fury of
the lions of the time, than to fall into the hands of your indignation;
although in truth it were hard to discern which of the two will be the
worst and most dangerous to me.

2ND CHAPTER.

Q. I could not dispense with granting the trade of Detroit to the Company of the Colony, which promised me to do everything in its power to
make that settlement a success.

A. If you had known [what] its power [was] you would have hoped
for nothing from it; it is the most beggarly and chimerical company that
ever existed. I had as lief see Harlequin emperor of the moon. It was
this company that entirely upset my scheme by consistently opposing
your intentions in an underhand manner, the whole being cunningly managed by the Jesuits of that country.

A. Since you wish to know it, here it is in few words. I agreed with the directors, by the concurrence and consent of the Governor-General and the Intendant, that I should be assigned the third part of the trade which should be done in that post, on which condition the Company should be relieved from [paying] any gratuity to the other officers. The most envious having obtained information of this treaty, made some commotion about it, and thought it burdensome to the company. Hence, another agreement was made by common consent, providing that the Company should pay me each year the sum of two thousand livres and supply me and my family with food; and that it should pay also to M. de Tonty thirteen hundred and thirty-three livres on condition of doing no trade directly or indirectly with the savages, and of preventing—as far as in me lay—anyone from doing any in that place, and of preventing—so far as my knowledge went—[any] frauds and malversations, the directors trusting also to my care and my conduct for their interests. That is the main part of the treaty which I made with the directors.

Q. That is in accordance with what I had written, the King wishing you to be given an increase of salary as it was not reasonable that you should carry on that settlement at your expense and be excluded from the trade of that place which was the only means of indemnifying you. This deed is apparently executed before a notary.

A. That is so; it is agreed to by the Governor-General and the Intendant and signed by all the directors and by me.

Q. You have done well to take all these precautions. Are there many savages at Detroit?

A. There are now more than 2,000 souls. This place becomes peopled and settled visibly; it can reckon four hundred good men bearing arms.

Q. How did you contrive to induce those people to leave their villages, their fields and their crops? That must have cost the King dear,—I am judging by the heavy expenditure made at Quebec and at Montreal for the savages there, since they are given the soldiers' ration, and are given it even down to the infants at the breast, besides considerable presents which are made to them every day.

A. I do not know how I did it; what I do know is that·I have not spent a farthing, and that the Governor-General and Intendant would not grant me even the value of one pistole to make use of on the occasion; that on the contrary, both of them, and above all the Jesuits, have employed every means and exhausted all their strength and their ingenuity to prevent the savages from coming to settle there. But all their efforts have been fruitless.

Q. But for these hindrances, it looks as if the greater part of the savages would have been mustered in that place.

A. That is beyond doubt for they knew the goodness of the lands and

Q. But why do you say it is such a good country and so fecund? If
that were so, would all the evil that is said of it, be said? I am even
informed that the land there is worth nothing; that it produces no grains,
that there is almost no hunting or fishing, and that there are only lands
enough to place a small number of inhabitants. These conditions have
obliged me to call for the fullest explanations before pressing this settlement further; and for this purpose the King wished that an assembly
should be called together at Quebec in which you should be present in
order to answer all these facts, not doubting that if they are true you
would have agreed to them in good faith, and that if they were false you
would have combatted them so keenly and clearly that they would have
been obliged to give in.

A. When a man wishes to kill his dog, he declares that he is mad
[? Give a dog a bad name, and hang him]. Do you not see once more
that this is a matter led and arranged by the cunning of the Jesuits who
have the power of attaching to their party the Governor-General and the
Intendant—the rest of the inhabitants give them no further trouble; and
their opinions are always the conclusions of the Epistles of the Apostles,
that is to say, Amen, of all, in all, and for all that the Society in this
country wishes. If you had wanted to know the truth, My Lord, and the
condition of that settlement, you could have attained your end by sending an honest man there, secretly and incognito. I say incognito, and an
honest man because if he had been known to have been chosen to give
you an account of this matter he would have had to have been furnished
with effective preservatives not to feel the contagion and the pestiferous
air of this country. If he had kept himself free from it, he would have
assured you, as I do, that in all New France there is no land so good;
that finer grains cannot be seen, nor larger crops. As regards the number
of inhabitants, there is room to place Asia and Persia there by spreading them out to the right and to the left in the depths of the lands; they
must have been very bold and rash to have dared to forward to you such
a falsehood. This proves how affairs are managed in that country. In
reference to the hunting, there is no district which approaches it; and it
cannot be denied that more than thirty thousand animals have been killed
there these three years. In short, in what habitable country is there more
hunting than at Detroit?

Q. I believe you are right. I now see plainly that they are acting out
of animosity against you, which makes me decide clearly that the King's
service suffers by it, and that it is necessary to look to this disorder. It
is not difficult to see that if the lands are good at Detroit, there will

me. Give me also a little explanation as to the offence this settlement gives to the Iroquois.

A. This is a trick of the opponents of this post who, having learnt that the Court wishes peace to be kept between us and the Iroquois, in order to make it waver as to the increase of this settlement, make it believe that the Iroquois are discontented because of it; and yet that is so untrue that there are at this very time at Detroit thirty families of that tribe who are settled there. Before establishing this place, we were given this reason; you have overcome it, the place is fortified, hence that objection is now out of date and no importance, and as long as Detroit is fortified by the French and by savages, the Iroquois will never make war upon us. The Jesuits know it well although they insinuate the contrary; but in order to attain their ends, they will cause the Iroquois, who wish for peace, to be attacked by our savages.

Q. Yet in the assembly which was held at Quebec it was agreed that that was the greatest obstacle to keeping up this post. Why did you not set forth your reasons for removing that difficulty?

A. I had no knowledge of that assembly; hence I could not object to what was said or done there; and the letter which you did me the honor to write to me, dated the 20th of June, 1703, was only handed to me in the month of July, 1704; I took action in consequence, having assembled all the people who were in Detroit, and they signed the contrary of all that was done in the assembly of Quebec (where the Governor-General guarded the door and would let no one go out who had not signed against this post.) All the people who were there asked me for permission to settle there, because of the knowledge they had of the goodness of the lands and of the country. You may see it in the resolutions which I take the liberty of sending you, dated the 14th of June of that year.

Q. I can no longer doubt that everything is done in that country by intrigue and cabal; and I understand that, if you had been summoned to that assembly as I wished and ordered, this matter would perhaps have turned out differently. I see clearly that the King's orders are altogether weakened beyond the Great Bank, but I will look to it. What surprised me this summer was that the Governor-General and the Intendant did not positively declare either for the preservation or the destruction of this post. Had they not some private reason for dealing with it thus of which you can inform me?

A. It is simply a counsel of the Jesuits. Neither of them wished to appear nor to declare himself against this settlement, for fear that exposing their prejudice you might have known that those who formed the assembly had given their opinions only to adhere to those of their superiors as they could not act otherwise without risking their wrath. That is why the Governor-General and the Intendant prudently pretended to maintain an apparent neutrality, contenting themselves with making the

public speak, who were made to sign the crucifixion of that post, making
use of the public voice without allowing it to appear that they had put
anything of theirs in it, in order the better to gild the pill for you.

Q. What you say there might well have been; you ought indeed rather
to have warned me of it; [but] yet it may well be that they had some
other reason for not declaring themselves openly against that post.

A. I am persuaded that they had other reasons and that they did not
show so much discretion except because of the fear they had that, in causing the fall of that post in a high-handed manner, the condition and management of the Colony might be upset by it, and that if it should happen
that our savages went over to the English, or rather if the latter came
and settled at Detroit, the Court would have reason to reproach them,
with justice. That is why they kept silent, and apparently neutral, so
that in case of an evil result, they could exculpate themselves and cast the
blame on the decision of the assembly held at Quebec by the order of the
Court. But my opinion is that the savages will not quit that post at all,
whatever may be done at Quebec; and that makes me anticipate that the
Jesuits, in despair at not being able to succeed, perhaps in league with the
Governor and Intendant, will cause war to be got up by our allies against
the Iroquois, so as in that case to take the final resolution to abandon
Detroit. That is an idea I have; it may be that I am mistaken.

Q. That is vexatious, that you were not present at this assembly which
I ordered only in order to inform myself thoroughly as to the necessity
of that settlement; nor am I at all pleased at my letter having been delivered to you too late.

A. You might well be still less so at the evil trick that was played
upon me, or rather at the insult that was offered to you, for, speaking of
letters, I may tell you that they intercepted and opened three which I had
the honor to write to you last year; that copies were taken of them which
have become public; and this shows how little respect they have in those
countries for His Majesty's ministers, besides which it is a violation of
the law of nations, and nothing more could be done by the enemies of the
State, during war.

which I have now upon my hands, from which I hope you will have the kindness to release me, by punishing the hatred, or rather the fury, of those who are plotting my ruin, [? hatred] founded on this, that I have maintained with so much vigor the [advisability of] preserving Fort Pontchartrain, the success of which they have been unable in any way to interrupt.

Q. I understand you, and it is not difficult, for me to recognize that, as a consequence of the letters you wrote to me having been opened, your personal enemies and those who have opposed that post would be much fluttered, because I remembered that in your letters you point out to me (as you do now) what their type of mind is, and the special and general reasons they had for opposing this settlement; and it appeared to me, from all you said concerning it, that those who clamored so against that place acted only with reference to their private interests, and on account of the hatred they bore you. I see that it increased in proportion as you made the settlement flourish and advance. I am very much mistaken, if your enemies would not have played their last stake this year in order to upset your scheme entirely, without considering that in doing so they were thwarting the will of the King, and sacrificing the Colony. I fear, as you have pointed out to me, that if the Iroquois are kept in awe because of the fort of Detroit, some tribes other than those of Fort Pontchartrain might be stirred up to make war on the Iroquois, in order to destroy that Post which, according to what I know of it, is not kept up by a strong garrison.

A. There is no other Minister so wise, so enlightened and so vigilant as you, who can see through the false zeal of the opponents of the settlement of Detroit, and who can distinguish the injustice of my enemies. You shall see the vileness of it from the manner in which I have behaved, and from their dishonesty.

3RD CHAPTER.

Q. Give me an exact account, and tell me without disguising anything whether you are guilty of all you are accused of, and as to the complaints which the directors of the Company have made against you, and whether it is true that you have transacted trade and been guilty of malversations at Detroit. If so, you have acted contrary to the King's orders, and also to the agreement you made with them; you will therefore be very culpable. But, if you are innocent, justify yourself and prove to me your integrity and your innocence; and be assured that, when once I know it, you shall have my protection, for I should be very sorry if any wrong were done you for having done your duty by supporting my intentions.

A. If I am guilty of any contravention of the orders of the King, if I have traded, or been guilty of malversation, it is just that I should be punished for it. But I can assure you, My Lord, that I am as innocent of all the calumnies imputed to me as the angels are of sin.

Q. But whence comes then this cause of hatred and animosity which people have against you, which causes so great an outcry against your conduct?

A. You shall see the origin of it; I am going to give you a detailed [account] of, it, so that you may know what stuff they are made of in that country, and how justice is rendered there.

Q. I am very glad to be informed, but I recommend or rather order you to speak with sincerity, and that truth shall be found in all its purity in everything you tell me, for if you distort it, far from finding in me all the protection your good right deserves, you must expect only my indignation and a double punishment.

A. I will take care not to commit so heinous a fault; it is only the force of the truth which I maintain, which gives me the strength to appear before you with so much perseverance and firmness. This then is the origin of my dispute. I convicted M. de Tonty and two clerks of the Company of having traded at Detroit, although they were bound by a valid contract not to do so.

Q. Has this trading been proved?

A. It is indisputable, [they] having been caught in the act, beyond the possibility of gainsaying it.

Q. No doubt you seized the skins which these clerks wished to smuggle.

A. That was so done; but what seems to me most heinous is that these skins were taken from the Company's own warehouse, or at least it appears that they come from merchandise belonging to the Company which they have sold to the savages, converting the payment to their own use.

Q. How and when did you find these packages of skins which you say you seized?

A. I found nineteen packages of them, of an important kind, which these two clerks had hidden in a hut in a village of the Hurons.

Q. Did you question these clerks, and did they agree that these nineteen packages belonged to them, and were the proceeds of their trading?

A. That is so; they did not deny the fact, and both signed their deposition and their own condemnation.

I seized even in the warehouse of the Company, marked with the mark of M. Armand the principal clerk.

Q. How did you come to discover the theft of these four packages in the warehouse?

A. This was discovered through two beaver-skins found marked with the mark of the Company's warehouse, with the number 229, which served as a wrapper for forty roe-buck skins passed [?=smuggled]. The beaver-skins were not yet spoilt although they had been thrown into a cellar full of water, in an empty house; and this made me conclude that the warehouse had been plundered. I went there to pay it a visit, and that was the cause of my finding these four packages which M. Armand, the principal clerk, had concealed there; and this proves beyond contradiction that it was he himself who took away the package number 229, and with that many others.

Q. Are you not aware that these clerks have been guilty of great malversations, though, however, those are quite enough to hang them?

A. Pardon me, I know they have smuggled or stolen about a hundred and eighteen packages.

Q. What! a hundred and eighteen packages! That is a great number. Explain to me a little the value of that quantity of skins, and the sum to which it may amount.

A. According to my reckoning, at the current price, each packet on an average is worth at least forty crowns; thus it is a loss to the Company of more than fourteen thousand livres.

Q. I have no doubt that you warned the Governor-General and the directors of the Company of all this, so as to remedy this irregularity, and to have Armand and Nolan, their two clerks, severely punished.

A. I did so only too well; it would have been better for me to abide by the proverb which says that everyone must live, thieves as well as others. I wrote about it to M. de Callière whom I thought to be living, but who was dead when my letter reached Montreal; consequently it was handed to M. de Vaudreuil. the General in command. I wrote also of it to Lotbinieres one of the directors; I begged him in my letter to send me his orders before the convoy left Fort Pontchartrain for Montreal, regarding this matter, which I had stated very circumstantially, notifying him that if they wished to arrange it I was content provided I was secured as regarded them and the board of directors thinking that my conscience would not be burdened with it after I had made my accusation, as I was bound to do by the agreement I had made with the directors.

Q. But whence comes it that you accused these two clerks to the Governor-General and Lotbinieres only, and that you did not at first inform all the board of directors of it?

A. I thought I ought to treat the matter thus for two reasons; the first because, an officer being mixed up in this dishonest affair, I ought to warn only the Governor-General of it in order to show my respect for him; and the other because M. Armand, the principal clerk who was in the case, and was the contriver of all this irregularity, was the son-in-law of M. Lotbinieres, and M. Lotbinieres, the uncle of M. de Vaudreuil.

Q. So far, I do not blame your conduct. But since M. de Calliere was dead, and M. de Vaudreuil, the general in command, received your letter, apparently he will have answered you and sent his instructions as to what you ought to have done.

A. He did so, writing to me not to do anything in a hurry because he first wished, he said, to see the Intendant who just then was at Quebec.

Q. But M. de Vaudreuil is wrong, for I observed that you asked in your letter that an answer might be given you before the departure of the convoy from Fort Pontchartrain, and that you were content that this matter should be arranged, provided you were secured as regards the board of directors. Hence this reply to do nothing hastily has no security for you from the claims which the board of directors might have had under the agreement which you had made with it, by which you undertook, as you have told me at the beginning, to prevent frauds and malversations; and I am anxious to know how you proceeded on the order of M. de Vaudreuil.

. A. When I had received this order, I was much embarrassed, because I should very much have liked to obey it; but several reflections which occurred to me weighed against it. The first was that, if I deferred warning the board of directors of the thefts of its clerks, on the departure of the convoy which was at the beginning of Sept., conducted by Nolan one of the clerks, it could not be informed of it and look to it until ten months later, and this would have been too long a delay which would have caused the interests of the Company to suffer. The second reflection was that when once the wages of the clerks had been paid to them there could no longer be any recovery from them, as they were two merchants, in debt and insolvent, who knew not which way to turn; and this would have given the board of directors cause for complaining justly against me, for the contract of these clerks contains a provision that they shall lose their wages if they are found in fault. The third reflection was that M. de Vaudreuil being as yet only the commanding [officer], his letter ordering that nothing was to be done hastily was no security for me, for two reasons; the first because this expression was not strong enough to exonerate me from the obligation I owed to the board of directors who could

fault with what had been written to me by M. de Vaudreuil, to do nothing hastily.

Q. I am no longer troubled now as to what you have done, for I see from what you have just said that you lodged information against the clerks with the board of directors, and that you forwarded the documentary proofs of it; you did well to act thus. I also approve the steps you took with the Governor-General; I likewise consider you did well to act on the considerations that occurred to you on reflection [lit. "on the reflections you made"]. You do not however tell me whether Lotbiniere replied to your letter.

A. Pardon me, [but] I should have done still better to have allowed the Company's warehouse to be pillaged and plundered without saying a word; the directors only kept their relatives there with this view. As regards Lotbinieres he replied stating that he was grieved at his son-in-law's fault, and he begged me to pardon him for it, and that he would arrange everything with Delino on account of Nolan his brother-in-law without anyone discovering it. M. Monseignat, also the brother-in-law of Armand wrote to me in the same manner; but when I received their letters it was too late because the convoy had set out from Detroit, and by it I had sent to the board of directors [an account of] the seizure made from their clerks.

Q. Explain again to me, shortly, who these two clerks of the Company, Armand and Nolan, are.

A. They were formerly two shopkeepers and managed their business so ill that they are both overwhelmed with debts. Armand is the son-in-law of Lofbinieres and the uncle of M. de Vaudreuil the Governor-General; Monseignat is Armand's brother-in-law. Nolan is the brother-in-law of Delino and of Louvigny; and Lofbinieres and Delino are directors, both councillors. The first has the complete protection of the Governor-General his nephew; and the other that of the Intendant although there is no relationship. As regards the last [? statement] I rely on the opinion of the public.

Q. That being so, I see that your lot is unfortunate and still worse in our affairs; there is no doubt that they had fixed on you some groundless quarrel. I am much mistaken if we shall not have to pay very dearly for all this at the post of Detroit.

A. Nothing can escape you; your penetration is unbounded, even into the most far off countries. It is true that I am suffering unheard of persecution for having done my duty; if you do not have compassion on me, I do not see how to extricate myself from it.

Q. Let us see what it is you are accused of. Who are they that complain? What have you done then so [wrong]?

A. I have done no wrong in this matter; it is the directors who make complaints against me; it is their clerks, whom I have convicted of fraud, theft and malversation, who are my accusers.

Q. Did these clerks accuse you before you denounced them to the Governor and the board of directors, and before you convicted them?

A. Not at all; it was ten months after I had sent the proceedings to the board of directors signed by themselves.

Q. Since that is so, their accusations ought to be rejected, and deserve no attention. Yet I am very glad to know what the board of directors accuses you of, apparently that must be written in the petition of their complaint.

A. This is then the first point of accusation, that I compelled their clerks to sell the goods to the savages at a low price and at a loss, and that it is a clear act of violence.

Q. Is that true? Have you dealt with them thus, premeditately?

A. It is the greatest falsehood in the world, for since 1702, the directors, so far from complaining of me concerning the interests of the Company, have been well pleased about them, which I can prove by their own writings which it is not possible for them to disown, and that it is also true that they paid me my gratuities up to the end of the year 1703, which proves that they were satisfied.

Q. If what you tell me is true, the directors must be mad, and must have lost their wits, to take proceedings of that kind against you, which appear to me, so far, without any foundation.

A. It is out of pure spite. It is a trick of Lofbinieres and Delino, who rule the three other directors, who, when they saw that I was pressing Armand and Nolan their near relatives, who deserve to be hanged, took it into their heads to protect them at the expense of my reputation and my uprightness, by causing me to be accused by these same clerks of having made them sell the Company's goods at a loss.

Q. That is called playing with cunning; but I find that Lotbinieres and Delino wish to extricate their relations from this false step by unworthy means. It is not right that your honesty should suffer by it. Leave it to me; their injustice shall be punished when you have completed the proof of what you have put forward. But as I have remarked, and according as you have just told me that the directors approved all that you did up to the end of 1703, I have reason to presume that you perhaps used violence towards their clerks in 1704, by compelling them to sell

Company to carry on its trade in skins, taking care to do so according to the orders of M. de Calliere, and to prevent [them] selling the goods sent to them to the savages any dearer, and that in concert with the clerks of the Company. This order is in reply to a paragraph contained in a long memorial presented to MM. de Vaudreuil and Beauharnois of which this is the purport. The board of directors thinks it well that the Company's clerks should consult the Commandants, and that they should confer with them on matters of importance concerning the Company's interests; but it thinks the principal clerk should decide in matters regarding the trade of the Company and this in accordance with the orders he may have from the board of directors, or with what he deems most advantageous, without the Commandant having the right to make him do what he orders.

Q. I see how it is; the Company would have liked to sell goods at excessive prices, without troubling whether the savages would be withdrawn from our interest or not by going with their trade to the English. I see that the Governor and the Intendant did well to reply to this paragraph as they did. Have you carefully followed their instructions on that, and have you caused the sale of the goods to go on according as you were ordered by the late M. de Calliere when you began to establish Detroit?

A. Not at all; the order of the late M. de Calliere is to see that goods are sold to the savages of Fort Frontenac at 25 p. c., and to those of Detroit at 50 p. c., which order he made with a view to treating them kindly on account of the general peace which he had just made both between us and our allies with the Iroquois, foreseeing that as a consequence of that peace our savages would think first of the trade which would be most advantageous to them, and that the sole means of retaining them in our interest was to give them goods at a reasonable price. And it appears that M. de Vaudreuil and M. de Beauharnois were entirely of his opinion from the orders which they gave me; even the board of directors agrees, writing to its clerks, that it cannot disapprove of the manner in which I acted and made them act. And finally in the last letter of M. de Vaudreuil of the 24th of April 1704, he writes to me in these terms:—Although I tell you, M., to allow M. Denoyer to carry out the orders which he has Denoyer from the board of directors, supposing always that the interests of the Company King's service are not concerned. I tell you also, Sir, that in some cases clerk of t the last pl it will not be amiss to trade on the old tariff. Try however to be careful of the Company's interests as far as may be possible.

Q. I cannot believe that, having the orders you have, and the letters from the board of directors, anyone could accuse you of violence in this matter. That would be folly on the part of the directors; and the carelessness of the Governor-General and the Intendant, if they suffered and permitted this count, and such a pettifogging charge against a Command-

you, not doubting that you have conformed to them and have had them carried out most scrupulously.

A. Pardon me, I thought I ought to allow something to my discretion, and by that means husband the funds of the Company; for instead of having had the goods sold, according to the orders of the late Chevalier de Calliere confirmed by those of M. de Vaudreuil, at the rate of fifty per cent., the Company's powder has been sold at Fort Pontchartrain at four hundred per cent., bullets at six hundred per cent., tombac at three hundred per cent., vermilion, glass beads, cutlery, iron-work, and other hardware, at two hundred per cent., and lastly all kinds of fabrics at a hundred per cent., the whole being based on the price of skins sold at Quebec, and [? if] it is, at the invoice rate, at forty sous per pound, we have sold it to the savages and even to the garrison [at] four times forty sous, that is, eight francs a pound; and so with the rest.

Q. You astonish me; I cannot exempt you from blame for having permitted the clerks of the Company to sell goods so dear to our savages at a time when it is necessary for us to keep them in good humor on account of the war we are waging against the English who do all they can to attract them to their side. I am very much afraid that the exorbitant price of the goods which the Company has sold them may induce them to take some inconvenient step against the service of the King and the Colony.

A. You should indeed, as it would seem, rather blame the Governor and the Intendant for permitting them to cavil at me on this point, when I had forgotten their orders and had acted in the interests of the Company beyond all they could expect from me in such a difficult conjuncture, for the English had sent necklaces* to Fort Pontchartrain and a list of the prices of their goods in which they promised to sell them to them two-thirds cheaper than the Company.

Q. But since the Company sold its goods so dear, it must have made a great profit out of the trade of that post.

A. By no means, very much the reverse. It has lost a great deal, because the directors positively conduct the affairs of the Company very

might perhaps have spoken; and are pretending to prosecute, having chosen a subdelegate to go and investigate at Detroit against them, or rather, against me; in order that by this trickery and protection, which it is impossible to resist, they may be able to extricate themselves and their relatives from this affair while laying to my charge atrocious calumnies which they cannot prove.

Q. Who is this [man] who has been sent to Detroit to investigate this matter?

A. It is the [man] called Vincelot whom the Intendant has subdelegated on the proposal of the directors. He is a man who has come of a race steeped in filth, whose father is a bastard and his mother illegitimate, a man of no capacity, and first cousin to M. Pinaud one of the directors, and consequently my adversary, which renders the proceedings void, the said Vincelot being liable to peremptory challenge under the ordinances.

Q. This count of the complaint alone is enough to show me the bad faith of the directors, and it makes me conjecture that their valid right consists in fact of the protection which they find in the authority of the Governor and the Intendant; and it is very easy to distinguish that the seizure you made of the skins [in possession] of their clerks, obtained by dishonest practices, has roused MM. Lofbinieres and Delino to action; and that M. de Vaudreuil, the general of that country, being mixed up with that alliance sets the whole in motion; but they shall not profit by it. It is not right that, having maintained like a good officer the interests of the King's service, and as an honest man the public good, you should be ruined by it. Although the proofs of which you have spoken to me are more than sufficient to clear you, and I am resolved at the same time to punish those who are thus using trickery against you, I should be very glad to know all and to have you tell me whether you have not any paper which shows that you have used no violence towards the clerks, for if that is so I shall perhaps be able to have the directors and their clerks prosecuted.

A. That would be well done. I have still a settlement with the clerks, drawn up by common consent, signed by them, by the almoner of the Fort, by M. de Tonty and by me which completes the proof that I have used no violence.

Q. That is enough, and more than was necessary on this point. I ought not to listen to any others, since the directors make such a bad beginning; I see plainly that there is neither rhyme nor reason in their procedure. Let us pass now to other matters and tell me whether they complain of any other violence on your part.

A. Yes, they impute to me as a capital offence having used abusive language to their clerks under the pretext, they say, that they did not

Q. Oh, indeed! Under the pretext of certain marks of respect which you claim to be due to you! Can the directors doubt that their clerks owe respect to you at the place where you are Commandant, and where you hold the authority of the King?

A. They doubt it so much that they claim it in this way. It is true that I have sometimes reproved their clerks: but this has only been when I have caught them *in flagrante delicto,* and after I had convicted them of malversation.

Q. That is very serious, and there is a fine cause of complaint on the part of the directors. Either they must be very silly, or very passionate to lay an information against a Commandant on such a point. Let us see whether there is not something else for, at present, I see nothing but folly in their action.

A. The third count of their complaint is that when they sent one, Denoyer, to replace the principal clerk, they say that on his arrival at Fort Pontchartrain I retained him for more than two hours in my room, under the pretence of reading and inveighing against the letter that had been written to me, in order that Radisson the other principal clerk, might have time to remove the papers which he and I wished not to be seen, and this is the cause of the board of directors not being able to obtain the information they need.

Q. This count has very much the look, to me, of being violently dragged in. and I feel that the whole of this case is founded on conjecture. for I foresee that there is no proof of all this. I mistrust also that this Denoyer, whom they sent there as their principal clerk, will put in an appearance on the reports, and will be of a fawning disposition; but no matter, it is well that I should be informed whether what they complain of is true.

A. You shall be informed of it in a few words. Denoyer having handed me the letters which the Governor-General, the Intendant, the directors, and other private persons wrote to me, I begged him to take breakfast (which he did) while I read my letters. The Governor-General's consisted of one sheet, the Intendant's of half a one, and that from the directors of fourteen pages; and this occupied me over half an hour, after which I dismissed this new clerk to go and carry out his orders,

Q. It is not true then that Radisson removed any papers?

A. I had no knowledge of it. Radisson maintains that it is a falsehood and a fabrication by Denoyer; and neither the latter nor the directors have been able to prove it. But indeed even if Radisson had taken some papers, by what right can the directors attribute to me that I did so by connivance with this clerk. All this is without proof, and exists only in their imagination, which supplies them with the means of adding one falsehood to another. That is why I hope you will be so good as to compel the directors to make reparation for so atrocious a wrong, for it is not permitted to insult a man in writing, who has the authority of the Commandant in so unfair a matter, and one which cannot be proved.

Q. You shall be satisfied, if that accusation is not proved; it is not sufficient to bring accusations and to allege duplicity, proofs are needed. These are wonderful complaints, that make me think that this will last a long time for, by allegations, a man could be kept on trial until the Day of Judgment. Never mind, continue to inform me, because I wish to know [about] that matter thoroughly.

A. Since you will really have patience for that, I feel assured of my justification and of the punishment you will mete out to the directors. This is the fourth count; they say that, after having accused Radisson of bad conduct in regard to the Company's interests, I became his protector and induced the savages to speak in his favor to ask that Denoyer might be dismissed; and that I also made them ask that my wife and Radisson's should remain at Fort Pontchartrain in order to insure my return and that of Radisson to my post.

Q. I see by what you have just told me that the directors could not find any valid proof against you; and that, seeing their case thus shattered, they had recourse to seeking for some among the savages and the pagans. But it seems to me, or I am much mistaken, that their evidence has never been admitted in [a court of] justice.

A. How could a judge trust to the evidence of people who have neither faith nor law, and whom any one can make say what he wishes provided he pays them, and who can equally be made to unsay [it] on payment; who would have themselves baptized a hundred times a day for a glass of brandy. They are people who are liable to no punishment when convicted of false witness, not being subject to our laws; when they kill each other, and, what is worse, when they kill us; and this has been seen only too often for some years past, they having killed more than twenty Frenchmen without having had any punishment for it, and outraged several Frenchwomen whom they killed after outraging them; and this has occurred this year even, near Three Rivers, without any example having been made of it. Now what likelihood is there that I should have caused the savages to apply to have Denoyer dismissed in favor of

the latter; and it is evident that Denoyer, whom I did not know, and whom I had never seen, had up to that time, done nothing and said nothing which could displease me; and since it is a fact that the savages demanded his dismissal the third day after his arrival, during which time I had made him eat at my table, which in truth he did not deserve. The directors are wrong and are speaking heedlessly when they ridiculously assert that I prompted the savages to speak to make my wife and Radisson's remain at Fort Pontchartrain in order to secure my own return to my post. There might have been some appearance of truth or probability if I had had an order from the Governor-General or the Court to leave it or to go down to Quebec or Montreal, to give an account of my acts, or for any other reason; but the fact is that I had asked leave to go down to Montreal the previous year for the latter [reason], and that it was granted me by the Governor-General, that is, by M. de Vaudreuil who, at the same time notified me in his letter his satisfaction with my conduct. What, therefore, should I have feared on his part? What reason could I have had for making the savages apply, to have my wife remain at Detroit, since she has ever been free, as I have, to remain there or to depart therefrom, neither she nor I having had any order or any threat, nor anything of the kind, to recall us from it.

Q. Your reasoning is good and very sound; and, as you very well say, there would be some probability in the thing if the Governor-General had given you an order to go down under some pretext which might show yòu that he was displeased with your conduct; but since it was you yourself who had asked permission [to do] so, that destroys in every way the evil inferences they wish to draw against you, and everything is after all founded on conjecture. Is that all that the directors have to say concerning the savages?

A. It is not all; in fact they state that I have prompted the savages to say that they will not allow the skins which are in the fort to leave it; that they do not see the warehouse stocked with goods; and that all the French have not the right to transact trade; and [the directors say] that that is a trail which proceeds from me, with the object of inducing the company to send large consignments to this post, in order to make myself master of them in the usual manner.

Q. Whence comes it that the savages have made this request, and that they have spoken in this way?

A. It is because Denoyer on his arrival, and the other clerks, and

them; hence it is not extraordinary that they should have demanded this freedom which they have had at all times and which they were promised when Detroit was established.

Q. But what do the directors mean when they assert that what you did was in order to compel them to make large consignments to that place so as to make yourself master of them in your usual manner?

A. Who can guess what they mean? One cannot tell from this talk whether they are awake or asleep; for, if I had appropriated their goods, or if I had wasted them, they would have had good grounds [for it], but these two things not being facts, it is talking contrary to common sense; and as to this, what does it matter to me whether the Company makes large consignments or not, since I have no interest in it? On the contrary, if it were true that I had been trading (as they have dared to assert) it would have been an advantage to me that they should send but few goods so as to sell mine (if I had had any) to better advantage and more readily.

Q. I see the directors continue to make the proceedings against you out of imaginings and conjectures. Will there not be any count of their complaint real or effective?

A. Pardon me, they cry out greatly against the audacity, they say, I had in having Denoyer committed to prison, whom they sent to Detroit to replace Radisson their principal clerk whom they recalled because I had accused him of bad conduct. This accusation they say, was brought by an agreement with Radisson, in order to cover his acts of dishonesty. Is not the reasoning of the directors altogether whimsical and anomalous? And is it not answered by itself? For it is not natural that Radisson should consent to my accusing him by agreement in order to have him recalled from his employment which was worth to him eighteen hundred livres a year and food, to lose his wages, to blacken his reputation and to sustain an action. I put it to the judgment [even] of infants at the breast; that would indeed be concerted action well contrived.

Q. The matter appears as you say; but let us see what was this imprisonment of Denoyer, the principal clerk. I should be very glad to know, before you proceed further, whether you have been forbidden to imprison [anyone], or whether you have the power to punish with imprisonment the officers or others in your post. If it was the case that you had this power, it must be said that the directors have lost their wits to lay an information against you on this point.

A. Yet that is my great crime, and they declare they will be even with me for having, as they call it, the audacity to imprison one of their servants whom they appointed as their principal clerk, a waif and a poor wretch who came here not knowing which way to turn on his arrival in this country. As to my powers, they are very ample, being to punish, by imprisonment, or by deprivation [of civil rights]; and in case of distinct disobedience, to run my sword through anyone who has [so] offended against me. It is by reason of the remoteness that these orders have always been given to me, and on account of the seditions and intrigues which have been attempted to be formed there, which I have known quite well how to repress.

Q. There is much more than is necessary for it. Tell me now the reason you had for having Denoyer, the principal clerk, imprisoned.

A. You shall see it. A soldier of the garrison having been killed by the enemy, the savages reported that they had found the stake to which he had been bound. On this report, a party of about a hundred savages of different tribes was instantly formed to pursue the enemy and try to avenge this soldier's death. They asked me for seven or eight Frenchmen to go with them, and having granted them this I ordered M. de Tonty to command eight good men, of the employés of the Company, to take those who voluntarily offered themselves, and to have provisions and ammunition given to them out of the Company's warehouse, according to custom. Denoyer, the principal clerk maintained that I could not form any detachment for the King's service out of the employés of the Company without his permission, and that they could not go outside the fort without telling him of it; that the matter should be so [arranged] or he would take strong measures. The Canadians engaged for the Company's service having complained to M. de Tonty who had commanded them, he came and made his complaint of it to me. Having heard him I sent for them and, after I had questioned them and they had deposed to what is above stated in the presence of witnesses, I sent for M. Denoyer. Having asked him whether it was true that he maintained that I had no power to detach the Company's employés from the King's service without telling him of it and without his leave, he had the impertinence to maintain to my face, M. de Tonty being present, that he did not claim it but that he did not belive I had this power. This reply made with all possible arrogance, compelled me to send him to prison with these words —'I will teach you, you little clerk, to swerve from your duty and to raise sedition by estranging minds from obedience.'

Q. Is it possible that this clerk had such insolence, and that a rebel should be supported and protected so far that they wish to impute to you as a crime having administered so small a punishment? If you had treated him otherwise you would yourself have deserved to be severely

allow the King's authority to be disparaged in anything whatsoever. But what is that prison, how long did you make this clerk remain there?

A. I reported it very carefully to the Governor-General as soon as I arrived at Montreal. He knew some time after that the directors were laying information against me on this matter without having given any sign of opposing it, which proves his connivance and protection as regards Lofbinieres, his uncle and the father-in-law of M. Arnaud, or at least (with all deference) his lack of ability in upholding the authority of the government and maintaining in it the officers who know the service. As regards the prison, it is nothing more than the sergeant's room, and this illustrious clerk Denoyer remained in it only about three hours.

Q. That is indeed a great punishment; be assured I will see right done to you for the lack of attention of the Governor-General in this matter. I should, however be very glad to learn whether this imprisonment took place before or after the savages demanded his dismissal.

A. This remark is very right and very good, you shall be plainly informed as to this difficulty. Thus I shall tell you that Denoyer arrived at Fort Pontchartrain on the 5th of June; that on the 8th the savages demanded his dismissal by a [*collar] which he himself accepted contrary to my judgment, I having made several representations to him, (and if I may make use of these terms) even remonstrances not to take the course of going back, at least so soon, because I would arrange that affair, not doubting that I should learn the reasons of the savages in time, undertaking moreover to persuade them out of the bad impressions they had formed of him personally, and after having several times repeated my representations to deter him from returning, he absolutely would not give it up; that is so true that he himself signed the things I have just told you. And this makes me think that Denoyer had instructions himself to make the savages demand his dismissal; causing me to be accused in my absence, the board of directors and their league having in view to stir up quarrels against me in order to procure the downfall of this post. Finally he was imprisoned on the 22nd of June, fourteen days therefore after the savages had demanded his dismissal, and all because he was rebellious.

Q. I am content; no conclusion against you can be drawn. that you made the savages speak. Something of it might have been believed if it had been after the imprisonment of that clerk. But I have heard it said that he had embarked with you and Radisson in the same boat to come together from there to Montreal without your having had any dispute with him.

A. That is quite true, the matter is publicly known; what caused us to

*See p. 216.

disembark and land was the news of the death of the soldier killed by the enemy, of which I have spoken to you, which compelled me to remain to give my orders and obtain information of that matter, which gave me occasion to imprison that clerk on account of the foolish claims (with all deference) which he made, and on account of the sedition he wished to occasion.

Q. According to the account you give me, it appears that the clerk Denoyer had given up all business, having already embarked with you to come to Montreal.

A. That speaks for itself. A long time ago he had handed over his instructions, all his papers, and in general the effects of the Company in his hands, to the man called Chatelerau, another clerk.

Q. That then was the reason of his imprisonment; he got off cheaply for it. Tell me shortly the reasons you had for doing it a second time.

A. I did so because it is laid down in my orders that nobody, officers or otherwise, is to set out from that post without my permission; yet the clerk Denoyer, to continue his disobedience, had his boat put in the water and loaded for Montreal (as he says) without speaking of it to me or saying anything to me about it, claiming always that he was not subordinate to me. On my departure he remained closeted with the other two clerks although everyone was under arms according to the custom in the distant posts; and finally, having found the boat of these clerks at the water's edge manned by eight men, without any information of it having been given to me, I sent Denoyer to prison and the other two clerks with him.

Q. It seems clear that there was some snake in the grass, and that these clerks only behaved so badly because they were incited to it. Were you removed from your command at that time? For I know well that it is not allowed to leave these places without permission of the Commandant, and if they ordered eight men [to do so] without speaking to you of it and without your leave, you have done well to punish them again. But was it the fault of Chateleraut, the second clerk?

A. Yes, for he was in charge of the instructions, papers, and effects of the Company, and it was for him to come and ask me for permission to send down this boat. This slight showed me the intrigue which was

Q. Are intrigues and revolts frequent in that country, and have you not a strong garrison to maintain good order there? It seems to me that you should have a hundred men in your fort, M. de Calliere having sent me word of it, and also several officers.

A. The preceding year the clerks and employés revolted against M. de Tonty who was then in command in my absence, although it was on account of a command for the King's service by the order which he had concerning it from the Governor-General; so that, since this rebellion remained unpunished, these clerks thought they had only to continue it, and I should not dare to punish them for it. Besides, there has been no commandant in that country who has subdued very strong rebellions. It is true that during all the time I have had the honor to command, that is to say, for twelve years, none has happened; but that is on account of having prevented them by prompt punishment for which I have been duly approved. As regards the garrison, the Governor-General, the Intendant and the Directors have so used their utmost endeavors that they have reduced it to fourteen soldiers who are treated there like convicts; since, for three years they have received no clothes nor their pay.

Q. I expect that at the time these clerks wanted to play the mutineer, the number of the employés was superior to [that of] your garrison.

A. That is wisely observed. There were at that time thirty men employed for the Company, and they could have raised a regular rebellion if they had desired to second the designs of the Company's clerks.

Q. Those then are all the counts of the complaint which the board of directors has made against you. What then are their contentions?

A. They say that all these acts of violence (it is thus they describe the punishment I inflicted on their clerks) prove that I have had interests opposed to those of the Company, and that on account of this fact they oppose my returning to Fort Pontchartrain of Detroit. and even my being present in Montreal at the time of the departure of the convoy, which should set out at once for the said post in order to prevent me from holding communication with the travellers because I might be able to imbue them with opinions contrary to the interests of the Company's business.

Q. I see from all you have just related that the directors draw conclusions from the very thoughts you might have. bringing an action against your intention by an examination into futurity. It was necessary to let you go to Montreal and have you watched; and if you had in fact given the advice which they imagined, or rather which they maliciously conceived, it would have been these facts on which they could have laid an information. But I consider it absurd to do so on facts which have no existence save in the imagination of the accusers, which is absolutely chimerical. I know also that if they have opposed your return to your post, it is in order to prevent the success of that settlement, or rather to work without hindrance at its destruction. Did they ask anything else in their petition?

A. Yes, the directors asked that I should be made to remain in this town to answer the questions which there may be put to me; and finally they conclude that they claim to make me responsible for all the wrongs I have caused to the Company and for the outrage I offered it in the person of its clerks, begging the Intendant to permit them to lay before him information on the above facts, circumstances and dependencies, and to order me to remain here in the town of Quebec until he shall order otherwise.

Q. The matter is rather ridiculous, to lay information against you as to facts which can at once be proved; for I have seen from the account you have given me that you hold documents justifying your conduct. As for all that concerns the interests of the Company, I know quite well that it approved of all you did, and was satisfied with you up to the end of 1703, since it paid you four thousand francs for your trouble, and for your care. But the directors are, no doubt, angry at the accusation you made against Arnaud and Nolan, their clerks convicted of knavery, the former being the son-in-law of Lofbinieres and the other the brother-in-law of Delino, both directors.

Therefore, if they have raised this storm against you, you are right in saying that it is in recrimination, in order to shelter these two dishonest men; and if they have laid information against you, it is for the purpose of eluding in this way their [own] condemnation, and the restitution they would have had to make to the Company. Moreover it is making themselves ridiculous, to lay information against a commandant regarding an act of imprisonment when he has power to order it on his own authority, especially when the offence tends to rebellion. I am anxious to know how the Governor-General and Intendant acted in this matter. I cannot believe that the latter has granted what they ask him for in their petition.

A. Excuse me, and you shall see. He has permitted the directors to lay information against me on all the counts contained in their petition; decreed that it should be communicated to me, for [me] to answer it;

know whether M. de Ramezay had you arrested at the request of the Intendant.

A. He did so, but not without protest, and without intimating several times to the Intendant that he saw nothing in the petition of the directors which was criminal; that, in short, it was only a complaint and not proven facts; and that therefore he did not think an officer ought to be arrested who was settled and domiciled in the country; and the commandant, by the orders of the Court. of Fort Pontchartrain, which is a distant post in the van-guard of the Colony. He added that he would write to the Governor-General about it, who was then at Montreal; which he did.

Q. I suppose he received an answer to his letter, and the Governor-General was of his opinion.

A. Not at all; he sent him word that he had done well to carry out the order of the Intendant and to have me arrested.

Q. I no longer doubt, now, that the Governor-Gen'l., the Intendant and the directors are in league together. All that they have done after all, has been only in order to save the two clerks at the expense of your reputation, and to overturn the post of Detroit by removing you from the command, because when [you] are no longer there, I clearly see that there will be no opposition to the measures they will take to destroy that post, so much the more that this is a matter directed by the Jesuits who are reported to have the power of the government and of justice. But be not discouraged; continue to inform me; be assured that I will not allow you to be destroyed thus, for having carried out my intentions, and for having observed strict integrity in all things. I have also learnt that on the petition of the directors, the Intendant has subdelegated M. Vincelot to collect information against you at Detroit, and that he has also been sent there to look after the business of the Company. But I should like to know whether you accept such a judge, and whether you have not anything to say against the proceedngs he will take.

A. It is sufficient that the said Vincelot is the first cousin of Pinaud, one of the directors, who is my adversary, to make him liable to challenge and his proceedings absolutely void and worth nothing. You can see what choice the board of directors makes of a clerk and the Intendant of a subdelegate, (for they were not unaware that Vincelot was nearly related to the director Pinaud, and that his father and mother are bastards and illegitimate, moreover that he is a grand-nephew of M. Beaulieu who took for his second wife the widow of Xaintes Armurier, now the wife of Lofbinieres); and this shows that they chose such unworthy men, all relatives or allies of the directors, only in order to ruin me if they could. On the other hand, the Governor-General has sent M. de Louvigny, a major of Quebec, to Detroit under the specious pretext of commanding the convoy, though the only [reason] was to go there to support Vincelot

against me and to cause that post to be abandoned; as I will prove in
·another place, and to shelter Armand and Nolan, the latter being also
brother-in-law to M. Louvigny. And, to omit nothing, it is important to
point out to you that MM. Lofbrinieres and Delino, when recalling their
two clerks Armand and Nolan, their relatives, replaced them by two
others also relatives, namely M. Chateleraut and Demeul; the former is
also related to Louvigny; a prettier family party was never seen.

Q. Stop there; by the way you are going on you would have me believe
that all those who have been employed at Detroit and still are so since
you have been kept at Quebec, are relatives or allies of the directors,
Lofbinieres, Delino and Pinaud, and therefore I see that this alliance
is connected with that of the Governor-General. I see you have not done
so badly in appealing in your case; for I know well that the Governor-
General, the Intendant and the Jesuits are so powerful in that country
that the best business in the world· is treated as atrocious, when they
intervene in it; but the King does not permit acts of injustice. Let us
pass again for a little to the reasons you had for appealing in this matter,
and finish this account.

A. You have seen them in what I have had the honor to communicate
to you. I have not yet spoken of the steps that have been taken to absolutely destroy Detroit; as I have just learnt some of them, I will inform
you of them after I have told you the reasons for my appeal.

Q. It is true that you have supplied me with enough of them, but the
number of the proofs can do no harm.

A. Since you wish it you shall be satisfied. I may tell you then that
I challenged [the competency of] the Intendant, because at the same time
that he gave the directors permission to give information against me, and
therefore without any such information having been made, he had me
arrested in this town, preventing me from returning to Fort Pontchartrain, which is my post, and this is absolutely contrary to the ordinances,
and is a clear act of violence, which proves that he is my adversary on
account of his so-called subdelegate, whom I committed to prison, as [I
did] the principal clerk, on account of his sedition. I claimed it also on
this ground, that he was quite unable to judge as to a fact which is not
within his competence, seeing the orders and the authority I had to imprison and punish according to circumstances, which I have always had
in the distant posts, and until now, in the twelve years I have commanded

of his debtor, and lastly that his evidence is necessary to me as he has private knowledge which will be denied by the directors; and finally because M. de Vaudreuil has told me that he will avenge the imprisonment of his subdelegate. I have also objected to M. de Vaudreuil on the ground that M. de Lofbinieres, who is my adversary and the chief director, is his uncle and the father-in-law of Arnaud one of the clerks convicted of malversation; and also because M. de Vaudreuil and M. Lofbinieres, especially the former, hold letters concerning the dishonest practices of the said Arnaud and Nolan, who is also the brother-in-law of Delino, another director, which they will not give up except after an order [from] superior [authority]. I have also protested against the validity of the proceedings taken by the [man] named Vincelot who was subdelegated by the Intendant, a man without character, whose father and mother were bastards and also of evil reputation; and because, moreover, the said Vincelot is liable to be challenged as being the first cousin of M. Pinaud another director, who is my adversary. To sum it all up, I have appealed in this matter on account of the conspiracy between the Governor-General, the Intendant, the Jesuits and the directors who, having been unable to find any means of upsetting the post of Detroit while I remained [there], believed that by keeping me here a prisoner under devilish pretexts they would succeed in it, and also in sheltering their guilty relations by imputing to me the same charge as I have convicted them of, [although] they can prove nothing against me with all their arbitrary power; and in order to complete a work so execrable that it passes the imagination, they have sent Louvigny, a major, from Quebec to Detroit to bribe the savages and make them give evidence against me; [a man] who has himself been convicted of trading and of contravening the orders of the King by decree of the sovereign council, deserving to be cashiered; which Louvigny is also the brother-in-law of Nolan, who is one of the dishonest clerks and of Delino the director, all three being brothers-in-law. Chateleraut who is now a clerk of the Company at Detroit is the cousin of Louvigny, Delino and Nolan. The Governor-General having chosen Louvigny on this occasion, to the prejudice of twenty-eight captains, proves his good will towards me. Demeul the other clerk now at Detroit is the grand-nephew of Lofbinieres, the uncle of M. Vaudreuil. Hence you can see and judge, My Lord. whether I am far wrong in having apparently attacked them by taking my case before the King where I hope it will be investigated with care and acuteness and not as they do in this country where there is neither faith, nor knowledge nor capability.

Q. You told me, I believe, that after you had explained to me the reasons for your appeal, you would inform me of the steps they have taken to destroy utterly the post of Detroit.

A. That is true; but I hope you will allow me first to make a few

Q. Very well, I am contented, make them.

A. The first is that the clerks Arnaud and Nolan, having accused me, set out from Quebec as soon as they learned of my arrival at Montreal. The 2nd is that they were sent away to Missilimakinak in a boat belonging to the Jesuit fathers loaded with a dummy load of goods; the whole in order to afford means to the said Arnaud, son-in-law of Lofbinieres, to get back his beaver and other skins from the said place of Missilimakinak where he conveyed them after having stolen them from the Company's warehouse at Detroit. The 3rd is that the beaver and other skins were in the house of the Jesuit fathers at Missilimakinak, which clearly proves the protection by the Governor-General of the Jesuits, and of the directors to their clerks. I spoke to the former about it one day, and he answered me that these clerks had gone to Missilimakinak unknown to him, the Jesuits having said nothing to him about it; a fine beginning for a Governor-General! What is one to think of it? The 4th observation is that almost all the witnesses who had, at Detroit, deposed to the knavery of the clerks, when they arrived at Montreal were sent up to the country of the Utavois in charge of goods in order to prevent confrontations and proofs. The 5th is that, having taken the depositions of those who have accused me, they have sent them to the Utavois to shelter them from [punishment for] their theft; and, in the meantime, they are bringing an action against me, keeping me in prison, persecuting me, destroying the little property I possess. And all that is put in practice to gain time for overturning Detroit from top to bottom; in order to weary me, to tire me out, to make me cry mercy! mercy! and ask pardon. But I shall do nothing of the kind. I expect everything from your justice and that of the King. I will pursue this matter to the end; my reputation has been attacked and I will have satisfaction for it. I have served the King with diligence, with zeal and with distinction; I have good certificates of it. All the letters of my superiors are filled with the satisfaction they have felt with my services and my conduct.

Q. One would have to be very narrow-minded not to know that it is, in effect, a conspiracy which has been formed against you. The Jesuits have long known of it and they have made use of the occasion, they have profited by the opportunity. I see clearly that they have embittered the Governor-General, Lofbiniere and Delino against you on account of your prosecution of their relatives; also that the Intendant, who is still a novice, has allowed himself to be led astray. I anticipate that you may

service of the King. If what I have had the honor to recount to you merits any attention, the matters you are about to be informed of deserve it entirely. This is now the actual plan that has been formed for the destruction of Detroit; yet I dare not proceed, unless you order me to do so.

Q. You may do so, and count on my protection, provided you make your indictment justly, and that you in no way distort the truth.

A. I will never depart from that rule. I have no other patron but truth itself, and so great is my confidence in it that I believe I shall be invincible so long as I fight under its standard. I am about, therefore, to state to you facts from which you can draw what conclusions you please; the public have drawn theirs. This is the first fact. M. de Tonty having come down last year from Detroit to Montreal and to Quebec, found himself accused, together with the clerks of the Company, of trading and malversation.

OBSERVATIONS TO BE MADE ON THIS 1ST FACT.

So far from punishing him and having him recalled, they sent him back to Detroit, having found him a very good tool to make use of for acting in an underhand way against me and against the post. And in order the better to encourage him they gave him a pension of six hundred livres a year by a document under private seal, on the pretext of making his wife come down; and this was done to make the savages understand that Detroit was being abandoned. On this news I made the same proposal to the board of directors for my [wife], but they would not hear of it. I acted in this way to get more information.

The 2nd fact is that at the same time M. de Mauthet was despatched to go to Missilimakinak with two boats loaded with merchandise and brandy and some presents for the savages, under the pretence of taking the amnesty there.

OBSERVATIONS TO BE MADE ON THE 2ND FACT.

M. de Mauthet set out for the Utayois before the amnesty had come, and more than a month or six weeks before the arrival of the ships.

The (third) 3rd fact is that they sent M. de la Decouverte to the Utavois and the Miamis with two boats loaded with merchandise and brandy on the pretence of arranging certain disputes that existed between our allies.

OBSERVATIONS ON THE 3RD FACT.

M. de Mauthet was charged (according to the confession of M. de Vaudreuil) with presents and [collars] to arrange this same dispute; the mission of M. de la Decouverte to the Miamis was only to prevent that tribe from coming to settle at Detroit and, in case of ill-success to throw

The 4th fact is that M. de Vincennes was sent to the Miamis with orders to pass through Detroit, addressed to M. de Tonty; the said M. de Vincennes having three boats laden with merchandise and more than four hundred jars of brandy; under the pretext of going to put an end to the war begun by the Miamis aouyatanouns against the tribes settled at Detroit and the Iroquois.

OBSERVATIONS ON THE 4TH FACT.

This quarrel had been put to an end, and the Governor-General and the Intendant had been informed of it; besides which it is not natural to send an ensign ad honores [i. e. honorary-unpaid] to adjust the dispute between the tribes at a post where there was a commandant nominated by the Court. Therefore, having questioned M. de Vincennes about his being sent. he told me that the Governor-General had his share in the merchandise he was taking, which I made known in speaking to him himself, and he answered that he should cashier him because he had allowed him to take only two boats.

The 5th fact is that Father Maret, Superior of Missilimakinak and of all the missions of the Utavois; Tonty the captain at Detroit, and Manthet were together at Quebec. It was there and then that the ruin of Detroit was arranged with the Superior of the Jesuits of Quebec, and with the General in command, and the Intendant, and with the board of directors, having planned to re-establish the Congés and the mission of Missilimakinak. And so that this business might not fail, Father Maret went up again with a boat full of merchandise; M. de Manthet with him in two other boats, and M. de Tonty to Detroit; and by the same means they induced the savages to ask for M. Boudor who took the Utavois more than twenty thousand franc's worth of goods and brandy.

The 6th fact is that M. de Louvigny:

Q. Wait a bit, you are passing the 5th fact without making any observation.

A. That is true. My Lord, I thought it was better to leave it to you to make. However, since you wish me to be another St. Jean Bouche d'Or, to say all that I know and all that concerns it, you shall have the satisfaction you ask.

OBSERVATIONS ON THE 5TH FACT.

dor one, and the savages at his disposal to bring up more than 20000 ♯ of goods. But as, up to the present, you might be troubled because they had not rewarded Tonty enough, I may tell you that he took up for himself to the Utavois three boats where they sold their merchandise. It is true that this permission was granted him under the pretext of going to the Illinois, and these boats had, like the others, a good supply of brandy. Thus there were twelve boats that went to the Utavois, besides the quantity of merchandise taken by the way of the savages.

The 6th fact is that it was forbidden throughout the Colony, to sell brandy to the savages under any pretext, on penalties laid down in the ordinances; and this was enforced with all possible severity.

The two b
which we
for M. de
to the Ut:
ty brough
M. de Vau
reuil two :
dren pisto

OBSERVATIONS ON THE 6TH FACT.

While they punish without mercy those who disobey the decrees concerning the sale of brandy to the savages, they allow (or perhaps do worse) an enormous quantity of that drink to be taken into the depth of the woods, without the Jesuits complaining of it. They maintain a great silence, after having made so much fuss about it in the time of the late Comte de Frontenac and M. de Calliere. That is because then they were not dominant in this country.

The 7th fact is that the fort of Detroit was set on fire, the fire having been put in a barn which was flanked by the two bastions and was full of corn and other crops; the flame by a strong wind burnt down the church, the house of the Recollet, that of M. de Tonty, and mine which cost me a loss of four hundred pistoles, which I could have saved, if I had been willing to let the Company's warehouse burn, and the King's ammunition. I even had one hand burnt, and I lost for the most part all my papers in it. I had the fort repaired in two or three days, all the savages having assisted me, and having done things with the best grace in the world. They showed their generosity to me on this occasion for, having lost all my provisions and those of the garrison and employés of the Company, they made a present to me personally of fifty minots of wheat; and as all our grains were burnt, they supplied all the food [we required] at the usual price, without taking advantage of our distress.

OBSERVATIONS ON THE 7TH FACT.

The garrison of a hundred men which had been given me at the beginning had been reduced to fourteen; it was therefore impossible for me to guard the four bastions of the fort. I could only guard two of them by laying heavy work on the soldiers, to whom neither pay nor clothing has been given for three years, which has greatly discouraged them. However, the savage who set fire to the barn was shot; we have never been able to learn who it was. We may be able to obtain some information about it hereafter. All the tribes settled at Detroit assert that it was a strange savage who did this deed, or rather—they say—some Frenchman who has been paid for doing this wicked act; God alone knows.

The 8th fact is that the Miamis aoüyatanoüns came and attacked the savages of Detroit; they killed one Outavois, two Hurons, and one Poutoüatanis. This act of hostility set all the tribes of Fort Pontchartrain in arms, but I made them suspend [action in] that matter. I sent to the Aoüyatanoüns, who number four hundred men, to tell them that if they did not come promptly and make atonement for that insult, I was going to set out, myself, to exterminate them; and I sent them a flag to serve as a passport for them during their journey. The tribe submitted; it sent chiefs to Detroit who replaced the dead men by living ones, according to their custom, and made large presents to the relatives of those who had been killed. In this way I put a stop to that war at its origin.

OBSERVATIONS ON THE 8TH FACT.

Father Mermet, a Jesuit, is the missionary of the village of the Aoyatanoüns Miamis. This attack was made after the Miamis of the St. Joseph river had set out from their village to come and settle at Detroit.

The 9th fact is that at the same time that the Aoyatanouns made an attack on Detroit, the Illinois came there on the war path with a party of fifteen warriors who, having been discovered, were made prisoners. We contented ourselves with whipping them with birch rods when they arrived at the fort, to make them understand that I was treating them like a father, saving their lives which they had deserved to lose, and so that they should not be rash enough to carry war into that place again. After this I sent four of them to the village of the Illinois to tell them to send a deputation of some [men of] importance, to learn from them the reasons they had had for declaring war aginst the tribes of Detroit; that matter was settled and peace maintained, in consequence. The Illinois said that Eloüaoüssé, one of the chiefs of the Utavois of Missilimakinak, had been amongst them to arrange a war against his own tribe which is at Detroit, and that he had gained over fifteen young men to begin it, who set out unknown to the older men, who were not implicated in that affair.

OBSERVATIONS ON THE 9TH.

aoussez, of whom I have spoken, set out from Missilimakinak for the Illinois some time after the arrival of Father Maret, and of M. de Mauthet at Missilimakinak.

The 10th fact is that the Hurons who had remained at Missilimakinak have quitted that place and have joined those at Detroit, so that the whole of that tribe is now settled there. I had the honor to assure you, in my letter last year, that that would happen also, in spite of the statements to the contrary made by this wonderful Father de Carheil who was the missionary to them. I stated to you also, that I would undertake to reduce this rector to not having the credit of keeping even one of his parishioners to bury him. The Utavois, also, of Missilimakinak have withdrawn to Detroit except sixty or eighty. This migration has surprised the whole body of the Jesuits in this country who were not expecting it any more than the Governor-General and the Intendant who had trusted to MM. de Mauthet, de la Decouvèrte, and above all to Fathers Marèt and de Carheil.

OBSERVATIONS ON THE 10TH FACT.

I had the honor to send you last year copies of the letters of the Jesuit fathers, especially those of Missilimakinak, in which they wrote to me that they would follow the savages if they came to Detroit. They have come; but the rectors have still remained fast in their parish without moving from it. I do not know what you will think of the following fact.

The 11th fact is that the sixty Utavois who remained at Missilimakinak came and took away about forty Iroquois under the curtains of Fort Frontenac, having killed one of them, on whom they placed a Huron tomahawk. This scheme is diabolical; it is to administer an emetic to Fort Pontchartrain, that is to say, to play double or quits.

OBSERVATIONS ON THE 11TH.

These 60 Utavois attacked the Iroquois who were at Fort Frontenac. They could not go into their villages and into the places where they are settled without passing through Detroit; that is a thing which we should not have permitted to the tribes who are there if they were enemies to one another. It was a very cunning trick to put a Huron tomahawk on the body of that Iroquois who was killed, so as to intimate that it is the Huron who kills them (that did not come out of *their* bag); but it was not he who thought of it. Those who induced the Utavois to make this attack had for their object to absolutely compel the tribes of Detroit to return so as to establish Missilimakinak, for they clearly foresaw that they could not maintain their [position] there without a settlement or a strong French garrison, for the number of the Iroquois is greater even

the audacity, of themselves, to declare war against the five tribes of the Iroquois, unless they had been set in motion by giving them hopes, almost certain, of the re-establishment of Missilimakinak. They have even taken these steps during the time I have been detained at Quebec a prisoner; and lastly, after this attack was made M. de Mauthet arrived at Montreal, and M. de la Decouverte came a fortnight after him, both having brought several boats loaded with beaver and [other skins] as a reward for so noble a mission.

The 12th fact is that M. de Vincennes is now at Detroit with four hundred jars of brandy, where he keeps a tavern, having been forerunner of M. de Louvigny, major of Quebec, brother-in-law of Delino the director, of Nolan the dishonest clerk, relative of Chaleleraut another clerk at Detroit, M. de Louvigny having himself been convicted of having contravened the King's orders by a decree of the Council. The said M. de Vincennes has also been the forerunner of M. Vincelot, subdelegated by the Intendant, who has given information against no one but me alone. Brandy has not been spared to bribe the savages; but they have not done what they wished nevertheless. This pretended subdelegate is first cousin to M. Pinaud, who is my adversary, being one of the directors and of a stock of which I have already spoken.

OBSERVATIONS ON THE 12TH FACT.

e Louvig-
was paid at
r pistoles a
, and
celot two
oles. The directors have paid to M. de Louvigny the sum of two thousand livres of France for making this journey on which he was only fifty-five days; a thing which has never been seen, for until now an officer has never been paid for escorting or conducting a convoy, which shows that the directors and the Governor-General have warmly recommended me to the attention of M. Louvigny.

M. Vincelot also had the sum of one thousand livres for this journey when he returned with M. de Louvigny. You see the bounties the board of directors are dispensing at a time when the Company is engulfed, and the Colony is in distress and without resources. The interpreter whom the late M. de Calliere and M. de Champigny had appointed at Detroit

evidence of that woman; and she stated that I had given [collars] conjointly with M. Radisson, who was at that time principal clerk, in order to have Denoyer dismissed, the women kept at Detroit, and [also] the skins until merchandise had been brought there.

OBSERVATION ON THE 13TH FACT.

Jean le Blanc, brother of this woman whose evidence M. de Mauthet took, said at Detroit in open council, like the other Utavois that he knew nothing except from the mouth of Quarante Sous, chief of the Hurons, who appears to have played me a trick in order the better to obtain his own ends. Therefore the evidence of Jean le Blanc at Detroit and that of his sister at Missilimakinak contradicted one another. Now M. de Mauthet is an officer, who served under my command at Missilimakinak where, having desired to raise a rebellion with MM. de Courtemanche and Delisle, they were put under arrest at Montreal and afterwards sent to prison at Quebec where they remained a month; and this is known to everyone, and I have the proofs of it in my possession. That is the way the Governor-General has corrupted his people in order to ruin me, not foreseeing that their evidence would be liable to be challenged; and it manifestly appears that that was a matter arranged between M. de Mauthet and Denoyer, the whole being managed by the agency of the Jesuits as transpired by a letter of Father de Carheil which he wrote at the latter place, dated. [no date given]

The 14th fact is that the Utavois accused Quarante Sous, the chief of the Hurons, of having told them that it was I who caused the dismissal of Denoyer, the retention of the women &c to be demanded.

OBSERVATIONS ON THE 14TH FACT.

Quarante Sous denied the act, and maintained in the presence of M. Louvigny, Vincelot and all the Frenchmen that it was false and that I had never spoken to him of it; and he said "I do not understand M. de Lamothe's language, he does not understand mine; where then is the interpreter?" The Utavois hung their heads and said they knew nothing about it. If therefore Quarante Sous has done wrong or spoken evil, and has made use of my name, am I to answer for it? Let them hang him if they like, what do I care? But I do not think there will be any disposition to do that.

The 15th fact is that it has been said that the wife of the man named

Techenet acted as my interpreter for speaking to Quarante Sous, and lastly they will have it that it was in a barn where that piece of *morforio* [? double dealing] was transacted.

OBSERVATIONS ON THE 15TH FACT.

The wife of Techenet is the daughter of a Frenchman and a savage woman. After she had been married with the rites of the Church, at the end of a year she left her husband and betook herself to the English where she got married again to a savage of the Loup tribe, with whom she remained twelve years, having had several children by him. During the last war this woman was captured among the English by our Iroquois from the Waterfall. She was ransomed by one of her brothers-in-law, a Frenchman named Maurice Menard, who took her to the Utavois where her first husband was, to whom she would not go back. At Missilimaki-nak she led a dissolute life and, her brother-in-law wishing to correct her, she accused him of having tried to seduce her with illicit intercourse with her and to take her back to the English. She brought her complaint thereon before me and, when proceedings were instituted, the imposture of that wicked woman was recognized. She afterwards enticed away two Canadians, to take them to the English, and when she set out with them I had her pursued. She was caught with these two young men, who confessed the fact, [and] I sent her under guard to the Chevalier de Calliere who sent her down to Quebec to send her to France. As no precautions were taken, the man Jean le Blanc, of whom we have spoken above, took her off, brought her back to Missilimakinak and married her. She left him to take another, and has been kept by more than a hundred men. That is the woman whom they pretended I made use of as an interpreter; and they quoted her in the hope that they would bribe her very easily. Yet she maintained strongly that she had no knowledge of this fact, and declared after she was questioned that they had threatened her on behalf of M. de Vaudreuil, and that they promised to reward her if she would accuse me. Thus they desired and in fact made use, in these proceedings of an interpreter related to my adversaries, and a perjurer [as declared] by decree; of a drunken savage; of a dissolute woman; of a sub-delegate whose kindred is full to overflowing with vileness, and a relative of di rector Pinaud; of an officer related to my adversaries, namely M. de Louvigny, himself declared by decree to be guilty of contravening the King's orders; of Tonty, whom I denounced two years ago for transacting trade and complicity with the clerks; of Mauthet, whom I had put under arrest and in prison at Quebec for a month. Further my adversaries are Lofbinieres, Delino and Pinaud, directors, all relatives of the clerks whom I convicted of malversation. For Arnaud, a clerk at Detroit, married a

the brother of Vincelot's mother; and the said [widow] of Xaintes married, the third time, M. de Lofbinieres and the latter is the maternal uncle of M. de Vaudreuil. For M. Jobert de Marson married the sister of Lofbinieres who was of low birth; M. Monseignat who is [their] son, and the brother of a master tailor of Paris, now a Councillor, also married one of the daughters of the said [widow] of Xaintes, wife of M. de Lofbiniere, and consequently stands in the same degree of relationship as M. Arnaud. Delino, Louvigny and Nolan, a clerk I have also convicted of malversation, are three brothers-in-law; for Louvigny and Delino married the two daughters of Nolan senior, who was a tavern keeper in Quebec. And in spite of all this, this relationshp, alliance, protection and expenditure, nothing has been proved against me; and if there is anything in the information against me it will surprise me, for all who have come from Detroit have said openly at Quebec that everything possible has been done to intimidate them but they have given no evidence except to clear me.

The 16th fact is that M. Vincelot has made the Utavois take oaths, and has made them swear by the share they claim in Paradise to speak the truth.

OBSERVATIONS ON THE 16TH FACT.

There has never been any precedent for this among the Outavois tribes and I will stake my life on it they cannot produce one. They would have raised their feet [as readily] as their hands, and they would have themselves baptised a hundred times for a hundred drinks of brandy; you can infer from that what their oath is. It is a fact which no one can dispute that there is not a hut but has its own private divinity, as the serpent, the bear, the eagle, and so of the other animals, to which they sacrifice in their need, and especially on occasions of war or sickness. Hence the only result or the only good the missionaries do consists in the baptism of infants who die after receiving it, or by chance that of some old man at the point of death. Where would you find an officer willing to command in that country if the evidence of the savages were received in courts of justice? It would have been more prudent in M. de Vaudreuil to recall me arbitrarily, since he wished to destroy that post and protect his relatives in their acts of injustice, than to allow such a proceeding as that. For the savages hereafter will threaten commanding officers, and will no longer have either respect or fear for them, which are two things essential for governing them well. M. de Vaudreuil has not taken care or foreseen the grievous consequences of that matter and the rude shocks such conduct gives to the King's authority. The late MM. de Frontenac and De Calliere would not have taken so false a step.

The 17th fact is that M. de Lacorne, a lieutenant of the troops, whom the Governor-General sent to command at Fort Frontenac, has given a war-feast to the Iroquois and has set the hatchet in their hands to go and

OBSERVATIONS ON THE 17TH FACT.

M. de Lacorne. who is a good officer and understands the service, has not caused war to be declared on the savages of Detroit without having an order to do so from the Governor-General either verbally or in writing. This latest attempt against Detroit is a gross one, and proves only too evidently that the war which the Illinois and the Aoyatanoüns began against the savages of Detroit proceeds from the same source; the blow struck by the sixty Utavois of Missilimakinak, in declaring war on the Iroquois who were at Fort Frontenac, comes and also proceeds only from the same quarter. It was only spoken of [before] on the evidence of the savages; but what M. de Lacorne has done on this last occasion completes the revelation and the disclosure of the mystery. This is surprising and you can easily observe, my lord, the tractableness of the tribes of Detroit and their good behavior. They knew as well as M. de Lamothe, that there was a grudge against them and that an attempt was being made to drive them from that post; for two tribes made war against them. They made peace at a time when they were victorious; their relatives of Missilimakinak had made prisoners, and it was they who made them let them go. Now as a reward for having behaved so well, someone has caused war to be declared against them.

The 18th fact is that M. de Vaudreuil has sent to the Utavois, with two boats, the man named Sansouci, formerly a soldier in his company, who was born on the land of Vaudreuil, under the pretext of dismissing a man called Ouendigo who is a savage of Missilimakinak where he took merchandise and brandy to the value of seven or eight hundred livres.

OBSERVATIONS ON THE 18TH FACT.

If pretexts like these are good [enough] to send to the Utavois, it is useless to suppress the 25 congés.* Can it be doubted that the said Sansouci has an interest in this trade together with the Governor-General.

The 19th fact is that M. St. Germain has rented the concession belonging to M. de Vaudreuil, which is the furthest advanced, and he gives him three thousand livres a year for it and has had a house built on it which must remain for M. de Vaudreuil.

OBSERVATIONS ON THE 19TH FACT.

The 20th fact is M. de la Decouverte who went up to the Utavois came down again with ten thousand franc's [worth] of beaver skins, as may be seen at the office for receiving the said beaver skins, [and] of this M. de Vaudreuil has had a thousand crowns; this point requires no further observation than what follows. If M. de Vaudreuil did not hold all authority [here], the proofs of it should be sent; but how can one go about that—*durum est contra stimulum calcitrare* ["it is hard to kick against the pricks"]. I see clearly that I am sacrificing myself on behalf of the public; but no matter, I must hope that God, the King and your Highness will see to it.

I beg you, my lord, to be good enough to grant me leave to go to France next year, in case you should not grant Detroit to me. But if you wish me to form a settlement there send me if you please a permit to go there when I think fit. I will hazard nothing, I will do everything for the best having no other wish but that of pleasing you, and of being with very deep respect

My Lord,

Your very humble and very obedient servant,

Lamothe Cadillac.

At Quebec, this 14th Nov. 1704.

The trade of Detroit was given to the Company of the Colony of Canada Oct. 31, 1701. See Western Literary Cabinet, vol. X, p. 122.

When Lewis Cass was Minister to France he obtained copies of various papers relating to the history of Detroit, from the French archives. Mrs. Electa M. Sheldon was then conducting a magazine, the Western Literary Cabinet, at Detroit and she made use of these documents in several articles on the Early History of Michigan. These articles were subsequently rearranged and enlarged and published in 1856 in Sheldon's Early History of Michigan. In editing and publishing the above dialogue between Count Pontchartrain and Cadillac, Mrs. Sheldon concluded, from its form, that the dialogue actually took place in the City of Quebec. Judge Campbell, in his History of Michigan, curiously fell into the same error. Attempts have been made by some writers to throw discredit upon all the writings of Cadillac by asserting that this dialogue was untruthful and never took place. (Mr. R. R. Elliott in an article in the United States Catholic Historical Mag. (Vol. IV. No. 2, p. 117.) There can be no contention, on the part of any student, that this is anything more than an imaginary dialogue, a form of narration not, at that time, uncommon, but it served to show Cadillac's side of the then pending controversy between himself and the Jesuits. Mr. John Gilmary Shea in a letter in the above article of Mr. Elliott, states that "His (Pontchartrain's) correspondence with the Governor and Intendant shows that he never came to Canada. This (dialogism) style of imaginary conversation is not uncommon," but it cannot be believed that because Cadillac used this form of reporting his troubles that he is unworthy of confidence. His quarrels with the Company and with the Jesuits were experienced by nearly every person of importance outside of their own ranks. The dialogue, upon its face, purports to be no more than a report to the Minister, and is signed in the usual manner of signing reports.—C. M. B.

31

ATTEMPT TO PREVENT TROUBLE BETWEEN THE HURONS AND OUTAVOIS.

Endorsed—Colonies.   M. de Vaudreuil, 5th May, 1705.

My Lord,

The Sieur de Beauharnois and I have had the honor to write you a joint letter by this opportunity; this one is only to thank you for the honor you have done me in granting me your protection, and to ask you to continue it, assuring you, My Lord, that I will apply myself so diligently to the discharge of my duties for the King's service, and to carrying out your orders, that you will never have occasion to repent having granted it me.

I have just learnt, My Lord, from a savage—an Iroquois—who escaped from Michilimakina, where he had been taken as a prisoner, and passed by Detroit, that the Hurons savages settled at that post are intending to withdraw and join the Iroquois, and that to this end they have sent a belt to the Sounoutonans in order that two or three hundred of them should come over and fetch them, as they dare not go away without this help, on account of the other tribes.

As this news, My Lord, only comes from a savage it needs confirmation; but it is not however unlikely, more especially as we have been informed for a long time of the just causes of complaint which the Hurons have against the Outavois savages of Michilimakina, and we know they are only waiting for an opportunity to fly at each other's throats. I am about to send at once to Detroit to ward off this blow; and I have no doubt that the Sr. de Tonty who is in command there will take every means to prevent this junction, if he has knowledge of it. I have every reason, My Lord, to be pleased with the manner in which he manages all these tribes.

I will not recite to you in detail, My Lord, what is going on in the country, leaving it to the joint letter which the Sr. de Beauharnois and

POSTS OF THE UPPER COUNTRIES.

Extract from the letter of M. de Pontchartrain of the 17th of June, 1705, at paragraph 8.

Canada.

When the settlement of Detroit is formed His Majesty will approve of your coming to France to give him an account of it; but this must not be, as long as the war lasts. Therefore even when the settlement is com- Index lett pleted, do not come without orders unless peace has been concluded.

MEMORANDUM ON THE POSTS OF THE UPPER COUNTRY.[1]

The number of posts established there in which there are Commandants and garrisons is the chief cause of the bad condition of the companies. The best soldiers are sent to these posts, and they first become traders and then desert, because it is so easy for them to go first to the Illinois and thence to Louisiana.

The necessity for sending to the Commandants, the Missionaries, and the soldiers forming the said garrisons, the articles they need, serves as a pretext for multiplying licenses or permissions [to trade].

Their trade is developed by settlers from the Colony who get so accustomed to the business of Voyageurs that they become incapable of devoting themselves to cultivating the land; and many of them do not return to their concessions, and become "coureurs de bois."

In order to succeed in carrying out His Majesty's orders forbidding the grant of licenses, it would be advisable to limit the number of such posts to those at Detroit and Michilimakinac, which it is indispensably necessary to keep up.

As regards the others, there appears no need to retain them; for the savages that are attracted to them could equally well go to trade at Michilimakinac or Detroit, and the Commandants could control the savages who are above the two posts.

It is also necessary that the number of boats for Detroit and Michilimakinac should be decided on by the Council, as they formerly were for the posts where there were commanding officers.

[1]Not dated. The text indicates that it was after the date of the trading grant given to Cadillac, 1704, and about the time of his first transfers of village lots, 1707. —C. M. B.

That the persons to whom they are granted should be bound to have them registered at the Registry of Montreal before they leave. That, on their return, they should hand them in to the Registry of the same juris-diction; that, when they hand them in, they shall be bound to declare to the Registry the day of their return, and to obtain a paper from the Reg-istrar to serve them as a quittance; that mention should be made of this document on the Register, which they shall be bound to sign, if they know how to do so; if not, it should be stated that they have declared that they cannot sign.

If the number of permits for Detroit were not limited, the Command-ant of this post, who holds the monopoly of the trade, could extend it into all the upper countries and it would be impossible to prevent it.

He alone would have power to trade for furs; and the suppression of licenses to trade would mean an increase of trade to him, as extensive as he might think fit. It appears, from the annexed list, that 56 permits have been registered this year for all the posts together.

The same rule should be observed as to the passports or permits which are granted for Orange and other places in New England. If this were done, it would not be necessary for me to examine the licenses, permits, or passports, for it would only be a question of examining into the times of departure and return, and whether the conditions laid down in the said permits had been carried out.

As, in accordance with His Majesty's memorandum of the 15th of June last, the monopoly of the trade at Detroit is granted to the Commandant of this post, on the condition that he shall be responsible for all expenses, and the French people who may settle there are forbidden to trade at all, except for their provisions, there is no likelihood of any other settlers going there except those whom it may be to the Commandant's interest to have there, to employ them in transacting his trade.

Those who are there now have acquired sites within the fort on which they have built houses, all living within the fort. They were only at-tracted there by the right of trading which M. de la Mothe Cadillac had granted them for ten livres rent a year. Most of them contented them-

They buy this permission in order to obtain the right of trading there, without which they would not undertake a journey of 300 leagues; for if they went up there without this permission they would incur great expense without any chance of profit.

The drawback that there will be no settlers at Detroit, does not appear great; for, if large settlements were made there, they would be destroyed in the first war against the savages, and for this reason it would be advisable to have no settled inhabitants either at Detroit or at Michilimakinac, and that only Voyageurs should go there.

The King might keep Commandants in these two posts without allowing them to do any trade, and without any expense to His Majesty beyond the officers salaries and the pay of the garrison.

The necessary funds for that expense might be found by selling, for His Majesty's profit, the limited number of licenses for the upper countries which it might be decided to grant. The proceeds of the sale of these licenses would suffice both for the additional pay which the Council might grant to the Commandants and for all the extraordinary expenses which would be incurred at these posts, if a condition were inserted in the licenses that each of the persons who make use of them should be bound to convey a certain quantity of the necessaries required by the garrisons, which is usual with regard to licenses in which these conditions are inserted.

AGREEMENT MADE BETWEEN THE DIRECTORS AND AGENTS OF THE COMPANY OF THE COLONY OF CANADA, AND M. DE LAMOTHE IN CONCERT WITH THE GOVERNOR-GENERAL AND THREE INTENDANTS, CONCERNING DETROIT OR FORT PONTCHARTRAIN.

Canada. Posts of the Upper Countries.

Before the Royal Notary in the provostship of Quebec, undersigned, there resident, and witnesses named below, there were present M. René Louis Chartier, Esquire seignior of Lotbiniere, Chief Councillor to the Supreme Council of this Country, and Master George Renard Duplessis, seignior of L'Auzon, Treasurer of the Navy, the general and special agents of the Company of the Colony of this Country, dwelling in this town of Quebec, of the one part, and Antoine de la Mothe Esquire, lord of Cadillac, Captain of a Company of the detachment of Marines kept up by His Majesty in this country and commandant for the King at Fort Pontchartrain of Detroit, at present in this town, of the other part; which parties to wit MM. de Lôbiniere [and] Duplessis in virtue of the orders of My Lord the Comte de Pontchartrain, Minister and Secretary of State, dated the fourteenth of June of last year, addressed to the board of directors,

consent of the high and puissant seignior Messire Philipes de Rigault, Marquis de Vaudreuil, Knight of the Military Order of St. Louis, Governor and Lieutenant General for His Majesty in this country of New France, Messire Jacques Raudot. Councillor of the King in his Councils, Intendant of Justice, Police and Finance in this country, Messire François de Beauharnois, knight, seignior of La Chaussoye Beaumont and other places, Councillor of the King in his Councils, Intendant-General of the Navy and formerly Intendant of New France, have agreed on what follows.

1st.

That the merchandise which is at Fort Pontchartrain of Detroit shall be handed over to M. de la Mothe, or to whomsoever commands there under his orders, as soon as he arrives at the place, on the first application he shall make for them to the clerks of the Company.

2nd.

That a general inventory shall be made by M. de Bourgmont, an officer, and M. de Grandmesnil, the agent of the said M. de la Mothe, and by the clerks of the Company at the said place, in the presence of M. de Tonty and of Father Constantin de Halle, Missionary, of all the merchandise and movable property, houses, warehouse, and cleared lands and generally of everything there may be at Detroit. In the inventories shall be noted what goods are neither spoilt nor damaged.

3rd.

That M. de la Mothe shall pay for the goods which are saleable, and which are neither spoilt nor damaged according to the invoice which shall at once be presented to him, it being understood that in the parcels which are damaged or spoilt he shall pay for what is found good in them as good merchandise.

4th.

Over and above the price of the said goods, M. de la Mothe offers the Company to grant it a premium of thirty per cent. Both parties have deferred, on this point, to what it may please My Lord the Comte de Pontchartrain to order.

5th.

That as soon as the general inventory is here two merchants shall be nominated, one by M. de la Mothe and the other by the Company, to note the said goods which are not saleable amongst the savages nor amongst the French people there; and also the waste goods there are. He shall not be bound to take over the said goods except according to the valuation which shall be made of them by the said two merchants to whom both agree to refer.

6th.

In case there should be any difficulty as to the price of the goods under the invoices, they shall refer the matter to two merchants whom they shall agree on together, and shall submit to their opinion.

7th.

That in regard to the houses. buildings, warehouses, cleared lands, and other useful and necessary expenditure which the Company claims to have incurred at the said place of Detroit, which the Company asks to be re-imbursed by the said M. de la Mothe, who claims that he owes it nothing for all these things, they have left this point open and beg My Lord the Comte de Pontchartrain to decide upon it.

8th.

That the said M. de la Mothe will pay the price of the said goods, and the premium according as it may be settled by My Lord, in money or bills of exchange to the Company, it being understood that compensation will be given for what may be found owing by it to the said M. de la Mothe with regard to the bills of exchange or the money; and, as to the term of the payment, they have both left the matter to what My Lord may be good enough to lay down on this point.

9th.

That M. de la Mothe may not supply to the Company more than fifteen or twenty thousand livres' worth of beaver-skins a year at most, which shall be accepted and paid for by the Company according as they are accepted and paid for at the Quebec office and at the same price.

10th.

That neither M. de la Mothe, nor the people who may be with him at Detroit, shall be permitted to trade except in Detroit. nor to send boats on the lakes.

11th.

That the Company shall be at liberty to send an inspector, whom it shall pay at its own expense, to Fort Pontchartrain of Detroit. to give information if the above article is not being infringed, and in case of in-

during the time it had the working of the said post. ·For, thus it has been agreed between the parties &c, under the obligations ·&c, Renouncing &c.

Drawn up and executed at the Chateau St. Louis at Quebec the twenty-eighth day of September, one thousand seven hundred and five, in the presence of MM. Pierre Huguet and Estienne Miranbeau, merchants, witnesses dwelling in the said Quebec, who have with my said lords the Governor-General and Intendant, my said MM. de Lotbiniere, Duplessis, De la Mothe, and the notary, signed thus. Signed to the draft as it stands,

R. L. Chartier de Lotbiniere.
Reynard du Plessis.

I declare that my present signature will in no way affect what concerns the twelfth and last paragraph Signed, La Mothe Cadillac, Vaudreuil, Raudot, Beauharnois, Huguet, Merambeau, and by us the Notary Royal undersigned; one word erased, is not worth signing; Signed thus, Chambalon.

True Copy.

La Mothe Cadillac.
I have the original here in my possession.

CADILLAC IN POSSESSION OF DETROIT.

Endorsed—Colonies.   M. Raudot, 19th Oct. 1705.

My Lord,

*   *   *   *

On my arrival here I found the subjects of dispute between the Sr. De la Mothe and the Board of Directors adjusted by a decree given by M. de Beauharnois and, in accordance with your orders, I caused the furs which had been seized from him by the Directors to be returned to him.

as he acted towards the clergy of St. Sulpice regarding the Island of Montreal.

*   *   *   *

I have made inquiry, My Lord, as to what might have laid the Jesuit Fathers open to the suspicion of trading in beaver-skins, as they are accused of doing. What has given rise to that is that they are obliged to make use of servants or hired men to take up the boats conveying to them their provisions and the other things they have need of at their mission. Notwithstanding all the precautions taken, these servants or hired men cannot be prevented from taking goods on their own account, which they trade in for their own profit; and as they take them in the boats belonging to these Fathers, people will have it that it is they who carry on this trade.

My Lord.
> Your most humble, most obedt. and most obliged Servant
>> Raudot.[1]

Quebec this 19th Oct. 1705.

————

CADILLAC'S REQUESTS TO THE GOVERNOR-GENERAL REGARDING THE SETTLEMENT OF DETROIT.

Endorsed—Memorandum by the Sr. de la Mothe Cadillac.

To the Marquis de Vaudreuil[2] Knight of the military order of St. Louis and Governor-General throughout New France.

As you have told me that you will not decide on my requests concerning the settlement of Detroit unless they are made to you in writing. I continue to comply with that.

I begged you by the requests which I had the honor to make to you on the 27th of January last, to which you replied on the 29th of the same month, to grant me two hundred men, including the sergeants and upper grades, for the safety of Fort Pontchartrain.

I also very humbly begged you to permit me to choose them and to take those who are most inclined to go.

This is what you decided regarding these three requests—"The Sr. de la Mothe may count on a hundred and fifty men."

---

[1]Jacques Raudot, Intendant, 1705 to 1711.—C. M. B.

[2]Philippe de Rigault, Seigneur de Vaudreuil, Governor-General, born 1643, son of Jean Louis Rigault and of Marie, his wife. He married Louise Elizabeth de Joybert at Quebec, Nov. 21, 1690, and had ten children. He was buried in the church of the Recollets, in Quebec, Oct. 13, 1725.—C. M. B.

In my opinion this order or decision states and clearly sets forth the number of men—that you will order to be detailed to accompany me to Fort Pontchartrain; and for that reason I could not doubt, and ought not to have doubted before I set out for Montreal, that you had given your orders to the Governors of the various places in order that this detachment might be formed and a muster-roll of it drawn up in due form, and advances taken.

What you decided before is also stated in the following words:—"And he shall have permission to choose from the Companies, well disposed men who wish to go with him."

This order states and also clearly means that I might choose from the companies those who were well affected without any restriction, exception, or reserve, up to the number of a hundred and fifty. Yet this order is annulled by what you laid down a little while ago in a counter-order which you sent to Governors de Ramezay and de Crizafix, by which they are enjoined to choose four of the best soldiers out of each company before letting me see the troops, and you made me the bearer of this order without saying anything to me about it.

This phrase again, to choose from the companies well disposed men to go to Detroit, in my opinion does not mean as they claim at Montreal, that I am obliged to take all those who offer themselves, of whatever sort they may be. If that were so it would exclude me from the permission you gave me to choose. I had understood that, amongst those who were favorably disposed, I could take the good ones and leave the rest; otherwise it would not be a choice.

I was equally bound to believe that the soldiers would be with their companies when these were shown me. But when I was at Three Rivers, I found there were only seventeen men in the company of Sr. St. Martin; eight in that of the Sr. de Tonty; and seven in that of the Sr. de Courtemanche; the soldiers having dispersed in the direction of Montreal and Quebec. It may be that those who were well-disposed towards Detroit had been sent away designedly. The Marquis de Crisafix tells me, with reason, that there were twenty-nine men in the company of the Sr. de Tonty, but that they had never come to Three Rivers, and that he had not seen more than fourteen of them since it had been there, including the two sergeants.

From that time I knew that I had undertaken my journey in vain, and that I should probably meet with just as many obstacles at Montreal as

This caused me to make up my mind finally to go no further, considering that this would be laboring in vain, for it was impossible on such conditions to carry out what I presumed you had decided. Hence my journey cost me five hundred livres, and yet I effected nothing towards the settlement of Fort Pontchartrain.

I made my remonstrances to you, Sir, in writing on the 27th of January last, together with my requests, supported and enforced by substantial reasons. I had the honor to represent to you that two hundred men were absolutely necessary for the security of Fort Pontchartrain. You had promised me them before the sailing of the véssels, and in accordance with that I wrote to the Comte de Pontchartrain. I had the honor of telling you so, when you reduced this number to one hundred and fifty, and you replied that you would take the responsibility of it.

I pointed out to you that the best soldiers were not good enough, because of the difficulties of that journey; and the risks there would be to that settlement if you gave me unskilful men. You yourself know that if it were a detachment of sickly or slovenly men, it would give the savage tribes occasion to despise the French nation. It is of infinite importance to prevent them from forming bad impressions of it; for it is necessary, in order to keep them in awe, to impress their imaginations by the sight of troops that would be capable of inspiring them with fear. That is a point which has always been most regularly observed in all the detachments for those posts.

Since you have had the four best soldiers in each company chosen for certain consignments you are to send to Fort Frontenac, a journey that is made on barges and in wooden boats, how would unskilful men manage to make the journey to Detroit in bark canoes, the journey to which is more difficult since it is three times as long, and consequently more laborious? I feel obliged to tell you that I have done my best to realize, with all my strength, the intention of the Court regarding the settlement of Fort Pontchartrain of Detroit, by buying such goods as are most necessary for the subsistence of the savages, the boats and other conveyances for taking the troops there. the provisions for the journey and the stores for taking them there, by making agreements with a certain number of families; which cannot be done without great expense. This should remove the bad impression people have tried to give concerning me, and put a stop to the false reports of my conduct—which have not only been spread in this country but have also been made to re-echo in the midst of the Court. wishing to insinuate that I had originated the scheme for this settlement only with a view to making my own private fortune there, while ruining the interests of the public as regards the trade of this upper colony of which I intended to make myself master, and the sole proprietor. As a matter of fact, it might well be that anyone but myself would

Comte de Pontchartrain to induce His Majesty to grant me by giving me the trade of Detroit, which this great Minister, has, no doubt, done only with the intention of enabling me (by means of the profits I could make thereby) to keep up this post in the manner desired by the King. But my true disinterestedness, my zeal. and my constant devotion to his service will, in the eyes of the wise, confound the malice of those who have sought to create the same prejudice in others; for it is certain that, far from keeping this right to myself, that is from appropriating the whole trade· of this post for myself alone, pursuant to the authority which I hold from His Majesty to do so, (and this at a time when I could make large profits because of the scarcity of goods through the country) I am, on the contrary, leaving and giving up all the trade of Detroit not only to the inhabitants, but also to the troops who may wish to transact it, with the object of inducing them both by this valuable privilege, to make a dwelling-place for themselves there which will give them the means of living in comfort. That will not prevent me from seeking else- where, and in other ways the means of procuring for that upper colony, and also in this one, trade which has never yet been thought of; but I consider it necessary to wait until the aspect of affairs changes, for private reasons.

When I had the honor to beg you to promise me the choice of the soldiers, it was with the object of succeeding in carrying out this enter- prise, and at the same time for the security and preservation of this post which is far away from all assistance. And when I requested you to grant me those who were well-disposed, that was with regard to the means of forming this post by these soldiers settling there. Therefore I beg you very humbly to decide in what manner you wish the detachment for Detroit to be made up, and to give me your orders so definitely that they will not be liable to interpretations which might delay their execu- tion, as has been done hitherto, seeing that it is a matter of the King's service, and is pressing.

you have decided to choose six officers who are willing to come with me by common consent I beg you to decide also that I may choose six sergeants from the troops, favorably disposed·or otherwise, as well as six corporals in the same manner, as this number is absolutely necessary to me for the good of the service and for the success of that enterprise.

After all the representations which I have had the honor of making to you heretofore and in this present memorandum, permit me to inform you that if, for want of the assistance you can give me, which I very humbly ask of you, I am unable to carry out the orders of the Court, I decline all responsibility for the evil consequences which may follow in this matter, and also on my journey and in all that concerns the settlement of Detroit.

Presented on the eighteenth of March 1706.

Signed, La Mothe Cadillac.

REPLY OF THE GOVERNOR-GENERAL TO THE MEMORIAL PRESENTED BY MONSIEUR DE LA MOTHE CADILLAC ON THE 31st OF MARCH, 1706.

To the Marquis de Vaudreuil Knight of the military order of St. Louis and Governor General of all New France.

The order of the Court is that I am to defray only the cost of conveyance to Fort Pontchartrain at Detroit of the soldiers I ask for; these are the word:—

"Besides that, His Majesty orders MM. de Vaudreuil and de Beauharnois to give you all the assistance in their power.

"He charges Monsieur [de Vaudreuil] to give you as many soldiers as you ask for, and Monsieur de Beauharnois to pay them their pay as usual, on condition that you defray the cost of their conveyance."

I therefore very humbly beg you, in conjunction with the Intendant, to cause me to be supplied with the articles most necessary for the use of the garrison of the said Fort Pontchartrain of Detroit viz. forty stoves weighing nine livres apiece, as it is absolutely necessary to put the soldiers in separate messes on account of the extreme heat of summer in that place.

2.

And forty dishes of wood or tin large enough to hold four men's food each.

1, 2, 3, 4, 5
The Sieur
la Mothe
apply to t
Intendant
these first
seven thi

3.

And a hundred and thirty-five ells of linen for thirty pairs of sheets for the said soldiers, so that we may be able to provide for them properly in case of sickness, as there is no hospital at that place.

4.

And a hundred and twenty-one ells of clochetterie or mattress cloth for the beds of the soldiers.

5.

And two candlesticks, two lanterns and a lamp for the guard-house.

6.

And fifty good axes weighing at least four full livres each, well fastened with good steel, for getting fire wood for the said guard-house.

7.

I also beg you to decide what payment you will have made for the cartage of each cord of wood burnt at the said guard-house.

8:
Governor
give or-
s for faulty
s to be ex-
nged for
150 soldiers
) form the
Fort Pont-
rtrain; also
der h°rí's,
swords or
onets shall
upplied to
se who are
hout them,
ch shall be
áined by
m on de-
tion from
ír pay ac-
ding to

8.

I also very humbly beg you to be good enough to give orders for faulty arms to be exchanged and good ones to be given to the soldiers who form this detachment also powder flasks or powder horns, and to give some bayonets gratuitously; the whole because this post is far from all succor, and at the further end of the country.

to be good enough to make some outlay on the King's account on behalf
of this church. Monsieur de Beauharnois had purchased a piece of tap-
estry, but when he learnt that the church had been burnt down he did
not give it.

11.

I beg you to instruct the Intendant to pay a Recollet for serving as
almoner to the troops at the said Fort Pontchartrain, since the officers
and soldiers cannot remain without spiritual aid.

11, 12
The Inter
will reply
these two
heads 11 a
concernir
the missic
ries asked
by the Si
de la Mot

12.

Also another Recollet to come with me in the convoy which will start
this spring, who will serve as missionary at the said place Detroit, for
this is necessary for that Settlement. That is in accordance with the
letter from Monseigneur in these terms:—"His Majesty also orders MM.
de Vaudreuil and de Beauharnois to see that the missionaries necessary
for that settlement are given to you, together with all the aid" &c. And
in another place it is said—"Things being thus ordered, you will have no
more quarrels with the Jesuits. If these Fathers (who are, however, able
assistants) do not suit you, other priests shall be given you" &c. Two
Recollets are therefore necessary at the said post, until their Superior can
grant more.

13:
As some
French fa
lies are to
up to sett'
Fort Pont
chartrain
Governor-
eral will t

13.

I also beg you very humbly to permit the soldiers who are to go to
Detroit, whose names I will give you, to be married here before their
departure, so they may be able to take their wives there and start this
settlement, seeing that there are none at Detroit. This is in accordance
with Monseigneur's letter in these words:—"His Majesty permits you"
&c "and that you may give permission to the soldiers and Canadians, who
wish to marry, to do so provided the priests who officiate as rectors see
no legitimate impediment."

permit th
soldiers to
married in
cordance
His Majes
intention.
however t
should be s
soldiers w
are settin
out, wish t
married ai
take their
wives with
them, the
ernor-Gen
will give p
missions tc
interests
that settle
ment.

14:
There should
be at Fort
Pontchartrain ·
at Detroit six
hundred livres
of the King's
powder, and
bullets in pro-
portion. The
Governor-Gen-
eral will give
orders for the
whole to be
handed over to
the Sieur de la
Mothe who is
not to use
them except
in case of an
attack, as the
said warlike
stores are only
for the preser-
vation of Fort
Pontchar-
train.

14.

As there ought always to be one thousand livres of powder and thousand livres of bullets at Detroit for the preservation of Fort Po chartrain, which warlike stores ought not to be touched except in c of attack or on other occasions of importance. I very humbly beg you give me your authority to take the quantity stated; and. in case the s stores are consumed, that you will have the aforesaid quantity of th supplied to me on the spot.

15.

15 and 16:
The Intendant
will reply to
these two par-
agraphs, 15
and 16

It is absolutely necessary to have two interpreters at Detroit, one the Hurons and Iroquois and the other for the Outaouais tongue. I lieve I shall find two for the pay of three hundred livres a year ea instead of 500# which has hitherto been paid to them.

16.

As the garrison will also be unable to do without a surgeon I beg t you will consent to have pay to the amount of three hundred livres iss to one whom I will propose to you, capable and suitable for that place

17.

EXTRACT FROM THE LETTER OF THE SAID MINISTER OF THE 9TH OF JUNE 1706 AT PARAGRAPH 6.

I am also writing to him that he should not prevent you *from coming* Index lett *to Quebec, nor from sending any of your officers there when the interests of your post* require it.

Extract from the same letter at paragraph 12.

You notify me that you will be obliged to *establish your settlement* in a different *place from that at which you lived at first.* It appears to me that your only grievance relates to the interior works which M. de Tonty constructed at your fort; if it were nothing more than that, it seems to me that you could remedy it by having them demolished, you could do so with less difficulty than [there would be] in constructing another elsewhere. That would be all the more unfortunate because in that way you would cause the Company to lose the cost of the first.

Extract from the same letter at paragraph 17.

His Majesty approves of your taking with you two priests from the seminary of Quebec, to have charge of spiritual matters there; and if anything should prevent them from being able to go there, he would approve of your taking a recollet as you propose. But it appears to *His Majesty that it is for you to supply these ecclesiastics with food as M. de Lassalle formerly did in the settlement he was permitted to turn to account for his own profit.*

Extract from the same letter, Paragraph 18.

You must not fear that His Majesty may change his opinion regarding Detroit, *and you may be satisfied that it will stand, His Majesty consenting to take it under his protection, and that I for my part, shall ever do all that may depend* on me to support it.

TALK BETWEEN MARQUIS DE VAUDREUIL AND ONASKIN, CHIEF OF THE OUTAVOIS.

Endorsed—

Replies of the Marquis de Vaudreuil to the words of the Outavois of Michili-makina, brought by the Sr. Boudor, and read in the presence of Companissé and Le Brochet on the first of August, 1706, in order to learn whether those were the sentiments of their people.

I have seen, O Companissé and Le Brochet, what Onaskin has sent to tell me in writing, which the Sr. Boudor has brought to me on his behalf; and I have had it read in your presence that I might learn whether it was indeed your sentiments; and as you have both assured me that it was the words of my children of Michilimakina, I am going to reply to them. Listen and hear me, O Champanissé, and thou, Le Brochet. I should have been very glad to see all of you here, to bring back the slaves you promised to hand over to me to give to your brothers the Iro-quois; and I had tried, by treating you well, to let you all know the difference I make between a disobedient child and

Words addressed to the Marquis de Vaudreuil by Onaskin, Chief of the Out-avas.

As our father directed us to bring him eight slaves to fulfill the promise which we had made to him last sum-mer, we had determined to bring down ten boats for that purpose; but the grievous news that has come from De-troit decides us not to bring down so many. We will only go in order to try · and set right these unfortunate affairs,

for the loss they have sustained at Detroit, or to an attack from your
enemies. I am convinced, and am willing to believe that, as you had no hand
in what took place at Detroit, you had
no other object in what you have done
except to prevent your brothers the
French from being insulted. But as I
look upon all that has taken place with
other eyes than you do, I cannot and
will not permit my young men to be
molested in any way; and if you had
really felt the sentiments you ought to
have felt for your brothers, the French
who are up there, and for me, who am
the Father of you all, you would have
come down with them as you ought to
have done; you would even had aided
them with the means of bringing their
furs. That is how you would have given
me proofs of your affection, and not
by keeping them among you like prisoners or like hostages while you await
my reply. I love my children the
French; I am their Father, and I will
spare nothing to avenge them. Listen
and hear me, O Companissé; and thou
also; O Le Brochet.

I am very glad to see that my children of Michilimakina, in spite of the
bad news from Detroit, still retain the
sentiments they ought to feel, and that
they remember the promise they gave
me last year. I receive with pleasure
the four slaves whom they send me to
return to their brothers, the Iroquois,
and I am satisfied that they will send
me the other four next year, and I ever
regard them as my true children; but
I also wish them to give me proofs of
their confidence by aiding all the
French people I have up there with the
means of coming down, and also by
their young men helping them to bring
their furs down here. That is the only
way in which they can testify to me
of their obedience; and it is also the
only means left to me to forget what

though we were only bound to give
four. But we are glad to make known
to our father, by this number, that we
are obedient children.

We will not fail, next year, to complete the number of slaves we are
bound to give. We beg our father to
look upon us as his children, to treat us
as a father, and to have pity on us in
the handling of this present affair in
which we have no part, and to have regard to the small number we muster
here.

are not quite free I cannot listen to anything.

I sent you last year a message by M. de Louvigny. I am rejoiced that it served you as a strong help in rejecting all the evil suggestions which have been made to you. You must have known that all he told you from me was true. I am a good father; do not oblige me to be severe.

I told you last year that you were my children, and so were the Iroquois, but that I held you always on the left side, as the nearest to my heart. Do not make yourself unworthy of a place which ought to be so dear to you, but imitate your brothers the Iroquois who, though they have just grounds of complaint, always remain obedient, and do not take any steps without consulting me.

I sympathize with you strongly in all the difficulties you may have; but I have already told you that, until I see my French people who are up there back again, and until you place yourselves entirely in my hands as true children ought to do, I cannot give you any answer, and I will never allow it to be said that a child is to lay down the law for his father.

I have seen what you tell me regarding your brothers of the Sault. I do not wish my children to have any difficul-

The message which Monsieur de Louvigny brought us last spring from our father has been a powerful aid to us in rejecting everything evil which could come to us, for we know that all he said to us on behalf of our fathers was true, and also his kindness in not taking rods to chastise his children who had disobeyed him but, on the contrary, overwhelming them with benefits.

We remember well that our fathers told us that we were in his bosom, and the Iroquois also, our brothers, but with this difference, that the latter were in the right side and we in the left; we are so safely lodged in his heart that no troubles, however bad they may be, will give him cause to drive us out.

We beg our father to take pity on our families, especially those who are mourning.

We learnt last year that the people of the Sault cherished bitterness in their hearts because they had lost the son

Miamis, our enemies into the fort and excluding us.

As regards what you say to me abóut my commander at Detroit, and the action he has taken in what has happened there, I am surprised that my children of Michilimakina can speak to me as you do.

The people of Detroit, for I ought not to call them my children any more, attacked the Miamis without cause, since thè Sieur de Tonty who was then in command, had settled the difficulty they had had with the Missisaguez, and I had even shown my pleasure thereat to the offender when he came down here. Yet in spite of that, the Outavois at Detroit attacked the Miamis, who are my children even as they are. But where did they attack them? At my door, in my very arms; for it was I who made them come within the bastions of my fort. And you complain that my commandant there received them in his fort, and gave them aid. You say that he killed some men; could he have done otherwise? And if the Outaoüas had been attacked by the Miamis, would you not have wished him to get you out of it in just the same way? His fort is fired upon; has he not grounds for thinking that they have designs on him as well as on the Miamis? And if he ordered the Outaouas to be fired at, was it he who sought the Outaouas to kill him, or the Outaouas who came to attack him. I think you are too wise, my children of Michilimakina, to take part in such a discreditable business. I am even willing to believe, as Maurice will have told you, that the Outaouas of Detroit had no direct intention of attacking me; but as they have sláin the

We beg our father to watch over our interests, so that we may return to our families in safety; and to be well assured that nothing will ever happen on our part which is not in conformity with his will.

We hope that all the tribes will know the good heart of their father, giving him their full confidence in negotiating this present trouble. We beg our father to have pity on us, being now compelled to fight our enemies, by giving us a little powder and some bullets, that we may remain on thè defensive.

follow the advice of Father Marest
whom I have sent you as a Missionary;
help my French people in the means of
coming down with their furs; help them
yourselves; come here with them, and
trade. You will find everything you
want here, for we have just received
goods in abundance, and you will always
find me with a father's heart, and arms
open to receive you. But, on the other
hand, if you offer the slightest insult
to my people, I will not only deny you
all the help you have a right to expect
from me, but I will also declare war
against you which will end only with
the complete destruction of your tribe.
Remember well O Companissé, and thou
also Le Brochet, all that I have said to
you, so that you may be able to repeat
it to your people when you return; and
you may assure them that it rests with
them alone whether they will be my true
children or will become my enemies.
And in order that you may forget nothing that I have just said to you, I am
sending a copy of it to Father Marest,
that he may put you in remembrance
of it.

LETTER FROM FATHER MAREST TO THE MARQUIS DE VAUDREUIL.

Endorsed.—Letter from Father Marest to the Marq. de Vaudreuil annexed to the letter of the 30th of Oct. 1706. This letter is marked E. in

and take the news themselves, thus showing us clearly how true they believed it. I must not weary you by a useless repetition of what I then wrote to you but I must give you an account of what has taken place since.

For my part, if I had regarded my personal and private interests, and even that of my mission, I should have taken advantage of the opportunity to give way as so many people advised us, and nothing could have been said against me; but I sacrificed both to the desire to satisfy you and fulfil the promise I had given you, together with my Superior. I believed and had reason to believe that I should please you by pushing on further and by making the others do so, but without violence, and by taking all the precautions necessary for our safety. I had no difficulty in making those who had hesitated a little, reflect that, after all, savages whoever they may be, always mix as it were the false with the true in their reports; and, if the tidings they had given us turned out to be false we should repent of having founded a resolve of such a kind on so unstable a basis, and of turning back as it were from the gates of Michilimakina without obtaining any certain knowledge of the condition of the French people there. The Sr. Shartier, whatever reason he had to fear Mishilimakina on account of the slaves you know of, was one of the first to say that it would be disgraceful if, on account of the talk of the savages, however probable it appeared, we failed to go all together, as we had promised you, either up to the village of Mishilimakina or to a spot whence we could obtain certain news of it, and afterwards endeavor to save the French people if they were still alive, as it appeared they were.

God himself gave us an opportunity, which we had not looked for, of avoiding all risk. Meravila the Sinago Outaouak of whom I have already spoken to you in my letter from Toupikanich, instead of returning to Detroit with the men of Toupikanich who wished to take them back with them on the war path to avenge the death of his brother who had just been slain the next day after he had been made a chief and had raised up the name of Ouichkouch Meravila requested us, on the contrary, to speak to the said savages of Toupikanich that they might consent to permit him to come with us to Mishilimakina, which we did; and this also shocked them, [seeming] as if he had no friendship towards his brother.

The Sieur Menard told him that everyone advised us to give way, and he replied that he desired to speak to the Sr. Menard and me on that subject. The parley took place the next morning. St. Ignatius' day, after the mass of this Saint had been said. The other Frenchmen who wished

culty and those at Mishilimakina also, if they were still alive. Then he
held out a beautiful belt, and said that he wished to give it to the men
of Mishilimakina as a present to get the French out of their difficulty if
they were there; that if anyone wanted to attack them, he would bare
his bosom and tell him to strike him first; that if matters were favorable,
he would return to us to bring us back news of it together with the reply
to a letter which we were to give him for the French; that as to the
French at Mishilimakina, if he found them dead, he would not say he had
seen us but would come at once and tell us everything, so that we might
retire as soon as possible; and if he were in danger from his own people
on our account, he would join us and would go down to the lower Colony;
that he would ask us for a flag, and a letter to take to the French, which
would serve him as evidence that he had refused to imbue his hands in
their blood. You can well imagine how his proposal was received (though
there is always a risk in placing one's life in the hands of a savage),
but we promised him so much, both on your account and our own, that
it was a strong inducement to him to keep his word. He was told that, on
his return, he should be abundantly rewarded, whether matters were
favorable or unfavorable; that we would inform you of the essential
service he was rendering us, and you would never forget it; and indeed
I do not see that any savage deserves better to be rewarded and esteemed
by the French than this one. You will oblige us all greatly, and me in
particular, if you reward him well for the way in which he has behaved
on this occasion, and make him feel what it is to do a service to Frenchmen who carry your orders, and to a missionary, without taking into
consideration that we have, each of us, already given him the value of
four beaver-skins which it is right that the King should repay us, since
we are only exposed to so many risks on behalf of his service. This man,
as a greater proof of his fidelity, left all his family with us as hostages,
and himself set out on the 3d in a boat to go to Mishilimakina. He carried
out his mission with all possible secrecy: he said nothing either to the

that, since the last news from Detroit, in which it was said that the
French had not taken part in the second attack on the Outaouak, matters
were more tolerable; that moreover, the day before they left Mishilimakina to come to us, all the Outaouaks who were in the village set out
for Detroit, to the number of 160 (including those from Detroit who had
come to invite them); and that if the French attacked them again, there
would be more reason to fear than ever for all the French who might be
at Mishilimakina.

Notwithstanding this news, we did not give up going together to Michilimakina; for I did not see that there would be any more risk for me,
either of remaining with the savages, as a hostage, or of falling a victim
to their resentment, than what had been foreseen·and must have been
foreseen before I set out from Montreal; and I knew moreover that my ·
presence would be of use to the French and would for a time restore the
temper of the savages if they thought a little. In fact, on our arrival on
the 9th of August, everyone seemed rejoiced, and the savages assured
me that they saw clearly from that that their father would not abandon
them; and that, whatever might happen at Detroit, the French would
always be in safety here; that they perceived that their father had no
part in the affair at Detroit and did not believe that they had taken part
in it since, despite his knowledge of it, he had sent his message, and their
missionary had returned, notwithstanding so many risks and the evil
reports he had heard on the way.

That has not prevented the French from setting to work to construct a
fort, apparently as a dwelling-place for me, (for it was very necessary
to adopt this pretence so that the savages should not oppose it) but in
reality to place the French in safety there with their property, for the
word of the savages cannot be relied on; the chiefs are not masters, and
in spite of the good will which the chiefs showed, and in spite of all the
efforts they have made, the French people have thought themselves in
danger for such a long time, and it was this which compelled them to
make so many presents.

Mons. Arnault made some [expenditures] on this occasion for the general good for which he certainly deserves to be repaid; he will himself
hand his bill to you and to the Intendant.

This para-
graph ref
to Mons.
Arnault.

You are not unaware how zealous Mons. Arnault is for the public good
on all occasions, and especially when he knows that what he is doing must
be pleasing to you. His zeal and generosity should not go without a
reward. The Sr. Menard and those who went up with me will also present their bills to you for what they have supplied for the King's service;
for it may be said that the journey which we have all made together was
made solely· because you considered it necessary for the good of the

country; they beg that you will be good enough to have it paid for* by
the Intendant, and I made you the same request out of affection for them; they have already been deprived of the greatest profit they might have made when, by the ingenuity of Mons de la Mothe, they were compelled to send back their lead and powder.

It is not right that they should also pay expenses which they have incurred solely for the King's service, who at such troublous times had given no presents for setting troublesome matters straight. The Sieur Caillierie is one of those who supplied most liberally, as the King's boat did not contain sufficient. As for me, I have supplied the value of about twenty beaver-skins, including my attendants. You will also allow me to say that, having come up as I did, solely by your orders, with the desire of doing a service for you and the King, amidst so many dangers, I might have been given some gratuity for my journey, and I hope that you will hereafter be good enough to pay some regard to that. Whether that takes place or not, I am still very glad to be here and to have shown you by my steadfastness that my inclination was not against coming here, and that nothing can stop me when it is a question of doing what you wish. I flatter myself also that my presence will not be useless; I believe that if we had arrived at Mishilimakina before the warriors set out for Detroit, we could have stopped them—the Sr. Menard and I—by telling them certain things we had heard on our way. But God did not permit us to arrive soon enough, by reason of the precautions it was necessary for us to take. Perchance He foresaw that we could not have succeeded in stopping them; and in that case it is better for us that we were not at Mishilimakina, so that M. de la Mothe could not impute it to us as a crime that we had permitted them to depart although [it would have been] in spite
of us. We reproached them severely for this action in the council; they told us that they were unable to hold their young men back after they had heard of the treachery of the Hurons, and that, moreover, they went to seek their relatives and supply them with provisions.

We hear from Toupikanich that a party of a hundred men was to come there on its way to Detroit, but they did not appear while we were there.

These people of Toupikanich begged me to bear witness to M. de la Mothe that they had not insulted us in any way. I did so although reluctantly, and requested him at the same time to look to the safety of our priests with the Miamis, if he perceived that they were in danger, and that in so doing he would be pleasing you. I believe that you will not disapprove of me [for doing so] for I consider that these priests are in great danger.

A party of warriors was to have set out from here which would have induced the Poux Sakis to fall upon the Miamis of the St. Joseph river. M. Arnault stopped it, first of all until our arrival; we then thought it advisable to stop it entirely. For that purpose we gave the belt which you had intended for speaking about Detroit, when the opportunity occurred, which we had not given because it did not seem to us reasonable to praise the men here for not having taken part in the affair at Detroit, while they were going on the war path with those from Detroit. This belt with some tobacco, had the effect of stopping Ounaskie and Koutaouililouo, and with them out of the village everything could easily be frustrated there; and although a few boats have gone since, [and] some young men have spoken of sending after them again, at least they will not be able to make an important attack. I asked the savages whether I could safely send a boat of Frenchmen to St. Joseph River; they replied that I could do so, and have even escorted me there, seeming to take an interest in the priests there; for, while they are there, they do not think they are at liberty to make war on the Miamis as they would like to do. For this reason they would be pleased to see the priests all out of this post; but I do not think that you should desire it, for it is the most important after Mishilimakina. If they were free to go there, they say that they would take so many men with them against the Miamis that, in a short time, they would drive them out of this beautiful country. I do not, however, think that they will undertake it without learning your wishes on the matter. I had spoken to some Frenchmen about taking news to the St. Joseph River, and helping our priests, and getting them out of their difficulties if they are there and enabling them to leave, but there are other French people who intimidated one of those I spoke to; it is not done to the savages.

I feel obliged to testify to you the pleasure I have had in those who have taken up our boats. It is the sole gratification I have had on the journey, to be in the company of minds so well formed. I have also every possible reason to be well satisfied with those who took up the King's boat. They have done us all sorts of services on the journey.

I thought, as well as the French people, that it was not advisable for the Sr. Menard to leave here until we were settled in the fort. I believe

be desirable that he should not leave until we have had news from Detroit; but at least he will tell you we are safe for a time, even if bad news should come from Detroit. You have certainly every reason to be pleased with the Sr. Menard who is beloved by the savages, who knows their ways; who has no difficulty in answering them, and that with a free and easy manner, ever cheerful. He discovers things which are done secretly; and, certainly, whether he comes here as commanding officer or not, he would render good service here. It costs him no small sum, as an interpreter, to get the savages to smoke, as the savages have now the upper hand over us. It appears that nothing can be done with them now except by keeping them on the terms we have put them on, acting by presents, which however settles nothing reliably. As for me, if it be desired that I should make any presents on behalf of the King, some must be sent to me, for I am destitute of everything. I do not know whether I shall have enough to live on this year.

All the old men of this village, including Koutaouilibono, have behaved so well towards the French in all the troubles that have arisen from Detroit, that they deserve to be rewarded for their zeal; it is not a thing of to-day, Koutaouilibono's declaring for the French, he has sufficient intelligence and influence, and is well-affected enough towards us, to deserve to be conciliated. He has begged me in private to tell you that he cannot, all by himself, arrange so many difficult affairs; he would like you to send him in the autumn, the French chief whom you intend to give them, also that beaver may be restored to its value again; that they can no longer find either martens or beavers; that they do not want to have any more disturbances in this village.

Ounaskie has requested me to write and tell you* that what made him give way was the fear that disturbances might happen in his absence and that no one would settle them; that while he was at the Huron island, La Picotte laid waste this village; that he had invited the Kiskakous from Detroit to return here; that they did not obey him and have been slain by the Hurons; that it was he who took the French people under his protection when the hearts of those who had come from Detroit were embittered against them; that I had seen that they were all right; that

turbances here; that it was enough that there should be any at Detroit.
He urges you always to regard his village with affection and to prevent
the word of Le Pesant proving true, who had given the Iroquois six
parcels [? of furs] to come with him to devour the village of Michilimakina; that you should continue to stop the Iroquois, since he keeps
his word so faithfully, and that you should urge the Iroquois not to
receive the Hurons if they want to withdraw to them. You will do what
you think fit about it.

I have at last found another Frenchman to go to the St. Joseph River,
and I hope four of them will set out to procure the safety of the fathers,
about which there is reason for much concern, on account of so many
parties of warriors, who are going in that direction. At the least, they
will bring us news of them, unless they find too much danger on the way.

There are several French people here whom one could wish not here.
The Sr. Menard knows them and will be able to name them to you.

We are expecting Mons. Boudor very soon with news from Detroit. I
am sending off a boat to the St. Joseph River at the same time as the
King's boat leaves to go down. There are, however, some French people
who oppose it; but I look upon that as a matter in which the public interest is concerned. I have however granted them three or four days' delay
to obtain news; it is necessary to humor them. I am in deep respect, Sir,.
Your most humble & most obedient servant,

Joseph J. Marest of the Company of Jesus.

J. M. J.

Mishilimakina this 27th Augt. 1706.

Sir

I did not think I should have the honor of writing you this second
letter by the Sr. Menard: but after our fort was finished, the time for
the return of the savages, who had gone from here to Detroit, being so
near, the French people again requested me to stop him so that he might
take you news of it, which beyond doubt, was the only important news,
and might give you the information necessary for settling matters up here.
God has since then permitted the wind to be contrary for his setting out
and favorable for the return of our savages, who had gone to Detroit; and
this gives me the means of writing to you again today.

I shall tell you then—1st. that the chiefs have always said that their
men were not going to fight but to withdraw their brothers from Detroit;
2nd that they found them on the way, and that they had already left
Detroit five or six days since, when they found them all gaunt with
the hunger they had endured; 3rd those from this place having taken the
lead in return, arrived at Mishilimakina on Monday the 23rd of August.

others; ten boats and Simon with them, have gone to look for food at Saguinan on the way; 4th Those who have arrived say that there was a final fight at Detroit, and that the French went out with the Miamis and Hurons to attack the Outaouaks in their fort; that two Frenchmen were killed there in this fight by a Miamis. 5th Some are afraid they have killed some Iroquois from the Sault, if it is true that there were some with the Hurons in their fort. 6th All say that the Miamis were the masters at the French fort; that they plundered their wheat, their ammunition, &c.; that they had burned an Outaouaks there. 7th. That the Hurons had burnt an Outaouaks woman in their fort; that they had sent four slaves to the Miamis of St. Joseph, and that two had escaped and had told their people that the Miamis had not ill-treated them and threw the whole [?blame] on Quarente Sols. 8th That the same Hurons were keeping two other Outaouaks prisoners, whom they wished to give either to the Miamis, who were very soon to come back from Detroit, or to M. de la Mothe. 9th That most of the fields at Detroit had been laid waste. 10th That there was no one remaining at Detroit but the few Miamis who were settled there before the attack. 11th That the Loup Indians had also retired. 12th That they had no news yet of Monsieur de la Mothe.

The Sr. Menard* will tell you everything and will explain it to you at more length; you may rely on his report. He has certainly done his duty, and has shown in everything, that he is in truth the King's servant and yours. If any one should make complaints to you about him I can assure you he would be very wrong, whether it be those who have gone up with him, or others. He will tell you how the people here have set their hearts on continuing the war against the Hurons and the Miamis, but you know how important it is to preserve the post with the Miamis. If M. de la Mothe should draw the Miamis away from it in order to attract them to Detroit, he would do a vital injury to the country and would draw down upon him war with all the tribes of the Lakes.

We are impatient for the return of M. Boudor with the Outaouaks chiefs. I have not yet sent to the St. Joseph River. I hope to do so very soon. I am being urged to finish, assuring you that I am respectfully, Sir, Your most humble and most obedt. servt. Joseph J. Marest, Missionary of the Company of Jesus.

Sir,

The Outaouaks, seeing the price they have had to pay for being divided, ought to endeavor effectually to unite permanently. To maintain this union and strengthen it, I will assist as far as I can. Koutaouileoné is a man to utilize for that purpose, and deserves that you should make him some good presents.

There is nowhere any list of the people who came to Detroit in 1706, after the exclusive control of the post was given to Cadillac. It was in that year that the greatest influx of new comers came—second only, in number, to those who came in 1749. From the records in the notarial offices of Montreal, the archives of Quebec and the church records of Detroit, the following list has been compiled, which, if not complete, is much fuller than anything heretofore compiled in this line.— C. M. B.

LIST OF THE PEOPLE WHO CAME TO DETROIT IN 1706.

Deny Baron

Jean Barthe (dit Belleville)

François Beauceron

René Besnard

Pierre Botquin dit St. André

Pierre Bourdon

Jean Bourg dit La Pierre

Gillis Chauvin

Jean Batiste Chauvin

Louis Chauvin

Robert Chevalier

Michel Colin dit La Liberté

Pierre Collet

Joseph Cusson

Nicolas Cusson

John Baptist Dutremble

Joseph Dutremble

Michel Filie, sieur de Therigo

Francois Chalut de Chanteloup

Martha, wife of last above. They were married in Montreal June 10, 1706

Louis Gatineau, sieur Duplessis

Pierre Hemart

Jacques Hubert, dit La croix

Marguerite La Forest married Antoine Levegir June 10, 1706

Lescuyer, Paul—brothers—They brought 10 head of cattle and 3 h‹
to Detroit in 1706. These were the first domestic animals in the we
Laurent Leveille—Panis Indian
Antoine Levroir dit Laferte
Jean Baptiste Magdeleyne dit Ladouceur
François Marquet and his wife Louise Galerneau, who were mai
April 26, 1706 at Quebec
Claude Martin
Jacques Maurisseau
Jacques Maurivan
Louis Maurivan
Marie Melain, wife of Blaise Fondurose
Blaise Fondurose
Jacques Minville, came with Paul and Jean Lescuyer
Louis Morisseau
Louis Normand, dit Labriere
Joseph Parent
Yves Pinet
Nicolas Rabillard
Louis Renaud dit Duval
François Robert

CADILLAC'S LETTER TO MARQUIS DE VAUDREUIL.

Copy of the letter written to the
quis De Vaudreuil by the Sieur ‹
Mothe Cadillac from Detroit Pont
train of 27th of August 1706.

The beginning of this letter from
Mons. de la Mothe shows that the Outaouas have always been attached to the
French; & although he maliciously says
that they have never declared them-

Sir,
I received on the way, the twc
ters which you did me the hono
writing to me on the 27th of June
3rd of July. You tell me in the

although it appeared that the Sr. de Bourmont had composed it, that was an Indian ruse to induce the Miamis not to mistrust them, and to come and fall into the snare of the. Outaouas, who have already been connected in interest with the Missisaguez. A proof of that is that, in the continuation of this letter, Mons. de la Mothe himself agrees that these Missisaguez, to the number of one hundred, came to the aid of the Outaouas, which is confirmed by the letter of Father Marest of the 14th of August last.

To pursue this matter it appears at first sight that the Outavois wanted to attack the French as well as the Miamis, but on looking into the reports of the soldiers who came to bring this news, they all agree that the Outaouas called to the French not to fire; and that, although the Father and the other soldier were killed, it was only after there had been firing on both sides, from the fort and from without. However that may be it does not make the Outaouas any less to blame, but it does not prove that they had any intention of attacking the fort when they began. And, with regard to the Father having been stabbed, those who came down only speak of his having been shot twice, which agrees with what Miscouaky said.

Miscouaky, the brother of Jean le Blanc, explains these points and says that it was the young men who came and fired while the elders were in council. The real fact is that they did not fight against the Fort any more after this affair; and if there was any fighting at Detroit afterwards, it was the Hurons and Miamis, who attacked the Outaouas, as appears from a council held on the 2nd of July by the Sieur de Bourgmont, and not the Outaouas who came to attack the Fort; and this is confirmed by Maurisseau, an Iroquois interpreter who came down from Detroit a few days ago, as well as by what

more especialy as the commandant of this post had composed and settled it; and in fact, as soon as the Outaouas had made their attack, the Missiaguez withdrew from Detroit so that they could not be suspected of having given any help to the Outaouas. They even came here, after I had arrived, to mourn over our dead, according to the custom. It appears that the action of the Outaouas against the Miamis was premeditated. But, in continuation of M. de Bougmont's letter, a copy of which he showed me, and concerning which you write to me. It appears that they bore ill-will also against the French, for it would have been very easy for them to have killed the former [?the Miamis] without killing the R. P. Constantin, and La Riviere the soldier who was outside the Fort; for they went and bound the former in his garden where he was stabbed with a knife which he could not ward off, and afterwards shot three or four times while he was escaping and approaching very slowly to the door of the Fort.

Who is there who does not know that savages employ stratagems and treachery. Our old men—say the Outaouas had no hand in this business, it was the young men. A fine excuse truly. And it would be a convenient one if we were foolish enough to accept it.

How comes it, then, Sir that after they had committed this wicked deed Jean le Blanc came to ask for peace, with a stick of porcelain, from Mons. de Bourmont who received him, granting his request and referring him to you as to what should be done about it, or to me on my arrival; and yet Jean le Blanc, who is the second chief and the elder of the village, four hours after, attacked the fort with a large number of his men, and that they fired and kept up a good fire on the Fort from five o'clock in the evening until midnight, and that in fact the fighting continued for forty or fifty days, up to the day of their retreat.

rons for the Outaouas. Yet M. de la Mothe says briefly that fighting continued for 40 or 50 days and does not say how the matter took place, thus maliciously leaving it to be understood that it was the Outaouas who kept coming to attack the Fort, which is not so, but it was the Hurons and Miamis who went to attack them.

This paragraph is much more malicious. M. de la Mothe would almost wish to give us to understand from what Jean le Blanc said, that the Outavouas acted as they did only on the order of Monsieur de Vaudreuil, as if what Jean Blanc said when he brought the flag, which Monsieur de Vaudreuil had given him at Montreal some time ago, did not mean that by coming to speak under the auspices of that flag he had nothing to fear, and that Monsieur de Vaudreuil had so assured him when he gave it to him.

What the Sr. de la Mothe says about the two Forts which the Outaouas and the Hurons made would seem very reasonable if the Sr. de Tonty and he had not agreed upon them in order to keep the Outaouas from quitting the post. It is for the Sr. de Tonty to defend this point, as well as that of the accusation against him of having forced Frenchmen to work at them. But as regards the powder, which the Sr. de la Mothe accuses him of having got rid of on purpose, Mons. de Vaudreuil must do him this justice. The Sr. de la Mothe knows, and so do all the French who were at Detroit at that time, that the

Again, what did this same Jean le Blanc mean when he returned to the Fort with a flag, and a walking stick in his hand and, approaching the bastion, said to Mons. Bourgmont "With what I hold in my hand I fear nothing because that comes from Monsieur de Vaudreuil. It will not be you who will arrange this affair, it will be he; I hearken to his words and do what he has told me to do." After which he entered the fort, having asked permission of M. de Bourmont to do so, and there he repeated the same thing. What language is that? Who indeed can understand it. Was it the young men or the old who were concerned in this act?

The whole course pursued by the elders, or rather by this tribe, proves only too clearly that this was not a resolution taken at the moment, nor would this scheme even have been carried out if Monsieur de Tonty had not been careful to plan and to have drawn out two large forts, one for this tribe and the other for the Hurons, at which he made the Frenchmen work against their will, contrary to the advice I had given him before I left Detroit to do nothing in the matter as it was not prudent to raise fortifications on his right hand and on his left for people on whom no reckoning can be made; on the contrary it

real necessity when the Sr. de Bourmont arrived, who indeed had left 200 #
of powder in a hiding place, and of this
he did not lose a single livre, for he
sent to look for it in the early spring.
This shows that the Sr. de la Mothe
does not care what statements he
makes, provided what he says has an
appearance of probability. It is the
same with the remark he makes, out of
malice, that there were only fifteen men
in the fort, without explaining that, up
to the 20th of April, there have always
been nearly forty men and that, although they were reduced to this number, that was the fault of the Sr. de
Bourmont for not having retained the
Company's servants or the soldiers he
gave to the Sr. de Tonty to go down
with him until he had received help
from below. It is also the fault of
Mons. de la Mothe for not having sent
five boats in the early spring, as he had
promised to do, for they could have got
to Detroit more than a month before
the trouble with the Outaouas happened.

The people who came down to bring
the news of the occurrences at Detroit
told Monsieur de Vaudreuil so; and as
regards what Monsieur de Vaudreuil
wrote to the Sr. de la Mothe about his
finding no Outaouas at Detroit, nothing was so probable, as Monsieur de
Vaudreuil explains in his letter.

What Mons. de la Mothe writes, as
to the departure of Father Marest is
no less malicious than all the rest of
his writings.

tests that he had left only 31 pounds,
and this again was priming-powder
which Mons. de Bourmont had to have
sifted to enable him to make use of
it; and had it not been for the 50
pounds which M. de Bourmont saved
out of what he had buried last autumn
when he came to Quebec, all the rest
being spoiled, would not the fort have
been taken, Sir; and whose fault would
it have been? A royal fort, a post established by the King's orders to be de-
nuded of powder! And the Outaouas
were well informed of that. Lastly,
there was a garrison of 15 men who had
to defend themselves with axes! But,
Sir, however it may be; whether the
savages were fortified or not; even if
there were only 15 men in the garrison;
whether there was any powder or not;
why did these savages kill Frenchmen,
why attack our fort, why kill the
Miamis who had been there for five
hundred years, who had eaten and
drunk with them every day, who had
been at war [with them] for twenty
or perhaps thirty years, who had no
quarrel with them. Was it the attack
made upon the Missisaguez? O! it was
the Missisaguez, who would not avenge
themselves, who withdrew, who would
not take part in the evil action of the
Outaouas, and disapprove of it!

No Sir, the Outaouas did not offer
themselves as hostages as you did me
the honor to write and tell me, to remain in the Fort until my arrival; they
were not sufficiently well-disposed to dis-
play such devotion. You believed very
justly, when you wrote to me that I
should not find any Outaouas here on
my arrival. I was of the same opinion
as soon as I learnt, on my way, while I
was still two days journey from Montreal, of the attack on the fort, and of
the death of this poor Father, the soldier, and the Miamis.

Nor did I fail to admire the zeal of
the Rev. Father Marest in hastening
with so much eagerness to repair to
Michilimakina, accompanied by only

boats to go up to his mission. Yet he feigns ignorance of it and says that he can never tire of admiring the zeal of this Missionary who, in spite of the news from Detroit, hastens with the zeal of the seraphim to go to Missilimakina after having abandoned it last year with at least as much zeal, and that that is a good many movements in one year for this missionary, meaning to insinuate that that covers some hidden design. The letter from Father Marest to Monsieur de Vaudreuil will explain this point.

The remainder of this letter is in the same strain. The Sr. de la Mothe agrees, because he cannot deny, that if he, or the Sr. de la Forest had been at Detroit, the affair with the Outaouas would perhaps never have happened; and at the same time throws the blame on the fact that he was kept at Quebec, as if Mons. de Vaudreuil could help arresting him on the request of Mons. de Beauharnois, and as if what happened in 1706 was a necessary consequence of the suit he held with the Company in 1704. And by way of proving his allegation he says that Mons. de Vaudreuil, after his case was decided, refused to allow him to go up to his post. But he does not say that his trial was not concluded until the 15th of June, 1705, and he did not go up to Montreal until a long time after; that from there he went down again to Quebec, on account of the illness of his wife, and did not go up finally until the 15th of August.

the Fort at Detroit, and that the Recollet Father, who was there, has been cruelly massacred and assassinated. That could only be in order to dispute with him the crown of martyrdom. It is true that this zealous return to that tribe seemed strange to me after his having abandoned it last year, and having reduced their church, their dwelling and possessions to ashes by fire; after they had themselves, with their own hands set fire to their church, and had gone down to Quebec. Such consuming zeal to leave! the zeal of the cherubim and seraphim for going up again! That makes a lot of movements for these holy missionaries, especially within one year.

It may also be, Sir, as you very well say, that if I or M. de la Forest had been on the spot this affair would not have happened. Let us both agree in some manner that that may be so; we should perhaps have seen through the plots which were not observed by Mons. de Bourmont. But if the disposition of the savages had changed so much for the worse, it might well, perhaps, be attributed to my unjust detention at Quebec by your orders, on the pretext of a complaint cleverly got up by the Company of the Colony. I am well aware that you may have believed me guilty; but after I had been absolved by the decision of the Intendant, I had the honor to demand of you, with all possible urgency, leave to return and to continue my duty at my post, for which the King had intended me (for I was not chosen for it by any Governor); and as you refused me at the time, I am bound to believe that you had

that when the ship, the "Hero," arrived on the 6th of Sept., it took two orders, one after another to make him come down; and that although Monsieur de Vaudreuil did not give him his orders until the 25th of September, that was because he was hoping that, having received his orders from Monseigneur the Comte de Pontchartrain, he would ask leave to go up; but, seeing that he remained silent, he gave him this order to make him speak, as in fact he did, by asking that he might send the Sr. de Bourmont there, which was granted him in view of the reasons alleged. It was not that Monsieur de Vaudreuil waited all this time before giving him his order, expressly in order to make it impossible for him to go. And as regards the Sr. de la'Mothe's statement that the Sr. de Bourmont, who is a young man, could not get there with six men in a boat, everyone knows how the matter happened, and we know from experience that three boats heavily laden, with only three men to each boat, have got there well enough, although starting later, which also happened this year, and that five of his boats have left Montreal and yet hope to get there all right.

the terms of your order to find out that I could not, or ought not to have set out after it was handed to me, for the conditions mentioned were not stated therein, and the memorandum containing them, of the 14th and 17th of June, 1704 and 1705 had neither been given me nor notified to me. It was this which compelled me to present to you, on this matter and for other reasons, a long remonstrance in writing, which I have sent to the Court, and we hope it has had its effect.

It was in this interval that it was decided that Mons. de Bourgmont should come and set out from Quebec to command at this place in my absence. The matter is very plausible, for the order you had given to Mons. de la Forest and me to set out at once is dated the 25th Sept., and the one you gave the Sr. de Boumont the 26th of the same month. This shows whether you really gave me leisure to think of my business and choose any officer other than the Sieur de Bourmont, if I had wished; lastly, it was necessary to settle and make a contract with the Company in two days, and no further delay was allowed me in which to make the contract, and I had everything against me, and was obliged to put up with a hundred rebuffs in trying to maintain my interests. The contract is dated the 28th of the same month. You also learnt, Sir, that M. de Bourmont who left Quebec on the 29th of Septr., did not arrive here by land until the 29th of January; and if that officer who is young and strong and vigorous, had some difficulty in managing it, do you indeed think that Mons. de la Forest who is between 50 and 60 would have come out of it well, considering the ill-health he was in at the time? I am more vigorous than he, because I am younger; but I am very glad I remained for I should have done badly to go for several reasons of which you approved and, if I may confess it to you, I shall keep the best reasons to myself, for another occasion.

together with the Hurons, have killed
three Loup Indians; I consider they did
well. On my way through Sonontouan
I came across the dangerous spirit Pim-
abauso; I saw some inclination to make
it hot for him; but he is a demon, and
always gets out of difficulties, for I
have just learnt that he is near here,
coming from Orange with a load of
brandy, as usual. Perhaps heaven will
guide us in working against him effectively, as you wrote to me to do.

This matter as to Montom is not so
great a difficulty to the Sr. de la Mothe
as he pretends. He is the brother-in-
law of Latishenotte who serves him as
an interpreter in his most secret business. Mons. de la Mothe will know very
well how to make use of that man
when he wants him.

Monsieur de Vaudreuil is sending
Monseigneur the Comte de Pontchartrain, an account of what he has done
in the matter of the deserters; and in
accordance with the orders from the
Court, he will send another 50 men to
the Sr. de la Mothe.

The man Montom is keeping Pim-
abausa company. Consider what you
wish me to do about that man. I am
told by everyone that he has always
been left at liberty down there, and that
not a word is said to him when he comes
and goes.

I feel sure that you will have some
of the deserters punished and that you
will send me back the others or, indeed
will replace them, so as to complete the
number you have granted me, and even
an increase of fifty over the three that
I have asked you for; in default of this
assistance, I beg leave to decline responsibility for all untoward events which
may happen at this post.

These two women could not be arrested, nor could the two soldiers of
M. de la Moth's company who have not
put in an appearance here. Monsieur
de Vaudreuil is sending Monseigneur
the Comte de Pontchartrain the decision
of the council of war, of which the Sr.
de la Mothe speaks.

I also hope you will send back the
wives of Chanteloup and La Roche de
St. Ours; also the men St. Jean and
Parisien of my company, with their
wives, these two rascals having deserted
or taken a holiday out of mere wanton-
ness. For, on this side of the bar I left
four or five boats which were not getting on so well as the others, and I
sent word to them by Mons. du Figuer
that I was going on in advance because
I should wait for them at the fort of
the Sables where they could come on
without any risk.

from the Iroquois that there were some Outaouas at the portage. They came indeed to the fort of the Sables because they knew very well that they would not find me there! However I had obtained a promise from the Iroqouis that, if they came there they would escort them up to the portage at Niagara. The Hurons, to the number of 7 or 8, passed by the fort of the Sables and offered to take them, as an escort, but they would have none of it. Hence they deserve to pass the winter in prison and to be sent back in the spring.

I send you the proceedings against St. Jean at Fort Frontenac. Whether the decision be good or bad, it is conditional. It was given in haste, as this man presented himself just when we were going to embark and depart.

I am very much obliged to you for having forbidden the four boats which have gone to Mishilimakina to take powder there. I do not know whether your orders were carried out, for a hundred Missisaguez have come here, well armed, with a letter which Father Marest writes me. Who then supplied them with powder? They say that no one would take their beaver-skins but that all their sables were bought. I have forbidden any trading for powder with them here for fear it might be on behalf of the Outaouas, or that they might consent to give them some of it.

There came, then, a hundred warriors, Sauteurs, Missisaguets and Amikouéque, whom Father Marest and Maurice had got together near Tanpicaniche, perhaps in order to come and succor the Outaouas and assist them in getting away to Mishilimakina. This is believed to be so, for the savages had with them two Outaouas and an Outaouas woman;

The letter of Father Marest testifies to this point as to the prohibition which Monsieur de Vaudreuil issued against taking powder, and at the same time vindicates this from the accusation which M. de la Mothe brings against him, of having given ammunition to these hundred Missisaguez, for he declares in that neither he nor Maurice Mesnard has seen them at all, that they only heard it said that they had set out with the intention of going on the war path; and if Mons. de la Mothe received a letter from Father Marest on this same occasion, it is the people from Topicamiche who have joined the former, and may also have induced them to change their first intention.

Regarding the two Outaouas prisoners given up to these Missisaguets, Mons. de la Mothe says it was the Hurons who gave them up without his knowledge; the Missisaguets say it was M. de la Mothe. Time will show how

As it appeared that they had had no hand in the affair of the Outaouas against us I had to support them and, after many councils, to come to high words about them; for the Hurons and Miamis, who are no fools, saw well enough that these men came there on this occasion to aid the Outaouas.

The reasons they gave were very good ones, viz: that if these men had come there in peace they would not have come equipped as warriors, nor in such a large party, and would ·not have brought with them two Outaouas who were recognized as having been among those who had fought against them, and even an Outaouas woman.

I made vain endeavors to dissipate this notion. I saw very well that our people had good reason. But at last I spoke authoratively and said I would not permit them to kill men whom I knew to be innocent, and that I would rather die with them. On that the Miamis went out of the Fort armed and repaired to the village of the Hurons; while I had the gates closed and the guard doubled. Finally they came to council and I settled the matter peacefully, and all were satisfied.

The Rev. Father Marest and Maurice had chosen their time badly and given bad advice to these poor people who would have fallen victims to their passions if I had not set matters right. The

of any arrangement with the Outaouas; on this point we do not listen to the Governor, nor to you either. If he were to give us all the goods in Quebec and Montreal, we should refuse them. (I very much doubt this, however.) We beg you to join your forces to ours. We have been killed for trying to keep your fort alive, and to avenge you. Mons. de Bourgmont had no powder, we gave him ours, for your defence. We will not have peace; that must not be spoken of; if you make peace with the Outaouas, we shall think bad thoughts. That is, in plain English, that if I make peace with the one set, I shall very likely have war with the other; but nothing can confound me, I shall succeed in my purpose but not without difficulty.

I have replied to them as follows.— We have been struck by the same hand. I will not make war in your way. I will make it in mine. You go in small parties and put small kettles on the fire often. But for my part I declare to you Hurons, Miamis, Onyatanous, Chavanons and Iroquois who hear my words, I will boil up only one big pot that I may plunge all the Outaouas in it at once. Hearken to me. If they discover our approach and take to flight, they will be unable to sow their corn; if they have already sown, we will ravage their crops. The Governor will not give them any powder; and those people will not be able to live by their bows and arrows, and are dead men without it costing you the loss of a single man. If they stand firm in their village and fortify themselves, I promise you to set fire to the palisade and get you in. I will myself be at the head of the French and your warriors, and I promise you not to let one Outaouas remain on the face of the earth.

Since that time we have had to pass day and night in council, and I am overwhelmed with it. I know not how I can ever find time to write you such

The scheme of warfare against the Outaouas, which the Sr. de la Mothe frames, is very good if its success were as easy. There is no doubt that the Outaouas would be unable to resist an army of 800 men, coming to fall upon them suddenly. But it is necessary to get them together for that purpose, for M. de la Mothe at the time he writes this letter, has only 75 savages altogether at his post, according to a letter from the Sr. de la Forest of the same date as his. He must get provisions and build boats, all without being perceived. After that he must go to Mishilimakina; and as that is 100 leagues from Detroit, at a point at the mouths of two great lakes, it is almost impossible to get there without being discovered. What are you to do then? If you have less than 800 or 1,000 men, they will keep on the defensive and laugh at you, and will prevent your disembarkation. If you go with men enough to overpower them what will your success be? It will be the success we had in the campaigns against the Sonnontouans and the Onnontaguez. They will burn their villages themselves and retire inland with their women and old men, whence they will

Nothing is more natural, nothing more necessary than not to allow the act of the Outaouas to go unpunished. It is a matter of importance to the French nation to expect vengeance for it, but the Sr. de la Moth's proposal is ill-timed. Le Pesant and three or four others must be put to death. For that purpose we must get hold of them; and we shall never do so unless we sow dissension among them, which can only be done by exciting jealousy between one part of them and another. It was with this object that Mons. de Vaudreuil began to act this year on Companissé who, being full of energy and finding that he is esteemed by the young men, and by the French, will keep his word and, in spite of the Outaouas who have come from Detroit, will send all the French people down or will at least divide the village; he assured Monsieur de Vaudreuil of that when he left. What Monsieur de Vaudreuil said to Miscouaky, brother of Jean le Blanc, was also said with the same purpose. Jean le Blanc is the only man who can openly oppose Le Pesant. Monsieur de Vaudreuil would not accept his submission through his brother, but neither would he take from him all hope of returning, for his object was, not only to separate the Outaouas chiefs of Michilimakina from those who came from Detroit, but also Jean le Blanc from Le Pezant. If this plan succeeds it is the only one by which we can obtain satisfaction from Le Pezant; for, but for that, the Outaouas will never abandon their chiefs, and so long as they are united, to ask that one of them should be put to death is to ask that the whole tribe should be destroyed. This act must not however be left unpunished; and if the Outaouas do not begin this year to return all our French people, Monsieur de

makina and to form a party of three hundred men, and they ask me to join them with a hundred Frenchmen. I have put off this party till next spring when they have decided to march with eight hundred men.

It is for you, Sir, to consider what you must do. You have time enough to let us hear from you by sending me your orders promptly in the autumn by a small boat which will hold on as long as it can, and if the winter overtakes it, the men can come by land.

My opinion is that we must not leave this action unpunished. I believe it will be necessary in order to settle everything peaceably, to shoot Le Pezant and three or four others, and to pardon the rest of the tribe. This punishment will make the chiefs of all the tribes wiser and more prudent, for they are the originators of the wrong that is done and of their [?the savages] disobedience. Besides Le Pezant is an old man, and his missionary will pray for him after his death, and will give him absolution if he asks for it.

I should have sent a strong boat with some men to inform you of all that has taken place here, so that you might take whatever steps you thought necessary, but the soldiers who were sent by Mons. de Bourgmont, as well as my correspondents at Montreal, had assured me that no one took any trouble to send them back nor to find a boat for them; and that, at least, it was necessary to supply them with one at my expense and even to advance them money. If you do not give me a definite assurance, Sir, that in future the parties I sent to inform you of what takes place within your command will be paid for by the King, I hope you will be pleased to content yourself with receiving news from me

it is almost impossible for him to write otherwise. He complains that his men are kept when he sends any one down here. Mons. de Vaudreuil's letters prove the contrary, for the boat sent by the Sieur de Bourgmont arrived at Montreal on the 26th of June and returned on the 3rd of July, the men having asked for this time to rest; yet the Sieur de la Mothe imprudently says that he will send no more, because no trouble is taken to send them back again. It is the same with all the Sieur de la Mothe's statements. Monsieur de Vaudreuil begs that the Comte de Pontcharatrain will observe this conduct and that of the Sieur de la Mothe, regarding the post of Detroit, and hopes that he will do him justice. The remainder of this letter consisting of points which concern Monsieur Raudot, or such as can only be settled by the Comte de Pontchartrain himself, Monsieur de Vaudreuil will not reply to them.

that you will be good enough to speak to the Intendant on three matters; the first, that I should be paid for the boat which the soldiers sent by M. de Bourgmont, took at Montreal, which they have made almost unfit for use. The second, that I should be supplied with a boat in place of that furnished by me (which was quite new) for conveying the 800 # of powder and 300 # of bullets which the Intendant issued for the defence of the Fort, and other occasions. The third, to let me decide on the reckoning with the soldiers. Since when has the soldier had only 3s for his food? Since the 1st of January this year, and it has not been at the same rate within the last ten years.

Why does not the Intendant undertake the supply of food to the troops in this garrison at the Quebec rate, as he maintains that I should do? Have I not made him the offer? Why has he refused to do so? Next year also I shall be very much pleased if he will accept it, I ask nothing better. It is so great a difficulty to me that I know of none greater, and it is the only trouble I have here.

I do not bind myself to discount with the soldiers at the same rate as they did four days ago, so to speak, at Quebec. If the Intendant were informed that the fat that is given to the soldiers, being better than bacon fat, is worth fifteen sols per pound, he would not decide so hastily as to the soldiers' discount. In a word, if he thinks the thing possible, he has only to do it; I agree to it most heartily. For when I undertook to feed the men for their pay, it was only to remove the objections which might have been made. I cannot but believe that you will, with the Intendant, pay attention to my requests and that you will be good enough to grant them.

I give you notice that the Hurons and Miamis are about to go on the road to Michilimackina to pillage any Frenchmen who go to that place, so as to pre-

there. Lastly, Sir, the acts of the Outaouas are of importance; you are well-informed and know the interests and the customs of the tribes, consider what you wish me to do. I beg you to allow M. Riverin a merchant of Quebec, and M. Hardouin of Montreal to send necessary articles to me and to the officers by such persons as they propose to you; also to permit those who wish to come and settle here to do so. But, as you are usually at Quebec, I also beg you, Sir, to give orders to Mons. de Ramezay on this matter, that this post may not suffer by the delay. Permit me to take the liberty of subscribing myself with very deep interest, Sir, your very humble and most obedient Servant.

My wife and daughter are most grateful for the honor of your remembrance of them; they present their very humble respects to you and to Mme. de Vaudreuil.

Mons. de Boucherville has requested me to ask you to be good enough to permit him to go down if his father wishes him to do so in order to help him; and to say that Mons. de Niverville, his brother, will come and take his place. For my part I shall be quite satisfied with that.

Since I had the honor of giving you a list of the soldiers who had deserted from the detachment at La Chine or Montreal, the man La Roche of St. Ours' company has deserted at the Cascades. He has carried off all his provisions and one of the King's axes. He is married

tion.[1] He replied that that was not just, and that the loss would be borne by the King, up to three months' pay. I hope therefore that he will allow them to me. Desmarests de St. Martin has been drowned. Savoyarde de Demay has been killed. As regards provisions, they had them at La Chine, and took them with them when they deserted. That was so much lost, but I am sure the Intendant will allow me for them; you know well that it is impossible to arrange differently. We have no ration officer on journeys of this sort.

Signed
Lamothe Cadillac.

TALK OF MARQUIS DE VAUDREUIL WITH THE SONNON-TOUANS.

Words of the Sonnontouans with the replies of the Marquis de Vaudreuil, annexed to the letter of the 4th Sept. 1706.

Replies of the Marquis de Vandreuil to the four Iroquois tribes on the 25th of August, 1796.

Words of the Sonnoutouans to the Marquis de Vaudreuil on the 23rd of August 1706.

First Belt.

I am very glad, my children, that you have not forgotten what I said last year to the Outaouas in your presence. I am still of the same mind.

First Speech.

Behold I have come here my father, with four tribes of the Iroqouis, to tell you we have not forgotten what you said to the Outaouas last year in our presence. You told them, O our father, that you were displeased with them, and that you had been, as it were, obliged to buy back the prisoners they had made at Fort Frontenac and elsewhere. You also told them that, if it ever happened that they attacked your children again, you would abandon them. I am very glad, my father, to show you that I have not forgotten your words.

[1]This is a literal translation of the original. It probably means that the soldier's pay would cease upon his death or desertion and that if advances were made to a soldier by Cadillac and the soldier should die or desert before making repayment, the advances would never be made good.—C. M. B.

Second Belt.

You are right to say that my fire is alight from here to Detroit, it is alight also among all the tribes which harken to my word. And I have learnt, as you have, that the Outaouas of Detroit, in attacking the Miamis and the Oniatanous, have slain a missionary and a soldier of mine. I am indebted to you for the feelings you show towards me; but as I am the father of you all, I am surprised that you should take up the axe against those who have attacked me without learning my will first. I am also surprised that you are unwilling for me to say anything as to the resolve you have formed. The Outauoas of Detroit have offended against me, and I am determined to take vengeance on them. But I want to know first how these things took place. Listen then well, as you have done hitherto; I am going to tell you my will. Remember that you have given six-and-twenty men to the man whom I have sent to Detroit, and they must be witnesses of what will take place there. I stay your axe until you and I are informed of everything; and there is my son Joncaire whom I am sending after you, and he shall tell you my final opinions, according to the manner in which the Outaouas of Detroit have behaved. In the meantime make no movement without learning my will.

Third belt by four slaves.

You have thanked me for having got back your kinsmen out of the hands of the Outaouas of Mishilimakina. It was a pleasure to me to give you, by that

Second Belt.

My father, your fire is alight from here even to Detroit. You know, as we do, that the Outaouas a little while ago killed a Recollet, a soldier and some Miamis and Oniatanous there. Remember, O our father what you said to them last year. Abandon the Outaouas to us, and hold us back no longer; our warriors are all ready. Make us no further reply, for we have already made up our minds; and the words which we bring you here we are making known at the same time to our brothers the English. It is thus a settled matter; make us no further reply.

Third Belt.

We come here, my father, not only to speak to you on business but also to thank you for the kindness you have shown us in keeping your promise to us,

came to bring me these four slaves which I give you, and assured me that neither he nor any of them at Mishilimakina had any share in what has taken place at Detroit, and that he would bring me next year, without fail, the remainder of the slaves he had promised you. Hence although difficulties have arisen at Detroit, I stay your axe as regards Mishilimakina, until they have had time to keep their word, or I have had time to withdraw the missionaries and French people I have there. After that I will let you know my will. Meanwhile as I do not wish to hide anything from you, I will show you at the conclusion of the Council what Campanissé and Le Brochet told me, with my replies.

Fourth Belt.

I thank you my children for sharing my grief concerning what took place at Detroit and my losing a missionary and a soldier there. I receive your present as a proof of your affection and, until my son Joncaire goes, on my behalf, to mourn on your mats your loss of the wide lands at Menade, I give you powder and bullets so that you can defend yourselves if you are attacked in returning; and I also give you tobacco that you may smoke in peace on your mats, until we are informed on all matters.

Fourth Belt by a dressed skin and some other skins.

The Outaouas of Detroit, O our father, have befouled your garments; they are still all stained with blood. Here are a dressed skin and some other skins which we give you to cover your dead, for it would be disgraceful for children to have no share in the grief of their father.

Fifth Belt.

A few days ago a number of Frenchmen passed by our village on their way to Detroit by your orders. The commander asked me for some men to escort them, and we said that he should wait for us at Lake Erie, and that we would be witnesses of what took place at Detroit. We sent him six and twenty men under the command of one Touatacoute by name, one of our chiefs.

Sixth Belt.

I have no doubt, my father that you are surprised at seeing such a large number of warriors here, escorting a

sary because of the fear we felt lest the ·
Outaouas should insult us in their
usual manner. We beg you, O our father,
to give us powder and bullets that we
may defend ourselves in case of attack
as we return.

SPEECH OF MISCOUAKY, CHIEF OF THE OUTAOUAS TO MAR-QUIS DE VAUDREUIL.

Endorsed—26th of Sept. 1706.

The words of Miscouaky, brother of Jean le Blanc chief of the Outa-oüas at Detroit, who came down from Michilimakina with Maurice Menard, to the Marquis de Vaudreuil on the 26th of September, 1706.

You will be surprised, My Father, at the evil matters I am about to inform you of, on behalf of Le Pezant and Jean le Blanc, concerning what has taken place at Detroit. I beg you my Father to open your door to me as to one of your children and to listen to what I have to say to you.

When I set out from Michilimakina, my Father, our old men did not think I should come so far as here, hoping you would still be at Montreal. I have but a short time left in which I can return; I beg you, my Father, graciously to hear me.

All the tribes of the Outavois that were at Detroit, the Kikakou, the Sinagault, and the Sand tribe, have been attacked; and the remnant which has got back to Michilimakina, has returned there in the last stage of wretchedness. It is the Miamis, my Father, who have fallen upon us.

The reason which compelled us to fight with the Miamis was that after we had set out on the war-path against the Sioux, in accordance with what we had told the Sr. de Bourmont, we were warned by a Poutouat-amis, who had encamped near the fort of the Hurons, that the Miamis at Detroit had resolved to let us go. and get three days on our march, and after that they would attack our village and destroy our women and children.

a Poutouamis called*   , who is married to a Miamis woman,
that the Miamis were to devour our village. On this news, my Father,
as we had already set out, the war chiefs of the three Outavois tribes
held a council and came to the conclusion that they ought not to give any
decision in a matter of this importance without the consent of Le Pezant
and Jean le Blanc their principal chiefs, whom they sent for at once.
When Le Pezant and Jean le Blanc had arrived, Le Pezant, after he had
heard the news which had been told us by the man called*............,
decided, stamping with his feet that since the Miamis had resolved to fall
upon us and boil us in their pot, we must be beforehand with them.

When Le Pezant said we must attack, we all saw clearly,—Jean le
Blanc, first of all,—that he was going to do a wrong act, but no one dared
to speak against it, both on account of his influence and because we should
thereby have exposed ourselves to the scorn of the young men.

My Father, my brother and I said at the time, what is Le Pezant thinking of to attack while our people are divided? We have some at war with
the Hurons, we have some at Montreal; what will the commandant at
Detroit say on seeing us fighting at his door?' This we said to Le Pezant,
but he would not listen to us; it is he, my Father, who is the cause of all
the evil that has happened.

Jean le Blanc, my Father, would have come here with me. but he was
despoiled of everything and dared not come like a beggar, and he told me
to come and learn your opinion. He would have come, my Father; but in
accordance with our custom, whenever we have engaged in war, being
at Detroit, he put all his belongings in the hands of the Sr. de Bourmont,
thinking they would be safer even than in our fort, and they have all
remained there in consequence of the troubles which have befallen us
since our departure to go to war with the Sioux. He had not come, my
Father, and all I can do is to offer you a belt on behalf of my tribe, which
is all that I have, which I also draw from my bag on purpose.

According to the decision we had come to, to attack the Miamis, we
took our way back to our fort; and, just as we came near to the fort of
the Hurons, we found eight Miami chiefs who were going there to a
feast. As we met them, Le Pezant said to us "There are our enemies:
these are the men who want to kill us, for it is they who command the
others; we must rid ourselves of them." On that he uttered a cry to
serve as a signal, encouraging us not to let one of them escape. The first
time no one moved; but Le Pezant having uttered a second cry, just as we
were walking on both sides of the road while they were in the middle,
they were fired at and only Pacamakona escaped, who withdrew to the
French fort. I venture to tell you something, my Father, which I have
not told anyone,—that, as he was a great friend of mine I signed to him

After those had been killed our young men began running to carry off whatever might remain in the huts; and as Le Pezant and Jean le Blanc could not go as fast as the others, I was one of the first who got there, so as to prevent any misunderstanding from arising between the French and us, as the Miamis were encamped near their fort. On my arrival I found that the Miamis had withdrawn into the fort of the French, and that one of our young men was killed, who had been recognized as a chief two days before; while our young men in despair at his death were determined to burn the fort. I threw myself into their midst and wrested from several of them the arrows, on which they had put [du toudre*] to carry out their purpose, showing them that they must not do harm to the French who were not at all included in the quarrels we had with the Miamis. While this was going on I heard a voice shouting that "the yellow robe had been seized." I ran there and saw my brother, who was sending the Recollet Father back to the fort, having unbound him and begged him to tell the Sr. de Bourmont not to fire on us, and not to give the Miamis any ammunition, but to put them out of his fort and let us alone. We did not know until next day, my Father, that the Recollet Father and the French soldier had been killed, for those who had fired at them did not boast of it. Then I reproached my brother severely for not having kept the Recollet Father, and he gave me, as his reasons for not doing so, that he thought he was doing well, and that he did not think he was safe at our fort because our young men were excited by the death of the chiefs whom we had lost.

Next day, my Father, my brother took a flag which you had given him, and we asked to speak to the Sr. de Bourmont, requesting that arms should be laid down on both sides, so that we might be able to explain matters to each other. He told us that he had no answer to make to us, but that the S. de la Forest, whom he had been expecting since the early

listen to us, putting us off always until the Sr. de la Forest arrived. Yet we had sure proofs that he desired to fight, for he uncovered his houses and fixed swords on the ends of poles. We continued for some time to hold conferences with him, and we went into the fort of the Hurons without fear, always reckoning them among our allies, but we never went except by boat, for fear of the Miamis.

My Father, the Hurons called the Sinago Outaouas and said to them: "My brothers, we have been brothers for a long time and have fought together against the Iroquois. In speaking to you, I speak to all the tribes of the Outavois, to the Poutouatamis, the Sakis the Sauteurs, and the Mississaquez. Here is a belt, my brothers which I produce to show to you; our old men have preserved it for a long time; six men have labored at this belt; this belt, my brothers, signifies many things, it never appears except when we wish to grant life, or deal death to those to whom we are speaking. I put it up again, and tell you on behalf of the French that they invite you to a feast; it will not be held in our dwellings as that might inspire you with fear, it shall be held in this meadow near here, where the French flag will be hoisted; it is there that you shall come to the feast.

On the morrow, which was the day on which the feast was to be held, Jean le Blanc, as his waste lands were close to the place where the flag was set up, came and walked there and saw a number of Frenchmen bringing Indian corn and spreading it on sail-cloths which had been stretched out in the meadow, the Huron women were doing the same,— bringing Indian corn also and spreading it on the sail-cloths. Thereupon my brother believed that the Hurons had told the truth, and flattering himself that we were going to arrange matters satisfactorily; but, Le Pezant having joined him, they both reflected that, as the French had never been willing to speak to them, it might well be that, under the guise of this feast, the Hurons wished to betray them and to make it easy for the Miamis to attack them. While the women and children went for Indian corn, they determined to send to find out, and despatched four young men, who returned and reported that they had seen several trails entering into the woods and seeming to surround those who were to go for Indian corn. As some of our men had already started, we recalled them, seeing clearly that it was a snare that had been spread for us; and we knew henceforth that the scheme of the French and the Miamis, as well as the Hurons, was, that as soon as we had left our fort to go for the Indian corn which was upon the sail-cloths, where they believed we should go in large numbers, when they knew that we had done [so], the greater part of the Miamis and Hurons, who had gone into the depths of the woods, should come and take the fort, and that the rest of the

pose among the corn opposite the place where the flag was, should come and fall upon us.

As we had recalled our people, and no one went for the Indian corn, they were all of them much mistaken; and the Miamis who had gone into the woods, believing that at least a large part of our men had gone out of our fort, came with loud shouts to take it. Our young men who were in the bastions descried them from afar and we fired at each other all day long, and we lost one of our men, who was shot through an opening in the wall. In the evening the Miamis retired while we were unable to learn how many of their men we had killed. In retiring they met the man Catalibona and his brother, whom they killed, and scalped.

When the Miamis attacked our fort they took the precaution to separate into two parties, and, one of them being kept by the water's edge, they cast adrift as many of our boats as possible, in order to deprive us, in that way, of the means of escaping.

Next day, my Father, we knew for certain that the Hurons had joined the Miamis. They came together to attack our fort; and, on that day a man of much importance among the Miamis, who had escaped us on the previous day, was killed.

The next day they came back again to attack us, and the Hurons began to shout insults at us, calling out that we were nothing but women; that apparently we had no more powder left as we dared not fire any more; that we should get still less henceforward since Onontio had abandoned us, and had indeed done so for a long time past. It was the brother of Quarente Sols who said that to us. Thereupon our young men, angry at the insults the Hurons addressed to us, made a sortie, and we fought outside, against them and the Miamis; the Hurons stood their ground a long time, but the Miamis turned tail; there were four hundred of them.

That very day one of our men, who had been on the war path with the Hurons against the Flatheads, arrived at our fort, and told us that the others who had set out with them, and had all returned, lay bound in the French fort and that it was the Hurons who had bound them, and that

to us a place within gun-shot of the French fort where they fixed up poles, enjoining us to take presents there commensurate with the favor they were doing us. Our men, believing they were acting in good faith, returned there and, everyone having done his utmost, even the necklaces of our children were brought. Hardly had they placed on the poles ten beautiful porcelain necklaces, twenty kettles, two parcels of beaverskins, and in fact all they had brought, when, even while Quarente Sols was giving his hand to Jean le Blanc, Jean le Blanc was shot. At the same time they fired from the fort on all our men who, as they had gone in confidence and without arms, counting on the good faith of the French, were compelled to take flight. The Hurons and the Miamis having sallied forth, the remainder of the men in our fort came to the relief of those who were in flight, and the rest of the day passed in fighting on both sides. By this treachery we lost two men killed on the spot by the fire from the French fort, and five wounded.

The last attack, my Father, which was made upon us by the Miamis, was made in our waste lands by some young men. They killed one woman on the spot and took another prisoner; and when we sent afterwards to learn what they were doing with her, our people heard her cries from the French fort where she was being burned.

Hunger, and the toils of war, compelled our people to send Onabemamtou, one of our chiefs, to speak to the Oniatanous; formerly the Oniatanous had danced a calumet dance of peace with him; our people employed this man to go and speak with the Miamis. He said to them, my Father, that the Oniatanous had treated us like sons by dancing this calumet dance, my Father. "I am surprised that you continue so long to slay us around our palisade. Are you not weary of slaying us and of being slain yourselves? Have you no pity on your young men?" The Oniatanou replied that it was not they who did that, but the Hurons and the French who wanted to make them remain there until the autumn, so as to cause the Outavois to perish of hunger in their fort. And as the Oniatanous, after this parley resolved to return home, the slaves were divided; two of our men were given to the Oniatanou, two to the tribe of La Grüe, who are Miamis from the St. Joseph River, one was burnt in the French fort, and another shot, while the son of Koutache, a Mississaguez was granted his life by the intervention of the French commandant. There is one of our men, married to a Loup woman, whom we have no news of; the Sr. de la Mothe has sent back the other two to the Missisaguez. That is all that I know, my Father; and the old men have charged me to tell you that after all the treachery with which the Hurons have treated them, they will have great difficulty in preventing their young men from going on the war-path against them as long as they remain at Detroit, from which place we have withdrawn only so that we may no longer be exposed to it.

escaped on the way and have come to rejoin our people, and have told them that they have not been ill-treated by the Onitanous. They report that the Miamis lost fifty in killed and wounded; and we lost twenty-six, including the men who returned from war, whom the Hurons bound treacherously.

My Father, I speak in the names of all the Outavois tribes, the Poutou-atamis the Sakis, the Outagamis, the Mastrowtins, the Kikapous, the Ouinipigos [?Winnipegs], the Malominys, the Sauteurs, the Mississa-guez, all the people of the districts bordering on the lake; finally all our allies are indignant against the Hurons because of their treachery to us. They all beg you, by my mouth, to let us fight against them. I pray you, my Father, to tell me your opinion that I may tell it to our people and that we may do naught but your will.

REPLIES OF M. DE VAUDREUIL TO MISCOUAKY, CHIEF OF THE OUTAOUAS.

Endorsed—Reply of M. de Vaudreuil to the chief of the Outaouas annexed to the letter of the 4th Nov., 1706.

Replies of the Marquis de Vaudreuil to Miscouaky, brother of Jean le Blanc chief of the Outaouas who were at Detroit, on the 28th of Sept. 1706.

I have listened quietly, Miscouaky, to all you have told me; and al-though I had already been informed of what took place at Detroit, I was surprised nevertheless at the account you gave me of it. I cannot give you a reply, for it does not appear to me that you have been sent by all the tribes, as you say you were, but only by your brother Jean le Blanc to sound me as to my opinion, and the proof of that is that you set out from Michilimakina with the intention of staying down here, and that it is only your brother's arrival which has made you desirous of going up again. However that may be, I am not sorry to have seen you, and I am very glad of what you have told me concerning your brother's conduct.

You wish to know my opinion, Miscouaky, you have begged me to tell

have always looked upon as my children, coming here to acknowledge their guilt and to ask for my pardon. I cannot forget that I lost a missionary and a soldier at Detroit, which is a matter of importance with us. That is what you may tell your brother and all the tribes from me, when you arrive there.

I have seen and examined the message which you have given me; as you have told me yourself that it was a belt which you had drawn from your bag, and that your people had not given you any when you set out, I return it to you and cannot receive it. Not that I scorn it because it comes from you, but I cannot answer it because it does not come directly from them; and I am very glad to return it to you, as a thing which belongs to you, in order that you may make use of it in arranging any troubles which may arise.

As regards what has taken place at Detroit, you will tell your people that I stay their axes and forbid them to go to war, whether against the Hurons, or the Miamis, or elsewhere; but that I order them to stand solely on the defensive at their homes until I am more fully informed of all matters. I am expecting news immediately from M. de la Mothe, and I will consider, during the winter, all that you have told me and the information he sends me, so that I may be able to arrange matters, if the account you have given me is true. And as in consequence of the troubles you have caused, it is impossible for you to go very far away for hunting this winter, your people will be able to come down here early, together with the French people I have up there, to learn my opinion. That is what they ought to have done this year, instead of sending you alone, and without a belt, on behalf of all the tribes.

It is not belts that I require, Miscouaky, nor presents. When my children have disobeyed me and have committed such a fault as yours; the blood of Frenchmen is not to be paid for by beaverskins. It is a great trust in my kindness that I demand, a real repentance for the fault that has been committed, and complete resignation to my will. When your people entertain these feelings I will arrange everything; but, for that purpose, they must come early next spring, or at least some of the chiefs must come; they must bring me all the French people, who must be assisted by your young men to bring down their furs; lastly, they must remain at peace on their mats, and not go to war either against the Miamis, or to the Hurons or elsewhere, but must remain simply on the defensive and not go to war even if any should come and attack them in their dwellings, contenting themselves with acting on the defensive until next year, and with coming to lay their complaints before me. That, Miscouaky, is my decision; that is what you may say from me to all the tribes.

I do not give you any present for your brother or for any of your chiefs, for it is not right that I should reward children as long as they are in a

have taken, and the trust you have reposed in me; I will give you a
blanket, a shirt of Mitasse, some powder, bullets and tobacco to spur you
on to use diligence in returning; and I shall have regard to you
according to your conduct up there, of which Father Marais will send me
word; and it rests with you alone to have proofs of my favor when you
return with the others.

AMOUNTS EXPENDED FOR THE KING'S SERVICE BY CADILLAC.

Endorsed—29th Sept., 1706.

Statement of sums spent for the King's service by Monsieur de la Mothe
in order to prevent the Miamis, Pepitakokia and Onyatonuns from going
to war against the Outavois this winter, and to prevent the tribe of the
Pchaugnissa from going to attack the Iroquois.

Three belts at 20#[1] each............................... #60:

Two hundred livres of powder at 4# per#.............. 800:

Six guns with their cases at 36# each.................. 216:

Thirty livres of tobacco at 40s. per livre................ 60:

Fifteen ounces of vermilion—total.................... 46:

Given to Quarante Sols, Chief of the Hurons, sent with
  Mons. Boucherville to support the orders of Mons. de la
  Mothe; ten livres of powder at 4# per livre........... 40:

A fine shirt with ruffles.............................. 12:

A red coat ornamented with imitation gold lace.......... 45:

1 linen bag to hold powder............................ 1:

A barrel of brandy holding 4 pots at 20# a pot.......... 80:

Given to Pakoumakouá, chief of the Miamis, to go with
  Mons. de Boucherville to support the orders of Mons.
  de la Mothe; ten livres of powder at 4# per livre...... 40:

Five livres of bullets at 40s. per #................... 10:

Two linen bags for the bullets and powder, at 20s. each... 2:

Given to Mons. de Boucherville for his journey with four
  soldiers, to go and carry the orders of the M. de la

Four roe-buck skins for making saddles for the soldiers
at 50s. each; total................................. #10:
Two livres of tobacco at forty sols a #................ 4:
Forty gun-flints 2:
One boat—total one hundred livres................... 100:
One sail made of six ells of Mélis* cloth for............. 30:
Tackle for the sail................................... 1:
Three linen bags to hold powder, bullets and lead........ 3:
A copper-kettle weighing five livres at six francs per #... 30:
One large axe.. 10:
1# of tobacco at 40s................................. 2:
1 barrel to hold powder for their journey............... 2:
One sponge 5:
Given to Pipouhet, a Loup Indian, who is going with M.
Boucherville to serve as interpreter, one gun and its
case, value 36 Livres................................ 36:
10 livres of powder at four francs per #................ 40:
A bag to hold the said powder......................... 1:
One ounce of vermilion............................... 3:2s.:6d.

                                        _____

            Total................................#1,931:2s.:6d.

We the undersigned certify that M. de la Mothe, Commandant, on behalf of the King of Detroit, Pontchartrain has spent the sums stated
above, and on the other side, as set down, for the service of the King,
and that the goods included in this statement are reckoned and priced
at the current values at the said place; given at Fort Pontchartrain this
29th Sept. 1706. And after that is written, We Antoine de la Mothe
Cadillac, commandant of Fort Pontchartrain, certify what is contained
above to be true; given on the day and year as above.

> (Signed) Lamothe Cadillac; De la Forest; Derané; Boucherville;
> Dufiguier; Brother Dominique de Lamarche, Lecturer
> in Theology and missionary of the said fort; and
> Grandmenil.

                            _____

MEMORIAL OF THE S. DE LA MOTHE CADILLAC, WITH THE REPLIES OF M. DE VAUDREUIL IN THE MARGIN.

Endorsed—Annexed to the letter of the 30th Oct. 1706.—

To the Marquis De Vaudreuil, Knight of the military order of St.
Louis, the Governor-General of all New France.

_____

*Sail cloth manufactured at Mélis.

As you would not give any decision on all my verbal requests as to matters concerning the establishment of Fort Pontchartrain at Detroit,

and have instructed me to prefer them to you in writing, I have complied with that, since you wish it.

I very humbly beg you, in conjunction with the Intendants, to grant me six of the King's boats to help me to take the soldiers up to La Gallette. or even to Niagara if necessary, as these boats were built solely to carry troops from one post to another. I have reason to hope that you will give me this assistance, which has very often been granted to officers, soldiers and settlers for their private needs, such as to convey corn, stone, hay &c. The late Monsieur de Callieres granted some to the Directors to go up to Niagara, to take my wife and family and that of Monsieur de Tonty there. This request is in accordance with one of the paragraphs in the letter to Monseigneur de Pontchartrain the terms of which are as follows:—"Besides that, His Majesty directs MM. de Vaudreuil and Beauharnois to give all the help and encouragement which lies in their

power."

As it is absolutely necessary for the security of Fort Pontchartrain to have two hundred soldiers there, including sergeants and upper grades, I very humbly beg you to grant me this number. This is in accordance with the order from the Court in these words:—"His Majesty enjoins Monsieur de Vaudreuil to give you as many soldiers as you ask for;" and in another paragraph is said: "I have informed you above that Monsieur de Vaudreuil will give you as many soldiers as you wish."

I also beg you to allow me to choose them, and to take those who are most favorably disposed. Two strong reasons compel me to prefer this request. The first is that even the best soldiers are scarcely good enough for taking up the boats, because of the difficulties of the route, which you know yourself; so that if I were obliged to take men who were unskilful or unwilling to go, that would mean incurring a real risk of losing all our warlike stores, our arms, and baggage; and would also be a very certain way of causing this settlement to fail. Moreover it is the in-

those who are willing to come, by mutual consent, whom I shall have the
honor to name to you at the time.

I may also add that Monseigneur does me the honor to write me that
the King directs you to allow all who wish to go and settle at Detroit to
do so. That being so, I beg you to decide this point in order to enable
me to give definite assurances to those who are now presenting themselves,
and those who may hereafter do so.

Since it is necessary for me to go to Montreal to get ready all the
vehicles and equipment required for the success of this undertaking, I
beg you to be good enough to decide as to my requests as promptly as
possible, so that all the equipment may be ready as soon as navigation is
open, and I may be able to repair to my post with diligence.

Presented on the 27th of January, 1706.

Signed Lamothe Cadillac.

---

¹REPLY TO THE MEMORIAL . OF .THE SR. DE LA MOTHE CADILLAC.

Endorsed—annexed to the letter of the 30th Oct. 1706.

Reply to the memorial presented to us by the Sieur de la Mothe Cadillac on the 18th of the present month.

Since His Majesty, in his memorandum of the 14th of June 1704, orders the Sieur de Beauharnois and me to give the Sieur de la Mothe all the assistance in our power for the establishment of Fort Pontchartrain on the strait ["detroit"] of Lake Erie; and also, if the said Sieur de la Mothe asks us for a larger number of soldiers, he wishes us to give him them provided that he has them conveyed there at his own expense, His Majesty merely having their ordinary pay issued to them.

As His Majesty does not prescribe, in this memorandum, the precise number of men that should be given to the Sieur de la Mothe, but only says "a large number," and the garrison of Detroit consisted of twenty-five men in 1703, concerning which matter this memorandum is a reply,

¹[In pencil "20th of March 1706" at the head of this document.]

yet, in order to conform to His Majesty's intentions, although the interests of his service does not permit us to deprive ourselves altogether of the troops in his service in this country, the said Sieur de la Mothe may count on a hundred and fifty men, including six sergeants and six corporals, as he has requested. And it seems strange to us that the said Sieur de la Mothe appears in doubt as to the number of men we are giving him, after our reply to his memorial of the 27th of January last, and after he set out, in accordance with it, to go to Montreal to see the troops and draw up a list of those who would suit him, in order to receive our final orders. For, to say that it was impossible for him to see the troops, because the soldiers were not with their companies, is an objection without foundation. In the first place, the said Sieur de la Mothe would not see those in the governorship of Montreal, according to the letter of Mons. de Ramezay of the 7th inst.; secondly, MM. de Ramezay and de Crisafix have orders from us to have the soldiers kept with their companies, and not to permit any of them to go away from them without an order in writing signed by us.

As there are twenty-eight companies in this country, and His Majesty's intention is not to break up one company entirely, but only to have detachments formed from each, the Sieur de la Mothe shall have his choice, taking five men from each company who are disposed to go, or on his selection; but only after we have had four taken out of each company whom we have need of for the King's service.

Besides the five men per company, as above, the said Sieur de la Mothe may choose six sergeants and four corporals to his liking out of the companies, to complete the number of a hundred and fifty men, subject to the condition that he may not take more than one of the two sergeants or one of the three corporals from a company.

Orders will be sent to Monsieur de Ramezay, or Monsieur de Crisafix in accordance with this memorandum, when the Sieur de la Mothe applies to us for them; and we declare to him that if his undertaking should fail by reason of delay we shall report it to the Court, and it is for him to use all diligence in the matter.

Given at Quebec this 20th of March 1706.

REPORT OF MARQUIS DE VAUDREUIL, GOVERNOR-GENERAL, REGARDING THE CONDITION OF THE COLONY.

'Endorsed—The Marquis de Vaudreuil, 4th Nov. 1706. Colonies.

My Lord,

I have received the two letters you did me the honor of writing to me on the ninth and twenty-third of June last, and also the one about the Sieur de Montigny; and, after thanking you for all your kindness to me and begging that you will continue it, I hope you will permit me, My Lord, to express my joy that you appear satisfied with the assurance I gave you last year, that I held MM. Raudot, senior and junior, in all possible esteem and regard. I hope, My Lord, that you will be no less content concerning us this year; and, for my part, I cannot be other than well pleased with the obliging behavior of these gentlemen.

* * * *

The portion not here translated is printed in Vol. IX, New York Colonial Documents, page 779.—C. M. B.

You can see, My Lord, from what Miscouaky says to me, that they neither desire peace nor fear war, but that they do not wish for war with us. I am temporizing until next year, not only for all the reasons I have had the honor of giving you above, but also because I have declared to them that I wish to have all the French people back who are up there, and I am very glad therefore to wait until this autumn when they are to come down, either to have a proof, from that, of the obedience of the Outtavois, if they do not retain my people, or if they do keep them, to have a fresh ground for declaring war, such that the other tribes will not be able to complain of it. For you may see, My Lord, from the words of Miscouaky, that we have not only the Outtavois to deal with but also eight or ten tribes of their allies.

I had the honor, My Lord, in 1704, to give you an account of the reasons I had for sending the Sieur de Vinseine to the Miamis is preference to anyone else, because they were very fond of him. In a letter I wrote you at that time, I set forth all the grounds of complaint I had against him, and you were good enough to send us word in the common letter of 1705, that His Majesty had pardoned him on account of what he had done at Detroit where he wrested six Iroquois prisoners by force, from the hands

of Campanisé, Chief of the Outtavois, who had had the audacity to parade
them, bound, in front of the French fort. But since His Majesty wishes
him to be punished this year, I see no course open but to suspend him
from his ensigncy until you are good enough to send us orders regarding
him.

As regards the man Neven, My Lord, it is true that when he arrived
here, some time before the other party, I had him put in prison, acting on
a declaration sent to me from Detroit by the Sr. de Tonty signed by five or
six Frenchmen, in which the said Neven was accused of having taken the
Sieur de Vinseine by the cravat and threatened to strike him after having
repeatedly insulted him; but as far from having kept him in prison
for six months because he gave information of the said Sieur de Vinseine's trading, I released him after a fortnight or three weeks, on being
assured that their quarrel was only on a money matter. If, My Lord, the
meddlesome people who write about these matters would tell them
straightforwardly, as I do, I should not be obliged to defend myself now;
but that is not their disposition. Beginning with ingratitude, it is but
natural that they should end with double dealing and lying.

Allow me, My Lord, to reply to you concerning the Sieur de Louvigny
that he has accomplished his journey with such care and exactitude as
might discredit the prohibitions I had laid upon him. In conjunction
with M. de Ramezay I took steps before his departure to prevent any
infraction of the orders about trading by careful examinations both by
the Sieur d'Aigremond at La Chine and by the Sieur de Beaubasin twenty
leagues above the town of Montreal, where the latter was to escort the
Sieur de Louvigny. These two gentlemen are both relatives of M. de
Ramezay, and were chosen and nominated by him. I can assure you, My
Lord, that at the present delicate juncture of affairs I had need of a man
with as much influence over the savages as the Sieur de Louvigny, and
knowing how to influence the minds of the Outtavois as he does, in order
to make them give up the Iroquois prisoners and give satisfaction for
those they have killed. They have told me they will do so, My Lord, and
if any other critical matter arose, I believe I could not do better than to
make use of him in it. But I protest that if I had known him to be
guilty of any fault I should never have ventured to ask Your Highness to
include him in the list of officers whom you proposed to His Majesty to
be made Knights of Saint Louis. I feel bound, My Lord, to do him justice,

nault,[1]—who is indeed the son-in-law of the Sieur de Lobiniere's second wife, but is not his son-in-law, and even the wife is dead now—is no better founded. It is true that he went up to Michilimakina in 1704 for the Jesuit Fathers, who asked me for his services to take care of their property on the way. He arrived at Michilimakina at the time when the Outtavois were returning from their fine expedition from Fort Frontenac against the Iroquois; and, according to the statement of these same missionaries, wished to sacrifice what little property he had to ransom the prisoners and when he could not procure this from the Outtavois he made them at least agree that in his absence, none of them should be put to death, and came down here with letters from the missionaries to bring us news of this, of which M. de Beauharnois and I had the honor, My Lord, to give you an account, at the time; but as the season was too far advanced for sending the said Arnault back and those who had come down with him, we allowed him to go up again in the summer of 1705 for his belongings. So true is this, My Lord, that I am forwarding to Mme. de Marson, my mother-in-law, the permit which M. de Beauharnois and I issued to him, and she will have the honor of presenting the original of it to you.

I am not speaking to you, My Lord, in favor of the said Arnault. Fortunately for him, in the account I am sending you of what took place at Michilimakinac, I have the honor of forwarding a copy of a letter from Father Marest, the original of which I am sending to Mme. de Marson. You will see, My Lord, from this letter, what sort of a man the said Arnault is, and that what I have the honor of stating to you is true. As regards any differences he may have with the Company I have no intention of justifying him. If he is guilty, it is for the directors, and the Sieur de la Mothe his adversary, to prosecute him. But as far as his departure from Michilimakina is concerned, and his being sent back there by M. de Beauharnois and me, we both acted in that matter only as simple justice compelled us to do.

I confess, My Lord, that the post I have the honor to hold, of Governor

[1]Bertrand Arnault, son of Bertrand Arnault and his wife Marguerite Du Munsay, was born in France and married 1st Jeanne Pellerin at Quebec, Nov. 26, 1685. She died Oct. 9, 1687. A few months later, Jan. 12, 1688, he married Louise De Xaintes at Quebec. It is in connection with this second marriage that reference is made in the report to the statement that Arnault was the son-in-law of Lotbiniere. Françoise Zaché (or Taché or Jaché) was married three times, 1st to Claude De Xaintes, 2d to Antoine Gourdeau and 3d to René Louis Chartier, Sieur de Lotbiniere. Louise De Xaintes was a daughter of the first marriage.

René Louis Chartier, Sieur de Lotbiniere, a member of the Council, was born in 1642 and died June 4, 1709. In 1678, Jan. 24, he married Marie Madeleine Lambert. She died Nov. 15, 1695, leaving several children. He married Francoise Zaché, above mentioned, May 16, 1701 and she died Oct. 24, 1718.

In the above report Vaudreuil states that the mother of Arnault's wife is dead. This was not a fact if the records of Tanguay are to be relied upon. I am unable to ascertain the date of the death of Louise de Xaintes. Her youngest child was

General of this country, does not permit me to remain unaware of anything which takes place here; but there are a thousand things which may
not come to my knowledge for which I am in no way responsible. All
that I can assure Your Highness is that I understand perfectly well how
to secure obedience without too much severity and without any weakness.
In the difficulty at Montreal in 1704, I believe, My Lord, I discharged my
duty thoroughly satisfactorily. For, as soon as I learnt that the inhabitants had held a meeting, I proceeded there in spite of the severity of
the weather; and if I did not make examples harshly, several reasons
withheld me from doing so. The first, My Lord, was that the Sr. de
Bellemont, Superior of the Seminary of Montreal, and also M. de Ramezay himself, wrote to me when I had only proceeded thirty leagues from
Quebec that all the people had returned to their obedience, and that want,
and the harshness of some of the merchants rather than any intention of
revolting had compelled them to hold a meeting to demand justice, but
that they had dispersed as soon as they learnt that meetings of this
kind were not permitted. The truth is, My Lord, that we have been too
greatly alarmed, and that the intentions of the people had been judged
of by the reasonable grounds of complaint which they were declared to
have. These I remedied as soon as I arrived, by seeing that justice was
done to them, but also by removing from them the tariff which the caprice
of certain persons, rather than any real reason, had fixed. And if, in order
to publish them, I had proclamation made on all sides, that was only in
order to prevent similar meetings of the inhabitants, and not to grant an
amnesty, being quite persuaded that it appertains to His Majesty alone
to do that. I venture also to tell you, My Lord, that after thoroughly
considering the whole matter, I saw no reason strong enough to admit
of inflicting exemplary punishment: nor could this be done last year,
although, according to some letters, the turbulence was greater then than
the first time. M. Raudot and I had the honor, My Lord, to send you an
account of it in the autumn; and although we have done so this year
we take pleasure in doing so again on this occasion.

I will not say, My Lord, that certain people, by instilling into these
poor wretches whatever ideas they please, induce them to use seditious
language, and then spread abroad rumors which suit the private objects
they have. It is certain, according to the letters from Montreal that they
had everything to fear from an insurrection, if the first affair can pass

down from Montreal were confronted with them, it was never possible, whatever application I made, for any one of them to be punished, or to find any charge strong enough to justify exemplary punishment. We are giving you an account of it in our joint letter; all that I can have the honor of telling you, My Lord, is that neither in the first nor in the second affair did I show any lack of firmness in my action; and that in all I have done, I have acted only as I believed to be demanded by the interests of the King's service. Finally, My Lord, if I made no severe example in the first affair at Montreal, it was because I did not think I ought to make one, and because I believed it to be the part of a Governor, as I am, to sympathise with the wretchedness of the people, rather than to reduce them to the last stage of necessity and despair. Moreover, at the same time, two reasons compelled me to put an end to that trouble; first, that I had news from the savages—as I have already had the honor of telling you—that the English were coming to attack us, by Lake Champlain; secondly, that M. de Beauharnois, and the Sr. de Louvigny who was then in command at Quebec, wrote to me that notes were being circulated, written in a disguised hand and without any signature, to stir up the people, and that some movement was also threatened on the coasts, and the Sieur de Louvigny begged me to send him three companies. This I did not think I ought to do, but when I was sure that the news about the English was false I made the declaration of which you do me the honor to speak; I had justice done to the inhabitants who were aggrieved; I suppressed the tariff, and went down to Quebec where, on my arrival, I found everything calm. And as, My Lord, I never wish to make any statement to you which I cannot prove, I am sending to Mme. de Marsan,[1] my mother-in-law, the originals of two letters from M. de Beauharnois, which she will have the honor of showing you, if you wish.

I had the honor, My Lord, to send you an account last year of the position in which I had placed the affairs of the savages, and of the difficulty there was to keep so many different tribes at peace. As the Sieur de la Mothe was unable to go up to Detroit last autumn, for several reasons which he gave us, of which I had the honor to send you an account, I permitted the Sieur de Bourmont, an ensign, to go there, for whose services he applied to me, until either he or the Sr. de la Forest could proceed there in the early spring; and I ordered the Sieur de Tonty to hand over the command of the post to the said Sieur de Bourmont as soon as he arrived there. While the Sieur de Tonty was at Detroit, My Lord, although he interfered with nothing, all was very quiet there; but when the Sieur de

---

[1]Louis Philippe De Rigault, Seigneur de Vaudreuil married Louise Elizabeth De Joybert at Quebec Nov. 21, 1690. She was a daughter of Pierre Jacques De Joybert de Marsan and his wife Marie Anne Bequart. Madam De Joybert de Marsan was probably visiting in Paris at this date, as her home was in Quebec. —C. M. B.

Bourmont was left alone, whether because the savages had no confidence
in him. or because, being still a young man he could not foresee what
would happen, the Outtavois attacked the Miamis near the palisade of
his fort. I will not tell you the motives of both parties, My Lord, you
were able to see those of the Outtavois from what Miscouaky said to me.
But whatever their motives were, they could never be sufficient for attacking the Miamis at the gate of our fort and killing some of our people. All
I can say is that, as the Sieur de Bourmont had the Recollet Father and
a soldier out of his fort, he might, while giving shelter to the Miamis, have
temporised a little before taking either side, so as to give these two men
time to withdraw either to his fort or that of the Hurons. For it does
not appear to be stated that the Outtavois had any intention, at first, of
firing on the French and taking the fort; it was only the course affairs
took which made them resolve on this, which is none the less criminal for
that, as regards the offence they have committed against us, but yet
admits of explanation. One proof, My Lord, that the Outtavois had no
intention of attacking the French, is that Miscouaky speaks plainly of it;
but a better one is that, even by the confession of the Sieur Bormond
and the report of the soldiers themselves who came down to bring me
news of this. Two days before this affair happened the Outtavois, to the
number of more than a hundred, with their arms passed in front of the
fort when half of the garrison were outside the fort looking at them as
they passed, and they did not offer the slightest insult though nothing
would have been easier than for them to take the fort. I say again, My
Lord, the course of affairs impelled the Outtavois to do what they did.
I do not consider them any the less to blame, whether for having killed
two of our men or for having attacked the Miamis at the gate of our fort.
But what am I to do? Am I to lose the whole of a tribe which was so
attached to us and so useful in the last war, because some of them have
done wrong? And am I, because I have lost a soldier and a missionary
at Detroit, to lose yet another missionary and about fifteen French people
who are at Michilimakina, and were only kept there because news came
that it was the French who had attacked the Outtavois at Detroit, for
they were all on the way with their belongings to come down here when
they were stopped. You will see, My Lord, from my speech to Campanissé how I have spoken to the Outtavois on the subject, and also regard-

lost anyone, we could have constituted ourselves arbiters of the dispute between these two tribes. The Hurons were more politic, for although they have long desired to avenge themselves on the Outtavois, as I have often had the honor to send you word, yet they did not declare themselves until they thought they were able to do so. This you will see, My Lord, from what Miscouaky said to me, and this was also confirmed by a man who came down from Detroit since these late occurrences.

· The Outtavois of Detroit having joined those of Michilimakina, Index lett B. according to a letter I have received from Father Marest, a copy of which I have the honor of sending you, I find myself in a greater difficulty than ever, for I want to withdraw the people I have at Michilimakina, to obtain satisfaction from the Outtavois of Detroit, and not to lose the whole of that tribe if I can help it. It is that which obliged me, My Lord, to reply to Campanissé as I did, and afterwards to Miscouaky; my intention being, after having got my people away, to sow jealousy first between the chiefs of the Outtavois of Michilimakina and those of the Outtavois who have come from Detroit, and secondly to divide the latter also, as I see a good chance of doing if what Miscouaky told me about his brother Jean le Blanc is true. That is the only means remaining to us, My Lord, of obtaining vengeance on the offender who is the only cause of this war; for, as for saying that by sending a large expedition we should compel the Outtavois to give him up to us, that is a thing they will never do unless we first sow dissension among them. I have written according to the Sieur de la Mothe, and told him to remain on the defensive only until next year and that I will acquaint him with my opinion; for, between now and that time, I hope to obtain reparation from the Outtavois, and that I cannot yet give any decision as to that war, until I am certain whether they will send me back my men, or keep them; and also what course the Iroquois will take, to whom I have now sent the Sr. de Joncaire.

I receive, as I ought, My Lord, the assurances you are good enough to give me of your support with His Majesty, and I should never forgive myself if I were to do the least thing which could make me unworthy of it. When I had the honor last year of informing you that Mme. de Vaudreuil had no relatives in this country except her uncle the Sr. de Lotbinier, three cousins, two of whom are in the Church, and three very young female cousins, I thought that would be enough to prevent anyone from being impudent enough to try and impose on you. Yet I see, My Lord, from the letter you do me the honor to write to me, that some one has gone further, for they have thought to get me into a difficulty by assuring you that Madame de Vaudreuil had other relations also, of whom I did not speak to you, as for example her brother's widow, his daughter, and the Sieurs d'Amours, des Chaufours and Deplaine. As regards the widow of the Sieur de Soulange, you know, My Lord, that I have never concealed it from you; for in the same letter in which I speak to you of the Sieur de Lotbiniere and his children, I have the honor of asking you, on behalf of the widow of the Sieur de Soulange, my brother-in-law, for the confirmation of an estate above Montreal, and I ask you for it for her granddaughter who is still only a child of three years of age. Concerning the Srs. d'Amour, Deschaufours[1] and Deplaine,[2] although I feel all the respect for them that one ought to have for very worthy men, yet I venture to assure Your Highness that they are not relatives of Mme. de Vaudreuil, and that I recognize no one as such in this country, except the Sieur de Lotbiniere and his family, the widow of the Sr. de Soulange and her grand-daughter. Not that I scorn the Sieur d'Amour,—for in all their actions they have never done anything but what very worthy men should do; but because that is not so, and Mme. de Marson, my mother-in-law can explain the matter to you. But even if it were true that they were related to Mme. de Vaudreuil, what have I done for them? The Sr. Deschaufours has the honor to serve the King as an ensign in Acadie, and for two years remained a prisoner at Baston; he has only been a director for about a month. As it was on the recommendation of the Sieur Brouillant that you were good enough to grant him this ensigncy, he will no doubt have sent you an account of his conduct. The Sieur de Clignancourt[3] who, according to the certificates he holds from the Sieurs de Villebon and de Brouillant, has always done his duty thoroughly well, both on the St. John River in the last war, where, at the head of some savages, he repulsed the English, and on other occasions in which he has been employed by the Sieur de Brouillant, set out three months ago for Port Royal.seeing that I did nothing here for him.

The Sr. Deplaine, who is the third person spoken of to you, My Lord, is no more fortunate than the others. He served with distinction under M. de Brouillant in the expedition to Newfoundland; he served under his

[1] Louis d'Amours, Sieur des Chaufours, Seigneur de Jernsec was the son of Mathieu D'Amours. He was born May 16, 1655 and married Marguerite Guyon at Quebec Oct. 1, 1686. He died at Annapolis (Port Royal), May 9, 1708.

[2] Bernard d'Amours, Sieur Desplaine et de Fresneuse, was a brother of Louis d'Amours. He was born Dec. 15, 1667 and married 1st Jeanne Le Borgne and 2d Elizabeth Couillard. He died at St. Thomas Dec. 15, 1749.

RECORD OF THE MARRIAGE OF ANTOINE DE LA MOTHE CADILLAC
AND MARIE THERESE GUYON.

(TRANSLATION.)

The 25th of the month of June, in the year 1687, after the betrothment and the publication of two banns of marriage, having obtained dispensation of the third of Monsieur de Bernieres, vicar-general of the Lord Bishop of Quebec, the first being published the 22d and the second the 24th of the present month between Antoine de Lamothe, esquire, Sieur de Cadillac of the village of Port Royal in Acadia, aged about 26 years, son of Mr. Jean de la Mothe, sieur of the place called Cadillac of Launay and Semontel, counsellor of the parliament of Toulouse, and of Madam Jeanne de Malenfant, his father and mother, of the one part; and of Marie Thereze Guyon, daughter of the deceased Denis Guyon, a citizen of this place, and Elizabeth Boucher, her father and mother, of the other part, aged about 17 years, and not finding any hindrance, I, François Dupre, cure of this parish, have solemnly married and given the nuptial benediction in the presence of the subscribing witnesses, Sieurs Berthelmi Desmarest, Michel Denys Guyon, Jacques Guyon, Denys le Maitre, who have signed with the husband and wife.

LAMOTHE LAUNAY.
MARIE THERESE GUYON.
JACQUES GUION.
MICHEL GUION.
DENIS LE MAITRE.

DEMAREST.
FRANCOIS DUPRE.

orders in the last affair with the English at Port Royal; and the only favor he has obtained is that I have permitted him to go and improve the lands which he and his brothers have at Acadie, a favor which I could not have refused him even if I had wished to do so. But after all, My Lord, even if I wished to do something for them, what good could I do them short of taking it out of my own pocket? There are no longer any gratuities which the Governors in this country can dispose of; altogether there is only the nomination to half pay ensigncies that are in the nomination of the Governors-General. And of the seven which have become vacant since I have had the honor to hold that office, to whom have I given them, My Lord? Except one, given to the son of Sr. de Lotbiniere, on the request, not to say the pressure of the Marquis d'Alogny, I have distributed the other six half-pay ensigncies among the relatives of those who are complaining.

I know too well, My Lord, that it is His Majesty's will that there should be no favoritism in this country. I also know that it is not for a Governor to form intrigues, nor do I form any, and I even hold that to be unworthy of me. And if anyone intrigues here, permit me to inform Your Highness that it is M. de Ramezay and the Sieur de la Mothe and d'Auteuil. The partnership of the Sr. de la Mothe with M. de Ramezay and others in the profits to be made at Detroit, a copy of which I am sending to M. de Marsan, is one proof of it; the writings which the Sieur de la Mothe has sent you against me, which are written by M. de Ramezay's secretary and have marginal notes in the hand of the Sr. de la Mothe, are another. But the greatest proof, My Lord, is that they act so openly that, even if I had not known through certain persons what the secretary of M. de Ramezay had written, it would have been almost impossible not to have discovered it. Allow me to say that in spite of all that, I have always coöperated with them for the interests of the service; and that I would not speak, even now, did not my honor force me to defend myself. No, My Lord, it is not the family of Madame de Vaudreuil that need be complained of; it is the families of these three gentlemen's wives, though I would nevertheless distinguish between Mme. de Ramezay's and the other two.

As I have no aspiration but the welfare of the King's service, My Lord, in all that I do, I make no attempt to conceal my action. The frank avowal I made to you of the reasons which induced M. de Beauharnois and me to send the Sieurs de Mauthe, Vinseine, and La Decouverte to the Outtavois and to allow them to send goods there in order to save the King's money seemed to us so natural that it appeared to me, My Lord, that you must do me the same justice as I should do myself. Since, however, His Majesty does not think consignments of this sort expedient, I will abstain from them, and I hope the interests of his service will not force us to incur these expenses, which we should have saved in that way. I will employ, as far as possible, men for whose fidelity I can answer; but allow me to say, My Lord, that if people make you suspect all whom I can make use of. I shall find myself in a very uncomfortable position.

I am under great obligation to you for having done me justice regarding the information, which had been given to you, that I had sold eight licenses to trade in the interior. I cannot prevent people from writing false statements against me, but if it can be proved that I have transacted trade, however little, I heartily consent to be exposed to your displeasure, however severe.

M. Raudot and I had the honor last spring of giving you particulars, in our joint letter, of all that has taken place between M. Dudley and us, since the King's ship left, regarding exchanges. I informed you in my private letter, also of last spring. a copy of which I have the honor to send you, that as the Sr. Dudley did not give any sufficient explanation as to the proposals which had been made to me by his son, and apparently wanted to gain time. I had despatched several small parties of savages to begin the war again, in his command. We sent you word, My Lord, that according to the information we received, both from M. Dudley and by the Frenchmen who came back from Boston, that he had sent back fifty of our prisoners from Accadie in a boat to Port Royal, we also sent back the like number of his whom we had forwarded to the Sieur de Bonnaventure, having made them proceed to Port Royal on purpose to learn whether M. Dudley had really sent back the number he stated to us. The Sr. de Bonnaventure having delayed replying to my letters until the 22nd of September, I was in a constant state of uncertainty as to what was going on at Boston regarding the exchange of prisoners. At last, a fortnight ago, the boat I had sent to Port Royal, which went on from there to Boston to take back the English prisoners, in accordance with the orders I had given it, and which it afterwards received from the Sieur de Bonnaventure, has returned and brought me letters from M. Dudley in reply to ex letters mine, in which he writes me that he cannot sign the last treaty I sent him, of which, as well as of my letter, I have the honor to send you a copy, because it contains clauses which he considers by no means advantageous to him; that he sends me, however, all the French prisoners he

me, regarding the Sieur de Courtemanche, that his illness had very much
the appearance of a feigned sickness and that under the pretence of bringing him back to Quebec, the Sieur Weiche[1] had only come for the purpose
of trading, I thought it my duty to take all possible precautions and, as
soon as this vessel arrived, M. Raudot and I had a very strict examination
made by the Sieur de Monseignac, comptroller of the navy, of what it contained, which we shall have done also when it leaves, and we have set
guards over it. I am also, My Lord, having the Englishmen who came in
it escorted wherever they go; and I shall send to M. Dudley by this vessel
all the English prisoners who are in the hands of the French here, who
wish to go back; but, as there are several of them, especially women, who
have become Catholics, who do not want to go back, I have no doubt that
that will create a difficulty between M. Dudley and me. I will also make
known to him, since he has not signed my last treaty concerning exchanges,
that henceforth I will not allow any of his ships in this river on any pretence whatever, more especially as the prisoners I am returning to him
are only to get back those from Acadie, for he has but five or six of mine,
and I am determined that henceforth, if we make exchanges, they shall
be made at Port Royal, and not here. I hope, My Lord, that the Sieur de
Subercasse will be more careful about sending me news than the Sieur de
Bonnaventure has been, and by the information he sends me I shall adjust my exchanges with the government of Baston. In the meantime I
shall keep it constantly harassed by our savages, if only to keep them
from forming any tie with the English, which was all the more necessary
as the small stock of goods we had left this summer from last year, and
the uncertainty felt in this country as to the price of beaver-skins, had
entirely ruined the trade of Montreal, and had compelled us—if we were
not to lose our savages altogether, who were dispersing without consulting us,—to let some of them go to Orange, just as the Iroquois from that
place come here; and we were compelled to do so, My Lord, for we could
not prevent them on account of the scarcity of goods, and the low price
of beaver-skins, for which we could not at that time fix any price, because
as we had not yet received any news. The English were desirous of profiting by this opportunity, and also by an attack which three of our savages
from the Sault had made on some Loup Indians in the district under the
governor of Orange, (killing one of their women and taking away three
little children), for the purpose of getting belts secretly conveyed to the
savages, which would have had untoward consequences, together with the
attack by the three savages of the Sault, if, after having made these same
Sault Indians atone for the latter transaction, I had not discovered the

---

[1]This name is spelled Veach in Collection de Manuscrits II, 439, and on page 439,
Vetch. He was captain of the vessel sent with the Boston prisoners to be exchanged.
—C. M. B.

secret by means of repeated instructions to M. de Ramezay to get hold of
these belts from the English. I owe M. de Ramezay this justice, My Lord,
to acknowledge that he has taken great pains in this matter, as well as
the missionaries of the Sault, those of Sault au Recolet, and the Sieur
de Bellemont. You will see from what the Abenakis of St. Francois
ex letter said to me here, that it was time a remedy was found for it. You will
also see, My Lord, from the answer of the same savages to those from
ex letter I. the Sault, that they were entirely of my opinion, making it a reproach to
them that the Dutchman was wrong in making them give up the axe as
long as I had it in my hand. I have written accordingly to Fathers La
Chasse and Aubry, who have gone back with the Abenakis to the seacoast,
and I notify them to have war against the English kept up by their
savages as long as they possibly can, unless they receive letters from M.
de Subercasse, or from the Sieur de Bonnaventure in his absence, requesting them for very strong reasons not to do so; in such case, to make the
savages hang up the axe and to send me word of it as soon as possible,
forwarding to me copies of the letters from these gentlemen, so that they
may afterwards get orders from me and learn my opinion.

      *   *   *   *

I have the honor to reply to you, in a second private letter, regarding
the Sieur de la Mothe and the post of Detroit. I beg to believe, My
Lord, that I shall follow your instructions most strictly.

      *   *   *   *

Hitherto, My Lord, I have believed, in common with the whole country,
that it was a savage who set fire to the barn at Detroit in 1703; but M.
de Ramezay has just sent me word that an inhabitant of Montreal, called
Campeau,' has told him that it was a soldier named La Ville' of Tonty's
company who set fire to it. I am going to have the inhabitant and the
soldier sent down, and I shall hand over this matter to the Intendant
to whom I have already given notice of it, so that he could have the
prosecution prepared.

The man Boudor has just arrived from the Outtavois with four boats.
He has brought me a letter from Father Marest which informs me that
he is beginning to get settled, and that it appears that the
savages will return to their duty, and that they will come down next

brought me messages which are only a repetition of what Miscouaky told me on behalf of Jean le Blanc, his brother, Father Marest notifies me that the offender, finding himself in disgrace with the French and with the savages on account of what he did at Detroit, is adopting the course of withdrawing to one of the tribes of his allies. He also writes me word that the Sieur de la Mothe has sent a savage, who is an ally of the Hurons and the Outtavois, who has made certain proposals and has returned with a Frenchman. I hope, My Lord, I may not be mistaken, and that the Sieur de la Mothe knowing how contrary to the welfare of his settlement war is, will do his best to ward it off. I will follow his action step by step, and if I can bring the Outtavois to my terms I will certainly not make war, for nothing is so injurious to this colony, which, as you will see, My Lord, from the census, only numbers altogether 842 men above 50 years of age, 2,054 below, and 1,828 below 15 years of age. Hence, taking away the 842 over fifty, who cannot serve, and the 1,828 below fifteen who are unfit to do so, I have only 2,054 men left, in which number the people at Detroit, for M. de la Mothe, are included, those whom we send in one direction or another for fishing, and elsewhere, which naturally causes a considerable reduction; so that I reckon, My Lord, that with the few troops I have here, if I were attacked I could not, after garrisoning my forts, put fifteen hundred men in the field without employing the savages. Your Highness will, I flatter myself, have regard to this point and will not blame me for not entering on war any earlier than I can help; I shall, however, do nothing unworthy about it, My Lord, and I assure you that you will be satisfied with my action.

I cannot conclude my letter better than by speaking of the Sieur de Joncaire who is now again with the Iroquois. He deserves, My Lord, that you should think of his promotion. We have the honor of writing to you about him in our joint letter.

*   *   *   *

The Sieur de Joncaire has arrived from the Iroquois; he assures me, My Lord, that these savages received with pleasure what he told them on my behalf, and that they will make no move against the Outtavois unless I place the axe in their hands. The letters from the missionaries corroborate this. And as it is of importance to this country to keep the Iroquois at peace, I shall send the Sieur de Joncaire back in the early spring. Allow me, My Lord, to renew my request to you for his promotion. He deserves it by the good services he does.

The large number of people that the Sieur de la Mothe has taken from this country, with another fifty soldiers that I must give him in

have had some cadets accepted in order to relieve the old soldiers; this will be all the more useful to our troops since I am not taking any who are not fit to serve.

          *   *   "

I am very devotedly, and with very deep respect
My Lord
Your most humble and most obedient servant,
Vaudreuil.

Quebec, this 4th of Nov. 1706.

STATEMENT OF SUMS EXPENDED BY ORDER OF M. DE LA MOTHE FOR THE IROQUOIS CHIEFS WHO CAME TO SPEAK TO HIM.

Endorsed—1706.

1706	Namely	#	s.	d.
October 21st	3¼ lbs. of tobacco at 40s. per lb......	6:	10	
	1 chopin of brandy at 20# a pot......	5	—:	—:
March 1707	1 pot of brandy at —20#.............	20:		
5th	1 lb. 11 oz. of tobacco at 2# per lb......	3:	7:	6:
	3 knives at 10s.....................	1:	10:	
	paid to Pinct for mending one gun....	5:	— 1	—:
	to Labriere for mending eight axes.....	10:	—	
		51:	7s.:	6

We the undersigned certify that Monsieur de la Mothe, commandant for the King at Detroit has expended the above sum for the King's service.

Given at Fort Pontchartrain at Detroit this 1st of April 1707; signed La Mothe Cadillac and Brother Dominique Lamarche, lecturer in theology and missionary to Fort Pontchartrain.

EXTRACT FROM THE LETTER OF M. DE PONTCHARTRAIN, 1707, AT PARAGRAPH 2.

I am very glad to learn your arrival at Detroit with the convoy you Index lett have taken there. The Marquis de Vaudreuil has informed me that he had the detachment of soldiers formed, which the King ordered him to grant you, and that he permitted all the inhabitants who wished to accompany you to set out with you. He also writes me word that he is prepared to afford you all the protection and all the *facilities that may be in his power in order to support your post;* nothing, therefore, can now hinder you from working for it successfully.

EXTRACT FROM THE SAME LETTER AT PARAGRAPH 4.

I do not see, from the letters of the said M. de Vaudreuil and M. Raudot, that they have any other intention *than to carry out the positive orders they have received to smooth the path of your settlement* (and lower down is written) *that it seems that you wished to warrant it against all the evil-disposed enemies of your settlement.* Continuation of the same paragraph. *MM. de Vaudreuil and Raudot acted straightforwardly in all that concerns your settlement, and it will not rest with them if it should not succeed.*

EXTRACT FROM THE TENTH PARAGRAPH OF THE SAME LETTER.

In which it is said, I am well assured you will manage these savages so that you will have no *war with them and that on the contrary they will help you to form your settlement.*

EXTRACT FROM THE SAID LETTER AT PARAGRAPH 12.

You should not fear that His Majesty may change his opinion regarding Detroit, and you should be assured that it will stand, His Majesty having taken it under his protection. For my part I will do what may depend on me to support it.

POINTS CONCERNING CANADA FOR THE YEAR 1707.

Endorsed—

*

Detroit.

The Sr. de la Motte settled down there again last summer, 1706, with his whole family. There are now 270 persons there, among which number are 25 families. It is stated that more than a hundred other households have written to go up there in the summer on which we are about to enter.

The Sr. de la Forest serves under him there, and makes a good second in command. He has passed the 32 years that he has been in Canada either in the explorations of the Sr. de la Salle, or with the Sr. de Tonty, or in trading on his own account in the woods or by voyages.

He is known and beloved by the savages: no one can manage them better. He is no less beloved by the French people because of his good nature and disinterestedness; but he is beginning to grow old and might be inclined to retire to Quebec. Some favor from Monseigneur might remove this idea.

The Sr. de la Motte went through many troubles before he set out for Detroit; they did all they could to draw his men away, they refused him many things, and raised many difficulties. The establishment of this post does not please everyone.

The Sr. de la Motte surmounted all these obstacles by dint of heavy expenditure, and by his steadfastness. The definite orders of Monseigneur, received last year by the "Hero" will encourage him, but similar orders are still required to strengthen this post against those who are evilly disposed towards it.

Those who come from the place, or write about it, speak of it as a fine and fertile country. The hundred families who are to go up there next summer will push forward this affair.

This year the Sr. de la Motte had horses and horned cattle taken over land. There are already a large number of pigs there, and a quantity of poultry. Still larger numbers are to be taken there this year, together

some day, in relation to the English and the savages whom this post will overawe.

The Sr. de Tonty at Fort Frontenac, the Sr. Jonquaire with the Sonnontouans and the younger Renaud at Missilimakinac, are great hinderances to the establishment of Detroit. It is pretended that they are at these posts by the order of their superiors; they are really taking the cream of the public and private trade there under false pretenses. It is for Monseigneur to avert the consequences of such posts.

The Sr. de la Motte needs protection at Quebec and Montreal. The deputy's brother transacts the business of the Sr. de la Motte at Quebec, and the latter left him his general power of attorney on his departure. He did not dare to fill in his name, nor to act under it, before the "Hero" arrived at Quebec, lest he should get himself into trouble with his superiors.

It is this deputy's brother who receives all the goods from Detroit at Quebec, and sends the Sr. de la Motte families and convoys in accordance with his orders. This agent stands in need of Monseigneur's protection to prevent him from being molested in matters so full of details.

In order to deter families from wishing to go up to Detroit, the idea is instilled into them that this post will not be kept up long, and that it will have to be abandoned at an early date. The best way of undeceiving people on that point would be to raise that post to a permanent governorship, but without any pay.

Paris the 11th of April 1707.

Riverin.

DRAFT OF THE MEASURES WHICH DAUTEUIL, PROCUREUR-
GÉNÉRAL OF THE KING TO THE SUPERIOR COUNCIL
OF QUEBEC, MOST HUMBLY PROPOSES TO THE
COMTE DE PONTCHARTRAIN, MINISTER
AND SECRETARY OF STATE FOR
CANADA.

Endorsed—

1st. that, in order to prevent the continuance of forbidden trading at
Missilimakinaq and among all the other tribes of the Outaouas and of the
great river, orders be given that all boats that may be necessarily sent
up to those places, even that of the Jesuit fathers, shall be obliged to go
by the lakes so that they may proceed to Fort Pontchartrain at Detroit
on the said lakes, going up and coming down, at which place they shall be
bound to produce their passports to the Commandant of that fort, and to
permit the goods in the said boats to be examined both going and returning. of which statements shall be drawn up which the chief man of each
boat shall be bound to sign, together with the agent in the said fort and
the Commandant, to be sent every year to the Court, as being the sole
and certain means whereby it may be informed of what goes on in this
matter.

2. That, if prohibited goods are found in the said boats, as brandy
when going up, or fresh beaverskins when going down during the five
years to complete the arrangement made with the St. Aubert and company, or any other which the Court may direct, they shall be seized and
confiscated for the benefit of the church or parish of the said Fort

to take necessary articles for such of the said fathers as are among those tribes, anything other than the said necessary articles, on pain of confiscation of whatever is found to have been put on board other than the said necessary articles, and, as against the said Reverend fathers, of being deprived of His Majesty's favors if it appears that they have contributed or consented to the said prohibited loading.

* * *

Versailles, the 15th of April, 1707.

Dauteuil.

WORDS OF THE OUTAVOIS, ON THE 18th OF JUNE WITH THE ANSWERS.

Endorsed—

Reply of the Marquis de Vaudreuil to Jean le Bland and twelve other chiefs, or men of importance, among the Outtavois on the 20th of June, 1707.

I am not surprised, Jean le Bland, after what has taken place at Detroit, to see you embarrassed in speaking to me. You must have foreseen at that time what is befalling you now; and if I would not receive you here on your arrival, as I did Le Brochet and Meyaouka and two others, that is because I looked upon them as obedient children who have always been well disposed even in troublous times. But, as for you, I can as yet only look upon you as a rebellious child who has displeased me by his bad behavior.

I know all that took place at Detroit, and how it took place. I have been informed of it by M. de la Mothe, by M. de Bourmond, by Father Marest, by Miscouaky and by you yourself.

You told me yesterday that you brought me your body to do with it what I pleased, and to boil it in the pot, if I thought fit.

You testified to me of your despair. What you have done is something, but it is not yet enough.

It is true that I am a good father; but

Words of the Outavois, twelve of whom came down from Michilimakina; four Kiskakoua, 4 Sinago Outaouas and 4 of the La Fourche tribe; on the 18th of June 1707, to the Governor-General.

Jean Le Bland speaks for himself and the rest.

My father, my father, I am so moved that I know not yet whether I shall have strength to speak to you.

Our custom, my father, is to come and pay our respects to you as soon as we land. We were astonished yesterday to see that you would not receive us.

My father, you see your children the Outtayois; we are all that are in a position to come down here. We have no old men left; and of all our chiefs whom you have formerly seen, none but Le Brochet remains who is able to come down here.

My father, my father, Monsieur de Vaudreuil, I beg you to hearken and to listen to me quietly. I have committed an offence which is a very great one; but I will not say that I was drunk, for I had not taken the Englishman's brandy to pledge me to make this wrongful attack. But I am going to tell you in very truth what is the cause of my misfortune.

Observat of M de l Mothe on words of Outavois, which M. Vaudreuil to him. I the first ti he has inf ed him of he has do Montreal.

He confes it was not English w incited hi act as he d He is right that is the opinion of de la Moth

the better I am, the greater is the offence, when I am offended against. By coming down here, you have given me a proof of your obedience; you also give me another by the trust which you place in my goodness.

But I have no proof yet of your real and sincere repentance and of your constancy. What can I count upon, when you have returned to Michilimakina? And who will be security to me that, on the first day, you will not all of you insult my children?

When you came here two years ago, Jean le Blanc, with Le Pesant, did you not tell me with him that the Outtavois of Detroit were not like those of Michilimakina who had attacked the Iroquois without cause? That, as for you, you were not like that, and that, although the Miamis had attacked you twice, your tomahawk had always been buried since the peace; and that you would not attack anyone unless you were attacked first, that then you would avenge yourselves.

Did I not tell you at that time that if any trouble arose, you must apply to whomever was in command at Detroit, and he, knowing my mind and having my orders would always tell you what my will was?

Have you done so? Did you tell M. de Bourmond, before you attacked the Miamis, that as the Miamis were to attack you, you were going to anticipate them?

You took care not to do so, for it was only a pretext which Le Pesant, that bear which is now up there on his bed, was very glad to make use of for creating mischief. Since you kept your word so badly at that time, what reliance can I place today on what you tell me here? And ought I not rather to be-

We had set out, as you have learnt my father, to go and make war on the Sioux, to avenge our allies the Sakes. After we had passed in front of the French Fort, when we were near that of the Hurons, a savage came and told us that our children were dead, and that after our warriors had been three days on the march, the Oyatanous would come and devour our wives and children. Then, my father, we said—let us attack the Miamis before they attack us or else we are dead men.

My father, you learnt from Miscouaky, and you must have seen by your letters, all that took place in this matter, and particularly, to increase our misfortune, how the grey robe and the soldier were killed, but unintentionally however.

When the fighting was over, that is, some days after we had attacked the Miamis, I went to the Fort alone, to speak to Bourmond—I took a stick of porcelain and begged him to consent to listen to me and that it could be wished that Onnontio, Monsieur de Vaudreuil, and also the great Onnontio, the King, could listen to me, that he should hear my reasons.

I asked him for the justicoat which you had given me when I came down here and I had left with him to take care of, as with the best of my friends. I asked him, my father, for this justicoat in order to use it, to go to the tribes clothed in the coat of my father, and to arrange all these evil affairs; but he would not listen to me.

The next day I went back there six times, and each time I took with me a man of different tribe with necklaces and beaver skins to be allowed to speak to him. He refused to listen to us as on the preceding day.

to serve as hostages. It is nothing but threats every day; and if I forbid you to go to war, that is enough to ensure that some among you should be on the watch to go.

Not but that, among your large numbers, there are some who hearken to my voice. I know that Meyaouta, who is present, likes to do what is right; Le Brochet also. I know that Sakima's mind is very well disposed, and that since he came down here he has aimed at doing my will.

I know there are also some others up there whose intentions are good; but who will guarantee me that, when you return, Le Pesant, that bear who is dreaming on his mat only of making mischief, who will be answerable to me, I say, that he will not again warp the minds of all of you, and will not once more induce you to commit a greater fault than the one you have already committed?

The wrong you have done is all the greater because not only did you attack the Miamis, my allies, under my protection, without cause, which you ought not to have done, but you have attacked me myself by killing a missionary, for which it is hardly possible to make amends, who, among us, is valued so highly that if Le Pesant, who has remained up there, and is the sole cause of all this trouble, had come down here, I do not know what I should have done. But I leave to you the task of avenging me; and it was his head which you should have brought me, to make the reparation due to me.

My blood is still flowing; I see it constantly before me; and although you are

There is my body, my father: do with it all that you wish, boil me in your pot, if you think fit. But I am not the most guilty one, for what I did, I did like a man without sense, for I was not the master; and the one who is the most to blame is Le Pesant, that bear who is up there on his bed and did not dare to come down. It was he who would not listen to all the reasons we were able to put to him to prevent him from forcing us to make this wrong attack.

I am beginning to speak, my father; I take courage again. I beg you to remember that it was my father Le Talon, my own father, who was the first of all the tribes of the upper country to come to the French. He came through the woods to go to Three Rivers where he was well received by him who commanded there.

The year after he came there again, he found M. de Coursels who gave him the name of Talon, and told him they must set up communications between them, and since the door was open they must continue to see one another; that he gave him a key of this door that he might open it whenever he thought fit, whatever trouble even might arise.

It is I, my father, that keep this key, being one of his children. I use it today to open your door. It is true that I have almost shut it on myself by my bad action; but then of what use would this key be, if it did not serve me in a matter of importance? And who is permitted to make use of it, if not I, to whom my father left it?

I set out from Michilimakina, my

all these words mea road and of peace. knows ve well that is flatterin the Gover ear, becau

I give you this necklace, my father, that this door may remain open to us.

In losing our old men we have lost all; we have no wit left to guide us. How should we have any, seeing that we have no commandant now. We have seen at Michilimakina M. Louvigny, M. de la Mothe, M. de Tonty, M. de Mauthet, M. de la Forest with the Illinois. While they were there we always did what was right and were always obedient to the word of our father.

The disaster which befel us at Detroit is indeed grievous; I can never forgive myself when I think of it. It is I myself whom I have slain, in killing the grey robe and the soldier, who is the child of my father who gives us life. Have pity on us, our father, for I am extremely grieved for the wrongful attack I made.

Behold all my children here present. Like me, they tell you the same thing. We have slain the grey robe, it is true; but we hope to bring him to life again.

When I say that we will revive the grey robe, it is not with necklaces nor with furs; for I know that, even if we had a house full of them, that could not make reparation for the blood of our father. What can I do then, to content you? I can only satisfy you, my father, by giving you these two slaves who are our own blood, since we have adopted them. Receive them, my father, to cover the blood of the Recollet father, or else take our bodies. Have pity on us.

Nothing else can I offer you. Give us tranquillity again on the lakes and rivers that all your children may be at peace, and we may be able to boil our pots and drink our broth in full security.

There are some of those, my father, who call themselves your children, who have tried to deceive me, drawing me by the tips of the fingers; but you, my father, have always held me by the hand. It is true that I was on the point

The Recollet father and the soldier you have killed, they are my blood, my own blood.

With us the blood of a Frenchman is generally only to be paid for by blood. You see that I cannot be content with what you have done, and that it is, as it were, impossible to satisfy me, after the loss I have sustained, without bringing me as a sacrifice the head of the man who has been the sole cause of it. You know him; he is a man who has always caused disturbances; you have told me so yourselves. It is he who is the cause of all your misfortunes, who as long as he lives will continue to lead you into quarrels with all the tribes, and will be the cause of your ruin. Reflect on what I tell you and give me your answer.

father, from your letters and from what
Miscouaky told you, how many tribes
Quarante Sols incited to devour us. I
own to you that the Hurons after having
been our friends so long, have basely
betrayed us. I am stricken to the heart,
and cannot recover except by telling
you, my father, all that is in my
thoughts. The Hurons have not only
killed us in fighting against us but,
which affects me more deeply, they have
killed our men who, merely out of
friendship for them, went with them to
war against the Flatheads.

The Hurons generously took up our quarrel and, without them, the French fort would have been taken. M. de Vaudreuil gave them, in his gratitude for this, five livres of powder which they threw into the river when they received it, and with reason.

Long ago the Hurons would have perished if I would have abandoned their
interests. Many a tribe has asked me
for this roebuck to tear its flesh, but
I would never give it up. Yet it is they
who now betray me.

The Hurons, my father, betrayed us
four times over, in what took place at
Detroit.

I know not how many of their men
I may have killed, but they have killed
thirty of mine.

It was I, my father,—it was the Outtavois—who killed the grey robe; unintentionally it is true, but still it was we
who killed him and the soldier, for it
was we who were the cause of all the
misfortune which happened at Detroit.
As for Tichenet, it was the Sr. Bourmond who killed him, by sending him to
fight against us. For indeed the father
and the soldier were killed in the first
fire, but all that happened afterwards
was ordered by Bourmond in cold blood.

My great offence, my father, with the
Miamis and Hurons is that they often
taunted me that I had a father no
longer, and that you abandoned me;
and that a proof of that was that I
had no more powder, while it was sold
to them in abundance. Why, said I to
myself, am I not the oldest of my

They were allowed at Montreal to trade [for powder] before peace was made, and they came back supplied for attacking' this post again if the desire should seize

in a short time. I have replied to l
de la Mothe that if I had two bodie
I would willingly divide myself in
two parts to go and see him; but tha
as I had but one, and had been sur
moned by my father, I was going
learn his will.

WORDS OF THE OUTTAVOIS ON THE 21st OF JUNE WITH TH ANSWERS.

Endorsed—

Index letter C.

Reply of the Governor-General to the
savages from Michilimakina on the 22nd
of June, 1707.

I have seen the reply you gave me yesterday. I am willing to believe that you
are unable to give me up the head of Le
Pezant as I asked of you.

I must however have blood to content
me. The death of a missionary cannot
be paid for except by blood.

I have pity on you.

As all the tribes knew of your wrong
doing and are in suspense awaiting

Words of the Outtavois from Michil
makina to the Governor-General on tl
21st of June, 1707.

Jean le Blan speaks.

My father, my father, I come to yc
again. The Comte de Frontenac alwa
told our forefathers that we were h
children.

Though they are dead, yet I speak
you as if they were present. We a
your children, my father, we come
you.

By a necklace

But, whatever arrangement M. de la Mothe may find for setting right the mischief you have done, and satisfying the tribes against whom you have offended, as well as against me, I shall give him orders not to include this Pezant in the pardon he extends to you in my name, if he does extend it, or in the arrangement he may make between you and the other tribes, for I do not pretend that Le Pezant will ever be included in the pardon I shall be willing to accord to your transgression. There, Jean le Blanc, is the door open to you; consider whether you wish to make use of it. I return you the necklace you gave me the day before yesterday. When you have done what I order you to do, and M. de la Mothe has hit upon expedients with you for obtaining pardon for your fault, and for settling matters between you and the tribes you have attacked, bring me back this necklace by the lakes or by the great river; these two roads shall be open to you. Then I will myself ratify the pardon which has been extended to you in my name, and I will forget your fault. But if all of you Outtavois of Michilimakina do not give me this proof of your obedience, you will have everything to fear from my just resentment.

I do not speak to Companissé here, for Father Marest tells me that he intends to bring me slaves to satisfy his brothers, the Iroqouis, and that he would have come down but for that; only I charge you, Brochet, to tell him from me that I count upon his word.

to keep my word with him, and I should be grieved to have lied to him. I dare not promise you, my father, to do what you ask of me, for this great bear is allied to all the tribes of the upper country.

It is not that I should fear him, if it were he only; nor that any of us love him, for it is he who is guilty. But as he has allies round all the lakes I fear, my father, the consequences of this affair, and that all his allies may not only prevent me from bringing it here to you, but may also do to me what I would do to him.

My consolation, my father, is that he is an old man and cannot go very far; and when he is dead we shall have absolutely no more wrong-doing. But, meanwhile, we promise you not to listen to him any more; and, if we can mollify your anger, we give you our word that he shall certainly not make us do any wrong again.

My father, my father, we are your children, we are all French. It is a terrible thing if we must perish for his sake.

That is the first fault we have committed; it is the first wrong-doing that the Outtavois can be reproached with. They have always been friends to the French. Why, my father, are we to perish for him?

All of us who are here, my father, are chiefs and men of importance; we are resolved to do your will. Pardon us, you who are our father; we promise you that you shall never be displeased with

[marginal notes, right edge:]
If he is th
allied he
in that w
be the mo
formidabl
but when
head is cu
he will cr
no more d
turbances
That mus
insisted o

No; but th
must put b
to death t
save them
selves T
is the opin
of M. de la
Mothe.
This is an
astonishin
thing. Bu
why does
not confes
what indu
them to dc
this act?
They dare
they know
they have
their pard

Although you have offended me in the most sensitive place, and have plunged your dagger into my breast, you see that I have pity on you still, giving you the means of settling the trouble you have caused. Take advantage of my pity, ye Outtavois. I am giving my orders to M. de la Mothe. Remember; all of you who are here present, Outtavois, Kiskakous, Sinagos, you of the Land tribe, and of La Fourche, remember all of you the promise you gave me yesterday, never to recognize Le Pezant again in anything, and to look upon him in future as a member withered and severed from your body. Remember that you have promised me to cause no further trouble and never to give me the least cause for displeasure.

Outtavois, the blood of Frenchmen is sacred; remember well all I have said.

WORDS OF JEAN LEBLANC TO THE GOVERNOR-GENERAL, ON THE 23rd OF JUNE, 1707.

servations M. de la- the.

My Father, I am sorry that M. de Bourmond is not here before you, to tell you his reasons, as I am doing mine. I think he is ashamed since he has not come, as I have, to tell you his reasons.

he had not en assured etty strong- he would ve feared come: in ot he knew de la Mothe s not so mpassion- e as M. de- udreuil.

My father, my father, I beg you to consent to hear me; and you, interpreters, take great care to forget nothing, and to explain properly what I say.

Last year I said to Father Marest, when I arrived at Michilimakina, that I had thought I should die at my father's door; but when I saw little Renaud come, I told him that I had no fear any longer, since my father called me, and that I would go and offer him my body.

is is the id from ssilimakina Montreal. is is pleas- t hearing to de Vau- euil for it s come to point of w, which s to remove e Outavois m Detroit.

My father, I see that my flesh is not to your taste. I go to obey your will; I am going to find Monsieur de la Mothe, and to die near my brother the Recollet father.

My father, as I am an obedient child, I am going to Detroit; I have already told you that I gave my body up to you. I am going to Detroit, and thence I will go to Michilimakina to make smooth the old road. I will

Vol. 7, p. 1354.

do your will, my father, but as I am doing what you ask of me, I beg you to grant me what I ask of you.

My father, we have not yet consulted as to those who are to go with me to Detroit; I have brought them here for that purpose, we will tell you presently. My father, I obey your will; I am going now to lay my requests before you.

My father, our people will be anxious concerning me, for when I left they were almost stupefied, despairing of seeing me again. I beg you, since I am obeying you, to send one of your men of importance to assure them that I have set out to do your will.

If I ask that of you, my father, it is because the boat that goes to Michilimakina will get there sooner than I, and will tell our people that I have gone to see Monsieur de la Mothe; and thereupon the old men will dispatch a canoe to inform the other tribes and to tell them the purpose of my journey.

The Sakis, Malominis, Mascoutins, Quiquapóus [Kikapoos], Outagamis, and Poutouatamis are the tribes who will come to listen to the good news; they are our allies, and it is they to whom our old men will send information.

Whence comes it that I say that to my father? It is because all the tribes come to seek me in the spring; they will be very glad of this good news.

My father, I beg you to listen well to what I say, to take pity on us, and to send a man of rank among your Frenchmen, who will be able to reach Michilimakina sooner than we, so that the land may be united.

I came to bring you my body. I always thought that I should return by the same road as I had come; but now I see the contrary. However, it was my intention all along to go and see Mons. de la Mothe after I had seen you, my father.

My father, my father, M. de la Mothe has done as the porcupine does who does not suckle its young. It was he who called us, the four Outtavois tribes, to Detroit, but after having made an opening in the tree, as the porcupine does, to give its young to suck, he left us. If I had been at Detroit, or Tonty, or La Forest, all these troubles would never have come

It is stran
that this r
quest also
not grante
and the S:
Louvigny
not make
journey.
He lies im
dently. M.
la Mothe b
separated
detached
these tribe
from the s
of the Uta
vois, and
would not
meddle wi
it. M. de
dreuil was
formed of

This matte
was strong
enjoined o
him, since
repeats it,
twice; and
man of ran
would hav
been, but
Raudot ju
was not of
that opinic

M. de la Mc
agrees as t
the fact. T
was why t
had him de
tained at C
bec for tw
years so as
have plent
time to co

THE OTTAWAS COME TO QUEBEC IN THE SPRING OF 1707.

Endorsed—M. de Vaudreuil. Quebec, this 24th July 1707.

My Lord,

M. Raudot and I had the honor of sending you a joint letter a week
ago by a small brigantine which came from Plaisance and has gone back
there. We have the honor of sending you a duplicate of the same letter
by this opportunity, namely a ship from Provence which came to Quebec
this year. But, as the letter which we have the honor of writing to you
only informs you generally of the present condition of the country, I
thought you would not disapprove of my taking the liberty of giving you
a statement on my own account of what concerns myself and the various
reasons I have had for my action according to the circumstances which
have presented themselves.

As the chief concern of this country, My Lord, according to what I have
always had the honor of telling you, and also according to your own instructions, is to keep the savages who are allied to us completely united,
I have always applied myself to that as far as it was possible.

*   *   *

[p. 2 of transcript, and p. 3 to end of first paragraph, omitted.]

The season being too far advanced prevented the Outavois from coming
down here, and prevented me at the same time from being able to take
all the steps I should like to have taken, either to punish the Outavois
or to find a way to pardon them, while making them give me such satisfaction as should make a stir among the savages; and I found no better
device, while awaiting the end of the winter, than to have all the tribes
kept in a kind of truce until I had declared my will. For that purpose I
sent orders to the Iroquois, to Detroit and to Michilimakina. They have
been strictly carried out by the Outavois and the Iroquois, and it was
only the Miamis and Hurons who, though they did not in fact move, yet
according to what the Sr. de la Mothe tells me, especially as regards the
latter [tribe], would have very much liked to destroy the Outavois.

The Outavois, My Lord, remained all winter extremely impatient to
learn what I thought. At last, in the early spring, they dispatched twelve
chiefs or head men from among them, Jean le Blanc being one of them, to
come and speak to me. They arrived at Montreal on the 16th of June,
and, after having put themselves in my hands, and having fully acknowledged their misdeeds,—Jean le Blanc speaking throughout for them all—
they presented me with two slaves, as substitutes for the Recollet father,

and protested that they would do nothing in future which could displease me, and begged me to forget the past.

I showed them, My Lord, by my answers, of which I will do myself the honor of sending you a copy this autumn, as well as what they said to me, how easy it was for me to take vengeace on them, how little confidence I ought to place in their word, and lastly how great the fault was which they had committed, and also how important it was for me to exact reparation for it. I demanded of them the head of Le Pezant, one of their chiefs, as it was he alone who was the cause of all that had occurred. They did not dare to promise me it, and Jean le Blanc, having shown me that it was impossible, seeing the various tribes to which Le Pezant is allied, who would not fail to avenge his death if they undertook to kill him, offered to give himself as a victim, rather than promise a thing which he could not perform.

The submissive, and apparently sincere manner in which he has always spoken to me, together with the blind obedience he has shown to my orders and in doing my will, in coming down merely on the message which his brother Miscouaky had taken to him from me, prevented me from pressing matters too far. Moreover it is not just to punish an innocent man for a guilty one, Le Pezant being the sole originator of all that has taken place at Detroit. I therefore took another course, My Lord, and as I knew that the Sr. de la Mothe had sent word to this same Jean Le Blanc, before he left Michilimakina to come to Montreal, to go to him at Detroit, I thought—as I did not wish to lose the Outavois—that I could not do better, for the purpose of making known to the Iroquois and all the other tribes that these savages had come to make their submission to me, than to make them go and make reparation on the very spot where they had offended against me. After I had said all I thought I ought to say to them, I referred this matter to the Sieur de la Mothe, and gave him orders to try and find expedients for making peace between them and the Hurons and the Miamis. And, in order that I might be more certain, My Lord, of all the Outavois did, and that the Iroquois also might be the sooner informed of the steps I was making them take, I sent them by way of the Lakes instead of by the great river, their ordinary route, and I sent along with them a boat in which I put an officer who had served as an interpreter for me at Montreal and will be a witness, at Detroit of all they have said to me, and all they say there, as well as all that passes on their return to Michilimakina, where I have ordered him to proceed with them, returning thence before the ships leave down here, so that I may be able to give you an account of it. And by way of making it impossible for anyone to accuse him of going to trade, I have forbidden him and those with him to take any goods, under any pretence whatever not even

going from Detroit to Michilimakina and for coming down here again.

I have no doubt, My Lord, that the Sr. de la Mothe will find it very easy to arrange this peace, all the more since—as I have already had the honor of telling you above,—he himself sent word to this same Jean le Blanc, whom I am sending to him to come to him. But what further makes me think that he will give every attention to it is that, in one of his letters of the 11th of May, which I received while the Outavois were at Montreal, he urges me to make peace for these savages with the other tribes, warning me, as I have already known a long while, and have also had the honor of notifying to you, that everything was to be feared from too close a connection between the Miamis and Hurons and the Iroquois. However, in referring this matter to him, as I would not belie myself in what I had said to these savages, and in order that this might serve as a rule in future with all the tribes, I notified to the Sieur de la Mothe, and I declared to the Outavois who were present when I spoke, that, whatever expedient he might decide upon for pacifying everything with them, I would not permit Le Pezant to be included in it in any way, for I would never pardon him, nor any others who should attack the French in future. I am doing so, My Lord, not that I hope they will bring me his head, but in order to destroy his influence with the tribe until such time as I may be able to make an opportunity of taking vengeance on him.

I am aware, My Lord, that I could very well have settled that matter myself without referring it to the Sr. de la Mothe. But, besides the fact that it would have cost the King enormous sums for bringing all the tribes down and assembling them at Montreal, I was very glad to give

wanted to give the Sieur de la Forest, whom the Sieur de la Mothe sent here this spring to look after matters concerning his post, the additional fifty soldiers whom you order me to send him. The Sieur de la Forest, on my wishing to include among these fifty men the rest of the Sieur de la Mothe's company and his, and on some difficulty arising as to the vehicles, requested me to await the reply to a letter which he wrote to the Sieur de la Mothe on this subject, assuring me that the post would not suffer in any way from the delay in sending these fifty men. Otherwise, My Lord, although the Sieur de la Mothe has no means of transport ready at Montreal for conveying these fifty men, I should nevertheless have sent them, leaving it to you to be good enough to give instructions yourself concerning the expense. I am with great respect,

My Lord

Your most humble and most obedient servant,

Vaudreuil.

Quebec, this 24th of July, 1707.

COUNCIL HELD AT DETROIT ON THE 6th OF AUGUST.

Endorsed—

Summary of the words of Monsieur de la Mothe Cadillac, Commandant of Fort Pontchartrain at Detroit, on the 6th of August, 1707, to Jean le Blanc, Kiñougé, Meatinan and Menukoueak four chiefs of the four Outta-vois tribes, sent to him by the Governor-General.

First Council.

Monsieur de la Mothe speaks: Otontagan, Kinongé and the rest of you, listen to me well. I will not repeat the words you said to Onontio, nor the answers he gave you; you know well enough what they were, and so do I.

Could I believe that an axe had been fastened to the summit of this great tree, an axe sharp and heavy, which I did not see because it was all covered with leaves?

While I was sleeping peacefully and dreaming of nothing but good things, a wicked bear, a malicious bear, got up to the very top of the tree; he shook it with all his strength, the axe which had been hung up there fell upon my hut and broke it. My heart was displaced, it was thrown and jerked to the right and to the left; it fell to the bottom of my belly, it rose up even to my throat. Then I said, I will cut down this tree, I will tear up even its roots, I will reduce it to ashes.

But after my heart had got back to its place, I said why should I destroy this tree, its leaves and its fruit? I take pity on the women and the children. It is that drunken bear who has wrought all the evil; he has intoxicated all the children, and has taken away all their wits. He is the author of all this mischief; he must die, and I must grant the others their lives. Hearken then Outtavois, to my final decision.

I demand of you that you hand over Le Pesant to me, whom today you call the evil bear, that you give him to me to dispose of here in this place where he offended against me. I wish him to be in my power, either to grant him his life, or to put him to death.

If he refuses to embark, I demand that you slay him in your village. That is the only means I have found for granting you peace. It is not I who kill him, it is he who kills himself. It is not I who have slain your men; it is he who has killed them. Avoid the danger which threatens you; save your lives; have pity on your wives, have pity on your children; fear your misfortune and want. Nothing can make me change my mind. It is your affair; think it over and consider among yourselves the course you have to take, and give me a reply a little before sundown.

For the rest, Onontio and I have but one heart and one mind. Those who tell you otherwise are liars. He will confirm all that I do, whether it be for peace or for war.

Replies of Otontagan.

2nd Council.

The demand you make of us, my father is surprising. The bear that you ask for is very powerful in our village; he has strong alliances with all the lake tribes. It is a great tree; where is the man who will be strong enough to uproot it? We have thought over this matter; it is difficult. But, after all, since nothing can soften you, and your heart is as hard as a rock, we must obey you; only we beg you to spare us the grief of bringing him to you ourselves. Send a boat with us to Michilimakina, and we will hand over Le Pesant as you require, and you shall be the arbiter of his

brother, my own brother; but what can we do? We must obey you.
That is what you have demanded of us, and what we have decided among
ourselves.

By this means you will obtain peace; your wives and children will
rejoice at it; and I will forget the wrong that you have done me. M. de la Mo speaks.

3rd Council on the 7th of August.

Sasterecy, Miamis, listen to me. I promised you that I would never
make peace with the Outtavois without putting Le Pesant to death, for
I have always regarded him as the cause of all the evil that has been
wrought here. You have always told me you would be content with this
reparation. That is how I have demanded it from the Outtavois, and you
shall hear what I said to them and their reply to me. Monsieur l Mothe spe to the Hur & Miamis. M. de la Mo repeats to them the whole con- tents of th preceding page.

Allow me to tell you that we cannot believe that the Outtavois will do
what they promise you; for in fact, who is there that will uproot such a
great tree, whose roots—as they themselves say— are so deep in the earth,
and whose branches or alliances stretch out over the lakes. There is
meat here; why go and seek it farther off? The one is certain, the other
uncertain. Sastarcy speaks. The Miami spoke as t Hurons di

You have always told me that you would be content if Le Pesant were
destroyed. I have promised you and it will be done. The more difficult
the matter appears to you, the more clearly it will show you, very soon,
how powerful Onontio and I are, and that nothing can resist the power
of the French. M. de la M speaks.

4th Council on the 7th of August.

Otontagan, hearken to me. Here are the Hurons and the Miamis who
listen to me and have regard to us. I have told them of the proposals
I have made to you, your answers, and the promise you have made M. da la M speaks to Outtavois.

justice of you; I demand justice, give it me. Our chiefs have been slain,
they still lie stretched out on the ground. all stained with blood.

-Sastarecy, my son, there is a little meat which I give you to revive your
dead a little—I do not say altogether. As soon as the Outtavois have
made the reparation I demand of them, I will cast water on the earth,
I will wash it completely, I will cover it so that there shall be no blood
left to be seen.

The Miamis Reply.

My father, I have already told you that Pkoumakoua was coming to
listen to you, and gave it up as he fell sick. He said to me—"My children,
go and see what our father wishes, and come and bring us news of it." I
will tell the old men that that is well, and that peace is made. I beg
you to let me leave this meat here; when the old men come, they will take
it if they think fit. As for me, I cannot consult on anything; I came only
to listen to you.

5th Council on the 8th of August.

What brings you here Onaské? Was it Onontio who told you to come?
Has peace been made? Are we friends? Have I been avenged?

Onaské replies.

My father, you have known me for a long time. I go everywhere with
my head erect because I have never done what was wrong; and I said
within myself, "M. de la Mothe, my father, knows me; I do not believe I
run any risk in going to see him, I have confidence in him."

How dare you say that you have never done what was wrong? Did not
your people, your tribe, come to the assistance of the Outtavois of Detroit
who killed my people? I think you are very bold to come here while my
land is still all smoking with my blood and that of my children. Formerly
you had sense; when men grow old, they become wise, but you have grown
foolish. Speak then, what was your intent? You must have had other
reasons than those you have yet told me, therefore speak.

What can I say to you my father? It is our want that has made me
throw myself in desperation into your arms. We are unfortunate, our
children have eaten grass all the summer long, like cattle. We have made
some boiled for them, and pounded it in a mortar, and have made them
swallow the juice; want is a strange thing. I have risked everything,
since I must needs die; and I said "I will die by the hand of my father,
it may be that he will take pity on me." We shall have no Indian corn
this year; our children will all die. But for me, everybody would have
come to Detroit; but I said to them. "Have patience, and await my
return."

Well and good! Heaven punish you. Very soon I will avenge myself in another way. Go! Be off! You are impudent indeed!

6th Council on the 9th of August.

Sasterecy my son, I have never kept anything hidden from you. To you I have ever carried my heart in the palm of my hand. I want you to tell me now your opinion; not entirely,—I shall be satisfied if you will let me but just see what your intention would be, whether peace or war. Make known your heart to me, open it now. *M. de la M speaks to Hurons. tells them what pass concernin Onaské & Koutaouli and adds.*

My father, we have always told you that we would follow in your footsteps; you will always be our guide. We are your obedient children, we are under your wing, you have given us a good land; we are greatly indebted to you. Be assured that nothing could make us quit this land, and that we shall never depart from what you wish of us. Make peace, or make war; we shall approve of all you do. It is not for a good child to find objections to what his father does. We have full confidence in you. *Sasterecy plies to M de la Mott after cons ing.*

I thank you, Sasterecy. It is true that the Outtavois was formerly my elder son, but, since he has removed his hearth from here, and has committed an act of outrageous disobedience, he will in future be my younger son, if he returns to good behavior. And you Hurons, may boast to-day that, by your obedience, you have taken the place of your elder brother in my heart, and my favors; you may boast of having gained a great inheritance. *M. de la M replies.*

7th Council.

Otontagan you are aware, together with Kinongé and the rest, of my determination and of the promise you have made to me. On the fulfilment of this promise depends the peace you have asked of me. Hearken, Onaské and Koutaouliboy, and consider what you are to do. Have pity on your children, who have eaten grass all the summer, your tenderness for whom has made you risk your lives by coming here. *M. de la M speaks to 4 Outtavoi chiefs who had come from Montreal, and Onaské an Koutaouli from Mich makina.*

Onaské speaks.

thank you, my brothers, for the promise you have made him. Either we must keep it, and *live in peace, or we must die.*

Cadillac's Reply.

I had resolved to make you take away your furs. I would not even have given you a bone to gnaw; and you would have had nothing for your children to live upon. But because of your words, I permit you to trade, and to take away what you require for food. Do not abuse my kindness. What you take away will not go far; you will fall back into greater want again, like your brothers, if you fail in your word to me and my ears would forever be stopped [against your prayers]. I should never think of making peace again.

Tell your people that they are not to come here any more until peace is concluded. When the reparation that I demand of you has been made, then you may all come here with your heads erect. I will make the whole land smooth and level.

CADILLAC COMPLAINS OF VAUDREUIL.

Endorsed—The Sieur de La Mothe Cadillac, the 10th and 15th of September and the 1st of October 1707.

id way of
ing; it is
duty to be
missive to
superior
ber, other-
e I shall at
get weary
upporting
with all
se [claims]
ndepend-
e.

M. de Vaudreuil has always been strongly opposed to the establishment of the post of Detroit; he does not act openly, but, takes advantage of every opportunity he can find to undo everything that he [De la Motte] does in the interests of that post, and to put difficulties in his way.

e Vau-
uil is right;
ust do so.

The said Sr. de Vaudreuil claims peremptorily that he should report to him in general on everything which takes place at that post, and that he should carry out blindly all the orders that he sends him, under the pretext that he is to be responsible for it.

his busi-
to keep
ood terms
ι M. de
dreuil, to
his confi-
ce and
ndship by
respect &
lience he
s him;
rwise he
be re-
d, his
will fall,
his honor
fortune
ch are
id up with

He says that if he were obliged to inform him of all his plans none of them would succeed; because he, and certain people surrounding him, seek only to thwart him, according to his experience of them; hence, when he has succeeded in any matter, then he informs the said Sr. de Vaudreuil of it, who complains that he gives him notice of what he does, too late.

e Vaud-
is right.

As regards the orders which the said Sr. de Vaudreuil sends him, they are always contrary to the well-being and progress of his new settlement. He says that the said Sr. de Vaudreuil had ordered him to set himself to taking vengeance on the Illinois Indians who killed a Frenchman and wounded a Jesuit missionary; but, as that tribe is a powerful one, and moreover what took place with them arose from a quarrel between private individuals, and since it was not advisable to run into a war which might have disastrous results, he composed the matter without compromising the national honor.

his right course is to address his remonstrances and representations, with due deference to M. de Vaudreuil and then to obey, to send word here, afterwards, etc., after all this fine talk, there is a Frenchman killed and a missionary wounded without either satisfaction or vengeance which is not honorable to the nation. To see to it as soon as possible. He ought to have explained how, so that we might know.

So that there is now peace all around with all the tribes of savages in the neighborhood of Detroit, which is altogether honorable, for he has compelled the Outaouacks to bring him the chief of their tribe, whose head the said Sr. de Vaudreuil demanded, to do what he might think fit with it.

good—continue.

good.

. This savage managed to get out of the fort at Detroit, where he was detained, and to take refuge in the woods; but as his tribe has deserted him, and he has therefore no voice or influence with it now, he was sorry for his escape because, if he had put him to death he might have made some undesirable relations.

good.

Sufficient, he ought not to have put him to death, but pardoned him.

The said Sr. de Vaudreuil claims that it was he who made the Outaouacks give the satisfaction which was required from them for the attack which this chief made at Detroit. It is easy to judge of that from the fact that these savages refused to give him the head of that chief.

childishness; he should always attribute the honor to his commanding officer, even if he had not done it.

It is true that the said Sr. de Vaudreuil referred this matter to him for adjustment, but he ought not to have allowed the envoys of the Outaouack savages who went to him at Montreal, to do any trade there, and to take away all the war stores they wanted, for that was putting that tribe in a position to take the post of Detroit.

he always tries to find fault with what M. de Vaudreuil does. a fine argument when they were suing for peace.

good.

He has induced the Miami Indians, who number 400 men bearing arms, and were a long way from Detroit to come and settle at the Maurepas[1] River which is only 12 leagues away; it is the finest land under heaven—fishing and hunting are most abundant there.

The Jesuit who was acting as missionary among these Miamis did all he could to prevent them from taking this step and would not follow them; this has obliged him to give this mission to a Recollet priest who will discharge the duty well.

As the Jesuits have refused to carry on the missions at the post of Detroit, he is determined not to receive any of them; he is convinced that they would thwart him in everything that they could.

The savages that are in these parts, and know the permanence and strength of his post, flock to it from all parts to settle there; and he was also expecting the Outaouacks.

He arranges all these savages so that they may not inconvenience one another, whether as regards lands or hunting.

He begs that no change may be introduced in anything that concerns his post without hearing what he has to say, because all that he does is

He ought to have had 200 men, and had made arrangements to take *good.*
them away, but he only gave him 150, and he now offers him the remain- *These are his terms; refer*
ing 50—whom he is absolutely in need of—on condition that he defrays *to them, and carry them*
the cost of their conveyance, which would not be just, for it is not his *out precisely, and do not de-*
fault that he was not granted, at first, the number of men that ought to *part from them either in*
have been supplied to him. *his interests or against him.*

An offer has been made to him to send him his company and the Sr. *They could not d° better*
de la Forest's; but as they are very weak, and are made up of old soldiers *for him.*
who are not suitable for his post, he has requested them to remove these *he is right in that.*
soldiers and to put Canadians in their place, giving them the same pay as *I do not under-stand the rea-*
the other soldiers; but the said Sr. de Vaudreuil and the Sr. Raudot *sons for refus-ing; find out*
would not do so. *from MM. de Vaudreuil & Raudot, who are wrong.*

They wrote to him that the said Sr. Raudot would have the soldiers *learn why.*
who are at Detroit, paid in provisions or goods; but that is not practicable, for it would put the soldier in possession of his pay for a whole
year, and that would give him an opportunity to desert.

He says that when he accepted the post of Detroit, it was agreed that *Carry out the agreements*
the soldiers should be paid in the usual manner, and that this should be *to the letter—no more and*
adhered to. *no less.*

He has sent the Sr. de la Forest to Quebec to represent to the said *good.*
Sieurs de Vaudreuil and Raudot the difficulties there would be in pur-
suing this plan, and to agree with the agent of the Company of the
Colony as to the goods which were left at Detroit.

It would not be just for him to be charged with the cost of the clergy *adhere to the arrangements*
at Detroit, nor of the surgeon, nor the medicines for the sick; because *and the agree-ments,—noth-*
that relates to His Majesty's troops. As regards the cost of the in- *ing either more or less.*
terpreters, with which also it is sought to charge him, it is for the inter- *Write clearly to him and to*
ests of Canada generally that they are maintained; therefore that cost *M. Raudot, to put an end*
ought not to fall upon him. *finally to all disputes. all this reduces*

.. Raudot maintains that he makes a large profit on tl
r which His Majesty directs to be supplied to him fr₁
e states that he sells it cheaply to the savages, and t
:e in powder and lead is not kept up it will produce
ong these savages. A sergeant of a company died at D
led the corporal of the same company in his place, ar
:orporal by a good private. M. de Vaudreuil maintain
ht to make such changes without orders from him.
. Raudot also maintains that it is his duty to pay for tl
e soldiers' clothing from Montreal to Detroit.
it the post of Detroit is now sufficiently settled to be
ship. The fort is strongly constructed; there are 120 I
1' it, and 1,200 savages in the neighborhood, and a
ttle; finally nothing is now wanting for keeping it '
more than forty thousand francs on establishing it
)ost of governor for himself, and that of King's lieut
la Forest, and the office of major for the Sr. du Figui₁
adopts this course, it would be important to exter
: governorship.

According to a memorandum which he sends, each company would cost 5,847 livres a year for their clothing and pay, reckoning 50 men to each company.

It is certain that to establish such a corps would be most advantageous in the interests of religion, and for attaching the savages to the French.

There would be nothing to fear then from the Iroquois, any more than the English; for, if they made any attempt against Canada, they would be within reach of the French and Indian troops, who could at once take all the villages of the Iroquois and carry off their women and children as slaves.

If M. de Vaudreuil would act in concert with him, he would not only reduce the savages of Detroit to order and make them obey the laws of the Kingdom, but also,—gradually—all the neighboring tribes.

He says that the Sr. Raudot had adopted the views of the said Sr. de Vaudreuil as to all that concerns the post of Detroit, and speaks of him with all sorts of rancour; and that is not consistent with the interests of the service that he should express himself, as he does, with aspersions injurious to his character. He begs us to write to him to be more guarded concerning him. He hopes that His Majesty will be pleased that his post is well established, and that all goes wonderfully well there, and that he has brought about complete peace among all the savages.

At Michilimakinac there are 20 of the Frenchmen who have been there with the Jesuits who carry on the forbidden trade there, through correspondents they have at Montreal. It would be important in the interests of the service that they should be arrested. He asks orders on that, and as to the punishment that must be given.

He also asks to whom their forfeited goods will belong.

The said Sr. de Vaudreuil has sent him notice that he would keep back the powder that has been granted to him, until the ships arrive from France; and this will be a great injury to him.

The man who set fire to the fort at Detroit has been discovered; but as the said Sieur de Vaudreuil and Raudot only seek to make difficulties for him, this affair has remained unpunished. It is important in the interests of the service that the Sr. de Tonty should be superseded at Fort Frontenac, and should not be employed in the further posts.

M. de Vaudreuil and Raudot to cuss th ro ly d'Aigre nt send

opinion w the easo for it. That see good.

How is th To expl it himself an agree wit M. de Vaudreuil.

Ridiculous finds fault with every thing. W him to beh himself pr erly, with solute sub nation and deference write to M Raudot als sharply. good, witt Ponnisnity

Stop entir write to M de Vaudre and Raudc about it. good—foll the decre the letter; is forbidde ditto—foll the decre find out w

have him t in due for write stro to M. Rauc —to be go enough to show no p judice and assist the tlement in

Endorsed—Colonies—MM. de Vaudreuil and Raudot, 15th Sept., 1707.

My Lord,

*　　　*　　　*

'The Sieurs de Vaudreuil and Raudot had the honor, My Lord, of informing you in their joint letter, of the month of July last, the third copy of which they annex hereto, of the position in which the affairs of the Outavois stood. You will see from that, that they came¹ down to Montreal to sue for pardon; that they brought slaves there to replace the dead. You will also see from it that the Sr. de Vaudreuil refused their slaves and would not grant them the pardon they asked for; and, as they had offended against all the tribes as well as the French, he referred them to Detroit where they were to seek expedients with the Sr. de la Mothe for reconciling them with the French and with all the tribes they had attacked. The Outavois arrived at Detroit with the Sr. de St. Pierre. The Sr. de la Mothe made the same demand from them which the Sr. de Vaudreuil had made here, viz., for Le Pezant, the cause of all the disturbance which occurred last year. They consented either to give him up to him or to shoot him in the village, if he would not go there. The Sr. de St. Pierre, who² was sent by the Sr. de Vaudreuil, and the Sr. D'Argenteuil, who was also sent to Michilimakina by the Sr. de la Mothe, saw that this promise was carried out by the Outavois, and he was given up to the said Sr. de St. Pierre who gave him to the said Sr. D'Argenteuil to deliver him into the hands of the said Sr. de la Mothe.

The Srs. de Vaudreuil and Raudot are convinced that, if the Sr. de Bourmont had acted as he ought to have done with the savages, he would have prevented the troubles which arose at Fort Pontchartrain at Detroit last year. He failed, My Lord, for want of experience.

The objections, My Lord, which the Sr. de la Mothe raised when he took over Fort Pontchartrain at Detroit, made it impossible for us to negotiate with him as with anyone else. He³ has always maintained that he ought to pay for nothing; and that the help and countenance which you ordered the Srs. de Vaudreuil and Raudot to give him consisted in granting him everything he asked for, telling them also that he had no need of it otherwise. They will follow the instructions which you give them, My Lord, as to the things which the said Sr. de la Mothe

od.

od: free-
, after
ing pun-
d him.

follow the
ditions to
letter, and
hing more
xplain to
Mothe.

---

¹The marginal notes marked 1 to 20 are supposed to have been written by the minister on this letter from MM. de Vaudreuil and Raudot.—Trans.

is to pay for, and will see that His Majesty is reimbursed the expenses he advanced for this post.

The provisions necessary for the troops have always been conveyed by the Company. It is true that it is asking to be reimbursed for it by His Majesty but, My Lord, the Sr. de la Mothe is making profit enough to be charged with this conveyance, and it will cost him nothing, for in every boat which he permits to go there, 300 lbs weight is taken up for him in order to obtain that permission, and the boats going down again also bring back 300lbs weight for him to this colony.

Before the Sr. de la Mothe set out, and in order to make him do so, the Sr. Raudot, junior, was obliged to promise[4] him to pay him for the presents he made to the savages at trading price, in accordance with the certificates of the almoners. He has sent him bills for presents made to the Miami savages, Pepikokia, and Onyatanous, to prevent them from going to war with the Outavois last winter, the prices of which are excessive, amounting to a total of 1982£ 7s. 6d. The said Sr. Raudot replied to him that these prices were too high, and that in future if he made presents he would request you, My Lord, in order to avoid any kind of dispute, to be good enough to decide on the prices. He has the honor to annex hereto the paragraph of the Sr. de la Mothe's letter in reply to his. You will see, My Lord, from the way in which he answers him, that the only pretext he catches at against your[5] being good enough to settle these matters is that he cannot wait for his money, although the Sr. Raudot, junior, has offered him goods from the store until such time as these matters should be settled.

He has sent the Sr. Raudot, junior, a bill for a gross amount of 905£ 19s. for expenses which have been incurred at Detroit[6] for the defence of that post which is only signed by the Sr. de Bourmont and the man named Grandmenil, agent of the said Sr. de la Mothe, and is not detailed at all. The Srs. de Vaudreuil and Raudot are convinced that no part of this bill is due to him, seeing that it is stated in it that this expense was incurred to keep the Miamis for the defence of that post, which cannot be, since it was the Miamis who were attacked by the Outavois, and it was not necessary to make them presents to induce them to defend their lives and those of their wives and children.

[4] ditto not to add.

[5] ditto.

[6] Do. to wi sharply to Mothe.

[9]undoubtedly. no one is allowed to sell any except at that place. [9]It ap
My Lord, that His Majesty certainly ought to be exempt fro[m]
tax which the said Sr. de la Mothe has imposed on the sale o[f]
He wanted to subject him to this tax like other people; for whe[n]

[10]to arrange all St. Pierre [10] required brandy at Detroit, and told the Sr. (
that; to recon-
cile the activi- that he found some at 11 livres a pot to be paid for at the St. [
ty and exces-
sive interest Montreal, he said he would not allow him to take that bran[d]
of La Mothe
with their con- forced him to get some at his shop, for which he made him g
tinual opposi-
tion. at the rate of 20 livres a pot, and against this the officer prot
interests of the King, who was to repay him the cost of his jo
have the honor of sending you a copy of this protest, begging
us your instructions on this point next year, and to be goo[d]
inform us also whether it is your will that he should exact
price from private persons, as it is not right to make them gi
for a pot of brandy when they can get it in other places for t[
livres.

The Srs. de Vaudreuil and Raudot think they are bound to
here of the course taken by the Sr. de la Mothe at Detroit. If h
it, he will make a fine domain for himself there. He make[s

[11]to learn come there to trade pay[11] rent for the land inclosed in the
[about this]—
and on what rate of 12 sols per foot, and the inhabitants a rate of 5 sols p[
founded. these sites they build houses there which are subjected to thes[
has granted lands cleared by the savages, which have been ab
the Outavis, at the rate of 20 sols per arpent in front by twen
and one crown per arpent frontage, instead of capons.

[12]do. to await [12] He gives the soldiers lands to clear for one year, and th
his explana-
tions and year he grants them at a rent. The agent of the said Sr. (
those of
Clairambault. is the Sr. Rané, an officer of the troops, and he gives hin
[13]certainly quantity of wheat, peas and butter for his lands. As to t
very bad. who have trades, he makes them give a sum of money every

away all the confidence the savages ought to have in them, and in that way, deprives these missionaries of the means of promoting religion.

The Srs. de Vaudreuil and Raudot have the honor of informing you [15to look i oppression] that when the Sr. de la Mothe went up to Detroit[15] in 1705 he took [thoroughl] some cattle, the conveyance of which was undertaken by a settler in this country. This settler was obliged to winter at Detroit, and under the pretence that he had done some trading there, for which the said settler even maintained that he had permission, when he wanted to go down to this colony the following year, the said Sr. de la Mothe would not permit him to do so until he had compelled him to give him a note for 93 livres, payable at Montreal. And when the said Sr. de la Mothe learnt that the said settler had stated publicly that he would complain to the Sr. Raudot about it, thinking that nothing would come of this affair, he forced him to pay him this sum before he left the fort, which appeared to the said Sr. Raudot to be so from the note which was laid before him by the said settler, endorsed the same day by the said Sr. de la Mothe. The said Sr. Raudot is unable to do this settler justice, the Sr. de la Forest having stated that he was not the Sr. de la Mothe's agent for matters of this kind. The Srs. de Vaudreuil and Raudot may be allowed to say that when a man behaves in this way he is acting despotically and taking the law into his own hands. The Srs. de Vaudreuil and Raudot will see to it that His Majesty is not charged with any of the expenses which the Company used to bear for Fort Pontchartrain at Detroit, and they will make the Sr. de la Mothe repay those which have been defrayed.

[16]The Sr. de Vaudreuil, with a view to carrying out the order which he [16to urge t all to settl] received from you, My Lord, last year, to grant fifty soldiers to the Sr. de [matters.] la Mothe, in which you did him the honor of sending him word that you thought his company and that of the Sr. de la Forest would suit him, offered these two companies to the Sr. de la Forest, the agent of the said Sr. de la Mothe here, with the remainder of the men from other companies if these two did not make up the number of fifty. The said Sr. de la Forest told the said Sr. de Vaudreuil that before he sent them off he would like to inform the Sr. de la Mothe of it, and he has made no reply on this point, according to what the said Sr. de la Forest has stated to the Sr. de Vaudreuil.

The Srs. de Vaudreuil and Raudot assure you, My Lord,[17] that they will [17good: th cannot do] give the Sr. de la Mothe all the help and all the facilities which lie in [much.] their power. If that settlement should fail, they can assure you that that [18to make responsibl] will certainly not proceed[18] from them but from the Sr. de la Mothe, who [for it.] pursues money-making far more than the interests of the settlement he has started.

The Sieurs de Vaudreuil and Raudot were not mistaken, My Lord, when they sent you word last year that, if there were an abuses in the brandy-

prevent
gether.

trade, they could only come through[19] Detroit. The Sr. de Boucherville, an officer of that post, tells them that a great trade in brandy was done at Detroit last year with the savages. This officer maintains that it was in order to prevent this that the Sr. de la Mothe has placed the whole of the brandy in the hands of one person only. But it is impossible to sell brandy at 20 livres a pot to the French unless trading goes on, and

od; ener-
ically.

moreover he assured us that more than 12 casks of it went[20] up in the first convoy of this year. They will not fail to see to the execution of the new decree you do them the honor of sending them, regarding the prohibition of brandy, and will send a copy of it to the Sr. de la Mothe.

The Sieurs de Vaudreuil and Raudot will have some men and a boat supplied to the Sr. D'Aigremont to make the round of the distant posts of Canada. They will also give him a copy of the agreement made by the Company with the Sr. de la Mothe, and an extract from the engagements entered into by the said Sr. de la Mothe. If they have any orders to send to any of these posts, they will avail themselves of him for taking them.

*

The Sieurs Raudot have the honor of giving you an account of Fort Frontenac in their private letter, and of assuring you here that they will pay great attention to the conduct of the Sr. de Tonty and, if they see that he is doing any trading they will inform you of it.

*   *   *

My Lord
        Your most humble and most obedient servants
                        Vaudreuil,
                Raudot,   Raudot.

Quebec the 15th of Novr. 1707.

WORDS OF THE OTTAWAS TO CADILLAC.

Words of the Outtavois to Monsieur de Lamothe on the 24th Sept. 1707.

O our father, M. de la Mothe, the Outtavois have obeyed you. We are sent by all the village to hearken to you. There is Le Pezant who came into our fort; you have the power to put him to death, but our old men beg you to grant him his life. He is your slave, you can make him eat under your table like a dog that picks up the bones, and the pieces you do not like.

Words of M. de la Mothe to Le Pezant, with three sticks of porcelain.

There you are, however, Pesant, before your father and your master. Is this that great chief, that was so well related and so highly esteemed? It was you, then, that ate my white bread every day at my table, that drank of my brandy and of my wine. Was it not you who had an incurable disease, of which I had you healed by my physician? Was it not you whom I helped in all your needs, and whose family I took care of? And, because of all these benefits, you have killed my people.

You hide yourself and droop your eyes. Was it not you, also, who went every day to the grey robe who used to caress you, who made you eat with him, and taught you? Yet it is you who have killed him.

There are reproaches, Pesant, which slay you; there is no longer life in your heart, and your eyes are half dead: you close them, they dare not look at the sun again. Go, my slave.

The Outtavois.

All the village asks you for the life of this slave, and we are commissioned to tell you that, if you level the land as it formerly was, the whole village of Michilimakina will take up their hearths and bring them here to Detroit. We love this place: we see our brethren in abundance while, where we are, our children go fasting; the ears of our corn are no longer than the little finger, but here they are a cubit long.

By a young slave.

The Outtavois apply to you alone. We fear you, open your door to us, do not keep it shut. May the rocks which have been rent asunder join together again; may there be no more trees fallen across the path, that all the children may be able to come and see their father, and their brethren who are near him. We have orders to ask you whether you will give us back our fields; that would be well. If you put us a little further away from you, that will be still better. Our old men await your reply; and, as soon as they receive it, part of the village will come this year and the rest next spring. The old men beg you to send the children beforehand a little wheat so as to enable them to eat sagamité.

M. de St. Pierre told us that we should be your slaves if we came to Detroit. He did not say so at the Council, but apart and in private. That made us think that he was a liar.

He also told us to ask Onontio for him to come and command at Michilimakina. No one wanted to go to Montreal with him, but he so strongly

old men, but they told me that they will leave without saying anything to him.

Council of the 25th of Sept. All that was said is not reported.

This council opened at 7 o'clock in the morning, and it was not over until 3 o'clock in the afternoon, and M. de la Mothe had not broken his fast. There were many difficulties on both sides. The tribes, however, always showing great deference to M. de la Mothe; but they told each other their faults point-blank without being able to avoid doing so, and we were not sorry for it.

M. Delamothe with a beautiful belt speaks to the Outtavois to put an end to their disputes.

I am satisfied and very much pleased with you Outtavois. I am a good father. Your submission has gained my heart; your obedience has made the axe fall from my hand and has saved your lives, and the lives of your wives and your children. Onontio and I are but one; he will love you now even as I love you.

And you, Pesant, why have you fled? You have no more courage than a child. Death has made you fearful, you who were so brave; you have trembled in the bosom of the father you had angered. But, learn that the obedience of the old men, your brothers, and all the young men, has disarmed me; and, for love of your brethren, your children and your wife, of your tribe and your allies, I give you your life. For I am your master now and could take you anywhere, because you are my slave; no one could find fault with it. But you have life once more; if you die in your flight, it is you who kill yourself.

M. De la Mothe speaks to all the tribes.

I thank all my children for having heard and obeyed me today. Behold they are all united in my bosom and under my wings. I greet them all, I embrace them. They have all cast out the poison which was in their hearts, their mouths are now cleansed.

Here I am in the midst of my beloved children; those who had gone astray have returned trustfully to their father. Their father receives them with joy, for he sees that they have repented of their transgression.

I am making a great bowl of soup to-day. I invite all the tribes that are the children of Onontio to sit down by this bowl, and I wish us all to eat of it together and drink the good broth. And, while we are seated near this bowl, who would be bold enough to come and shake it to spill the broth?

I had pity on your dead and covered them; their blood no longer shows upon the ground. I have buried my tomahawk; I had only kept the end of the handle until I obtained reparation from the Outtavois. I have obtained it; they have obeyed me; and I bury this tomahawk entirely. Today I set over it for good this great rock which rises up to the sun when it is noon. Who will ever be strong enough to take away so lofty a rock? Who, even, bold enough to think of moving it?

With this belt, Outtavois, I open for you the gate of my village. You shall enter it and your elbows shall not be rubbed against the posts of this gate. There were no longer rocks in the river, level with the surface of the water; they shall not split your boats; I join up again those which had been rent asunder.

The sun was but one cubit high, and lo! it is now at its meridian. The mists are scattered, the waters are calm, they will no longer flood our boats. You walk no more through the night, the fallen trees will no longer graze your legs, and see, the rugged earth is as smooth as the palm of the hand. I will give you lands when the old men are here, we will consider together the place where your fire shall be kindled. I will send wheat to my grandsons so that they may clasp their grandfather about the neck when they see him.

The Outtavois speak, with a package of beaver-skins.

Our men had lost their spirit; all the land was stupefied, and want had taken possession of our bones. The children had lost their senses, but their father puts them right, and sets them on a good path. We beg you to have what we need given to us, and to sell us goods as to your true children. If we dared we would pass our hands gently over you from head to foot, to show you that we are very grateful for the favors you are bestowing upon us; but our hands are still dirty, and we must first wash them.

O all ye Hurons and Miamis and others, who is there who will not hearken? Can anyone stop his ears when our father speaks? Let us take one another by the hand again, and let us again be friends even as we were before. Let us never again have evil thoughts when we see boats on the lakes or smoke on land. Let us not say they are men of evil disposition but let us approach those boats and go towards that smoke, and let us say "these are brothers of ours, they are the children of De la Mothe and Onontio."

Monsieur de la Mothe, with three sticks of porcelain, speaks to the Outtavois; this porcelain represents the black robe, as if it were present

stealth. This is a proof that you are a liar; for, if you were telling them the truth, you would tell them it at a council where there would be Frenchmen and chiefs. But you would not dare, for you well know that the King wishes the Outtavois to come and settle at Detroit. Would you state the contrary,. before me, black robe? Speak; you dare not; for if you did so I would send you to the King for disobedience.

What are you meddling with, black robe? Are you a man of war, have you a sword at your side? You are all tied up with your long robe that reaches down to your heels. Is it for you to settle matters? Speak of prayer and I will hearken to you; the Outtavois may hearken. Go and enter your church and pray to God, you are the director of prayer; go into the huts, clasp your hands and teach them to pray; that is your duty. Prayer is your concern, but not the affairs which there are between the tribes. Onontio is the ruler of all the land, and I am.ruler here.

COPY OF MONSIEUR DE LA MOTHE'S LETTER WRITTEN TO THE MARQUIS DE VAUDREUIL FROM FORT PONTCHARTRAIN ON THE FIRST OF OCTOBER, 1707.

Sir,

I received by Malet[1] the letter which you did me the honor to write me on the 3rd of August.

You will have been informed as to everything by the return of M. de St. Pierre[2] from Repentigny. He will perhaps not have told you that he almost forced Sakima and the other two to go down, and to go and ask for him as commandant over them at Michilmakina.

I am sorry for the differences which he is said to have had with the savages who had gone down to Montreal, who came up again by the great

It is true, the twelve hundred marten-skins, which he is said to have taken away, may indemnify him to some extent.

Le Pesant was brought to me here by the Sr. D'Argenteuil with an 3rd. escort of ten Outtavois for greater security.

When the French and savages saw this boat in the distance, they gave 4th. a great shout. They went to the river when he landed, making a great uproar; and this poor wretch, while he was still in the boat, stretched out his hand to a Canadian and said to him—"I see I am a dead man." His teeth chattered so violently that you would have said he was tormented with ague though I think, if he had had it, he would have been healed of it.

I gave orders for him to be brought into the fort. He passed the night 5th. there in a house with his people, but escaped at daybreak over the palisade of the fort without being observed by the sentinels. He left his shoes, his knife and his shabby hat. He is so thin, and so altered that it would be hard to recognize him; and apparently he will perish in the woods. I had search made for him by the Hurons, the French, and also by the Outtavois, who were very much afraid of being put in his place, during one day when I kept the whole ten of them in prison.

What does it matter? The Outtavois have submitted and made the repa- 6th. ration demanded of them. Among the savages a man in this position is reckoned as dead, and remains without the right to speak, and without influence. He is my slave.

Peace has been established, and that firmly. We are now in a condi- 7th. tion of great quiet. I pray Heaven it may last. Having made peace here with the savages, I should like to be at peace with everyone. I hope you may be satisfied with my action. 1 believed I was doing well and carrying out what you wished.

The arrival of the Doge of Genoa in France was regarded throughout 8th. Europe with astonishment; that of Le Pesant, here, with surprise by all our tribes, who were never able to believe that the Outtavois would submit in this way. It is, indeed, a haughty tribe, and this man really has strong alliances. For this reason, this peace will be all the more advantageous and glorious to us, and will be a matter for reflection for all the chiefs, and still more for the others.

I have gone over my letter of the 15th of June; I have observed noth- 9th. ing like what you refer to. I see nothing in it which savors of menace. There is only one place where these words occur—"that will not hinder me from availing myself," perchance, of certain documents "at a suitable time."

who claim to have an intimate understanding of {
but are completely ignorant of them. I confess
because I felt from all your letters that you wisł
from the Outtavois, but that you might give wɛ
quest of many people who are always harassing
the state, which they do on account of their own
some other hidden purpose.

I have indeed, Sir, on certain occasions, acted :
Monsieur de Frontenac and M. de Callières. '
that, if my style was not that of a courtier, for {
less of worth.

If it be desired that I should write and flatter,
it will cost me dear, for at such times one outraɟ

;b.   I shall always speak my mind plainly in wha·
King's service. For example, it appeared to me
you· have taken in this affair, the only aim you
with the Outtavois, as if there were no tribe to bɛ
it was this tribe that trembled, with reason, t
fingers.

b.   When a man has been killed unjustly, it is not ·
ply to, to learn from him whether he would like to
the relatives of the dead man, for the murderer ₁
to arrange matters—that is not to be expected.]
Aoyatanous have been·attacked; you have said ₁
not know their minds, and as soon as the blow wa
for them with the Outtavois, while they were brɛ
& had been attacked.

ь.   The letters you wrote me were ambiguous and
purposes—am I to guess them? Tribes are not
way. You certainly put me in very great diff

mand, and you returned the ball to me to see how I should play it, and how I should extricate myself from this business. I also observed that, although you had no security that we should succeed in making peace, you allowed the Outtavois who went down to trade at Montreal and load themselves with ammunition, and by this means to put themselves in a position to refuse to submit. That amounts to saying to me on the one hand—"find means of making peace," while, [on the other hand] "I give your enemies the means of making war against you." I will stop, and give up a multitude of remarks that might be made as to your orders. Pardon me that I explain my meaning so freely; it is a proof of my open dealing, and of the sincerity of my opinions.

For the rest, Sir, since you desire that your orders should be carried out, I beg you will make those you send me quite plain and let them be free from ambiguity; for, otherwise, I take the liberty of telling you that I should delay their execution, as well as if they were not advisable, in the interests of this post and of this new colony.

M. de la Forest is not my agent down there, Sir. That would by no means befit his dignity, except in a certain contingency. He is detached by the Court, as you know, to serve as second in command at this post. I have sent him down there for the good of this settlement in accordance with the authority which the Court has given me to do so, to carry out my orders there; of this he acquits himself thoroughly well, and I am greatly obliged to him for it, and am well satisfied with him in other ways. He will still continue to represent to you—whatever concerns this new colony.

The men Chale, Chateleraud, and Tienel have gone to Michilmakina. M. de la Forest has, I believe, taken the proper steps in the matter; and I have nothing more to do with it. I am with deep respect, Sir, your most humble and most obedient servant.

[Signed]   La Mothe Cadillac.

45

ho claim to have an intimate understanding of the interests of the tribes,
it are completely ignorant of them. I confess, Sir, I insisted strongly
cause I felt from all your letters that you wished to obtain satisfaction
om the Outtavois, but that you might give way a good deal at the re-
iest of many people who are always harassing the man at the helm of
e state, which they do on account of their own private interests, or for
me other hidden purpose.

I have indeed, Sir, on certain occasions, acted in the same way towards
onsieur de Frontenac and M. de Callières. The result showed them
at, if my style was not that of a courtier, for the time, it was none the
ss of worth.

If it be desired that I should write and flatter, or flatter when I wrote,
will cost me dear, for at such times one outrages one's sincerity.

I shall always speak my mind plainly in what I think to concern the
ing's service. For example, it appeared to me, in adopting the course
u have taken in this affair, the only aim you had was to make peace
th the Outtavois, as if there were no tribe to be feared but this; and yet
was this tribe that trembled, with reason, to the very tips of their
gers.

When a man has been killed unjustly, it is not the murderer that we ap-
ʏ to, to learn from him whether he would like to arrange matters; it is to
e relatives of the dead man, for the murderer will make no great effort
arrange matters—that is not to be expected. The Hurons, Miamis, and
ıyatanous have been attacked; you have said nothing to them; you do
t know their minds, and as soon as the blow was struck you made peace
: them with the Outtavois, while they were breathing nothing but war,
had been attacked.

mand, and you returned the ball to me to see how I should play it, and how I should extricate myself from this business. I also observed that, although you had no security that we should succeed in making peace, you allowed the Outtavois who went down to trade at Montreal and load themselves with ammunition, and by this means to put themselves in a position to refuse to submit. That amounts to saying to me on the one hand—"find means of making peace," while, [on the other hand] "I give your enemies the means of making war against you." I will stop, and give up a multitude of remarks that might be made as to your orders. Pardon me that I explain my meaning so freely; it is a proof of my open dealing, and of the sincerity of my opinions.

For the rest, Sir, since you desire that your orders should be carried out, I beg you will make those you send me quite plain and let them be free from ambiguity; for, otherwise, I take the liberty of telling you that I should delay their execution, as well as if they were not advisable, in the interests of this post and of this new colony.

M. de la Forest is not my agent down there, Sir. That would by no means befit his dignity, except in a certain contingency. He is detached by the Court, as you know, to serve as second in command at this post. I have sent him down there for the good of this settlement in accordance with the authority which the Court has given me to do so, to carry out my orders there; of this he acquits himself thoroughly well, and I am greatly obliged to him for it, and am well satisfied with him in other ways. He will still continue to represent to you—whatever concerns this new colony.

The men Chale, Chateleraud, and Tienel have gone to Michilmakina. M. de la Forest has, I believe, taken the proper steps in the matter; and I have nothing more to do with it. I am with deep respect, Sir, your most humble and most obedient servant.

[Signed]   La Mothe Cadillac.

45

OBSERVATIONS OF THE MARQUIS DE VAUDREUIL ON THE LETTER FROM DE LAMOTHE OF THE 1ST OF OCTOBER, 1707.

The Sieur de la Mothe. My Lord, begins his letter by informing me that the Sr. de St. Pierre induced Sakima, Kataoulibois and the other savages who came down with them, almost by force, to come and speak to me, "in order" he says—"that they might ask for him as commandant at Michilimakina." The talk of these savages to me on the 7th of October, a copy of which I have the honor of sending you marked "F," settles this point and proves that it was of their own accord that they came down, to give me an account of all that had taken place, and not to ask me for the Sr. de St. Pierre as commandant, since they did not ask me for anyone.

The Sr. de la Mothe, fearing lest I may have complied with the supposed request of the savages, goes on to try and make me suspect the Sr. de St. Pierre, by accusing him of having engaged in trade. As I have the honor of sending you annexed hereto a copy of the order I gave the said Sr. de St. Pierre on his departure, you will see, My Lord, that I could not have taken any more suitable steps for preventing this boat from doing any trading. If the Sr. de Lamothe has proofs of what he alleges, he has but to produce them and I will deal with the Sieur de St. Pierre as he deserves.

When the Sieur de la Mothe says that Le Pesant was escorted by ten

x letter

his arrival, it needed but little more to make a man's teeth chatter, especially those of a savage.

The Sieur de La Mothe is too clever a man not to have taken all pos- 5th. sible precautions for securing Le Pesant, if he had not wished to let him escape. But, as he did not dare to put him to death, nor to keep him in his fort without making an example of him, and did not find out the mistake he had made in bringing him there until he saw him, he was very glad to set a Huron on to frighten him, so as to induce him—as he did—to escape. For to say that a man of at least seventy years of age, bulky and corpulent like Le Pesant, who bears that name only on account of his obesity, escaped over the palisade without their having consented to it, in a fort filled with people and provided with sentinels, is not at all probable. It is much truer to say, which is indeed the fact, that the Sr de La Mothe aided him to escape; for two reasons. The first, because he was very glad to get rid of him; and the second, because he was very glad to humor the Outtavois; and, whether Le Pesant returns to Michilimakina or whether he perishes—as he says—of hunger in the woods, he is no longer responsible, as he has declared to the Outtavois that if he had stayed he would have pardoned him.

"What does it matter" says the Sr. de La Mothe "the Outtavois have 6th. submitted and made the reparation we demanded from them. With the savages, a man in this position is considered as dead, he remains without the right to speak and without influence. He is my slave."

I do not intend, My Lord, in any way to disparage what the Sr. de La Mothe may do for the benefit of His Majesty's service. I am even very glad that he found an easy means of making peace for the Outtavois with us—both with us and with the other tribes. As I have already had the honor of writing to you, I only referred this affair to him with that object, and also to give him authority with the savages. But when the Sr. de la Mothe attributes the honor of it to himself alone, while I have labored for a whole year in taking steps to succeed in making this peace; when I see him saying and writing to everybody that it is he who has at last brought tranquility to the upper countries; that it was he only who compelled the Outtavois to submit absolutely to his will, and that without him I did not know where I was; I confess, Sir, that I cannot refrain from looking into his conduct, and following closely all that has taken place so as to give you an account of it. "Peace has 7th. been established, and that firmly" &c, says the Sr. de La Mothe in this paragraph; and, lower down, "I believed I was doing well and carrying out your will."

This news, my Lord, cannot but please me; and I should be wrong to complain of this letter if all its contents corresponded with this para-

"The arrival of the Doge of Genoa in France was regarded with astonishment throughout Europe; that of Le Pesant, here with surprise by
all our tribes," &c.

This paragraph throughout shows, my Lord, that I was not mistaken
in informing you in all my letters that it was more difficult than it
was thought to be, to have Le Pesant killed, looking to his alliances and
his importance among the tribes. But as regards what M. de la Mothe
says, that his arrival at Detroit was regarded with surprise by all the
tribes, it would not have been very great if they had known, as I know,
that Le Pesant had a promise from the Sr. d' Argenteuil, who was sent
for him by M. de la Mothe, that no harm should be done to him. Yet
that is a fact, which it is easy to prove, not only by the Frenchmen who
were at Michilimakina while the affair took place, but also from a diary
of the journey of the Sr. d' Argenteuil and the Sr. de St. Pierre to
Michilimakina, which has been sent me, and is in the handwriting of
the Sieur d' Argenteuil. It is stated, My Lord, in a paragraph of this
diary, speaking of Le Pesant, "We sent for him into a hut outside the
fort, and both told him that we had come for him and that he was to
embark to go to Detroit, to be given into the hands of M. de la Mothe.
I repeated to him emphatically to embark and said to him 'Things are
going well all round; you see the tribes are going away well satisfied,
believing that a general peace has been concluded; and if you do not
embark, you will upset the whole country once more.' "

Is it natural, my Lord, to advise a man to go and get put to death
for the welfare of his tribe? And is it not more likely, as I have been
assured, that he had been promised that no harm should be done to him.
If this paragraph is not sufficient, what follows in the same diary is a
proof of the promise which had been given him—"Meiavila and Katalaouibois gave him a thousand good reasons to convince him, asking him
whether, at his age, he was afraid to die and whether he did not think

la Mothe would have us believe, that Le Pesant went and gave himself into his hands. What is true is that the Sr. de la Mothe took advantage of the opportunity; and that, as the tribes were not informed of the tacit promise which had been made to this savage, his arrival is certain always to add to our reputation with them. God grant that his flight may not do us harm. Finally the Sr. de La Mothe believed he was acting for the best, at least I am convinced of it; and moreover I do not intend, in anything I have the honor of writing to you here, to disparage anything which may be to his advantage. I only wish to reply to the paragraphs of his letter and to let you know his disposition, which is to set himself up above everyone, to make capital out of everything, and invariably to blame the conduct of others.

The Sieur de la Mothe, My Lord, in the ninth paragraph of this 9th. letter, says that he has gone over the one he wrote me on the 19th of June last, and has seen nothing approaching threatening; that there is nothing but a passage in which are these words "that will not hinder me from availing myself, perchance, of certain documents at a suitable time;" but that this does not refer to me and only relates to the people whose names I ask him for. I am willing to believe this since he gives me this explanation; it appears to me nevertheless, on reading the whole passage, that it is of me he is speaking. It is in his letter of the 19th of June 1707, where he writes—"You also tell me, Sir, that I ought to have sent you the names of those who opposed the giving up of Le Pesant to me, and the proofs. I will only reply that I am too far away to bring law suits; it would be necessary first for me to know what form you wish these proofs to take, and when I have examples of them I will consider what I should do. That will not hinder me from availing myself of certain documents at a suitable time."

I do not know, Sir, whether it is of me he is speaking, or of the persons whose names I ask him for. But if this passage as a whole is not clear enough for me to be able to take it to myself, I cannot be unaware that he is referring to me when he says in the same letter—

"No secret intrigue is necessary for causing the originator of the attack which was made on this fort, to be punished with death—I mean Le Pesant, his head and his life must answer for it. His tribe must be compelled to hand him over to me alive; in order to leave me to deal with him; and if that is done, I answer for it that his head will not remain long on his shoulders. Can you exact any less reparation for the deaths of the Reverend Father Constantin and other Frenchmen, and for such an outrage on the King's fort? The thing would have been done long ago if your orders had not been opposed to it."

According to that letter, my Lord, it is I who hinder the reparation

Le Pesant at his disposal and that solely because I referred all these matters to him. Whence comes it, then, that he has not had him executed, as he ought—according to this letter—to have done, and has contented himself with simply making him jump over the palisade of his fort? It is because he never properly understood the importance of this affair until he saw it ready to be accomplished.

The Sieur de La Mothe says, in his tenth paragraph, that, as regards his style, he only expresses his feelings, because he knows an endless number of flatterers who claim to have an intimate understanding of the interests of the tribes, but are completely ignorant of them; and, lower down, "I have indeed, Sir, acted in the same way on certain occasions, towards Messrs. de Frontenac and de Callieres; the sequel showed that if my style was not that of a courtier at the time, it was none the less valuable for that."

· I do not know, my Lord, who these flatterers are, of whom the Sr. de La Mothe would speak; I cannot therefore reply on that point. But, as to what he says of the manner in which he wrote in former times to MM. de Frontenac and de Callières, and that they did not take exception to it, I had the honor of knowing those gentlemen, and I have seen all the letters he wrote to them. I can tell you, my Lord, that if he had had the effrontery to make use of the expressions with which, for a year past, he has filled all the letters he has written to me, they would certainly have brought him to a sense of his duty; and I should certainly have done so too, had not my knowledge of the favor you have been graciously pleased to honor him with, held me back, as it were, until I was able to bring you my complaints about it myself, and show you how far he departs from his duty to me.

"I shall always speak my mind plainly in what I believe concerns my King's service; for example," says the Sr. de la Mothe in this 11th paragraph of his letter, "in adopting the course you have taken in this affair, the only aim you had was to make peace with the Outtavois, as if there were no tribe to be feared but this; and yet it was this tribe which trembled, with reason, to the very tips of their fingers."

Even if I had had no other object but to make peace for the Outtavois with us and with the other tribes, I should consider I had done a good thing; for the Sieur de La Mothe himself cannot help saying, with a sort of joy, and writing word to all his friends, "Peace is concluded and that firmly; we are now in a state of great tranquility here, I pray heaven it may last."

That makes me believe that he is persuaded that this peace is of greater importance than he pretends. But he knows very well, and I had the honor also of informing you last year, that if I looked after the Outtavois and prevented them from being destroyed, it was not on their account, but on account of the Iroquois who would be too formidable, in case of any quarrel with them, if I were without the Outtavois to divert their attention. As I have had the honor my Lord, of explaining my reasons to you more fully, I will not repeat them any further. 12th.

In the 12th paragraph of the Sr. de la Mothe's letter he says, "when a man has been unjustly killed, it is not to the murderer that we apply, to learn from him whether he would like to arrange matters;" and afterwards, that the Hurons, Miamis, and Ayoatanous have been attacked; and that without knowing their minds, as soon as the blow was struck, I made their peace with the Outtavois, while they were breathing nothing but war, and had been attacked." If we could debate with the savages, as is done in Europe, on the interests and contentions of each tribe, it would perhaps not be very difficult to prove that if the Outtavois were the agressors in the Detroit affair, in attacking the Miamis, yet they only anticipated what was to be done to them. But as that would be out of place, it is sufficient for me to reply to the Sr. de la Mothe's point that I did not seek out the Outtavois, for it was they themselves who came to me; and I did not make peace with them without learning the attitude of the tribes they had offended against, for I referred them to Detroit to find means of satisfying me and, at the same time to make their peace with the other tribes.

The Sieur de La Mothe complains in the 13th paragraph that my let- 13th. ters were vague and ambiguous; and afterwards that, as he was unable to find out my purpose, I put him in a real difficulty, more especially as I had made the Outtavois go down to Montreal without summoning any of the parties interested there, which put him in the unpleasant dilemma of being compelled either to join the savages in making war on the Outtavois, in spite of my orders, or to draw down on himself war with these same savages if, in pursuance of my orders, he refused to side with them. What the Sieur de La Mothe says in this paragraph would be very reasonable if it were true. This much is certain, that my letters are not ambiguous, and if there is any vagueness in them, that can only be because he gave me no news of his post from which I could gather his real opinions, and I was afraid of having any steps taken which might injure his settlement. But, as regards the Sieur de la Mothe's statement that I sent for the Outtavois without summoning any of the other tribes concerned, that, my Lord, saving the respect I owe to you, is a very great falsehood. I did not send and invite the Outtavois to come to Montreal, though I was not sorry to see them come down there. However, one proof that I would do nothing without the concurrence of the other tribes, is that I referred these same Outtavois to him at Detroit, and would not settle anything with them.

your mind all the time to send the Outtavois to the spot, to make reparation there;" and afterwards he replies that this cannot have been my
intention, and, as proof, he says that he saw from my words to the
Outtavois that after I had demanded Le Pesant and his head, upon
their raising objections I returned the ball to him to see how he would
play it, and how he would extricate himself from the affair. I had the
honor of explaining to you, My Lord, at sufficient length, in my letter of
the 24th of July, all the reasons for my action. It is true that the last
reason, which I have not yet had the honor of telling you, is, that I
know the evil disposition of the Sr. de La Mothe, and that I was not
sorry therefore—seeing that it was compatible with the welfare of the
King's service—to lay upon him the necessity of making peace himself,
leaving him free regarding it to a great degree so that, if he failed to make
peace, at least he could not say that I was only seeking opportunities
for injuring his post.

He also observed, he says, that I had permitted the Outtavois to trade
at Montreal and to load themselves with ammunition without having
any security that peace would be made. I might, indeed, tell him that
it was he himself who allowed Onaskin and Catalaonibois to trade at
Detroit without having any certainty of what was to happen. But I
prefer to assure you at once, My Lord, that what he says about the
Outtavois, who came down to Montreal with Jean le Blanc and loaded
themselves there with ammunition, is a tale he has invented. That is
no difficult matter for the Sieur de La Mothe; he has had the privilege
of doing so for a long time.

For the rest, he kindly warns me, My Lord, to make the orders I
send him quite plain and free from ambiguity, for otherwise—he says—
he will not carry out any of them. That will not prevent me, nevertheless, from sending him orders whenever I think it advantageous and
necessary for the welfare of the service; and whatever the Sieur de La
Mothe may say, I know what my duty requires of me.

Everything offends him, My Lord, in what I write to him; and his
touchiness goes so far that because I mentioned to him in a letter that
the Sieur de la Forest, his agent down here, had told me certain things
concerning his post, he takes up the cudgels in his behalf and writes—

"M. de la Forest is not my 'agent' down there Sir. That would by no
means befit his dignity, except in a certain contingency. He is detached

I do not know, My Lord, whether it is the Sr. de La Mothe, a captain of the troops and commandant at Detroit, who speaks in this paragraph; or a Governor General of the Upper country. At all events, having seen his power of attorney to the wife of the Sieur de la Forest when she left for France, and seeing the Sieur de la Forest here transacting the Sieur de la Mothe's business and looking after all his interests, I did not think I was doing him any injury by calling him his agent; and I thought I was the more justified in doing so, and that I could not be wronging the dignity of the said Sr. de la Forest, because I have received word from Detroit that the Sieur de la Mothe has taken the Sieur de Roenne, a lieutenant of the troops, as his bailiff. That being so, it seems to me, My Lord, that this title of bailiff is far less befitting for an officer of His Majesty's troops than that of attorney or agent.

This last paragraph of the Sieur de la Mothe's letter makes me take notice of the manner in which he speaks to the savages up there in the councils that he holds; and, as I am doing myself the honor of sending you annexed hereto a copy of the last one he forwarded to me, within the last few days, concerning the peace he concluded with the savage tribes, on the arrival of Le Pesant. I also take the liberty of telling you that it does not accord with the rank which I have the honor to hold, that the Sieur de La Mothe should put himself in comparison with me, sometimes saying "Onnontio and I are one," sometimes having the savages told that if they see smoke on their way they may go to the place without fear, feeling sure that it can only be the children of M. de la Mothe and Onnontio—as if they were two separate governors—and lastly, hinting to them, as far as he can, that he is the absolute master up there, and he can regulate all matters by himself at will. That is not a proper thing for him to do, My Lord, nor is it expedient in the interests of the service.

M. de Ramezay has a different reputation in this country from the Sr. de la Mothe. I should be wrong if I complained of his conduct in this respect. He never speaks to the savages without letting them know that the Governor General is the sole master. It has been an established custom from all times, and is one which even leads the savages to have great respect for the Governor General. The Sr. de la Mothe has his reasons for behaving differently, in order the better to maintain the independence he affects.

I hope, My Lord, that you will be so good as to set this right; and in the meantime I shall always maintain as I am bound to do, the position which you have done me the honor to procure for me.

46

SPEECHES OF THREE INDIANS FROM MICHILIMAKINA.

Words of Three Savages from Michilimakina, who arrived at Quebec on the 7th of October, 1707, with the Sr. de St. Pierre, to the Governor General.

Kataolaouibois, one of the chiefs of the tribe of the Kiskakous, spoke for Sakima and himself, and also in the name of the Kiskakous and Sinagoux.

My father, behold we have at last come before you, Sakima and I, in order to show you how obedient we are to your orders, and to give you an account, at the same time, of all that passed at Michilimakina and Detroit during the course of the summer.

When Otontagon, that is, Jean le Blanc, had come down here, my father, with the others whom we had sent with him to try and appease your anger, we were impatient for their return, all the more as they had promised us to make as great dispatch as possible, so as to let us know your will as soon as they could. But, as you did not think fit to send them all back by the great river, and Jean le Blanc, with the greater part of them, proceeded by Detroit, the rest of those whom you sent back by the great river, when they arrived at Michilimakina and gave us an account of their journey, informed us at the same time that St. Pierre, whom you have sent to Detroit with Jean le Blanc, was to come through Michilimakina on his return from Detroit, in order to speak to the tribes.

Then I arose, my father (for you know that I have ever been French at heart) and I asked the young men as well as the old men whether they were drunken or asleep, and whether they did not understand the news that was brought to them from Montreal. "What!" I said to them, "St. Pierre is at Detroit with Jean le Blanc, he is to come by here in order to speak to the tribes, and you do not pay the least attention to the message of your father. Come! set out, young men, and bear this news to the Saulteurs, the Noquets, the Folles Avoines, the Poutouatamis, the Sakis, the Puants, and the Outagamis, so that St. Pierre may find them all here on his arrival, and nothing may hinder Onontio's will."

When I saw that St. Pierre was long in coming, I said to the old man, "What does that mean? Can any accident have happened to St. Pierre, and the message of our father be delayed on the way? I am going to Detroit to meet St. Pierre, if he has not arrived I will wait for him."

When I arrived at Detroit, my father, I found St. Pierre, and he, serving as an interpreter for M. de la Mothe, asked me in an angry tone, "Where are you going?" My heart was frozen within me, seeing the manner in which St. Pierre spoke to me; me, who only went to Detroit with good intentions, and had only left Michilimakina in order to be informed sooner of the will of my father. But as St. Pierre continued to ask me where I was going, while important business was going on at Detroit, and whether I came to prevent it from succeeding, I replied that, so far from having any evil design or wishing to spoil anything, I only came to tell him that a boat had set out to assemble the tribes, in accordance with the will of our father.

The next day M. de la Mothe sent me word by St. Pierre that I could go back with Onnaskin if I wished, but that as to the woman and children and my furs, all those were to remain until matters had been settled.

I answered M. de la Mothe that the matters on which Onontio had sent St. Pierre were important, but that, as for what related to my furs, that was of no importance; and that, as I had come to Detroit in good faith, if he would not allow me to sell them there I could very well take them away again.

When I saw, my father, that M. de La Mothe would not receive my furs, I suspected that there was something special which was being kept from me, for our men had not confessed to us at Michilimakina that you had demanded the head of Le Pesant at Montreal. I applied to one of our young men who knew all the news, as he had gone down with Jean le Blanc. He asked me whether Jean le Blanc had told me nothing, and when I replied "No" he said to me "There are many matters, you will hear about them."

Then I applied to Jean le Blanc and I asked him whence it came that I, whom myself am French, as well as all the Kiskakous, was detained at Detroit while he, who was among those who had caused the troubles at Detroit, appeared to be completely at liberty there. I told him at least to let me know, since he had seen Onontio, what had been decided at Montreal.

He told me that he was very glad to see me, and that, since I wished to learn the news, he would conceal nothing from me, and that Onontio at Montreal had demanded the head of Le Pesant to wash out the blood of the Recollet father; that, since he had been unable to promise him absolutely to make this reparation, for this evil-minded bear was like a great tree which has strong roots and is very hard to tear up, Onontio had referred him to M. de La Mothe to seek with him the means of complying with it, at Detroit itself, and at the same time to make his peace with the other tribes; but that he had declared to him that he

which M. de La Mothe might grant to him and all the Outtavois in his name; that M. de La Mothe, who has orders from Onontio, and is as another self to him at Detroit, had demanded Le Pesant from him absolutely, in order to have him at his disposal; and lastly that, seeing that it was the will of Onontio; and that there was no other means of satisfying him, he had promised M. de La Mothe to send him this great bear, or to kill him himself if he refused to embark; that those were the important matters which had at first been concealed from me; that this was the will of Onontio, and he had been unable to excuse himself from doing it. Then, my father, I took Jean le Blanc by the arm and said to him—"Good, that is a good thing, and is as it should be."

The next day Ottontagan and Kinougé, that is, Jean le Blanc and Le Brochet, took Onaskin and me before Mons. de La Mothe and said to us—"My brothers! we told you yesterday that we had given our word to Onontio to deliver Le Pesant up to him, that we had promised M. de La Mothe to do so. We are very much pleased to repeat the same thing to you to-day in his presence, and we tell you also that, if Le Pesant will not come to Detroit, we will kill him in the village." "Good" said I, "that is well." Then M. de La Mothe told me that I might trade with my furs. What, then, was M. de La Mothe thinking? Did he believe that by keeping back my furs he could make me do his will more readily? Did he not know that self-interest is nothing to me, but that I am ever obedient to my father?

I told M. de La Mothe,—and St. Pierre who is here can tell you so, my father, for it was he who acted as interpreter—I told M. de La Mothe that Le Pesant was not related to us, so that it was for Jean le Blanc and Kinougé to give him up; that as for us, we should be always ready to give them all the help they might need for the success of that matter, and that it was sufficient that it was the will of Onontio.

M. de La Mothe said to us in the evening, "St. Pierre is to set out to-morrow; embark and keep constantly under his flag, for there are three

portance, too many precautions cannot be taken in it. Look at M. de Louvigny when he came for the Iroquois; before taking them away it was very necessary that he should know all hearts and should listen calmly to all arguments.

I will not tell you, my father, everything that took place when St. Pierre arrived at Michilimakina; it is for him to give you an account of it.

* *

Three days after our arrival at Michilimakina, the outlying tribes having departed to return to their own homes, we put the affair of Le Pesant before a Council; for we had not dared to speak of it as long as the tribes were gathered together, because he is allied to almost all the tribes. I will not tell you further, My Lord, all that took place concerning him; it is for St. Pierre to inform you of it. But I will say to you boldly, in his presence, that it was Onnaskin, Sakima, Meyavila and I, in fact, that it was the Kiskakous and the Sinagaux who compelled Le Pesant to embark to go to M. de La Mothe at Detroit in accordance with your will. If there had been no one but Jean le Blanc, he would never have dared to attack this great tree; but as for your children of Michilimakina, we were all resolved to kill him if he had refused to embark, rather than find ourselves exposed to your anger for love of him.

My father, our dread is lest M. de La Mothe should not put him to death; and lest, remembering that we had given him up to you, he may seek to avenge himself.

That, my father, is all that we have to say to you. Only Sakima now remains [to be heard] and he begs you to excuse him for not having brought you slaves to give his brothers the Iroquois. He would not have come down had not his desire to bear witness to you of his obedience overborne the fear he felt that you would reproach him for having failed in his word. He gives you his word again, my father, and you shall not have reason to complain of him.

REPLY OF THE MARQUIS DE VAUDREUIL TO CATALAOUIBOIS
ON THE 8TH OCTOBER.

Endorsed.—Reply of the Governor General to Koutaoulibois; Sakima, and Makatepilé who came down from Michilimakina with the Sr. de St. Pierre, who arrived at Quebec on the 7th October, 1707.

I have seen, Kataoulibois, from what you told me yesterday, and what the Sr. de St. Pierre told me on his arrival, also from the letters of Monsieur de Lamothe, all that took place at Detroit and Michilimakina concerning Le Pesant, that bear who has caused troubles for such a long time. I am very glad that my children of Michilimakina have at last opened their eyes to their own interests and have, in accordance with my will, sent to M. de La Mothe the man who was the only cause that I could not make a true peace with them.

M. de La Mothe being at Detroit is my other self, since he has my orders. I am quite sure he will follow them in every detail, and, having Le Pesant in his hands, he will dispose of him as may be necessary, in the best interests of peace.

I am delighted to see you here. I know that Kataouliboué's mind has always been well disposed, and his heart French; I have therefore a real esteem for him. I have no less esteem for Sakima; and although he has not brought any slaves here with him this journey, for me to give to his brothers the Iroquois, in accordance with his promise, I will not say anything to him about it, on condition that he brings them to me as soon as he possibly can next year, that the Iroquois may not be able to reproach me with being a liar, and with seeking only to deceive them.

I will not delay you, my children. The season is far advanced. You may therefore depart when you please. Take to your brothers the good news that peace has been made, and that they have entirely disarmed my anger by their submission, in sending Le Pesant to M. de La Mothe to dispose of.

You may go now to Detroit, or come to Montreal; these two doors are

me, also, that after everyone had given expression to the feelings of his heart in his presence, you were all united together as true brothers ought to be. Continue in this mind, which is so much to your advantage; and since the land is thus once more united, take care to do nothing in future which might spoil it. Always obey your word; hearken to what M. de La Mothe says to you when you go to Detroit, and he speaks to you in my name; listen to Father Marest, when he brings you word from me: then you will never do anything but what is right.

As I am convinced that you only seek to do my will, and that your heart is with the French. In giving you these proofs of my liberality and of the regard I have for you, I recommend Father Marest to all three of you, but especially to you Katalaouibois and Sakima, that you may both take him under your care, and may prevent anyone whomsoever from offering him any insult. I will have two coverlets of scarlet cloth given to you for you two at Montreal, and also before you leave Montreal you shall be given enough provisions, powder, lead and tobacco for your journey. Ten livres of tobacco will also be given you for Father Marest; take great care of it, and remember well all I have said to you.

' SIEUR DE TONTY IN COMMAND OF FORT FRONTENAC.

Endorsed—Minutes. Canada 1707.

The Sr. de Tonty.   4th October.

M. de Vaudreuil has put him in command of Fort Frontenac; he manages the Iroquois so as to keep them always on the side of the French.

He begs that no credence may be given to what the Sr. de La Mothe has written as to his conduct, while he was in command at Detroit for the Company of the Colony. He says that he has always strictly obeyed the orders of the said Sr. de Vaudreuil, and that he has never been wanting in zeal for His Majesty's service.

REPORT FROM MARQUIS DE VAUDREUIL.

The Marquis de Vaudreuil, 8th of November.[1]

He takes all possible care to maintain the good understanding that has existed up to the present time between M. Raudot and him, being convinced that it is for the advantage of the Colony of Canada.

As the chief concern of this country is to maintain also a firm union among the savage tribes allied to the French, he has always devoted himself to that as far as he possibly could.

It appeared to him of great importance not to allow the act which the Outaouack savages committed at Detroit de Pontchartrain to go unpunished, so as to keep all the other savage tribes in awe; but, as it was not advisable to make use of the Iroquois, nor of the Huron and Miami Indians to destroy that tribe, he has sought for a means of compelling the Outaouacks to make reparation for this act, and he has succeeded.

These savages came to him at Montreal while he was there, to apologize and ask for pardon, and he thought it advisable to be hard with them, and to send them back to the Sr. de La Motte to seek means for adjusting the affair, and making their peace with the Huron and Miami Indians, who were concerned in the fight at Detroit.

Two chief reasons induced him to deal with it in this way; the first to inform the Iroquois of all the proceedings of these savages; and the second, to show the said Sr. de La Motte that, far from being in any way opposed to the settlement of Detroit, he sought only to make him influential among all the tribes in the neighborhood of that post.

He succeeded in his first object; for the Ouctaouacks, impressed by what he had told them at Montreal,—that he could not pardon them if they did not find means, with the said Sr. la Motte, to make peace all round at Detroit,—not only promised the said Sr. de La Motte all that he wished of them, but have even sent him the Ouctaouack chief who

As the said Sr. de La Motte skilfully hints that it is to him alone that these savages have conceded the point of sending him the chief who committed the act at Detroit, he thought he ought to state that it was the demand which he made on this point at Montreal, in the presence of M. Raudot and several officers that decided the savages to send this chief to the said Sr. de La Motte.

He was expecting that the said Sr. de La Motte would reflect upon the reasons which had induced him to refer that matter to him, to settle it himself, and that that would induce him to return to the path of duty; yet he continues to say things about him which injure his dignity; he ill-treats all who are devoted to him, threatening every day to ruin them; he has the impudence to make false statements in his letters, and to make the savages say things which are not at all probable; and lastly he considers himself independent of him, hinting to all the savages in the vicinity of his post that they have no ruler but him and should know no one else.

The said Sr. de La Motte was malicious enough to tell the Ouctaouacks of Missilimakinac, in the councils which he held at Detroit, that the Jesuit Father Maret, who is with them, dissuaded them from settling at Detroit, which is certainly quite unfounded.

As the said Sr. de La Motte said unpleasant things in these councils to the prejudice of this priest, because he cannot tolerate Jesuits, it would, be advisable to order him to speak more guardedly about missionaries, because that course destroys all the confidence in the minds of the savages which they may have in the missionaries, and consequently does harm to religion.

He also begs that this officer may be ordered to show more respect in speaking of him.

As he wishes nothing but good to the settlement at the post of Detroit, apart from all the reasons he has to complain of the said Sr. de La Motte, he has ordered all the savages in the neighborhood of his post to obey him in everything he tells them from him, and he has written to Father Maret to leave all the savages of his mission at liberty to go and settle at Detroit, and to follow them there rather than give the said Sr. de La Motte occasion to say that any of them have been dissuaded from doing so.

The said Sr. de La Motte has taken away the mission to the Miamis from the Jesuits and has given it to the Recollets, claiming that he has the power to do so. He would not give any decision as to that, leaving it to what His Majesty may order; he is, however, bound to say that the Jesuits are much better fitted for carrying on missions to the savages than the Recollets are.

47

The Sr. de Joncaire[1], who has returned from the Iroquis country, has assured him that everything was quite quiet there. This officer is held in esteem by all that tribe; he understands their languages thoroughly, and talks to them with great firmness.

He asserts that he sends no boats to the upper country except when it is absolutely necessary.

*   *   *

The news that was received, that the Illinois Indians had attacked those at Detroit was not found to be true.

He has learned that the said Sr. de La Motte sent a Frenchman to the Illinois with goods, in order to attract them to him.

He had ordered the said Sr. de la Motte to compel all the *courcurs de bois* who were in his neighborhood to come down to Montreal; but instead of that he has had a proclamation made at Missilimakina setting forth that all *voyageurs* who betake themselves to Detroit will be well received. The said Sr. de La Motte has not written anything to him about this proclamation, and he is therefore not aware of the reasons he had for issuing it.

SIEUR DE LA FOREST SENT TO QUEBEC BY CADILLAC.

The Sr. de la Forest.   10th Nov.[2]

d.

The Sr. de La Motte has sent him to Quebec to look after the forwarding to Detroit of the reinforcements he requires.

‹ at the eement.

The said Sr. de La Motte counted on 200 soldiers, but M. de Vaudreuil maintains that he promised only 150; that if he supplies the further 50 that he is asked for, it is for the said Sr. de La Motte to defray the cost of their conveyance.

It is certain that, if the said Sr. de Vaudreuil had granted these 200 men at first, it would have cost him no more to take them to Detroit; for he had prepared the boats necessary for that purpose, which have fallen to pieces at the places where they were brought together.

The said Sr. de Vaudreuil intended to give them the said Sr. de La Motte's company and his to make up the 50 men remaining to be supplied. ^{good.}

good.

He says that the chief part of these companies is made up of old men, the youngest of whom is over 60 years of age, and therefore they are not fit for a new colony.

already se tled.

He represents that he had been a captain in Canada for 24 years, that he has been five years without receiving his pay; that he has incurred great expense for journeys he has had to make on duty; and that all his commanding officers have always been satisfied with him.

dealt with

consider.

He begs that he may be granted a pension.

Recommended b p. la Tour

LETTER FROM M. DE VAUDREUIL EXPRESSING HIS CONTEMPT FOR CADILLAC.

Endorsed—M: de Vaudreuil.   12th November, 1707.

My Lord,

I had the honor, in my letter of the 8th of this month, of giving you an account of all that had taken place in this country since last year. I had also contented myself with notifying to you, rather briefly, that the Sieur de La Mothe, making bad use of the favor you are good enough to show him, behaved very badly towards me.

The honor I had done him in referring the affair of the Outavois to him, together with what you do me the honor of writing to me regarding him this year, made me almost hope that he would reflect and would change his ways; and I should not have troubled you any more about it, My Lord, but for the last letter he wrote me, of which I take the liberty of sending you a copy with observations or replies I have made to it.

Index lett Q.

Index lett R.

The haughty manner, My Lord, in which he treats all who are attached to me, saying no less than that he would ruin them with Your Highness, together with his audacity in making false statements whether in his letters or at his councils, attributing to the savages things which

right that a man like the Sieur de La Mothe should be allowed to ruin the whole country with you in order to gratify his passions.

What he makes the savages say in his council concerning Father Marest is so false, and so easy to disprove from all this Father's letters, that I feel obliged, My Lord, to do him justice by assuring you in advance of the contrary. What the Sieur de. La Mothe himself says, afterwards, at this council about this Father is not only contrary to the interests of the King's service, but is also adverse to religion, for he destroys all the confidence the savages might feel in their missionaries. It is of the utmost importance, My Lord, that the Sieur de La Mothe should speak with more reserve of these missionaries. It is also of extreme importance that he should show more respect in speaking of me; for, although I have sufficient contempt for him to have no fear of anything he can say, that may, notwithstanding, withdraw the people from the true respect they owe to me; all the more because it is sufficient for obtaining the support of the Sieur de La Mothe, to have deserved punishment of any kind here. I hope, My Lord, that you will do me justice; and in spite of all the grounds for complaint, and all the reasons which the Sieur de La Mothe gives me for it, that shall not prevent me from granting him, in pursuance of your orders, all the help he may require for his settlement, and it is also a pleasure to me, as I have already had the honor of telling you in my other letters, to show your Highness that it is not passion which directs my actions, but the interests of the service alone.

I am with very deep respect

My Lord

Your very humble and most obedient servant

Vaudreuil.

Quebec this 12th Novr. 1707.

CADILLAC GRANTS CONTRACTS TO DETROIT CITIZENS.

Lists of the contracts granted by M. de La Mothe Cadillac to the inhabitants of Detroit, under the authority which he had received from His Majesty in 1704, 1705, and 1706.

To Wit.

To [one] Pierre Chesne by name, a site within the fort Pontchartrain of Detroit, having thirty feet frontage to Ste. Anne street and twenty-two feet wide, adjoining on one side M. Joseph Depré, and on the other Estienne Bontron, on condition of paying three livres quit-rent and rent, and moreover and over and above [that], for other rights, which we have given up, the sum of ten livres each year on the 20th of March [payable] in good furs or, at first, in [any] coined money which there shall be current in this place. 1. Sites wit the fort 1 of March

Also to André Chouet called Camiraud a site of thirty feet frontage on Ste. Anne street and twenty feet wide, adjoining on one side Michel Massé and on the other a soldiers' house belonging to us, at three livres quit-rent and rent, and also ten livres for other rights as set down above. 2. 10th of M 1707.

Also to Pierre Faverau called Le Grandeur a site of nineteen feet on Ste. Anne street and twenty-two feet wide adjoining on one side M. Du Fuguier and on the François Marqué, in consideration of thirty-eight sols quit-rent and rent, and moreover ten livres for other rights as stated above. The site has been sold to Robert Germain. 3. 10th of M 1707.

To M. Joseph Despré a site with twenty feet frontage to Ste. Anne street, and twenty-two wide, adjoining on one side Guilleaume Bouet, and on the other Pierre. Chesne, in consideration of two livres quit-rent and rent and ten livres for other rights which we have given up. 4. 10th of M 1707.

To Salomon Joseph Du Vestin a site of twelve feet on Ste. Anne street and twenty-five feet on St. Antoine street in consideration of forty sols quit-rent and rent, and also ten livres for other rights which we have given up; sold to Richard le Michel Bizaillon. 5. 10th of M 1707.

To Pierre Leger called Parisien a site with twenty feet frontage to Ste. Anne street and twenty-two feet wide, adjoining M. Boucherville on one side and St. François street on the other, in consideration of forty solos quit-rent and rent, and also 10# for other rights which we have given up; sold to Jacques Cardinal. 6. 10th of M 1707.

To Bonnaventure Compien called L' Esperance a site with twelve feet frontage to Ste. Anne street and twenty feet wide adjoining Pierre Mallet on one side, and on the other a soldiers' house belonging to us, 7. 10th of M 1707.

at twenty-four sols quit-rent and rent, and also 10# for other righ
which we have relinquished; sold to François Livernois.

8.
1 of March
1707.
To Jacob De Marsac called Desrocher a site with thirty-one feet from
age to St. Louis street, and twenty-two feet wide adjoining Jacques I
Moine on one side and François Livernois on the other, for three livr.
two sols rent, and also 10# for other rights which we have given up.

9.
of March
1707.
To M. D'Argenteuil a site having twenty feet frontage to St. Lou
street, and twenty-two feet wide, adjoining us on one side and Jeron
Marsac on the other, on condition of paying fifty sols quit-rent an
rent besides 10# for other rights which we have given up; sold 1
Nicolas Rose.

10.
of March
1707.
To Jean Richard a site of twenty feet in Ste. Anne street and twent:
two wide, adjoining M. René le-Moine on one side and us on the othe
on condition of paying us forty sols quit-rent and rent, 10# for othe
rights we have given up. The said site has been abandoned and grante
again by M. de La Mote to Jacques Lubert.

11.
of March
1707.
To Jean Labatier called Champagne a site of twenty feet in St.
Anne street and twenty-two deep, adjoining on one side M. Jacque
Langlois and on the other Estienne Bontran in consideration of tw
livres quit-rent and rent and also 10# for other rights which we hav
given up; this site reverted to M. de La Mote by [his] permission o
the 27th of March, 1709.

12.
of March
1707.
To Estienne Bontran, called major, a site thirty feet in Ste. Ann
street, and twenty-two wide, adjoining on one side Jean Abatis an
on the other Pierre Chesne at three livres quit-rent and rent, and als
10# for other rights which we have given up; this site reverted t
M. de La. Mothe by [his] desire on paying for it what he had receive
for it [literally, what it had produced to him], and was given to Antoin
Magnant.

13.
1 of March
1707.
To Pierre Hemard a site with twenty-five feet frontage situated i
Ste. Anne street, and twenty feet wide, adjoining on one side M. d
Rancé, in consideration of fifty sols quit-rent and rent, besides 10;
for other rights given up by us; sold to Jacques Hubert.

14.
1 of March
1707.
To Antoine Dupuis, called Beauregard, a site with thirty feet fron
age and twenty-two wide situated in Ste. Anne street, adjoining o
one side Jean Serond, called L'Eveillé, and on the other a plot of lan

To Guillaume Bovet called Deliard a site with twenty-five feet frontage to Ste. Anne street and twenty-two wide, adjoining on one side a
soldiers' house belonging to us, and on the other, Joseph Depré, in consideration of 2# 10s quit-rent and rent, and also 10# for other rights
which we have given up; sold to Pierre Robert.

To Michael Massé a site with thirty feet frontage to Ste. Anne Street
and forty-two feet to St. François street, and twenty-six feet to St.
Louis street, adjoining on one side, André Chouet, in consideration of
8# 8s quit-rent and rent, and moreover 10# for other rights which
we have given up.

To Michel Campo a site fifty-three feet long in St. Antoine Street and
seventeen feet in Ste. Anne Street, and on one side bordering on a
soldiers' ground belonging to us, for five livres six sols, and also 10#
for other rights.

To Louis Normand a site of twenty-five feet in Ste. Anne Street and
twenty-four feet deep, adjoining on one side Bonnaventure Compiens,
and on the other Pierre Hemand, at two livres ten sols quit-rent and
rent, and also 10# for other rights; sold to Alexis Lemoine.

To François Tesée a site of twenty-five feet in Ste. Anne Street and
twenty-two wide adjoining Antoine Dupuis on one side and land belonging to us on the other, [at] 40s, quit-rent. and rent, and also
10# for the rights we have given up; sold to Antoine. Carriere on the
20th of June, 1710.

To Pierre Chantelon a site having twenty-eight feet frontage to St.
François street and sixteen deep, adjoining a soldiers' house belonging
to us, and on the other [side] us also, in consideration of fifty-six
sols quit-rent and rent, and also 10# for other rights; sold to Jean
Leséeur.

To François Bienvenu called de L'Isle a site with thirty feet frontage to St. Louis Street and twenty-two feet wide adjoining Desroches,
on one side and M. Michel Massé on the other, for 3# quit-rent and
rent and 10# for other rights which we have given up.

To Pierre Esteve a site with 25 feet frontage to St. Louis street and
twenty-two wide, adjoining Jerôme Marsac on one side, and us on the
other; for fifty sols quit-rent and rent and 10# for other rights.

To Blaise Surgere a site of thirty feet in St. Francois street and
twenty-six feet deep, adjoining Jacob de Marsac on one side and Antoine Ferron on the other, for three livres rent and 10# for other
rights.

To Pierre Poirier a site of twenty-five feet in St. Joachim street and
22 feet wide adjoining Guilleaume Aguenet on one side, and on the
other a soldiers' house belonging to us, for fifty sols quit-rent and rent,
and 10# for other rights.

26.
of March
1707.

To Antoine Ferron a site of 20 feet in St. Francois street, and 26 feet wide, adjoining on one side Pierre Leger and on the other Blaise Surgere, for forty sols quit-rent and rent, and also 10# for other rights.

27.
the 10th of
March
1707.

To Pierre Tacet a site of 25 feet in St. Joachim street and 22 feet wide adjoining on one side Martin Sirier and on the other Pierre Pichet, for fifty sols rent, and also 10# for other rights; sold to Jean Content.

28
the 10th
f March
1707.

To François Fafard de Lorme a site having forty five feet frontage to St. Louis street, and twenty-two wide, adjoining St. Antoine street on one side, and us on the other, at 4# 10s quit-rent and rent, and 10# for other rights.

29.
the 10th of
March
1707.

To Michel Disier of 25 feet in St. Joachim street and 22 feet deep, adjoining Pierre Pichet on one side and us on the other, at fifty sols rent and 10# for other. rights, sold to Louis du Charnie.

30.
of March
1707.

To Jacob de Marsac a site of 20 feet in St. Francis street, and 26 feet wide, adjoining Blaise Surgere on one side, and us on the other, at forty sols rent and 10# for other rights; sold to Charles Charon.

31.
of March
1707.

To Rencontre, a site having twenty-five feet frontage and 22 feet deep adjoining Salomon and, on the other [side]) us, at fifty sols rent and 10# for other rights; sold to Andre Marsille.

32.
of March
1708.

To Desloriers a site of twenty-five feet in St. Joachim street, and 22 feet wide, adjoining Langlois on one side and Guilleaume Aguenet on the other, at fifty sols rent and also 10 for other rights; sold to Pierre Cornie.

33.
of March
1708.

To Xaintonge a site of twenty-five feet in St. Joachim street and twenty-two feet deep, adjoining on one side Michel Dizier and on the other Pierre Tachet, at fifty sols rent and 10# for other rights; sold to Bouché.

34.
of March
1708.

To Jacques Du Moulin a site of thirty feet in St. Louis street and sixteen feet deep, adjoining Quilenchivé on one side and us on the other, at three livres quit-rent and rent and 10# for other rights.

35.
of the
of March
1708.

To Guilleaume Aguet called Laporte a site having twenty-five feet frontage to St. Joachim street and twenty feet .wide, adjoining on one side Pierre Poirier and on the other Jean Ferland, at fifty sols rent and 10# for other rights; sold to Pierre Chesne.

livres quit-rent and rent, and 10# for other rights; sold to Nicolas Rivard.

To Quilenchivé a site of twenty-five feet [frontage] and fourteen wide, adjoining Deslories, on one side, and Jacques Du Moulin on the other, at fifty sols rent and 10# for other rights; sold to Juliën Dervisseau. 39. 10th of M 1707.

To M. Derancé a site of 15 feet in Ste. Anne street and eighteen feet wide, adjoining on one side M. Boucherville and Rencontre street on the other, at thirty sols quit-rent and rent and 10# for other rights. 40. 10th of M 1707.

To M. du Figuier a site of twenty-seven feet in Ste. Anne street and twenty-five feet deep, adjoining us on both sides, at fifty-four sols rent and 10# for other rights; surrendered by said the M. [du Figuier] and granted to Paul Guillet. 41. 10th of M 1707.

To La Montagne, called Pierre Monet a site of thirty feet on the Square and twenty-four feet wide, adjoining us on all sides, at 4#, 10s rent and 10# for other rights; sold to Baptiste Trudeau. 42. 10th of M 1707.

To Pierre Mallet a site of forty feet in Ste. Anne street and about seventy feet wide bordering on St. Joachim street and adjoining Antoine Dufresne and us, at 8# rent and 10# for other rights. 43. of the 10th of M 1707.

To Antoine Dufresne a site of twenty-five feet in Ste. Anne street and seventy feet or thereabouts deep, bordering on St. Joachim street, adjoining Pierre Mallet, and us on the other side, at 5# rent and 10# for other rights. 44. 14th of M 1708.

To Jean Baptiste Chornic a site of sixteen feet in St. Louis street and fourteen wide, adjoining on one side Jacques Du Moulin, and us on the other, at thirty-two sols rent and 10# for other rights; sold to Jean Chevalier. 45. 10th of M 1708

To Jean Casse a site of twenty-five feet in Rencontre street, and twenty-two wide, adjoining us on both sides, at fifty sols, and 10# for other rights; sold to Zacharie Plante. 46. 10th of M 1708.

To Paul L'Anglois a site with twenty-five feet frontage to St. Joachim street and twenty-two feet wide, adjoining on one side Jacques L'Anglois and, on the other, Jean Ferland, at fifty sols rent and 10# for other rights. 47. of the 10th of M 1707.

To Jerome Marliard a site of twenty feet on St. Louis street and twenty feet wide, adjoining on one side Mis. d'Argenteuil and on the other Pierre Estevé, at forty sols rent and 10# for other rights. 48. 10th of M 1707.

To André Bombardié a site of twenty-five feet to St. Joachim and twenty-two feet wide adjoining us on both sides, at fifty sols rent and 10# for other rights;—sold to Pierre L'Ecuyer. 49. of the 10th of M 1707.

To Pierre Du Roy a site of thirty feet in St. Louis street and fourteen feet wide, adjoining Quilenchivé on one side and us on the other, at 3# rent and 10# for rights. 50. 10th of M 1707.

51.
of March
1707.

To Pierre Roy a site of twenty-six feet in Ste. Anne street and 27 feet wide adjoining Pierre La Montagne on one side and us on the other, at 3# 18s and 10# for other rights.

52.
ı of March
1707.

To François Margue a site of thirteen feet in Ste. Anne street and twenty-five feet deep, adjoining on one side Faverau, and Salomon on the other, at 26s rent and 10# for other rights; sold to Jean Paquet.

53.
ı of March
1708.

To Antoine Magnant a site of twenty-five feet in Ste. Anne street and seventy feet or thereabouts wide, adjoining Antoine Dufresne on one side, and us on the other; at 5# rent and 10# for other rights.

54.
of the
h of July
1708.

To François Bonne a site of twenty-five feet in Ste. Anne street and seventy feet or thereabouts wide, adjoining Magnant on one side, and us on the other, at 5# rent and 10# for other rights.

55,
Of the
of March
1708.

To Touissaints Dardennes a site of fifteen feet in St. Louis street and fourteen wide, adjoining St. Aubin on one side and us on the other, at thirty sols rent and 10# for other rights.

56.
Of the
of March
1708.

To Pierre Bassinet a site of 10 feet in St. Louis street and fourteen wide, adjoining Louis Gastineau and Robert La Chappelle, at 20s rent and 10# for other rights.

57.
Of the
h of June
1708.

To François Brunet a site of 20 feet in Ste. Anne street and twenty-two wide, adjoining us on both sides, at forty sols rent and 10# for other rights.

58. .
Of the
th of July
1708.

To Antoine Beauregard a site of about seventy feet in Ste. Anne street and the same width, adjoining on one side Magnant and on the. other Antoine du Fresne, at twelve livres rent and 10# for other rights; returned to M. de La Motte, for the said Dupuis.

59.
Of the
of March
1707.

To Marie Le Page a site of twenty-four feet in St. Antoine street and 22 wide, adjoining one side on St. Louis street and, the other, on the Square and us, at three livres twelve sols, and 10# for other rights; sold to Joseph Seneval.

60.
. of March
1709.

To Jacques Campo a site of twenty feet in Ste. Anne street, and 20 feet wide adjoining on one side René Le Moine and on the other François Tesée, at 40s rent and 10# for other rights.

61.,
Of the
ı of March
1707.

To Jean Serond a site of twenty-five feet in Ste. Anne street 22 wide, adjoining Antoine Dupuis and Grandmenil, at fifty sols rent and 10# for other rights; sold to Joseph Trudeau.

62.
ı of March
1709.

To Pierre Robert a site of thirty feet in Ste. Anne street and about seventy wide, and.bordering on St. Joseph street, adjoining Pierre Mallet

To René Le Moine a site of twenty feet in Ste. Anne street and 22 feet wide, adjoining Jean Richard on one side, and Jacques Campo on the other, at forty sols rent and 10# for other rights. 64.
Of the
20th of M
1709.

To Jacques Le Moine a site of twenty-four feet in St. Louis street and twenty-two wide, adjoining on one side Jacob de Marsac and us on the other; at forty sols rent, and 10# for other rights. 65.
1st of Se
1706.

To Paul Guillet a site of thirty feet in the main street by seventy feet or thereabouts wide, adjoining Magnant on one side and us, at six livres rent and 10# for other rights. 66.
10th of D
1709.

To Joseph Rinaud a site of fifteen feet and a half in the main street, Ste. Anne, and eight wide, adjoining on one side Jacques Cardinal, and us on the other, at thirty sols rent and 10# for other rights. 67.
27th of J
1710.

To Antoine Tuffé, called du Fresne, a site of twenty-two feet in Ste. Anne street and twenty-five feet wide, adjoining on one side M. Dufiguier and, on the other, Camerand, at two livres four sols rent and ten livres for other rights. 68.
28th of J
1710.

Gardens.

To Beauregard half an arpent of land, adjoining, towards the north Michel Dizier and François Bienvenu and us on the south, and on the other [side] Pierre Estevé, following the boundaries, on the terms and at the rate of one sol a foot, making four livres ten sols.

To [one] called De L'Isle a like quantity of land for the same price and on the same conditions.

Lands granted.

To Pierre Mallet an extent of land of two arpents in front by twenty arpents deep, adjoining on one side Estienne Bontron and on the other Joseph Parent and on the south the great river for which piece of ground he shall pay five livres quit-rent and rent, and this for all dues, and if he has no site within the fort he shall pay ten livres for the rights which we have given up. 1.
of the
10th of M
1707.

To François Fafard de Lorme a piece of ground of two arpents in front by twenty arpents deep, adjoining on one side our domain, and on the other François Bosserou, and on the south the great river, at five livres rent. 2.
Of th
10th of M
1707.

To Baptiste Gorion a piece of ground of two arpents in front by twenty arpents deep, adjoining on one side François Bosserou and on the other Jacob de Marsac, and on the south [the great river]. 3.
Of th
10th of M
1707.

To Jacob de Marsac a piece of ground of two arpents in front by twenty deep, adjoining on one, side Jean Baptiste Gorion, and on the south the great river; five livres quit-rent and rent. 4.
Of th
10th of M
1707.

5.
Of the of March 1707. To André Bombardie a piece of ground of two arpents in front by twenty deep, adjoining on one side Jacob de Marsac and on the other Pierre Hemard, for five livres quit-rent and rent.

6.
Of the of March 1707. To Pierre Hemard a piece of land of two arpents in front by twenty arpents deep, adjoining on one side André Bombardié, and Compien on the other, for five livres quit-rent and rent.

7.
Of the of March 1707. To Bonnaventure Compien a piece of land of one arpent in front by twenty arpents deep, adjoining on one side Pierre Hemard and on the other Estienne Bontron; three livres fifteen sols quit-rent and rent.

8.
Of the of March 1707. To Jerome Marliard a piece of land of two arpents in front by twenty deep, adjoining on one side Pierre Estevé, and on the other François Marque, for five livres quit-rent and rent.

9.
Of the of March 1707. To Pierre Estevé a piece of land of two arpents in front by twenty deep, adjoining on one side Blaise Surgere, and on the other Jerome Marliard, for five livres quit-rent and rent.

10.
Of the of March 1707. To Estienne Bontron a piece of land of one arpent and a half in front by twenty deep, adjoining on one side Bonnaventure Compien and on the other Pierre Mallet, for three livres fifteen sols quit-rent and rent.

11.
of March 1707. To Antoine Dupuis, of two arpents in front by twenty deep, adjoining on one side M. Joseph Parent and on the other Blaise Surgere, for five livres quit-rent and rent.

12.
of March 1707. To Joseph Parent a piece of land of two arpents in front by twenty deep, adjoining on one side Pierre Mallet, and on the other Antoine Dupuis, for five livres quit-rent and rent.

13.
of March 1707. To Michel Dizier a piece of land of two arpents in front by twenty deep, adjoining on one side François Marqué and Jacques L'Anglois, for five livres quit-rent and rent.

14.
Of the of March 1707. To François Bosserou, two arpents in front by twenty deep, adjoining on one side François Fafard, and on the other Jean Baptiste Gorion, for five livres quit-rent and rent.

15.
Of the of March 1707. To Jacob de Marsac, two arpents in front by twenty deep, adjoining on one side Jean Baptiste Gorion, and on the other André Bombardié, five livres quit-rent and rent.

16.
of the of March 1707. To Antoine Dupuis, two arpents in front by twenty deep, adjoining on one side Joseph Parant, and on the other Blaise Surgere, for five livres quit-rent and rent.

17.
of the of March 1707. To François Marqué, two arpents in front by twenty deep, adjoining on one side Jerome Marlier and on the other Michel Disier, for five livres quit-rent and rent.

18.
of the of March 1707. To Jacques L'Anglois, two arpents in front by twenty deep, adjoining Paul L'Anglois on one side, and Disier on the other, for five livres quit-rent and rent.

To Paul L'Anglois, two arpents in front by twenty deep, adjoining on one side Jacques L'Anglois, and on the other Antoine Ferron, for five livres quit-rent and rent. 19.
10th of M
1707.

To Antoine Texier, two arpents in front by twenty deep, adjoining Paul L'Anglois, and François Jardis, called Rencontre, for five livres quit-rent and rent. 20.
of the
10th of M
1707.

To François Jardis, two arpents in front by twenty deep, adjoining on one side Antoine Ferron, and Pierre Chantelon, for five livres quit-rent and rent. 21.
10th of M
1707.

To Pierre Chantelon, two arpents in front by twenty deep, adjoining one side François Jardis, and us on the other for five livres quit-rent and rent. 22.
of the
10th of M
1707.

To Jean Richard, two arpents in front by twenty deep adjoining on one side Pierre Robert, and on the other Pierre Leger, for five livres quit-rent and rent. 23.
of the
10th of M
1709.

To Laloire, for two arpents of land in front by twenty deep, adjoining on one side Pierre Poirier, and on the other Jean Richard. for five livres quit rent and rent. 24.
of the
10th of M
1707.

To Pierre Leger, two arpents in front by twenty deep, ajoining on one side Jean Richard and on the other Jean Durand, for five livres quit-rent and rent. 25.
of the
10th of M
1707.

To Lafleur, two arpents in front by twenty deep, adjoining on one side Robert, and us on the other, for five livres quit-rent and rent. 26.
of the
10th of M
1707.

To Michel Campos, four arpents in front by twenty deep, adjoining Jean Durand on one side and us on the other, for ten livres quit-rent and rent. 27.
of the
10th of M
1707.

To Jean Durant, two arpents in front by twenty deep, adjoining on one side Pierre Leger, and on the other Michel Campo, for five livres quit-rent and rent. 28.
of the
10th of M
1707.

To Blaise Surgere, two arpents in front by twenty deep, adjoining on one side Antoine Dupuis, and on the other Pierre Estevé, for five livres quit-rent and rent. 29.
of the
10th of M
1707.

To François Massé, two arpents in front by twenty deep, adjoining on one side Pierre Chantelon, and us on the other, for five livres quit-rent and rent. 30.
of the
10th of M
1707.

To Damoiselle Magdalaine de La Motte a stretch of land with three leagues frontage to the great river of Detroit, to extend from the river Ecorse inclining towards the Lake Erié, with Grosse Isle and other islets which there are in the front of the Concession, and in depth five leagues in a straight line; the right of hunting, of fishing and trading; the whole as a fief, with right of the intermediate [and] lower jurisdiction. 31.

of those who have had contracts for gardens around the fort.

M. D'Argenteuil	one arpent of land
Pierre Mallett	half arpent
Jacob De Marsac	half arpent
Jacques L'Anglois	half arpent
Louis Normand	half arpent
Pierre Estevé	half arpent
Jerome Marliar	half arpent
Michel Disier	half arpent
Estienne Bontron	half arpent
Bonnaventure Compiens	half arpent
Chantelon	half arpent
Pierre Porrier	half arpent
Pierre Leger	half arpent

For copy

Begon

THE JESUITS' COMPLAINT AGAINST CADILLAC.

rsed—25th of March, 1708. f.

THE JESUITS OF CANADA.

They represent that His Majesty has permitted them to establish them- that is not settled. selves wherever they can in Canada, in order to preach the Gospel there, with orders to commanding officers to support them in their missions; and that it is very hard on them, after having sacrificed themselves to to concilia one aⁿoth teach the savage tribes, and subject them to the rule of France, that they should be robbed of their labor in favor of Recollets who do not know the language of these savages; and that the said Sr. de la Mothe Cadillac, self-love. for that purpose, makes use of His Majesty's authority, of which he says he is the sole depository in Canada.

They also say that this officer is audacious and aggressive; that he rightly. thinks his power unlimited; that he always acts without waiting for bad. authority; and that he gives everyone to understand that he is the master of the Jesuits, and will send them to France whenever he thinks fit to give an account of their actions. They beg that they may not be they must under him left at the mercy of this commandant, who thinks he can do whatever they are t let them g he pleases, and openly displays his animosity against them everywhere. away.

They also beg that they may be reinstated in possession of the mission good docile und to the Miamis savages, and the others of which the said Sr. de La Mothe La Mothe. has deprived them, and to order him to let them carry on their missions, as they think fit, when they are within the limits of his command, and not harass them as he has done hitherto.

FATHER MAREST'S COMPLAINT AGAINST CADILLAC.

Copy of a letter from Father Marest, missionary of the Society of Jesus at Michilimakina, written to the Marquis de Vaudreuil on the 4th of June, 1708.

Sir,

　　　*　　　　　.ﾞ.　　　　　*

The short time they give me for writing does not allow me to give you full details. I shall content myself with stating concisely what seems to me most essential.

1st. Last Autumn, Monsieur de La Mothe, when he granted le Pezant his life, employed the Outtavois who had accompanied him to Detroit and brought him back here, to invite not only those of le Pezant's tribe, or those who had already been at Detroit, but all the Outtavois of Mich-

sieur de La Mothe opened for the Outtavois the road to Detroit, saying that they had disarmed him by sending Le Pezant to him, proceeded to hang up two strings of wampum threaded, and said that one was to invite and bind all the Outtavois, and the other for me to follow them with all the French people from Michilimakina. But Monsieur de La Mothe did not deign, in a matter which concerned me so nearly, to honor me with even a word in writing. He had his reasons; his spokesman claimed that he was a living letter. It is, however, true that he said things which ought in no way to have been said nor permitted, contrary both to your authority as Governor and to my position as missionary.

3rd. If Monsieur de La Mothe had promised Ouakesson a crown as a reward for the mission he charged him with, he could not have acquitted himself better in it. Besides the earnestness and boldness with which he spoke, he employed every means to succeed in his purpose,—promises, threats, even of death, to anyone who would not go to Detroit; presents, visits, persuasions, offers of services, truths, falsehoods—everything has been employed. Monsieur de La Mothe could not have been better served than he was by this savage. Nevertheless he met with resistance from many, especially the Kiskakous and what vexed him more —from Le Brochet, who belongs to his own tribe, the Sand tribe.

4th. For my part, in accordance with what you have done me the honor to tell me in your letters, I did not propose[b] to those who resolved to go to Detroit. I did more, for I gave them a belt to make known to them that I would not abandon them, and that I would go with them if I could divide myself up; that, although I could not do so, I was expecting another missionary at once who would be another self to me, and when there were two of us one could go with them, the other remaining here; but that this could not be done until you had been informed of it, since you fill the place of His Majesty here. I gave them in writing a statement of what this necklace signified, as they re quested me to do so.

5th. Matters being in this position, they set out for their winter quarters. Those who were for Detroit, and also others who were undecided, went by Monsieur de La Mothe's orders to winter in the direction

over land to the great river and stopped the young men, saying they must not attack without speaking to you and obeying your will.

7th. At the same time that they arrived we had news by boat from Sakinang that three Frenchmen had been killed, or captured at Detroit, by the Miamis, and that it was believed they had also captured five Outtavois at Sakinang, which we were sorry for.

8th. In spite of this news, which completely destroyed the assurance which Monsieur de La Mothe had given through Ouakesson against enemies of all kinds, Monsieur d'Argenteuil took all the Outtavois he found at Sakinang to Detroit, making them a present of ten sols' worth of corn. He invited them to come and avenge themselves on the Miamis; but about five or six boatloads, who have come back here, say that if it was really to go to war, they ought to have sent the women and children to Michilimakina where they would be safer.

9th. It is said that what annoyed the Miamis was that Monsieur de La Mothe did not show your firmness regarding Le Pezant; and that although he had promised the Miamis to boil him in the pot, he had granted him his life and had invited him to come and settle at Detroit with his tribe. It is added that the Miamis have made large presents to the Iroquois, and that it is this that makes them so bold; that it is to be feared that it may reopen the war between the Iroquois and the French. That is the opinion of the Outtavois here who say that those at Detroit will be obliged to retire to Michilimakina again as a refuge. Monsieur d'Argenteuil holds a different opinion and writes from Sakinang that he hopes to return here this summer, bringing good news from Detroit; but he did not know when he wrote, in what condition he would find things. As for Monsieur de La Mothe, we see no letters from him.

10th. The Outtavois of Michilimakina are working hard at their field, and are all sowing seed.

11th   *   *   *

I forgot to tell you that, as I did not doubt that Monsieur de La Mothe would use all his skill to prevent the people of Detroit from making any attack, and believed that there was more to be feared from the Outtavois, especially from one whose brother had been cruelly burned by the Miamis, I gave him one of your necklaces to appease him, and keep him from stirring up troubles in the land. But the evil arose from a source from which it ought least to have come. It is believed that the Huron had a large share in it.

     *   *   *   *

The men who arrived to-day from the Bay say that the Poutouatamis who remained there, and with them several Sakis, were to go and rejoin at the St. Joseph River with Ouilamez, where the land is excellent and

49   .

there are animals in abundance. It is probable that the bad news from Detroit may make them change their minds; and they may also make the Poutouatamis depart, which would be a great pity.

I was ready to close my letter when Onaskié and Sakima came and requested me to tell you that they were sending this boat, in advance, in order to inform you of the attack which the Miamis made upon them at the great river; that you said that the first who made an attack should be punished; that they wished to act according to your will.

They also requested me to tell you at the same time—1st. that this winter some savages brought a piece of wampum, threaded, from Detroit to Sakinang, which denoted a message from Monsieur de La Mothe closing the great river [to them]. They ask whether it is in his power to do so, and whether he has greater authority than you, who declared to them that the paths to Montreal and to Detroit were equally free to them.

2nd. That he had threatened them with disease, which would spare them even less than the small-pox which had afflicted them so heavily when they refused his first invitation. This threat has frightened several of them and drawn them away; but there are some now who say "if Monsieur de la Mothe has control over the disease, why does he not launch it at the Miamis, who attacked him, and not at us who are all for the French although we remain at Michilimakina."

3rd. These same savages wish me to inform you, Sir, that Mons. d'Argenteuil wanted to give a letter to a Kiskakou named Sipy to take to Sakima, and, as he would not take charge of it, he ordered him to tell Sakima by word of mouth to come to Detroit as soon as he could, or else a hundred soldiers would come and take me away from here and bring me by force; on which Sakima added that whoever came to invite him to go to Detroit would waste his labor, that he saw plainly that they were annoyed with me at Detroit because I was dwelling with them.

4th. He says that Mons. d'Argenteuil is to go from here to the Bay and the North, to invite all the savages to make war against the Miamis, or for some other purpose that he does not know. Almost all the savages say that M. de La Mothe ought not to have given them so complete

in disobedience to your orders, and are living scandalous lives. I am, with deep respect, Sir, Your most humble and obedient servant—

[Signed] Joseph Marest, missionary of the Society of Jesus.

EXTRACT FROM THE LETTER OF THE SAID MINISTER OF THE 6TH OF JUNE, 1708, AT PARAGRAPH 6.

I am satisfied that you have none but worthy aims in all you are doing to establish the settlement of Detroit firmly; but it is not sufficient to tell me that you will give an account of your conduct when you are here. You must inform me clearly and and in detail, in all your letters, of everything you are doing; for His Majesty will not permit you to come here before that settlement is completely established.

Index lett C.

LIST OF THE OFFICERS WHO WERE IN THE EXPEDITION COMMANDED BY MM. DE LESCHAILLONS AND ROUVILLE.

'The Sieurs de Leschaillons' and Rouville' Lieutenants and Commanders of the expedition.

Index lett G.

The Sieurs		
Chev. de St. Ours		
La Gauchetiere, major		
Fabert	Ensigns of fort.	
de Tavenne		
de Contre coeur		
de Terches'		

The Sieurs		was killed
Dupuis, adjutant		
Croisil		
de Normanville	Ensigns on half pay.	
Cizard		
de Livetot		
de Chambly'		was killed

---

(1) The above report refers to the attack on Haverhill, Mass., July, 1708.

Although all these gentlemen discharged their duty thoroughly well, I can assure you, My Lord, that the Sieurs de Croisil and Dupuis greatly distinguished themselves.

Vaudreuil,
P. T. O.

[On 4th page *verso*.]

List of the officers who were in the expedition commanded by Messieurs de L'Eschaillons and Rouville.

———

SPEECH OF THE OUTTAVOIS OF MICHILIMAKINA WITH RE-PLIES OF M. DE VAUDREUIL.

*　　　　*　　　　*

Endorsed—Words of the Outtavois of Michilimakina to Monsieur de Vaudreuil, with his replies, on the 23rd of July, 1708.

*　　　　*　　　　*

Index letter D.

By a necklace.

My father, my father, this spring Monsieur de La Mothe sent us word that he barred the great river [to us], that he set a barrier there as high as the trees, that no one might make use of this way to come down here. But I said, why does Monsieur de La Mothe block up this way against me? Is it not the way by which I go to see my father? What have I to

·no one to guide me; judge, my father, whether I have done well. However, it seems to me that Monsieur de La Mothe ought to be content with having divided our village. As those of our people who are with him, were settled with him before, we do not regret that; but as for us, who have always lived at Michilimakina, why does he annoy us, why does he not leave us in peace where we are, since we do not wish to abandon Michilimakina? That will not prevent us from having dealings with the savages of Detroit. They will give us some of their corn when they have any, and we will give them our beaver-skins in exchange. But as for going to dwell there, we will not do so.

* *

REPLY OF THE MARQUIS DE VAUDREUIL TO THE WORDS OF THE OUTTAVOIS FROM MICHILIMAKINA.

* * *

I have no news yet from Monsieur de La Mothe, but it cannot be long before I get news. I am sorry also that you are going so soon; but, no matter, whatever news I receive I will let you know it as soon as I possibly can. Therefore I stay your axe until you have been more fully informed of my will. I have considered what you told me as to the barrier which Monsieur de La Mothe has set on the great river, to prevent you from coming down here. It must have been people who were misinformed as to his intentions and mine, who told you that. I mean the way to be free in both directions. I sent you word of this last autumn by Sakima and Koutaouliboa; I tell you so again. As long as you act obediently, and do nothing against my will, you may go to Detroit to settle there, or to do your trading, or you may come here; you will always be received alike, I put no restraint upon you in that matter, nor do I wish anyone whomsoever to restrain you.

* *

REMARKS ON LETTERS OF CADILLAC.

good. following on the whole your notes; he explains well and too truly the infinite harm caused by the "Conges" and the abuses which arise from them, which are the presents of the Governor, all the trade [being] in his hand, and the brandy scandal. Reflect on it. I beg you; but let us finish. we will speak of it if we think fit, but that would injure him.

Endorsed—1708. M. de la Mothe Cadillac at Detroit, the 15th of Se 1708.

He attributes to the Jesuit Fathers most of the difficulties which finds in his post of Detroit because, he says, they have perceived the fulness of them and have desired to profit by them, and that that can be reconciled with his own interests,—Thus he says it is necessary t he should quit this post, or that they should abandon it, which [latt he is prepared to arrange, granting them compensation [for it].

Apparently the missionary father is mistaken in the date; M. de la Mothe discourses at great length on that, and he says that the Jesuits will prove whenever they wish, that this letter was written thirty years ago, without anyone daring to contradict them.

He says further that it is these Fathers who have prevented the O vois from going to settle there; he claims to prove it by a letter wb Father Malet, a missionary of Missilimakina, wrote to him; this lette dated the 23rd of October, 1677. He did not, however, receive it u 1707.

True but impossible make him understand the absurdity of it.

In order to establish Detroit firmly it would be necessary to settle or six hundred inhabitants there and troops in proportion; to erec strong fort of earth there and a small one on the other side of the ri by which means we should be certainly masters of the passage of tribes.

With five or six hundred Frenchmen there would be nothing to 1 either from the Iroquois or from any other tribe, because as soon as th were any one of them that wished to declare itself against [us] we co set ten others on to them.

It would also be necessary to destroy the fort at Frontenac and b a new one twenty-five leagues lower down, at a place called La Pale which would form an intermediate post, good in all respects, betw Montreal and Detroit.

As he says that there is no one but himself who knows it and can verify it. ask him about it.

And lastly it would be necessary to make a junction between Lake and Lake Ontario. He says that he knows, for that [purpose], a and a canal which has remained unknown to everyone else until now.

It would be necessary also to carry out the proposal which he has made to form Companies of the savages, but that this plan meets with opposition because everyone is interested in gainsaying all that relates to Detroit.

Bad.

The great scheme of the people of Canada is to settle Missilimakina with *"Congez"* and scouts.

True, but least bad he puts it.

That is the great attraction for the Governor General which makes him, as it were, master of the trading; without Missilimakina the border line of the savages at Montreal would not exist, nor, consequently, the presents which the governor general draws therefrom. So greatly does Canada regard Detroit as an obstacle to the re-instatement of the *"Congez"* that it need cause no surprise if they clamor against [us]; but if they are reinstated we shall see a rise again, at the same time, abomination-, blasphemy and debauch, infamy and evil quarrels.

True, but necessary

True. he exagge ates like a Gascon.

It has been objected against him that he could not maintain his post, if he had war with the Iroquois, because he could not communicate with Montreal. He says that that would not embarass him, that he will go to Montreal as often as he wishes, and that whenever it pleases him he will set so many enemies on to the Iroquois that they will leave him in peace.

That did n appear in affair he h with the Miamis.

He complains that M. de Vaudreuil has given him only 150 soldiers in place of 200 which he ought to have given him; that, in fact, he offered him all his company, and that of M. de la Forest, but that they are most of them old men or settlers in Canada. He had asked that he might be permitted to marry some Frenchmen to Indian women, after the latter had been taught, because that would be so many guarantees of the fidelity of the Indians. M. de Vaudreuil has forbidden him [to do] it and he has obeyed. He complains that the Company, in whose place he is, has always had permission to draw from Canada the corn it required, but that M. de Vaudreuil has refused him this, leaving him only liberty to go and seek it among the Iroquois, which is impossible. The said M. de Vaudreuil has forbidden him to receive French fugitives at Detroit, of whom he might usefully have availed himself, under the pretext that they are *in reatu* [i. e. persons accused of crime] : yet he has granted them leave to go down to Montreal, and always allows the merchants of Montreal to supply

He will nc need so m there.

that migh good to p mit it.

M. de Vau dreuil's reasons ar not knowr unless tha would ple the Frenc men to liv among the dians, whi would cau a loss of m Think it o

owes to him. He was put in charge of Detroit according to the clauses and conditions contained in a memorandum which I sent him on the 14th of June, 1704. He says that in this memorandum nothing at all is said of a surgeon, of medicines, of interpreters, of missionaries, of refreshments for the sick, nor of the conveyance of provisions; that, accordingly, he did not think he was obliged, and that now they wished to oblige him to defray the cost of them. He notes that, having accepted this post at his own risk, he does not think that by that word could be understood all the expenses to be defrayed, and that that clause would subject him only to all the disadvantageous events which might happen concerning this post.

Nor does he think that it could be brought against him that the Company defrayed these expenses; because, for that, it would be very necessary that he should have the advantages of the Company.

He was not at all obliged to construct, at his expense, the fort which he has had built at this place, any more than the church. He offers however to have the choir of the church built, and to give a piece of ground for it, provided he may have the patronage of it; and he says that, if His Majesty will not give anything for the nave, he will be able to order the inhabitants and the foreign merchants to do so; for his part he offers five hundred livres.

It is stated that he has made a large profit since he has been at Detroit; and he thinks that, even if that were so, no fault ought to be found with it, looking to the trouble and care he has taken, but that he is ready to render an account to anyone we please of all the expenses he has been put to for this post, and of the small amount of trade he has done, and it will be seen that he is twenty thousand livres out of pocket; not that he regards that as a loss, because the rents and revenues created there remain to him. Everything is extremely dear at Detroit; he thinks it would be convenient if the king would lay down the price per day for the soldier, if His Majesty wishes him set to work on the fortifications.

And in order to pay for this staff, and all the other expenses [named] above, on account of which there is a dispute, he asks that there may be granted to him, as governor, six thousand pounds of powder, four thousand pounds of musket balls, and two thousand pounds of Royal shot [or, lead] each year, on the condition that the King pays for them, and without [charge for] freight; besides that, his Company with its pay. To M. de La Forest, as King's Lieutenant, his Company and its pay, and the pay of eight soldiers which it would be necessary to reduce in that Company; and as the pay of the Majority, M. du Figuier might be given the Company of M. de la Jemerais, or some other, with the pay of eight soldiers in addition to that Company. In establishing this government it would be necessary to settle its boundaries, and he thinks that it could be pushed forward as far as the Illinois. He proposes to take for the other expenses above, with which they wish to charge him, and which he does not think due [from him], the funds intended for the marriages of the girls of Canada.

This fund been abolished.

He says that the great aim of France should be to make herself mistress of all the coast of North America; that that would be possible wtih a fund of a hundred thousand crowns, which he undertakes to find if we will permit him to come to France, provided he is not thwarted as he has been accustomed to be.

good. we will ta it to ask for it.

He complains much of the irregular conduct of M. de Bourgmont, Ensign of infantry, who has quitted the country; he applies for his post for his younger son.

a bad cha acter. has he cas iered the brother?

The King granted him the trade of Detroit to the exclusion of all others. He believed that, for the advancement of this post, it would be expedient that he should give up his right to everybody; and, as he was thus deprived of a certain revenue, he thought that he could impose a tax on all those whom he permitted to carry on this trade, to take the place of the favor which was granted to him by His Majesty.

M. d'Aigre mont note that this t which he establishe 10 livres a head. is that goc

He complains that M. Raudot makes him pay for powder more than he ought, and that he does not give him shot or lead of suitable qualities. He begs that he may be ordered to treat him better in this respect.

M. Raudot does not concernin

In case His Majesty should not think fit to do what he proposes for setting up this country as a government, he begs [me] to send him, through M. Raudot, three thousand pounds of powder a year, four thousand pounds of musket bullets, and two thousand pounds of Royal lead; but he asks me to fix the price myself, so that that may not be done at Quebec.

He says that Detroit being in the midst of the savage tribes, one half of the funds intended by the States of Canada for communications with

It is very essary to on one's g against dr

In Canada officers draw the pay of the soldiers who work; he treat: them the same way at Detroit. He has made an estimate of it, amountin$ to a small sum which might be used for refreshments for the sick.

He asks for orders on that; he says that a soldier who works at Detroi· is by no means to be pitied, and that he can earn from seven hundred t< 1000# and more, a year.

His intention has been to make over the land at Detroit to the King again, after he has established it. For the two years he has been ther< it has produced 1025# a year in quit-rent and rent; if the estate, th< mill and the cattle were established, it would yield now 4000#; and h< is still of opinion that, if he is not interferred with at all it will yield i1 ten years 25,000# a year.

But in order to succeed with his design to make Detroit a profitabl< place, nothing must be conceded to the Jesuits nor to the other societies because they possess the secret of attracting everything to themselves and it is that which causes the lords of Canada to remain poor.

He has given to his daughter, who. is 18 years old, a grant with right: of intermediate and lower jurisdiction, and another to his son, who is a1 Ensign. He begs me to send him the ratification of them, his intentio1 is to re-unite them some day to the principal fief, to which will be give1 whatever title we please.

He has reserved for himself five leagues of territory on both sides of th< river of Detroit, with five leagues in the depths of the lands, and th< powers of higher, intermediate and lower jurisdiction with all the pre rogatives given in Canada.

He begs [us] to consider whether we think fit to send him the gran· ut of it; afterwards we can raise it into an earldom or a marquisate, as w< think best, and he will resign it if it be desired.

LETTER FROM M. RAUDOT, JR.

Endorsed—M. Raudot, junior.

Quebec, the 25th of Octr. 1708

My Lord,

*   *   *

Detroit has brought the savages only too near the English. Almost all the beaver skins produced go to Orange, and we see hardly any here from that post.

My Lord,

Your very humble and most obedient servant,

Raudot.

LETTER FROM M. DE VAUDREUIL.

Endorsed—M. de la Touche, M. de Vaudreuil,

Quebec, the 5th of Novr. 1708.   Colonies.

M. de Vaudreuil.

My Lord,

*   *   *   *

I annex to this second letter copies of three letters which I received at the same time from Father D'heu[1], missionary to the Annontagues, Father Marest, missionary at Michilimakina and Father Chardon[2], missionary to the Poutouatamis. These three letters will show you, My Lord, the state of things at the time; and it is partly on this first news that I have been obliged to act up to the present time.

MM. Raudot and I have the honor of giving you an account, in our joint letter, of everything concerning Detroit, and of the result of the affair of Pesant. If the Sr. de La Mothe had pursued my first objects, and had been content to leave this savage at Michilimakina as an outlaw, instead of inducing him, as he did, to come to Detroit, the savage would

---

[1]Father Jacques D'Heu, S. J., came to Canada, June 14, 1706, and was drowned Sept., 1728. Rep. Gen. 85.—C. M. B.
[2]Pierre Jean Chardon (or, according to Jes. Rel. & All. Doc. LXXI. 129, Jean Baptiste Chardon) S. J. born at Rouen, arrived in Canada Aug. 27, 1693, and went to the Illinois. Died at Quebec, April 21, 1743. Rep. Gen. 76.—C. M. B.

have remained among his tribe disgraced, and the Miamis would never
have dreamt of attacking the French, for they only did so in order to
revenge themselves on the Sr. de La Mothe, who had deceived them by
promising them that he would put the offender to death, and not doing
so. The Miamis, My Lord, would never have attacked the French if the
Sr. de La Mothe had not, last year, prevented Father D'Aveneau, their
missionary, from returning with them, with the view of putting a Recollet
there. It is certain that this missionary by his influence would have
diverted the savages of his mission from doing anything contrary to the
welfare of the service. The Sr. de La Mothe will not agree to that, for,
far from doing that, he defames them to your Highness as far as he can,
and injures them in the minds of the French and of the Savages.

What he has written to you, My Lord, concerning Father Marest is a
falsehood. Hitherto this missionary appears to me to have been strongly
inclined to carry out your orders in detail, as he himself writes to me in
his letter of the 4th of June, a copy of which I have the honor to send you.
Nothing keeps these savages of Michilimakina from going to Detroit
except that they have a natural aversion to that post, of which they informed me again this year in their speeches when they came to bring back
to me the rest of the slaves which they were to hand over to me, to give to
the Iroquois. From these speeches, My Lord, you will learn their true
feelings. The carelessness which the Sr. de La Mothe shows about giving
me news from him, places me in a serious difficulty, and when the savages
come to speak with me I do not know what I ought to answer them, especially at the present juncture when it is no less dangerous to declare war
than not to do so. The extraordinary thing, My Lord, is that the Sr. de
La Mothe pretends that it is I who prevents war from being made; whereas it is he himself who keeps me in a constant state of uncertainty by fur-
nishing me with no news of his post; and prevents me from saying anything definite in reply to the savages, lest I should cause any action contrary to the welfare of his settlement, to be taken. It would be well if he
would act with as much sincerity and uprightness as I. The King would
thereby be better served, and our reputation with the savages would be
different from what it is.

*   *   *   *

So far, the Iroquois appear very well disposed towards us, in spite of
the desire of the English to make them mistrust us. It was not the fault

that this young man believed he was right in killing this soldier, because
with us a deserter is accounted dead, and I had even said so two years
ago to the Senontouans when they requested me to pardon two deserters,
and that no one but the King could do so. You will see, My Lord, from
their speeches and my replies, all that took place in this matter; they
promised me a slave in place of this soldier. I would, indeed, have demanded from them the surrender of the savage who committed the deed,
but, as the soldier was a deserter, and that was all the English were
waiting for to make their party at Onontagués rise in favor of this young
savage, I thought it was better to accept their submission than to persist
obstinately and risk war for an unfortunate man who was shot only because he was a deserter. I thought that might frighten the other soldiers
who wanted to follow the same course. Notwithstanding, I forbade the
Iroquois ever to do such a thing again, telling them that a deserter is none
the less a Frenchman, and that if that happened any more I should be
obliged to demand revenge for their death, as I should do for the death of
anyone else. They assured me that I should have no reason to complain
of them: and I promised them for my part, that, if they would arrest
deserters and bring them to me here, or at Fort de Frontenac, I would
have them rewarded.

*   *   *

The Sieur de Tonty has the honor to write to you, to beg you graciously
to grant him permission to go and pay a visit to France where he has not
been in all the twenty years he has served in this country. I had him relieved at Fort de Frontenac, upon his being suspected of having given a
measure of brandy to a savage. That has been found to be false; but, as
he has been accused before, of being fond of trading, I was very glad for
his own sake to remove him from a place where anyone, who was ill-dis-
posed towards him, would always have the opportunity of creating difficulties for him by bringing false accusations against him. The Sr. de
Tonty is a very capable man and one of the best we have here for ruling
the savages; and, but for the faults he had committed before, which he
hopes to atone for, I assure you, My Lord, I should not have superseded
him at the present juncture unless you had ordered me to do so. I have
replaced him by the Sieur de Fresniere Hertel[1], a lieutenant on half-pay
who understands very well the languages of the Iroquois and the Alkon-
kin, and even that of the Abenaki.

*   *   *

Whatever ground of complaint I may have against the Sr. de La Mothe,
it will never prevent me from acting in harmony with him on all matters

---

[1] Zacharie François Hertel, Sieur de Le Freniere, a lieutenant on half pay, born
1665, married Marie Charlotte Godfroy Jan. 17, 1695, died at Montreal June 20,

that may contribute to the welfare of the King's service; that is a matter
of fact, and I give my whole mind to it, for I have no aim but to carry
out your orders punctiliously. The Sieur de La Mothe, My Lord, takes a
course opposite to mine; and instead of sending me news of him as he
might and ought to do, it was as late as the 20th of August before I received a single letter from him, although several boats had come from his
post. This affectation of not writing has not failed to embarrass me, for
I was unable to give any definite answer to the Outtavois concerning the
affair with the Miamis. This is the way in which the Sr. de La Mothe
behaves, and he does so to show everyone that he is independent. And
as he does not doubt that I shall complain of this neglect, he prejudices
you by assuring you that, if I would act in concert with him, he would
not only bring the savages at Detroit into order and to obedience to the
laws of the kingdom, but also, gradually, all the surrounding tribes. I
hope that is so, My Lord, though I am strongly persuaded of the contrary;
and if, for that purpose, it is only necessary to act in concert with him,
he may count on everything [I can do] and which, naturally, I ought to
do.

I do not know what he means by the powder I have refused him; I have
not done so, nor have I ever had any such intention. It is the same with
his statement that he proposed to me, that the old soldiers, who are not
suitable for his post, should be withdrawn from his company, and that of
the Sieur de la Forest, and that Canadians should be put in their place
with the same pay. He never, in his life, made this proposal to me; and it
would be desirable that this should be done, not only in the companies of
the Sr. de La Mothe and the Sr. de la Forest, but also in all the companies
in this country.

I have hitherto, My Lord, abstained from mentioning to you an abuse
which arises in connection with the permissions I am obliged to grant to
all those who wish to go to Detroit. This is that the Sieur de La Mothe's
agent, or attorney at Montreal applies to me for these permissions whenever he thinks fit, sometimes for two boats, sometimes for three, and
occasionally for one; and when once these *voyageurs* have left Montreal,
they do as they like, since there is no one to prevent them. Some stop on
the road to sell their goods, under the pretext of not being able to get
there; others go to the Outtavois although they are not allowed to do so;
and it was also in this way that we had two soldiers desert, one of whom
was killed by an Iroquois, of which I had the honor of sending you an
account. I cannot, however, without orders from you, refuse these per-

not be able to say that I make use of these same permissions to send to the Outtavois. It appears to me that, if these *voyageurs* set out all together and returned in like manner, desertions of this kind would not occur, and it would also have a wholesome effect on the savages, whereas, since these boats often proceed alone, whether going or returning, that makes no impression on their minds.

      *   *   *

The Sieur de Brussy having died on his way to France, the Sieur de Bourmont having deserted from Detroit, and the Sr. de Verehive having been killed by the English I have had the Sieurs de l'Inetot¹ and Dussy taken in place of the two latter.

      *   *   *

Your most humble and most obedient servant,

Vaudreuil.

Quebec, this 5th of Novr. 1708.

MEMORANDUM BY MM. DE VAUDREUIL AND RAUDOT, ON THE PROPOSAL OF THE SR. DE LA MOTHE TO ESTABLISH FOUR COMPANIES OF SAVAGES AT DETROIT.

Endorsed—1708.

The Sieur de La Mothe proposes to My Lord, to establish four companies of savages at Detroit, or two at least in addition to the French Companies there. He contends that this would be very advantageous to the Colony, because these savages would be attached to the French, and we should have nothing more to fear from the Iroquois, nor from the English; for if they made any attempt against Canada, it would be within the reach of the French and savage troops to pillage the villages of the Iroquois at once, and take away their wives and children as slaves. His scheme would be to place these companies on the same footing as those of the French; to have them commanded by the savages who have the most influence among the tribes; to make a separate corps of them by ordering that the last French captain, etc.

The proposal of the Sieur de La Mothe to form the savages into companies cannot be expedient for the Colony; for, even if the savages could be formed into companies, it would appear to the Sieurs de Vaudreuil and Raudot that we ought not to do so, seeing that these savages by educating themselves up to discipline would become more formidable to the Colony than they are already.

The savages would not be more attached to the French service by these companies. We saw no example of that in the savages who received officers' pay in this country and afterwards withdrew into the woods. These companies would not shield this country from attacks by the Iroquois and the English; on the contrary, it is more likely that, as Detroit brings the savages nearer to the English, they will be attracted by the good trade they will find with our enemies; the pay they will receive from the King will not attach them to us more. The savages being near the Iroquois will be able to form alliances with them; they will all become related to one another, and if the Colony should be at war with the Iroquois we should have great difficulty in making them declare it.

They are not within such easy reach as the Sr. de La Mothe assures him, for falling upon the village of the Iroquois. They could not go in a large party, for making a great attack, all of a sudden; moreover, before such an attack could be made, the French and savages at Detroit, would have perished of hunger, seeing that they would have the Iroquois to contend with every day, and that hardly any assistance could be furnished to Detroit from this country.

Since the savages are all on an equality with one another, they could not be formed into companies, for the captains would have very little authority. It is true that these savages have chiefs among themselves, but these chiefs have no absolute command; they only say a certain thing must be done, and after that the others do it if they like. As there is no punishment among them, there can be no discipline; that is how the savages arrange matters.

MM. DE VAUDREUIL AND RAUDOT REPORT OF THE COLONIES, AND CRITICISE CADILLAC.

Endorsed—M. de la Touche. MM. de Vaudreuil and Raudot. Quebec, the 14th Novr. 1708. Colonies.

My Lord,

The Sieurs de Vaudreuil and Raudot have received the memorandum of the King, dated the 6th of June of this year, which you were pleased to address to them.

They have the honor to assure you that they will ever be found perfectly at one in all that concerns the good of the service of His Majesty and the welfare of this Colony, and that neither of them have any other object but to obey, strictly, the orders you are good enough to give them.

This Colony, My Lord, is truly in a pitiable condition because of the fall in the price of beaverskins and the high price of goods. They are constantly seeking means to reduce this evil, but it seems impossible except by an increase in the price of beaverskins, which the agents might grant to the extent of forty sols. This rise would tend to attract the savages to us, and would prevent them from going to Orange. But as regards the price of goods, peace alone would remedy that.

The Sieurs de Vaudreuil and Raudot have the honor to assure you that they are giving all the orders necessary for carrying out the contracts of the Sieur Aubert[1], which has enabled this colony to pay its debts, and has secured to him its trade in future.

They will pay special attention to the matter about which you do them the honor of writing to them, concerning the beaverskins of the Sieur Aubert. They will have them embarked in preference to all others on His Majesty's ship, when he is good enough to approve of one being sent on his account to this country, unless the said Sieur Aubert consents to their remaining here. If they find any room left after putting these on board, they will have the furs of the merchants loaded.

---

[1]Charles Aubert Sieur de la Chenaye, at one time agent of the West India company, engaged in a very extensive trade on his own account and was sometimes termed the king of Canadian merchants. Born in Picardy, he came to Canada about 1655. His first wife was a daughter of William Couillard, and his second wife was Marie Louise Juchereau. He died in Quebec in 1702. Gagon's Bib. Can. 534. It is probable that the Aubert referred to in this document was one of the sons of Charles. Charles was married three times. The wife not mentioned by Gagnon was Marie Angelique Denys. By the first marriage there was one son, Charles; by the second marriage there were six children, and by the third marriage there were ten children, or 17 in all. There is a letter from Sieur Aubert in Collection de Manuscrits relatifs a la Nouvelle France, III. 494, dated June 25, 1708, but the full name of the writer is not given.—C. M. B.

'e the honor to represent to you that a vessel from His Majesty,
ing the number of those that come to this country, brings it
; and to beg you to be good enough to send one every year.

and flatter themselves, that you would not discontinue this
is Colony, which only exists and is maintained by the benefits
eigned to bestow upon it, which you will graciously continue.
chants of this country have suffered heavily from the loss of
s, but that has been a general misfortune; as this loss is now
ced, that will tend to make trade a little better. The bills of
'or beaverskins, which the Sieur Aubert pays for in ready
1 do the country good and will induce the merchants to buy
rom the savages at a rather better price.

ir de Vaudreuil applies himself as far as he can, My Lord, to
ι cordial alliance with all the savages; only this alliance can
happiness and safety of this Colony. War with these tribes is
ns expedient for the French; they have nothing to gain by it.
s are to be found everywhere in the country; and they will
hiding behind a tree trunk ten days until they can assassinate
'oman, living in this condition on an ear of Indian corn. More-
warfare is the cruellest in the world, for, not content with
uses, they also burn the prisoners they take, and they do not
o death until they have kept them constantly in the most cruel
hey can devise. The Sieurs de Vaudreuil and Raudot cannot
lis good understanding, nor prevent these tribes from allying
with the English, without making them presents; it is a neces-
They would be very glad not to be obliged to make any; and
do give is so small a matter compared with the large quantity
vhich the English make them presents of, besides the cheap
offer them, and the brandy they give them at Orange as they
the heavy prices they put on beaverskins, that the said Sieurs
uil and Raudot cannot help being constantly in fear of too
ιderstanding between these savages and the English, who prac-
art to attract them. They also, on their side, use every means

in the year 1706, when they killed three Frenchmen. The Sr. de Vaudreuil proposed that they should hand over to him the offending savage,
who had been the cause of this deed; and, as these savages represented to
·him that they had not sufficient control over one another to be able to
give up one of their men, which is true, and that the offender was allied to
several tribes of savages which would never suffer him to be surrendered
to the French, the Sr. de Vaudreuil answered that he would believe that
it was not in their power to deliver him the man he demanded of them;
but that, as when they killed the Frenchmen, they had killed some of the
savage tribes, it was necessary for them to go up to Detroit where they
would find the Sr. de La Mothe and all those tribes, and that there the
said Sieur de La Mothe would, in accordance with his orders, find means
by which they might atone for the evil deeds they had committed; but
that he would warn them beforehand, that if ever they killed any Frenchman, they would have to bring him the head of the murderer, and that
the blood of Frenchmen was not to be wiped out by beaverskins nor by
slaves. The Srs. de Vaudreuil and Raudot, with the Srs. de Ramezay
and la Forest, whom they consulted on this occasion, thought that they
could not take any more prudent course than they did; for, although they
had risked the proposal of demanding the offender, they were almost
certain that it would not be granted; the savages have no sufficient
authority over each other to be able to hand anyone over. If they had
been absolutely determined on it, they would have had to wage war,
and consequently to abandon the Outavois to the Iroquois. This course
would have been by no means expedient, seeing that the only policy that
can be pursued in regard to the savages is to prevent any connection
between the natives of the upper country, namely the Outavois, and the
peoples round the Lakes, with the Iroquois, so that, in the event of one
of the two tribes wanting to make war on this Colony, we could set the
other against it. This was carried out at the time of the war with the
Iroquois, and was the cause of its coming to an end, from the various
parties that the Outavois always kept in the field. It is in order to
prevent the latter from being destroyed by the Iroquois, that we have
tried to compose all disturbances; for, if the Iroquois could have destroyed the Outavois, as they would then have had nothing more to fear
from the people of the upper country, they would afterwards have made
war on this country. The Sieurs de Vaudreuil and Raudot also thought
that this affair ought to be adjusted at Detroit, since the Miamis and
the Hurons were concerned; they felt sure they had done all they could
in the matter. The Sr. de Vaudreuil had issued his orders to the Sieur
de La Mothe, but he, thinking to do something brilliant which he believed
must do him honor, has spoilt everything; and he was the cause of the
attack which the Miamis made on the French at Detroit this year. The

them that he would have the offender, and that this was the only way to
atone for their misdeeds. The Outavois set out from Detroit, with the
Sr. d'Argenteuil to Michilimackinac; and when they got there, after
great councils had been held, the offender gave himself up to them, but
at this time he was quite sure of his life being spared, and that he
would be secure, provided he and his family came and settled at Detroit,
this having been promised him by the emissaries of the Sr. de La Mothe,
whom he had sent with the said Sieur d'Argenteuil. When the offender
came to Detroit, the said Sr. de La Mothe held great councils with the
Hurons and the Miamis. They wanted the death of the offender, but he
wished to save him, and it would not have suited him to put him to death,
because the family of the said offender would not have come and settled
at Detroit. He hit upon a plan which was to make him escape; and the
offender did, in fact, escape. The said Sr. de La Mothe immediately
called the savages together and told them that there was no need for the
offender to escape, nor to fear, for he gave him his life. Since then the
offender has returned to Detroit with all his family. That affair, and
the sight of the said offender at that place, irritated the Hurons and the
Miamis to such a degree that this spring they plotted with 20 Iroquois,
who were returning from war against the Têtes Plattes [Flat heads]
to murder the said Sr. de La Mothe and all the French who were at the
Fort with the Outavois savages settled there. This scheme would have
been carried out if they had had enough men to seize on all the houses and
huts; but as they had not a sufficiently large number, it was put off, and
this caused it to be discovered, by the greatest good fortune possible.
The Miamis, enraged at their plan having been found out, made an
attack on three Frenchmen, whom they killed, and brought disgrace on
the Sieur de La Mothe. They afterwards came back to make amends
for that wrong-doing. The said Sr. de La Mothe demanded from them
those who had made the attack, and payment for the cattle. The savages paid him for the cattle and promised to hand over to him, in twenty
days, the Miamis who had made the attack. They did not keep their
word, so that the Sieur de La Mothe thought himself bound to go and
attack the Miamis in their forts. He did this because he fancied they

ing all this time, the said Sr. de La Mothe, for fear he should get wounded, stationed himself behind a tree which was eighteen feet in circumfer- ence, nor did he venture out except to go and get out of the range of the shot. This is such a public matter, and the Sr. de la Mothe makes so little effort to hide it, to his very great disgrace, that they feel they cannot help informing you of it. If the said Sr. de La Mothe had wished, he could have carried this fort at the point of the sword, for sixty men headed by a good sergeant could have done so, according to those who were present at that attack. Such an act would have created a great stir among the tribes and made them respect the French name; it would also have punished the Miamis, by the large number of them that would have been killed, for the evil deed they had done in killing the Frenchmen. But the said Sr. de La Mothe, more prudent, contented himself with letting his men fire on the fort, so that the heavy musketry fire com- pelled the Miamis to hoist a French flag. An arrangement was talked of; and the Miamis got quit of the matter by giving him three hostages with a promise to deliver to him those who had slain the Frenchmen, and on giving him furs to the value of a thousand crowns, five or six packets of which he had kept, apparently to pay him for the trouble he was put to in proceeding to that fort.

The hostages were taken to Detroit where they have complete free- dom, and are in a position to escape whenever they like; and the Sieurs de Vaudreuil and Raudot have not heard that these savages have kept their word with the said Sr. de la Mothe, but are convinced of the con- trary. The Sieur de Vaudreuil always pays great attention to keeping all the savage tribes on good terms with one another. The Iroquois still observe the same neutrality, and he hopes that it will continue, notwith- standing the arts which the English constantly practice to make that tribe break it. We did not begin last year to prepare to resist the Eng- lish until we heard the news that the armament had set out from Baston. The work which has been done on the batteries, by reconstructing all the platforms which were quite rotten, was absolutely necessary. We could not have served a single gun. The citadel battery was constructed entirely of walls, without mortar, a foot and a half thick, and the em- brasures of part of it were too high and too narrow, and were constructed like windows so that a gun could not be leveled properly there; it has been necessary to cover the whole of this battery with gabions, without which it would have been impossible to serve it, because the enemy's can- non shots, coming and striking against this wall, would have wounded everyone who was there, with splinters. The said Srs. de Vaudreuil and Raudot have tried to save expense as far as possible, and have only had done what was absolutely necessary on this occasion, according to the decisions of the councils of war which have been held here, for putting

this town in a state of defence. It is true that they will delay the fortifications a little. On the representations of Sr. de Vasseur, who said
that the masonry of the bastion that had been begun might be spoilt,
they have had ten thousand livres out of the funds for next year employed on it. This bastion has already cost the King forty-one thousand
livres, and they hope it may be finished for fifteen; that will make fifty-
six thousand livres it will have cost His Majesty. They also hope that
sufficient clay may be found for them to be able to use it, as well as for
the other works. The Sieurs de Vaudreuil and Raudot, in conjunction
with the Sr. de Vasseur, have also considered the devices he has for continuing these fortifications, without their being too much of a burden to
His Majesty. All these plans, My Lord, which he has for continuing
these fortifications, simply come to placing taxes on this country, which
might cause it to be abandoned, or prevent its expansion, which would
destroy the towns and entirely ruin trade. This country cannot bear
heavier taxes than it has already on wines and brandy; it cannot pay
on any other provisions, as it is very poor and very hard and goods are
very dear there. It may be said that there is no one rich here, and
all who have been in this country can assure you, My Lord, that its inhabitants have great difficulty in obtaining food and clothing. There are
however a few persons here who, because they have gained wealth, and
want to get more, believe that everyone must be rich and ought to enrich
them.

They will give the said Sr. la Vasseur, as you direct, all the help and
countenance he may need.

The Sieurs de Vaudreuil and Raudot have re-annexed to His Majesty's
domain all the lands in the lower town, as they have not been built
upon, and have at the same time given notice that all who would buy
lands must come and make their offers at the Intendant's office. These
lands re-annexed are places which are covered by the tide, and a great
deal of money is necessary for building on them, seeing that walls five or
six feet thick are required; hence, as no one is in a position to incur that

built which cost three thousand livres; they hope, My Lord, that you will be good enough to send this money next year. In future they will be very careful not to undertake anything without your orders; but this work appeared to them most indispensable, and they have the honor to inform you that it is built as strongly as possible, and will last an indefinite time.

The Sieurs de Vaudreuil and Raudot had the honor of sending you their advice regarding the redoubts which the Sr. le Vasseur proposes. They assure you that they think this work useless, and cannot understand what good they can be; the forts that are built have a better effect, as the inhabitants have their houses built within them and can retire to them in time of war. They have the honor of informing you that these redoubts cannot cover the land of this country, nor prevent the savages from passing them. Besides this, the inhabitants cannot, at the present time, labor at works of this kind, when they have great difficulty in earning enough to clothe themselves; the expense His Majesty would incur on this account would be useless, as well as that which would have to be met in paying for the Sieur le Vasseur's journeys, who does not travel cheaply, and demands that an overseer and a man to take measurements should be sent with him in these journeys, as was done in M. de Beauharnois' time. Perhaps if he were not paid for his journeys he would not seek to rebuild these redoubts; like the Sr. de Reygayard,[1] who asks to go to Three Rivers, Montreal and Chambly to visit the arsenals, where there are about twenty 6- and 11-pounders altogether, and a thousand weight of shot, only in order to be paid for his journeys. There are good gunners at these places who render exact accounts. The Srs. de Vaudreuil and Raudot proposed to the said Sr. Gayard to go without getting paid for his journey, but the desire to go left him at once. If they were to let these two men make as many journeys as they liked, in order to be paid for them, both of them would deplete the King's funds in this way as much as they could.

If the work of the redoubts were good, the Srs. de Vaudreuil and Raudot would be more interested in its being done than other men, since it is the duty of both of them to seek only to render the Colony safe, which you, My Lord, have been good enough to intrust to their care.

The Srs. de Vaudreuil and Raudot have the honor herewith to enclose the memorandum which you do them the honor of sending them regarding the proposal of the Sr. le Vasseur, for doing work to the extent of one-sixth more than the sum allotted, together with their opinion thereon. They will prevent any irregularity in connection with the fortifications, and will punish those who are found at fault.

---

[1] Pierre Rey-Gaillard, commissary of artillery, born 1656, married Françoise

The Sieur de Vaudreuil does not at present see any probability of a treaty of neutrality with the Governor of Baston; if, however, one should be made, he will scrupulously adhere to the instructions you give him on this matter.

The Sieurs de Vaudreuil and Raudot will utilize, so far as they can, the opportunities which the junctures of affairs may give rise to, for sending their orders into the interior of the country. They are taking every precaution to prevent the prohibited trade. They have the honor to annex hereto the memorandum which the Sr. d'Aigremont has sent them in compliance with his instructions. As he is a very upright man, they are convinced that he will do himself the honor of informing you of the truth in all things.

They received last year, in the memorandum of His Majesty, the orders you were pleased to give them concerning the claims of the Sieur de La Mothe. The Sieur Raudot, junior, wrote to him about it, and has the honor to inclose the answer he received. You will see from it, My Lord, that he has no intention of carrying out the order you sent him on your behalf.

Permit the Sieurs de Vaudreuil and Raudot to represent to you that, if the Sr. de La Mothe were at liberty to make presents, he would use up all His Majesty's funds; moreover all the presents he makes are given simply to induce the savages to come and settle at Detroit, and they bring him considerable profit through the trade he does with them.

The Sr. de La Mothe has changed the management of his brandy office, but it is still sold at twenty livres. Each boat that goes up has permission to take twelve pots only, but the Sr. de La Mothe gets as much taken up as he wishes. The Srs. de Vaudreuil and Raudot will regulate the price of what has been used for the service, as you direct them to do.

The Sieurs de Vaudreuil and Raudot do themselves the honor of informing you of all they have learnt regarding the behavior of the Sr. de La Mothe. He is equally detested by the troops, the settlers and the savages, who have neither respect nor regard for him, looking upon him as a very selfish man, to say nothing more. He has granted all the lands of the fort, at the rate of two sols a foot frontage on each street, so that those who border on two streets pay four. He has granted the land at 50 s

lated, it would be found that it cost him less than those that are built in this colony, for three hundred weight is conveyed for him, free, going, and the same returning, by each boat; and all the workmen who have done this work have had only half a pint of brandy a day as payment, which is worth five or six sols here. Hé still continues to make gun-smiths and blacksmiths pay for the right of working; this oppression, to which he subjects workmen, will not encourage them to go and settle where he is.

He grants licenses for hunting, and with these licenses he sends out boats to go and trade in the further parts of the lakes, contrary to what is definitely laid down in his agreement. The Sieurs de Vaudreuil and Raudot do not know what becomes of the beaverskins they bring back, nor of those obtained at Detroit; for only a very small quantity is supplied from this post to the agency, and the Sr. de La Mothe, who has bound himself, by his agreement, not to supply more than 15 to 20 thousand livres' worth, has supplied 600# worth this year.

That, My Lord, is the way in which the Sr. dé La Mothe conducts himself. He tries to make as much money as he can, and that in whatever way he can.

The Sieur de Vaudreuil offered him his Company, and that of the Sr. de la Forest, as he had the honor of informing you. It would appear that he did not think he required them, since he has not sent for them.

The Sieurs de Vaudreuil and Raudot beg that you will be good enough to send them a decree forbidding the trade in brandy, and containing a penalty of 500# against those who disobey it. The one you did them the honor to send them, ordered, for the first offense, only the confiscation of the liquors; those who carry on the villainous trade with the savages, having generally only one or two pints of brandy, incur no great punishment. The Sr. de La Mothe has the trade publicly carried on at Detroit, at his office, charging 20# a pot. It may be that he does not let the savages have enough at a time to get intoxicated, but the expense they go to for this drink—which is served them regularly every day—ruins them and prevents them from getting what they need.

The Sieurs de Vaudreuil and Raudot will give the Sr. de La Mothe all the help, and the facilities which may lie in their power for the settlement of Detroit. They hope it is going on as well as the said Sr. de La Mothe states. Those who come from that post every day, to this colony, speak quite differently of it.

It is true, My Lord, that the Sr. de La Mothe has inveighed most bitterly against the Jesuit Fathers, and that he has spoken of them in the presence of the Outtavois in terms which are by no means seemly. He has, by his authority, and without any reason, taken from them the mis-

with these savages for nineteen years and knew their language and customs, in order to place a Recollet there who did not understand them. They hope that what you have done him the honor to write to him will keep him from destroying these fathers who do useful and fruitful service. It is certain that the language he has used about them may do harm among the savages, to religion, for they have wit enough about them to see how little respect he bears the priests.

The Sieurs de Vaudreuil and Raudot are convinced that, if this Jesuit missionary had remained with the Miamis, they would never have entered upon the attack they made on the French at Detroit this year.

If the man Boudor returns to Montreal, they will not fail to have him arrested and put on his trial.

The Sieurs de Vaudreuil and Raudot will give their attention as you order them, My Lord, to the conduct of the two settlers who have been accused of having carried on the forbidden trade.

They will have the pay of the Sr. de Meuthet withheld, according as you do them the honor to direct them: they cannot, however, help leaving him half of it to live on until further orders, as he has a very large family.

The Sieur de Courtemanche has succeeded very well this year on the coast of Labrador in fishing for sea-wolves; the cod-fishery is very abundant there. This post would be a very good one if the said Sr. de Courtemanche could bear the necessary expenses; first establishments are always difficult and cost a great deal. The Sieurs de Vaudreuil and Raudot have the honor to assure you that he merits the gratuity you have been good enough to grant him, and to ask you to continue it to him.

The Sieurs de Vaudreuil and Raudot will prevent those who take up the boats of the Jesuits, from carrying on trade, and they will comply with the orders you do them the honor to give them, regarding the man Despins who is still at Detroit. They have taken all possible care this year to prevent the trade from the end of the island; they have sent detachments there to make the savages go down. They will continue in future, as you

to them without obtaining a receipt for them, which they forward to Mons. Begon. nor without warning these captains to have all possible care taken of them.

The sentence which has been given against a sergeant and a private, who had fought a duel, was one of outlawry; they will see carefully to it that such crimes are punished.

The Sieurs de Vaudreuil and Raudot would have been greatly obliged to you, My Lord, if you had been willing to put the companies of this country up to the strength of fifty men; they hope you will be so good as to do this for a Colony which stands in need of it. They thank you for the recruits you have graciously directed to be sent to them by the King's ship from Accadie, but they fear lest the Sr. de Subercasse, under the pretext of always having need of some, may keep them. No soldiers arrived by the ship L'Affriquain, which anchored in the roadstead of this town on the sixteenth of last month; the twenty soldiers who were to have embarked in it, embarked with the others in the Loire. They are expecting them next year by a ship which they hope the Sieur de Subercasse will send here to bring them; it would cost too much to send them overland.

Mons. Begon has sent the Sieur Raudot a copy of the agreement he has made with the Sr. Plassant, and they will see it is carried out.

The Sieurs de Vaudreuil and Raudot can assure you, My Lord, that the merchants of this country bestir themselves with all possible activity to try and revive the trade of this colony. Times are so bad, money is so rare, and insurances are so heavy, that they cannot maintain their trade unaided; they need relief in every way, My Lord, to enable them to keep up. The fishery of the Sieurs Hazeur and Peire has succeeded better this year; they have obtained a hundred barrels of oil. Although the said Sr. Hazeur died this summer, the Sieurs de Vaudreuil and Raudot beg you to be good enough to continue to grant the same gratuity to the St. Peire, or to the heirs, or the creditors of the Sr. Hazeur, who will prosecute this fishery in future.

They are greatly obliged to you, My Lord, for continuing the gratuity which you were so good as to grant to Madame de Repentigny. The lady takes great pains, and deserves the honor of your bounty. The small fabrics which she has made, will do no harm to those of France, which will always be preferred, on account of their good quality and manufacture, to those she makes, as soon as they become cheap enough for all the people to be able to purchase them.

The Sieurs de Vaudreuil and Raudot will look to the due execution of the decree you were good enough to send them last year, regarding the tithes. They thank you for it, in the name of all the inhabitants of this country, and beg you, on their behalf to be good enough to leave matters always as they now stand.

The Sieurs de Vaudreuil and Raudot are most obliged to you, My Lord, for the good will which you are always graciously pleased to inform them that you bear this country; they hope, and beg you to be good enough to have five hundred Tulle muskets sent to them gratis, to replace the five hundred which have been kept in the stock of this country. These guns will serve them for exchanging the bad arms still remaining among the troops, and for arming the reinforcement which will come from Accadie this spring. They hope for this favor from you, My Lord, and flatter themselves that you will be good enough to grant it.

They will carefully comply with what you do them the honor to write to them regarding the arms.

The Sieurs de Vaudreuil and Raudot have not yet changed all the bills of M. de Champigny; they will proceed with that this winter; they are so bad that they cannot be used any longer. They can, both of them, assure you that they will not issue any without having the funds of the King as security for these bills, nor without the treasurer being charged to withdraw them, as you were good enough to permit them to do in your letter to them both of 1705. In case funds should be wanting, in lieu of the bills on the treasurer, of which the Sieurs Raudot had the honor to inform you in their private letters, they have prepared bills of thirty-two livres, in accordance with the report annexed, in which the reasons which have inclined them to take this course are set forth. They antici pate, My Lord, that you will approve of their action, since these bills in no way pledge His Majesty, being secured on a fund which the treasurer general of the Navy has in his hands. They will burn them after the departure of the vessels, the Sieur Petit being obliged to return them to them within that time.

The Sieurs de Vaudreuil and Raudot have the honor to inform you

Colony; together with the Sieur de Vaudreuil, they will give their atten-tion to inducing the young people to marry. If His Majesty would be good enough to replace marriages on the list of charges, that would still further induce the settlers to marry. They hope, My Lord, that you will graciously accord this new favor to this country, as well as that of making up the number of the garrisons again, since they have learnt that the agent was paying the same price for the agency as he gave for it in the past. ·

The Sieurs de Vaudreuil and Raudot thank you, My Lord, for the regard you have been good enough to pay to the recommendation which they had the honor of making to you in favor of the Jesuit Fathers, to fill the place of the Sieur Deshayes. They can assure you that they will always provide one of them, capable of filling that post in order to keep school, and will take precautions against the country being in want of any, and that they will do a service on this occasion which will be very useful to this Colony.

The Sieurs de Vaudreuil and Raudot will comply, My Lord, with what you do them the honor of ordering them to do, concerning the general hospital. The Sieurs de Vaudreuil and Raudot beg that you will not permit them, My Lord, to represent to you that, if the services rendered to His Majesty by the Sr. Hertel, senior, are not important enough to obtain from his kindness the letters of nobility he asks for, those of his children, all of whom are in the service, who are all brave and upright men; the death of one of his sons in the party which went against the English this year; the bravery and good conduct of the Sr. de Rouville, one of his children, in command of this expedition, which he held jointly with the Sr. Deschaillons; might decide you, My Lord, to obtain this favor for them. The Sieurs de Vaudreuil and Raudot can assure you that all this family are brave and very devoted to the service of His Majesty, and that they will never show themselves unworthy of the favors you may deign to obtain for them.

The Sieurs de Vaudreuil and Raudot could not, during the stay of the vessels in this roadstead last year, carry out the order regarding the Sr. Giton's powder; they did so after their departure and have the honor to inclose the report thereon.

The Sieur Petit will be reimbursed, My Lord, for the advance he made on the statement of charges for 1704, by the letters of exchange which will be handed to him by the agents, and they will take care to carry out what has been arranged on that matter.

The Sieurs de Vaudreuil and Raudot are convinced, My Lord, that little interest should be shown in the lead mines until the peace, when His Majesty will be able to have them worked. If they should be found to

They will promise, as you do them the honor to tell them, that those who have discovered them shall be rewarded when His Majesty has the mines worked.

The Sieurs de Vaudreuil and Raudot will do themselves the honor of informing you further on in this letter, of the expedition which was sent against the English this year. They hope His Majesty will be pleased with the valor of his troops, of the settlers, and of the savages who were in this expedition.

His Majesty, My Lord, grants so little for the extraordinary expenses of the war, of which we have to use a part for presents to the savages, which go much further than they are thought to do; another part for the fortifications, the workmen, the traveling and journeys, the hospitals, and other matters laid down in the statement, that almost nothing remains. And expeditions cost so much that the Sieurs de Vaudreuil and Raudot cannot despatch as many as they would like to do. In the past they have induced the savages to make expeditions, which cost much less. That despatches this year have greatly diminished the funds, as to which they have to represent to you, My Lord, that you caused the freight of the salt sent to them in 1706 by the "Hero" and the store-ship "La Holland" to be retained. They hope, of your kindness to this country, My Lord, that you will be good enough to countermand this order, and have the said funds remitted to them.

The Sieurs de Vaudreuil and Raudot beg you, My Lord, to be so good as to cause the pension of her father to be sent to Madame de la Chesnaye' in her name; he died this year. They can assue you that this lady is very badly in need of it, being burdened with many children.

The Sieurs de Vaudreuil and Raudot will have the honor of informing you that there are only sixty-three houses at Detroit instead of 120, as the said Sr. de La Mothe tells you there are, that as regards the savages, there are about a hundred and fifty huts, in place of 1,200 as the said Sr. de La Mothe informs you; that the whole of the settlers number sixty-three, twenty-nine of whom are married soldiers, while the others are *voyageurs* of the country, and settled here, who go up every year and only have houses within the fort for the purpose of trading.

mattock, there is a large quantity of wheat which he makes into bread and sells for 10 and 15s the livre to the French and the savages.

The said Sr. de La Mothe deceived your confidence in him when he wrote you that there was a large number of cattle at Detroit. There are three cows, six or seven bulls and calves, and one horse. It would not be to the advantage of the said Sr. de La Mothe that there should be a greater number of them, for he would not sell them as he does, milk at twenty sols the pot, and would not let out his horse at ten livres a day, if he had more animals. The Sieurs de Vaudreuil and Raudot are greatly surprised that the said Sr. de La Mothe should have ventured to propose to you to set up a jurisdiction at Detroit, for the said Sr. de La Mothe is not sure of having twenty settlers, and that place is not at all well established, and will have great difficulty in becoming so under the command of the said Sr. de La Mothe. They are also surprised that the said Sr. de La Mothe proposes to My Lord to set up a notary there; he would in that way reduce the rights he has acquired, since he exacts the payment of four livres for every contract of concession he executes himself, which is the fee paid to notaries in this country.

The Sieur de La Mothe proposes to My Lord to form companies of savages at Detroit. This is only with the object of profiting by the funds which would be set apart for their pay. The Sieurs de Vaudreuil and Raudot find this proposal impossible, after having discussed it with the Sr. D'Agremond. They have the honor to annex hereto a detailed memorandum thereon, with their opinion.

The best way, My Lord, to range all the savages on the side of the English is to establish a port at Niagara; those who are capable of making such a proposal to you are more the friends than the enemies of the English. As for the Sieurs de Vaudreuil and Raudot, to whom you have done the honor of entrusting the care of this Colony, they would deem themselves unworthy of this favor if they did not notify you of all the difficulties which may arise if this post is established, which would afterwards end in entirely destroying this colony. There need be no fear, My Lord, of the English seizing this post; the Iroquois is too skillful, and understands his interests too well, to permit it. If the Englishman were settled there, the Iroquois would find himself deprived of the profit he makes out of the people of the lakes who pass through their territory to go to the English, or from the beaver-skins they trade in with them on which they make a profit out of the Englishman.

There is yet another reason which would cause the Iroquois to oppose it, namely, that if the English were settled there, the people of the lakes would no longer have need of the Iroquois for trading with the English, who would attract to them all the tribes of the lakes, so that, in this

would always side with the English because they would be attracted by
the trade they would do with that nation.

Is it not the same thing with the French, My Lord? If they were
settled there, they could never—whatever effort they might make—compete with the price of the English goods: so that, were this post established by the French, and the savages of the lakes attracted near to the
Iroquois, tempted by the cheap prices at Orange, they would pass over
the lands of the Iroquois to go there. It is certain that the nearer we
bring the savages of the lakes to the Iroquois, the fewer furs we shall get,
seeing that the Iroquois will trade with them for them all with English
goods.

Our great policy should be to always keep the intercourse of these
savages with the Iroquois distant, and to foster in them continual interest of the latter, which cannot be done if we bring them near to one
another.

There would also be oppression from the Iroquois, if the French were
to establish a post there. The Iroquois have not spoken of it to the Sieur
de Vaudreuil, but he learnt that the English having expressed a desire
to establish a post on the River Donnontagué near the Lake Ontario, and
another on Lake d'Onoyonte, alleging to them as a pretext that the French
wanted to set up posts at Niagara and La Gallete, they replied to the
English, who had made the proposal to them, that they absolutely would
not have them settle at either of these posts, and that they would oppose
those which the French wanted to establish as far as they could.

The Iroquois, perturbed by this news, spoke to the Sieur de Joncaire
about it, who told them that he knew nothing of the matter, but that he
was sure that, if it were desired to establish these posts, we should speak
to them about it first.

The Iroquois do not understand their interests this time; for, if we
establish this post, it can only do good to them and harm to us. Hence

success of the expedition which the Sr. de Vandreuil sent against the English this year, and hope, My Lord, that you will be pleased with the good management of the commanders, with the valor and steadiness of all the officers, soldiers and settlers of this country, and of some of the savages who composed it.

This expedition appeared to the Sieur de Vaudreuil to be very necessary in order to break up all the intrigues which the English at Orange were carrying on with our savages to prevent them from making war on those of Baston. They have learnt, by an experience sad for them, that although our savages are attracted by the advantages they offer them, they are still faithful to us. The valor of the French on this occasion will attract them to us still more strongly and will give them a respect for our nation which they absolutely refuse to the English.

This expedition was made up of one hundred French, soldiers and settlers, and sixty savages, under the command of the Sieurs Deschaillons and Rouville and of the Sr. de la Perriere, ensign, who commanded the savages. They set out as follows—the said Srs. Deschaillons and Rouville by St. François, with all the French and the Abenaki and Nepissingue savages, and the Sr. de la Perriere by Lake Champlain with those from Sault and La Montagne, before all to meet at a lake near the English. But the savages whom the said Sr. de la Perriere commanded either bribed by the English, or wishing to cover our nation with shame, by making the expedition retire, returned to their huts, so that the Sr. de la Perriere was obliged to fall back, being unable to find among these savages two men who would show him the way, so that he could join the expedition. These savages have excused themselves for this desertion on the ground of an illness which was running through their village.

The French and the remaining savages, not discouraged by the difficulty they experienced every day from the small quantity of water in the rivers, which was constantly causing injury to their boats and compelling them to drag them, and in no way disconcerted at not finding the other savages at the meeting-place, continued their journey and fell upon an English village called Heûreil, consisting of twenty-five or thirty houses, besides that of the governor, who was in the fort, in which were about thirty soldiers, with ten or twelve in each of the houses. These troops had been sent to reinforce this village, by the governor of Baston, on the information he had received of the expedition. They attacked the village half-an-hour after day break. They found great resistance; and in order to make themselves masters of the houses and the fort, after they had tried firing for a long time, and had only succeeded in forcing a part of it, they were compelled to set fire to it, as well as to the fort, before they could make themselves masters of them. There were about a hundred

h.

achievement, when they fell into an ambush of sixty to seventy Englishmen who were in the woods, whom they did not discover until the enemy opened fire on them. Immediately throwing away the provisions they carried, they rushed straight on the ambush and gave their enemies so little time to prepare themselves that they destroyed them all, except ten or twelve who were.chased up to the first houses. This second action, My Lord, was much warmer than the first; and the commanding officer took the only course open, to send them on this occasion to save their men and have but few wounded.

In these two engagements there were killed the Sr. de Vercheres, ensign, and the Sr. de Chambly petty officer, five Frenchmen and three savages; and we had eighteen men, Frenchmen and savages, wounded.

The Sieur de Vaudreuil incloses with his private letter a list of the officers who were with this expedition, all of whom acted with all possible prudence and valor.

May the Sieurs de Vaudreuil and Raudot be permitted, My Lord, to propose to you that rewards should be given to those who have distinguished themselves in it? Nothing encourages the officers of this country to do well more than promoting them in proportion to the good work they do. The Sr. Deschaillons was rewarded on his arrival here, by the company of the Sr. de St. Ours, his father, which you were good enough to grant him.

The Sr. de Rouville, My Lord, deserves to be promoted; he led this expedition with all possible prudence, valor and resolution. The Sieurs de Vaudreuil and Raudot beg that you will be good enough to grant him the Company of the Sr. de la Jesmeray who died this summer. It may be said that he labored for the glory of God and of the King, on this occasion; for, before ordering them into action he thought he ought to make a short speech to the party, telling them that they were very soon going to fall upon the enemy, and before entering upon that, if there had been any quarrel between them they should all forgive one another, and embrace each other, which they did; after that he told them that on this occasion they ought all to expect to conquer, or to die, for retreat would be very difficult if they did not succeed against their enemies. Fired by this speech they succeeded as the Sieurs de Vaudreuil and Raudot have already had the honor to inform you.

They have also the honor to propose to you the Sr. de la Gauchetiere for the lieutenancy of the Sr. Rouville which will be vacant if you consent to make him a captain. He has been an unattached ensign for fourteen years; he acted as Major to this party, and behaved as on all occasions when he has been present in this country, like a brave and upright

CONTRACT MADE BETWEEN CADILLAC AND HAZEUR, 1694.
FROM THE BURTON LIBRARY IN DETROIT.

that the savages of Le Sault and Le Sault au Recollet, should take from the Sr. de la Periere the reward which would be due to him on account of his bravery and good conduct, if they had not compelled him to retire in spite of himself. He has so many good actions to his credit, during the twenty-one years he has been an ensign that they are guarantees that he would have done as well in this expedition as he has done in the past, in all those in which he has been. The Sieurs de Vaudreuil and Raudot are therefore obliged, My Lord, to ask you to give him the lieutenancy of the Sr. de Montigny, who became a captain on the death of the Sr. de Grand-ville, as they have already had the honor of informing you.

The Sieurs de Vaudreuil and Raudot have the honor to lay before you here, My Lord, the services of the Sr. de la Chassagne, and can assure you that he deserves the honor of your patronage. For a long time he has served without promotion; and they would beg you to deign to grant him the cross of the Knight of St. Louis. This mark of distinction, which he deserves, will fully convince him that you have not forgotten him, and that you would be willing to take the opportunities which may pre-sent themselves for his promotion.

You were kind enough, My Lord, in the King's letter of the year 1704, addressed to the Sieurs de Vaudreuil and Beauharnois, to inform them that you had granted to Madame de Varenne, widow of a governor of Three Rivers, the pension which was vacant by the death of one Landron. Madame de Varenne has learnt that this pension used to be paid at Rochefort, and is sending her power of attorney there by the vessels. She and the Sieurs de Vaudreuil and Raudot, beg you to be so good as to direct that it shall be paid there, since you have accorded her that favor.

The Sieur Hazeur, law officer to the Great Superior Council, and of of this town, died this summer regretted by everyone on account of his merit, his virtue and his uprightness. He has left a son who is a barrister at the Paris courts, who will fill his place, if you will graciously grant me this favor; he will make himself more worthy of it every day by his dil-igence and research. The Sieurs de Vaudreuil and Raudot beg to be permitted to represent to you, My Lord, that in this case the father's ser-vices should induce you to obtain from His Majesty's favor this post for the son.

Captain the Sr. de la Jaymeraye died this summer and the Sieurs de Vaudreuil and Raudot have had the honor of asking you to give the Sr. Rouville his company. He leaves a wife and six children to beggary. It is a pity, My Lord, to see this family in distress, and with no means of subsistence for the future, unless you will be so good as to aid them. As you will not make any appointment to her husband's company until next year, if you would of your charity, let her receive the pay until then, this

Madame de Muy has lost her husband, My Lord, just when you were beginning to make him feel the advantage of your favors. She hopes that in default of him you will consent to bestow them on her and her family, who need them. The Sieurs de Vaudreuil and Raudot inclose with this letter a petition which she has the honor to present to you. •

The Sieur Longueuil who is in command at Montreal in the absence of the Sr. de Ramezay, who came down to Quebec for the arrival of the ships, was informed that there were some Loups from Orange with English goods to trade for beaver skins. He despatched the Sr. Clerin into the woods, who found neither Loups nor goods there, but only a hidden store of 343# of beaver-skins, with an Indian woman looking after it, which beaver-skins were brought into Montreal. The savages from Sault claim this store, saying that it belongs neither to the English nor the French. The said Sieur de Longueuil gave an account of this matter to the Sieurs de Vaudreuil and Raudot, who have sent him word to give up these beaver-skins to the savages, unless it could be proved to them that they belonged to Frenchmen or to Englishmen. That is the only account they can give you of this matter before the sailing of the vessels, but they will do themselves the honor of informing you on this subject, that, if we continue to harass the savages to this degree, they would fear very ill results from it. This matter originated with the Sr. de Ramezay having written to the Sieur de Vaudreuil to learn whether he should order the arrest of savages from Orange who came to trade for beaver-skins with English goods. The said Sieur de Vaudreuil replied that this trade was on no account to be permitted, and that he should approve of everything he did on this matter; and when the Sr. de Ramezay set out, he left this reply with the said Sr. de Longueüil, with orders that, if he learnt that any of them had come, he was to have their goods confiscated. This would have succeeded if they had found any goods; but to go and take away beaver-skins from the savages in the woods is by no means advisable, as matters stand in the country, and a trifle of this kind might lay the Colony open to the risk of war. It is absolutely impossible to

the ensigncy, which would thus become vacant, to pass to a younger son who, by his diligence and careful performance of his duty, would endeavor to make himself worthy of the favor you would be so good as to bestow upon him in that case.

The Sieurs de Vaudreuil and Raudot annex to this letter a petition which the Sieur de Lotbiniere, chief counsellor to the Superior Council of this town, has the honor to present to you, begging you to grant to his son the reversion of the office with which you honor them, or of that of lieutenant-general of the provostship which has been in his family for a long time. They have the honor to assure you that the said Sieur de Lotbiniere, junior, is very prudent and has much capacity, and will succeed thoroughly well in all the offices you may be good enough to grant him.

The same point arises, My Lord, with regard to the younger son of the Sr. Dupuis, for whom the father has the honor to ask of you in the petition annexed to this letter, the reversion of the office of local lieutenant of the provostship of this town. As for him, he also is very prudent and has ability, and he will succeed well in that office if you are so kind as to grant it to him. Nothing, My Lord, will be a better encouragement to the young Sieurs de Lotbiniere and Dupuis to learn than for you to be so good as to grant them the favor which the Sieurs de Vaudreuil and Raudot have the honor of asking you for them. Their fathers will labor to make them capable and to instruct them in the practical part of the work.

The officers are so badly off at Detroit, My Lord, that those who wrote to you most strongly in favor of this post are now forced by their distress to speak differently of it. It is thus that the Sieur de la Forest speaks, My Lord, begging the Sieurs de Vaudreuil and Raudot to represent to you on his behalf that he is unable to live at that post with a servant on the pay which His Majesty is good enough to give him; that when the Company had that post, it used to provide food for the junior officers, and gave a gratuity of 1,300 livres to the Sieur de Tonty, who was there in the same capacity as he is now; and that it would appear to him right that Sieur de La Mothe, who has the rights of the said Company, should treat him in the same way. His request, My Lord, seems to the said Sieurs de Vaudreuil and Raudot very reasonable, more especially

[margin note: Refuse all versions, pecially t one, for a reason.]

Formerly, My Lord, we used to send the pay to the soldiers in goods, to those who were in garrison at Michilimackina; but the boats that went up there under the licenses, carried them free of charge. In this case, the Sr de La Mothe would not let them load the goods of the soldiers, instead of the three hundred weight which is taken free for him in every boat he allows to go up there. It would be necessary to send boats on purpose, which would cost a great deal, and this would reduce the pay of the men to a very small matter, or, rather, to nothing.

There are no profitable goods at Detroit, except brandy. Powder and bullets are sold a little there; but, as regards all other articles, they are cheaper than at Montreal. Hence, to provide food for the soldiers, we should have to send brandy, which the Sieurs de Vaudreuil and Raudot could not, considering your orders; or powder or lead, but as the Sieur de La Mothe has three hundred weight free in each boat, he will be in a position to offer his cheaper, and make the goods run down until he brings them under cost price; he can then buy them and when he has the sole possession of them sell them very dear.

The Sr. de la Mothe has yet another plan, namely to get possession of all the corn, as he did this year, and then fix what price he likes for it. He makes no secret of this to the Sieur D'Aigremont, who told the younger Sieur Raudot, saying that the Sieur de La Mothe would not supply the soldiers with food any longer; that the said Sr. de La Mothe had told him that he had lost a great deal by doing so, for he would only have to get hold of all the corn to be able to sell it at whatever price he liked; that this made him a loser by more than forty thousand livres. That, My Lord, is how the Sr. de la Mothe pursues his own interests; thus, at this rate, and from the way in which he wants to proceed, an officer's pay would be necessary to provide food for each soldier, unless the said Sr. de La Mothe provides them with food, as he has done hitherto, although that has been very badly.

The Sieurs de Vaudreuil and Raudot will send word to the Sr. de La Mothe that he is to continue to supply food to the soldiers and will deal

they greatly distinguished themselves, and the Sieurs de Vaudreuil and Raudot have the honor of assuring you that they will both make very good officers, fit to undertake anything we want to order them to do. It is people of this sort, My Lord, that are absolutely necessary in this country, where war is conducted quite differently from what it is in France.

The Sr. de la Noüe, My Lord, is one of the officers who have done the best service in this country, having served in nearly all the expeditions, of which he bears marks, for he has been wounded. He has been a lieutenant on half pay for fifteen years. The Sieurs De Vaudreuil and Raudot have the honor to assure you that he is worthy of your patronage.

The Sieurs de Vaudreuil and Raudot hardly dare at the present time, My Lord, beg you to observe that the post of King's lieutenant at Quebec bears two hundred livres less than that of Montreal although the occupant of it is obliged to spend more than the other, seeing that he remains in command all the summer at this town, the said Sieur de Vaudreuil being at Montreal. It is the Sieur de L'Angloiserie who would ask of you this small increase. The Srs. de Vaudreuil and Raudot can assure you that he deserves it for his good service, and that he will always discharge well all the duties you may be good enough to procure for him.

In the joint letter of 1707, My Lord, you did the Srs. de Vaudreuil and Raudot the honor of telling them you would be good enough to grant letters of naturalization to the English Hamburghers and Flemings who are in this colony. They have the honor to send you, herewith, two detailed lists of those foreigners, to whom they hope you will grant the favor you were so good as to promise them, which they have now the honor of asking you for again.

The Sieurs de Vaudreuil and Raudot have the honor of annexing a concession made by the Sieur de la Bouteillerie by Mons. Talon in 1672, and one made to the Sieur de l'Epinay by MM. de Caillieres and Champigny in 1701, the ratification of which they beg you to be good enough to grant them, as they did not get it in time. They have also the honor of annexing those they made this year to M. de Ramezay, to the Sieurs Dumontier and Bernard Damour, and to Marie Joseph Fezeret of which they likewise beg you to be good enough to grant them the ratification.

If you grant these ratifications, My Lord, as the Srs. de Vaudreuil and Raudot beg you to do, one of them will bring about a marriage,—that of the lady named Fezeret. Her brothers died in the King's service, her father and mother without any property; so that unless you extend your favor to her on this occasion, she will be unable to establish herself in this country.

The hospitallers of Quebec are very grateful, My Lord, for your graciously gran   h   h   h   Srs de Vaudreuil and Raudot gave them of certain streams which fall from the Cap au Diamant now on to their ground.

* * * * * * * * * * *

The Srs. Aubert and Pacaut, interested in the equipment of the King's ship "L'Affriquain," on their friend's account, have almost forced the Sr. Plassant to take the said vessel back to France, instead of going to the islands. He could not go to Plaisance without running a risk of getting lost, on account of the season being too far advanced. They were all heartily inclined towards this return, thus preferring the public, to their private interests. If it had not returned, My Lord, this colony would have done nothing in France, and next year no goods would have come here. That would have alienated from us all the savages who are only too strongly attracted towards Orange by the abundance, and the cheap price of the goods of the English.

The Sieurs de Vaudreuil and Raudot beg that you will permit them to ask you still to continue your aid to this colony which exists and is maintained only by the continual favors you deign to bestow upon it. They also ask of you for themselves the same protection and the same favors; and have the honor to be with the deepest respect,

My Lord,

Your most humble, most obedient, and most obliged servants.

Vaudreuil

Raudot.

Quebec, the 14th Novr., 1708.

'LETTER FROM SR. D'AIGREMONT DENOUNCING CADILLAC METHODS.

Endorsed—Colonies. The Sr. d'Aigremont.

14th Novr., 1708.

My Lord,

90 leagues long. I arrived at Fort Pontchartrain on the 15th of July. During the time I remained there, namely 19 days, I had occasion to observe that M. de la Mothe, who commands there, was generally hated by all the French people and by the savages. One might except three or four of the former whom he makes use of for the secret trade he carries on, whom, for this reason, he treats better than the rest. Moreover I can assure you, My Lord, that this aversion does not exist without cause, and that he is not detested for nothing; the tyranny he uses towards both of them is more than sufficient for that. He exacts from the man Parent, a blacksmith, for permission to work at his trade, the sum of 600 livres, and two barrels of beer, and he is compelled to shoe all his horses for him, however many he may have, although at this present time he has only one.

From one Pinet, an armorer, 300 livres a year, and he has to repair 12 guns a month for him, of any sort that are offered him, and whatever the work he may have to do to them, even when they have to be remounted. Twelve guns a month make 144 a year, which must be worth, one with another, a pistole each to M. de la Mothe, or 1,440 livres for the 144 guns; and this, added to the 300 livres make 1,740 livres which he draws every year from this armorer's labor. But I do not think that will last long, for it will not be possible for this workman to make a living at Detroit on these terms. He made a man named Michel Massé, a blacksmith, pay 150 livres for having worked at his trade, merely in passing. Those, My Lord, are outrageous exactions. He has had a windmill built, and takes, as his charge, the 8th minot. The proprietors of all those in existence throughout the Colony, only take the 14th minot. He gives as his reason for this that the mill cost him more than 6,000 livres. But, My Lord, I know that he never paid more than 600 livres to the carpenter who constructed it, and 800 days' work of a man he provided for this carpenter, for which 800 days' work he gave 800 demi-aids of brandy, making about a barrel which did not cost him 200 livres because he has 300 livres weight conveyed for him by each boat.

I have had measurements made of the lands of Detroit which have been turned to account. There are 353 arpents: M. de La Mothe has 157 arpents, all the inhabitants together 46 arpents and the Hurons 150. These 157 arpents of M. de La Mothe's are made up of lands which had been cleared by several soldiers and savages, and 19 arpents by the company, and all of these 157 arpents together, have not cost him one sou to bring into their present condition. Therefore, My Lord, it became him very ill to write to you that, on his arrival, he found the company's lands either uncultivated or in the possession of the savages, for these savages have never held any lands but those they have cleared, and even the

If M. de La Mothe had intended to establish a settlement at Detroit quickly, instead of keeping these lands which the soldiers and the savages cleared, he would have granted them to the first inhabitants who settled there, and it would have been a great advantage to them when they began to settle there. But the public weal, My Lord, affects him little; he has therefore added these lands to his own domain, which has thirty arpents frontage, in the midst of which stands the fort. In this stretch of thirty arpents frontage are included several pieces of land cleared by the Outavois for which they demand payment, because they say that he lets them, and that is true, even at 8 livres per arpent of 100 square perches a year.

These savages complain that he keeps their belts and furs, which they give him as presents to speak with him although he does not grant the request they make to him, which is contrary to the usual practice with those people, and neither the one nor the other ought to be kept unless the request is granted.

They are so discontented with M. de La Mothe that they say plainly that if he remains in command at Detroit, they will not settle there.

They ask for lieutenant the Sr. d'Argenteuil, to command them. He has as much influence over savages as anyone can have, especially over these, so that he makes them do every thing that he wishes; but, in other ways, he has little discretion. These savages requested me to tell you, My Lord, that they would always be faithful to the King; and that they begged His Majesty ever to regard them as such.

M. de La Mothe has only granted lands to the inhabitants of Detroit that have not been cleared, beginning where his domain ends on the upper side.

The whole of the inhabitants of Detroit number 63, who have all taken sites within the fort on which each of them has had a small house built of stakes plastered with mud, and thatched with grass. Of these 63 inhabitants there are only 29 who have taken lands, for the others—except the officers, the Sieurs de Rané, d'Argenteuil and Du Figuier—are only at Detroit for trading. Still less, therefore, ought the latter to be regarded as settlers than the others, or I should rather say it is impossible to make sure of any; and I am convinced, My Lord, that if M. de La Mothe did not connive at trading in brandy, very few of these latter would remain there. I go further, and say that no one would go there; for there is nothing but that commodity, powder and lead which has any value there. Everything else is supplied by the English. So true is this,

y ought to be regarded as settled, for they only marshalled soldiers, of whom in at Detroit perforce and they still in the companies and guard the rest.

it in rotation by a private individual, at the rate of 20 livres a pot. The man who used to sell it is one Robert La Chapelle who accounted for it so badly that many a man has lost a third of his quantity by leakage. Those who want to get any are obliged to go and drink it in this warehouse, whether Frenchmen or savages; and, to prevent intoxication, each person is only given the third of a demi-aid on each occasion, that is the 24th part of a pot. It is true that, in this way, the savages do not get intoxicated; but, nevertheless, My Lord, much harm arises from this trade, for they waste the greater part of their furs on brandy, and they have almost nothing left for buying clothes, kettles, arms, powder or lead, and this is the reason why very often some of them die of want. I left in this storehouse more than a dozen barrels of brandy; ten boats have gone up this year to Detroit which have also taken a good deal there. As this brandy is sold in rotation, and there are some who have a larger quantity of it than others, it has happened that the brandy of many of these traders (St. Germain, Jacques Philipe, Beaubien, Dudois), could not be sold by the time at which they were obliged to go down, which compelled them to sell 104 pots to M. de La Mothe at the rate of 4 livres a pot. He is accused of having bought some from other persons besides those named in the margin, but I have no complete assurance of it. In this way he makes a gain of 4-5 on the brandy he puts into this office, which makes 16 livres a pot or 1,664 livres on 104 pots.

The said inhabitants of Detroit pay M. de La Mothe as follows:

For each arpent of land frontage by 20 in depth, 40 sols. For the sites within the fort. 2 sols for each foot frontage; when the site abuts on two streets, he made them pay double, viz.: four sols. The whole of these 63 inhabitants also pay M. de La Mothe 10 livres a year for rights which he says he has given up. I asked him what these rights were. He told me that the most important was the right which every inhabitant had, to carry on trade. It is to be observed, My Lord, that as regards the married soldiers this is a real oppression; for what trade can they do when he only gives to those whom he does not supply with food one livre of powder and one of bullets per month as their pay, out of which it is then necessary for them to feed themselves. I do not think the remainder leaves them in a very good position for exercising this wonderful right.

Those whom he does supply with food are in no better position to take advantage of it, for he makes them pay 5 livres 5 sols a month for provisions, so they have only 24 sols net pay for which he gives them six or seven bullets and a roquille of brandy which is the 16th part of a pot.

As regards all other persons, who have neither lands nor houses, they may not go to trade at Detroit without conveying 300 livres weight for him in each boat, and bringing the same quantity back for him to go down, every boat that goes down.' From the man Jacques Cardinal, he even exacted conveyance for a weight of 800 livres, because he knew that this man was to take a large quantity of brandy.

He makes them pay 4 livres for every contract of concession. The officers who have had houses built within the fort pay the same as the other inhabitants.

M. de la Forest had asked him for a site in front of the fort for making a garden, and he had promised it to him. But when an inhabitant asked him for the same site to hold for three years, on condition that he should enclose it with stakes, he withdrew the promise he had given to M. de la Forest, and granted it to this inhabitant, in the hope—as I believe—of letting it to him at a very high price after that time.

The stakes of the fort are almost all rotten, and in such a manner that I saw one of them fall in front of me. It is the soldiers who cut, and carry on their shoulders, the stakes which it is necessary to replace at this fort, and he does not give them anything for that.

As they have been obliged to enlarge this fort in some places on account of the houses that have been built within it, M. de La Mothe has compelled the owners of these houses to do this work, or have it done, each within the limits of the land he occupies, so that this fort does not cost him a sol.

There are two bastions which are so small and of such an extraordinary outline that you would not know what they were. That is because, when the curtains were pushed forward, these bastions were not advanced, but only shortened and contracted, as you will see, My Lord, from the plan which I have the honor to annex hereto.

These 29 inhabitants who, as I have already said, have only 46 arpents of cleared lands, have been unable to work at those which have been granted to them, since there has been war with the Miamis, because these lands are too far from the fort, and they will therefore run too much risk of being killed by these savages. M. de La Mothe has given several of them lands to clear in his domain, with possession of them for three years without paying anything; yet he has made each of them, from the first year, give four days' work per arpent at tilling some ground which he dug for sowing, in the places where the plow could not go, by reason of tree stumps. It is true that he says that it was the Sr. de Rané, a lieutenant, who was his agent at that time, who exacted that work from the inhabitants, and that he did not authorize him to do so;

per month for each man.   But M. de La Mothe only gave them a minot of corn every five weeks and 6 livres of fat per month.

He only pays [the soldiers] 24 sols as net pay, at a time when 39 sols is paid at Quebec and Montreal.   He states as his reason that wheat is worth 12 livres per minot and fat 10 sols a livre.   But, My Lord, when he puts up the price of wheat so high; it is with reference to that of brandy which he apparently puts at 24 livres a pot, for I know that he obtained 30 minots from the Hurons, at the time when this wheat was dearest, for 15 pots of brandy.   And if M. de La Mothe put this brandy at the price it cost him, he would find that this wheat would not stand him in 20 sols a minot, since the brandy should not cost him more than 40 sols a pot, as he has paid nothing for carriage on account of the 300 weight that every boat which has hitherto gone up, has conveyed for him. As for the fat, I know he did not buy it dearer that four sols a livre.

Hence you may know, My Lord, that far from losing on the food of these troops he makes a profit on it of more than half their pay.   It is to be observed that, at most, he only provides food for one-half of the soldiers, leaving the others at liberty to feed themselves; but he makes a still better thing out of those whom he pays in powder and lead, than by the other, for he sells them powder at a crown a livre and bullets at a crown a livre, so that he gains three-fourths on that, at the very least.   But, My Lord, he says he does not wish to be charged with the pay of these troops any longer, nor with feeding them.   I believe I can divine the reason of it from what he said to me—that he was sorry he had supplied them with food, and if he had not done so he could have bought all the Indian corn from the Hurons and could have made 40 livres a minot by it.   It may be, My Lord, that he has the same design, and would in that way make it necessary for His Majesty to buy from him at whatever price he likes.

Last autumn he called together the inhabitants of Detroit and said to them that, as several of them wanted Indian corn, and he also wanted some for the troops, they need not all go to the Hurons to trade for it; for, if they saw many people asking them for it, they would not fail to run up the price; but he would send four or five people to trade for it and would then give it to them at the same price that it had cost him.   But, after he had this purchase made, he had the inhabitants told that he had no more than he required for supplying the troops with food, and that they could trade for it for themselves; but this permission was useless to them, since there was none left

The margin note: The Merchants se neither of them for than 45 or sols a livre

He has permitted several soldiers who, for the same reason, found themselves without provisions, to go and pass the winter in the woods, on the condition that they should leave them their pay almost at net rates; and upon my telling him that this did not seem to me to be right, he replied that he was making profits out of it for the King. God knows whether this was his intention.

He told me that he had proposed to you, My Lord, to form whole companies of savages, on which I could not help telling him that I thought him very daring to have made such a proposal to you, and that it seemed strange to me to wish to undertake the discipline of men who have no subordination amongst themselves, and that their chiefs have no right to say to the others—"Do so and so," but only—"It would be advisable to do such and such a thing," without naming anyone, for otherwise they would not do it at all, as they hate all compulsion. Moreover those people have no idea of His Majesty's greatness, nor of the power which superiors have over inferiors; and that there would be no emulation among them and no desire to reach these steps of advancement, and consequently nothing to bind them to the discharge of their duties. Nor would they be induced thereto by fear of punishment, for, since they do not put up with any amongst themselves, they would still less bear any being administered to them by others. Finally, My Lord, men are great among those people only so far as they are well skilled in slaying others by surprise, and hunting well. As these qualifications do not remain in old men, they have the greatest scorn for them, so much indeed that, as I have heard that an Outavois, called Jean le Blanc, one day had the impudence to tell the late Comte de Frontenac that he was a poor sickly creature, who was fit for nothing, since he had to have a horse to carry him.

I am convinced that if one of these would-be captains were to give any command on the King's service to the junior officers, or the soldiers of his company, they would tell him plainly that they would not do it, and that he should do it himself. That would be indeed a very fine example for the French troops. But, My Lord, even if it were possible to teach those people to be obedient one to another, I believe that as a matter of policy it would be preparing for this Colony the greatest misfortune which could befall it, to teach the savages discipline; for it is

be set apart for these companies, or at the very least by three-quarters of them.

It was the same principle that he put into practice when he proposed the establishment of Detroit, for he knew, as everyone else does, that this post is most injurious to the Colony of Canada.

His most notable plea was that of bringing together all the tribes around lakes Erie, Huron, Michigan and Superior, namely the Outaois, Miamis, Hurons, Sauteurs, Mississaqueto, Amicoüets, and others who live by the rivers falling into Lake Superior, and to induce them to form villages in the neighborhood of Detroit. But the troubles which have arisen since the beginning of the establishment show clearly how wrong it was to bring the savages who were allies of this colony, so near to the Iroquois. The Hurons, whose language and customs have a great resemblance to theirs, and with whom they have close relations, constantly pass through their districts to take their beaver-skins to the English. They were not content with doing this trade alone; they have also introduced the Miamis to it, who were formerly the enemies of the Iroquois, and did the best service in the war we had against them. The Hurons did not stop there. They made them form a very close alliance with the said Iroquois by belts which they gave to each other, which, among these tribes, is an undertaking always to join forces together as soon as one of them is attacked by any other. This shows that the Iroquois have taken advantage of the time since Detroit was established, to attract our allies so that they may have them on their side in case of war, which would undoubtedly occur. Moreover, how can this collection of several tribes at the same place, who have been at enmity live without fighting? Nothing more is needed to start it but to treat one of them more favorably than the others, or merely for that, to appear to them to do so. Jealousy infallibly seizes on their minds at once and induces them to make an attack on the tribe they believe to be favored, and even on the French people that are at the post, as has happened.

This, then, My Lord, appears to me the best place in which to inform you of the occurrences, which led to the attack of the Outaois on the fort at Detroit in 1706.

Motives w gave rise t the attack of theOuta on the for Detroit in

It was reported to me, by five savages of this tribe whom I had ques-

me there, but be not surprised, I shall overthrow those who have tried
to ruin me,"—looking at M. de Tonty and at the Recollet father Constantin who were present, M. de la Mothe said to them again,
"Although I am going away, have no fear so long as my wife
remains here; but if you see her go down, then you will have reason to
fear." When Madam de La Mothe went down, two months after, they
were greatly alarmed, and thought of the attack which their people
from Missilimakinac had made on Fort Frontenac, and mistrust then
sprang up in their minds inasmuch as M. de Tonty, who had remained
at Detroit as commandant, did not give them justice in any way for
the insult which the Miamis had put upon them, any more than M. de
La Mothe. In 1706 the Sr. Bourgmont was sent by M. de La Mothe to
Detroit to relieve M. de Tonty. The savages assembled and went to greet
him, and asked him what news he brought. He replied to them in an
angry manner "I know of none except to tell you that M. de La Mothe
will come next spring with a large number of people, and that all the
French are already under orders." This bad reception, together with
the fact that nothing was said to them as to all their men that the
Miamis had killed, was the means of renewing their distrust. They continued however to go and see M. de Tonty but did not carry any complaints to him. But M. de Tonty said to them "the world must be turned
upside down, they send me a private soldier to command me." These
words redoubled their uneasiness, of which the Sr. de Bourgmont was
warned by a woman named Le Chenette whom he kept. On this, the said
Sr. de Bourgmont called these savages together and said to them, "I
have learnt that you asked M. de Tonty to go and make war on the
Sioux. I declare to you that I do not prevent you from doing so, and if
you wish we will also join with you the Hurons, who left their dead
there, the Miamis and the Iroquois, and you shall form but one corps.
But, while we send Quarantesou to speak to the Miamis, send some of
your young men with the Hurons to war on the Flatheads." This was
settled and ratified. They spoke to Quarantesou, to whom a present
was given, to which the Outaois had largely contributed, to take it
to the Miamis, and the Onyatanous, and tell them when presenting it to
them, that this present was to induce them all to go against their enemies.

e than 200
ues from
oit to-
is the
th.

Chenette, have told me so. The Outaois do not suspect us now; let us turn our arms against them," to which the Miamis consented. There were then some Iroquois, who also offered to join the party, having the attack, which the Outaois of Missilimackinac had made upon their people at Fort Frontenac, still quite fresh in their memories. During this space of time the Outaois had sent some of their men with the Hurons against the Flatheads, and another party in the direction of the Sioux, commanded by Outchipouak, a Sinagan Outaois and a war chief, to get together the savages in the direction of Puants Bay, 80 leagues from Missilimakinac, while waiting for Quarantesou's return to Detroit. This chief was much surprised when he saw the Saquis and the Poutcouatamis coming to him, who said to him, "We give you meat to eat, and it is the meat of the Kikapous." These Kikapous were among those he was looking for to reinforce him for going against the Sioux. "What are you saying to me, my brother Saquis and Poutcouatamis?" said this chief, "you give me meat to eat of those from those from whom I was hoping for help." Then the Poutcouatamis and the Saquis replied, "Do you not know the news, and the result of the embassy of Quarantesou? He made presents to the Miamis, the Onyatanous and the Kikapous, to induce them to tomahawk us all, instead of exhorting them to go with us against the Sioux." M. de Tonty was then still at Detroit. The brother of the Outaois who had been killed two years ago went to him and said—"What justice are they giving me for the death of my brother? I do not hear anything said about it. Does Onontio intend us to be always killed and never avenged? Yet we are his old children, while the Miamis have only known him as their father for a short time." The man who spoke in this way is called Quilengouché, a capable and important man, who is master of the Huron, Iroquois and Miamis languages. After this speech he said "I am going, my father, to fight against the Miamis;" whereon M. de Tonty said to him "Do nothing of the kind, you will have enough to do in protecting your village in a little while," without giving him any explanation. At that time M. de Tonty set out to go to Montreal, and before he left he warned four or five families of the Nipissingues and Sinagan Outaois that as soon as he had left to go down, they should withdraw because he had received letters from the Sr. Joncaire from Sonnontouan, which alleged that matters were not going well for them, and in fact a part of those people did retire as soon as M. de Tonty had set out. Some time after, Outchipouac, the war chief of whom mention has been made above, on his return from Ouisconsin reported all that the Poutcouatamis and Saquis had told him, and that that was why he had given up his first design against the Sioux, and said that they must not wait for help from the Hurons or the Miamis, and that they must not divide [their forces], but that the misfortune was that they

had some of their men with the Hurons in the country of the Flatheads,
and others trading near Lake Huron and Lake Superior; that if
they would trust to him, they would begin the attack on the Miamis
without giving them warning and before they had all got together again.
His advice was not followed, although it was true that they increased
every day in numbers. All these items of news put together, which were
all connected with one another, kept them in great uneasiness, but it was
prodigiously increased by what was said by a Sonnontouan woman who
arrived at Detroit, whose life the Outaois had saved. This woman said
to them—"My fathers, you saved my life, and I have left my country
that I, in my turn, might save yours. I did not depart in secret, but
neither did I say that I was coming here; they think I am hunting with
my family. You must know then, my fathers, that Joncaire arrived
this last autumn, and he said that the tribes were being lured on to
destroy you all, and that the French were to go to Missilimakinac to kill
those who are there; and I am surprised that M. de Tonty did not warn
you of it, for he knows it well; as for me I am come to warn you. Be
secret, and say nothing of what I am telling you." After this speech the
most important men of each of the Outaois tribes held a council and
decided to attack the Miamis. Two chiefs at the council, the one called
Ouaguescau of the Sable tribe, and [the other] Meaouana a Sinago, said
that they must not make an attack like that without warning the French
of it, and telling them that they should not interfere in their quarrel.
The rest were of the opposite opinion, saying that the French had concealed everything from them. "Recall everything to your minds," said
they; "do you not remember what Joncaire said at Sonnontouan, that the
French would never forgive us for the death of the soldier who was killed
on Hog Island; that M. de La Mothe told us when he embarked that if we
saw his wife leave we should have reason for fear; that Bourgmont, on his
arrival, did not speak to us except with a threat; that M. de Tonty secretly
told some of our people to withdraw as quickly as possible after he had left;
and you see that this Sonnontouan woman confirms all that for us. The
Poutcouatamis and Saquis have told Outchipouak that Quarantesou betrayed us, together with Bourgmont and La Chenette." "What do you

they had heard was true, was that when a dog bit one of their men, and the man struck the dog, the Sr. Bourgmont fell upon him and beat him so severely that he died some time after. They went out, therefore, from the Sr. Bourgmont's house greatly displeased, and decided that they would set out the next day, saying that they were going against the Sioux. This they did; and when they were in the woods they announced their scheme to the young men, which was to return upon their trail with all possible dispatch, and attack the Miamis, but not to touch either the French or the Hurons.

They therefore attacked the Miamis vigorously. Some of them went to the Missionary's garden, where they found him, and they took him and bound him. Jean le Blanc unbound him and said to him, "My father, go to the fort and tell the French people not to fire at us and that we have no designs against them." The father, as he went away, joined some Miamis whom the Outaois attacked; and while they were firing, and being fired upon from the fort, the father was shot. And at another place there was a soldier killed in the fray; and at that time the French had already killed or wounded five men. Next day they wished to take presents to pacify the French; but the latter fired on them, and they left their presents near the fort, and the French took them. I feel sure, My Lord, that this long discourse of the savages must be tedious to you; but I thought it my duty to repeat it at full length, that I might leave it to your sagacity to decide who were the persons who contributed most to this action.

This is what I have learnt from certain Frenchmen about that. They say that the Outaois left their fort in the morning with the intention of making an attack on the Miamis, and came along a narrow strip of forest opposite the French fort to fall upon their village; and having then caught sight of six Miamis who were going to the fort of the Hurons, Le Pesant said to his band that they had better begin by attacking these six men, and when they were mingled together he would cry "ho!" three times, and this should be the signal for killing them. This was carried out as planned; there were five of them killed and one escaped to the French fort; and as he shouted that the Outaois were attacking them, all the Miamis, who were in their village retired to the French fort where the Outaois pursued them up to the entrance of the fort; and the Sr. Bourgmont who was in command there, then ordered them to fire at the Outaois, two of whom were killed. The missionary, Father Constantin, who was in his garden outside the fort, and knew nothing of what was going on, was seized there and bound by the Outaois and taken into their camp. Jean le Blanc unbound him and said to him—"Go and tell Bourgmont not to let them fire at us, that we have no designs against the French." As the Father was returning, it happened that a young Out-

aois was shot dead by the Sr. Bourgmont or some other Frenchman, and
at that moment another Outaois, a relative of the one who was killed,
shot the Father as he was about to enter the fort, from which shot he
instantly died. A soldier who was on his way back from the Huron
fort, intending to go into the French fort, was also slain by the Outaois.
Then the Sr. Bourgmont ordered the gates of the fort to be closed and
the men to fire on the Outaois, of whom about thirty were killed by the
Miamis and Hurons.

This disturbance is not the only one which has occurred at Detroit
since it was first established, and one of which I have the honor of informing you, My Lord, will not be the last, if this post is long in existence.
In the month of April last, when the Miamis had killed three Frenchmen,
one league from the fort, M. de La Mothe sent a boat after the Sr.
d'Argenteuil, whom he had sent to Saguinau to take the provisions which
had been promised to the Outaois in the winter, to give him information
as to what had taken place. He requested him to make as much despatch
as he could, and to send to his assistance all the Outaois he found on his
way. He informed the Sr. d'Argenteuil in his letter that he could assure
the said savages that he would never make peace with the Miamis, and
therefore they need only come and he would not fail them. On this statement, the Sr. d'Argenteuil went on day and night, and in a short time
reached Saguinau, where he found some of the Outaois and Sauteurs,
the remainder being still far inland. He sent for them and took them all
to Detroit, to the number of about 1,300 persons. Among this number
there were 300 men, besides those whom he had found on the road and
had sent to M. de La Mothe's assistance, amounting to nearly 150. On
his way back he met with another boat which M. de La Mothe sent him,
through which he requested him to be as speedy as possible. The reason
of his urgency was that he had many enemies around him, consisting of
Hurons, Iroquois and Miamis, as these three tribes had determined to
slay him with all the French people at Detroit; and this would have
been carried out but for the Onyatanous who warned him of it at a council, giving him five bundles of furs. It was the Miamis of La Grue who

that they saw very well that he valued an ox and a cow higher than a man.

4th, to return what they had stolen from the French people in their country.

As the Miamis did not send back within the 15 days the young Outaois they have taken, M. de La Mothe determined to go and attack them in their fort, and to that end he had a flag hoisted, to which he had had a tomahawk fastened, without consulting either the officers or the savages, about it. Both of these were rather discontented, especially the latter, who complained, saying that M. de La Mothe was a cheat to go and attack the Miamis before the 40 days he had given them, for they did not think that the young Outaois, whom they had promised to return in 15 days, was sufficient reason why he should not wait this time. Notwithstanding this discontent, they decided to follow him. He ordered a war feast, but it was held at the expense of the French people, each of whom had contributed to it, even the soldiers. Three days later he resolved to begin the march. The Outaois begged him to delay one day more so that they might have time to shut up their wives and children in the fort; he made them no reply, and embarked while they were making them go in. The Sr. d'Argenteuil having pointed out to him that it was dangerous to leave such a large number of Outaois alone, he ordered him to stay with them and bring them as soon as he could, and he would wait for him on the way, but he did not tell him where. The Sr. d'Argenteuil remained and took them all next morning. On his way, four leagues from the fort, he met a boat which M. de La Mothe had sent for the powder, which he had forgotten—a proof of his lack of foresight and of the confused state of his mind. While waiting for this powder, he spoke to the French and the savages who were then with him, of the small value he set upon the Miamis, and how easy it would be to take them and destroy them. It was represented to him that he should not despise them so much, and that those people fought well, and he ought to take all the precautions necessary against surprise; upon which M. de La Mothe replied that they need not give advice to him. They remained there that day, and went next day to encamp close to the enemy's lands. They represented to M. de La Mothe that it was advisable to send scouts in boats and by land to find out whether the enemy were making any movements, but he would not do so. Next day he set out at noon just as if he were traveling in the midst of profound peace. The savages again represented to him that it would be well to lower the flags and go through the reeds so as not to be discovered, but again he would do nothing of the kind. He stopped about two leagues from the entrance to the enemy's river in broad daylight, where fires were lit, which made many people say that apparently he did not believe they were in the fort. He called

they must start and enter the river and that he would go on all night. On this the chief men of all the tribes pointed out to him that it was not necessary to go by night because it was still a long way from there to the enemy's fort; that their men were very tired and the savages were dying of hunger; but he took no notice of anything they could say. He went on therefore all the night, which was a very dark one. Some of them split their canoes and were abandoned. He was again begged to encamp because they could not possibly fail to lose their way, but still he refused to do so.

He abandoned both parties, who were so tired that most of them threw themselves on the ground to rest, and for fear of splitting their boats. In the morning they found themselves at the foot of the rapids of the river, but none of them knew what had become of M. de La Mothe, which made them decide to go to meet him. He was found on land on such a bad path, and walking so slowly that he would not have got to the foot of the rapids for four days, but for the help of those who had come to meet him. He arrived there, like the others, at the rapids. He then ordered them to march in order, and after marching for some hours, the savages, thinking they were near the enemy's fort, shouted according to their custom. This made those who were behind with M. de La Mothe think they had taken the fort, but they were undeceived a short time after by the firing that they heard. M. de La Mothe went forward and took shelter behind a tree of enormous girth and never quitted it until very late in the afternoon when he betook himself out of cannon-shot range from the enemy's fort, although they had no cannon. From the morning until one o'clock in the afternoon the savages only fired with the small quantity of powder and bullets which the French gave them during the action; for M. de La Mothe had not taken the precaution to give them any the night before, and if the French people had had no more forethought than he, they would have appeared in front of the fort without powder or bullets; and this made them say that he did not believe he would find the enemy there.

The Sr. d'Argenteuil asked to go to the palisade with such as wished to follow him, among whom would have been many of the savages, as he has very great influence over those people. It cannot be doubted that

ried off, and afterwards went to join him with the few people who had remained with him. Just then it was observed that the Miamis were showing a flag which M. de La Mothe had given them in the spring. When that was reported to him, he said they must be given a hearing. For that purpose he sent to them a Frenchman and a savage who spoke their language, with whom they agreed upon a place to parley in, to which these savages repaired and M. de La Mothe also; about 200 men were concealed on their flank, in case of treachery on the part of the Miamis. It was settled that a Miami chief should come and speak to M. de La Mothe, and that he should bring the flag which he had given him in the spring, and that the one who had brought the messengers should remain at the meeting-place in token of safety. After that the messengers departed and brought a chief of the Miamis to M. de La Mothe's camp. This chief reproached him severely, asserting that he had failed in his promise and had violated the law of nations, the forty days he had given them not having expired yet. But M. de La Mothe replied that, as they had not delivered the young Outaois to him within the time they had promised, he had been in the right in attacking them. It was then arranged that the Sr. d'Argenteuil should go for the young Outaois, who was a prisoner among the Miamis, which was done at once, and he was taken into the French camp. They then gave M. de La Mothe about 50 bundles of different furs for distribution among all those who had followed him in this fine expedition, and to stay the tomahawk. I was assured that they were not all distributed according to the intention of these savages, and that he had kept a good part of them for himself. The man Chauvin[1], who seemed to me the most devoted to him and is also related to him, confessed to me that he had kept four bundles. They also gave M. de La Mothe three slaves to replace the dead. The savages promised him that they would bring the murderers in six weeks if they could, and if they were unable to do so they would go and settle at Detroit, after they had gathered in their harvest; and, as security for their word, they gave M. de La Mothe three Miami chiefs as hostages, after which each side withdrew. That, My Lord, is the report given me by several persons who went through this glorious campaign. All the French and the savages say that M. de La Mothe did not act as he ought to have done on this occasion; that until then they had believed him to be a very brave man, because he had told them so many times that he was so; that every one felt a conscientious scruple about doubting it. Moreover,

---

[1] D' Aigremont calls Chauvin a relative of Cadillac. The relationship was not very close. Jean Guyon had among his children two sons, Denis and Michel. Marie Therese Guyon, a daughter of Denis Guyon, born April 9, 1671, at Quebec, married Antoine de La Mothe Cadillac, June 25, 1687. Gilles Chauvin married Angelique Guyon, a daughter of Michel Guyon, November 24, 1700. Thus it will be seen that the wife of Cadillac and the wife of Gilles Chauvin were cousins.

it is a very astonishing thing that more than 400 men, French and savages, did not take such a wretched fort as that of the Miamis, with no
more than 60 men in it, and two breaches which, it appears M. de La
Mothe had not seen. And if the Miamis had remained some time longer
without showing their flag M. de La Mothe would have raised the siege
in a disgraceful manner. There were seven Frenchmen wounded on this
occasion, four of whom were soldiers; four savages killed and two
wounded. He only took care of these wounded men for four or five days
although some of them were wounded very severely. He even had the
cruelty to sell them bread at 10 sols a livre. They have themselves attended to at their own expense. It will cost the man Richard, the one
who had most wounds, more than 100 pistoles, and the rest in proportion
to their wounds.

Heretofore he has not taken any more care of the sick soldiers. I have,
however, obtained from the almoner a memorandum of what he has supplied for the sick from the month of June, 1706, when he went up to
Detroit, to the month of July in the present year, which amounts to
410 livres; and if this were reduced to its true value it would not amount
to 30 livres; for brandy is set down at 24 livres a pot, bread at 15 and
20 sols a livre, and the powder which served to pay for a part of what
was supplied at one crown a livre.

As the Superior of the Hospitallers of Montreal is in France, I believe
he will have the honor of conversing with you, My Lord, as to the
request which M. de La Mothe makes for some brothers of his community
to take care of the sick at Detroit. When a month had elapsed and M.
de La Mothe had heard nothing from the Miamis, he sent a boat to them
with four Frenchmen. The said Miamis kept two of them and sent
back two Miamis to M. de Lamothe again assuring him that they would
do what they had promised him; but there is no ground for believing
it for they have withdrawn from their fort and two months have passed
by without any news having been received from them. I have no doubt
My Lord, that it is the impunity of Le Pesant which has given rise to this
war, and that it will be the cause of many others that will occur at
Detroit. But the private interest of M. de La Mothe prevailed in that
over the justice he ought to have done; for if he had put this savage to
death, those of the Outaois who came and settled at Detroit would not

the Iroquois would gain over all these tribes to the side of the English by the cheapness of their goods, and would induce them to take all their beaver-skins to them; and the Iroquois themselves would do some of this trade by means of these goods which they would obtain from the English. Moreover that is done now, and to such an extent that De troit has not supplied 700 livres of beaver-skins to the agency while Missilimakina has supplied more than 40 thousand-weight. M. de La Mothe has sent only four bundles, making about 200 livres. The remainder of the trade he has done must therefore have passed to the English; and this must have been of no small extent even if it had been only that which he has sent men to trade for, outside the limits of Detroit.

The man St. Germain, an armorer, has been to the Bay of Saguinau under the pretext of a permit to hunt, and saw three boat-loads of furs taken. Another armorer, Sarrasin, was with the said St. Germain.

A man named Trudaut confessed to me that he had also been there under the pretext of a hunting license, and had brought back 8 bundles of furs as his share.

The man Langlois also went there, on the pretence of going to look for hidden treasure. He had taken vermilion, powder, bullets, and even Indian corn.

The man Gignières is at Ouabache among the Onyatanous, under the pretext of obtaining from these savages what they owe him. He sent M. de La Mothe six canoes laden with furs, which he brought into the fort during the night.

M. de La Mothe told me that he had been accused of trading with the English, and of employing the Sr. Bourgmont for that purpose; but there is no ground for believing that that is so. He is too clever to put his interests in the hands of a man so dissolute as the Sr. Bourgmont, who deserted from Detroit to go after a woman called La Chenette, referred to above, with whom he is living in the woods like a savage.

In accordance with what has been said above, it is certain that, if the post of Missilimakinac were given up entirely, and all the Outaois there were to go and settle at Detroit, the greater part of the beaver-skins of Canada would go to the English, by the agency of the Iroquois. For the savages, and all others who were settled there, could not be compelled to sell their beaver-skins to us, except by our making our goods as cheap to them as the Iroquois sell those of the English; and this we could never do, whatever measures we might adopt. If any one thought he could compel them by force to do so, he would make the greatest of all possible mistakes.

It is also to be observed, My Lord, that if all the Outaois settled at Detroit, we should lose the trade of the northern part of Lake Superior altogether, which would also go to the English, through Hudson's Bay, for Detroit is too far away to be able to transact it.

This trade in the north is the only good trade there is in Canada, on account of the good quality of the furs obtained from there.

Those of Detroit and all other places to the south, on the contrary, are of very poor quality. The beaver skins obtained there have thick leather and are but sparsely covered with hair. The other furs are no better; the beaver-skins there are not so well covered with hair as those in the.north. There are no skins there but those of the roebuck only which are worth anything, and that again is only for the use of the settlers of Canada, most of whom make capotes of them; for, as far as their value in France is concerned, I do not think they are worth much there. It is certain therefore, My Lord, that the furs of the South are not as valuable as those of the North; but the beaver on the mainland here is especially to be preferred in every way to that of the South, and I venture to assert that two livres of the latter are not worth one livre of the other; that from the South having, as I said above, thick leather and scanty hair while the other has very fine leather and plenty of hair. For all of these reasons the northern trade is preferable to the southern.

The officers of Detroit who have. sent you word, My Lord, that,there was no better or more beautiful country in the world have imposed on you. The whole surface of the land, for about nine or ten inches in depth, is nothing but sand; and under this sand is a clay soil, so strong and so unbroken in its extent that water never passes through it. From this it follows that places which are quite on a level could never be drained, and that the further parts of the woods, where the slope leads down, are completely soaked, as well as the greater part of the prairies which are of enormous extent, and should rather, for this reason, be called marshes. Such of these lands as can be drained will grow wheat for a few years, because new lands, however bad they may be, always yield for the first few years; but that can only last so long as the manure arising from the rotting of the leaves from the trees continues, after which they will not continue to yield, unless they are manured again. There was occasion to observe this, this year, for the wheat was not so fine as that

birds fly out from the great marshes by millions, at the time when the latter is still soft, and swoop down upon it to such an extent that, if it were not watched continually, they would not leave a single grain. They do not touch the autumn crop, for then the grain is too hard. It may be that if they found none that was soft they would go to work on the hard grain, doing in that as men do, who eat biscuit when they have no soft bread. A clear proof of the bad quality of the lands at Detroit is that a single horse plows them; it is also seen from the sort of trees there, which for the most part are only small stunted oaks and hard walnut trees.

Although these lands do not produce a large quantity of wheat, they nevertheless bring M. de La Mothe in a large income; for as there is no one but him who is in a position to sell any wheat, he puts whatever price he likes on it, and that price will always be high, in accordance with his praiseworthy bent towards making large profits. This year he may have gathered 200 minots of wheat from the 38 he had sown. He does not require 100 minots for his house. So that he will have over 100 minots to sell. He will get at least 30 livres of bread out of each minot, which he will sell at ten sols a livre; and at this rate he will obtain 25 livres for a minot of wheat, or 2,500 livres for 100 minots. He will also have more than 80 minots of peas to sell, which he will sell for at least 10 livres a minot.

As regards the settlers, it will be long before they are in a position to sell either corn or peas, or even to obtain as much as they need for their food, for they could not cultivate their lands except with a mattock, as they have neither horses or oxen to plough them. M. de La Mothe would be very sorry if it were otherwise; and also if they had cows, for then he could not sell milk for 20 sols a pot, as he does, so that the three cows he has bring him in, at this rate, more than 500 crowns a year.

There were a few settlers who asked him for his horse, on hire, to plough their lands, but he would not let them have him for less than one pistole a day. Very few have used it at this price, of which he was very glad.

These settlers had a few pigs on the islands in the neighborhood of the fort, all of which the savages have killed. M. de La Mothe has still a few left which he has kept out of sight, for otherwise the savages would not spare them any more than those belonging to the settlers.

Formerly they had counted a good deal on hunting the animals with which this country has always abounded, especially oxen and roe-bucks. But since this place has been established, My Lord, there are none left in the neighborhood of the fort, so that they have to go 26 leagues lower down to find any of these animals, and I believe that, in future, it will be necessary to go more than 30 leagues. How, then, will such a large

hunting ground already so far away from it? Moreover it is to be observed that the place where these animals are is really only a tongue of land which will very soon be exhausted by such a large number of tribes.

From what I have the honor of stating to you herein, My Lord, you will readily gather that the settlers in that country are most unfortunate, and the junior officers more than the rest, for they are reduced for the most part to eating nothing but Indian corn cooked with fat from the ox, roebuck and bear, except M. de La Forest who took the precaution of having a small quantity of flour and bacon taken there at his own expense; for, as to the flesh of the ox or roebuck, they could not get any without paying more than 10 sols a livre, unless it were smoked, and even the latter costs them nearly as much.

As the subsoil of the lands at Detroit is nothing but clay, I do not think any fruits can ever be introduced there; and it does not seem to me that those that grow naturally should be relied on much. These are grapes, apples, and plums, the taste of which is detestable, according to what I have been told by many people. I drank some cider which had been made from these apples, and it seemed to me as bitter as gall. There are indeed some chestnuts which, though small, have a tolerably good flavor.

It might perhaps be said that, since these fruits grow wild in this district, it would be easy to grow good ones there; but this would be an erroneous inference, for the trees which bear these fruits, except the vine, have water almost up to the bottoms of their trunks. Now I am convinced that, on such lands, no fruits will ever be grown such as those eaten in France.

It is also to be observed that fruits get ripe only at their tips, at Detroit, especially apples and plums, although it is a very warm climate, its latitude being only about 43 degrees. That, My Lord, arises from the coolness of the land, which is always saturated with water.

The locusts eat up all the young growths in the gardens, so that the same crops have to be sown and planted as many as four times.

They even eat the trees and vines in these gardens.

and got 30, would be as rich as one who required only the same quantity but had 200.

Looking at this country from the point of view of the fur trade it seems to offer no more advantages. The only skins that can be obtained from it are bear skins of poor quality, and the skins of cats, stags, and roebucks which are of little value in France. As for the beaver, we must not count upon it, as the savages settled there have adopted the course of taking it to the English. They will never be prevented from doing so except by giving them goods at the same price as they let them have them, which is impossible.

It follows from all that has been said above, My Lord, that Detroit is a post that is a great burden to the Colony of Canada, and will bring about its complete ruin if we continue to keep it up. It will perhaps be said that this is true, but if we abandon it the English will seize upon it. I know nothing about that, but I can certainly assure you that it is far more to their advantage for us to have it, than if they had it themselves, for it costs them nothing and they do all the trade there. Even if it were true that the English would wish to take possession of this post if we abandoned it, I do not think the Iroquois would permit it, for if they were masters there, they would do the whole trade independently of the Iroquois, which would certainly not suit them. They are quite willing for the English to do this trade, but want it to be done through them, so that they may share the profit on it with them.

It did not prove to be true that M. de La Mothe took 15 barrels of brandy to Detroit when he went up there. I have ascertained, My Lord, beyond a doubt that he did not have two barrels of it. Even that quantity would not have been sufficient if he had given it to all to whom he ought to have given it.

As to powder and lead, he took a large quantity of them; and it may have been that which occasioned people to say that he had taken such a large quantity of brandy.

It is certain that M. de La Mothe had asked the Marquis de Vaudreuil for 200 men, and that he only gave him 150. But, My Lord, he has since offered him his company, and that of M. de la Forest. I do not think he can reasonably claim anything else on that head, more especially as the soldiers remaining in the colony are so poor that a sufficient number of good men can hardly be found for the parties it is advisable to despatch for the King's service.

It is true, My Lord, that M. de Tonty had sold almost all the powder belonging to the fort of Detroit, so that M. de La Mothe found only 40 livres of it when he arrived.

It appears from the formal statement of the Sr. de Grandmenil, formerly agent to the Company and now to M. de La Mothe, dated the 2nd of June, 1706, the time at which the Outaois fired on the French fort, that the Miamis and Onyatanous who had taken refuge there, broke open the Company's warehouse and took from it,—6 guns intended for trading, two carbines, 34 sword-blades, 32 gun cases, and 6 dozen knives [Statines].

The Sr. Bourgmont, fearing that the Outaois might set fire to the houses in the fort, had the chapel, the Recollet's house, and the Company's warehouse, unroofed and covered with the skins of hinds, which skins were much damaged by the rains which followed during almost all the time the said Outaois fired at the fort. I have, however, been assured that this damage was not very great.

M. de La Mothe had these houses roofed again with bark from the trees which he sent soldiers to fetch out of the woods, to whom he paid nothing. He gets almost all his other work done at the same price.

The brother of the secretary to the Marquis de Vaudreuil left Detroit a long time ago, My Lord, and the man whom he relieved, who is called Delorme has returned there. The truth is that the latter is a cleverer man than the other, and bears the reputation of an honest man.

MISSILIMAKINAC.

After I had remained at Detroit 19 days, I left there on the 3rd of August to go to Missilimakinac, which is at a distance of 130 leagues where I did not arrive until the 19th of the said month, on account of contrary winds. I only remained there four days, during which I observed that it was the most important of all the advance posts of Canada, both on account of its advantageous position—because of the difficulty of approaching it without being discovered—and from the trade that can be done there. This post is the resort of all the tribes that come down from Lake Superior, from the Bay des Puants, from the St. Joseph river and from Topicaniche. It is the way for any tribes which might intend making war on each other, so that it is easy for the Outaois to stay their axes and become the mediators in all their quarrels, as they have been in the past. It is inaccessible to the most powerful of their enemies, the Miamis and Onyatanous, as they are not boatmen.

The fishing is very abundant there, and the fish, the most excellent

terprise in this direction, for no more provisions can be carried than the quantity necessary for going up there.

It has been remarked above that all the beaver skins that go to Detroit are taken to the English. It is therefore necessary, in order to prevent that, to stop the savages at Missilimakinac. This can only be done by putting a commandant there with garrison of nearly 30 men, as the Outaois request. It would be necessary that the garrison should not sow grains of any kind, for that would often cause disputes to arise between the soldiers of that garrison and the savages. The later used, formerly, to get many furs with their Indian corn which they sold to the savages of the upper country; but, since they have been urged by M. de La Mothe to go and settle at Detroit, many of their people have been in a constant state of hesitation and have employed the whole time in journeys to and fro, and this has resulted in their growing very little Indian corn, and has made it extraordinarily dear. This dearness of price also arises from the fact that the Hurons are no longer there. They used also to grow a great deal of Indian corn, being the tribe of all others that applied itself most diligently to cultivating land. They would never have left Missilimakinac if there had been a French commandant there, and only left this post because of the natural dislike they had of the Outaois, and because the latter held them in a sort of slavery, which would never have been the case, if there had been a commandant there, as he would have taken cognizance of all their disputes, and would have acted as mediator in them. If this post were established they would very quickly go back there. I only judge of that from what they told me at Detroit, viz., that they were much better off, at Missilimakinac. I believe, My Lord, that if this post were re-established, it would be necessary as a matter of policy to make them return to it; for beside the fact that they are very industrious people, it is certain that their dislike for the Outaois would attach them completely to the French, which would make the latter more absolute at this post; but, nevertheless, there is nothing to be feared from the Outaois, for these people appear to me to be fond of the French.

If a commandant and a garrison are not placed at Missilimakinac it is to be feared that the Hurons may settle with the Iroquois on account of their discontent with M. de La Mothe. Moreover they would have been there already if the Iroquois had been willing for them to form a village there, but they will not receive them except on condition that they shall settle in the village of the five Iroquois tribes, and that their tribe shall be mingled with them, and the Huron name become extinct.

Since there are no Frenchmen left at Missilimakinac, or at least only a few fugitives, the greater part of the furs from the north are taken to Hudson's Bay' to the English; for the savages who obtain these beauti-

ful furs, who are called Crics and land tribes, used formerly to take them
to the junction of two rivers which fall into Lake Lemepigon, and to the
junction of the Manestigoyac and Le Pic rivers which fall into Lake
Superior at the end of Michipicoton Bay, where the French used to go
for them. But as the latter do not go now, these savages are obliged to
take them to the English. This trade cannot be kept up by the Outaois
for two reasons; the first, that these savages from the north are extremely
timid and fear them greatly—that is not within reason, for they have
often plundered them, or at least have only given them a very little for
their beaverskins. The second is that the Outaois are not careful enough
to justify us in trusting them with goods.

It is certain, therefore, that we cannot get these furs without going
for them. For that purpose it would only be necessary to grant twelve
licenses to the French for the first year, for the whole of the savages
who might come to those places would not come the first year, seeing that
they could not all be notified of our intention of going there. For this
reason a larger number of licenses would be required afterwards; it
might even go so far as twenty, but it would not be necessary to exceed this number, which would be sufficient for obtaining as many
beaverskins as we wished. These licenses should be sold at a fixed price,
and the proceeds handed over to poor families, as used formerly to be
done.

*   *

But, My Lord, since the beaver from the north is far better than that
from the south,—it might even be said that [one livre of] the former
is worth two livres of the latter—it would be very reasonable for the
traders to [be required to] pay more than 30 sols a livre for it.

It is certain that, if they would give 40 sols a livre for it, they would
obtain as much of this beautiful beaver-skin as they wanted.

As all the beaverskin from this trading would come to Missilimakinac,
it would be necessary, in order to prevent those who are charged with
taking it to Montreal, from sending any to the English through the
savages settled amongst us, that the commandant at this post should
draw up a most careful statement of the quantity of beaverskin loaded
into each boat, which statement would be sent to the Intendant. In this

These merchants are not the only people who send goods to these fugitives. Since 1703, many boats have been sent under various pretexts, all of which have taken their full load of goods there. As the people who were in charge of these boats have been, for the most part, creatures of the Marquis de Vaudreuil, it is certain that he has had a large share in this trade. I will not go further into details, My Lord, without first knowing whether you wish me to do so. But I think I am bound to tell you, My Lord, that a man named Boisseau, a Canadian, and a soldier in Esgly's¹ company, traded last year at Puants Bay, 80 leagues from Missilimakinac, to the extent of about 500 crowns' worth of goods. He had gone up in the autumn with the Sr. de St. Pierre, a lieutenant and interpreter of the Outaois tongue, for the purpose of going to Detroit and Missilimakinac to induce the Outaois to deliver Le Pesant to him to take to M. de La Mothe. It appears that the said Boisseau could not sell the goods he had taken, during the short time the Sr. de St. Pierre remained at Missilimakina, for he did not return with him. His pretext for remaining was that he was ill. The said Boisseau's mother came to Montreal, when the Sr. de St. Pierre arrived there, and she asked him for news of her son. When the said Sr. de St. Pierre replied that he had remained at Missilimakina sick, she was much alarmed, and went to the Marquis de Vaudreuil who consoled her greatly by assuring her that her son would not die of it, and that his illness was a small matter.

The Montreal merchant who does the most trade of all with the Frenchmen at Missilimakinac is the Sr. Soumande. On my return to Montreal from Missilimakinac I even found, on the spot where I set foot on land, a letter which a man named Chasles wrote to him, in which he asks him for a quantity of goods and sends him the names of the Outaois savages to whom he may give them. It appears that this letter had been forgotten by a savage.

But it is true, My Lord, that if these Frenchmen were not there, hardly any beaverskin would come to Montreal for we should only have what the Outaois might bring there, which would be a small quantity, because they would sell more than half of it on their way down, to the savages settled among us, who then take it to the English. I draw from that the inference that it is absolutely necessary to place a commandant at Missilimakinac with a garrison of thirty men, and to issue the twelve licenses spoken of above, by which means, and by taking the precautions there set forth, we should get all the fine beaverskins of Canada. For, as it is not possible to prevent goods from being sent to these outlaws every year, under various pretences, it would be much better to grant licenses. This advantage, at least, would result from doing so, namely, that the poor families would profit by a part of this trade, and this would relieve them to that extent; whereas, as matters now stand, the people who profit by it are those best able to do without it.

From all that has been said above, it may be seen that Missilimakinac is the most advantageous post in Canada; and, to show its superiority over Detroit, I may tell you that even if all the savages in Canada were settled there we should not obtain one tenth of the quantity of beaver-skin that we can get from Missilimakinac, for it would almost all go to the English by the agency of the Iroquois, the Hurons, and even many other savages who have gone that way. I say [it would be] the same even if we were able to sell goods to these savages at the said post of Detroit at the same price as we let them have them at Montreal, and the best proof that can be given of it is that the savages settled amongst us constantly come into the town of Montreal to trade for the beaver-skins of the merchants, with English goods, for the purpose of taking them afterwards to Orange. This ought once more to bring us to the conclusion, My Lord, that Detroit is a post which is very disadvantageous to the Colony, because it is so easy for the savages to go to the English by means of the Iroquois. *Note.* There is a point to be observed My Lord, in regard to the savages settled amongst us coming to Montreal to trade for the beaverskins of the merchants with English goods, which seems to me most important; this is, that we cannot prevent these savages from doing this trade except by using a great deal of force against them, and it is to be feared that this will so irritate them that they will declare against us if they find the Iroquois ever so little disposed to make war on us, which would be extremely unfortunate for this Colony. There is only one remedy for that, My Lord, which would be to compel traders in beaverskins to give 40 sols a livre for them; for if that were done, not only would the savages settled with us give up coming to trade for the beaver-skins of the Montreal merchants, but they would also bring them those they obtained in hunting. Moreover, we should, in that way, deprive the English of an almost certain means of making all the savages quarrel with us, and there can be no doubt that they will succeed in doing so if the price of beaverskin remains at 30 sols.

of their huts, and their fort, for they still had a great deal of brandy left. I assure you, My Lord, that the missionaries are in great danger at those times. These savages might have been prevented, at Montreal, from taking away such a large quantity of brandy. I have been told that they were only permitted to take such a large quantity on condition that they made large presents to the Governor-General. I do not know whether that is true; but I know from a good source that the presents which have been made to him by the savages this year are worth more than five hundred pistoles. The interpreters who are charged with arranging these matters with the said savages take very great advantage of it, and no one dares to disapprove; that is to say, they sell as much brandy as they like to the said savages, over and above what the Governor General permits them to take. From this, My Lord, a great deal of harm results, of which it is not the worst that it gives these savages occasion to get intoxicated; although this is very great, for, when they are in that condition, they take to burning their huts, quarreling with one another, tearing one another to pieces, killing one another and, finally, to every evil act men can be capable of. Another evil arises, the consequences of which are still more disastrous, namely, that when the savages have squandered the greater part of their furs on presents and brandy, the remainder is not sufficient, by a great deal, for them to get the things they need, that is, 'blankets, *mitasses,* guns, powder, lead, tobacco and kettles, and they fall into very great want; this leads them into using very unruly language about the Governor General, even so far as saying that he is a miser who has robbed them. From this contempt, the greatest misfortunes may arise for the Colony. What I am telling you has accordingly happened to them this year, for I know they have not taken back from the sale of their furs one-third of what they needed.

A large quantity of goods is also sent to Missilimakinac by the boats which take the missionaries the things they need; not that these good fathers have any share in that, for these goods belong to the boatmen who are employed for that purpose, under the authority of the Governor General.

*　　*　　*

Onaouyelo, a Kiscacou Outaois, who used formerly to live at Detroit, and is now at Missilimakinac, says that he left with the Sr. de Grandmenil, M. de La Mothe's agent, a large porcelain necklace and a great feast-kettle, which M. de La Mothe refuses to have given back to him, although he has offered the agent ten beaver-skins for the five beaver-skins' worth for which he had given him credit, and as security for which his kettle and necklace had been given to him. This savage says that, when he asked M. de La Mothe for this necklace and kettle, he replied that he had given them to the Miamis to speak to them.

That M. de La Mothe had invited him to go to Detroit, and as he would not go there, he believes it is for that reason that he refused to give him back the kettle and necklace.

That he also threatened him and many others of his tribe that if they did not go back and settle at Detroit they would all die. It is true, My Lord, that he said that to them, for he knows they are very superstitious. so that now they believe that it is M. de La Mothe who kills all those of their people who die. There are even many who have gone to settle at Detroit in order to avoid their imaginary death.

Those, My Lord, are all the observations I have been able to make on my journey. Some of them are against my inclination, all the more because in my private capacity I had no reason to complain of the persons against whom they are made. It needed no less than an order from you, My Lord, to compel me to make them. Your kindness in telling me that you would not expose me did not induce me to make up my mind to it more easily; I know too well that it is my duty to obey you without any conditions. Whenever, therefore, it is a question of doing that, I shall follow no rule but your will to which, all my life, I shall show a blind and respectful obedience.

  I am, with the deepest respect, My Lord,
      Your most humble, most obedient, and obliged servant.
                                                  D'Aigremont.
Quebec, the 14th of November, 1708.

EXTRACT FROM THE LETTER OF THE SAID MINISTER OF THE 6TH OF JULY, 1709.
PAR. 8 AND 9.

exletterG. However, as His Majesty has decided that he will bear no expense on account of that settlement, it will be very necessary that you should in

throughout the Colony, that is to say, the rate of the fourteenth minot instead of the eighth.

EXTRACT FROM THE SAME LETTER AT PARAGRAPH 18.

I have reported to the King the proposal you make to return [to him] the land of Detroit when you have brought *it into the condition you intend. His Majesty will not require that of you; but, far from wishing that you should study to draw from that land a large revenue, his will is that you should labor to render his post of service to the general welfare of the Colony, and to make the inhabitants there happy, while preserving your own interests as far as justice will permit.*

LETTER FROM MM. DE VAUDREUIL AND RAUDOT.

Endorsed—MM. de Vaudreuil and Raudot.
    Duplicate.

14th Novr., 1709.

My Lord:

The Sieurs de Vaudreuil and Raudot felt quite sure that the Sr. d'Aigremont would give you an exact and faithful account of the journey he made by our orders to the further posts of this Colony; they are also quite satisfied, My Lord, of the reasons which should induce His Majesty to keep up Fort Frontenac at the present juncture; but they hope you will permit them to represent to you that, if this Colony were unfortunately at war with the Iroquois, it would be impossible to keep this post up, for at least eight or nine hundred men would be necessary to escort every convoy of provisions that went up there.

They have the honor of assuring you that they will not establish any new post in this country without orders from you.

The Sr. de Vaudreuil will strictly carry out the orders which you do him the honor of giving him, My Lord, as to ordering down the troops that are at Detroit, and the Sieurs Raudot will see to their subsistence as to that of the other soldiers.

It is true, My Lord, that the Sr. de Vaudreuil, by the order he gave to the Sr. de La Mothe in 1706 when he went up to Detroit, forbade him to let French people marry savages until such time as he should receive order from you to the contrary. He did so as he is convinced that bad should never be mixed with good. Our experience of them in this country

Frenchmen who have married savages have been licentious, lazy and intolerably independent; and their children have been characterized by as great slothfulness as the savages themselves.

You will see, My Lord, from the private letter of the Sr. de Vaudreuil that he has been obliged to order the Sr. de Joncaire.to get rid of the man Montour who is the offspring of such a marriage. It seems that all children born of them try to create as many difficulties as possible for the French.

If the Sr. de La Mothe had thought that his prohibition was injuring his settlement, he could have done himself the honor, My Lord, of writing to you to obtain permission for this. The Sr. de Vaudreuil had the honor of sending you at the time a copy of the order which he handed to the Sr. de La Mothe before he departed, and you sent him word that you approved of it.

The presents which the Sr. de La Mothe receives from the savages at Detroit, My Lord, ought to recoup him for what he gives them, which amounts to very little, being nothing but a few livres of powder and bullets, of which His Majesty has graciously given him a quantity free; but the Srs. de Vaudreuil and Raudot, My Lord, will do what you order them to do as to this.

The Srs. de Vaudreuil and Raudot, after considering the matter, find no one among the officers who serve His Majesty in this country, more suitable for re-establishing the post of Michilimakina than the Sr. de Louvigny, who formerly commanded there during the last war, and was much respected and beloved by these savages. They have the honor, My Lord, to nominate him to you for this post, but that ought not to stand in the way of his appointment to the King's lieutenancy, which is about to become vacant, as he is the senior major and moreover a most intelligent and vigilant officer. It would be very hard on him if, by rendering him the justice due to him as regards the post of Michilimakina they should prejudice his promotion.

The confidence the savages have in the Sr. de Louvigny make them believe that nothing could be better at the present juncture than to send him to this post; for, with the English straining every nerve to raise the Iroquois against us, it is of the utmost importance in case that should happen to set all the Outavois tribes against them, as the Comte de Frontenac did, who made use of the said Sr. de Louvigny for that purpose and was very much pleased with him because of the constant expeditions he got up against the enemy, which prevented those they might have made against this Colony.

If His Majesty adheres to the intention of having this post re-established it will be essential, in order to make the savages understand that it is a permanent one, to have a fort and some houses built there, as there

After this post has been re-established, the Sr. de Lonvigny could return and take up the appointment you may have been good enough to obtain for him; for his journey to Michilimakina ought not to interfere with the promotion which he deserves.

The Sr. Boudor having died at Michilimakina was unable to take advantage of the favor which His Majesty was graciously pleased to grant him. Four or five of these backwoods traders came down, on hearing rumors of war, and having arrived while M. de Ramezay was in the field, they went and joined him at once; and he was well pleased with them and has written to the Srs. de Vaudreuil and Raudot to request them to ask you to pardon them, hence they have not prosecuted any of them on account of the war with which the Colony was threatened. All of them are most repentant for the wrong they have done, as well as some who remained at Michilimakina, of whom they have the honor of sending you a list, begging that you will graciously pardon them, sending them a general amnesty for all the backwoods traders.

Three brothers who were backwoods traders belonging to this country were found by the expedition to the north. The Sr. de Lanoüe had them arrested, and while they were on an island, with the detachment which had captured them, they escaped in the boats. The Sr. de Croisil who caught sight of them took up his gun and called them to return, or he would fire on them; and as they did not come back and he had no boat to go after them, he killed one of them.

*   *   *

The Srs. de Vaudreuil and Raudot will see to it carefully that all the beaverskins that are bought by Canadians are taken to the office. They would be very glad if fifty or sixty thousand of them could be supplied every year; but they fear, My Lord, that that cannot be done without the licenses, which they believe it absolutely necessary to begin issuing again. When His Majesty has a commandant at Michilimakina on whom he can depend to make sure that no trade in brandy is carried on there, and all the boats of the *Voyageurs* are obliged to go there, an examination shall there be made to see that they have no brandy; or the same shall be done with those boats before they leave here.

In accordance with the decree they have received, they will see to it strictly that there is no trade in brandy carried on with the savages.

*   *   *   *

My Lord,
        Your most humble and most obedient servants,
                            Vaudreuil.
                            Raudot.
                            Raudot.

REMARKS ON REPORT OF RAUDOT.

Endorsed—M: Raudot. M. de Frontenac.

14th Novr. 1709. We must ask M. Raudot for these plans; I should be very glad to see them. Discuss with him rather thoroughly the town of Cape Breton; it is one of the most important matters affecting the Colony.

It is absolutely necessary to settle, once for all, the affairs of Madame de Verchere; pray look into it with MM. de Viene and de Chagnais, and enable me to settle it.

To set right the excessive size of concessions, we must despatch for that country a decree similar to the one sent regarding the American islands and St. Dominique. That is important.

As regards the hospital of the St. Charron and the Sisters of the Congregation, I do not know that the decision can be changed in any way, and the consequences of too large a body of ecclesiastics are to be feared. It is only necessary to prevent it from receiving legacies, which might disturb families. There are moreover several important matters in this letter.

LETTER FROM RAUDOT.

MM. Raudot.   Quebec 14th of Novr. 1709.
Duplicate.
My Lord,

The Sieurs Raudot have received the letter which you were pleased to write to them, dated the 6th of July this year.

The settlers are devoting themselves more and more to cultivating the ground. They are beginning to know that that is the best thing they can do, its fruits being a certain possession. But they have been distracted from it by the different expeditions, and all the compulsory work they have done this year on the fortifications of this town. The Srs. Raudot urge them constantly to increase their spare lands, and

devoting themselves to growing hemp; as time goes on they will begin cultivating it, and it is only little by little, and, as it were, of themselves that the districts can be formed.

The Srs. Raudot agree, My Lord, that the timber trade of this country can scarcely be carried on without expense to the person undertaking it. His Majesty would have assisted this Colony by sending a storeship, because of the market it would have created. They believe there would have been no profit in fitting this out, but also that there would have been no loss, or a very small one. But if it be desired that matters should be equalized, or that there should even be some profit, they are convinced that it is too soon yet to embark on this trade which, as time passes and the country becomes more populous and consequently richer, will bring in profit; and it will easily be carried on when a large number of vessels come here to trade in it. The merchants are not in a position to undertake this trade and could only do so by applying to His Majesty for extensive privileges; therefore, My Lord, they cannot be looked to for this undertaking. The Sieurs Raudot beg leave to say, My Lord, that Mons. Begon has not had a proper examination made of the statements of the consignments which were sent from the port of Rochefort in the year 1705, and 1706; otherwise he would have observed that, in the year 1705, one hundred and twenty-nine guns were sent to this country, which were supplied by the Sr. Froüant at 19# each, for which 2451# were retained out of the funds which you were pleased to grant us at this time; and that in the following year also 356 guns were sent at the same price, taken from the warehouse at Rochefort, for which 6754# was deducted. These two consignments make up the number of 475 guns, for which the Srs. Raudot gave acknowledgments to the treasurers to the amount of 9215# which had been retained by the port Rochefort for these two consignments. They have the honor to annex hereto a copy of the invoices of these consignments certified by the keeper of the armory at Quebec, who received them and gave his certificate for the payment; by the controller of the Navy, as this sum was employed in the discharge of the treasury in payment for these guns; and by the treasurers as it was retained by them out of the funds of this country by the treasury of the said port of Rochefort. These guns have been used to change those of the troops which had become unserviceable, as they had had them for 20 years, and to arm the men who were without any.

The Srs. Raudot beg you, My Lord, to be good enough to have these guns replaced for them, and therefore to order Mons. Begon to have 475 of the said guns from Tulles sent to them without deducting the cost of them from the funds of this Colony. They can assure you that they

ies, as it has been necessary to distribute many to the settlers and savages, on account of all the alarms there have been this year in this country. The said Srs. Raudot do all they can to call them in, but there are always a number of them lost, or returned unserviceable.

In accordance with the orders you do them the honor to give them, the Srs. Raudot will take care that no useless expenditure is incurred when one of His Majesty's ships comes here. It is not their fault that any such expense is incurred in this country; but, My Lord, they cannot apply a remedy for that. They resist so far as they can, and in pursuing that object, bring on themselves the ill-will of many people; but, in the end, they have to give way. For, if matters chance to turn out differently from what they had anticipated, and turned out badly, they would be accused to you, of the greatest crimes. The accusation which M. de Vaudreuil made against M. de Ramezay, that he had exchanged good men and given him bad ones in the expedition of last year, must make everyone tremble who serves under such a government as this.

The Srs. Raudot had the honor last year of sending you maps of the government of Montreal, which were presented to you by the Sieur de Marigny. They have the honor, this year, of sending you maps of the governments of Three Rivers, and Quebec. The Sr. de Catalagne (Catalorgne), Lieutenant of the troops of this country, who has drawn up all these maps, has taken all possible pains and care in order to make them correct and exact. They can assure you that he deserves the honor of your favor, and that you should be good enough graciously to include him in the promotions that are to be made in this country. His services, My Lord, and all the trouble he has taken over these maps, make them hope that you will grant him an appointment as captain. This reward, which he deserves in many ways, will save you, My Lord, the pension which he would deserve for this work, which has cost him two years' labor, during which time he has been obliged to visit all parts of this country, even in the roughest and hardest weather. This work, My Lord, has drawn down on him the indignation of the Sieur Le Vasseur, engineer in this country, who asked him at the castle, in the presence of the Governor's wife, by what orders he was working, and appeared very angry that he was doing so by the orders which you had

them so, so much so indeed that several people wish to have copies made from the originals which remain here.

The Sieur Robert has copied all these maps, and those which are to be presented to you are all from his hands; he has worked at this task all summer. The Srs. Raudot hope that you will consent to grant him a gratuity on this account.

The Srs. Raudot expect next year the church ornaments which His Majesty has graciously granted to the Sr. Brelay. They have the honor to beg that you will order M. Begon to have them sent by the ship you may be pleased to grant for this Colony.

The Nuns of the general hospital are greatly indebted to you for the attention you were good enough to pay to the request which they had the honor of making to you last year for conveyance of mill machinery; they hope that at a more favorable time you will graciously grant them that favor. The said Srs. Raudot begged you at the same time to be good enough to grant them permission to take two lay sisters, besides the two they are allowed to have, informing you of the need they had of them; they are so convinced of this need that they repeat the request which they made to you about it.

The man Boisseau, a soldier in the company of De Desgly, was given to the Srs. Raudot by M. de Vaudreuil to go up in the boat of the Sr. de St. Piere, who was going to Detroit to accompany the Outaouois chiefs who had come to Montreal to ask for pardon for the attack they had made on the said fort of Detroit, where the Sieur de La Mothe was to seek for means of arranging that matter. The said Sr. de St. Piere repaired at once to that fort; but, as the said Sr. de La Mothe would not accept this pardon of the Outaouois unless they would hand over to him Le Pezan, a savage of their tribe who had been the cause of the attack, he set out to go to Missilimakinac with the Sr. D'Argenteuil. That, My Lord, is how the soldier came to be at Missilimakinac where he remained, not returning until the year after. M. de Vaudreuil says publicly that he fell ill there, and that prevented him from returning; he even recommended him on leaving, to the Sr. D'Aigremont; who, having made inquiries about him, learnt that instead of having been ill, he had been trading all the winter in the Bay des Puants. When this was told to the Sr. Raudot junior, he did not pay him for his journey.

The Srs. Raudot, My Lord, had the honor of informing you last year that the merchants of Quebec had rented a house to establish an Exchange, and had, amongst them, provided a three year fund for that purpose; hence it is costing His Majesty nothing.

On the petition presented to him by the St. Aubert, the Sr. Raudot

such goods confiscated to the said St. Aubert, or his agents, and permitting them to make an examination of the goods in the shops of
the merchants. The truth is that they learnt that boats had come with
some Agniers, last autumn, from Orange to Montreal full of these
goods, which these savages had traded there. The Srs. Raudot were
not there at that time, and M. de Vaudreuil, who was there, did not
prevent that trading. The Sr. Raudot junior spoke to him about it
here on his return, and told him that it appeared to him that we ought
not to allow the savages to come and trade publicly in foreign goods
in one of the towns of this Colony, and that he ought to have sent
these savages back again with all their goods, and had them conducted
as far as beyond Chambly so that they could not have traded them.
But he told him that he had known nothing about it, and that if he
had been aware of it he would have prevented it, and that such things
as this must not be permitted. This answer however was only moderately plausible; for it seems impossible that a matter of that kind, which
lasted for five days, could go on publicly in a town, without a Governor
being told of it, especially since he has interpreters whose whole business is to watch for the arrival of savages and speak with them, in
order to obtain permission for them to begin trading. The Srs. Raudot
did not think they ought to inform you of this, as they were satisfied
that it would not happen again, and left it until it should happen a
second time, to do so.

It may be said that there are hardly any English goods which can
be of value in this country, except one, namely scarlet, which is a cloth
that the savages are very fond of, and they make themselves coverings
of it. They are great admirers of this stuff, and it is to be feared that
if they do not find it at our merchants' they will go to Orange for it;
and that the savages of Sault, who are great traders, will themselves
trade for the English or for Frenchmen, in this article, and by teaching themselves still more about business than they knew already, they
may transact the whole trade themselves. The beaver-skins, which they
trade in for this material, will most certainly be taken to Orange and it
will not be possible for us to prevent it. If, on the contrary, the
French have this stuff, the savages will prefer to trade with them rather
than with other savages, because they find other goods in their shops
which they wish to have as well as this scarlet. They [the Srs. Raudot]

sider that they could help granting the St. Aubert the decree which they have had the honor of mentioning to you above. They have received, in the common letter, the one His Majesty has been pleased to give on this subject, which they will see carried out strictly. But they should think, My Lord, that if, for the good of this country, in order not to withdraw the trade of the savages from it, and not to make the English receive a large part of their beaverskins by driving the savages away, His Majesty could remove this prohibition against the sale of any English goods, at the same time forbidding Frenchmen to wear and dress themselves in English stuffs, or even to use things coming from Orange in any way, on pain of confiscation, with such fine as it may please you to order, payable to the informer. In this way nothing would come to this country except scarlet and blue cloth, which appear to the said Srs. Raudot to be absolutely required for the trade with the savages. That, My Lord, would not prevent the prohibition against sending beaver skins to the English from being still kept in force, and being made more rigorous.

If the Sieur de La Mothe were a little less fond of gain, My Lord, he would not complain to you of the Sieurs Raudot, who have ever done him justice in all things, in accordance with the orders which you were graciously pleased to give them regarding him.

When the Sr. de La Mothe went up to Detroit, they were obliged to grant him all he demanded of them on the condition that, if you did not agree with what they did in this respect, he should be obliged to reimburse His Majesty such expenses as were not approved thereon. They had the honor of giving you an account of them, and in the common letter of the year 1707, you were good enough to notify them that His Majesty did not see fit to pay in full the wages of the two interpreters at Detroit, and that therefore, if the Company of the Colony used to pay them, the said Sr. de La Mothe must do the same.

The Company of the Colony always paid the interpreters at Detroit. It is true that, in its claims on His Majesty, it is asking for half of what it paid for the said wages; but nothing has been decided in that matter. Hence the utmost that the said Sr. de La Mothe could claim would be to pay only half of them.

You were also good enough to write to them regarding the pay of the surgeon, the medicine chest, and the pay of the almoner and the missionary, that all that was the said Sr. de La Mothe's concern, and that therefore His Majesty would not bear any expense for it.

The Sr. Raudot, junior, wrote to the Sr. de La Mothe on the subject, in accordance with that letter, and it is that, My Lord, which causes his complaints. If the said Sr. de La Mothe had been a different man,

)ute on either side. But he is a man who wants everything his own
', who is full of ingenuity, and would have taken it as entitling him
to go to Detroit if he had been refused anything. The said Sieurs
ıdot beg to represent to you that an Intendant is occasionally placed
ı difficulty, especially when he has an order from you to give a post
ı man who always knows how to explain adroitly all the proposals
ıas the honor to make to you. ·They have been a good deal exposed
ıis bad temper since they refused him the money he wished the King
end him, and some goods· which we were unable to supply, nor had
Srs. Raudot the right to risk the King's property in that way; and
said Sr. de La Mothe told them that they had orders to give him
r support, and all the assistance in their power in establishing the
: which had been given him, and that if this support and assistance
not include what he asked for, he had none. What is to be done?
at to be said to this talk? The best course is to listen, to say nothing,
to take the honor of informing you of it.
he Sr. de La Mothe has complained to you, My Lord, that the Srs.
ıdot have raised the price of the powder and lead they had sent him.
y had expected this complaint, knowing the said Sr. de La Mothe
hey do, from the letter which the Sr. Raudot, junior, received from
, dated the 21st of July of this year, in which he writes to him in
ıe ·terms. "You know well, Sir, that I have never complained either
ʒou or.to Monseigneur, as to the price of the goods you have had
ded over to me from the stores of His Majesty, and you also know
: that was settled by common consent, and that you have received
ment for them on delivery. Yet Monseigneur writes to me as if
·e had been disputes on this subject and adds that if Ɩ think the
:e too great I am to write to him about it and His Majesty will cer-
ıly set it right."
he said Sieurs Raudot hope they may be permitted to beg you to
ice that he states in this letter that he does not know who has com-
ned to you, My Lord, but notwithstanding that it was he, as you
:hem the honor to tell them, & that, by all appearances, he is stating
ely that he received a letter from you on this subject,. since it was
ɣ this year that you did the said Srs. Raudot the honor to write
:hem about his complaints. What opinion can one have, My. Lord,
ıt respect can one feel. for a man who is such an adept in lving. and

price as they were sold to other people. They also beg you graciously to believe that they would be very sorry to deal with the Sr. de La Mothe except as justice dictates, and they beg you to notice that, had they not the King's interests so much at heart, the said Sr. de La Mothe would not bring so many complaints to you as he does. He deserves, in true justice, My Lord, to pay all the expenses wholly, if only as a punishment for all the pettifogging squabbles he got up before his departure, both regarding his agreement with the Company and as to the demand he made. He held an order from you, My Lord, for that post to be given him; and as soon as anyone refused him anything, his cry was that people would not let him go up to it, that people were opposing that post, and that he had orders to establish it. A mere nothing stopped him; the desire for the settlement of Detroit had left him, for he said at that time, to the Sr. Raudot, junior, that it would give him great pleasure if he could find a means of preventing him from going up. The said Sieur Raudot answered him that it was his business; that, as he had received that post by your orders and had had the honor of asking you for it, nothing but other orders from you could prevent him from carrying out the first. He wanted nothing but a plausible objection, with some appearance of reason in it, to throw everything up, so that, on his asking the said Sr. Raudot, junior, for an assurance in writing that he should be paid for the presents he made to the savages for the King's service, he gave it him to quiet him. Since then he has sent him bills for presents, a copy of which is annexed hereto. Before ordering him to be paid for them, the said Sr. Raudot thought it his duty to ascertain from the Sr. D'Aigremont, who was at Detroit last year, whether these presents were made for the service or in the private interests of the Sr. de La Mothe. The said Sr. D'Aigremont gave him the original of the message of the said Sr. de La Mothe, which the Sr. Boucherville took to the Miamis, a copy of which is annexed, from which you will see, My Lord, that although he puts in the heading of the bill for these presents, that they are to prevent these savages from making war on the Outaouois, he does not mention it to them; he only urges them to come and settle at Detroit, and that in order to increase his trade. As the Srs. Raudot think that the expense which the Sr. de La Mothe may have incurred in order to attract savages to the post he is at, should not be included in the King's business, as that only concerns the trade of the said Sr. de La Mothe, they are putting off the payment of this bill until they have received your orders on this matter. It also seems to them that they ought not, after the prejudice which this bill inspires them with, to believe the others of the Sr. de La Mothe to be correct.

to be recalled from Detroit, the Sieurs Raudot think that His Majesty should no longer bear any expense there; all the expenditure for which the Company asks to be reimbursed is only that connected with the troops that were there, and it appears to them that His Majesty ought not to be put to expense for a post where there are no troops left, and there is no one remaining, except the Sr. de La Mothe, who will carry on trade there. The Srs. Raudot, My Lord, in making any new concessions, will take care to grant seigniories of less extent than those that have been granted in the past. It appears to them that no remedy can be applied as to what has taken place regarding this in this country, because of the different hands through which all these lands have passed. The Srs. Raudot, My Lord, will have the claims of the Sr. Dauteuil looked into, as to the arpent of ground which he maintained has been taken from him in this town for fortifications, and will have the honor of sending you an account of them; but they may tell you that the said Sieur Dauteuil has benefited by a stone redoubt, which belonged to the King, which he uses, and it is now included in the enclosure of his house.

They take care to insert in all the concessions they grant, that, in case His Majesty should want land for building forts and fortifications, he will make no payment to the owner for them; hence His Majesty will not be exposed any more to these claims, when he requires land.

It is as just as anything can be, My Lord, that payment should be made to Madame de la Forest, and the proprietors of the boats, for the loss the said boat suffered by the journey it made to the Isle of Orleans to take troops there. The Sieurs Raudot will have it made, on the parties taking the necessary receipts to the treasurer; but they cannot help pointing out to you that the money out of which you order them to have this payment made, will never be realized if the goods which are sent next year for this Colony are as dear as the awards that have already been given at the post of Rochefort, for we have learnt that the supply of mazamet was priced at $3\#$ 18s per ell, and this same stuff is not so dear among the merchants in this country, to whom it costs only thirty-seven or thirty-eight sols per ell in France. They quite understand that, looking to the delay in payment, they can-

seems to them useless to cause His Majesty to run risks for goods which cost him as much in France as in this country, on which there would be a loss rather than a profit when resold) ; also the additional articles they need. They have, therefore, the honor of begging you to be good enough to make provision for this boat, which amounts to the sum of 1125#. They will take care to withhold the 200# which you were pleased to have paid Mme de la Forest in advance.

The course you have taken, My Lord of forbidding M. de Vaudreuil to receive presents from the savages, and directing him at the same time to prevent the interpreters and other people whom he employs from abusing the authority he entrusts to them in that way, was in order to remove all the abuses which might arise as to the savages in regard to their trade.

The Srs. Raudot can assure you that for their part they will see to that, and that they will inform you carefully of all that takes place on that head. This prohibition, My Lord, is that the savages are no longer to be pressed to make large presents, and the Governors of this country in future, will not sink into contempt which the said Sr. de Vaudreuil has brought upon himself among the savages by the greediness he has shown in the negotiation entered into by the interpreters, for them to be increased.

When the Sr. D'Auteuil went to France, the Council consisted of so few members that it was obliged to appoint the Sr. Haymard to act as deputy Procureur-général. He did the work from the time the said Sr. D'Auteuil left until the arrival of the King's ship the following year, when you ordered that the junior councillor should perform the duties of the Procureur-général. The Srs. Raudot considered that, as the said Sr. Haymard holds no appointment from His Majesty, he ought to be paid for the time he had served, and have therefore included him in the statement as employed, for it did not seem right to require work from a man for nothing. They have also had the Sr. Macard paid, the Councillor who has done duty as Procureur-général since your orders; the said Sr. Macard, although a Councillor, is one of the junior members and unpaid. It therefore appeared to the said Srs. Raudot that it was just that he should be paid the salary of an office which he was carrying on, in which there is much more work than that of Councillor; and it did not seem to them reasonable that a man who is in France, on his own business, should receive his pay to the exclusion of the one who was performing the duties of his office. That, My Lord, is the action which the said Srs. Raudot have taken as to these payments, which appeared to them reasonable, and which they hope that you will graciously approve.

France had this year, and the grievous effects it has caused. They learn
from the letter you do them the honor to write them what want there
is in the kingdom, and the extremity to which the people have been
reduced by that want. What happiness it would be to this country, My
Lord, on occasions of this sort, to be able to assist the kingdom from
which it derives everything! It is greatly indebted to you for your
having been good enough to observe that to send a ship from France
to seek flour here would have exhausted the stock too far, because the
quantity it has furnished this year to the various ships that have come
from La Rochelle, and have left for the Islands, to those from Plaisance,
and to those from this Colony which have gone to the latter place. We
could not have supplied it with flour, except by taking it from the
cargo of the other vessels which make purchases of wheat in winter in
this country to make up their cargo. They have the honor to annex a
statement of the vessels that have left and arrived in this Colony, of
the quantities of flour and vegetables they have taken on board, and the
places they were bound for. You will see from that, My Lord, that 9589
quintals 55 livres of flour were exported from this country, including
coarse and fine. The harvest of this year has been at least as good as
that of last year, in the opinion of everybody, so that a like quantity
can be exported next year; it will not be the same as regards peas, for
the turtle doves have eaten the greater part of them.

It is only in this way, My Lord, that the Srs. Raudot will be able to
inform you, year by year, of the yield of each harvest. It is impossible
for the settlers to know, at present, how much wheat they have, for
they do not thresh it till winter, and all the sheaves do not give an
equal quantity. They would have incurred a heavy expense by sending
all through the Colony to collect statements from all the settlers, and
the latter would not have made them correctly, for they all take offence
at requests of that kind; whereas, in this way, they have the honor of
informing you with certainty and without any expense, of what you
wish to know.

exports by his purchases, and procures trade for the country, and of those who do not raise wheat and are obliged to buy it. This order against exporting flour during the summer is productive of great good at a time of scarcity in France, when we could not fall back upon the kingdom, since by this means there is always wheat between one harvest and another, and if the last harvest turns out a failure no export would be allowed. It seems to the said Srs. Raudot at this time absolutely necessary; but when sowing has been carried out in favorable weather, and the wheat appears good, we can let a small quantity go, but only in order to avoid offense, to a ship coming to this Colony, as an encouragement.

The Srs. Raudot would be very glad if this country could produce a greater quantity of corn than it does, and for the settlers to add to their spare lands. Allow them to tell you that you can do everything in that matter, My Lord, and without cost to His Majesty, if you are good enough to re-introduce the licenses. By applying these licenses, or rather the money which would accrue from selling them, to assist the settlers, so as to encourage them and give them the means of turning their lands to account, we should see all their spare lands increasing, and this country becoming much more fertile than it is. To this end it would be essential, My Lord, that this distribution should be made by an upright man who should set himself to know the country, the settlers who are in need, and those who want nothing but the means for improving their lands. For example, there are several who have no oxen for ploughing, and are compelled to work with the pick axe. These gifts would give them the means and opportunity, in that way, to raise more wheat than they do. It would also be necessary to study to give rather to increase good lands than poor ones. It is, as it were, trouble and money lost, to add to lands where the soil is poor. It would also be necessary to give gratuities to those who were commencing work on lands, and even to those who had lands well cleared and well cultivated, by way of encouraging the other settlers to do the same. It is gifts like these, if they are well applied, which will increase the size of this country visibly, and will make it a very fruitful one. That result, My Lord, if you are so good as to approve of this proposal, will rest entirely with the man to whom you commit this distribution. It is certain that the strength of this Colony will always lie in its settlers; that they will support it and extend it by their labors. The townspeople would like to see them sacrificed to them, for the sake of the low price at which they want to get their provisions. The Srs. Raudot have had an instance of it this year; for, on permission being given to export flour from this country, there was an outcry in this town because it was foreseen that this export would always keep wheat at a rather higher price than it would be if none were exported. The people who speak of these things would like to get it at 20s. per minot, because they are buyers of it; but it is very necessary, in order to encourage the settlers to produce it, and to cultivate the land easily, that it should always be worth from 40 to 45 sols per minot, French money.

As regards what you do the Srs. Raudot the honor to tell them, My Lord, that the settlers should be prevented from trading at their homes with the savages, there were old regulations in this Colony which confine trading with the savages to the three towns of this country. Since then they have heard say that the Court had permitted all the inhabitants of the Island of Montreal to carry on trade, so that they might by this means set themselves up again, after the war they had endured against the Iroquois. That lasted for some years until, on your doing them the honor of sending them word in the common letter of 1706 that the inhabitants of Montreal complained that a large trade was done at the end of that Island by a few private individuals, which was enough to ruin that of the other inhabitants of the Island, and that it was necessary that the Srs. de Vaudreuil and Raudot should look into it in order to apply the remedy needful, if the matter required it, they had the honor to answer you that it was true that trade was carried on at the end of the Island of Montreal, that this trade had been suffered, and even sanctioned in part, by you in order to restore the said Island, after the war with the Iroquois which it went through, that this Island had now partly recovered, and that [if] this trade continued where it was it would cause considerable injury to the town, and that the said Srs de Vaudreuil and Raudot would in future give distinct orders that it was not to be carried on there any longer. In reply, you did them the honor of writing to them, My Lord, in the common letter of 1707, that His Majesty had seen what they wrote as to the complaints which the inhabitants of Montreal had made of the

accordance with these orders, My Lord, the Sr. Raudot issued a decree for preventing this trade at the end of the Island; but he did not intend to include the Sr. Guenet, who holds a special permit from His Majesty to trade, for he has by no means the right to interfere with that permit without a special order. Nevertheless, the said Sr. de Vaudreuil has had the said Sr. Guenet prevented from trading, by his detachments. He does not know for what reason; but it appears to him he ought to respect permits of this kind, and not interfere therewith in any way. The trade of one single man cannot cause any great injury; and it appears to the Srs. Raudot that the said Sr. Guenet lost so much in the war with the Iroquois that His Majesty might consent to order the said Sr. de Vaudreuil to let him enjoy this permit to the full, and not to send soldiers to his house any more.

The Srs. Raudot are still convinced, My Lord, that the trade of the savages ought to be confined to the three towns; also that it is not sacrificing the interests of the country settlers to forbid them to trade, for all the traders are generally bad laborers, who forget to care for the land and think of that trade only. But it also appears to them that His Majesty ought not to bear any expense for the prevention of trading at the end of the Island of Montreal; and therefore ought not to send any detachment there. As this prohibition is for the benefit of the merchants of the town it is for them to bear the cost of carrying it out. But the King is only made to bear it in order to obtain presents from the savages, who do not give any when they stay at the end of the Island, and in order to have the power of conferring favors—which are not given free—by permitting some people to trade and forbidding others. Hence, My Lord, the advice of the said Srs. Raudot would be to forbid the sending of this detachment, since it is the business of the inhabitants of the town of Montreal to prevent this trade if it does them harm. A detachment is also sent every year to the great falls, which seems to them useless, for though it is done only to prevent people from going up to the Outaouois, it has never stopped anyone but, on the contrary, has helped in bringing down the furs of certain persons who were there, contrary to the King's orders. On arrival in a country, My Lord, one cannot tell either what is good or what bad, more especially in this country where everyone speaks simply in accordance with his own interests, and never with regard to the public welfare; after remaining some time there, experience is gained which shows, in their true colors, many things which we have not exposed.

As the Sr. du Tisnet is not in this town, being in garrison at Montreal, the Srs. Raudot cannot have the honor of informing you this year of what the man Deniset demands from him. They will have that honor next year.

The Srs. Raudot are most obliged to you for the proofs of your favor which you give them in the care you are so good as to take in notifying them that it was impossible for you to grant the Sr. Fleury, their agent in La Rochelle, conveyance of twenty tons, which he had the honor to ask you for on their behalf, in the "Affriquain," which was to come at that time to this Colony, but afterwards, My Lord, could not be fitted out, in spite of all the care which you were good enough to exercise for that purpose. The said Srs. Raudot fully understood the hard times and the distress in France, but they have the honor of pointing out to you that the absence of goods belonging to the King in this country will cause great expense, although they cut down expenses as far as they can, for their part, and it is not their fault that others do not do likewise. They will have the honor of informing you in more detail, in the joint letter, concerning the items of expenditure, and the injury which has been caused to this country by this vessel not coming. As they are ever confident of the good-will which you are kind enough to feel towards them, they have the honor to point out to you that, for want of this ship, they have suffered considerable injury through their property having remained at La Rochelle, for they have been obliged to buy all they are in want of here, at a very heavy price; that since you have honored them with the appointment they hold they have always been paid one-half of their salary in notes, on which they have lost one-half, so that they have only drawn from 8000 to 9000# out of the 12,000# which His Majesty is good enough to grant them; that, moreover, they have always paid freight on their goods, and the taxes on their wines every year, while their predecessors, My Lord, did not pay for any of these things. They hope you will graciously have regard to all the losses they suffer, and grant them next year freight for these 20 tons in the ship you are pleased to grant for this Colony. But despite all these losses, My Lord, they will be only too happy if you will deign to approve of their conduct in this country. They can assure you that it is founded on justice and equity, and that it can stir up no one against them except those who are unjust, and cannot bear in others what they are themselves without.

that that had occurred with him. He has sometimes given certain persons the name which their bad conduct deserved. Can it be said that it is quarrelling when one takes such a course? As for him, he cannot think so. It is true that he has often been sharp with those who are of this character, and it is necessary in order to show them the nature of their acts. He confesses, My Lord, that that did occur, not long ago, with a petty seigneur of this country called La Chevrottiere; one of his tenants had brought complaints against him last year concerning a grant which he enjoyed, on having some measures of corn given to him, that when he gave him some capons for his rent he maintained they were not fat enough. As, in his contract, it was stated that he should give him some of this quality, the said Sr. Raudot regarded that as something so bad that he thought, since the said La Chevrottiere maintained before him that he had a right to do so, that he could assume a high tone to let him know that he looked upon that as an extortion condemned by the laws and quite opposed to good behavior. This year, another of his tenants has come to complain that he had made him pay the rent for the ten years previous, of two perches of land which he had over and above what was laid down in his concession contract, although this tenant had possessed it for more than ten years and had not paid him any other rent than that laid down therein, the said three arpents, which are included in it, having been marked out by him at that time. In the same tone he showed him his injustice, the possession which this tenant had had for more than ten years protecting him from this wrongful inquiry, which, if it were admitted, would give rise to as many lawsuits as there are holdings in this country. The said Sr. Raudot, My Lord, looks upon things of this kind as oppressions which the superior wishes to deal out to the inferior, and thinks he is bound to raise his tone somewhat when affairs of this kind come before him, being incited thereto by his character which makes him naturally hate injustice and oppression, and wish to keep all those to their duty who, in similar circumstances, might take advantage of weakness, as we see him do on such occasions. It would be easier for him to keep quiet; but he thinks he is bound to take upon himself to show his displeasure, in order to give peace to the whole country, in which he does his best to set up justice, a good conduct, and peace, instead of injustice, wrongful acts and the civil strife which reigned there. Up to the present time, My Lord, the said Sr. Raudot has omitted nothing to make this good intention succeed; but since evil-disposed persons have no fault to find with his conduct but that, he will be obliged hereafter to treat good acts and bad ones alike; but he has conducted himself thus for four years, and it appears to him, in common with all upright men, that the country has not been dissatisfied with it. The wrong-doers complain because

Last year, My Lord, you did the Sr. Raudot the honor of ordering him to determine the dispute between Madame de Verchere and Madame Dejordy; and at the same time added to the paragraph in your letter the petition which the said Madame de Verchere had presented to you, in which she set forth the whole truth as to her case, doing herself the honor of informing you that Mons. de Meulles, formerly Intendant of this country, had given a decree against her, but that the Sieur de Beccaucour had left her in peaceful possession up to 1706, at which time she was disturbed by the Sieur Dejordy (as he had married ·the daughter of the late Sr. de Beccaucour), suing before the said Sr. Raudot who, having no right to interfere with a decree of one of his predecessors, confirmed it by another decree, against which the said Madame de Verchere declared that she would appeal. She has appealed to you, My Lord, and has set the whole case·before you in her petition, and you afterwards ordered the said Sr. Raudot to determine that matter, and send you an account of it. He has tried the case, although he was well aware that a decree of the Council was necessary, not because he had already given a decision in that matter, for he can receive a petition for consideration against that, but because of the decision of Mons. de Meulles, which he could not have interfered with without your orders. He has the honor to annex thereto a copy of his decision with an extract from the letter which you did him the honor to write to him, and a copy of Madame de Verchere's petition. He also has the honor to inform you that he cannot change his opinion on this matter. It is true that, in order to make it quite regular, a decree should first have been obtained from the Council cancelling the order of the said Sr. de Meulles, and the one he made in consequence of it, and referring the substance of the case to him for decision. But on your orders, given on the true statement of the whole case, which was set forth in the petition of the said Madame de Verchere, he thought he could pass over this and (try the case) in accordance with His Majesty's good pleasure, as he informed you in the letter which he had the honor of writing to you last year. Allow him, My Lord, to point out to you that, from the way in which the said order was framed, it cannot be attacked again as regards formalities, but only as the substance [of the case]; and this will be a very good thing for the parties. If it were decided on technical points, it would be necessary to send the parties before him again to try it all over again, whereas in considering it in substance the Council would

has been found of moderately good quality; they will try and have it better in future. They have received the memorandum of the Sr. Gobert which you were good enough to send them, and will make use of it to perfect this manufacture, and they will send all the pitch they have from the manufacture here, to the port of Rochefort.

It appeared to the Sr. Raudot, from the agreement made with the Sieurs Aubert, Neret and Gayot, that the company of the Colony ought to pay the Sr. Demaure and the packers their wages, as their agent maintained, but the latter would not pay them, until the dispute was settled, without having a pledge in his hands. This compelled the said Sr. Raudot to issue an order for the six thousand fresh beaver-skins to be handed over to him as security; which order he had all the less scruple in issuing as it did not deprive the said Company of the ownership of its beaver-skins. In accordance with your orders, he will have them returned to the said Company to be used for the purpose you direct, when the parties request it.

The said Srs. Raudot have the honor to point out to you that, though they do not have the honor of sending you the numbers of this Colony every year, it is not for want of diligence on their part. They apply to the seigneurs for it, but they act so slowly that when the vessels have come they are still without the numbers. The Sr. Duplessis, Treasurer of the Navy, who is also a seigneur in this country, contends that it is not his duty to take the census, but that of the captain of the coast; and as he is not a man to give in easily, we cannot succeed in it. If the King had to have the census of this Colony taken every year at his expense it would cost him at least 2000#; and it seems to them right that the seigneurs, who had their lands for nothing, should do this sort of compulsory work. They will always do it reluctantly unless you are good enough to send the Srs. Raudot an order from His Majesty to compel all seigneurs holding the higher jurisdiction, or receiving quit-rent in this Colony, to forward, every year in the month of May, to their subdelegates in the three towns of this country the census of the seigneures they hold in the government of each town, under a penalty of 200# declared to be incurred after the said month, which sum shall be paid in preference to all debts on their seigneures and employed in paying a man to take the census of their said seigneures. In this way, My Lord, we shall be able to succeed with the seigneurs who will have no more to say when they see an order from the King.

Although the Sr. Raudot, senior, had the honor to write to you that the Sr. de Boishebert was at first employed very uselessly on the fortifications by M. de Vaudreuil, and in spite of them; also that the said Sr. de Boishebert acted badly towards them about it, as the works

use on them, they have had him paid and have not even deducted the time he was of no use, so as not to expose themselves to the ill-will of M. de Vaudreuil, with whom the Sr. Raudot, junior, was working at that time on the affairs of this Colony. It is necessary to purchase his good will, if you want it, by constant acts of defence; for when you refuse him anything you find yourself always at odds with him.

Although there is no doubt that the nomination of inspectors is a matter for the Intendant, since they are the police of the fortifications, the said Sieurs Raudot beg you to be good enough to decide the matter definitely. For, in this country, people try and raise disputes on all points, even those which are least doubtful.

They have just learned that the Sr. de Vasseur, the engineer, is going to France and that M. de Vaudreuil is giving him his bundle of letters, that he may have the honor of presenting them to you. They should have thought that, at the present time, the said Sr. Le Vasseur ought not to have been permitted to go, for, as this country may be exposed next year to the same alarms as this, we shall in that case have to take other advice, which will have to be paid for. This causes them to beg you to be good enough not to have the said Sr. Le Vasseur paid in France, for it appears to them that his pay should be given to the man who serves in his place.

They did not think they ought to give him their letters, so as to show still more plainly they have not consented to his journey. They have entrusted them to the Sr. Aubert, a member of the Superior Council of this country, who is going to France, and will have the honor of presenting them to you, as well as the maps of the governments of Three Rivers, and of this town. They have the honor to beg that you will graciously cause him to be paid for his journey.

        *   *   *

The said Sr. de Lamozandiere was very busy all summer, having been obliged to come in default of the Sr. D'Aigremont who has been ill with

putes with them. However that has always been done, My Lord, in this country, but there is moreover a laxity which needs remedying. Hence they beg you to be good enough to give orders that officers who go on expeditions shall be responsible both for the boat which is given them, and for its rigging, and shall be obliged to return the whole into store when they come back.

*   *   *   *

The Sr. Raudot, senior, has also the honor to annex thereto the order he made for handing over to the Sr. Demaure the fresh beaver-skins belonging to the Company of the Colony which he had previously ordered to be handed as security to the Sr. Aubert agent of the Srs. Aubert, Neret and Gayot. The said beaverskins will remain in the hands of the said Sr. Demaure, My Lord, until you are pleased to order whether they are to be sold by auction or whether the Beaver Company shall take them, and at what price. In either case, he will order the sum of money proceeding from the sale of the said beaver-skins to be handed over according to the instructions you have laid down for him regarding that.

The Srs. Raudot also annex, My Lord, the statement which you have done them the honor of sending them as to what is due to the Company of the Colony of this country, with the necessary explanations by the side of each paragraph. They are taking special care to have all that is due to the said Company paid to it.

Your humble, most obedient and most obliged Servants,

Raudot.

Quebec, the 14th of Novr., 1709.

COPY OF A LETTER WRITTEN BY MONSEIGNEUR DE PONTCHARTRAIN TO MONSIEUR RAUDOT.

Versailles, the 23rd of May, 1710.

You know that the Sieur Riverin has been here in the capacity of a delegate from the Colony, since the year 1702, in accordance with the unanimous decision of the assembly held at Quebec on the 17th of Octr. in the said year. Up to the year 1706, he has been paid by his salary at the rate of 6000# a year, as laid down by the said resolution. The Beaver Company having at that time completed its agreement with the Colony, the said Sieur Riverin was kept on as delegate by a resolution of the twelfth of October, 1706, in order to superintend the carrying

ony. This resolution sets forth that as the Company of Canada has no
longer any funds to pay the salary of the said Sieur Riverin, it places
itself in my hands to decide upon them and as to the funds on which
they are to be charged. As there has been no opportunity up to the
present time of finding a fund for the payment of his salary, the said
Sieur Riverin has been unable to obtain any, and has been obliged to
live on his own means since that time and to advance the money for the
cost of all the journeys he has been obliged to make to follow the Court,
and for other necessary expenses; so that he has been losing heavily
for a long while. As the increase in the price of beaverskins ought not
to produce money for the Colony, and is an extra payment to it which
it had no right to expect, it seems to me right that the Sieur Riverin
should be paid out of this money at least a large part of what is owing
to him; and I think it indispensable to settle his salary and to grant
him from 8,000# to 10,000# on account, out of the sum that the 4s
will yield in the year 1712. I do not see that there can be any difficulty
even as to that. I was, however, very glad, before giving any decision
on this matter, to write to you about it, so that you might explain the
justice of paying the said Sieur Riverin to the Colonial Assembly, and
that it might give its consent, and His Majesty on that might issue a
decree authorizing it. I am writing to Mons. de Vaudreuil accordingly,
and you will take care to arrange with him about that, I must tell you
that you, for your part, should facilitate the matter in every way and
should make them clearly understand the pains he has taken and is
taking every day to preserve the interests of the Colony.

EXTRACT FROM THE MEMORANDUM OF THE KING CONCERNING CANADA.

Marly, the 7th of July, 1711.

His Majesty has seen the resolution which was passed in the Colonial
Assembly, as to the salary of the Sieur Riverin, its delegate. He had
observed that the greater part of the good merchants of the Colony have
not signed it, which gives ground for the belief that there was a good
deal of strong feeling on the part of some who signed, and of complai-
sance on the part of others. The reason which induced the said Sieur

had as much to do as he had before, and has worked at it with great advantage to the Colony. As the latter did not accept the proposal which the Sieur Riverin made in his letter of the 5th of July, 1706, it is not right that it should obtain any advantage therefrom; moreover the dearness of provisions in France for some years past has more than doubled the cost [of living]. Hence it does not appear that the offer which the Colony makes to give the said Sieur Riverin 1500# a year, is reasonable, and he cannot be given less than 3000# a year, at which rate His Majesty has fixed his salary, counting from the 17th Oct. 1706, as he has been paid up to that date.

· The said Sieur Riverin agrees to credit the Colony with the sum of 2701# for the two letters of exchange which are in his possession, which are not payable until the beginning of next year; and as regards the other sums in the statement annexed to the resolution, the said Sieur de Vandreuil will see from the answers in the margin of the said state· ment that the Sieur Riverin has received nothing on behalf of the Colony, and it was out of place to ask him for an accout of them. The said Sieur Riverin has asked leave to go back to Canada; but as it was seen that his presence in France is still necessary, His Majesty has directed that it be explained to him that it it is his will that he should remain there, and continue to look to the affairs of the Colony as he has done in the past; we shall see next year whether it is advisable to send him back to Canada. His Majesty wishes the said Sieur de Vaudreuil to explain to the Colonial Assembly his will in this matter.

EXTRACT FROM REPORTS OF MM. DE VAUDREUIL AND RAUDOT.

Endorsed—Colonies. MM. de Vaudreuil and Raudot.

2nd Septr., 1710.

[45 pages]

My Lord,

[page 34]

The Sieurs de Vaudreuil and Raudot have sent for the troops from Detroit, as you were good enough to order them to do. They did so at His Majesty's expense; but it appears to them that the Sr. de La Mothe ought to reimburse the King for that expense, since they went up only at his request, and came down only because he refused to supply them with food.

[page 35, *verso*]

The savages, My Lord, have retracted and now say that the Sr. de Tonty, whom they had accused of having sold them brandy, never did so. He is very unfortunate in having been accused on this occasion. and having thus incurred your displeasure. He hopes, My Lord, that his vindication will restore to him the honor of your patronage, from which he has already experienced so many benefits.

*   *   *

Yours most humble, &c.,

Vaudreuil, Raudot.

Quebec, the 2nd of November, 1710.

EXTRACT FROM A RESOLUTION PASSED AS BETWEEN M. DE LA MOTHE AND HIS SETTLERS OF DETROIT ON THE 7TH OF JUNE, 1710.

This day, the 7th of June, 1710, M. de La Mothe, the commandant for the King of the Fort Pontchartrain of Detroit, having called together the inhabitants of the said place to inform them that His Majesty was withdrawing his troops to Montreal on his having refused to supply them with food, and that therefore His Majesty would defray no expense at the said place; and M. de La Mothe having, on this, set forth to his settlers that it was absolutely necessary to have a priest to officiate in the parish, [it was decided] firstly, that M. de La Mothe should write to the Lord Bishop of Quebec or, in his absence, to his vicar-general, both on his behalf and in the name of all the inhabitants and

of the said sum of five hundred livres, in accordance with the rules which are made at Quebec about it.

5th that M. de La Mothe binds himself to pay, as his personal share of it, the sum of one hundred livres, so that only the sum of four hundred livres will remain to be paid by the inhabitants; which said sum of 500# shall be sent this year to M. Grandmenil, the agent of M. de La Mothe, resident at Montreal, and the following years as ordered by the priest or friar who officiates in the said parish.

6th that all the *voyageurs* and others who may come to trade at this place shall be bound to pay proportionately towards the said five hundred livres for the said priest or friar, and this before beginning their trade; for it is right that, since they share in the profits of the place, they should take part in the expenses of all that concerns the spiritual man. Executed *in triplicate at Fort Pontchartrain on the day and year as above.* Names of inhabitants Robert, Lafontaine, Joseph Parant, François Fafart, Pierre Roy, Francois Picard, Francois Livernois, Antoine Dufrene, Alexis Germain, Joseph Trudaux, Toussain, Dardene, Jacques Gaudet, Michel Campant, Guillaume Boucher, Jacques Campant, Jean Chevalier, Pierre St. Yoe, Baptiste Trudaux, Mathieu Perrin, Paul Guillet, Antoine Magnan, Pierre Mallett, Chesne, Jacques Hubert, Antoine Carriere, Laurens Trubo, Alexis Lemoine, Pierre Lebeuf, Nicholas Vozé, Garvan, Jacques L'Anglois, Jacques Cardinal, Jean Casse, Jean Tabant, Jean le Scieur, Jean Paquet, André Chauvet, Michel Bizaillon, François Bienvenu, Pierre Esteve, Jacques Demoulin, Ducharme, St. Servin, L'Espagnol, De Martal, Michel Massé, Jean Baptiste Turpin.

I certify the above copy to be in accordance with the original which I have in my possession.

At Paris, this 8th of July, 1720.

La Mothe Cadillac.

NECESSITY FOR RE-ESTABLISHING MACKINAC.

Endorsed—Colonies. M. de Vaudreuil 3rd Septr. 1710.

[Note of minister]—I can see that the post of Missilimaquina must be re-established; but I feel a good deal of doubt as to the licenses.

My Lord,

I have received all the letters which you have done me the honor of writing me since the 15th of October last year. I have also received, together with MM. Raudot the memorandum from His Majesty of the

In accordance with your order, My Lord, I have had the honor of writing you several letters by way of Plaisance. Two of my despatches were cast into the sea, as the vessel which should have taken them to M. de Costebelle, had the misfortune to be captured by a pirate.

    ＊   ＊   ＊

Thus far I have had the honor of giving you an account of what has taken place in this country from the departure of the ship "La Bellonne" last year up to the arrival of the King's ship "L'Affriquain."

The Sieurs de Gallifet, de Longüeil, de Langlosiere, de la Chassaigne, and all the officers who have been promoted, are all most obliged for your kindness in procuring them their promotion from His Majesty. They thank you very humbly for it.

The Sr. de la Forest, My Lord, being at Quebec on the Sr. de La Mothe's business, I gave him the orders which you did me the honor to forward to me for him, on the arrival of the King's ship "L'Affriquain"; and, as you direct me to send the Sr. de La Mothe Cadillac his without delay, I have despatched them to him, by a boat with four soldiers and an officer, to whom I have given orders to hand them to the son of the Sr. de La Mothe, who is starting at the same time, if his boat should get on better than the other.

As the Sr. de la Forest is obliged to remain at Quebec until next spring, in order to take proper measures with regard to the post of Detroit, he has requested me to agree to permit him to send an officer there in his place, and has selected the Sr. Dubuisson, a lieutenant, to whom I have given the annexed instructions. The Sr. de la Forest, My Lord, has the honor of writing to you. On the 25th of August last M. de Subercasse sent a boat to M. Raudot and me, to ask us to carry out a memorandum which he sent us, provided we had not had word that one of the King's ships was going to Accadie. I made use of this boat when it returned, to send him the despatch which you did me the honor to forward to me for him. One could wish that you had graciously done the same for M. de Costebelle. He writes me, in a letter which I received a few days ago, that a merchant vessel which left La Rochelle

ex letter
L.

turned three or four days afterwards to Detroit, where M. de La Mothe received them, being unable—he says—to do otherwise, because he had no one to put them under arrest. I do him justice, and am satisfied that he had no share in the desertion of these ten men. It is not every one here who does him so much justice, and many believe that these ten soldiers acted only under his orders.

I have seen the memorandum of the Sr. de Remouville, My Lord. The small number of settlers residing at Detroit, which consists I believe of seven men, the rest being voluntary residents who do not remain there, cannot be of much assistance to the establishment of Louisiana. If, however, his Majesty thinks fit to send these settlers there, this country will sustain no great loss.

The proposal of the Sr. de Remouville to let these settlers establish a post at Ouabache might be carried out, if a silver mine, a small sample from which was shown to me this year, shall be found to be productive. I have sent there, My Lord, or rather have given a settler at Detroit permission to go there, with orders to bring me as great a quantity of it as he possibly can, so that I may send you some next year. This mine, from which I have seen a piece of pure silver worth about five sols, produced in the gross like a musket bullet from the marcasite or stone of this mine, is among the heights of Ouabache, about a hundred leagues from Detroit, and in, or at least near, the same spot where it is stated that there are also very productive coppermines. If that is true, as there is reason to hope, it would be more to the purpose to place the settlers who are at Detroit there rather than to send them to La Mobile. The Ouabache river, from its source to the place where it loses itself in the Mississipy is nearly two hundred leagues in length; and it is to be observed that, from the sea up to the head of this river is navigable throughout for large boats. There is likewise a very fine river from the heights of Ouabache to go to Detroit, by which very complete and easy communications could be kept up with the settlers who were established there. As I am hoping, My Lord, next year, to have a number of samples from this mine, I shall have the honor of sending you some, and at the same time of informing you fully of all the facilities there will be for success in this matter, either for this country or for La Mobile.

In accordance with your orders, My Lord, I have the honor to send back to you the commissions of the Sr. Bernapré as captain on half pay and naval second lieutenant, as the said Sr. Bernapré has not returned to this country.

M. Raudot and I have the honor of sending you, in our joint letter, the remonstrances of the Company of this country as to the salary

France], will have the honor of informing you as to the interests of the said Company.

The Sieurs de Martelly and Datisné are taking advantage of the licenses which His Majesty was good enough to grant them. The Sr. Martelly has informed me that his family affairs absolutely required his presence in France. He is a very good officer.

The Sr. de Persillon, a man of rank, but in very straightened circumstances, as I had the honor of stating to you last year, is proceeding to France to beg you to graciously order to be issued to him, in his country, the pay of a half-pay lieutenant, which His Majesty has been so good as to grant him as a pension in the room and stead of his lieutenancy which he vacates here.

The Sr. de Scelle, a Lieutenant, having suffered much from nostalgia for three or four years, and being unable to find relief in this country, I had the honor of asking you last year for a leave for him. I could not refuse him, this year the permission which he requested of me to go [to France].   ·

The Sr. de Sabrevois, a Captain, begs you, My Lord, to graciously send him a permit to go next year. He has been in this country from 24 to 25 years, and has never yet asked permission to pay a visit to his family; moreover he only asks for it in case peace has been made, or his presence is not required here. He is one of the best officers we have here, who devotes himself closely to the service, and is well suited for the campaigns of this country.

The Sr. Dufiguier, an ensign, asks for leave for next year. He has arrived from Detroit, where he performed the duties of major all the while the troops were there.

The Sr. de la Descouverte has the honor of writing to you. It is grievous to him, after twenty-five years service and two severe wounds, to find him still a junior officer. As he is desirous of honor rather than money, having sufficient to live upon, he would ask as a favor, a commission to do duty as a lieutenant without any other emoluments than

honor of thanking you for your kindness in thinking of him. If it had lain with me to decide as to the distribution of appointments, My Lord, I confess I should have made the Sr. de Senneville captain, for the reasons which I had the honor of notifying you in my letter of last year.

In accordance with your orders, I annex hereto a memorandum show- Index lett ing the names of the officers of the troops serving in this country, their M. ages, places of birth, seniority of service, and their various capabilities. I venture to assure you, My Lord, that I do justice to those who deserve it, and that I have shown no favor.

*   *

CADILLAC APPOINTED GOVERNOR OF LOUISIANA AND DE LA FOREST COMMANDANT AT DETROIT.

Index letter J.   At Quebec, the 13th Septr. 1710.

His Majesty, Sir, *having appointed you to the governorship of Louisiana, and having at the same time chosen M. de la Forest as commandant at Detroit* on the same footing as you have held it until now, I could not refuse M. de la Forest [the services of] M. Dubuisson, a lieutenant of the company of Le Vasseur, for whom he has applied to me to go and take possession of the post this autumn in his place, until he may himself be able to repair there next spring; and this *all the more because, from the orders I receive, it appears that the will of His Majesty is that you should go at once to Louisiana overland.* M. Dubuisson has the honor of being known to you, Sir, as a very upright man; and I have every reason to believe that if your affairs do not permit of your setting out so soon, you will be good enough to give him your advice as to the course he will have to take in the absence of M. de la Forest, both as to what concerns the good of the service, and as to the interests of

absence will by no means diminish any services I may be able to render
you here in [all] that relates to your interests. My compliments to
Made. and Mdlle de La Mothe. I am, Sir, most entirely your very
humble and very obedient servant.

                                                                Vaudreuil.

DUBUISSON[1] ORDERED TO ACT AS COMMANDANT AT DETROIT.

Order given to the Sieur Dubuisson, Lieutenant of the troops, to act
as commandant at Fort Pontchartrain at Detroit in the absence of the
Sr. de la Forest, dated 13th of September, 1710.

His Majesty having thought fit, for the welfare of his service, to
grant to the Sr. de La Mothe Cadillac the governorship of Louisiana,
and having chosen the Sieur de la Forest, Captain of the troops, to command at Detroit Pontchartrain and hold it on the same terms as the
Sr. de La Mothe Cadillac has had it hereto. We, in pursuance of, and
in conformity with the orders of His Majesty, and upon the request
which the Sr. de la Forest has made to us to grant him the Sieur
Dubuisson to go to Detroit Pontchartrain, to watch over his interests
and to act as commandant there in his stead until he shall be able to
go there himself.

Order all Frenchmen, *voyageurs* and others who are at Detroit
Pontchartrain, or who may go there, to recognize the said Sieur Dubuisson, Lieutenant of the troops maintained by His Majesty in this country, as their Commandant in the absence of the Sr. de la Forest. Enjoining them to obey him in everything that he may command them
for the interests of the King's service and for the execution of our
orders, which will be given to him by the said Sr. de la Forest in ac-

MEMORANDUM FOR SIEUR DUBUISSON.

Memorandum for the Sieur Dubuisson Lieutenant of the troops main-tained by His Majesty in this country, and Commandant on behalf of the King of Fort Pontchartrain at Detroit, in the absence of M. de la Forest. Index letter K.

The Sieur Dubuisson, before leaving Montreal, will take full instruc-tion from the Sr. de la Forest as to matters concerning his interests.

As soon as he arrives at Detroit he will give M. de La Mothe the packet which we have given him from the Court, addressed to M. de La Mothe; he will also hand him the letter which we have given him for M. de La Mothe, to whom he will communicate the order we have given him to take command at Detroit Pontchartrain in the absence of the Sr. de la Forest, and request that he will cause him to be recog-nized as commandant, so that no one may be able to plead ignorance of the matter.

So long as M. de La Mothe remains at Detroit, the Sieur Dubuisson will show him all the respect which his character deserves; he will per-mit all the men whom M. de La Mothe thinks fit to take with him to Louisiana, to assist him on his journey, to go there, provided M. de La Mothe gives him a certificate as it is he who is taking them away, and on condition also that the said *voyageurs* shall complete all the busi-ness they may have with their partners, or with the merchants down here, before leaving Detroit. If M. de La Mothe's affairs do not permit of his setting out this autumn to go to his government, the Sr. Dubuisson will take his advice as long as he is at Detroit, on all matters concern-ing the welfare of His Majesty's service, and will also request him to be good enough to assist him at his councils.

The Sieur Dubuisson will take all possible care to prevent the savages allied to us from making war against one another, and will also take every possible means to prevent them from making any attack on the Iroquois.

The Sieur Dubuisson will be very careful to prevent drunkenness, either among the French or the savages, and will pursue the same course in that matter as M. de La Mothe has hitherto taken to prevent it. For the rest, we leave it to the experience, the skill and the wise discretion of the Sr. Dubuisson to do what he may think best for the interests of His Majesty's service, in the execution of our orders.

Given at Quebec this 13th day of September, 1710.

Vaudreuil.

EXTRACT FROM THE LETTER OF M. DE LA FOREST, WRITTEN
TO M. DE LA MOTHE AT DETROIT, AT PARAGRAPHS
1, 2 AND 3.

Endorsed—Cotte K.

Sir,

M. Dubuisson, who will bring you this letter, is also the bearer of that
from the Court for you and of that of M. the Marquis de Vaudreuil.
You cannot be more surprised than I was when I received the order from
the King to go and take command of Detroit de Pontchartrain in your
place, His Majesty having made you Governor of Louisiana. I must
the less have anticipated it, that I had strongly represented to the
minister that my health was so bad that I was no longer in a condition
to undertake long journeys; but that is [a matter] to which he has paid
no attention, & he apparently wishes me to end my life in uncivilized
countries.

My health having prevented me from setting out this autumn, I have
nevertheless been obliged to send on M. Dubuisson to command at fort
Pontchartrain in my absence because I have been assured that the Court
ordered you to go as soon as its orders were received, to proceed to your
government; but knowing the impossibility, as I believe you will find it,
of your setting out this autumn, and that according to all appearances

LETTER FROM SR. D'AIGREMONT.

Endorsed—Canada. M. d'Aigremont, 18th Oct. 1710.

M. de ——————— show Father Lamberville what he says about the licenses: for the rest, rebuke him about M. de Ramezay, who abuses the influence he thinks he has. The Sr. d'Aigremont, Quebec, 18th Octr., 1710.

My Lord,

Last year I received the letter of the 6th of July of the said year, which you were pleased to honor me with, and the duplicate this year. I had the honor of replying to it, but my letter met with the same fate as many others which were thrown into the sea. This letter will be the same as the former one, except for a few additional paragraphs.

Your graciousness, My Lord, in writing me that you were satisfied with the account which I had the honor of giving you of the journey which I made by your orders to the advance posts of Canada, gave me inexpressible pleasure.

I very humbly ask your pardon, My Lord, for not having sent you in 1708, the statement as to the trade transacted annually at Fort Frontenac. That arose from my being in want of an explanation on a minor point, in order to make up that statement, when the ship left. I have the honor to annex two statements regarding this trade, one for the said year 1708 and the other for this year and last, from which you will see, My Lord, what profit it has yielded. It cannot be doubted that, if goods have to be brought here to carry it on, or if those that come from France are as dear in future as those that came in the "Afriquain" this year, there will hereafter be a loss on this trade.

If I had believed that a longer stay at Detroit could have given me any fuller knowledge of that post, I would not have left there so soon.

As regards the complaint which M. de La Mothe has made to you, that I had not conversed with him long enough to learn thoroughly the reasons which have governed his action, I thought, My Lord, that any

Lake Erie could be made, it could only be done with very great expense and it would not follow from that, that Detroit would be able to obtain from Montreal any help it might need in case of war with the Iroquois; for such help could not even be given to Fort Frontenac, which has to be passed through on the way to Detroit.

*   *   *

I feel greatly honored, My Lord, that you have sufficient confidence in me to ask me which of the officers in Canada would be the best fitted to take command at Michilimakinak.

The Sr. d'Argenteuil, who has recently been made a Captain, is the one that seems to me to have the greatest influence of all the officers, over the minds of the Outaois, and moreover they ask for him as Commandant, but, in other respects, he has but little wisdom.

The Sr. de Lignery is a wise and brave officer, and the one I should rely on most of all those in Canada, for honesty and uprightness. He has not much knowledge of the tribes of the upper country, but, My Lord, I am satisfied that, if you did him the honor to nominate him to command at that post he would succeed there; the savages are very fond of men of his disposition.

The Sr. de la Noüe, his wife's brother, recently made a lieutenant, is nearly of his disposition, but smarter and capable of the greatest things.

I will see to the carrying out of the two new decrees as far as I can, one of which forbids illicit-trading in brandy, and the other the conveyance of beaver skins to the English.

But few savages have come down to Montreal this year and last, so that the interpreters have not had an opportunity of doing their usual trade in brandy.

The man Petit Renaud, called Velvet Mitasse, came down from

or 60 stakes in the inclosure of the town. He charged M. de Ramezay
to tell the said Sr. Deschambaut to have them supplied by the inhabitants of the said town, in accordance with the usual practice. M.
de Ramezay having spoken to the said Sr. Deschambaut about it, the
latter replied that he believed he could not do that without an order
from the Intendant. When the Governor General learnt this, he became
furiously angry against the said Sr. Deschambaut, saying that he would
certainly make him do it, and that that should permit of no delay.
Being with the Governor General at the time, I took the liberty of saying that it appeared to me that, in fact, they ought not to await the order
of the Intendant to have these stakes supplied, since, while waiting for
this order, the snows might melt, so that it would become impossible to
draw them; and I offered to speak to the said Sr. Deschambaut about
it, saying that I was sure he would make no difficulty about having
these stakes supplied as soon as possible. I therefore went to his house
next morning where I found no one but his wife. When I went back
to the Governor General's in the afternoon, he asked me whether I had
seen him; I told him I had been to his house, and had only found Mme.
Deschambaut there, but that I would go there again the next day, so
early that I hoped not to miss him. Mons. Deschambaut, having been
informed of what I had to say to him about these stakes, came to me
in my room, in the morning, where I had no great difficulty in inducing
him to have this supply of stakes furnished immediately. I went to
the Governor General's again in the afternoon. I found him in his reception room, where he was watching Lieutenant the Sr. de Martelly,
and the Sr. de Senneville, a Canadian gentleman, play piquet; and a
moment after he said to me, "Well, have you seen Deschambaut?" upon
which I replied "Yes, sir, and he will do what you wish." Notwithstanding that, he sent for the said Sr. Deschambaut next day, and
treated him with such ignominy that those who were present were quite
shocked at it.

The Governor General has adopted as a pretext for his violence [the
excuse] that I had not told him that that the said Sieur Deschambaut
had agreed to have these stakes supplied without waiting for the Intendant's orders. As to this I can assure you, My Lord, that nothing
in the world is more true than that he asked of me and I replied what
I have the honor of reporting to you above. But, My Lord, even if it
were true that he thought I had not given him an account of the inclination of the said Sr. Deschambaut, why did he not find out about it

treat the said Sr. Deschambaut and nothing could prevent him. For the Governor General has this good quality that, when he has once begun to hate anyone, it is for his whole life, and always more and more. The hatred he has for M. de Ramezay, for example, has reached a height at which it is easy to see that he is seeking every means of ruining him. It went so far that he accused him, two years ago, of having taken 40 good men from the expedition commanded by the Sieurs Deschaillons and de Rouville and included 40 bad ones in it, in order to cause it to fail. Anyone must be extremely malicious to accuse M. de Ramezay of such a thing, for there is no man more zealous or more bent on fulfilling his duty, and anyone but the Governor-General would be pleased with him, and with his scrupulous compliance with his orders, and his care in giving account to him of the affairs of his governor-ship, and that with a diligence so great that it goes so far as to rob him of rest. But, My Lord, nothing good that he can do has any merit with him, because he is not in a state of grace. I most humbly beg you, My Lord, to believe that the relationship which exists between M. de Ramezay and me has not changed my heart nor corrupted my judgment concerning him, and that it will never bring me to take advantage of the confidence with which it has pleased you to honor me, by attributing these good qualities to him if he did not possess them; and if M. de Ramezay had been capable of an action so base as that of which he was accused, I would denounce him to you, My Lord. The Intendants, who are just and enlightened, will always do him—as well as all the worthy men of the country—the justice which is due to him, as to his zeal and care in the King's service. It is this strict care which constitutes his crime with the Governor General, because he is offended by this conduct in the most sensitive part, namely, his cupidity, which might be called extreme avarice. The report, My Lord, which I shall have the honor of making to you as follows, will show it to you to its full extent.

M. de Longueil was sent to the Iroquois last autumn to learn how they were disposed towards us, because we had received information that they were to declare for the English against us. They asserted that that was not so, and that they would preserve perfect neutrality; and, in order to give us greater proofs of it, this tribe sent sixteen of their people, both men and women, to Montreal in the month of March, over the ice. They

that M. de Ramaezay had kept these belts and had sold them to the store, which he could have done according to the practice in the time of the Conte de Frontenac, for M. de Callieres never sent him the belts presented to him in his absence, but only the messages. As regards the time when M. de Callieres was Governor General, M. de Vaudreuil never received any, because he had so little confidence in him that he had forbidden him to interfere in anything. As the Governor General did not receive these belts, instead of replying to the messages and sending the savages back over the ice, he gave M. de Ramezay orders to detain them until he arrived at Montreal, because he wished to speak to them himself. All the chief officers at Montreal were greatly astonished at such an answer, not being able to understand what reason he could have for detaining these savages who were asking to go back over the ice. For my part I guessed in a moment what it was, namely, that he wanted the belts to be presented over again to him, and the same speeches delivered to him which had been made to M. de Ramezay, so that he might make a profit by these belts. And this turned out correct; for, as soon as he arrived at Montreal, which was not until nearly the end of May, he sent for the store-keeper to ask him whether M. de Ramezay had not sent him these six belts, and whether he had not received the money for them; and when the store-keeper said to him "No," that they had been sent to Fort Frontenac, he told him that he must keep an account of them for him, and took very little trouble to speak to the savages. Hence, My Lord, the Governor General, because he wanted to obtain these six belts which were worth about 130 livres, entailed an expense of more than 800 livres on the King for the food of these savages for more than two months, while they were detained against their will.

I will take the liberty of pointing out to you, My Lord, that there is an abuse in connection with these belts which does not fail to put the King to expense. For as the Governor General sells to His Majesty all those he receives from the savages, while all that he gives them cost him nothing, since he takes them from His Majesty's stores, he makes this communication between him and the savages as frequent as possible; that is to say he gives the savages belts for the smallest things he has to say to them, in order that they may answer him with other belts, so that one belt will have been sold by the Governor General to the King more than four times in one year. I am very sorry, My Lord, to be obliged to make remarks so discreditable to the one who represents the King's person here; but I thought this frankness due to the confidence with which you have been pleased to honor me, and to the deep respect I have for your orders. I am with the same feelings

PETITION FOR PENSION FOR CAPTAIN DE GRANDVILLE'S WIDOW.

Quebec, this 31st of Octr., 1710..

MM. Raudot and I had the honor, My Lord, in 1708 to beg you to be good enough to grant to the widow of the Sr. de Grandville, captain, who died in that year, the pension which her husband had from the state. I have the honor to beg you very urgently not to refuse me this favor. Madame de Grandville has remained a widow, with four children and no property. They will all pray to God for your health and prosperity; and for my part, My Lord, I shall accept this favor as if you granted it to me personally.

The Sr. d'Ervilliers, a Lieutenant, asks for a permit to go [to France] next year.

CENSUS OF DETROIT DE PONTCHARTRAIN IN THE YEAR 1710.

The inhabitants' who cultivate the land are

---

[1]The names of the inhabitants of Detroit in 1710, given in full, are as follows:

François Fafard dit Delorme, farmer and interpreter. He died January 28, 1734, aged about 80 years. His first wife was Magdeleine Marguerite Jobin and his second wife was Barbe Loisel.

Jacques Langlois, farmer and blacksmith. Born 1767; married Marie Dussault. He lived sometime in Detroit, but returned to Montreal and died there January 30, 1733.

Joseph Parent, farmer, master toolmaker and brewer. His wife was Magdeleine Marette, whom he married at Beauport, January 30, 1690.

Jacob de Marsac de Cobtrion, Sieur Desrochers. He was a sergeant in the marine department. He married Therese David. He was buried April 27, 1747 at Detroit, aged 80 years.

Delorme ⎫
Langlois ⎪
Parent ⎪ They are all married, and have
Des Rochers ⎰ their wives and children at Detroit.
La Jeunesse ⎪
Malet ⎭

Jacques Hubert dit La Croix lived in Detroit in 1709. His wife was Marie Cardinal.

Pierre Roy. He married a Miami Indian named Marguerite Ouabankikoue. It has been claimed that he lived with the Indians on or near the site of Detroit before Cadillac came.

François Masse, farmer. His wife was Marguerite Couk dit Lafleur, widow of Jean Fafard. They were married in 1702.

Jean Baptiste Turpin, son of Alexander Turpin and Charlotte Beauvais. In 1710 he married Marguerite Fafard, daughter of Jean Fafard and his wife Marguerite Comique (or Couk mentioned above).

Vin Despagne (cannot make out this name at present—the meaning of the two words would indicate a slang expression).

Pierre Chesne, so far as the church records show, he had no wife at this time. He married Jeanne Baili, but she died in 1700.

Pierre Gareau dit St. Onge, born at Boucherville, May 1, 1673. He was sometimes called Xaintonge.

Louis Gastineau, Sieur de Ste. Anne, born 1674, married Marie Jeanne Le Moine at Batiscan, January 22, 1710, died February 20, 1750. While living at Detroit he got into trouble with Cadillac and commenced a suit against him in Quebec.

Bonaventure Compien dit L'Esperance, soldier and farmer. His wife was Catherine Laplante.

Michel Campau, farmer. His wife was Jeanne Masse. She must have come to Detroit after this date (1710). He got into trouble on account of accusing another Detroit citizen of setting fire to the fort in 1703.

There were three men of the Le Moyne family in Detroit at this time, viz.; Alexis Le Moyne, Sieur de Monier; Jacques Le Moyne and René or René Alexander Le Moyne. The last named married Marie Renée Le Boulanger February 2, 1712

Despers (cannot make out this name at present).

François Benoit dit Livernois, married Angelique Chagnon in 1710.

Pierre Robert dit Lafontaine, came to Detroit with his wife and family May 19. 1708. His wife's name was Angelique Ptolomée or Tholmé. Pierre had brothers Prudent, Francois and Joseph, all of whom lived in Detroit.

Blondin dit Chevalier. Pierre Chevalier acted as God-father to an Indian baptized in Detroit, March 22, 1711. Fabeau.

Joseph Touteau, came in April, 1702, and died in Montreal in 1745. He was a carpenter.

Jean Baptist Touteau, brother of Joseph, came to Detroit with him. He married Magdeleine Parent September 1, 1715, and died in 1754.

Nicolas Rose, a soldier. He was born in 1674 and died in 1746.

Toussaint Dardennes, came to Detroit in 1707.

Joseph Despré (or Depré). There was a Jean Baptiste Despré in Detroit at a somewhat later period.

Michel Bizaillon, married Marguerite Fafard dit Delorme, June 30, 1710.

There were several people by the name of Cardinal. The only one who appears to have been a bachelor at this time was Pierre Cardinal. He came September 6.

Those who have houses only, within and without the fort, and would not take lands, are—

St. Aubin he has his wife at Detroit ⎫
Lafleur he has his wife at Detroit ⎬ Soldiers
De Lisle he has his wife at Detroit ⎭

La Croix ⎫
Le Roy ⎪
Massé ⎬ Canadians. They have their wives at Detroit.
Turpin ⎭

Vin Despagne, widower, a Canadian.

Chesne ⎫
St. Onge ⎭ Frenchmen; their wives will not go to Detroit.

　　　　　 ⎧ Gastineau ⎫ he has his wife at Three Rivers
Canadians ⎨ Lesperance ⎬ he is a bachelor
　　　　　 ⎩ Le Moyne ⎭ bachelor

Michel Campau, Canadian; his wife is at Montreal.

Mounier, bachelor
Despens, bachelor
Livernois au Gaudet, bachelor
Roberts, his wife is at Detroit
Blondin, called Chevalier, bachelor
Fabeau, his wife is at Montreal
The two brothers Trudeaux, bachelors

has damaged it severely, bad as it was before; it is a good gun-shot from the fort, between the fort of Detroit and that of the Hurons. It is absolutely necessary to rebuild the fort entirely, from one end to another. *"Hoc opus, hic labor est."*

INSTRUCTIONS GIVEN DUBUISSON BY M. DE LA FOREST.

Canada
Posts of the   Endorsed Cott L. 1711, Jan. 17.
Upper Provinces

As it is necessary that M. Dubuisson should apply himself to carry out what is contained in these instructions as to what concerns M. de La Mothe and M. de la Forest, for their interests. The said M. [Dubuisson], so that he may have nothing to reproach himself with and may not be accused of neglecting the affairs of M. de la Forest, is compelled, in order to acquit himself as a man of honor of what is due from him, to present to M. de La Mothe this memorandum, which I beg [him] very humbly to accept.

First article contained in the instructions which M. de la Forest gave M. Dubuisson.

If M. de La Mothe should ask him how I intended to act regarding his mill, his cattle and *other effects* belonging to him, *he will tell him* that *I will take over* everything that he leaves *at the fort according* to the valuation which will be made of them by skilled persons, and in case of objection on his side or mine, that we will refer it to Monseigneur de Pontchartrain, we obeying whatever order he shall make thereon.

M. Dubuisson will have only the fourteenth minot taken as *payment for grinding,* in accordance with the orders of His Majesty, which *M. de La Mothe* must have received last year, since Monseigneur de Pontchartrain sent me word about it this year.

Regarding the houses, the rents of which M. de La Mothe causes to be paid to him, *he will inquire who live in them and will tell them that it*

will tell the soldier who has charge of it that I have put him in the number of the soldiers at fort Pontchartrain.

M. de La Mothe no longer carrying on trade, I think you may make use of the warehouse in which he used to put his goods. If you should find the least objection to it, and that M. de La Mothe still wants it, it need not be thought of. It will be necessary to have wheat and peas sown .as extensively as possible this spring, supposing that they have not been sufficiently sown this autumn.

I give notice that the articles mentioned above are the same as are contained in the instructions which M. de la Forest gave me for his interests.

Executed at Fort Pontchartrain this 10th of January, 1711.

Dubuisson.

As I have learnt, Sir some days ago that you were granting contracts *for lands and places within the fort to those who asked you for them,* I am compelled, Sir, to beg you to await the arrival of M. de la Forest, and to remember that I have had the honor to show you the articles which make mention of the claims which M. de la Forest has in this post. I have shown you the letter which Mgr. de Pontchartrain wrote to him; moreover I have the honor to inform you that he must divide up the fort in a different manner from what it now is, and on a smaller scale.

I have also been warned, Sir, that you had told the inhabitants that you would grant them *arable lands to sow* [in] *the spring; permit me, Sir, if you please, to have the honor to inform you that* the thing is impossible, these lands being domains of this place, and moreover you would take away from me the means of having seed sown in accordance with my orders concerning it from M. de la Forest; it is of too great

the honor to deduce for you, so much the more because the King's service demands it, to speak to them about payment for the animals, that is to overcome them. You know that we are not in a condition to go with them so quickly.

I beg you also, Sir, to be good enough to keep 10 minots of wheat for me, in order to make the said sowings, on paying you a reasonable price for them, seeing that you alone have French wheat to sell.

I am also obliged to inform you, Sir, that I have a verbal order from, M. Raudot to caution you on no account to sell the animals you possess, as it is necessary that they should be attached to the domain of this place, and to oppose it in case you should wish to disregard [this order].

As also to hand over to me some powder and shot for the defense of the fort, in case of attack. Of these, you have received, Sir, 800# from the King, and 500# of shot, as it is laid down in the order of M. Baudot, which has been given me; and that you should hand over to me the remainder, and an account of the quantities you have consumed of them, on giving you a receipt for those you hand over to me.

Given at the Fort Pontchartrain this 17th of January, 1711.

Dubuisson.

MEMORANDUM TO SERVE AS INSTRUCTIONS FROM THE MARQUIS DE VAUDREUIL TO THE OFFICERS AND *VOYAGEURS* DESPATCHED TO BRING DOWN TO MONTREAL THE SAVAGES OF THE UPPER COUNTRY.

Endorsed—10th of March 1711 (Detroit.)

Philippe de Rigaud Marquis de Vaudreuil, Knight of the Military order of St. Louis, Governor and Lieutenant General for the King throughout all New France.

The various movements of our enemies, and the false reports they spread abroad among the savages settled with us, with the object of alienating them from us, show that they intend to make an effort to come to this country this year; it has therefore appeared to us of the utmost importance, and we have thought it to be of consequence to the interests of the King's service, to bring the savages of the upper country allied to us down here, not only to obtain reinforcements of men in this way, but also to show the Iroquois that the moment they declare themselves against us the tribes of the upper country will fall upon them. This consideration having made it necessary for us to make choice of

various persons of influence with the savages, to take our orders at the
same time to the different posts it is necessary to go to, we have chosen
the Sr d'Argenteuil, captain of the troops maintained by His Majesty
in this country, to go to Fort Pontchartrain at Detroit and to Saquinau
and to bring here as many of the savages as possible; and as our will
is that he should also bring the Mississagues, Sauteurs and other savages whom he may meet, we have thought fit to send him by the French
River, so that, on his way to Detroit Pontchartrain by Lake Huron, he
may meet these savages who, according to the last news we received and
(after) the attack of Paskoüé, have retired to these parts.

Since the Fort Pontchartrain at Detroit is now, as it were, the centre
of affairs and the place where almost all the tribes assemble, because
of the goods they find there and the ease with which they can go from
that place to the English, the Sr d'Argenteuil should use every endeavor
to attract all the savages here if possible, and particularly as many
as he can of the chiefs and important men of the Outtavois and Hurons
and also the warriors, and, in order to avoid the belts which the English
might send in an underhand way among these savages, if they proceeded
by the lakes, the Sr. d'Argenteuil will take them by the French River,
informing them that that is the general place of assembly of all the
tribes, and that there they will receive further orders from us; if we
have any to send them before they arrive down here.

The Sr. d'Argenteuil will inform all these savages that our war with
the English is not only a war of religion for those who love to pray,
but also that it is to their interest not to allow the English to become
the sole masters of this continent, because they would not fail to make

together, especially when they meet at the French River to come down here and all take one and the same road.

As the sole reason which makes it necessary for us to despatch the messengers we are sending is to arrange for the savages generally who are allied to us to come down here, nothing could be so opposed to it as for those who go up, to take goods with them; for, if the savages find goods to be traded for up there, there would be a good many of them who would not come down. Moreover it is likewise probable that if the French people who go up have goods to get rid of, they would delay the savages up there in coming down as long as they could, so that they might succeed in selling their goods, which would be most inconsistent with the welfare of the King's service and with our object, viz: to bring down all the savages. Therefore, under penalty of being punished for disobedience and of being deprived of the privilege of going up there again as a recompense for this present journey, we forbid any *voyageur* and also the officers and those in command of the boats that go up, to take any goods on their own account, except those we issue to them from the King's stores, for making presents to the savages, and goods to the value of sixty livres for each *voyageur* personally for the purpose of obtaining provisions up there, and also boats, if they come to be in need of them, permission being given to the Sr. d'Argenteuil, to the Sr. de St. Pierre, and to the other officers, and to those in command of boats, in view of certain expenses which they will necessarily be obliged to incur, to take goods on their own account to the value of forty livres each, in addition. And, in order that this present permission of ours may not give rise to any irregularity, we command the Sr. d'Argenteuil, the Sr. de St. Pierre, and the Sieurs de Vincenne and Desliettes, and the Sieurs Reaume and Le Moyne, and all the *voyageurs* who are to go on this journey, each to give M. de Ramezay, before leaving, an invoice, signed and certified as true, of the goods they are taking on their own account, so that a strict examination may be made of them at such places as Mons. de Ramezay may think fit to have it made, in accordance with our orders; and we also make the Sr. d'Argenteuil, and the others in command of boats, responsible for any frauds that may be committed by the *voyageurs* who go with them, if they do not give notice of them.

The same reason which makes us order the Sr. d'Argenteuil to return with the savages he brings from Detroit, by the French River, induces us likewise to direct all whom we are sending up there with our orders to come back to that river, and it is desirable that, before they set out with the Sr. d'Argenteuil, they should all agree on the time, approximately, at which they will be able to get back there, and on a spot for a meeting place so that those who get there first can wait for the

others. The Sr. de St. Pierre, having orders from us to go to Michilimakina as soon as he leaves the Sr. d'Argenteuil at the lower part of
the French River, will proceed to the said place as speedily as possible
and will communicate our orders to the reverend Father Marest there,
and will make known our intentions to the savages he finds there, and
will then go to the settlement of Longekam and to the Bay where the
Folles Avoines are, and in accordance with our orders above for the Sr.
d'Argenteuil, will use every means to bring to us here the largest possible number of these savages, and especially chiefs and important persons, but above all a large number of warriors.

He will do the same at Michilimakina; and in accordance with the
arrangement made, he will proceed within the time stated to the lower
part of the French River with all the savages whom he has succeeded
in inducing to come down with him.

The Sr. Reaume, having been chosen by us to take our orders to Lake
Superior, to the Ste. Marie falls, to Kiouanan and Chagouamigon and
other places on the said lake, will comply with our orders as above,
and will likewise proceed to the lower part of the French River to the
general meeting place, like the rest.

As the Sr. Lemoyne is sent to the Fox Indians only, he will go to
Michilimakina in company with the Sr. de St. Pierre, unless he obtains
reliable information on the way that these savages have settled at Fort
Pontchartrain at Detroit, in which case, without going to Michilimakina
he will proceed with the Sr. d'Argenteuil, but, if he obtains no certain
information of the said Fox Indians on the way, he will go to Michilimakina, and having arrived there he will ascertain the place where these
savages now are, and on finding out for certain whether their settlement is at Detroit, the St. Joseph River, or at their old quarters, he will
go there with his boat, and will use all his tact for the purpose of bring-

the upper part of Lake St. François, and having arrived there will wait until the navigation is free, if it is not so on their arrival; they will proceed to Fort Frontenac to obtain news, and will deliver our letters there, and will then repair, as speedily as possible, to Fort Pontchartrain at Detroit; and if they fall in with any Mississagues, Saulteurs or other savages allied to us, they will tell them that the Sr. d'Argenteuil has gone to Fort Pontchartrain at Detroit by the great river, and that there is news of importance to be told there, and will write them to go and hear it there, without giving them any further explanation.

When the Sr. de Vincenne reaches Detroit he will find out the place where the Miamis are now settled, and if he can go to it in his boat by the great river, which is in Lake Erie, he will go; if not, he will proceed overland, sending his boat, together with that of the Sr. Desliettes, to the St. Joseph River to wait for him. In this case the Sr. Desliettes will put a man from his boat into the Sr. de Vincenne's so that the said Sr. de Vincenne may take two of his men with him by land, to accompany him and to carry part of the King's presents, if necessary.

The Sr. de Vincenne, being fully aware of our intentions, and of the necessity that exists for bringing some of the Miamis to us here, so that the other tribes may not have reason to fear them during their absence, will leave no stone unturned to bring some of them down here, especially chiefs and men of importance; and if he thinks, when he is at Detroit, that the children of St. Souanne would be of use to him for the success of our orders, he may employ them, our will being that the Sr. d'Argenteuil and the Sr. Dubuisson, to whom we are writing, should act in concert with him in this matter.

The Sr. de Vincenne will induce the Miamis and other savages whom he may meet, to come by the St. Joseph River, so as to avoid passing through the Lakes, for the reasons we have stated above, and also that they may join the rest of the tribes who are to go by the French River, in accordance with our orders, to come down here.

The Sr. Desliettes, being appointed to take our orders to the great river, where Companissé is, and to the Sakis, Poutouatamis and other savages settled on the St. Joseph River, will set out from Detroit as soon as the Sr. de Vincenne has taken his detachment, and will go to the great river, where Companissé is, and will invite him to come to Montreal, as well as the other savages with him. He will afterwards go to the St. Joseph River to explain our orders to the savages there, and will there act in concert with the Reverend Father Chardon who is there, and with the Sieur de Vincenne when he arrives. Above all he will not forget to bring Oulamek down here, and in going back by the great river he will take Companissé and the others who have promised to come with him, and will go, together with the Sr. de Vincenne, to the French River as soon as they possibly can, according to the time agreed on.

It would be preferable for all the tribes to be assembled at Michilimakina or the French River, before making the presents; but, as that appears to be impossible, those who are charged with the duty of giving them must at least do so in such a manner that the savages may feel obliged to us for·them, and that it may cause no jealousy between them. It is also necessary to manage so that no dispute may arise on the way between the various tribes assembled,· and they may not renew any old quarrel. This is a matter to which those who are charged with our orders must give most particular attention; and if they should find, on their arrival up there that any of the tribes are at war with one another, they must all, with one mind, act in concert to heal the troubles so that that may cause no delay to our purpose of bringing the savages down here.

As His Majesty forbids trading in brandy with the savages, we forbid anyone whosoever he may be, to take any brandy to give to the savages under any pretext whatever, on pain of incurring the utmost rigor of His Majesty's decrees on this point; provided only that, in view of the somewhat late season and the coldness of the water, each *voyageur* shall be permitted to take four pots to drink on the journey, on condition·that they do not give any to the savages; and if they take any larger quantity they shall be deprived of the right of going up there again, besides being punished on their return for the wrong use they have made· of it.

His Majesty having consented, at our request and that of the Intendant, to grant an amnesty to the recalcitrant *voyageurs* in the upper country, the Sr. d'Argenteuil, the Sr. de St. Pierre and all who are charged with carrying our orders, will notify the said *voyageurs* of it at the various posts they go to, and will inform them that if they do not take advantage of this pardon which His Majesty consents to grant them, and if they do not come here with them at once to take service in the Colony, there will be no hopes of pardon left to them, and we shall send next year in pursuit of them in accordance with the King's order, to whatever places they may withdraw.

This order of ours, being a general one, will be common to the Sr.

WHO CAME DOWN FROM THE UPPER COUNTRY.

Index letter F.

Endorsed—

Words of the Governor General to the savages who came down from the upper country.

I am greatly pleased, Outtavois of Michilimakina, Saulteurs, Malominy, Sakis, people of Longekain, Poutouatamis, Outtavois of Detroit, Hurons, Miamis, Outtagamis, land folk, and generally, all the tribes here present, who have come down to hearken to my word. I am greatly pleased to see you assembled before me, and to know that you have all come down on the invitations which were given to you by the officers and others of my French people whom I sent to the upper country to bring you down.

Since the season is advancing, I have resolved to send you back in a short time; but I am very glad first to explain to you what my opinions are. I am also very glad to make known to you all that it is not the assistance I have claimed from you, which compelled me to bring you down. My intention was, seeing you all here, to reunite your minds and to induce you to live together as brothers, so that forming but one and the same body, you may henceforth have but one and the same mind.

I will not repeat, what I have already said several times to you all separately, how much trouble and care I have taken, since the general peace was concluded, to keep you at peace and in union with one another, or between you and your brothers, the Iroquois. You all know quite well of what I am speaking, and there are none of you here to whom I have not made known, either in public or in private, how greatly your dissensions affected me. I desire to open my heart to you again; and, that no one may be able to complain, I shall speak to you all, tribe by tribe, one after another.

*   *   *

Words to savages of Detroit.

You, Outtavois of Detroit and Hurons, were witnesses of the culpable attack which the Mississagues, who were returning from trading with the English, made upon the Miamis, who, like you, were coming down to hear my word. You know that those who made this attack were not intoxicated, and this should satisfy you that those men were hired by the English to stir up quarrels and to prevent you from coming to listen to me.

I look upon this murder as a matter that has occurred to me myself, for I was taking my children, the Miamis, by the hand to bring them here. Therefore, as you have always joined the chiefs of the French, since you have been at Detroit, in adjusting troublesome affairs, I exhort you Otonsu, you Eleouaoucassé, and you Outchipouat, and you, people of Sastoressy, together with all the chiefs of your villages, I exhort you all, when you get back, to join with M. Dubuisson to compel Skou-tache and Makouamité, who were witnesses of the affair, to give up the man Sipy, the murderer, into the hands of M. Dubuisson, in order that he may give him to the Miamis and in that way give them satisfaction for the evil deed that has been done to them, just as Paskoué did here when he gave up one of his children to me in reparation for his tribe having murdered an Iroquois last year.

Besides this first attack which the Missisagués made on the Miamis, I have informed you of what M. Dubuisson wrote to me regarding the two Miamis who were slain by the Renards' at Detroit. I am writing to him to inquire into this matter in order to have reparation made to the one who is entitled to it. I therefore exhort you my children, Outtavois and Hurons, to support M. Dubuisson in this matter so that the land may be at peace at Detroit, and not in future to permit any tribe to disturb it. It is with you my children Sasteressy and Outtavois, to whom I am speaking, you who, together with the French, started the settlement at Detroit, who like myself had no other object in forming that settlement save peace and rest only, I say it is with yourselves, my children, that you must begin. Cast off, then, and put far from you the evil suspicions you may have entertained, one of another, so that together with M. Dubuisson you may inspire with your spirit the people who have recently come to dwell in our lands.

that he may have reparation made by the one who is wrong to the one who is in the right. My will is that both of you remain in peace upon your mats, for I do not approve of the attack which the Outtagamis made upon you any more than of that which the Oyatanon made on them.

I learnt last year, Outtagamis, that you had come to take up your abode with my children at Detroit. I thought you would at the same time, adopt their spirit and would obey the will of him whom I have set there to command and to rule all the tribes of those districts. Words to Outagami

I learnt today from the mouth of all men, that you think yourselves masters of that place, and, far from having brought peace there, you have brought nothing but disorder, and have shed the blood of my children there. I am ordering M. Dubuisson, who is in command, to inquire into the matter of which he has written to me, so that he may see that reparation is made to the party injured, for I do not approve of the attack which the Oyatanous made on you any more than that which you made on them and on the Peauguichia.

I have moreover learned from the letter which M. Dubuisson has written me that certain evil-disposed persons among the Outtagamis had formed the intention of preparing ambushes for the return of my children, the Miamis and Hurons, who have come here to listen to my word. If they are attacked on the way, I rely on you, Outtavois, who are returning with them, that the Frenchmen who are to accompany the Miamis, the Outtagamis and the Hurons who are going up again may enter in peace into the fort of Detroit, and that you may all form but one company together.

I am very glad to tell you, Outtagamis, that I wish the country of Detroit to be peaceful, that I encourage all my children there to take all possible care to that end, and to unite with me to succeed in it. It will only depend on you, Outtagamis, whether there shall be rest and peace in these parts.

I also intend the war you have with the Ilinois to be stopped, for you should not doubt that the Ilinois are among the number of my children. To this end I stay your axe with this belt, not only against my children of Detroit and its surroundings, but also against the Ilinois. And as the Kikapoos are united with you in one and the same body, I arrest their axe also by this belt, and give you both this tobacco that

Pay attention, Outtagamis, to what I have just said to you; do not draw down upon you all the tribes in the land. My opinion is that you would do better to go back to your old village, where the bones of your fathers are, and a great part of your people also, rather than try to settle in a strange land where you may be insulted by all the tribes. Reflect once more, Outtagamis, on what I have just said to you, for it is for your preservation.

ds to
kepia a
pou

I praise you, Kakikepia for having prevented your tribe from continuing the war against the Ilinois. M. de Tonty has assured me that you told him that your men would remain at peace in your village. To induce you to remain always of the same disposition, there is some tobacco which I give you, for them to smoke when you get back.

*　　　*　　　*　　·

CADILLAC ASKS TO KNOW THE WILL OF HIS MAJESTY.

To the Marquis de Vaudreuil, Knight of the military order of Saint Louis, Governor and Lieutenant General of New France.

Sir, ·

Having been in possession of Detroit since the 28th of September, 1705, I beg that you will explain to me the will of His Majesty in regard to the letter which you did me the honor to write me on the 13th of September last.

The following is a summary of the said letter.—His Majesty having invested you with the government of Louisianna, and having chosen, at the same time, M. de la Forest as commander at Detroit on the same condition as [those on which] you have held it until now, I was unable to refuse M. de la Forest [the services of] M. Dubuisson, Lieutenant of the company of Vasseur, for which he applied to me, to go and take

I beg you will explain it to me so that I may be able to comply with it.

M. Dubuisson who commands at the said Detroit in the absence of M. de la Forest, has claimed that the lands [here] belong to him, the mill, the cattle and generally all my goods, movable or otherwise which are at the said place Detroit, according to the valuation of them which is to be made by skilled men; and to that end without more preliminaries, he has prohibited the miller from paying me for the grinding of the mill, the inhabitants from paying me the income of my estates or the rent of my houses, and from buying my cattle; claiming that I have no right either to sell or enjoy them.

M. Dubuisson relies on his instructions from M. de la Forest for all his acts of violence, availing himself of the authority of his office, without being willing either to pay for all these things or to give security for the payment; a course which is quite contrary both to reason and to justice. M. de la Forest in the letter he wrote me on the 1st of October last, takes upon himself to appropriate all the possessions remaining to me at Detroit, according to a valuation which is to be made by skilled persons, and in case of any objection either on my part or on his, he states that he will refer the matter to Monseigneur. He makes a similar offer in the first paragraph of the instructions he has given to the said M. Dubuisson, who has forwarded it to me certified and signed by him and several others.

Moreover, Sir, the said M. de la Forest enjoys all the revenues and profits of the whole of Detroit, monopolizes commerce there, forbids and excludes from trading those who have trading rights, and will make no arrangement with me, which does me a great injury especially as I have to withdraw from this country in accordance with the King's commands and go and rule at Louisianna. On the statement which I have the honor to make to you, I beg you Sir to settle immediately on what terms and in what manner the said M. de la Forest is to possess and enjoy Detroit, and whether he is not bound to accept it on the conditions which were laid down for me by His Majesty on the 14th of June 1704, and by the contract made with the agents of the said Company of the colony on the 28th of September, 1705; further to restrain him from taking over the mill, my cattle, animals and generally all my goods according to his offers as before stated; and, in default of his paying me for them or giving me security for payment, to [compel him] to abandon the said place Detroit and any claims he may have to it, and to repay me the money he has received from those who have been in trade at the said Detroit, also to those who hold the right to trade there under their contracts; to forbid him likewise to disturb me in my possession, as also the inhabitants who are settled there and who may

Since you have promised me eight men to send for my family, I beg you Sir to put an end to this matter at once, so that I may send my orders by the same opportunity. You will permit me moreover to warn you that that post is in much danger and that it will be very necessary for M. de la Forest to reside there if he intends to accept this arrangement.

I cannot, Sir, proceed in this matter at law because no judge can be informed as to the will of His Majesty; you alone know it and can interpret it.

At Montreal this 15th of June, 1711.

[Signed]　La Motte Cadillac.

CADILLAC TRIES TO SELL HIS PERSONAL EFFECTS TO DE LA FOREST.

Endorsed—Cotte N. 1st of July, 1711.

I, Antoine de La Mothe Cadillac, formerly Commander for the King and now governor of Louisiana, having received a letter from the Marquis de Vaudreuil on the 13th of Sept., 1710, by which he informs me that His Majesty has granted the said fort of Pontchartrain to M. de la Forest on the same terms as I have held it until now, which said M. de la Forest has sent M. Dubuisson, Lieutenant of the King's forces, to the said fort to take possession of it; the said M. Dubuisson being also charged with instructions from M. de la Forest, as appears from the memorandum of the said M. Dubuisson which was given to me on the 17th of January of the present year and likewise [from his] having sent me a letter of M. de la Forest of the first of October, *1710*; which instructions of M. Dubuisson [and] the said letter of M. de la Forest declare that the said M. de la Forest will come to terms with me concerning my mill, my animals, and generally all the effects belonging to me which I leave at the said fort *according to the valuation which*

buisson, on the 19th of January of the present year, to learn from him
whether he holds full power from the said M. de la Forest to treat
with me for all my property, both real and personal, *and whether he
can pay me ready money for my said property, or at least give me a
bail or security for payment for it, and likewise to be good enough to
give me a copy of the order of the King under which it was decided
that I stand dispossessed of all my said property;* afterwards I made
my protest against it on the 15th of April of this present year, having
come into the town of Montreal where I found the Governor general,
to whom I presented a memorandum of the 16th of June last by which
I beg him to explain to me the intentions of the King as to the letter
which he wrote me on the 13th of Sept. 1710, with the other reasons
contained in the said memorandum, to which my said M. de Vaudreuil
replied to me on the 18th of June last that His Majesty put M. de la
Forest in possession of Detroit on the same conditions as I have had
it, and *it is for the minister himself to settle the differences unless we
refer them to the Intendant* who is appointed in order to administer
justice to everyone in this country; after which I went down to Quebec
where I presented an explanatory memorandum to M. Raudot which
he returned to me without being pleased to settle anything between
me and the said M. de la Forest, [I] having made an offer in his presence
to said M. de la Forest to hand over to him my mill, my animals and,
generally, all the belongings which I have at the said Detroit according to the valuation which will be made of them, on his paying me in
ready money or in furs; to which the said M. de la Forest replied that
he had no money at all, and thereupon I answered him that I would
grant him proper time [to pay] on giving me security for my payment, on account of the large sums he owes, in which [payment] his
creditors might [otherwise] share at so many shillings in the pound;
to which the said M. de la Forest said that he had sought everywhere
for securities and he had found but few. On this declaration I begged
the Intendant to permit me to sell my said belongings on the spot; to
which the said M. de la Forest replied that he opposed it, and immediately I demanded of him that he should have the animals and all
my said property taken to Montreal at his expense and at his risk,
reserving all expenses, damages and interest against him. After all
these disputes, the Intendant having declined to settle anything, sent
me back to Mgr. the Comte de Pontchartrain. The said M. de la Forest
availing himself of the interest he had with the persons who had the
right to judge us, has made proposals to me which he has drawn up in
writing; and having examined them, in consequence of the refusal and
denial of justice by the Governor general and the Intendant, I am com-

erty at Detroit, to subscribe and sign the said agreement or proposals against the validity of which I protest, [claiming] all expenses, damages and interest from the said M. de la Forest and others, as compulsory and obtained by violence and against all those [agreements] that I may hereafter sign on the subject of the disputes between the said M. de la Forest and me, regarding the said post of Detroit.

At Quebec, this 1st of July, 1711.

Signed   La Mothe Cadillac.

AGREEMENT MADE BETWEEN MM. DE LA MOTHE AND DE LA FOREST.

Endorsed—Annexed to the letter of M. de Vaudreuil of the 7th and 8th of Nov. 1711.

Cotte F.

Proposals, considered between MM. De La Mothe and de la Forest to put an end to the misunderstandings which have arisen between them on the subject of the command of the fort of Detroit Pontchartrain, granted to my said M. de la Forest, and of the property at the said Detroit belonging to my said M. De La Mothe, the parties being agreed moreover to refer the matter to the orders of the Comte de Pontchartrain.

As my said M. De la Forest is not in a condition to pay my said M. De La Mothe for the property which he has at the said Detroit, whether in animals or in merchandise and movables, which he values at more than thirty thousand livres, nor to find anyone here who will guarantee for him the payment for them, and that yet it will be difficult for my said M. De la Forest to keep up that post this year on the conditions laid down in his instructions if he cannot make use of the said goods believing that he is acting in accordance with the will of His Majesty, he has offered the said M. de la Forest to give him a gratuity of two hundred French crowns payable on the arrival of the ships in 1712, the time at which the differences between them concerning the property, real and personal, which the said M. de La Mothe possesses at the said fort of Detroit, will be settled by the Minister; consenting also that the said M. de la Forest, who has this autumn sent up by M. Dubuisson some goods in order to trade with them at Detroit, may do so, [it being] well understood that he will not send up any other [goods] in future, and that the officers who go up to Detroit by the consent of the Governor General shall carry on trade for the profit of the said M. de La Mothe, as he has carried it on until now.

And if, on the arrival of the ships of next year, there shall remain at Detroit goods belonging to M. de La Mothe or agents of his, he shall bring them down at his cost and expense without M. de la Forest being obliged to take them over, nor shall it be permitted to the said M. de La Mothe to negotiate about them, or to sell them either to Frenchmen or to savages, if he does not prefer to sell them to the said M. de la Forest at Montreal prices, provided always that the said goods are good and saleable.

The said M. de la Forest, ever ready to obey the King's commands, has entered into all these motives, not only because that puts an end to all differences which might exist between the said M. de La Mothe and him, being very glad for the said M. de La Mothe to have all his securities for the effects which may belong to him, but also on account of his health, which he knows to be so bad in consequence of the ailments by which it is now attacked and which may cease next year, and so [he may] be in a fit state to obey the order of Monseigneur and go in person to command at Detroit de Pontchartrain.

All the proposals above will be presented by MM. de la Mothe and de la Forest to the Governor general, in order to obtain his consent and to do nothing except by his good pleasure; the Intendant to whom they have been communicated having agreed to them, being persuaded that they are in no way contrary to [the interests of] the King's service, but on the contrary that they are in accordance with such interests, whether as regards the health of the said M. de la Forest, or the development of the post, or further because that ends all the differences which the said MM. de La Mothe and de la Forest could have one with another; my said Intendant having also declared that it would be a

Approved by us the undersigned [including] the part in the margin
of the second page, the interlineation, also in the said page and the
interlineation in the same way in the third [page]. Signed, La Mothe.
Cadillac and De la Forest. And below is written:

We, the Intendant, certify that we have seen the above writing which
we have found to agree with our opinion. Made out in duplicate at
Quebec in our house.

The 3rd of July 1711.   Signed—Raudot.

MEMORANDUM OF M. DE LA FOREST IN WHICH HE ASKS [PERMISSION] TO GO TO HIS POST.

Endorsed—annexed to the letter of M. de Vaudreuil of the 7th, &
8th November, 1711.

Cotte f.

To M...... M. the Marquis de Vaudreuil, Governor and Lieutenant-
general of New France:

Sir, In consequence of the news, which I learn on arrival at this
town, from the Frenchmen who come down from Detroit, and from the
letters I receive from that place, that all is in [a state of] conflagration
there and that our savages settled [there], and our allies who are at a
distance are waging a cruel war against each other and kill each other
every day, in consequence of this news, which shows me the necessity
for my presence at that post, I beg your to approve of my proceeding
there at once. The agreement which I made at Quebec with M. de La
Mothe being only conditional, and having been made at a time when
we were both at liberty to think that all would be quiet at Detroit,
ought not to affect prejudicially the interests of the Service.

At Montreal this 14th of July, 1711.

Signed. De la Forest.

ANSWER OF M. DE LA MOTHE TO THE MEMORANDUM OF M. DE LA FOREST OF THE 14TH JULY 1711.

Cotte G.

To the Marquis de Vaudreuil, Knight of the military order of Saint Louis, and Governor general of New France.

Sir, I had the honor to present a memorandum to you in which I begged you to be good enough to explain to me the will of His Majesty, and in what manner Detroit was granted to M. de la Forest, Monseigneur the Comte de Pontchartrain having done me the honor to write to me that the King had given the command of it to him in my stead and place.

The answer which you made to my said memorandum lays down, Sir, that His Majesty granted the said Detroit to M. de la Forest on the same footing and under the same conditions as I had it, and not being willing to decide anything, you referred me and the said M. de la Forest, as to what concerns our interests in regard to the said post, to M. Raudot, Intendant of this country, as being appointed here to dispense justice to everyone.

In accordance with your answer I went down to Quebec and I, as well as the said M. de la Forest, applied to M. Raudot, Intendant; and, after we had each pleaded our own cause, this matter was drawn out in the form of proposals which, having been examined both on the part of the said M. de la Forest and on my part, we agreed to, copied out fair, and signed in good and proper form, and on being presented to the Intendant he agreed to them and declared them to be in accordance with his opinion, as you have seen.

As you did not wish, Sir, to take cognizance of what concerns my interests and those of M. de la Forest regarding our disputes as to Detroit, having sent us to the Intendant to adjust them, it appears that the Intendant approved of the plan we adopted of presenting our agreement to you in order to obtain your approval which involves only what concerns the nomination of the officers and the command, which cannot be understood in any other way without giving offence, if it appears [to be] the intention of the Intendant, to whom M. de la Forest and I have been referred by you, Sir, in order to obtain a settlement concerning our claims as to our interests:—

It happens, Sir, notwithstanding, that you are sending M. de la Forest to Detroit to command there, to the detriment of the said agreement. You hold all authority in this country; therefore we can only, and ought only to obey you and abstain from opposition. Yet I hope you will not think it wrong that I beg you to forbid the said M. de la Forest to have any merchandise taken to the said Detroit in the future, to give up the trading to me entirely, in whatever way it can be done, in a word, to enjoy peaceably all the property whether personal or real at Detroit, in the manner, and just as it is explained in the agreement made and settled at Quebec on the 3rd of this month, I obeying, however, the intentions of His Majesty in all that concerns the said trading.

The question, Sir, is now no longer one of explaining or interpreting the intentions of the Court as to my claims and those of M. de la Forest. For the present that difficulty is removed, the matter is of a different nature; it is a question of giving judgment on an agreement made between M. de la Forest and me. If he wishes to return, contrary to it, he should make application before the Intendant, whom he has recognized as the judge, as well as I, regarding what concerns our interests, in accordance with the reference you made, not wishing to take cognizance of it all. I do not think the said M. de la Forest can return, in the face of his signature; he is not a minor, nor under the care of a guardian. Hence our agreement must hold; and, if he wishes now to go to Detroit because of his honor, why did he not entertain this same sentiment ten or twelve days ago, when the said agreement was made; his honor, then, must have been asleep for the time. And since he declared himself in his said agreement to be unable to make the journey to Detroit on account of his bad health which he did not expect to be re-established until next year, by what miracle does he find himself healed in a week, [and] so much better than [he has been] for nearly a year, since when he has [had] his orders to go to his post, but has not set about repairing thither; yet he has been going and coming as he does now.

Be that as it may, Sir, he can go and take command at Detroit; I must not oppose your will, but only beg you to take in hand the execution of our said agreement in what concerns our interests, and to prevent M. de la Forest from going beyond [it] until the Intendant has given his judgment, before whom you sent us, offering to pay the sum to which I bound myself towards him in the time prescribed, the whole until Monseigneur has settled the other claims we both have, regarding Detroit.

having voluntarily withdrawn from it by the agreement which he made with me, it being always understood that the said M. de Marigny will be invested with my rights according to and in conformity with the conditions laid down in the said agreement made between the said M. de la Forest and me, on the third of this month. If you grant me this just and reasonable request, you will give me the means of receiving payment for all the property I have at the said Detroit, without losing anything, because the said M. De Marigny pays me ready money according to the arrangement we have made, giving me securities for the said payment on the return of my family and their arrival at this place, which will be towards the end of September, according to the inventory which will be made of it; with which surety and security I am content and satisfied, the said M. De Marigny binding himself moreover to do all that may be necessary for the development and preservation of the post.

And in case, Sir, you should refuse me the just favors I ask from you, which are to enjoy the profit of my agreement of the third of this month made with M. de la Forest, permit me to abandon Detroit to you [with] all my property in general that I possess at the said place, being unable to act otherwise as I am compelled to yield to your authority, hoping that His Majesty will have regard to the great loss I am sustaining and will provide means of compensating me.

Given at Montreal this sixteenth of July 1711.

Signed.   La Mothe Cadillac.

REPLY TO CADILLAC'S CLAIMS.

To the Marquis de Vaudreuil, Knight of the Military order of St. Louis, and Governor general of New France.

Sir, In reply to the claims of M. de La Mothe, which you have been good enough to communicate to me, on the subject of the agreement which we made together regarding the command and the trade of Detroit:

I told you, Sir, that this agreement was made between M. de La Mothe and me in order to settle and end certain disputes between us on the subject of the remaining goods which he says he left at Detroit, and because we thought everything quite tranquil at Detroit, and also so as not to expose me, without strong reasons, to the fatigue of so long and laborious a journey as that to Detroit, on account of my ill health :—

But having learnt on my arrival at Montreal from the letters written to me from Detroit and from all the travelers who come from there, the great disorder and the misunderstanding there is between the French and the savages at Detroit, and the war that there is between the savages settled there and the savages our allies, who are at a distance, and who are killing each other everyday, I thought that in order to remedy all these evils I ought not to hesitate to ask you, Sir, for your permission to go and take command of my post, where, without vanity, I absolutely believe my presence necessary, and that it is for the service of the King and my duty for the preservation of this post in the conditions in which things [now] are, that I should at once proceed there, which you have had the goodness to grant me.

When the Intendant is informed of the troubles and disorders that there are at Detroit, as you are Sir, and of the reasons which I have for going there, I am quite convinced that he will have no regard to the agreement which we have made, M. de La Mothe and I, partly on account of my ill-health, and that on the contrary he will be pleased with my intention to go there as soon as ever I can, in order to put an end to all these disturbances, which, if not promptly set right, might cause the ruin of that post, and cause it to be abandoned by the French inhabitants and traders there. And as I am going presently to develop that post, and as it is necessary that I bear the expense of it, how can M. de La Mothe take it into his head that I shall let him carry on the trading. He need not think he will impress people by the specious and elaborate arguments which he uses only for the purpose of perpetuating his hold on Detroit.

With reference to what my said M. de La Mothe says, that I ask now to go to Detroit because my honor demands it, and how is it I did not entertain the same feeling ten or twelve days ago when our agreement was made, and that my honor must then have been asleep:—

I have already had the honor of informing you, Sir, that when we

should send any clerk that he thinks fit, to sell the goods that are left, and which he has been unable hitherto to dispose of. That, Sir, is what I hope you will give serious attention to, as well as the Intendant.

At Montreal, the 17th of July, 1711.[1]

PORTION OF REV. FATHER CHERUBIN DE NIAN'S LETTER TO CADILLAC.

Canada
Posts
of the
Upper Provinces.

Paragraph from the letter of the Revd. Father Cherubin de Nian,[2] recollet and missionary at the fort of Detroit, written to M. de La Mothe, who was at Quebec, dated the 24th of August, 1711.

In fact, Sir, Detroit is all in commotion, both within and without; order and subordination, whether spiritual or civil no longer exist, nor respect for authority, political or ecclesiastical. M. Dubuisson has had the fort cut into halves, has turned Madame out and also the Church, and, consequently, me with the six chief families here, namely de Lorme, Parent, Mallet, Roy, Robert and Campos. I have forgotten the surgeon, who is not less necessary than the interpreter. It seems, from the bearing this M. Dubuisson adopts towards us, that he is infallible, invulnerable, and invincible. I do not say more on this subject, for, if I were to tell you all, and to sketch the portrait of Detroit for you as it is, it is terrible, it would affright you. As for me, I no longer live there. I languish and suffer there beyond everything that could be imagined, seeing its desolation and being unable to go away from it. Yet God be praised for all things, since nothing happens to us in this life but by the will of adorable Providence, and for our santification; when we do not oppose its designs.

---

[1] (Not signed.)—C. M. B.
[2] Franciscan friar.—G. M. B.

INVENTORY OF CADILLAC'S DETROIT PROPERTY.

Inventory to be attached to the papers of M. de La Mothe.
Inventory made at Detroit of the property, personal and real
of M. de La Motte
Cotté F.

General Inventory of the buildings, the mill, the animals, the merchandise, the tools, furniture, fixtures and other effects belonging to
the M. de La Mothe Cadillac, Governor of Louisiana, which are now at
Detroit in the hands of M. Roy, an inhabitant of that place.

To wit.

A mill of wood, about thirty-four feet high and thirty feet eight inches
in diameter with all its rigging except the sail-cloths which are worth
nothing.

1 stout cable for raising the grinding-stone of the mill
1 ditto of medium thickness for turning to the wind
46# of plaster
an S-piece of iron weighing ten livres
1 crow-bar of iron for raising the millstone, weighing 15#
2 hammers weighing together 21#
1 sledge-hammer of iron weighing ten livres.
1 small hatchet with a hammer
1 large [ditto] of iron for *piyer Lenyard.*
1 sieve
1 half-minot
3 Bolts.

The Buildings.

A warehouse thirty-seven and a half feet long and twenty-two feet
wide, eight feet high; boarded top and bottom with thick planks of oak,

four cabinets with their doors and locks closing with keys; the said house having window-shutters and a door closing with a key.

Also a small cellar adjoining the said house boarded below with split stakes, with a shutter and a door closing with a key.

Also a porch at the door of the said house, with its door and lock.

Also another house of stakes in earth, eighteen feet long, twelve feet and a half wide, six and a half high; boarded with split stakes above, and below, half of sawn beams with square joints and the other half without boarding; with its shutters, and a door closing with a key.

Also a cabinet in the house with a door and its hinges.

Also a postern outside the house framed, with its lock.

Also a cellar twelve and a half feet long by six wide, adjoining the house, with a door and its iron-work.

Also another, inferior, house of stakes in earth, sixteen feet long, twelve wide; without either door or shutters; serving as a shed for cattle.

Also a barn fifty feet long by twenty-seven wide and eleven high; the top roofed with wood, having its tenons broken, with its [*battrier*] of thirty-four joists and partly worn-out, surrounded with stakes in earth, joined together.

Also another house thirty-three feet long, twenty-one wide, nine high, boarded above with split stakes, surrounded with stakes in earth, neither closing by a door nor by shutters, having only the four sashes of the shutters and the two side timbers of the door.

Also a dove-cot raised on four wooden posts, six feet high, ten square, surrounded with oak beams two inches thick with square joints, covered with straw, and two gable ends of earth; its door with its hinges.

Also and ice-house fifteen feet square and six high out of the ground, and fifteen feet deep in the ground, boarded with split beams, with its door closing with a key.

Also a building, used as a church, thirty-five feet long, twenty-four and a half feet wide, ten high; boarded entirely above, with oak joists in a good ridge, and below of beams with square joints; with its doors window and shutters, and sash-frames between of twenty squares each; the whole closing with a key.

Also a heavy bell.

Ornaments of the Church.

A chalice with its paten of silver; gilt inside.

A Monstrance of silver, without a stand.

3 caps of flax.

2 missals, one large and one small.

A silver box for keeping the extreme unction in.

1 white chasuble.

1 ditto satin of mingled colors, a little worn.

1 ditto green, half worn out.

1 white stole.

1 white maniple.

1 white veil variegated.

1 bag for holding the communion-cloths, covered with satin.

1 satin stole.

1 ditto maniple.

1 ditto veil.

1 green stole.

1 ditto maniple.

1 black veil.

3 albs, one of which [is] half worn out.

4 girdles of which there are two of thread and two of wool.

2 large altar cloths.

3 other fine cloths half worn-out.

6 amices half worn out.

1 small fine cloth for communicants.

15 purificatories

9 communion cloths, half-worn.

6 lavabos (napkins) half-worn.

2 surplices.

1 scarf of red taffeta.

2 white pals [covers for chalice]

3 altar-fronts of which 1 white, 1 ditto of mockadoes, 1 ditto of mixed colors.

2 Agnus Dei.
2 small copper candlesticks.
4 ditto of red wood.
1 pyx-cloth, ornamented with violet paper.
10 large candlesticks of painted wood.
16 ditto of black [wood].
2 cushions of mockadoes.
1 green carpet.
1 old turning-box of mockadoes, above the altar, with fringe.
2 small credence tables of French walnut-wood, closing with a small bolt.
1 altar of French walnut-wood with its steps and a stool with two-steps, and a tabernacle closing with a key.
1 large wooden cross.
1 confessional.
1 armchair.
1 chair.

Joiner's tools.

2 large trying planes, fitted.
4 plough-planes, fitted, two called [or ditto] for beams and two for planks.
2 fillister-planes put together.
1 holdfast.
2 mortise-chisels, one large and one small.
1 large chisel without handle.
1 large ditto with a handle.
1 small chisel.
3 wimbles [or braces].
2 plough-plane irons.
7 quadrant irons.
1 trying-plane iron.
1 scraper.
1 large mortise-chisel.

Carpenters tools.

2 troy-bills.
1 hand-saw.
1 mattock.
2 iron set-squares.
2 axe-hammers, with heads.
1 round axe-hammer with head.
1 large chisel.

3 augers, two called large and one small.
2 cross saws put together.
4 cross saws unmounted.

Mason's tools.

2 iron hammers.
1 trowel.
5 iron punches weighing, in all, six livres and a quarter.
3 chisels, together weighing three livres and three quarters.
1 pick-axe weighing five and a quarter livres.
Also several kinds of other tools.
1 fly-wheel weighing three livres and a half.
2 large wheelweights' ladles.
1 cooper's scraper.
1 calking-iron.
1 pick-axe of poor quality.
1 small ink-stand.
2 new seals and four old ones.
6 rings for lanterns.
4 cases for seals.
1 calking chisel.
3 pairs of cramp-irons.
4 wrenches.
2 files.
1 pit saw unmounted.
3 pit saws mounted.
1 pair iron handcuffs.
8 hinges which have seen service.
1 cast iron mould weighing fourteen livres, making seventeen balls on one side and, on the other, moulded flat.

3 hinges not matched.

26 dozen fire-beaters.

1050 large fishing-hooks, barbed.

94 [pairs of] tongs.

120 worm-screws with sockets.

3 dozen and 2 flemish knives.

1 dozen and a half of large wood-cutter's knives.

5 dozen and a half Siamese knives with cane handles.

3 dozen and a half large Z with ball handles.

4 dozen and two large knives Z with yellow handles.

' 3 dozen small knives Z black handles.

8 planished knives.

6 dozen and a half [dalleinnes].

2 dozen and a half crucifixes.

19 dozen and a half red rosaries.

6 ounces weight of large needles.

29 packets of small aniseseed, weighing with the paper, three livres and a half.

100 small trumpets.

6 calumets.

36# of medium [size] black glass beads.

76¾# of large black beads.

8¾# ditto green, streaked.

33#, 6 oz. glass beads in strings, of all colors.

13 dozen small tin mirrors.

4 wooden combs.

7 dozen small horse-hair buttons.

7 dozen ditto medium, silk.

¾ [livres] of alum.

1 bed-valance of white serge, bordered, ornamented with a small yellow silk ribbon, without iron-work, containing generally all its fittings.

2¼# copperas and nut gall mixed together.

22# of brass wire of one kind.

7¼# of sorted thread, a little eaten by mice.

12¼# of Holland thread.

12¼# of thread for vests.

5# all but an ounce, ditto.

1 ounce of [empille].

2¾# of [ampille] spoilt.

11¾# of thread for vests.

13¼# of gold thread spoilt.

8¼ of small iron wire.

2¾# of [taiselle] of all colors.
24# of thread for vests, spoilt.
30 [? livres] wall nails.
148 nails [a connerir].
725 gun flints.
3 large muskets, English make.
4 large muskets, French.
1 ditto, newly put together, without a trigger-guard.
2 ditto spoilt.
3 gun-cases blue.
3 ditto, poor, spoilt.
200# of lead and bullets together.
740# of lead.
1 white cover with two points.
1 wooden trunk without a lock, with a roebuck's skin at the bottom.
2 dozen shirts for women, of Lyons cloth.
2 small shirts, part-worn.
2 small ditto of hempen cloth, half-worn out.
14¾ ells of mockadoes.
9½ ells of mockadoes.
36 lace calottes [priest's caps] red and blue.
2 pairs of fine stockings for a man.
1½ dozen napkins of hempen cloth and
3 table-cloths.
2 pairs of sleeves, one blue and the other red bordered with [taiselle].
8½ ells of red stuff [a mitasse].
4¾ ells of red swan-skin buttoned.
6 ells, all but an eighth, of red cloth.
A branding-iron.
1 set of steps with two steps of oak planks.
1 medicine chest with eleven leaden bullets, and a box of tin with its

1 ditto black and white.

1 white shell with two divisions of blue porcelain.

22 canons of porcelain, medium.

14 : ou of porcelain and [with] divisions, mixed black and white.

1 small white shell, with 1 red girdle [*meamise*].

4 large calumets of red stone with their stems and plumes and stands to hold them.

2 locks, one large and one small.

1 half minot.

2 large shutters with three hinges.

1 door with a latch, a lock without a key.

1 door with its hinges and a latch.

2 main masts and two rails for à cutter [boat].

2 large [*apaconee*] stretched out in the warehouse.

1 third of a minot.

1 sieve to cleanse corn.

1 bed with a green border, ornamented with rings, with all its furniture new.

1 lead inkstand weighing 2¾.

1 sable, half worn out.

1 large [*grif*] with seven branches.

1 small ditto half worn out.

2 square mats of rushes, with a girdle and a tomahawk.

20 minots of soda.

16 buckets, some large and some small.

1 large pirogue.

33# of tin [*en sepplats*].

3¾# of soap.

1 oven.

1 large cloth bag quite new.

Another of horsehair.

1 leather bag weighing 50# full of flour marked with a +

1 bag   " of 44 " + a little [spoiled by the heat] .

1 bag weighing 60 " + a little   "   " " "

1 bag weighing 70 " ⊖ a fine

1 bag   · or   66 " +·a little

1 bag _____ 53 " + a little

1 bag _____ 66 " marked G

Animals.

4 large oxen.

4 large bulls of the same age, rising four years.

3 bulls rising three years.

3 bulls rising two years.

3 bulls rising one year.

2 heifers rising one year.

9 large cows.

1 heifer rising four years.

1 horse called Colin, 8 years old or thereabouts.

Harness of the horse.

1 collar with the breeching and the ridge-band and the bridle.

1 bridle bitten.

1 of serge, half worn.

An old curry-comb.

2 old irons.

1 plough.

1 bag and a centre-punch.

1 pair of old rowels with their iron hoops.

1 iron chain for a plough.

2 iron bolts.

1 gauge.

2 small irons for ploughs.

1 new large cart for carting wood.

1 cart fitted up for carting corn, with its wheels.

1 ox-wagon.

1 old pair of rowels.

2 traces.

Also 1 feather bed with its bolster, weighing, with the skins, forty-six livres, with ten roebuck skins, buccaned.

1 barrel of powder weighing about 60# tare 7#.

1 barrel _____ 56# _____ 7#.

1 barrel _____ 58# _____ 8#.

241# of lead in five bags.

164# of shot in three bags.

76# of salt with the barrel in which it is.

1 iron [grif] with seven branches.

2 iron spits for roasting, one large and one medium.

2 andirons weighing nineteen livres.

1 large couch of walnut wood.

2 ditto medium.

1 large walnut-wood table.

2 small ditto.

9 chairs, two of which are not covered [or seated] with straw.

2 frying-pans half worn out.

1 fire-shovel.

1 iron pepper-mill.

1 large walnut-wood cupboard, with two panels, six feet high or thereabouts.

1 small, with two panels and two drawers.

2 armchairs, one of them covered with ox-hide and the other ornamented with elm-bark.

2 pots all but a gill, of white vinegar.

3 pots and 3 chopins of red vinegar.

1 tin funnel.

2 watering-pots.

2 old chains, weighing nineteen livres.

1 shaft, wood.

1 weight of iron of 25#.

1 mass of iron serving as a weight of 8#.

1 iron wedge, serving as a weight, weighing 6#.

1 pair of scales, copper, with iron chains and a wooden beam ornamented with iron.

1 copper stamp weighing 8#.

1 iron lamp, plain.

1 copper tart-dish.

1 slice.

1 small iron porridge-pot with its lid.

3 small bottles.

1 large bottle.

2 copper candle-sticks and snuffers and snuffers pan.

5 dozen candles.

A dozen table napkins and 2 table cloths of hempen cloth, measuring an ell and a half or thereabouts.

4 ounces of pepper, cloves and nutmegs.

4 dishes of different kinds, one with the edge cracked, weighing three livres and a half.

An old tin basin weighing 3#—

We the undersigned, Pierre Chesne and Antoine Magnant, both inhabitants of this place of Detroit Pontchartrain, declare and certify that we have assisted at the present inventory, have seen measured, weighed and counted all the effects included in the said inventory except the flour, wheat, peas and oats laid down above, and in the memorandum of M. Marigny, which effects have been handed over to custody of M. Pierre Roy, an inhabitant of the said place, to keep them and to take care of [them] as his own property, without however running any risk, and to return them to M. de La Mothe or to his order when required; in proof of which we have signed—

Executed at the said fort Pontchartrain, the 25th of August, 1711.

Pierre Roy declared that he did not know how to sign.

Signed in the original,   Chesne and Magnant.

I the undersigned Priest, Recollet Missionary at the fort Pontchartrain du Detroit, certify the contents of the above to be true, having assisted at the said Inventory, in proof of which I have signed at the said fort this 25th of *August,* 1711.

Fr. Cherubin Deniaux,
Priest, Missionary, Recollet.

REPORT FROM M. DE VAUDREUIL OF THE CONDITION OF THE COLONY.

Endorsed—M. de Vaudreuil, 8th of Septr. 1711.

My Lord,

approved of the manoeuvers I made in 1709, in order to compel our enemies to retire and to burn their forts themselves, which they had constructed along the Orange River, their boats, canoes, and almost all their
stores. I have reason to flatter myself that His Majesty will also approve
those I have made this year; and I think M. de Nicholson very lucky—
after having boasted to the savages that the fall of the leaf would find
not a single Frenchman left in Canada—. I shall consider him very lucky
if he saves all his transport in the direction of the upper country. I have
too much humility to speak of the disaster which befell his fleet in our
river. I know that it is to God alone that we should give thanks for
that; but as regards the upper country affair, I think I may set down
his precipitate retreat somewhat to myself.

The English having spared nothing to induce the Iroquois to declare
against us, and having even spent large sums for that purpose, I heard
from several sources that as many as six hundred of them had been in
their camp; but that before they had news of the fleet beating back, they
had almost all gone back and that there were not a hundred left with M.
de Nicholson when he resolved to return himself. I had the honor of
informing you in my other letter of the steps I had taken with such of
those savages as were at Montreal, to induce the others not to take either
side in the quarrel between the English and us. I have no doubt that
when they returned they used every endeavor to keep their promise to
me, and I am persuaded that it will not be long before they come to me
to make excuses for the others.

It is a matter of importance to us, My Lord, not to be at war with
that tribe if we can possibly help it, and the five Iroquois villages are
more to be feared than the whole of New England. If they come I shall
take care to speak to them in such a manner as to show them that I am
not obdurate, but I beg you in advance to induce His Majesty to approve
of the course I shall take at this meeting. The experience of more than
24 years shows me clearly enough that this sort of war is by no means
advisable for this Colony. I know only too well how dearly it has cost
us, and how much difficulty the people have had in recovering from it.

I had the honor, in my letter of last year, to give you an account of
the plans Mr. Dudley had for attracting the Abenaki savages of the seacoast of Baston, to bring their beaver skins there and buy goods. Hitherto I have found means, somehow or other, of preventing them from taking
their course, but I cannot answer for the future. It is very unfortunate
that it was impossible to do what I had the honor of writing to you
about last year, and that His Majesty was unable to send to this country
goods to the value of twelve or fifteen thousand livres to be given to these
savages at a low price. It is true that these goods would have to be
bought at the price at which the merchants buy them in France, and

the King; but then His Majesty would only advance this sum once, at the beginning, and every year the same amount would return to his stores. I have the honor of informing you, My Lord, that this point deserves very serious consideration.

As the Sr. de la Forest was continually hoping that we should have news from France early, in accordance with the promise which M. Raudot, junior, made him on his departure, and that you would do him the honor of replying to the letter he had taken the liberty of writing to you, he did not go up to Detroit this spring, having indeed been ill almost all winter. He was however making preparations to go up in the month of June when M. de La Mothe Cadillac arrived from that place.

M. de La Mothe, who only came down from that post with the intention of proceeding to France, at once made several proposals to me; but as it is well to be on one's guard with him I told him to put them to me in writing.

I have the honor of sending you herewith his first requests of the 15th of June, and also my reply concerning the forty men he asked me for to conduct him to Louisiana.

The next day he made other proposals which he also dates the 15th of June. I have the honor, My Lord, to send you them, together with the reply I made.

The Srs. de La Mothe and de la For t h

point this spring; that in regard to the agreements which the Sr. de la
Forest and he had made together at Quebec in the presence of the Intendant, that they did not amount to a decision given by the Intendant
but were only conditional agreements which the Sr. de la Forest had
nullified by adopting the course of proceeding to his post himself;
that the proposal that the command should be given to the Sr. de Marigny
was not advisable in the interests of the service, for although he was personally a very worthy man he was still too young and too little acquainted
with the affairs of the savages; that I found it hard to believe that the
command of that post and its trade could be separated from one another;
that, in order to make certain matters easier for him, the Sr. de la
Forest pledged himself, in writing, to permit him to send any agent he
might think fit up there to sell the goods which he says that he has
there; that as regards the other points in dispute, it appeared to me
that there was no one who could decide upon them but you alone, My
Lord, since no one could know your intentions but yourself; that it
had appeared to me and did still appear from the Intendant's letters,
that this was his opinion, and as for me, I could only obey the orders
I had received; that my orders were to have the command and the trade
of Detroit transferred to the Sr. de la Forest; that I could make no
change in that without receiving fresh orders. That, My Lord, was the
reply I made to the Sr. de La Mothe as to his last memorial. Since
then the news came about the English, and I found it impossible for me
to allow the Sr. de la Forest to go up to his post. I had, however, given
him permission to go up this autumn in two lighters with twelve men;
but on the news that the enemy had entered the river, M. de Ramezay
stopped him at Montreal because his going would have served many of
the savages as a pretext for disbanding. M. de Ramezay reported it to
me on his arrival, and I approved. Moreover, from my last letters from
Detroit, it appears to me that things are much quieter there than they
have been. The Sr. de la Forest will go there in the early spring and I
will grant him any two officers he may ask me for. As for M. de La
Mothe, since he is going to France with his family, he will have the
honor of stating to you himself the reasons which prevented him from
proceeding to his governorship overland.

I had the honor of writing to you last year about a silver mine which
a settler at Detroit believed he could discover towards the heights of
Ouabache. That has had no result, for this settler could not succeed in
finding what he was looking for; but as to copper mines, it is certain
that there are plenty of them in those parts. I am sending Madame

to me that it will be much easier to convey it by the Ouabache River
and then by the Mississipy. As I was obliged to send an escort back
with these savages, one of their men having been killed on the way by
some Mississagues returning from Orange, I gave orders to the Sr. de
Vincenne. for whom they asked me, to go to the place where these mines
are, if possible, and to examine thoroughly the facilities there might be
for conveying it here or through Ouabache.

I saw from the memorandum of His Majesty the reasons he has for not
deciding to grant the re-establishment of the licenses at once. I venture
to assure you, My Lord, that nothing is more essential if we would prevent the tribes allied to us in the upper country from going to trade
with the English. It is certain that there is no time to be lost, and that
before long, if we do not take care, the English will be more the masters
of these tribes than we ourselves. I am sending Madame de Vaudreuil
a letter from Father Chardon, the missionary at St. Joseph's River, which
will show how greatly the savages at his mission are disposed to go there.
The savages from Lake Superior go there every year; and this year the
Frenchmen, whom I sent to the upper country to send down the savages there, met two boats returning from Orange, laden with very fine
goods, and with several belts to give to the other tribes. The Foxes,
who came to settle at Detroit, only did so in order to get nearer to the
English, because they are people who do not use canoes, and it is even to
be feared that they may form a settlement near the Iroquois, to become
afterwards embodied with them. It was this which compelled me to
speak as I did to those who came to Montreal. I have the honor of informing you of it in my letter of the 25th of October.

With regard to the irregularities which the licenses formerly gave rise
to, that can easily be remedied; and as for the loss in numbers that that
would cause the Colony, it is certain that the number of savages it would
attract to us at Montreal every year, as compared with the French for
whom they would come down, or with whom they would come, would
amply replace the French who would be employed in managing these
licenses. It is nothing but the welfare of the service, My Lord, that
makes me speak thus; and, if I were not afraid of saying too much, I
would say that those who present memorials against it do not know the
country, or else have objects which I cannot discern.

The Sr. de. Louvigny, My Lord, has not gone up to Michilimakina;
I have had too much need of him here, and he is too good a man for me

he stayed at Montreal in assisting me to control these restless spirits who rarely fail to give a good deal of trouble. It appeared to me that they had a genuine regard for him, and there is every reason to hope that he will succeed in establishing the post at Michilimakina if His Majesty wishes it, provided that His Majesty will grant him the number of soldiers he asks for, or that he will at least be good enough to sanction the re-introduction of the licenses; for, to send a commandant alone to Michilimakina, without any Frenchmen with him, is a most useless proceeding, and so far from inspiring respect in the savages it will only serve to make them despise us. The Sr. de Louvigny, My Lord, is not the man to go to that place on those terms, any more than the Sr. de Lignery. M. Raudot, junior, who has a complete acquaintance with the affairs of this country, can tell you better than any one else, how necessary it is to re-establish the post of Michilimakina if we do not wish to lose the savages who are allied to us in the upper country, and that can only be done by sending Frenchmen there, and goods which can also be sold to them at a reasonable price, to prevent them from going to the English any more. While awaiting your orders, My Lord, which I beg you to communicate to me in the early spring through Plaisance or Labrador, the Sieurs de Louvigny and Lignery will be of some service to me here, and, if I find occasion for employing them in making any attack on Acadia, I will not lose the opportunity.

It is grevious, My Lord, that I was unable to give the inhabitants of Acadia the reinforcements they asked me for. You would have censured me if I had sent my men away at a time when I was receiving threats from all quarters that I was to be attacked in this country, both at Quebec and Montreal, by very large numbers. Yet it was with genuine pain that I refrained from doing so, although the reinforcements I could have given them would have been quite useless; for the English, retiring from this country with a fleet as strong as they had, would still have been able to retake the fort if they had desired ever so little to do so.

I have learnt that the inhabitants of the outskirts of Port Royal have come to terms with the English. They have, however, sent me word by an express that they had only done so, that they might not be disturbed in their harvesting, and might be able to obtain their corn; that, moreover, since they were entirely destitute of ammunition, they could not have done anything else. As to the inhabitants of Les Mines and Beaubassin, they seem still to be quite faithfud. I have the honor of send- Index lett

no news of him, nor of the Vermandois, nor of another small vessel called the St. Jean, which was to come to this country. I have given the Sr. de Beaujeu the captain's commission which you were pleased to send me for him. I have also, in accordance with His Majesty's orders of last year, had the Sr. de la Fresniére admitted as Lieutenant, in the room and stead of the Sr. de Plané (or Rané) who died at Detroit; the Sr. de Senneville in succession to the Sr. de Chalus, who held a captain's commission for the first vacant company, and had that of the Sr. d'Argenteuil, who died of apoplexy this spring, as I had the honor of informing you in my other letter. The Sr. Dumesnil Norey, junior, has been accepted as an ensign *vice* the Sr. Veyeard, and the Sr. Dupuis *vice* the Sr. Aubrey, who gave in his resignation on coming to this country last year. They all have the honor of thanking you for your favors to them. Allow me, My Lord, to mention to you again the Sr. de la Chauvignerie; I ask you as a favor for him for an ensign's commission for the first vacancy.

I had the honor of informing you, My Lord, in 1709, that it would be advisable for His Majesty to send me an order permitting me to appoint any officers I thought fit to the command of the expeditions I sent into the field, to prevent the possibility of captains refusing to obey a King's Lieutenant, or a Major of a place, who might command the party. That was because, My Lord, officers in this country maintain that a King's Lieutenant and a Major of any place, other than that where they are, have no higher rank; yet there might be some occasions on which I should be very glad to make use of these gentlemen in preference to many others; and this country is organized in such a manner that, if even a moderately large expedition is fitted out, it is necessary that in one way or another all should go well.

It was with deep gratitude, My Lord, that M. de Ramezay, M. de Galisset and I saw that His Majesty had graciously decided, on our behalf, to bring up the garrisons of Quebec, Montreal and Three Rivers to their proper strength. We have the honor of thanking you, being all of us convinced that it was you who obtained this favor for us from His Majesty. For my part, My Lord, I cannot but be ever deeply sensible of all the favors you are good enough to show me and my family, and am most grateful for them.

I have seen the complaints which the Sr. de Courtemanche has laid before you against the man Constentin. I will take care, My Lord, to follow the instructions you give me on that.

I had the honor of replying to you above, as to the two officers that the Sieur de la Forest has asked you for. I will give them to him in accordance with your orders, and I will take care to explain to him that it is His Majesty's will that he should pay them. The Sr. Dubuisson is

and difficult a time as that at which he went up there, he has not got through it badly.

I gave the command of the Fort de Chambly, last year, to the Sr. de Jordy; it must long ago have come to your knowledge, My Lord, that he is a very good officer.

The Sieurs de Sabrevois, du Figuier and d'Ervilliers will not avail themselves this year of the permission you gave me to grant them leave to make a journey to France. They would be very sorry for anyone to be able to reproach them with having left this country at a time when the war may be fiercer than ever; but they again ask you for permission for next year provided there is nothing to be feared here. I have the honor of sending you herewith a list of the officers of this country who are in France. The Sr. Duplessis Fabert, junior, has, according to all appearances, been unfortunate enough to be captured again this year; the Sr. de Beaubassin the same. As to the Sr. de Monzens, he writes me, and I am assured in several letters that he was unable to embark, and was very ill when the ships left. I must humbly beg you graciously to grant him the honor of your patronage; he has need of it for he sustained heavy losses in the ship in which he was captured last year.

I now find myself obliged to represent to you, My Lord, how necessary it is that you should give orders to the treasurers of the navy to pay the letters of exchange drawn by their agent here on preceding years, so that that may give some little support to our paper-money. Without that, My Lord, this country will fall into the utmost extremity of poverty, and no one will continue to send us any goods; then the savages, disgusted with our trading, will give us up altogether and attach themselves to the English, as they are already only too strongly inclined to do. May it please you to be good enough to consider that this country has now no return cargo to offer but that of flour; that in default of the vessels that come here and take it on board, we cannot find a market for it; that the small quantity of furs that the traders send to France is not sufficient for the needs of this country; that the expenses even eat up the greater part of their value. This makes me hope, My Lord, that, on giving your attention to what I have the honor of writing to you, you will give orders that letters of exchange drawn in the preceding years are to be accepted and paid in the first six months of the year we are about to enter on. M. Raudot who is going to France, as well as his son, can tell you better than anyone else that what I am asserting is true, and how necessary it is to re-establish the credit of our letters of exchange on the treasurer.

One could wish it were possible to have our merchant vessels con-

remained in our waters, to make some attack on the fort of Port Royal.
I particularly beg you to have sent to us here early, some powder, guns
and kettles, some cloth for making bags and other necessary things
when we go into the field. There is the utmost necessity for that; and,
if it is such a great expense to the King every year, as soon as I am
obliged to make any military expedition, it is because a great many of
those things are lacking in his stores, and we are obliged to buy them
from the merchants at an exorbitant price; even so, some are not to be
found. It is also very necessary to send here some coarse blankets to
give to the savages, and also some linen for sale, to make them shirts.
I have reason to believe that the Intendant may have thought of all that
in his memorandum. If he has forgotten it I beg you, My Lord, to see
that it is attended to. We are also in want of gun-flints, a matter of
absolute necessity.

The Sr. de Talaise and the other officers from Acadia, who arrived
here in the King's ship, "the Hero," expressed to me a great desire that
they could go back to Port Royal, if I can find any opportunity to make
an attack on that post. I have long known the Sieur de Talaise as a
very good officer, he having served here under my orders; I feel obliged
to do him that justice.

The Sr, Duplessis, the treasurer, has requested me to give you an account of his conduct. I am able to say that he discharges his duties
here in such a manner as to satisfy everyone. I have told him I would
give him the memorandum you addressed to me, after the departure of
the vessels, in order that he might make notes on it, as it is not possible
for him to do so now since he is fully occupied with his accounts of
expenditure for the year 1710, and also with the preparation of the
new paper money which we were obliged to make before the departure
of M. Raudot, as we had the honor of informing you in our joint letter.
The Sr. Duplessis, whom I notified that you had ordered me to tell him
not to send any more memoranda or documents concerning the affairs
of the Company, assured me that he had never meant to grow importun-
ate, but had thought it his duty to give you an account of the matters
which had been intrusted to him by your orders; but, that, as he was
relieved of the Company's affairs, he would take great care in future
to write nothing on this subject which could displease you, and begs you
to continue to honor him with your patronage.

*   *   *

I am, with very deep respect,

> My Lord,
>> Your most humble and most obedient servant
>>> Vaudreuil.

Quebec, this 7th of November, 1711.

REPORT OF SR. DUBUISSON TO M. DE VAUDREUIL.[1]

Endorsed—(Letter from the Sr. Dubuisson to the Marquis de Vaudreuil of the 15th of June, 1712.)

Sir,

As I thought it a matter of very great importance to send a boat as speedily as possible to inform you of the condition of this post, I requested Mònsr. de Vincennes to undertake the journey, and assured him that that would give you pleasure, as I am convinced, Sir, that you are impatient to know what is taking place here. The overwhelming work I have, day and night, in the public and private councils I hold with the savages, prevents me from giving you full details in the report which I have the honor of making to you. Monsr. de Vincennes has promised me faithfully to forget nothing of all that has passed, so that he may be able to give you full information about it.

The destruction of two villages of the Maskoutins and Outagamis is one of the strongest reasons which induces me to despatch this boat; it is Heaven which has allowed these two audacious tribes to perish. They had received many presents and belts from the English to destroy the post of Fort Pontchartrain, by slaughtering us, and then certain tribes allied to us, to which the Hurons and Outauois settled at Detroit Pontchartrain were to be no exceptions; and then these wretches were to withdraw to the English, to be at their disposal for creating constant disturbances. It is asserted that Quinetónant's band, and Makatemangoua's have been received by the Iróquois to form a village among them. Three boats of Outagamis have been destroyed four miles from this post by the Saulteurs, who have brought us the news.

I am much afraid for M. de la Forest, as I have no doubt he has started on his journey up here, since he may meet with a party of these Outagamis out of those who are to set up a village among the Iroquois. The bands of the great chiefs Lamyma and Pemaussa came in the early spring and encamped, in spite of my opposition, within fifty paces of my fort. for they would not listen to me at all, and always spoke most insolently, speaking of themselves as the masters of all the land. It was necessary for me to speak to them fair, for I have only thirty Frenchmen with me, as you know Sir, and I wished to preserve those of the Miamis—to the number of eight—who were with Monsr. de Vincennes, and also to sow

---

[1] This report was printed in pamphlet form by Harsha & Willcox, Detroit, 1845. See also Smith's Hist. Wis. III. 315, and Wis. His. Col. XVI. 267.—C. M. B.

seed and have the cattle pastured. Moreover the Outtauois and their
Hurons had not got back from their winter quarters. I was constantly
exposed to a thousand insults; they killed hens, pigeons, and other creatures belonging to the French, and yet I dared not say a word, as I was
not yet in a position to speak my mind. Some of them came into my
fort to assassinate a settler named La Jeunesse, and a big girl belonging
to the man Roy, another settler; but I could not restrain myself so far.
I took up arms to resist them in this evil act against me, and compelled
them promptly to retire, so as not to give them time to increase their
numbers. For they also on their side, were waiting for their allies, the
Kikapoos, so that they might all together carry out their detestable
project and be sufficiently strong to retire to the English and Iroquois,
without fearing anything. These wretches were only waiting until the
moment they could set fire to our houses to overwhelm us. It was quite
a different matter when they heard that the Maskoutins, who had wintered in the upper part of the St. Joseph's River, had been destroyed,
to the number of a hundred and fifty souls, men, women and children,
by Saguina, war chief of the Outtavois and the Poutouatamis. They
wanted instantly to destroy an Outtavois hut which was at the gate of
my fort. I was warned of this by the man Joseph, an Outagami who has
long abandoned his tribe to devote himself entirely to the French. It
is through him that I have learnt all that has taken place in the village
of the Outagamis and Mascoutins. He has the honor of being known to
you Sir; he went down to Montreal last year. It was he also who
warned me that I was to be burned in my fort, which made me immediately send a boat with some Frenchmen to the place where the Outtavois and Hurons had wintered to tell them to hasten to come and join

put a better face on things than the circumstances warranted, constantly encouraging the French who were in a state of consternation, and looked upon their destruction as a certainty. As I was afraid lest anything might happen to the Frenchmen who had not yet arrived and as it was necessary to sow seed, and pasture the cattle, I dared not speak my mind nor refuse to let them enter the fort and trade, for fear they should perceive that I knew their wicked designs. All that I could do was to tell them I was afraid of the Miamis who, when they knew I was keeping them near me, would make war on me, and that was why I was going to set my fort in order; but they did not pay much heed to my reasons. We had to skirmish to get stakes, which were outside the fort, and they had got possession of them. I devoted myself to have my fort repaired as speedily as possible with what stakes I could get hold of, and I doubled it perfectly well with the materials from the houses. I employed a ruse to obtain a dove cote which they wanted to keep, which would have given us trouble and caused us to lose some men. I had it set up at once opposite to their fort, with good loop holes; I had two swivel-guns mounted on two great logs to serve me as cannon in case of need, which they did.

On the 13th of May, when I was anxious for the arrival of my allies, whom I had sent for, which was the only succor I could hope for, Monsr. de Vincennes arrived from the Miamis with seven or eight Frenchmen, bringing me no news of the savages whom I was expecting. This troubled me greatly, for I hardly know which way to turn.

But Heaven was keeping watch over our safety for us. When I was least expecting it, a Huron entered my house, quite out of breath, and said to me—"My father, I ask to speak to you in secret." He said to me—"I come from our old men." There were only seven or eight Hurons in their village at that time; it seems that everything has occurred here as by a miracle, for the remainder arrived two hours after, and the Outtauois also. This messenger said to me—"God has pity on us, He wishes your enemies and ours to perish. The news I bring you is that four men have just arrived at our fort, who dared not enter yours, because of the Fox Indians and Mascoutins around you. They are Maquisabé, war chief of the Poutauatamis, and the brother of Ickamasimon and two others; he asks to speak to you." I requested Monsr. de Vincennes to go; and when he got there he recognized the four savages. An hour after, he came to bring me an answer and told me from Makisabé that six hundred men would arrive very soon, to come to my help and devour these miserable tribes who had disturbed the peace of the whole land; that I must be on my guard to avoid being taken by surprise by the Outagamis and Mascoutins, who might hear of the arrival of this assistance. I requested Monsr. de Vincennes to go back to the Hurons'

content ourselves with driving the Mascoutins and Outagamis away and
compelling them to return to their old villages, since that Sir was your
will; but there was nothing to be done. The Hurons were too highly excited, and this important business had been too well planned during all
the autumn and winter, with all the tribes, and presents given. Monsr.
de Vincennes saw that it would only be irritating them to speak to them
of any arrangement, and went on further with it, more especially as the
savages said that all these evil people had never kept their word. We
had, therefore, to say nothing and go through with the matter with a
good grace, fighting with them against our common enemies. The Hurons
even asked us, in reproach, whether we were weary of life since we had
learnt the wicked scheme of the Outagamis and Mascoutins; and said
that it was absolutely necessary to destroy them and extinguish their
race; that it was your will that they should perish; that they had learnt
your mind on this matter at Montreal. Monsr. de Vincennes returned
and said to me—"It is useless to speak of any arrangement." I well
knew, indeed, that there was ground for fear in attracting so many
tribes to us, not knowing whether they were well disposed towards us.
Then it was that I had the gates of my fort closed. I divided the few
Frenchmen into four divisions, each having its commander; I examined
their arms and got the ammunition all ready. I posted them on each of
the bastions; I put four men in the redoubt which I had just made. I reserved some whom I stationed at the two curtains, where there was most
danger of attack, with swords fitted in shafts, my two pieces of cannon
all ready with wedges of iron to put in them which I had had made by
the blacksmith. Our reverend father, for his part, busied himself holding
himself ready to give general absolution in case of need, and to succor
the wounded, if perchance there were any; he also prepared the consecrated host. Everything being well arranged, when we were only awaiting a good fight. I was presently informed that a number of people were
appearing. I got up on a bastion, and casting my eyes in the direction
of the wood, I saw the army of the tribes from the South coming out,
namely, the Illinois, the Missouri, the Osages and other tribes still more
distant; with them was also Saguina, the Outtavois chief, and also the

are burning, and your wife is among them." There was no need to say more, they uttered a great cry, and at the same time they attacked with all speed, the Hurons at their head, as well as the Outtavois of this place. The Outagamis and Miscoutins also shouted their cry, and about forty of them came out of their fort all naked and painted, with their arms waving everywhere, to come and reconnoitre our men and defy them so as to make them believe they were not afraid of them; they were, however, obliged to retire very quickly and go into their village again. Our men asked leave to go into my fort, and I allowed them to do so, seeing they were too excited. My intention had been to make them encamp outside, near the wood, so that we should not be inconvenienced.

The chiefs of all these savages assembled in the square of my fort, and addressed me in these terms: "My father, I speak to you on behalf of all your children, the tribes that are before you. What you did for them last year, in saving their flesh from the fire when the Outagamis wanted to roast and eat it, well deserves that we should bring you our bodies that you may be the master of them and make us do whatever you desire. We do not fear to die when it is necessary to face death for you. We only ask that you will beg the father of all the tribes to have compassion on our wives and children in case we should lose our lives with you; and we ask you to throw a little grass on our bones, to protect them from the flies.

You see, my father, that we have left our villages, our wives and our children that we might come and join you as quickly as possible. We hope you will take pity on us and will give us food, and a little tobacco to smoke; we come from afar and are destitute of everything. We hope you will give us lead and powder that we may fight with you. We will not make a long talk; we perceive that we are wearying you and your Frenchmen because of your earnest desire to fight." I answered them at once, and in few words: "I thank you, my children; your desire to come and offer yourselves to die with me is very gratifying to me and gives me great pleasure. I recognize you as the true children of the Governor; I will not fail to report to him all you do for me to-day. Doubt not that when your interests are in question he will look after them with great zeal; these are the orders which I always receive from him—to watch unceasingly over the safety of his children. As regards your needs, I know that you are in want of everything. The fire which broke out is a misfortune both for you and for me, but I will do my best to see that you have what is most necessary. I invite all the tribes that are assembled here to live in peace, union and good understanding with one

your bows and arrows, and especially your guns; I am going to have some powder and bullets given out to you presently, and then we will attack. That is what I have to say to you.'

All the savages gave a great shout of joy and gratitude saying, "Our enemies are dead men; now the sky begins to shine upon us, and the master of life to take pity on us."

All the old men delivered harangues all round the fort to encourage the warriors to listen attentively to my words, and obey me in all the movements I would have them make.

I distributed lead and powder to them at once; and then all together, we shouted the war cry, the very earth trembled with it. The enemy, who were only a pistol-shot distant, shouted their cry also, and at the same time the musket shots began on both sides and the bullets came like hail. We also had to do as our savages did, in order to encourage them; the powder and bullets, which you were good enough to send me, Sir, last autumn, did not last long; we were obliged to have recourse to the three barrels which Monsieur de La Mothe had left with the man Roy to sell, for he did not leave me a single grain when he set out for the defence of the fort, in case of attack. All mine went also, and was not sufficient with the other powder which I was obliged to buy from the French people. I kept the Outagamis and Mascoutins besieged for nineteen days, wearing them out by a continuous fire, night and day; in order to avoid the heavy fire they were obliged to place themselves four or five feet deep in the ground. I had had two large platforms constructed, to a height of twenty feet, in order to fight with them better in their village; they could not get to the water, and were overwhelmed with hunger and thirst. I had four or five hundred men blockading their village day and night so that no one could get out to go for help. All our savages went scouting in the outskirts of the wood, and constantly brought back prisoners with them who were coming to join their people, not thinking they were besieged. They amused themselves by shooting them with guns or bows and arrows, and by burning some of them.

The enemy, whom I was holding in siege, thinking to intimidate me and thus compel me to let them go free, hung their palisade round with

on one of my platforms and spoke to them in the name of all our tribes in these terms.

"Wicked tribes that you are! You think to make us afraid with all this red you are putting on your village, but be you sure, if the earth is dyed with blood, that it will be with yours alone. You speak to us of the Englishman; it is he who is the cause of your loss for your listened to his evil counsel. He is the enemy of prayer, that is why the master of life chastises him as well as you, evil men that you are. Have you not learnt, as well as we, that the father of all the tribes who is at Montreal, continually sends parties of his children to the English to make war on them and brings back prisoners in such large numbers that they know not where to put them? The English, who are cowards, defend themselves only in an underhand way by killing men with that evil drink, brandy, which has made so many die a moment after drinking it. We shall see, therefore, what will become of you for having listened to their words.

I was obliged to put a stop to the conversation as I preceived that the enemy had only asked to speak to me in order to divert our attention and get a little time to go for water, as thirst was afflicting them heavily. I gave orders for our heavy fire to begin again, and it was so violent that we killed more than thirty of their men and some who had stolen away to go to the water. That day I lost twelve men in my fort, killed by our enemies; in spite of my efforts, they had taken possession of a house on which they had set up a platform behind the gable which was made of earth so that our musket bullets could not pierce it. Hence they killed some of our men every day from this place. This obliged me to set up, on one of my platforms, two great logs on which my two mortars were mounted. I loaded them with the wedges and had them fired at this gable which was annoying me so much. The first two shots succeeded so well that we heard the platform, which they had set up behind it, tumble down, and some of them were killed. They were so terrified by these cannon shots that we heard them giving vent to terrible cries and howls, and in the evening they cried out and asked whether I would consent to grant them permission to come and speak to me. Then I called together all the chiefs of the tribes who were with me to learn their opinions, and we all agreed together that it was necessary to let them come so that we might attempt by a ruse to get back from them three women belonging to our people whom they had made prisoners a few days before the siege, one of whom was the wife of the great war

It was the great chief Pemoussa who constituted this first embassy. He came out of his village with two other savages, with a white flag in his hand. I sent my interpreter forward to bring him to me, and to protect him from attack by any young warrior. He entered my fort; I had him conducted to the middle of the square, and then I called together all the chiefs of the tribe that were with me to listen all together to our ambassador. Here are his words:

By a necklace and two slaves.

"My father, I am a dead man. I see clearly that the sky is fair and bright for you alone, while for me it is all black. When I came out from my village, I hoped that you would consent to listen to me. I ask you, my father, by this necklace which I lay at your feet, to have compassion on your children and not to refuse them the two days they ask you for, during which there shall be no firing on your side or on ours, so that our old men may hold council, to find means to soften your heart.

"It is to you that I speak now, children who obey the word of our father. This belt is to beg you to remember that we are your allies. If you shed our blood, know that it is yours also. I beg you then to try to soften the heart of our father whom we have so often offended.

"These two slaves are to replace, it may be, a little blood which you have perhaps shed. These few words are all that I say to you until our old men speak, if you grant us the two days that I ask of you."

This, Sir, is what I replied to them: "If your heart were a little touched, and you did, in truth, recognize the Governor as your father, you would have begun by bringing me the three women whom you have as prisoners among you. That you have not done that, makes me think that your heart is still bad. If you wish me to listen to you, begin by bringing them to me. That is all I have to say to you."

All the chiefs who were with me cried aloud—"My father, after what you have just said, we have no reply to make to this ambassador. Let him be of your mind if he wishes to live."

would call us to account for them. Now do with them, my father, as you wish; you are the master of them. Behold we, the Mascoutins and Outagamis ask you to make all the tribes that are with you retire, so that we may go free to seek the means of subsistence for our women and our children; many are dying every day of hunger and want. All our village repents of having angered you; if you are a good father, as your children who surround you say, you will not refuse us the favor that we ask of you."

As I had the three women I demanded, I no longer cared about humoring them. I replied to them—"If you had devoured this flesh of mine which you have brought me, you would not be alive now; you would instantly have had such heavy blows that they would have beaten you into the earth so deep that you would never be heard of again. As it is, although I love the flesh of the father of all the tribes, as regards the freedom you ask of me I leave it to my children to answer you. Therefore I have no more to say."

The great chief of the Illinois, called Makouâandely was appointed to speak by the chiefs of the other tribes: in these terms—

"My father, we all thank you for your goodness to us, we thank you that you give us leave to speak; we are going to do so"— And, addressing the hostile chiefs,—"Now hear me, therefore, you tribes that have troubled the whole earth. We see clearly, from all that you say, that you are only seeking to impose upon our father and to deceive him again, when you demand of him that we should retire. As soon as we did so you would molest our father again and would certainly shed his blood. You are dogs, who have always bitten him; you have never been grateful for the benefits you have received from all the French. You thought, wretches that you are, that we did not know all the messages that you have received from the English to slaughter our father and the children here, and then to take them there. Therefore retire; for our part we will not move from here, we wish to die with our father, and if he told us to go away we should disobey him because he knew your evil heart, for we will not leave him alone with you. We must therefore see now who are to be masters, you or us. You have only to retire; as soon

men so much that they thought they were all lost. I reassured them all, telling them that that was nothing and that it was necessary to provide a remedy as soon as possible. "Come!" I said to them, "take courage, let us quickly remove the coverings of the houses and put bear and roebuck skins in their place." The savages assisted us. With the assistance of a large number of men, I had two large wooden boats brought in, in which I had twenty barrels of water put, with swabs at the end of rods to put out the fire when it caught in any place, and hooks to pull out the arrows. I had four or five French people wounded. I fell into another difficulty much greater than the first; my savages became discouraged and wished to depart, some saying that that tribe would never be conquered, that they knew well that they were braver than any other, and that moreover, I was no longer able to give them provisions enough for their subsistence. The fickleness of these tribes should teach us that it is dangerous to leave such a distant post without troops. I found myself therefore, in consequence of this, on the eve of being deserted and left a prey to our enemies, who would have given me very little quarter; and the English would have triumphed. The Frenchmen were so scared that they said to me that they saw that it was necessary to retire as quickly as possible to Michilimaquina. I said to them—"What are you thinking of? Can such base sentiments be entertained? And why abandon a post in such a cowardly manner? Drive from your minds, my friends, such an evil project. What is it then that seems to you so bad as to put you in such fear? You may be sure that if you had done such a thing as to abandon me, the Governor General would have had you pursued everywhere, to punish you for your cowardice. What the savages have just said to me ought not to frighten you; I am going to speak privately to all the chiefs and put heart into them again. Change your minds therefore, and leave me to act, and you will see that all will go well." They replied that they did not intend to retire without my consent, with me at their head, as they did think we

source of expense to me at Quebec. When I had gained over all the savages in private, I held a general council to which I summoned all the tribes. I said to them, "How is it, my children, when you are on the eve of destroying that wicked tribe, that you are thinking of flying disgracefully, after having begun so well? Would you ever be able to hold up your heads again? You would always be weighed down with shame. All the other tribes would say—'Those are the brave warriors who fled in so cowardly a manner and deserted the French.' Be not troubled: take courage. We will try and find a little food yet; the Hurons and the Outtavois, your brethren, offer you some for me, and I will do my best to relieve you and assist you. Do you not see that our enemies are only holding on by a thread? Hunger and thirst are overpowering them; we shall very soon be masters of their lives. Will you not be greatly pleased after their great overthrow, when you are at Montreal and receive so many caresses and tokens of friendship from the father of all the tribes, who will look with favor on you for having risked your lives with me? For, doubt not that when I send him my report of all this, I will do justice to each of you individually for all that you have done for me. You must know also that, in destroying this tribe, you are giving life and peace to your wives and children who have never yet experienced it."

The young war chiefs whom I had gained over, scarcely gave me time to finish and said to me, "My father, permit us to interrupt you. We think some liar must have come and given you a false report. Know that every one of us loves you too much to desert you, and we are not such cowards as they would represent us. We are determined even if we have to fast still more, not to leave you until your enemies and ours have been destroyed." All the old men and the others applauded this saying, "Come! Let us hasten and take arms, and give the lie to those who have given this false report to our father." The great shout was raised and they sang, and danced the war dance, while a large number fought.

Every day some Sakis came out, who had formerly set up a village among the Outagamis, and returned to their people who were with me, who received them with pleasure. They informed us of the state the enemy's village was in, assuring us that they were in a state of utter ruin; that more than from sixty to eighty women and children had died

moussa. With them were also two great Mascoutin chiefs, one named Kisis and the other Ouabimanitou. The great chief Pemoussa was at the head of three others, and had a crown of porcelain on his head, several necklaces of porcelain hanging round his body, and several others like shoulder-belts; he was painted with green earth. He was supported by seven women slaves who were also painted and bedecked with porcelain; the other three chiefs each had a chichicoy in his hand. In this manner they all marched in order, singing and howling with all their might to the sound of their chichicoys, calling all the demons to their aid, to have compassion on them. They also had small figures of demons hung from their belts. They came into my fort thus bedecked; and, in the midst of all the tribes allied to us, they spoke as follows:

"My father, I speak to you and to all the tribes who are before you. I ask you for life; it is ours no longer, you are the masters of it. All the Manitous have deserted us. I bring you my flesh by the seven slaves that I place at your feet: but do not think that I fear to die, it is the life of the women and children that I ask for. I beg you to make the sun shine that the sky may be fair, so that we may be able to see the light of day, and that we may do nothing but what is good in the future. There are six necklaces which we give you; which hold us attached to you as your true slaves. We beg you to detach them as a sign that you grant us our lives. Remember, all of you, how long you have been of one family with us. Tell us something, I beg of you, that may give pleasure when we go back to our village."

I left it to our savages to reply to these envoys. They had become so full of anger against them in such a short time that they answered them nothing. They only asked me, to the number of eight or ten chiefs, to speak to me in private. "My father, we come to ask you to kill these four great chiefs. Is is they who prevent our enemies from surrendering to us at discretion. When they no longer have them at their head, they will be in a great difficulty and will surrender." I replied that they must

had come to ask us. These poor wretches well knew that there was no hope for them. I confess, Sir, that I was touched with compassion for their unhappy lot; but as war and pity do not go together, and more especially as I was well informed that they were paid by the English to destroy us, I abandoned them to their sad fate. On the contrary, I has-tened to put an end to this tragedy, so that this example might strike terror into the allies of the English, and the English themselves.

The heavy fire began again worse and worse; the enemy, being at bay, fought constantly in their village, and outside when they wanted to go for water, or to snatch a little grass to relieve their hunger. The only chance they had left was that of a dark night with rain falling, in which to escape. They awaited it with great impatience; it came on the nine-teenth day of the siege, and they did not fail to take advantage of it. They fled at midnight and we did not find it out till daybreak. I en-couraged our men and they went after them most energetically. Mon-sieur de Vincennes went, with a few Frenchmen, which pleased our sav-ages greatly.

The enemy, suspecting that they would be pursued, stopped at a pen-insula, which was opposite the end of Hog Island, near to Lake St. Clair, four leagues from the fort.[1] They cut forked branches and laid them crosswise above, and had stakes set up all along. Our people did not perceive them and fell into their intrenchment, losing more than twenty men there killed and wounded. They had to encamp also, and besiege them a second time. It was a regularly constituted camp: every day a hundred canoes were seen carrying provisions for the Outtavois, Hurons, Saulteurs and Mississagues. The chiefs sent to me to ask for my two pieces ordnance, all the axes and mattocks that I might have, for cutting the woods and penetrating them in order to approach the enemy's in-trenchment, and still to supply them with powder and bullets; as for Indian corn, tobacco, and condiments, it was the usual thing, without reckoning all the kettles of the French people which have been lost, and I have had to pay for. The enemy held out for four days longer, fighting with great courage. At the end of that time, being unable to do any more, they surrendered at discretion to our people, who gave them no quarter. All were destroyed except the women and children whose lives were granted them; a hundred and fifty men escaped who were bound. All the tribes allied to us returned to my fort with all their slaves, think-ing to infect us [? with their cruelty]. Their amusement was to shoot four or five of them every day; the Hurons did not give quarter to a single one of theirs. That, Sir, was the end of those two wicked tribes, with such evil designs, who disturbed the whole land. Our reverend father celebrated a high mass to give thanks to God for having preserved us from this enemy.

The Outtagamis and Mascoutins had, as I said before, constructed a very good fort within a pistol-shot of mine. Our men did not dare to attempt to storm them in it, say what I could to them; there were three hundred men to defend it and we should certainly have lost a large number, but the siege would not have been so long. Our savages lost sixty men killed and wounded, of whom I had indeed about thirty killed in my fort, and a Frenchman named Germain, with five or six others wounded by arrows. The enemy lost a thousand souls, men, women and children.

I must not forget to inform you that there were about twenty-five Iroquois in this fight, who had joined the Hurons from the foot of the lake. These two tribes together distinguished themselves above all the others, and also lost more men. They were made much of by all the savages, more especially by the Poutouatamis who made them reparation for their old ground of complaint, by slaves and calumets. It was I who induced them to make friends as to this matter.

I venture to assure you, Sir, that this general assembly of all the tribes has put them all at peace with one another, and has renewed their former alliance. They all count on large presents, which they say, Sir, you have promised them.

With the consent of his tribe, I have detained the great chief of the Illinois, from the village of Le Roche, to send him down, (his name is Chachagouache, and he is a good man, with much influence) in order that you may compel him, Sir, to make peace with the Miamis. This matter is of very great importance, the Miamis having sent me word that, if it is not made, they are going to abandon their village and form another at the Oyau River at the end of Lake Erie. That is just where the English are to build a fort, according to the belts they have given to the tribes. They have also sent me word that they would feel safe if you sent them back a garrison, and a reverend Jesuit father, with some presents which they say you promised them. Maquisabé, the Poutouatami chief is also going down; he has great influence over the mind

came to Detroit to speak to the three villages, was destroyed by the Hurons and Outtavois; there was a great chief whose head was brought to me with three others. This attack was made out of revenge, because he had bound some Hurons and an Iroquois last winter; moreover they looked upon him as really an Outagamy. I do not know whether the Kikapoos would not have put the two Hurons and the Iroquois to death even, if Mons. de Vincennes had not been at the mouth of the River of the Miamis; it looked very much like it. Those same people also arrested Langlois, who was on his way back from the Miamis, charged with many letters from the reverend Jesuit fathers in the villages of the Illinois. All these letters were torn up, which annoyed me very much as I felt sure that there were some for you, Sir, coming from Louisiana. They sent back this Langlois, a settler here, keeping all the furs we had, and charged him to go back and learn the news; but he has no great desire to do so, nor have I to let go. The Outtavois however might send there; the Kikapoos have with them one of their wives and her children. I will contrive that the Outtavois shall join with the Hurons in making some arrangement with this tribe, so that we may have peace here.

All the tribes have retired in peace, with all their slaves. Saguina has abandoned his village, and is going to Michilimaquina. The Poutouatamis are also abandoning theirs, and are to come here or go to the Illinois. More than half of the Outtauois of this place are also withdrawing to Michilimaquina. The Saulteurs and Mississagues are going to Topicanich; they would on no account hear of making reparation to the Miamis for the murder of last year when Monsr de Tonty was here; the Miamis loudly demand justice from me. I am sparing no pains to make them have patience and understand that I am still working in their interests. I have the honor of telling you, Sir, that I arranged a matter last autumn which Monsr. de La Mothe was never able to succeed in doing, during the whole time he was here, viz. to compel the Outtavois to make a firm peace with the Miamis, and induce them to go to them·which they would never do. I succeeded most happily; the Miamis could not have received them better, and they made a strong alliance with one another. I flatter myself, Sir, that you will approve of my doing myself the honor to assure you that Mons. de Vincennes has done his duty thoroughly well, and has taken great pains as well as in his journey to the Miamis and Ouyatanous last winter. If I am so fortunate, Sir, as to have pleased you by my conduct, I shall have cause to console myself for all my troubles with which I could not have been more overwhelmed. I have extricated myself from these difficulties by the great influence I have over the tribes. Monsr. de Vincennes

possession, in what a state my finances must be; but I venture to put
my hopes in your goodness that a poor devil will not be thrown on
charity. I have the honor to be with very deep respect,

      Sir,

           Your most humble and most obedient Servant,

                                  Dubuisson.

At the fort of Detroit Pontchartrain the 15th of June 1712.

1703

———

LIST OF INDIAN TRIBES IN THE WEST.

Numbers of the Savage Tribes who are in connection with the government of Canada; of the warriors of each with their coats of arms.

*   *   *

Lake Erie   there are no tribes settled on the coast of
                         this lake.

*   *

Detroit   between Lake Erie and Lake Huron
300 leagues from
Montreal

The Poutcouatamis   The Poutcouatamis have a village there
                         of 180 warriors...................... 180

coat of arms   their arms are a golden carp, a frog.

The Hurons   The Huron tribe, formerly so numerous, is
                         reduced—if I except those at Quebec—to

At the farther end of Lake Huron is the post of Missilimakinak of which I have spoken, on the road of the river of the Outaouas. I believe. therefore, that I have gone through all the districts in which we are acquainted with any settlements of savages—of those who are connected with the government of Canada. If your curiosity is not satisfied as to the hieroglyphics or coats of arms of the savages, do not accuse me of negligence therein. I have been as desirous as possible to inform myself upon them, and to give you the explanations you ask me for. But, Sir, how few men,—even of those who have passed almost their whole lives among these tribes,—have devoted themselves to this study! I should say, not one, if La Honton had not written about them, still, what he says of them is but a dream and a romance. As for me, I have devoted myself to it; and, as regards the Iroquois,—the only tribe thoroughly well known to me,—I sent you some years ago several drawings of their coat of arms which must content you; from that you can judge of the other tribes. For the rest, had I not been unaware of the object of your research, and had you communicated your ideas to me I should have been better able to have assisted in your objects.[1]

I have the honor to be, &c.

INDIANS ON THE ST. JOSEPH RIVER.

Endorsed—Annexed to the letter from the Marquis de Vaudreuil of the 6th of Nov. 1712.

Letter from the Revd. Father Joseph Marest, missionary at Michilli-makinac, to the Marquis de Vaudreuil dated the 21st of June, 1712.

My Lord,

If Koutaouiliboé had been listened to I should have had the honor of replying earlier to the two kind letters I received from you, one of the 4th of September last year, and the other of the 23rd of March this year; but he was advised not to be in a hurry to send you a boat because we had as yet no certain news to tell you except that the Outaouas of the Grand river with the Poutouatamis of the St. Joseph River had made a great attack upon the Maskoutins. Since then, indeed, other things have happened, which you have doubtless already heard of through Detroit,

---

[1] The above document is not dated, or signed and there is no way of fixing its proper

of which this first attack was as it were the seed. I hope to say something about them after I have dealt with the two letters you honored me with.

1st, I thank you for having had regard for the persons whom I had. recommended to you. It was in the public interest rather than my own, that I made recommendations of this kind to you; but I may also assure you that you succeeded in pleasing all the savages who went down, difficult as they are to satisfy.

2nd, Thanks again for having spoken in favor of the missionaries in open council. I have experienced the effects of that; and I assure you that your zeal in favoring the cause of religion and those who labor to extend it, has contributed in no small degree to calling down upon you and all the . country you govern, such a miraculous evidence of Divine protection as that which delivered us all from two powerful armies without our striking a blow.

3rd, Although you had reasons for sending the savages back before the enemy came, their coming down was, nevertheless, a great advantage since it showed the English and their allies that you can get them down again when you wish as soon as you invite them to come.

4th, I think Ouenamek is going down. He will tell you himself what he has done, and how the Poutouatamis at St. Joseph behaved in his absence, as they are obliged to leave that river.

5th, Villeneuve gave me the gift you had entrusted to him for La Blanche, and I gave it to her from you. She is a woman of some capacity, who assists at all the councils; she is the daughter of a chief and has hitherto been a close adherent of the French. Villeneuve still continues to behave well, and so does his wife; would to God there were many in the village

greater part of them together again at Michillimakinac. If we do not keep our word with them, it might have awkward consequences. It is unfortunate to have to make any confession to the savages which gives them occasion to say that their father has deceived them, that he has lied to them, for this is their term, etc.

8th, You request me to present your compliments to Father Chardon; I have done so at Michillimakinac. This Father and Brother Haren were obliged to withdraw here, as the war did not permit them to remain at St. Joseph nor with the Poutouatamis. It seems as if Providence had permitted that on purpose to furnish me with assistance which was absolutely necessary in the present state of affairs.

I now come to the news. The most important you have heard already from a boat which was despatched to you from Detroit. The Reverend Recollet Father at Detroit sends me word that eight hundred Fox Indians and Maskoutins have been destroyed, men, women and children. No doubt he does not include the forty Maskoutins who, with sixty women and more than a hundred children, are said to have been killed in the direction of the Grand river. As I can only tell you of it from the report of others, and as Saguina is going down, the man who took the principal part in it with Makisabé, a Poutouatami, who also went down from Detroit, it is for them to make known to you that they were right to attack the Maskoutins so as not to be attacked by them first, and how the French at Detroit obliged them to attack the Fox Indians also, because they were in fear of them themselves.

For the rest, although the number slain is large, yet it cannot be said that the Fox tribe is destroyed; without counting those who have gone to the Iroquois, for we do not know what will become of them, there is a large number left in the direction of the Bay—some say there are still two hundred warriors. The Kikapoos, their brothers, to whom ten households of Maskoutins retreated, have more than a hundred good warriors; the Sakis, who use canoes, have eighty men; the Puants, sixty brave men, also boatmen. If they were to unite together,—and that would be only natural,—they might very well spread terror everywhere up here even yet; and they would be all the more to be feared from being allied with tribes who use canoes. Then Michillimakinac would no longer be a place of safety as it used to be; for it is not far from here to the Bay, and they could come here both by water and by land, and that not only to attack the savages, but the French, also, as the chief cause of this war, and for having joined the savages in order to destroy the Fox Indians. It is thought, however, that, when the Fox Indians at the Bay hear of the

the French, from the direction of Detroit, the Bay, Michillimakinac, the
Illinois, &c., if they will go, as their custom is, two men only in a boat,
to go all round the Lake, &c. This tribe of the Foxes, Kikapoos, and
Maskoutins is found everywhere when they are least expected, and they
are people who will listen to no reason, and have no pity, &c. If the
savages ever wished for Monsieur de Louvigny it is now; and they say it
is absolutely necessary for him to come for the safety of the country, to
reconcile them with one another, to keep together those whom the war has
already brought back to Michillimakinac, namely all those from the Grand
River, almost all from Saguinan and many from Detroit. It is true that
a few from Saguinan and Detroit have gone to Maintoualin with Le
Pesant: but if Monsieur de Louvigny returned here, no one doubts that
they would leave Maintoualin, where they have only made very small
sowings, and would come and join the others here. I have been told that
all the Outaouas of Detroit would have come here but for the arrival—
they say—of fifty or sixty Frenchmen at Detroit quite recently; who,
they add, are to be followed by a hundred others. This news (which is
doubtless not true in its entirety) has, I was told, made many of those
who wished to leave Detroit change their minds. The Outaouas and the
Poutouatamis have been invited to go and settle at Detroit; but Saguina
-has got out of that, with all the Outaouas whether from here or the Grand
River. I do not know what course the Poutouatamis have taken, nor, even

I do not know whether I am forgetting anything, but my letter is too long already. I will, however, add that Saguina told me to beg of you, if you wish to honor him with any present, to address it to me, so that the savages may not plunder it so easily, to give it to a man called Ountino from Longekam's village or indeed to any Frenchman. I am, with deep respect, Sir, Your most humble and most obedient servant.

Joseph J. Marest, of the Company of Jesus.

LETTER FROM FATHER MAREST—COMPLAINTS OF THE INDIANS.

Endorsed—Annexed to the letter from the Marquis de Vaudreuil of the 6th of July, 1712.

Letter from Father Joseph Marest, missionary at Michillimakinac, to the Marquis de Vaudreuil, dated the 2nd of July, 1712.

Sir,

· This morning, before he set out, Koutaouiliboé came and picked a quarrel with me. "What does our father Onontio mean by it?" he said to me; "it is five years already since he promised to send us Monsieur de Louvigny, and he wants to deceive us again this year as he did all the other years. He tells us that the great Onontio, the King, loves his children, the savages of Michillimackinac above all; yet he seems to abandon them entirely. Formerly, before Detroit was established, we who had settled at Michillimakinac were people of importance. All the tribes respected us because they were obliged to come here for what they had need of; there were no unseemly affairs as there now are, when the fiercest and most senseless tribes such as the Foxes, Kikapous, Maskoutins, Miamis, &c. who do not know how to use canoes, are able to go on foot to Detroit in as large numbers as they like, to buy powder there and to disturb all their allies; yet see," he adds, "how they want to make a larger settlement than ever at Detroit. A boat which arrived here yesterday from Detroit brought us news that Monsieur de la Forest had already arrived there with fifty Frenchmen; but Monsieur de la Forest is not coming to remain there, he is only coming in advance to speak to the savages. In a short time from now, another French chief is to come who is a young man who has bought all the property of Monsieur de La Mothe, his silver

ant nor Frenchman is to go up there; at the most, only two boats will
go up, and some men who get away by stealth to come there, &c.   Is
that then the preference which is shown to the people of Michilli-
mâkinac?   Is it because Detroit has always been a battle-ground, and
always will be, that its settlement alone is thought of?   Does our father
wish us to leave a place of safety like the one we are in to go with our
children to be slain at Detroit?   If our Father loves us, why does he
not think of establishing this place for us. and of sending us the man
that has been promised us for such a long time, to give spirit to those
who have none, to strengthen us against our enemies if they attack us,
and to prevent us from scattering again now we are come together?
Does not our father know that all the Outaouas from the great river
have returned here, almost all those from Saguinan, and the most important men from Detroit except Jean le Blanc whose wife is also here?
Does he not know also that all the Outaouas of Detroit had already
tarred their boats for coming here also, with half of the Hurons.   The
other half would have (?) fled to the Iroquois if they had not heard the
news of the coming arrival of the French, for they did not think themselves safe at Detroit, nor did the Saulteurs and Missisaghez who all
left there after the attack made upon the Fox tribe." In answer to all
that, I told him that you would be able to reply to him when he had
the honor of seeing you; on which he answered that the only reply for
his father to make to him is to grant him the man that has been promised to them for so long, whom he is going to seek: that otherwise he
does not know what will happen.

He also told me that the plague was down there, and I refuted it by
the last French people who came from there. He added another fine

bec, and that he had assured the people of Detroit, when he set out, that he was not leaving them forever: that at the end of four years they would see him again. That is the way the savages manufacture tales according to their interests or inclinations.

The attack which the Folles Avoines made at Chagouamigoun was on the intended brother-in-law of Durivage and his intended wife; they killed the former and carried off the other. Durivage is coming here to get back the said prisoner. They say that the people of Detroit are to go and fight against the Kikapoos, and that they have sent to invite the Saulteurs to join in this fighting. Excuse me, Sir, for only sending you news of the savages. Koutaouiliboé will be able to tell you still more of them; but he will not fail to remind you that he was the only one who obeyed your words, and that he was right when he told you last year that all your children would forget them as soon as they got out of the lands of Montreal, and that they would not fail to kill each other. I am with deep respect, Sir,

Your most humble and most obedient Servant

Joseph J. Marest,

of the Company of Jesus.

REPORTS FROM THE UPPER COUNTRY.

Endorsed—Colonies. M. de Vaudreuil 6th of Septr. 1712.

My Lord,

I received through Monsieur Begon the memorandum from the King dated the 15th of June of this present year, to which we both have the honor of replying. I also received from him all the letters you did me the honor to write to me dated the 19th of February, 25th of March, 23rd of April, 11th and 15th of May, 22nd, 25th, 26th, 28th, and 29th of June and 5th and 7th of July.

I have ever, My Lord, to thank you afresh for all the favors you are good enough to show me and all my family. I beg you to continue them.

* * *

I annex hereto, My Lord, a copy of two letters which the Reverend Father Marest, the Superior of the Outaouais' missions, writes me on this subject, and also on the necessity for sending the Sieur de Louvigny to Michillimakinac as soon as possible with a number of Frenchmen,

tins and the Outagamis until they have entirely destroyed them, and those who wish to side with them. It was this that the man Koutaouiliboé came down to Montreal to ask of me, on the 18th of July, in the name of all the rest, when he informed me that they were only waiting for his return to start and fall upon the Outagamis who are at the Bay in their old dwelling place. The man Ouilamek who came down with Koutaouiliboé represented to me, on the contrary, that the Outagamis were closely allied with the Sakis and it was to be feared that the latter would side with them if one tried to drive matters to extremes with them; that he himself, although he was always most obedient to my commands could not conceal from me that he, and the man Pilemont, also another chief of the Poutouatamis, would be most perplexed if the Sakis joined the Outagamis; that it was not right to try and destroy the Outagamis of the further part of the Bay, who had no share in all that took place at Detroit. That the matter was not such a simple one as Koutaouiliboé represented it to be; that those savages were brave, and many in number; and that they had alliances among many tribes who perchance were already sorry for having attacked them; that he named nobody, but he knew the feelings of many; that it was also to be feared that those Outagamis who had fled to the Iroquois might induce them to avenge them; that he was not afraid that anyone would accuse him of fear, that he had deeds enough of his own not to dread

these savages have been asking me for the said Sieur Desliettes as the only Frenchman who is capable of setting these tribes in the right path again.

The Sieur Dubuisson, My Lord, deserves that you should be pleased to have regard to the manner in which he has conducted himself throughout that affair which was none the easiest, and in which he had need of great firmness and disinterestedness to complete it satisfactorily; moreover he stripped himself entirely of everything he possessed in order to succeed in it. He has the honor of sending you herewith a memorandum of the expenses he was obliged to incur, which it seems to me right that His Majesty should deign to consider. He might, My Lord, be indemnified for a part of these expenses by making him a captain; that would reduce to some extent what His Majesty might be good enough to grant him for the remainder, and would serve as a recompense to this officer for his services.

*　　　　*　　　　*

I also sent off the Sr. Desliettes to the Illinois, and the Sieur de Vincennes to the Miamis, as the Sieur de la Forest wrote to me in one of his letters dated the 10th of July, that it was a matter of the utmost importance to send the said Sieur de Vincennes there, both in order to make peace between these savages and the Ilinois, and to prevent them from approaching the English as they have long wished to do. I also sent the convoy for Detroit by way of the great river, upon the Sonontouans informing me that the band of Le Tonnerre, an Outagami chief who has not joined them, might wait for the convoy at the portage at Niagara, or on Lake Erie. I did so, My Lord, both to avoid their meeting these savages and that this convoy might not be exposed to being pillaged by the Iroquois who under the pretext that they were conveying stores to their enemies, might by an act of this sort begin war against us. I flatter myself that His Majesty will approve of the precautions I am taking. I also flatter myself that—knowing how necessary it is to get together all the Outaouais tribes at Michilimakinac, so as to put them in a position to resist the Iroquois, if they should declare war on them—I flatter myself, I say, that you will approve of my sending the Sieur de Louvigny there in the early spring, for whom these tribes are waiting with the utmost impatience.

I now reply, My Lord, to all the letters which you have done me the honor of writing me.

It was with great pleasure that I saw from the one of the 28th of June that you approve of the reply I made last year to the Sr. de Nicholson as to the letter he had written to me from Port Royal in

I gave the Baron de St. Castin the commission as supernumerary lieutenant which His Majesty was pleased to grant him; he seemed very grateful for that favor.

I will continue, My Lord, to employ the Baron de Longeuil when I have any negotiation to conduct with the Iroquois. As he understands their language better than he speaks it, he cannot, when he goes to these tribes, do without the Sieur de Joncaire or the Sieur de la Chauvignerie or sometimes without both, according to the business in hand.

The Sieur de Beaucourt is most obliged to you, My Lord, for the assurance you are good enough to give him that His Majesty is satisfied with his services; he most humbly thanks you for the cross of St. Louis which you were pleased to obtain for him, as well as the appointment of engineer at Quebec, formerly held by the Sieur Le Vasseur. He will continue his services with the same diligence as he has done in the past. He has the honor of giving you an account of the works that have been executed this year.

The Sieur de Louvigny still continues to discharge his duties in such a manner as to deserve the honor of your patronge. He is very grateful for your having been good enough to send him word that His Majesty

will remember him when occasion serves. I recognized the merits of everyone in this country last year, My Lord, because everyone deserved it. The people of this country were delighted to hear that I had given you an account of their conduct and of their good disposition. I shall keep them always in the greatest harmony, as far as I can, for I am quite convinced that it is by kindness rather than severity that men are best managed..

It is fortunate, My Lord, as I had the honor of writing to you last year, that the enemies fleet was destroyed by the gales without costing this Colony a single drop of blood; we gave thanks to God for it, convinced that it was a visible proof of his protection. I am most obliged to you for my part, for having done me the justice of believing that I should have made a vigorous defence.

It will be very difficult, My Lord, if the war lasts, to prevent the Abenaki Indians on the sea coast from holding intercourse with the

the honor of writing to you, and I, that of forwarding his letter. If his
health does not permit of his remaining there, or this post does not suit
him on the conditions His Majesty has granted him, I will send the
Sieur de Sabrevois there.

. It is quite certain, My Lord, that there are a number of copper mines
among the heights of the Ouabache River. I have again obtained several
samples from them this year, through the savages; but I do not think
it would be easy to obtain the output from them through this place at
least in the present condition of affairs at Detroit; perhaps hereafter
we shall find it easier. I shall have the honor of informing you of it in
due course. As regards sending the Sieur de Vincennes, it was a matter
of the utmost necessity to do so, not only to conduct the Miamis to their
homes and prevent them from being attacked by the Missisaguez on the
road but also to prevent them themselves from going to the English and
taking their furs there, which would have served as an example for
many others. The orders I gave him about the mines were only given
in case it might be possible for him to go to the spot where they are,
to get information about them.

good--pro
vid..d no f
pense fall
the king i
making th
discoverie

I have nothing to add, My Lord, to the reasons I had the honor of
stating to you last year as to the re-establishment of the licenses. The
two letters from Father Marest, copies of which I have the honor of
sending you, will show you better than anything I could say how necessary it is that they should be re-established as soon as possible. I will
comply with your orders regarding the Sieurs de Louvigny and Lignery,
and will only incur the smallest expense I possibly can in re-establishing
Michillimakinac; but it is absolutely necessary to give them some soldiers, as well as the Sieur de la Forest, otherwise it will be impossible
to keep these two posts in order, or to prevent *voyageurs* from turning
aside from them and going there without license, as some have done
this year both at Detroit and Michillimakinac, despite the precaution I
have taken.

I had the honor of giving you an account last year, of the proceedings
of the inhabitants of Acadia, and of the causes which had prevented me
from giving them the help they had asked me for. This year I have
given them all the assistance in my power. They send me word in a
letter which Father Felix, the missionary at Les Mines writes me, dated
the 29th of August, that the English are ill-treating them greatly and
are always threatening to rob them of all they possess. If I had received your orders sooner I could have made some attack on the fort of
Port Royal, but I only received the letters you did me the honor to write

that one'c
wish he h
received i
letters, bu
that he m
not now c

earlier, he would have been seized, with his Lieutenant Governor, his Major, and several other officers who all went to bathe at a place near the fort without any escort.   If His Majesty had been able to send only one of the two vessels I had asked him for last year, to serve as an escort to our merchant ships and afterwards cruise in the bay of Baston, I should have been able, with this help and what I could have done here, to retake this fort; but without such assistance, the thing is not possible; that is what the Sieur Gaulin tells me in a letter he writes to me from Beaubassin on the 15th of August last. He still holds out in his mission, My Lord, as well as he can, but he sends me word that, as he has not
atuity was ated to him year. received any help from France for a long while, he will very soon be obliged to give up everything as he finds himself heavily in debt in consequence of having been obliged to borrow in one direction and another. It is unfortunate for him that the greater part of the goods which Monsieur de Costebelle sent him last year was seized by the English; they would have been of great assistance to him.   I certainly do my best to give him some from here, as well as all the missions; but that, when divided among so many different places, seems but little although it makes a considerable expense.   The English, for their part, spare nothing to let the savages know that their want proceeds only from their own fault, that we are not in a position to support them for long, and that we shall be forced to abandon them in a short time; and to make them understand still better the difference there is between them and us, within the last few days after a party from Noventehouac of fifty men had fought against a much larger party of English and had killed several of them and taken two prisoners, the English ransomed them with forty-

The Sieur d'Esgly would be greatly indebted to you, if you would be graciously pleased to obtain a cross of St. Louis for him.

We received by the King's ship the goods and stores which were embarked for this Colony. The Tulle guns are very good; we should have been glad if more of them could have been sent, and a larger quantity of powder also. Allow me, My Lord, to point out that, if the war continues, it will be impossible to send too large a quantity of either, and especially powder of which we were very short last year. *A quantit goods rem ed at Roc fort, whic could not taken on board, and this has caused us great loss.*

Monsieur Begon and I will do what we can, My Lord, to arrange so that the troops may be satisfied with what they have this year; it will however be very difficult, seeing all the various posts where I find I am compelled to keep a stock. Monsieur Begon, Monsieur Dallogny and I will consider everything that can be done. I will always see to it, My Lord, as far as I can, that no brandy is given to the savages; and no change shall be made in the decision which binds the inns of Montreal and Three Rivers to supply them with beer. *See whet we have t statement what was at Rochef if not, ask them. good.*

I have explained your wishes to the Marquis Dallogny and the Sieur Dumesnil as to the settlers in this country, that they should hold a review of them twice a year in order to teach this militia military discipline, and to ascertain the condition of their arms and compel those who have none to supply themselves with some according to their means. They will carry out your orders as soon as the fine season will let them. *good.*

I have given the eldest son of the widow Du Sablé a commission as junior officer in accordance with your instructions. I will look after his brother when an opportunity occurs. *good. All has pleased m*

We received in this country this year a reinforcement of forty-five men, viz. thirty by the "Heros," nine by the "Louise" and six by the "Heureux Retour." None of these soldiers are more than children, and it will require at least three or four years before they can be in a condition to do any service. Monsieur Philippeaux did us a great injury by detaining at Martinique the soldiers who had been embarked for us last year in the "Vermandois." He could have sent them to us here by a prize which that vessel had made, which arrived safely in harbor; at least he might have sent us the arms and ammunition with which this vessel was loaded for us. Monsieur Costebelle sent us this spring one thousand livres of powder, fifty guns, and eight thousand gun-flints out of the stores which had been left with him by the "Loire" in 1710. By the same opportunity he writes me that you had given orders last year to Monsieur Begon to send him from this country the provisions necessary for the food of his garrison; and on that ground requested *Ask M. de Beanharnc for the list arms and a munition e barked on the "Ver mandois". good. well done.*

took one of our boats on the coast of the Chapeau Rouge in which were a hundred quintals of peas and forty "quartes" of flour which will certainly be a misfortune for him. Monsieur Begon has sent him some peas.

I will explain your orders, My Lord, to the officers of militia and to the seigniors of parishes in this country, and I will inform the latter that they have no right to insist on captains of militia communicating to them the orders they receive from the governors and intendants before they execute them. I will also acquaint the others that they should do so out of courtesy when that would not interfere with the service.

Monsieur Begon and I will reply, My Lord, to the petition which the Sieur d'Artigny had the honor of sending you last year. We will do ourselves the honor of sending you our opinion thereon.

The Sieurs Gayot and Company have sent the Sieur La Nouilliere here with an authority to take cognizance of their affairs and to adjust them. Monsieur Begon and I, My Lord, will give him all the assistance he may desire, as also to the person he entrusts with the interests of these gentlemen.

It was with extreme grief, My Lord, that we heard of the death of Monseigneur Le Dauphin and of Madame La Dauphine, and that of Monseigneur Le Dauphin their eldest son. All the people of this country testified their keen sorrow at this occurrence, and we joined our prayers to theirs in a solemn service which was held in the cathedral of this town at which we were present—the Intendant and I—together with the Superior Council. We shall continue our prayers, My Lord, for the preservation of His Majesty and of Monseigneur Le Dauphin.

In your last letter, My Lord, of the 7th of July, you do me the honor of sending me word that His Majesty has thought fit for the good of his service to grant the Sieur de La Mothe fifty men from this country,

I have also allowed Captain the Sieur de la Pipardiere to do the same, as his father is dead, and his relations have notified him that it is advisable for him to come and settle his affairs himself.

In the early spring, My Lord, I sent the small prize, which the Sieur Beaumont had left us last year, to Plaisance to obtain news; no expense was caused to the King for this journey. When it came back, on the information I received from the islands that the enemy were threatening us again, I had it fitted out for cruising and put a hundred men on it, including three officers and twenty-five soldiers, with orders to return on the first news they could get that the enemy wanted to make any attack on this country or Plaisance. They captured a prize which was worth eighteen to twenty thousand livres, and besides that they took a privateer with thirty men, which was infesting the coasts of Acadia. I had news two days ago that they should be here in a short time and that they had been left at Green Bay.

I have intrusted our joint letter and my private ones to Captain the Sieur de Beaujeu who will have the honor of giving them to you. I can assure you he is a very good officer.

I have the honor to be with deep respect

   My Lord

    Your most humble and most obedient servant

       Vaudreuil.

Quebec this 6th of November, 1712.

I have the honor to annex to this letter, My Lord, a memorandum which the Sieur de Beaucours has given me of the expenditure to be made for completing the works which have been executed this year. I take the liberty of pointing out to you that if they are not finished as soon as possible, it will cost double the money in less than two years, as the winters in this country completely ruin works that are not finished.

I have received the cipher you sent me, My Lord, and will use it when I have any matter of importance to send you word of. I will take great care to keep it under lock and key.

       Vaudreuil.

EXPENSES OF THE POST AT DETROIT.

Statement of what Mons. Dubuisson expended for the service of the
King to attract the tribes to him and attach them to his interests to
support him against the Outagamis and Mascoutins who had been paid
by the English to destroy the post of Fort Pontchartrain at Detroit.

To Wit.

4 barrels of powder of 50 livres each, to distribute to the savages
 for the defence of Fort Pontchartrain, and to attack the fort of
 the Outagamis and Mascoutins: the powder having been
 bought from *voyageurs* at 4 franc per livre makes the sum of.. 800#

Item, 300 livres of bullets for the same purpose, at 50 sols per
 livre .... 450#

Item, 60 sacks of Indian corn at 8# a sack to assist in feeding the
 savages .... 480#

Item, 300 gun flints at 7# a hundred........................... 21#

Item, 5 guns to give to five chiefs to attach them to Mons. Dubuisson's interests, each valued at 30#.......................... 150#

Item, 8 coverlets to cover certain important men killed with M.
 Dubuisson valued at 30# each............................... 240#

Item, 8 pairs of mitasses for the same purpose at 7 livres 10 sols
 a pair .... 60#

. FOX INDIANS ATTACK DETROIT.

Endorsed—Colonies.   The Marq. de Vaudreuil 15th of Octr. 1712.

My Lord,   ·

I have the honor of writing to you by way of Plaisance to inform you of the safe arrival in this country of the King's ship, which anchored in this roadstead on the 7th of this month. Monsieur and Madame Begon disembarked in perfect health, and I venture to assure you in advance of the good understanding that will always exist between Mons. Begon and me. The whole country felt a genuine pleasure in seeing him, and I, My Lord, much more than any one else.

I have already had the honor of writing to you three times since this spring, and, in these three letters, of giving you an account of all that has taken place in this country since the departure of the King's ship last year, up to the 23rd of July of this present year.

In my first letter, of the 28th of April, I informed you, My Lord, of the reasons which made it necessary for me to send the small ship, which Mons. de Beaumont left here for us, to Plaisance, on the melting of the ice, in order to obtain news. I informed you in the same letter of the reasons which compelled me at the same time to go up to Montreal where three Iroquois envoys awaited me, as well as a Fleming sent by the Council of Orange to demand back his wife and certain other prisoners made by our savages of Sault aux Recolets last autumn.

. In my second, of the 27th of June, I gave you an account, My Lord, of the departure of the Sieur de la Forest for Fort Pontchartrain at Detroit, with ten boats and forty men. I informed you, My Lord, how well-disposed the inhabitants of this country still remained and that, being most grateful for the visible protection of God over them last year, they were more than ever inclined to give proofs of their fidelity to His Majesty. I told you, My Lord, how I received the Iroquois envoys at Montreal, and how—after having reprimanded them for having allowed themselves to be beguiled by the English—I had shown them how important it was to them not to take sides either with the English or us. I told you, My Lord, in the same letter the reasons which had made it necessary for me to go down to Quebec again to press forward by my presence the stone works which the Sieur de Beaucourt was having executed in .accordance with His Majesty's orders and yours.

for this year. As I shall have the honor of giving you an account of
everything, My Lord, by the King's ship, I content myself here with
assuring you that no one could take more pains or show more diligence
than the Sieur de Beaucourt does, and that the inhabitants could not
possibly show more good-will.

At the same time, My Lord, that I had the honor of writing you that
letter I received one from Michillimakinac in which the missionaries of
that place informed me that the Fox Indians who came last year to
settle at Detroit had tried to offer an insult to the Sieur Dubuisson who
was in command there in the absence of the Sieur de la Forest; that
this made it necessary for him to intrench himself in half of his fort,
which was too large for the number of Frenchmen he had with him;
that he had not only defended himself against them, but had called the
other tribes allied to us to his aid, and the Fox Indians had almost all
been destroyed and had lost nearly a thousand souls, including two
hundred prisoners. This news, having been confirmed by the letters of
the Sieur de la Forest, and by the Sieur Dubuisson who arrived a short
time after with a convoy of fifteen to twenty boats, French and Indians,
made me resolve to go up to Montreal to be within easier reach for giving my orders; more especially as the Foxes, Maskoutins and other
savages concerned in the affair at Detroit are allied to several tribes
of the upper country, and it was to be feared that they might take their
side, as Ouilamek, a chief of the Poutouatamis, came all the way to
Quebec to tell me and as Fathers Marest and Chardon, the Missionaries
at Michilimakina also wrote me. These reasons, My Lord, made it necessary for me to go up to Montreal, and my presence there was much more
necessary than I had at first thought; for, scarcely had I arrived before
I learnt from the Sieur de la Fresniere, and afterwards from the Sieur
de Joncaire, whom I had sent to Fort Frontenac as commandant in the
absence of the former who had gone down to Montreal, suffering from
fever, as well as some of his garrison—I say I learnt, My Lord, that
the Sieur Pitreseul had made two journeys one after another to

at Onontagué to the number of a thousand or twelve hundred men, and having made their boats on the very spot where they made them in the time of the Marquis de Denonville, when they came to lay waste the neighborhood of La Chine and other places above Montreal, I stood upon my guard and spared nothing to obtain news from all quarters. At the same time I had the tribes allied to us warned, as far as possible, so that they might be upon their guard, enjoining on them however not to begin war first lest they should draw down on them a war which could not but be most fatal to both sides, letting them know at the same time that I have grounds for believing that the Iroquois would reflect seriously before entering upon any attack, more especially as the Sonnontoüans would not join with them in this war, and forty-five chiefs and important men of this tribe had even come all the way to Montreal to assure me of this. I waited for your orders, My Lord, until the 25th of September. As the season being so far advanced did not allow of my waiting any longer, I thought,—looking to the interests of the service, and for other reasons of which I shall have the honor to send you an explanation by the King's ship,—I thought, I say, that I ought to make no further delay, My Lord, in sending the Sieur de Lignery to Michillimakinac until I could send the Sieur de Louvigny there next spring. I ordered him to set out with three boats, besides two that I sent to the Ilinois and one to the Miamis. I also despatched the convoy for Detroit by the Grand river as I did not think it would be safe by the Lake route, the Sonontouans having told me that a company of Fox Indians might wait for them at the portage of Niagara or on Lake Erie. I am only sending you a summary of everything My Lord, leaving it until I have the honor of writing to you more fully by the Heros which is to return to France from this place. I have the honor to thank you in advance, My Lord, for all the favors you are good enough to show me. I beg you to continue to honor me with your patronage, and to believe that I am, with all possible gratitude and respect,

My Lord

Your most humble and most obedient servant

Vaudreuil.

Quebec, this 15th of October, 1712.

DEATH OF LA FOREST.

Endorsed—Colonies. MM. de Ramezay and Begon. 12th of Nov.

on the affairs of this country since the 20th of Septr. the day on which the Marquis de Vaudreuil left on the King's ship l'Affriquain.

Since that time we have received news from Orange, which a Missiagué Indian had brought back from there, that five boats have been destroyed by a party of Fox Indians towards Chicago, in which were twelve Frenchmen, including a Jesuit friar, who had set out from Michilimakina on the 15th of August last to go to the Ilinois, to the mission of the Jesuit Father Deville.

This new insult makes us feel, My Lord, that they are not much disposed to listen to proposals of peace, and that we shall be compelled to force them on with arms in our hands; for, if we remain inactive, they will become more and more insolent, and will alienate the savages allied to us either through fear or at the instigation of the English who are endeavoring in every way to get a footing among the Outavois tribe, having sent necklaces and presents to them by the man Itacougik, a Mississagué savage, their emissary, to induce them to act in accordance with their will. This will make the said Sieurs de Ramezay and Begon take all the steps necessary for carrying out the plan explained in the joint letter of the 20th of September last; and they will do themselves the honor to report to you the success of this undertaking, to which they will devote their whole attention.

Captain M. de la Forest, commandant at the fort of Detroit, died on the 16th of last month; and M. de Sabrevois will succeed him in accordance with your orders, but he will not be able to set out till next spring. This will cause no trouble since Captain the Sieur Dubuisson is now here.

We have given the Chevalier de Chalus, My Lord, the other despatches which we have the honor of sending you, as well as this one, and we beg that you will graciously show him the same favor as the officers who have at other times been entrusted with them.

WAR AGAINST THE FOX INDIANS AND AMNESTY TO THE
. "COUREURS DE BOIS."

Endorsed—Canada. To be laid before the Council of Regency—28th April, 1716.

The Fox Indians have killed Frenchmen on. several occasions and would have deserved to be punished for all the attacks they made upon us; but as war is not advisable in the Colony of Canada and any war that can be waged against these savages can have no other advantage except that of making them remain at peace, the Council considers it advisable to give orders in Canada to make peace with these savages, but without compromising the national honor; and at the same time to act as if we were preparing for war, to call together the "Coureurs de bois" for that purpose at Michilimakina, and to send settlers up there.

An amnesty was granted by the late King to these "coureurs de bois" on condition they should serve in this war if it were determined upon. The advice of the Council is to renew this and, as it is not consistent with the interests of the Colony that settlers should remain in the backwoods in future, or go up there without permission, the Council considers it necessary to add the penalty of the lash to that of the galleys imposed against these "coureurs de bois" by the Proclamation of 1696.

Also to assign cognizance of their disobedience to the Governor-General, the Intendant, the local governor of the town in which the trial is prepared, the King's Lieutenant, the Major, the two senior Captains and the Procureur de Roi of the ordinary jurisdiction, who will act in the capacity of Procureur-Général, with authority to any seven of them to adjudicate in the matter.

It appears necessary to withdraw matters of this kind from the ordinary courts, where the proceedings are protracted, and where little justice can be hoped for against men like these because of their relationships or the trade they do with those who dispense justice.

The Council also thinks it advisable to make it compulsory for settlers who go up to the backwoods, to have their permits registered in the registry of the jurisdiction of Montreal; and, on their return, the certificate of the commandant of the post to which they have been.

In this way the Procureur de Roy will be informed of all those who

Decision o the Court Regency agreed. L. M

the confiscation of the goods and of the furs returned—to furnish goods suitable for trading to any persons who are going into the back-woods, unless they have permission to go up there; also to forbid them—under the like penalty—to supply any goods to those who have remained there without permission.

Given and decreed by the Council of the Navy held at the Louvre on the 28th of April, 1716.

L. A. de Bourbon
Marshal D'estrees.

By the Council
La chapelle

THE SETTLEMENT AT DETROIT.

Endorsed—28th of March, 1716.· Canada.

Report and decisions in the margin of the Council of the Navy.

Detroit is a post at the entrance of Lake Erie where the Huron savages and some Outavois and Missisagues are settled. The Miamis go to trade at this post. The first settlement was made 30 years ago under the governorship of M. d'Henonville. It was abandoned in consequence of the war with the Iroquois, and was afterwards re-established by M. de Callieres.

The King ceded it to the Company of the Colony, to carry on trade there. The Company gave two thousand crowns a year for the poor families of Canada.

The affairs of this Company, which had accumulated no funds, having got into a bad state, the post was granted by the King to the Sr. de la Mothe Cadillac with the monopoly of the trade.

When that officer was appointed Governor of Louisiana, this post was

doned. He will issue orders to the 25 Frenchmen who have gone up in these boats to join M. de Louvigny and to obey his orders.

They add that, as this post is too important for them to leave it un-defended, the Sr. de Ramezay will send 10 soldiers there, including the 5 who are already there, and that they will be furnished with the same supplies as those at Michilimakinac; and that, in consideration of this, as the Sr. de Sabrevois is not obliged to go to any expense, he ought to. be satisfied if the King is pleased to grant him [permits for] two boats, which will enable him to live in more comfort than he used to do at Montreal.

The advice of M. de Vaudreuil is to put a garrison of 15 or 20 sol- The Coun approves the advice M. de Vau reuil. L L. M diers in this post as it is for the interests and welfare of this Colony to maintain it in order to open up communication with Louisiana, and prevent the English from settling there. Ditto. L. L. M

To grant the commandant of this post the monopoly of the trade, as he has always had it, but only at his post; prohibiting sending to the tribes, and obliging him to provide conveyance for whatever may be necessary for the garrison, and to keep an almoner, a surgeon and an interpreter there at his own expense, so that it may cost the King nothing.

From the letters which M. de Vaudreuil has received from Canada, he M. de Vau reuil must propose another officer and explain w new empl ment shou in his opin be given t the Sr. de Sabrevois L. B L. M is informed that the Sr. de Sabrevois, although a very agreeable man, does not possess the faculty of making himself liked by the savages. He therefore asks the Council's permission to appoint another officer there when he arrives in Canada.

M. Begon, in the duplicate of his letter of the 12th of November, 1714— States that it appears, from the concessions which were granted by the Sr. de la Motte to private persons at Detroit, to the number of over 60, which are in accordance with the one of which he sends a copy, that he made them in pursuance of the authority which he had from the King in the despatches dated the 14th, 17th, and 19th of June, 1706, The Coun wished to these dis-patches before de-termining this term. L. B L. M to grant the lands at Detroit as he might think fit, and that he has made them as if he had been the Seignior and owner by length of possession.

But that it does not appear that His Majesty intended to grant him the proprietorship, for in that case he would have given him letters of concession which would have been registered before the Superior Coun-cil of Quebec, which has not been done. It is therefore to be presumed that His Majesty, in the authority he gave him, only wished to enable him to grant lands in His Majesty's name, in order to establish settlers there; and, consequently, he ought not to have made them in his own

which he is unaware of, having seen no order from His Majesty on this subject.

The Sr. de la Motte cannot have had the post of Detroit except to develop it, in the room and stead of the Company, which did not possess the domain.

This leads to the conclusion that the Sr. de la Motte's concessions ought no longer to stand, especially as the persons to whom they were granted have been obliged to abandon them, fearing lest they should be killed by the savages; and for that reason no other settlements should be made there save those [necessary] for keeping up a garrison to preserve the understanding between the French and the savages.

That those who hold these concessions do not intend to use them to settle on at Detroit but only for taking goods there to sell them to the savages, and bring back furs, which is desiring to share with the commandant of this post the trade which has been granted to him by the King to the exclusion of everyone else.

It does not seem to him that the concessions which he made to two of his children should hold good any more than the others.

The opinion of M. de Vaudreuil is that these concessions ought not to stand.

Given and decreed by the Council of the Navy held at the Louvre on the 28th of March, 1716.

L. A. de Bourbon
Le Marèchal d'Etrées

By the Council
Lachapelle.

PEACE WITH THE FOX INDIANS.

the Northern tribes at Chicago, went to Rocher, one of the villages of the Illinois, thinking they would find the Sieurs de Ramezay Mannoir and de Longueil d'Adoncour there. They were both at the Cascacias, exceedingly ill, so that they could neither walk nor write. .The Sr. de Mannoir ordered a man named Bizaillon who belonged to the Illinois to induce as many of the savages of that tribe as he could to join the other party so that they might all go together, on the news he had received, and attack seventy huts of the Mascoutins and Quikapous, allies of the Fox Indians, who were hunting at a certain river.

They did in fact join them on the 20th of November, and, after a most obstinate fight, they broke through them on a steep rock where they had intrenched themselves, killed more than a hundred of them and took forty-seven prisoners without counting woman and children.

After [inflicting] this defeat, our savages went down in boats on the same river nearly 25 leagues, in order to cover up their trail. But, in spite of this precaution, on the eleventh day at daybreak, they were met by four hundred of the pick of the Fox Indians; and, although there were only eighty of them, thirty being on guard at a redoubt which they made every evening, in which were their wounded and prisoners, they defended themselves so vigorously from daybreak until three o'clock in the afternoon that they forced the enemy to retire with very heavy loss. They took seven of their heads, and saw signs of very great slaughter when they pursued them for some hours. Our people had 26 men killed and 18 wounded in these two actions. There are nine savages from the St. Louis falls, and eight Hurons dead; the others belong to the other tribes.

These two distinct actions produced most beneficial effects on the minds of our savages, and animated their courage while it damped that of the Fox Indians.

The Sr. de Ramezay has been informed that the chief of the Quikapoos came to declare to the first French people he met in the upper 'country that both his tribe and that of the Mascoutins threw themselves into the arms of their father, declaring themselves his slaves for him to disperse among whatever tribe he might think fit; that, moreover, if the Fox tribe would not adopt the same attitude, they would deliver them up to the pot.

The Sr. Pachot, a Canadian who is a cadet in the army and was formerly an interpreter at Detroit in the Huron tongue, the son of Madame de la Forest, and a man named Bizaillon, a settler, were the only two Frenchmen in these actions. By all reports, they did their duty thor-

and Begon, and the Sr. de Louvigny, the latter set out from Montreal on the 1st of May with 225 French and was afterwards joined at Detroit and Mishilimakina by 200 more, who were already there. The warlike stores, presents, and provisions requsite were taken by these Frenchmen at their own expense, without any cost to the King.

The Sr. de Louvigny arrived at Quebec on the 12th of this month after he had forced this haughty tribe to ask for peace. He reduced them to this necessity after having opened a trench 70 yards from their fort. The first night he carried it forward 20 yards; the second, sixteen. At last the enemy, seeing that he was connecting it with the center of the place, in order to mine it and blow it up, besides having two pieces of ordnance and a grenade mortar which kept up a heavy fire day and night, resolved to ask for a parley and to crave the clemency of the French. They were not given a hearing until advice had been taken from all the tribes who accompanied the Sr. de Louvigny, and their opinions gathered. He proposed conditions to them so stringent that all these tribes thought they would not consent to them. The conditions are—

1st, That they shall make peace with all the tribes subject to the King with whom the French trade.

2nd, That, either by force or by friendly means, they will induce the Kikapous and Mascoutins, their allies, and our enemies, to make peace like them with all the tribes in general.

3rd, That they will give back, or cause to be given back, all the prisoners they have from all the tribes. This they have carried out.

4th, That they will go on the war path in the further districts to make slaves in order to replace all the dead who had been killed in the course of the war.

5th, That they will hunt in order to pay the cost of the preparations made for this war; and, that as security for the fulfilment of the above conditions, they should give the Sr. de Louvigny six chiefs, or sons of chiefs, to be taken to the Marquis de Vaudreuil as guarantees for the conditions of the treaty. This has been carried out, the Sr. de Louvigny having brought with him to Quebec these six chiefs and children of chiefs.

This proud tribe, which ravaged the whole of the upper country and made it tremble, has been reduced to complying with all these conditions, although they had 500 warriors and more than 3000 women who, on

This action was conducted very vigorously, and the officers who were present gave proofs of their alertness and energy by working at the trenches like the meanest soldier, in order to set an example and urge on the small numbers that accompanied the Sr. de Louvigny, which only amounted to 800 men, to press on an action which was important in itself and one where delay might have involved failure because of the proximity of the allies of the Fox tribe to whom they had sent word and from whom they had demanded help.

The Sr. de Louvigny, although his eyesight is slightly affected after such a long journey, hopes before the last ships sail to be able to draw up a report of what took place during this expedition, which is the first military operation that has occurred in His Majesty's reign, and is glorious to the King's arms, and most advantageous to this colony.

Vaudreuil.

REMARKS ON THE WAR WITH THE FOX INDIANS.

By the King's proclamation of the 21st of May, 1696, His Majesty prohibited all persons from going to trade among the savages on pain of the galleys. The reasons for this prohibition were that too many Frenchmen went up among the savage tribes, which had brought in too many beaver-skins, and the excesses these same Frenchmen committed among these savages. At the same time, the King withdrew all the officers and garrisons he had among these tribes. But, on the representations which were made the same year, as to the necessity for having officers and garrisons at Fort Frontenac, Michilimakina and St. Joseph of the Miamis, the King decreed that those posts should be preserved with the same officers and troops, trading being forbidden. Fort Frontenac was re-established; and the Iroquois having asked that trade should be carried on for them to obtain what they needed, it was set up there, and it is the King who now carries it on.

The posts of Michilimakina and St. Joseph of the Miamis were not re-established; it would have cost very large sums to have sent the necessary things for those who would have been in garrison there, by boats which could not have traded.

Despite the prohibition against going to trade among the savages, there have always been some Frenchmen who have gone there, and, not daring to return to the Colony, have remained among the tribes. They are called *"courcurs de bois."*

And as the   were men lost to the Colony. the Governors and Intendants proposed to grant them amnesties, in order to get them back. There were two granted up to 1710, and the third was granted in the month of March, 1714 in connection with the war with the Fox Indians, a copy of which is annexed. It sets forth that these *coureurs de bois* may take advantage of the amnesty, provided always that, before returning to their homes, they repair to the Fort of Michilimakina and serve there in accordance with the orders given them by the officers in command there, in case it may be deemed advisable, for the interests and peace of .the country to make war on any savage tribes, in which event they will be bound to supply themselves with provisions, arms, powder, lead and boats for the said war; and in consideration of this they shall bring back certificates from the said officer proving that they have presented themselves, and have carried out his orders, which certificates they shall be bound to have registered before the Superior Council of Quebec in the year 1715, at latest, in order to possess the privileges contained in the present decree, in which the King again repeats the prohibitions against going trading in the woods.

This war led to the decision to send an officer to Michilimakina with a garrison, to maintain our alliance with the Outavois, Sauteurs, Miamis, Ilinois, Puants and Folles Avoines, who have always been on our side, and served us very effectively in the war we had against the Iroquois, and to induce these savages to join us against the Fox Indians, in case we should be obliged to make war against them.

Word has always been .sent Canada to prefer peace to war, as peace suits the Colony better for all sorts of reasons.

And in case we could not succeed in that, and were obliged to make war, to make use of the *coureurs de bois* for that purpose, to whom the amnesty was granted only on that condition.

Also to permit some Frenchmen to go up with goods, on condition that they go against these savages.

This course was taken because the King was not in a position to defray all the expenses necessary for this war. They are very large when a number of Frenchmen have to be equipped.

Also to send 200 Frenchmen up to Michilimakinac with goods, in order that it may cost the King nothing, on condition that they shall serve in this war if they require them, we supplying them with powder and bullets on the spot, if they are going to the war.

To renew the amnesty, on condition that the *courcurs de bois* shall serve in this war.

And at the same time to have all prisoners given up to the Fox Indians, which the French have of theirs, and to make every effort to obtain peace while, however, arranging everything as if we wished to make war.

The proposal which M. de Louvigny makes, to send five or six hundred men equipped solely for this war, does not appear practicable, and it would cost forty or fifty thousand crowns to do so.

M. de Vaudreuil thinks the same on this matter; and asks that, to the penalty of the galleys imposed by the King's proclamation of the 21st of May, 1696, on the *coureurs de bois,* may be added that of the lash; which will make more impression on the minds of the people of Canada than the former; and that examples are absolutely necessary to put a stop to the disobedience of these *coureurs de bois.*

He also asks that these *coureurs de bois* shall be tried by court-martial, and not by the ordinary courts, and afterwards by the council, on the ground that there is no end to these formalities, and moreover, since those judges are nearly all merchants, there is no reason to expect much justice from them against people who have been trading for them, or their relations, or partners.

Remark.

It is certain that the penalty of the galleys makes little impression in Canada, and that it is necessary that examples should be made as to the *coureurs de bois.* It is true that they would be obtained more easily if the matter went to a court-martial; but as that does not appear to be a matter for a court-martial, it is thought that it would be better to give cognizance of matters of this kind to special judges, who should include the Governor General, the Intendant, the local Governor of the town where the trial was brought, the commanding officer of the troops, the King's Lieutenant, the Major, the judges of the ordinary jurisdiction, the two senior captains in the garrison of the town, and the Procureur de Roy who shall discharge the duty of Procureur-Général, and give them authority, to the number of seven, to give judgment; and for this purpose to issue a new proclamation adding the penalty of the lash against the *coureurs de bois,* and at the same time granting an amnesty to all who are in the woods, provided always that, before

officer ,in command there, in case it may be thought fit to make war on
.any savage tribes, in which event they shall be bound to supply themselves with provisions, arms, powder, lead, and boats for the said war,
in consideration of which they shall obtain certificates from the said
commanding officer, providing that they have presented themselves and
carried out his orders, which certificates they shall be bound to have
registered at the registry of the jurisdiction of Montreal eight days
after their arrival in the Colony, and within a year from the day of
the publication of the present edict, the whole on pain of being punished as *coureurs de bois*. And as it will be necessary for a number
of people to go to the upper country on account of the war with the Fox
Indians to permit them to go up there after obtaining the Governor
General's permission countersigned by the Intendant; that those to whom
such permission shall be granted shall be bound to have it registered at
the registry of the jurisdiction of Montreal; and at the same time to
oblige them to· present themselves to the commandant of the post to
which they have permission to go, and to obtain a certificate from him
showing that they had presented themselves and carried out his orders;
which certificates they shall also be bound to have registered at the
registry of the jurisdiction of Montreal .eight days after their arrival,
and within 1S months from the day on which their permission is dated;
the whole on pain of being punished as *coureurs de bois*.[1]

ENGLISH ENTICE THE INDIANS TO LEAVE THE FRENCH.

Endorsed—Index letter C.

Extract from the letter of M. de Sabrevois to the Marquis de Vaudreuil.

Detroit, 8th of April, 1717.

I have already had the honor of sending you some account of what

do as well as I can, and will not answer for any troubles that may arise. We set out. A long time after, Ouytaouikigik arrives with some barrels of rum. It was this wretch who, as I was told, took away La Turpin to the English. He brought a necklace, on behalf of the English, to all the tribes here, telling them by that necklace that they are very foolish to adhere to the French, that they rob them; that they should come to them and they will give them two yards of cloth for two beaver-skins, and that now they will receive all their furs, as the French do; that when they died it was the French who gave them medicine; that the Governor of Canada was always asking them for medicine and they could not refuse to sell him any, and that it was in order to cast it on them. If I had had my interpreter, all that would not have happened, for as soon as I learnt that he was approaching I should have sent him to meet him, and he would have learnt all, and I should have upset all that. But I did not hear of it until this winter. I have also learnt that councils were held this winter between the Poux and Outaovast, arranging to go to the English for goods because the French sold them too dear. When I heard that, I immediately labored to defeat all their plans and I could answer for it that they will not go; but I made known to the savage who brought all that news, that if he went to the English any more, and came back here, I would have him shot. And I will not fail to do so.

[extract ends thus.]

A TALK WITH THE OTTAWAS AND THEIR REPLY.

Endorsed—Index letter B.

Reply of the Marquis de Vaudreuil to the words of the Outavas.

I am sorry you have lost your old men who. were sensible men and capable of making you do what was right.

I am well aware of this loss, from the account that has been given me of the wrongful acts you committed against the French.

But I know there are well disposed men among you; Chamgonueschi and Makakous are such men, for last year they prevented Maurice my interpreter from being stabbed and put a stop to the evil purpose of those who wanted to take away a barrel of brandy by force from M. de la Noüe, a chief of great importance in my eyes. Reflect well on that, and see that no such thing occurs in future, if you wish me to look upon you as my children.

What you have told me about M. de Sabrevois surprises me greatly. I have also seen what you said to M. de Tonty, about him, when you met him. I strongly approve of all that M. de Tonty said to you, and of what he did to bring you to your senses; and I am very glad that you hearkened to his words, which are mine.

You knew before you left Detroit that M. de Sabrevois had been recalled, and that M. de Tonty was going to command there instead of him. You ought therefore to have awaited his arrival at Detroit. He is a good man and would have contented you; or, if you did not wish

Words of the Outavas from Saguinan and of the Poutevatamis who arrived at Montreal on the 24th of June, 1717, coming from Detroit whence they had set out, to the number of 17 boats, to go and trade at Orange, of which 17 boats, six came to Montreal and the rest returned with M. de Tonty to Detroit.

Shamgoueschi, an Outevas chief, speaks for those from Saguinan.

My father, I beg you to hear me. What can I say to you now? We have no longer my chiefs left, all those who had sense are dead.

Since M. de Sabrevois arrived at Detroit, matters have altered very much. He has not followed the example of his predecessor, he has dealt badly with us. He has treated us harshly. He was never accustomed to feast a single chief, nor give them a morsel of tobacco, which has offended us a little. This is the treatment we have received from M. de Sabrevois. He has sold us blankets at as dear a price as fifteen beaverskins and has refused to give us suck, (that is brandy to drink).

I am not a man of any rank, I am nothing; and if I speak I only do so in obedience to the chiefs who are present, and in order to explain their feelings to you. We have brought nothing here but what M. de Sabrevois has rejected, a few worn out skins all torn, and a few ox-hides; what more we have is very little.

The bad treatment we have received from M. de Sabrevois, whom we

to wait for him, you should have come to me at Montreal to make known your troubles.

Nothing should have made you take the course of going to the English. If you had carried out your intention I should have been very angry, and I should not have looked upon you as my children any longer, for you would have deserted a father who loves you and has always supported you, to apply to a stranger who has never done anything for you but, on the contrary, has always urged the Iroquois to make war on you. I have spoken to the merchants and they have assured me they will give you goods cheaper than they sell them to the French. I hope you will have cause to go back pleased with that.

M. de Tonty writes to me, as to the brandy you ask for, that you assured him that you would not get intoxicated and that you would drink it quietly in your homes. I consent to permit you to take a little away; and, if M. de Tonty informs me next year that you have made good use of it, I promise to give you some more.

I advise you to take as little brandy as possible in order to husband your resources, so that you may have the means of dressing yourselves, and covering your women and children.

I was pleased to hear that you removed your homes last year from Saguinan and had gone to rejoin your old men and your brothers at Missilimakina. I counted on re-establishing your village there, as completely as it was formerly. M. de Louvigny has gone there for that purpose, but I learn to-day that you have returned to Saguinan.

That troubles me greatly, for I am convinced that you would be much better off than you are if your tribe were all re-united at Missilimakina; and that, in the event of war, you would be better able to defend yourselves if you were all together.

I regard you, at Saguinan, as wandering children who must have forgotten looked upon as our father at Detroit, but who did not look upon us as his children, has offended our old men extremely, and has driven us to adopt the course—to the number of 17 boats of various tribes—of going in the direction of Orange, being convinced that we should get goods there on far better terms than at Detroit.

We met M. de Tonti who was going to Detroit to be our father there. He dissuaded us from our purpose of going to the English and induced those of us who are here to come to Montreal, assuring us that we should be well treated, and that goods would be given us on favorable terms.

My father, I speak once again on behalf of the chiefs who are here. They beg you to see that they meet with good treatment in the little trade they have to do.

We beg you, my father, to permit us to take away a little brandy; we want some to entertain our young men in our country. Point out to us one, two, or three houses where they may give us some. We will limit ourselves to what you think fit to grant us.

I forgot to tell you that we have been warned that the disease was here, and that, by coming here, there was reason to fear lest we might meet with the same fate as so many others who have died of it. But we risked coming here in order to see our father; and we hope that, as this epidemic has ceased, we shall find the road smooth and without danger for us to return.

TALK OF THE POUTOUATAMIS AND THE REPLY OF M. DE VAUDREUIL.

Reply of M. de Vaudreuil to the words of the Poutouatamis from Detroit.

I know, my children of the Poutouatamis, that you have always hearkened to my words; but the steps which you were going to take when you met M. de Tonty was not that of a child who is much attached to his father.

You complain of the bad treatment of M. de Sabrevois. It is true that it was I who sent him to Detroit; I hoped that it would please you. But if he has made you uncomfortable, it is to me that you ought to have complained and you ought not to have gone to the English. If he sold you goods dear it was because they were scarce. You have done well to listen to the words of M. de Tonti, who has gone to Detroit instead of M. de Sabrevois. He is a good man; he is taking a quantity of goods; and I am sure he will deal kindly with all the tribes there.

I am glad, my children, that you are rejoiced to see me; I am no less pleased to see you here, and that you have forgotten all the vexations you felt.

I am willing to believe that you had no intention of seeking another father, when you purposed to go to the English, and that it was only the ease in obtaining brandy and the idea of finding cheap goods which made you take this course. If you had pursued it, you would have run many risks and would have exposed yourselves to the loss of a father who loves you, who has never abandoned you.

As regards the cheapness of the goods you have heard what I have just said to your brothers, the Outavas.

You are right in regarding me as your true father, for I have never acted to-

Otchik, a chief of the Poutouatamis, speaks for those belonging to his tribe.

My father I beg you to listen to me. I am an old man of no importance, and am unfit to be a spokesman.

I have never failed to obey the words of my father, I have always hearkened to them; but I confess that on this occasion, being indignant at the bad treatment of M. de Sabrevois, I took a course quite opposed to those words.

It was you, my father, who sent M. de Sabrevois to govern Detroit; but I have reason to think that he has not obeyed your orders for he has taken from us as much as three bear skins for the worth of one beaver skin. That was what made me decide to go to the English and offer them my body as a sacrifice, and try to get a small quantity of their goods.

M. de Sabrevois gave us to understand that he treated us in this way only by the orders of the King and M. de Vaudreuil.

When I met M. de Tonty, whom you have sent to Detroit, he asked me where I was going. I replied that, being disgusted with the bad treatment I received at Detroit, I was going to seek better treatment from the English. He informed me that that would make you angry; he induced me to come and see you here and assured me that I should be well treated.

We are greatly rejoiced to have the honor of seeing M. de Vaudreuil, and his presence makes us forget all the annoyance we have felt.

We beg you, my father, to take pity on your children, who never intended to go

ward you otherwise than as a father acts to his children. I consent, therefore, to have regard to the request you make to me that you may take away a little milk, to give your children to suck.

Take as little as you can, for you will then have less expense and will be better able to supply your needs. Use it with moderation, when you get back to your homes. It is only my pity for you and my fear lest any harm should befall you, which makes me say what I am saying to you.

and look elsewhere for another father. We hope that you will consent to arrange matters so that we may obtain good terms in the trading we have to do; that we may get from it the means of clothing ourselves, and may get blankets for three beaverskins.

As you are really our father and we are your true children we hope you will consent to give us suck, by permitting us to take away some brandy, in order to rejoice our young men.

REPORT OF THE DEATH OF THE SONS OF RAMEZAY AND DE LONGUEUIL.

Endorsed—Colonies M. de Vaudreuil, 12th Octr. 1717. This letter requires no answer—resolved, 5th. Jany. 1718. La Chapelle.

Quebec, 12th of October, 1717.

I have caused the two pieces of scarlet cloth, which had been seized at Madame de la Pipardière's house, to be given up to the Iroquois from St. Louis' falls who claimed them, this savage having informed me that they belonged to him.

The report which was current here last year, that M. de Ramezay's son and M. de Longueuil's had been killed, has not turned out to be false. We have learnt from a letter from the Revd. Father de Villers, a Jesuit missionary with the Kaskacias, which has been sent to me from Detroit, that these two officers started to return to Detroit by the Ouabache with several other Frenchmen accompanying them. They fell in with a large party of Cherokees, a savage tribe from the neighborhood of Carolina. When they wanted to reconnoitre this party, their troop was surrounded by them; and, on the first fire, these two officers were killed with some of their men; the remainder were captured, and these savages took away prisoners. Six of them escaped and returned to the village of the Kaskacias bringing this sad news.

I have taken care to make public the Council's decision as to the claim

ıcil for having graciously granted me a gratuity of 6000 livres, and
ng informed me that it will always be inclined to gratify me when
sion offers.

Vaudreuil.

_____

VIGNY SENT ON AN EXPEDITION TO THE FOX INDIANS.

ıdorsed— Canada. The Marquis de Vaudreuil 12th Oct. 1717. Coun-
ıs to the journey of M. de Louvigny and the Fox Indians. Lay
ʹe the Duke of Orleans: resolved 5th of Jany. 1718. La Chapelle.

Quebec, 12th of October, 1717.

had the honor of informing the Council in my letter of the 20th of
.l that, having completely regained my health, I went up to Mon-
in the month of March over the ice; and that M. de Louvigny, who
mpanied me was to return to Missilimakina to see that the Fox In-
s carried out the conditions of the peace with them; to that end, to
ζ to Montreal the chiefs of that tribe and of the other tribes who
· to come there; and to make all the *coureurs de bois* come down.
ıe said Sr. de Louvigny set out from the Isle of Montreal at the
of May, as the length of the winter did not permit of his leaving
er. All the boats of the *voyageurs* who were going to Missilimakina
their goods left at the same time and under his orders, and I sent
ʹ them the Sr. de St. Pierre, captain of a company of the troops,
went to the end of Chagouamigon on Lake Superior to inform the

This disease, the report of which had spread into the upper countries, had created so much terror there among all the tribes, who fear it like death, that none of the Fox chiefs, nor those of the other tribes, dared to set out to come to Montreal.

As there was some ground for fearing lest the death of these two hostages might disturb the Fox tribe, and might be made a ground for breaking the peace (for these savages, as well as those of other tribes, are somewhat disposed to think that, when any of their men die while with us, it is we who have caused their illness) I sent with the said Sieur de Louvigny the chief of the three hostages who had escaped the disease, so that he might go and inform his tribe of the good treatment which they had received and make known to them that, although two of the hostages had died, it was by a misfortune which they had shared with many of the French, and the result of the epidemic which raged throughout all this country, from which the five Iroquois tribes had not escaped, that nothing had been spared to save their lives, and that this accident ought not to disurb the peace which has been made nor prevent them from fulfilling the promises which Ouechala, their head chief, made in the name of the whole tribe.

When the Sr. de Louvigny arrived at Missilimakina, he sent this hostage into his own country with his wife and child. With them he sent the men Memard and Reaume, interpreters, and gave into their charge some presents which I had given him to cover the dead hostages. This ceremony was performed by the interpreters as soon as they arrived at the village of the Fox Indians, after which the Fox Indians testified that they retained no resentment for the death of Pemoussa and Michiouaouigan because they were laid in the bed of their father Onontio: that they had not forgotten the punishment they received last year; and that they recognized that they could not sufficiently thank their father for having given them their lives. The returned hostage, Okimaouasen, expressed his surprise at not having found them setting out to fulfil the promise they had given. "How ungrateful you are!" added he, "you have shown little remembrance of the favor our father extended to you in sparing your lives. You cover me with shame this day, for you make me a liar. What am I going to do down there? For I see naught of what you have promised."

Ouechala agreed that the hostage was right; he excused himself as well as he could, and said he would go down without fail next year, and would never forget their father's kindness to him and his tribe. Okimaouasen afterwards set out to return with the Frenchmen who had ac-

he was going to stay in his country in order to make them remember it, and induce them to fulfil it next year.

As this hostage seemed to me very well disposed towards us, I feel sure he will endeavor with success to make his tribe carry out what they have promised. The Sr. Tamorandiere, whom I have sent to take command at the Bay, has orders to persuade them to do so; and Ouenamek, a Poutouatami chief of great influence with the Sakis and the Fox Indians, who came to Montreal this year, promised me for his part to assist in it. I hope, therefore, that the chiefs of all the tribes will come down to Montreal next year to ratify this peace and put the finishing touch to it. When this labor is completed, the only difficulty will be to keep it up. I will devote my whole attention to this, and will neglect nothing which may contribute to making all the tribes of the upper country live on good terms with one another.

Vaudreuil.

ON THE SAVAGES OF DETROIT.

Endorsed—Canada.   The Marquis de Vaudreuil 12th Octr. 1717.

Quebec, 12th of October, 1717.

I have the honor to acknowledge the receipt of the letter from the Council, dated the 7th of July last, regarding the permission granted

with the same purpose. This dispersing [of the Indians] astonished him; and, in order to stop it, he called together the officers that accompanied him, and the chief men of the French boats which were going up with him, and pointed out to them the disadvantage of allowing these savages to establish relations with the English prejudicial to the Colony; that they must use every endeavor to stop them, that they were all interested in doing so, and that they ought all to contribute to the present which it would be advisable to give them. All agreed, and the Sr. de Tonty, having summoned all the chiefs of this body of savages, spoke to them in these terms. "It would have been a pleasure to me to have seen you all at Detroit, to speak to you on behalf of your father who has charged me with his message; and I should have much pleasure in meeting you here, but that I am informed that you are going to the English. I am surprised that you could have taken this course, for you know well that you are going against the will of your father, and that you cannot take this step without displeasing him. You must change your mind, for you cannot have two fathers. The English have never done anything for you; on the contrary, they have constantly incited the Iroquois to make war on you; whereas, your father has supported you for more than a hundred years, has always supplied your needs, and defended you against your enemies." The Outavois and Poutouatamis replied that the high price of goods at Detroit, and the refusal to give them any brandy had induced them to do this; that, as it was the first time they had gone this way, they felt sure that we would have pity on them and let them go their way; and that they wanted to appease their thirst for it; that their fathers had given them to understand that the breasts of Onontio their father would never be drained, and that they would always get milk, that is, brandy; but now they were experiencing the contrary. They were most obstinately set on going on their way but, after many councils which had to be held, during three days, the Sr. de Tonty managed so well with the aid of three Canadians, Guillet, Loranger and Mallet who had influence over these savages' minds, that he succeeded in making them give up their purpose. To effect this, he had to promise them that the price of goods at Detroit should be reduced and that I would have brandy given to them. Ten boats followed the Sr. de Tonty to Detroit, and seven proceeded to Montreal. Loranger, the interpreter, was chosen to accompany the latter party and prevent them from going to the English. He was unable to get more than six to Montreal, the seventh escaping to go to Orange just when they were at the mouth of the river of the Onontagues, as I have already told you in my letter on

cheap, and that I would let them take some brandy, I induced the merchants to give them good bargains, and they were well pleased with them.
I also allowed them to buy two or three pots of brandy a piece to take
to their village, and appointed a reliable person to see it distributed
to them, so that they should not take more. I could not avoid letting
them have some, for they demanded it urgently, and if I had refused
them they would have resorted to going to the English for it. I found
myself obliged to do the same for six other boats of savages from the
Bay,—Sakis, Folles Avoines, and Nokes,—who came to Montreal this
summer. I put the quantity I allow them to have very low: this small
quantity contents them, and keeps them from going to the English for
it, who would supply them abundantly. Moreover, they do not drink it
at Montreal, nor on their journey; they keep it to make a feast with
it in their villages, and brandy is a drink which the savages are so pas-
sionately fond of that it is impossible to keep it from them altogether;
for, if they don't get it from the French they will from the English: and,
as it is extremely important that the savages of the upper country should
not trade with them (for if they once began to do so, the profit they
would find would induce them to continue it, which would absolutely
ruin the trade of the Colony) I have reason to believe that the Council

roved,
rided he
tinues to
e precau-
ary meas-
s.
will not disapprove of what I have done, nor of my continuing to take
the same course, according to circumstances; for I have no other object
in doing so save to avoid alienating our savages.

sidered,
of Jan.
, La Cha-
e.
The Sr. de Tonty, who arrived at Detroit on the 3rd of July, spoke
to the tribes settled there in my name that their chiefs might come to
Montreal to be witnesses of what took place regarding the Fox Indians;
but they excused themselves on the ground of a disturbance which occurred a short time ago, which prevented them from leaving their villages, saying that they would go down next year without fail. They
went on to complain that for some years the prices of the goods sold to
them had been too dear; observing however, that they hoped that the
change of commandants would be to their advantage and the Sr. de Tonty
would let everything be given to them cheaper. But they declared that,
if the price of goods were not reduced, they would all go to the English
for what they required next spring.

The Sr. de Tonty thereupon called all the French people together and,
after he had conferred with them, a price was agreed upon for certain
goods with which the savages testified that they were well pleased.

The trouble which prevented the principal chiefs of the Detroit tribes
from coming to Montreal, was created by an Outaouac of that post and
four others from Saguinan. These five men pretended they were going
to war against the Flatheads; they proceeded to the river of the Miamis
and there slew an Iroquois and his wife, who was a Miami woman, and

man who was killed was of their tribe. It also concerns the Miamis, for the man was married and living with them. This matter must be settled, and the Iroquois and Miamis must be prevented from taking vengeance on the Outavois and the other tribes of Detroit.

The Sr. de Tonty has already begun, for his part, to take action with the Miamis through the Sr. de Vincennes to dissuade them from their intention of avenging themselves and to remove every pretext for their pursuing this course which would give rise to a war between them and the people at Detroit and Saguinan, which it would be difficult to stop. He has induced the tribes of Detroit to join him in sending to Saguinan to seize these murderers and deliver them up to the Miamis.

The Outaouacs and Poutouatamis each sent a boat of their men, to which the Sr. de Tonty added a boat of Frenchmen under the command of the Sr. de Bragelongue, a Lieutenant, who brought back the three murderers to Detroit where the Sr. de Tonty had them under guard until he received news from the Miamis, to whom he had taken care, to make known the amends, which it was proposed to make to them. He hopes that they will be satisfied with this action and will accept as a complete reparation the presents which the tribes of Detroit, and the French also, are preparing to make them, and that this disturbance may be suppressed by this means. I hope so, too; but I shall not be able to get any news about it until next spring.

As regards the Iroquois, if they move in this matter, I shall find means to settle it with them, as they will not fail to bring their complaints to me before taking any action.

[Signed]   Vaudreuil.

TONTY PREVENTS THE SAVAGES FROM TRADING WITH THE ENGLISH.

Endorsed—Annexed to the letter of MM. de Vaudreuil and Begon of the 8th November, 1718—No. 2.

Canada. Colonies.

Statement of the expenses incurred by Monsieur de Tonty in order to stop seventeen boats of Outavois and Poutouatamis whom he met on Lake Ontario, who were going to the English.

To wit

For sixty coverings of cloth which the savages obliged him to give
them for five beaverskins each, at which price they were at the
English post, on which he lost three hundred beaverskins at
three livres apiece... 900#

                                                           1180#.
We, the undersigned, certify that Monsieur de Tonty, Commandant for
the King at the fort of Detroit incurred the expense above mentioned in
order to stop the savages who were-going to the English, whom we met
on Lake Ontario. Given at the Fort of Detroit this 25th of August 1717.
                                                      Dumont
                                                        L.'Orangée.
De Bragecongue
   Montandre.

A LETTER FROM SABREVOIS TO CADILLAC.

Endorsed—M. Raudot.   R. par GOG.

Copy of the letter of M. de Sabrevois, commandant at Chambily; written to M. de la Mothe.

I have the honor to write to you in order to send you word that M.
de Tonty has sent away all the inhabitants of Detroit, those to whom you
had granted contracts of concession, not allowing them to sow the land
nor [even] to sow one seed of wheat or other grains. More than half of
them have come down, and the other [half] without fail will come next
spring, and the interpreter also, being unable to endure it; as he is unwilling that anyone should do any trading there besides himself, he is
sending them all to the devil. The common opinion is that Detroit will
be abandoned in a short time, that the Savages will give it up to the
English, and that they will poignard Tonty and the rest of the Frenchmen who remain there. The Savages of Detroit generally go to the English now.

All these poor inhabitants who have actually come from Detroit beg

have been annulled. Do something for these unfortunates and give to all a little comfort.

Those who have now come have told me that he is not rearing calves and is eating the oxen and cows, that there is a great scarcity of them, that he has never had so many of them there as when I left. If you wish to make any communication to them [i. e. the inhabitants] you have only to send me word and I will tell them. Detroit is a hell; the Savages have brandy like water, and never was there such disorder there; that is enough. I beg you, &c.

Signed—Sabrevois.

TONTY PREVENTS A WAR BETWEEN THE MIAMIS AND OTTAWAS.

Endorsed—Colonies. MM. de Vaudreuil and Begon 8th Novr. 1718. & Council. Several requests.

Quebec, 8th of Novr. 1718.

We have the honor to forward to the Council a memorial from the Bishop and the Lady Superior of the general hospital, in which the nuns offer to have a certain number of arpents of standing wood cleared at their expense every year on the islets—whatever number it may please the Council to fix—provided that the ownership of one half of such lands is granted to them to indemnify them for the expense of clearing them.

As the Bishop, in founding this hospital, gave these lands to the poor, not to be alienated from them for any reason whatsoever, we have told him that we could not authorize the alienation he proposed making for the profit of the nuns of this hospital, of half the lands they might get cleared at their own expense, although it appeared to us, as it did to them, that it would be an advantage that these forest lands which yield nothing for the poor of the general hospital, should be given up on the conditions proposed. For the poor, though losing half of the property which the nuns ask for, would obtain an assured income from the other half; and we believe there would be nothing objectionable in granting the nuns the decree they ask for, for this alienation, provided it was ordered that the whole of the [? cleared] lands of the seigniory of the islets should first be measured and their boundaries marked out, and a report of them drawn up, so that they might remain the property of the poor of the said hospital, and the nuns could not take advantage of the decree to appropri-

tion has been made to us, one by the Sr. Dejordy, a captain of the troops,. the other by the Sr. de la Valterie, the son of a former captain. On these we await orders from the Council, as the King again ordered us, in his memornadum of the 15th of June, 1716, not to grant lands in future except in socage, and to allow in these concessions, (on good lands), only three arpents frontage by 40 deep.

The fathers of the Seminary of Foreign Missions in this town have requested us to represent to the Council that the condition of their affairs is very bad in consequence of their heavy losses in the two fires they have had, and that they have run heavily in debt in order to rebuild; that they have, however, continued their services to the Colony by educating children—uninterrupetedly since it was established more than 50 years ago, for it is from this seminary that most of the priests and missionaries have been obtained, and the other pupils have been employed in various posts and have founded respectable families:

That the former Bishop, now deceased, used to make up the deficiency in the cost of maintaining the Seminary with the gratuities from the late King, who had promised to give them emoluments of from 4000 to 5000 livres, but these have not been granted them, and the gratuities which they used then to get have been withheld so that theirs is the only community in this country which receives none from His Majesty, although it is the most heavily burdened. That they have been obliged to incur a heavy debt in order to carry on this work; and they beg the Council, in order firmly to establish the benefit which the Church and the Colony gain from it, to grant them the emoluments which had been promised them, or to obtain from His Majesty, the renewal of the gratuity of 4000 livres which they used formerly to receive, as appears from the deed of allowance of the 4th of Septr. 1689, annexed, which they handed to us.

We cannot refuse to bear witness to the Council as to the benefits which the seminary has conferred on the Colony, and that it deserves the gratuities from His Majesty.

We send a statement of the buildings belonging to the Sr. Hertel which were pulled down at Chambly in 1709 by the orders of M. de Ramezay because there was a danger that the English, who were expected to come that year, would set fire to them and that this fire would spread to the fort which at that time was one of the stakes only. The Sr. de Vaudreuil charged M. de Chaussegros, when he went to Chambly, to find out what those buildings were worth at that time; and he estimated them at

for want of payment of this pension. We beg the Council to be good enough to have it paid to him for the past years.

We send a memorandum from the Sr. Peire on the establishments for the porpoise fishery which he is working. This year he has only made 22 barrels of oil, because the herring and small fish which attract the porpoises to land have not been abundant. We beg the Council graciously to continue to give him the gratuity of 400 livres granted to him on this account, as he takes great pains to maintain these establishments; and following his example, a fishery has this year been established, at the little river, near La Malbaye by the inhabitants of that place, who have caught 42 porpoises from which they have obtained about 32 barrels of oil.

We beg the Council to be good enough to continue the Sr. Sarrasin's gratuity of 500 livres which was granted him in 1716 on account of the studious research to which he applies himself in the intervals of his duties as physician, which he continues to fulfil with perfect ability and with his usual care. This year he has dissected a white shark and is sending an account of it to the Academie des Sciences; he is also raising several plants for the Jardin Royal which he will not be sending till next year as they have not yet taken root since he transplated them.

We beg the Council to continue M. de Longueuil's gratuity of 200 livres granted to him in consideration of his lodging at his house the Iroquois savages; also that of M. de Martinière, chief councillor, of 200 livres, in consideration of his long and good service, and of the bad state of his affairs.

We are sending the Council a memorial from the Sr. Desgly, major of Three Rivers, as to the claim that has been made against him for 240 livres for 3 tons freight which were granted to him in 1716 on a brigantine belonging to the Sr. Butler of Rochelle, which had been chartered by the King to convey His Majesty's effects for this Colony, which could not be taken in the ship "Le François." We beg the Council to dispense with his paying this sum, having regard to the bad state of his affairs and the money he is obliged to spend since M. de Gallifet's absence, as Commandant at Three Rivers, which is a place through which many people pass, being on the road from Quebec to Montreal.

The Sr. de Tonty, commandant at Detroit, last year settled two very difficult affairs, in which he was successful, which might have been very prejudicial to the Colony. He has represented to us that he was obliged to incur extraordinary expenses on this account which he asks to be reimbursed.

The first is a matter he adjusted on his way up to Detroit when, having met seventeen boats full of savages on Lake Ontario, from Detroit and Saguinan, who were going to Orange, he dissuaded them from doing so,

Orange, where the English try to attract them by the low price of goods and by the presents they make to them; there would have been a danger of others going there, following their example which, after a time, might detach them from our side. This affair cost him 1180 livres, according to the annexed memorandum he has given of them.

He also spent 1574 livres on the other affair, that is the arrangement he contrived between the Miamis and the Outaouais when the former were preparing to go on the war path against the latter, on which the said Sr. de Vaudreuil is sending a separate report.

As expenses of this kind are very different from those which the said Sr. de Tonty is responsible for, for keeping up his post, and the two matters which caused them were of great importance to the Colony, we beg that the Council will take this into consideration and grant him the reimbursement of these expenses in accordance with the statements of them, a copy of which is annexed.

We send a petition from the nuns hospitalers of Montreal regarding the freight for four tons which they beg the Council to grant them gratis in consideration of their very heavy expenses. As they have, in part, the care of the sick soldiers who are received in this hospital, and the latter are very well treated, we are induced to ask this favor for them from the Council.

Vaudreuil
Begon

CADILLAC PETITIONS FOR COMPENSATION FOR HIS LOSSES AT DETROIT.

Endorsed—Colonies. 1718. M. de La Motte Cadillac. Council.

all the goods that were at the said fort Pontchartrain; and this has been carried out on both sides.

The Company of the Colony, finding itself in debt over the trading of that post, by its bad management and through the onerous obligations to the King to which it was subjected, without knowing the reason, being unable any longer to bear the loss it was making on it, abandoned it to the King who was not able to keep up that post on account of the war; whereupon M. de La Mothe who knew its importance for compelling the Iroquois to make peace, and having made it that they might be obliged to observe and keep it as a matter of necessity, as the event shows, and who also knew very well that by this means there would be taken away from the English a considerable trade which reverted to the French Colony, and for several other good reasons: All these views and considerations compelled him to make offers to His Majesty who granted him a monopoly of the trade as the Company had had it, with the direction of that affair, and left the command to him as he had had it when the post was established; it is true that he did not at all submit to the conditions of the said Company, since those on which it is held [? by him] are very clearly set forth in the letter from the Court, written to him, dated the 14th of June, 1704; it is that letter which forms his title and which is his contract; moreover, it is therein clearly and distinctly explained and precisely laid down; a copy is annexed.

The said M. de La Mothe, in order to carry out his said contract made an agreement with the said Company of the Colony on the 28th of September, 1705, (a copy of which is attached) M. de Vaudreuil, Governor-General, and MM. Raudot and de Beauharnois, Intendants, being present, which has been complied with on his part, he having even paid for the goods which the said Company had at Detroit with a premium of 40 per cent, according as it was settled by the letter of M. the Comte de Pontchartrain of the 9th of June, 1706.

In pursuance of the said letter or contract, made by M. de La Mothe with the King, and of the agreement made likewise with the Company, M. de La Mothe, in order to comply with the wish of the Majesty, began by expending a considerable sum in the purchase of cutters for the conveyance of two hundred soldiers, in paying substantial wages to sixty Canadians for taking up his cutters and boats; he took there nearly forty families, a part at his expense and some on making advances to them for which he has not been paid; he had horned cattle, oxen, cows and nearly all sorts of domestic animals taken there by way of the lakes, and a quantity of fruit trees in boxes: he had a wind-mill built, which cost him a great deal; enlarged the fort by four other bastions; he has had houses, barns, ice houses and beer breweries built; in

M. de La Mothe did to establish a colony quickly, having regard to the
·distance of *three hundred leagues* which there is from Montreal to Detroit, and to the difficulties of the journey. When he left that post to
·come to France, and afterwards to go to Louisiana, according to the
inventory which has been made of them, he left there a fort with eight
bastions, houses, warehouses, goods, munitions of war belonging to him,
400 arpents of land cleared and cultivated, a good mill which produces
five hundred crowns rent, thirty horned cattle, oxen or cows, which were
valued at *a hundred crowns each,* a horse worth four hundred livres, 143
inhabitants paying quit rent and rent as shown on the register of the
fort Pontchartrain.

M. de La Mothe points out to the Council that, when he was selected
for the governorship of Louisiana, M. de la Forêt a former Captain,
who was serving under his command and as second at the said Detroit,
was also chosen by His Majesty who sent him a commission as Com-
·mandant in the place and stead of the said M. de La Mothe.

The commission of the said M. de la Forêt was quite simple and con-
·cerned only the command. He proposed to M. de La Mothe that if he
would give up to him his claims he would reimburse him for them, and
this was granted him; that is proved by various documents. But when
it was a question of paying the total of this sum to M. de La Mothe,
the said M. de la Forêt found he was not in a position to do so; and,
·as he was overwhelmed with debts, he could not even find anyone who
would be security for him; so that M. Raudot, at that time Intendant
·of New France, seeing on one side the just claims of the M. de La
Mothe and on the other the impossibility of M. de la Forêt meeting the
payment of the sum due to M. de la Mothe or of giving him securities,
·and being moreover a witness of the ill-health of the said M. de la Forest
who was unable to go to Detroit, found an expedient which was agreed
to by the parties.

This arrangment was that M. de la Foret should withdraw from the
·command of the fort Pontchartrain of Detroit in favor of the Chevalier
de Marigny, another Captain with whom M. de La Mothe had made an
agreement both for the enjoyment of the exclusive right of trading and
·of his lands, houses, warehouses, mills, brewery &c, and likewise of the
corn, animals, movables, merchandise and the rest; by the terms of
which the said M. de La Mothe was to pay to the said M. de la Foret
a gratuity of 600#. All that was signed at Quebec, also by M. Raudot

the [proper] time and place, which sets forth the violence done to him by no other law than that of arbitrary authority taking advantage of the fact that M. de La Mothe was obliged to go to Louisiana being without employment, because when he was made governor of that place, the King gave his company to the eldest son of M. de Vaudreuil and his command to M. de la Foret, who was an invalid and at that time not fit to go to his Post.

The said M. de La Mothe having learnt on his return from Louisiana that the King has reannexed to his domain the fort Pontchartrain of Detroit with all its appurtenances and dependencies, also the exclusive right of trading; and that His Majesty has granted both to M. de Tonty, Captain in Canada, he has every reason for hoping that His Majesty will reimburse him and will cause him to be paid for the expenses and outlay that he made for the purpose of forming that Colony, and for the value of his lands, houses, animals, brewery, mills, corn, goods, movables, &c. according to the inventory which was made of them in good and proper form before his departure from Detroit; also compensation for the exclusive right of trading taken away from him, as well as the restitution or the value of his rents, and that the concessions granted to the inhabitants by M. de La Mothe according to his authority shall hold good which M. de Tonty has taken away from them contrary to all justice.

He hopes also that His Majesty will take into account that he had at Acadie a seigniory of two leagues with an island, by 14 leagues, with the right of higher, middle, and lower jurisdiction, and a fief at Port Royal, and that he has abandoned all in order to serve His Majesty; by the capture of that province which the English made in the year 1690, M. de La Mothe was plundered without being left even the value of 30s, being at the time on the vessels of the squadron commanded by M. de la Caffiniere, ordered to go and take New York.

He hopes likewise that His Majesty will cause him to be paid for the advances he has made for his service according to the lists certified in the form prescribed for it, of which he is the bearer.

76

Endorsed—Colonies, 1718.

To His Most Serene Highness, Monseigneur the Comte de Toulouse.

Monseigneur,

M. de La Motte Cadillac has the honor to represent to His Most Serene Highness that one of the decisions of His Royal Highness lays down that he shall be paid for the property which has been taken from him at Detroit for the King's service. That must be understood at the price they were worth at the time at Detroit with the savages, it not being just to pay him for them at Quebec prices since he has run the risk and paid the cost of their transport.

There has been sent to the Petitioner this year, a certificate from M. Dubuisson, the first in command at Detroit by the order of M. de Vaudreuil; this certificate sets forth that he has taken for His Majesty's service eleven bags of lead or bullets, three barrels of powder and ten sword-blades belonging to the Petitioner. The certificate, a copy of which is annexed hereto, gives proof of it.

M. Dubuisson took these munitions without paying for them; yet this commander made the calculation of the quantity of lead or bullets, and likewise of the powder a year later to the very day, as is proved under his certificate of the 9th of June, 1712, by that of the 9th of June, 1713.

It is to be observed that at Quebec and Montreal they have bought powder from the King's magazines, the barrels of which coming from France are of 100# weight, and the bags of lead or bullets which the merchants send for trading with the Savages, usually weigh 100# each for the convenience of the portages.

M. Dubuisson in his certificate declares that the above goods belong to the Petitioner, that they were in the hands of one Roy by name, an inhabitant of Detroit, and that he took them for His Majesty's service. Yet this commander has drawn the payment for them from M. Begon as things belonging to him; on which His Most Serene Highness is very humbly entreated to give his attention to the remarks which the Petitioner has the honor to make to him on the subject of this said certificate.

1st, All expenditure which is made in Canada for the King's service in the Further Posts where the Governor-general and the Intendant are not present, has to be certified by the Commandant and by the missionaries or the almoner of the said Post; after that this expenditure is paid for at Quebec on the certificate of the Governor-general by an order of the Intendant. Without this formality it should never be passed by the Chamber of Accounts.

2nd, Under this rule, established in New France, why has M. Begon caused M. Dubuisson to be paid for the powder, lead and bullets and the ten sword-blades belonging to the Petitioner, who most certainly has not given this commander authority to receive this sum for him, having on the contrary protested against him in writing on his arrival at Detroit, against his acts of violence and for having seized on all that belonged to the Petitioner in Detroit, to which this commander declared in writing that he had made use of them in this manner by the order of his superiors.

3rd, Why did not M. Begon, when paying this sum, receive from the hands of Dubuisson this certificate of expenditure, since the man called Roy had charge of these goods and others of which he was despoiled after the departure of the Petitioner. If it may be thought that it is through forgetfulness, the Petitioner has the honor to point out to His Most Serene Highness that this officer nevertheless professes to have an exceedingly good memory since after the lapse of a year he appears to have stated the weight of the eleven bags of lead or bullets and the three barrels of powder which had been used up a year before for the King's service. His memory was even so good that he did not forget to cause payment to be made to himself for them by M. Begon, who cannot have made this payment or re-imbursement except on the certificate of the Governor-general. This proves that these gentlemen thought that they had the right, because of the absence of the Petitioner, to seize on everything that he possessed in Detroit; lands, mill, animals and other property; and that they would be clear of responsibility for them by writing to the Council as they have done, that it would be just to bestow upon the Petitioner a grant which should stand to him in lieu of all indemnification and even of being paid for the re-imbursement which he made to the company of the Colony; and this is in fact very just as regards him, since all his property has been taken from him by authority and he is so oppressed that, if His Majesty pays no regard to it, his family will be reduced to beggary.

4th, The Petitioner proves his oppression by the conduct of this commandant—of which he was informed at Quebec by the Almoner of the fort, according to the annexed extract from his letter—and this is the manner of it. M. Dubuisson, coming to command at Detroit, brought to the Petitioner his appointment as Governor of Louisiana, with a letter from the Court ordering him to repair there by land; invincible obstacles were met with to the execution of this order, the detail of

wanting for nothing. M. Dubuisson, in order to drive them out of it,
cut the fort in two, put the house and family of the Petitioner outside
its shelter, as well as that of the Almoner, of the Surgeon, of the Troops,
of the King's interpreter, and of several of the most well-to-do inhabitants; so that the family of M. de La Motte, finding themselves exposed to the insults of the Savages wrote to him of it at Quebec, and
the Almoner did the same. Conduct so outrageous on M. Dubuisson's
part compelled the Petitioner to lodge his complaint of it with M. de
Vaudreuil who paid no attention to it. He also complained to M.
Raudot senior who was the Intendant, and he—with all Canada—found
this action so astonishing that he fulminated against M. Dubuission
with much vehemence, and certainly did not spare M. de Vaudreuil on
this occasion because that Intendant who was an acute man saw clearly
whence the blow came. The Petitioner believed that there was no other
course but to send to Detroit for his family to prevent it from being
sacrificed, and to take it with him to France and afterwards to Louisiana, abandoning all his possessions in order to go and serve His Majesty
according to his orders, after having made his protest in the form of
a remonstrance to the M. de Vaudreuil and later on, his private protest
before a notary.

5th, These terrible molestations compel M. de La Motte, with reason,
very respectfully to beg His Most Serene Highness to have the goodness to cause the answer of MM. de Vaudreuil and Begon to be communicated to him in writing so far as it concerns him alone, since the
first has always been really and in fact his enemy, so that he may be
able to reply to their answers if necessary, seeing that they may be
colored, and that the Petitioner may be in a position to throw light
on the truth. This demand is according to rule and to equity since he
has claimed justice from the King.

6th, It is not a question of redressing the wrongs and the injury the
Petitioner has suffered and still suffers by reprimands; that is a matter
of indifference to him. He demands the justice which is due to him
and the restitution of property which has been taken from him; he can
never obtain it in Canada because there is no tribunal in that country which dares to take cognizance of that suit. Moreover the Petitioner has made his appeal to the Council of the Navy, and H. R. H.
on the demands of the Petitioner has given several decisions which form
an interlocutory; and on that it is natural that the Petitioner should

him. Afterwards, being recalled, he was replaced by M. de Tonty who seized on all that remained belonging to the Petitioner saying boldly and in public that all which had belonged to M. de La Motte now belonged to him, without excepting anything; and that officer persecuted the man named Roy so sharply that he compelled him to withdraw to Montreal, where he was so ill-treated by the Governor-general in revenge for his having taken care of the Petitioner's property, for some time, that this poor man was forced to quit the Colony and betake himself to the Savages.

8th, The inhabitants of Detroit were not better treated than the Petitioner. M. de Tonty revoked their contracts and drove them from their lands, having put on crying taxes for the right of trading which had been granted to them by the Petitioner's contracts, on the faith of which these inhabitants had settled at Detroit.

9th, His Most Serene Highness is very humbly begged to observe that His Majesty, by his decree of the month of August 1716, annulled the grants made to the said inhabitants; that the grounds of that annulment expressed in the said declaration were that the said grants were not in the form usual in Canada. Thereupon His said Majesty permitted the Governor-General and the Intendant to make other grants to the inhabitants of Detroit; but they took care not to do so because, to conform to the King's intentions it would have been necessary to make these grants with rights of hunting, fishing and trading, such being the usual form in Canada. So that the intended alteration of the grants which M. de Vaudreuil and M. de Tonty made use of in France in 1716 as a pretext (in which way they abused the confidences of H. R. H. and of His Most Serene Highness) has not been able to be carried out in accordance with the said intention of the King's declaration, M. de Vaudreuil having taken care not to make grants at Detroit with trading rights. That is the essential point which touches him most nearly; one need not be a Seer to divine the reason of it.

10th, When M. de La Motte asked His Most Serene Highness for the lands at Detroit with the title of Seigniory and rights of hunting, fishing and trading, he did so with a view to fulfilling the intention of His Majesty, that is to say, of granting contracts in the said usual form of Canada, and in that way of conforming to the intentions set forth in the said declaration of the King.

11th, His Majesty made an exception in the said declaration of 1716, in which he declares that the inhabitants of Detroit shall enjoy their grants if they have conformed to their contracts. Yet their contracts, their lands and their houses have been taken away from them without any other legal formality, by which they have suffered to some extent the same fate as the Petitioner who has been completely informed of

12th, The Colony of Detroit was not established until after its importance was well considered by the late King; it was not on the decision of a Minister, as usually happens. This matter was settled by the King himself and his Privy Council on the report of the late M. Daguesseau, councillor of state; is it right that those who have settled there should be ruined with impunity? M. de La Motte speaks of it because it concerns his interests, being informed by them of the persecutions M. de Tonty inflicts on them, which have been so outrageous that he has compelled them to pay to him the quit-rents and rents which were due to the Petitioner, and yet will not leave them in the enjoyment of the provisions and conditions of their contracts, particularly as regards trading.

13th, The Council of the Navy has made known to the inhabitants of the Colonies that they may address their complaints to it in case injustice should be done to them by those in authority; of what use would their complaints be if they are not redressed at the expense of those who commit it, when it is proved? They would only end in causing themselves to be ill-treated more harshly.

14th, The Petitioner, finding himself independent of the M. de Vaudreuil as he had returned from Louisiana to France, and having been informed of the manner in which his property had been taken away, carried his complaint to the Council of the Navy. He claims its jurisdiction in order to be judged on the facts and the demands which he had made or shall hereafter make; and he cannot be so in proper form until he has had communicated to him the answer made to the Council by the party opposed to him, in order that, on his replies, whatever is just may be ordained by a decree, seeing that the decisions already given are an interlocutory and, loose documents and out of his hands, are liable to be lost in course of time. And in case the truth cannot be made clear enough, he begs the Council to permit him to supply proof of it by sending a commissioner on the spot to Quebec, Montreal and Detroit at the expense of [the person] who ought to pay for it, in order that right may be done to the parties after the inquiry is made and reported; the Governor General and Intendant and others being forbidden to trouble or disturb the said commissioner or to oppose his making the said inquiry; and in the meantime [he begs the Council] to grant him the lands he has asked for as a seignory with fishing, hunting and trading rights on the condition that he shall make grants.

Endorsed—Colonies—M. Vaudreuil.

Quebec, the 15th of October
1719.

I have received the letter which the Council did me the honor to write me on the 6th of July, 1718.

This inspection of the posts every two years, proposed to the Council by the Sr. de Louvigny, seems to me most desirable for maintaining good order and peace among the tribes. As he is perfectly familiar with their dispositions and interests, no one can discharge this duty better than he, for which purpose I consider he requires an appointment as Commander-General in the districts where the French trade. But at the same time, I think I ought to point out to the Council that this duty will become useless if the licenses are suppressed; for, in that case, being unable to get the necessary articles conveyed to the posts for their maintenance and the food of the garrison, we shall be compelled to abandon them. That, if this is carried too far, His Majesty will be burdened with a new expense which will be a considerable one, by the presents the said Sr. de Louvigny will be obliged to make to the tribes where he goes: and by the two boats which he will require for making each inspection, the equipment of which, with the provisions and wages of four men to each, will cost more than a thousand crowns, —without counting the provisions that will be necessary for the said Sr. de Louvigny, and a gratuity which he will not fail to ask for on his return from each journey. Finally that if His Majesty is not willing to bear this expense, he will not be able to refuse him a sufficient number of permits [to trade] for defraying it.

Two Jesuit missionaries came this year who set out from Missilimakina at the end of August in two boats. As one of these missionaries is intended for the Ilinois, and the other must remain at Missilimakina where there was no one but Father Marest who is advanced in years and very infirm, the other posts will not be able to have one until some more come. I very humbly beg the Council graciously to arrange for at least four to come over next year for the missions of the upper country.

The suit of the Sr. de Morienne for the bill he had from the Sr. de Bellestre has been arranged. M. de Ramezay, who was concerned in that arrangement will be able to give you an account of it.

Speak to M
le Regent.
The Counc
thinks ord
should be
given for
these insp
tions, and
they shoul
made at th
King's ex-
pense, wit
out any lic
ses.

Good, as r
gards the
pointment
Commdt.
Gen'l. of t
advance p

Write to t
Procureur
about it.

last year on a certificate from the surgeon major of the troops showing
that he was unfit to serve the King: and he went to France at the same
time.

The man Jammier de Flavaucourt alias Deschamps was also given
his discharge last year, on a letter which I received from the Marshal
D'estees concerning him.

I have looked into the memorial containing the claims of the Sr. de
Sabrevois for the time that he was in command at Detroit, but I find
no reason therein why the Sr. de Tonty should be made to give him
any compensation. The fact of his not enjoying the privilege of trading
at Detroit exclusively during the years 1715 and 1716, which is alleged
by the said Sr. de Sabrevois, is one I was not able to have any knowledge of as I was in France at that time; and a thing for which, even if
it were as stated, he can have no claim as against the Sr. de Tonty
since the latter did not contribute to the trouble of which the said Sr.
de Sabrevois complains, and since he has enjoyed this privilege he has
borne all the expenses for which the Sr. de Sabrevois was responsible.
Moreover I induced the said Sr. de Tonty, at the time when he was
going to start for Detroit, in the month of May 1717, to grant two
permits for two boats, which the agent of the said Sr. de Sabrevois sent
there, which were free to transact their trade there, although it interfered with that of the said Sr. de Tonty, to the extent of 1800 livres
of France in paper money which those who turned them to account
paid to the said Sr. de Sabrevois, to whom the said Sr. de Tonty was

As I was informed that the Sieurs de Monnoir and d'Adoncourt, whom
M. de Ramezay despatched in 1715 loaded with presents to invite all the
tribes of the south to this war, went to Detroit the same year and made
presents to the tribes settled there; and as M. de Louvigny assured
me that when he proceeded to that place to go on his expedition in
1716, he gave them some also, of which he has a statement certified by
the said Sr. de Sabrevois; I do not see that the latter was right in
making any himself on the occasion of that war. Moreover, if we were
to judge of the matter by what was said to me in public by the Outaou-
ouast chief from Saguinan and by those of the Poutouatamis from Detroit who came to Montreal in 1717, whose words I annex hereto,—
index letter B—the said Sr. de Sabrevois was far from being as liberal
towards the savages as he would have the Council understand. From
the complaints which these savages then made to me (of which I thought
I ought not to inform the Council, so as to spare the said Sr. de Sabrevois), and from a second extract from his letter of the 8th of April
1717, marked C, and the copy of the one of the 17th of May in the same
year, marked D, it will be easy to see how little capacity he had for
governing them with the tact advisable so as not to alienate them. What
ever the credence that should be given to the certificates which he has
written and annexed to the memorial which he has presented to the
Council, this is certain, that the greater part of the settlers who have
signed that of the 11th of July 1717 for him were the people against
whom the said Sr. de Sabrevois had made great complaints to me on
several occasions, and men whom I should have had imprisoned if they
had come down at that time; who, for their part complained loudly of
him in writing to their relatives and friends to whom they wrote that
their own crime lay in their refusal to submit to the exactions of the
said Sieur de Sabrevois who made friends with them when he was ready
to leave Detroit in order to induce them to sign this certificate. Although, in my reply to the talk of the savages from Detroit, I agree
that it was I who sent the said Sr. de Sabrevois there, I had, however,
no share in his nomination for the command of that post. Mons. de
Pontchartrain, who had nominated him, forwarded to me the order from
the King to send him there, and I complied with it; but I should have
taken great care not to propose that, for I knew that he was a very
grasping man. I do not really think that he made any large profits
at Detroit; but it is certain that he lost nothing, for, after he had paid
back all the money which had been advanced to him by the merchants
and whatever he owed those who were in his pay, he found he had more
than eighty bundles of furs left.

fort we have ever had in this country. As the Sieur de Tonty has spared no expense to make it substantial and to put himself in security in it from every attack, and as it has cost him more than two thousand livres, French money, I consider it just that the Council should grant him a gratuity.

I will take care to let this officer know, next spring, what the Council notifies me concerning his demands.

Vaudreuil.

CADILLAC SHOULD BE REIMBURSED FOR HIS LOSSES AT DETROIT.

M. Raudot. Canada: as to M. de La Mothe Cadillac. MM. de Vaudreuil and Begon. 14th of Novr. 1719, Council Index letter C. Colonies.

Quebec, the 14 of Novr., 1719.

We have received this year the letter from the Council of the 6th of July, 1718, with the documents and the two petitions of M. de La Mothe Cadillac annexed thereto.

We have also received the letter from the Council of the 3rd of June, 1719, with the extract from the memorial of the said Sr. de La Mothe regarding his claims to Fort Pontchartrain of Detroit.

From the examination we have made of these documents, we consider that the King should reimburse him for the expenses he has incurred for presents to the savages and for refreshments to sick soldiers, because His Majesty was charged with them, as appears from the letter of M. Raudot of the 18th of March 1707, and from that of M. de Pontchartrain of the 6th of June 1708. But the expenses for the pay of the

by the valuation of the merchandise and articles of value which the Company had at this place, which amounted to 18716£. 12s. 4d. local currency, making 14037£. 9s. 3d. French money, and by the payment of this sum in accordance with M. Raudot's decree of the 21st of Dec. 1707. All these documents simply prove that he entered upon the privilege which the Company of the Colony had concerning the trade, and not on the ownership since the Company did not possess it, and it could not have been granted except by a deed of concession or a decree of the Council of State.

The inventory which was made when the Sr. de La Mothe left Detroit to go to the country of Louisiana, a copy of which is annexed, which was forwarded to us by his agent the Sr. de Grandmenil, proves that he left at this post a quantity of goods, tools, property, cattle and buildings. *this docum has been a tached to original of letter.*

The said Sr. de Grandmenil said that out of all these buildings none remains except the mill; that the people who have been in command of that post have demolished them, and have used the iron work and materials for building others.

In order to clear this point up, it would be necessary to hear the Commandants of this post in their defence; and as there are none of them here now, we can say nothing definite on this subject.

It seems right that His Majesty should repay the Sr. de La Mothe for the powder and lead which have been taken from the warehouse of the said Sr. de La Mothe for His Majesty's service on his producing the orders from the Commandants, without which this expense should not be repaid to him by His Majesty; also no decision can be given as to these certificates until they have been examined to ascertain whether the stores have not been replaced from the warehouse of the King.

It seems right also that he should be reimbursed the cost of his other goods, effects, implements and buildings by those who have profited by them. But as, since he left, there have been various Commandants at this post, we think that in order to avoid the lawsuits which he would be obliged to bring, it would be advisable not to allow him any remedy against any person, but for His Majesty to accord him some favor which would stand in lieu of all indemnification to him, both for the sum he re-imbursed the Company of the Colony and for the money he advanced

of experience there, the Sr. de Vaudreuil thinks that the Sr. de La Mothe's son has not experience enough to rule the minds of the savages.

Vaudreuil

Begon.

CADILLAC COMPLAINS OF TONTY.

Endorsed—Colonies. La Mothe Cadillac.

To his Most Serene Highness the Count of Toulouse, Admiral of France.

La Mothe Cadillac has the honor to represent to His Most Serene Highness that the answer of MM. de Vaudreuil and Begon is founded only on the report that M. de Tonty made to them; consequently it deserves no attention.

The large sum of money the Petitioner has spent cannot honestly be disputed; even the letter of MM. de Vaudreuil and Begon of the 14th of Novr., 1719, written to the Council, proves it. And if this year they should write otherwise about it that can only be for reasons of private interest, inspired by M. de Tonty whom the Petitioner caused to be suspended by His Majesty with prohibitions to M. de Vaudreuil against giving him in future any command in the Upper Posts; but after the death of Louis 14th M. de Vaudreuil sent him to Detroit where he has frightfully molested the inhabitants of that place, and so long as he commands there it will be very difficult for the inhabitants to be at

And as, by one of the decisions of His Royal Highness the petitioner has his remedy against the commanders of Detroit and others, and to sue before anyone he thinks fit concerning the wrongs which have been done him, which consist in pulling down his warehouses built of good oak timber and the timber of the church and other houses, with which the fort has been repaired and redoubts built, his cattle have been killed and eaten, his lands and his mill taken possession of, and the rents received from the inhabitants; the petitioner has the honor to represent to H. S. H. that it is not at all fitting for old officers to go to law, more especially since the Governor-General and the Intendant would be necessarily involved in this trial; and that it would be more beneficial to both parties that His Majesty should accord a favor to the petitioner by granting him a pension of a thousand livres on the Order of St. Louis and a pension of a like amount to his family on the navy or elsewhere by preferment; and in default of the two pensions named, an abbacy on a benefice for M. Joseph de La Mothe, who was born at Detroit, son of the petitioner, aged 21 years and an ecclesiastic.

The petitioner hopes for the favors he asks as a recompense for the above losses and for the long service he has given the King for 40 years, and which he wishes to continue until his death. And as it is settled also by one of H. R. H.'s decisions that any property taken for the King's service, belonging to the petitioner, shall be paid for, it is just that this payment should be according to the value at Detroit, namely, the powder at 5# a pound, the lead at 3# a pound, the ten swords wanting handles and the ironwork at 100#, and also two portable chapels consisting of two silver chalices, gilded, two pyxes, two monstrances, with all the assortment of chasubles, &c., which cost him 1500#.

That moreover the petitioner may be able to take his property whether personal or real which may be found at Detroit in kind, according to the decision of H. R. H.

And as there is now vacant the priory of St. Beat in Begorre, by the death of M. de Villespassau, provost of the Cathedral of St. Etienne de Thé, which yields an income of about two thousand livres, if H. R. H. had the kindness to grant it to the son of the petitioner, the pension asked for, for his family might remain at one thousand livres; and this would be a recompense for the services rendered to the King by the petitioner and his children. It is on this occasion that the promise which H. R. H. had the goodness to make to the petitioner might be carried out, having said to him in public and aloud several times that he would like to do something concerning him and on his behalf, and the above arrangement might be made.

CADILLAC RELATES OF THE FOUNDING OF DETROIT.

Endorsed—M. Raudot—Colonies.   Read to the Council.   M. de La Mothe Cadillac 1719.

The Council can give no decision on these questions until after receiving the answers which come from Canada to the memorandum which it will remit to him only in order to be sent there.   All that the Council can do is to ask for all necessary explanations from Canada as to the facts, and to order that no damage should be done to the property or the cattle which he claims belong to him.

Monseigneur,

M. Raudot told me two days ago that I had not explained myself clearly enough as to my claims on Detroit at Fort Pontchartrain; the cause of this was my fear of giving annoyance by prolixity.   But foreseeing that justice cannot be done me, if I do not acquaint the Council with my case, I take the liberty of writing this letter to His Most Serene Highness, begging him to have the patience to read it, from the same spirit with which he is filled, of doing justice to whom it is due.

It was I, Monseigneur, who proposed the establishment of Detroit, at a time when the trade of New France was much shaken.   Although to recount this matter from its commencement until now would be very advantageous to my claim, I forego it because it would be necessary to write a volume.   I restrict myself as far as I can, and, so far as I know it, to what is most essential; and to saying that the Beaver Company obtained the exclusive right of trading in 1702 of the Fort Pontchartrain of Detroit on the condition that it should reimburse His Majesty for the expense he had incurred for that Post; this was carried out on the part of that Company.   H. S. H. will, if it please him, observe that this expense consisted only in the cost of the equipment, and of the mer-

doubt, I made offers to His Majesty with a detailed account, repeated and enforced, as to the utility of that Post. It was that which decided His said Majesty to order me to reside there during the war, and to repeat in his letter his intentions, in which he explains to me clearly the conditions on which he grants me that Post. This letter is dated the 14th of June 1704, confirmed by another in 1705 a copy of which I have sent to H. S. H.; this is the reason I do not now send it, since it is apparently in the office. The following is an abstract of the conditions:—

The first is that His Majesty appoints me to the rights of the Company and puts me in charge of that Post at my own risk.

The second compels me to pay the said Company for the goods which are at the said Post, and to reimburse it for the useful erections.

The 3rd gives me the command which I had already.

The 4th grants me the exclusive right of trading with the restriction of making only twenty thousand pounds of castoreum a year, with liberty to trade in all other skins; it being understood that I am not to transact trade outside Detroit; granting power to the Beaver Company to keep an inspector there at its own expense.

The 5th directs the Governor-General to give me the number of soldiers I ask for, on condition that I defray the cost of their conveyance.

The 6th is to permit all who wish to go and settle at Detroit to do so.

The 7th directs the Governor-General and the Intendant to give me the missionaries necessary for that Post.

The 8th is that His Majesty leaves me the absolute master of everything at Detroit.

The 9th permits me to grant lands at Detroit in the manner I find to be good and suited to the interests of the new colony.

The 10th is to allow the soldiers and Canadians at Detroit to marry.

The 11th consists of high promises.

This letter, Monseigneur, having been forwarded to me, and orders on this subject having at the same time been sent to the Marquis de Vaudreuil, Governor-General, and to M. Raudot senior, the Intendant, they began by telling me that it was necessary to make an agreement with the Company because it was in possession of Detroit and would not give up its claim unless I first carried out chiefly the first and second

accordance with my said letter, and in the execution of their orders, the Company retired in my favor, and the Governor-General, as representing the King's person, put me in possession of Detroit on the 25th of Sept., 1705.

Up to this point, Monseigneur, this matter was conducted in a proper manner; to the King, who had defrayed the first cost of that Post, was reserved the exclusive right of trading, until he was entirely repaid; neither would the Company withdraw until after having taken securities from me, and after I had satisfied the said Company concerning them. For the same reason it is indisputable that no one can be appointed to my rights until after having made an agreement with me concerning them, following the same rule; and if the Governor-General had taken the same course in my favor, he would never have put M. de la Foret in possession of Detroit as he did; and these are the grounds on which he based his action.

In 1710, His Majesty did me the honor to grant me the Governorship of Louisiana, and M. de Pontchartrain wrote to me in these terms. "His Majesty having selected M. de la Foret to command at Detroit in your place, I am sending him orders about it; it is necessary that you should instruct him in all that concerns that Post."   .

That appears to be a simple notice on the part of the Minister, which confers no other right on M. de la Foret but that of taking command, and does not confer on him either my exclusive right of trading, nor my lands, nor my cattle, nor other property or merchandise; and it seems to me that M. de Vaudreuil had no right to put M. de la Foret in possession except only by the force of his authority. It is true that he had a right to give him the command, which is a matter quite distinct and

was not obliged to settle any inhabitants there; it was nothing more than a trading post. But it is apparent from the conditions of my said letter that the King intends to form a new colony at Detroit, and wishes me to grant concessions to those who will settle there, and also to the soldiers who wish to marry there; and that I should direct this matter as absolute master. In fact, you have only to look at the register at Detroit and you will find there at least four hundred grants of which I have given copies to the inhabitants; and if the greater part of them had not been driven away or harrassed, it would now be a very fine colony. It is deplorable to see families, which had sold everything at Quebec or elsewhere in order to settle at Detroit, being driven from it by the greed of certain persons who have profited and still profit, by what lawfully belongs to them.

M. de Vaudreuil has always declared that the exclusive trade is inseparable from the command; M. Raudot senior well knows that that was his great theory. It is easy to see his reasons for it and that he will no doubt endeavor to uphold them to the end; but they cannot prevail except in a mind blinded by passion, since we see the contrary in practice every day.

However this may be, Monseigneur, M. de la Foret enjoyed all my property; afterwards, M. de Sabrevoir. But as he went there by the order of the Court, he did not stay there long, M. de Vaudreuil, having gone to France, caused that Post to fall to M. de Tonty who, all his life, has been his slave, as every one in Canada knows very well.

Can it be possible, Monseigneur, that after having served His Majesty so long, a post, the scheme for which I put forward, is to be taken away from me; a post, which I formed at my own cost and expense, since there was no settlement there when the King granted it to me. MM. Raudot, senior and junior, having come to L'achine to view my detachment of two hundred soldiers, eight officers, two almoners and missionaries, and forty families which I took with mine, were witnesses of this large equipment of cutters and the troop boats, having taken to Detroit domestic animals of all kinds, all sorts of grains and seeds, even to fruit-trees in boxes, all tools for carpentry, for joinery, axes, and locks of all kinds, and even the materials for building a wind-mill which in truth cost a thousand pistoles, a barge, in a word, all the ironwork for the fort, which I had built with eight bastions, all the lodging places for the troops, a church, a very suitable building and well ornamented, a fine warehouse, another for powder, a pigeon-house, a very fine ice-house, a brewery for beer, a barn eighty feet long. I took a hundred

to set it forth in detail; for it is well to observe that there are 360 leagues between Quebec and Detroit through very difficult roads.

I remained there only four years during which I did nothing but pay out money; and at the time I was about to recoup myself I was sent to Louisiana, though I had never asked to be; but as I have always made it a point of honor to obey, I did not hesitate to quit a Post which would have become very valuable to me.

It has returned to my mind that M. de Vaudreuil maintained that, not having a grant in due form from the King, the ownership of it did not belong to me.

To this objection I reply that I was obliged to be content with the security which His Majesty gave me by his said letter, which is a good title, since, under a declaration of His said Majesty, those who clear lands not already granted, hold the ownership of them, without anyone having the power to take them away from them; the rule being so favorable to the inhabitants of Canada, ought indeed to be more so for me, since I hold a title as appears particularly in the 6th, 8th, and 9th clauses of my letter which is my contract. One of these states that His Majesty leaves me absolute master of all matters at Detroit; he who says "all" excepts nothing, hence, that must be understood of everything except the conditions made with me. Consequently I was the master of all the rest which the King gave me: a country which was not inhabited either by the savages or by any other nation, only by a prodigious quantity of fallow-deer; a country which was absolutely uncultivated; a place, concerning which the Court was informed, by the Comte d'Arvaux who was in England, that that country wished to seize upon. It is true that the King desired and permitted me to make grants to the inhabitants. I did so, as I have already said; I also granted them as Seignor of Detroit. I sent to the Court a copy of the said grants; the Governor-General and the Intendants read them; the King found no fault with me concerning them, through his Minister. I had reason, therefore, for thinking that under this 8th clause I was the Seignor & had seignorial rights; for, if that had not been the King's intention, there would have been a restriction in my authority as to what concerns me in my pri-

an objection, where is the justice and the good faith in taking from me 400 arpents of cleared land, in a word all that I kept for myself and that I granted to others, after I have made it valuable in the hope of enjoying it, and of making of it an inheritance for my children.

If there is no difficulty to get over except this, of having a grant in due form, I must hope from the kindness of His Most Serene Highness that he will obtain the grant of it for me from His Majesty, accompanied also by an honorable title; especially since the English are now in possession of my estate at L'Acadie which I held with rights of higher, middle and lower jurisdiction, which had a frontage of two leagues to the sea, and a depth of two inland with an island of 14 leagues; and also a fief at Port Royal which I had bought for ready money.

I say, moreover, Monseigneur, that I had an agreement with M. de Laforest who, seeing that he was unable to pay me, or to find security, consented that the Chevalier de Marigny, another Captain, should take his place in the command, in consideration of a gratuity; and I had made an arrangement with the said M. Marigny for the exclusive trade, of all my goods and other property which I had at Detroit, and of all my buildings. This was confirmed by a judgment, after hearing all the parties in their justification, by M. Raudot, the Intendant, dated the 22nd of July, 1711, on account of the opposition M. de Vaudreuil made thereto, against which I protested without withdrawing from the respect I owed him, declaring that I should appeal at a suitable time and place, and that since he prevented that arrangement from being carried out, he could by force and authority do what seemed good to him at Detroit.

I have every reason to hope that His Most Serene Highness having found, by the details of my letter, that I was put in possession of Detroit at Fort Pontchartrain on the Beaver Company relinquishing it to the King in my favor, after I had paid it and satisfied it; and consequently my taking possession of the said Post by the order of the Governor-General; and that I never for my part gave up the said Post, nor received any payment from M. de la Foret who was appointed to the command in my place, nor from M. de Sabrevoir, nor from M. de Tonty; that consequently my title continues to hold good. And I beg that to this end prohibitions may be issued to M. de Tonty and to all others against troubling or disturbing me in the ownership and land of Detroit, of my personal and real property; and in order to avoid disputes in future, to grant me a concession of the said Detroit in due form, to decree that I am to be paid for the goods which the officers commanding or others, have taken from me at the prices they were worth at Detroit; also for the cattle, the milking, the enjoyment of the lands, houses, the payment for the grinding of the mill, the rents of the houses, quit-rents, rents & revenues; and that I am likewise to be paid for the powder, lead, bullets, arms, &c., which the said Commandants of the said Fort have caused to be taken for the service of the King, at the price they were worth at the said time at Detroit, since it is not just to pay me for them as for the same kinds [of stores] at Quebec, seeing that it costs a great deal to convey them & that there are considerable risks in doing so.

If H. S. H. thinks it advisable to re-annex Detroit to the domain of His Majesty, I beg him to have my claims settled in accordance with the inventory which was made at Detroit in 1711, in the presence of the Almoner of the Fort and certain inhabitants, which I have left in the hands of M. Grandmenil who transacts my business, and this according to the valuation to be made of them at the place by upright men; to be paid for them in France in money, with compensation for not enjoying them from the 1st of January, 1712, up to the date when the said reannexation is made.

If this proposal is not agreeable to H. S. H. I very humbly beg him to decree that whoever enjoys Detroit and the exclusive trade shall be bound to reimburse me for all my buildings, for all my goods, my cattle, personalty and realty according to and in conformity with the said inventory of 1711, at the price that the goods, personalty and realty, were worth at the said time, & that the valuation of them shall be made by upright men who know the condition in which I left the said goods when I was recalled from Detroit to go and serve at Louisiana; which experts shall be chosen by the person entrusted with my authority and others in like number by him who is to possess the property, who shall be bound to make the said payment in the manner agreed upon; and in case he cannot pay the whole, he shall give solvent security to my attorney, the deed for which shall be executed before a notary.

These three decisions are apparently just; by the first I ask to be given back what has been taken away from me, because it belongs to me, and to be paid for what has been taken from me, because it is due to me.

CADILLAC'S PROPERTY AT DETROIT DESTROYED.

Endorsed—Colonies. M. de La Mothe Cadillac 1719.

To His Most Serene Highness Monseigneur the Comte de Toulouse, Admiral of France.

La Mothe Cadillac, Monseigneur, very humbly represents to you that his attorney in Canada writes to him this year, that, from the month of August 1711 until now, the Commandants of the fort Pontchartrain have, one after another, seized upon the exclusive right of trading at the said Post, which belongs to M. de La Mothe, and likewise on his lands and revenues, on his mill, houses, and cattle *the greater part of which they have had slaughtered; M. de Sabrevoir also has had some killed to the value of 300# for which he has given his acknowledgement.* This considered, may it please you, Monseigneur, to order M. *Sabrevoir to pay him the said sum of 300#,* and to forbid the Commandants of the said fort and others to disturb the said M. de La Mothe, or others put in charge by him, in his said exclusive trading, and in the possession of his lands, mills, houses, cattle; and that the contracts he has granted to the inhabitants under the authority he had received from His Majesty shall hold good, until his rights and claims, and the damages he has suffered for eight or nine years, are settled, and in the meantime to enjoin on the Governor General and Intendant of Canada to stay their hands.

To communicate with de Sabrevoir as to the acknowledgement for 3 livre. to order that Canada the said c are not to destroyed. to ask M. de Cadillac for his titles.

MEMORIAL OF CADILLAC TO THE COUNCIL.

Endorsed.—Colonies.   M. de La Mothe Cadillac 1719.

Memorial presented to the Council by M. de La Mothe Cadillac, Chevr. de St. Louis, and formerly Governor of Louisiana.

La Mothe has the honor to state to the Council that he was in France in 1700, and put before the Court the project of the establishment of Detroit. It is a river receiving the waters of three lakes which are fourteen hundred leagues in circumference, and which proceed to discharge themselves into Lake Erie. This stretch of river is 25 leagues long, and it is that which is called Detroit in New France while the fort is called Pontchartrain.

His Majesty, having the said project considered by his royal council, approved it; and the same year sent to Canada M. de La Mothe who was selected for that expedition & had command of it.

He set out from Quebec in 1702 and arrived at Detroit on the 26th of the month of August in the said year. The same year a Company was formed in the Colony which, having taken over the beaver-farm, obtained likewise the monopoly of the trade of Detroit and, at the same time, of that of fort Frontenac on Lake Ontario, and made its agreements with MM. the Chevalier de Calliere and de Champigny, the first the Governor General and the other the Intendant; and this was done according to the orders of the King. That is shown by the arrangement which was entered into between the seven directors of that Company and the said Governor and Intendant, dated the 31st Octr., 1701, that is to say two months after the said M. de La Mothe arrived at the said Detroit. By that said arrangement that Company undertook to pay the King for the merchandise which had been sent to Detroit to be sold for the profit of His Majesty, and at the same time to reimburse him for all the outlay made in connection with the said Post. According to all appearances that condition has been carried out.

the seven directors of the said Company, when they treated with MM. de Calliere and de Champigny were in a position to discuss their rights and to enforce their arguments, which M. de La Mothe was not able to do, being then at Detroit, since the Comte de Pontchartrain, Secretary of State, settled in the King's name the provisions and conditions laid down in the said letter of the 14th of June, 1704, which the said M. de La Mothe was obliged to accept without reply, and to take thereon the orders of MM. de Vaudreuil and de Beauharnois, the one Governor General and the other the Intendant. This was executed and is proved by the agreement made between the general and special agents of the said Company and M. de La Mothe, dated the 28th of Septr., 1705, the whole in the presence of the Governor-General and of three Intendants. M. de La Mothe points out to the Council that nothing was forgotten in that said agreement. The general agent of the Company was the Lieutenant-General of the provost-ship of Kebék, and the special agent the treasurer of the Navy; also, there were four persons whose capacity cannot be questioned without offending against the respect due to the persons placed in authority and governing all New France at that time.

It is advisable to consider what that agreement contains or to see what is laid down in three clauses. By the first, M. de La Mothe is obliged to pay the Company for the goods it had at Detroit. In the second is contained the manner in which he was to make the payment. These two clauses have been carried out; this is proved by a decree of M. Raudot dated the 21st of Octr. 1707, which orders the said M. de La Mothe to pay for the said goods with interest, and by the receipt in accordance therewith dated the 6th Novr. 1709 for the sum of 10,339 livres, 12 sous, 2 deniers signed Monseignat, and this was in reimbursement of what the said Company owed to the King for the said Detroit. This was done in virtue of the first article of the letter of the 14th of June, 1704, which compels the said M. de La Mothe to pay the Company for the goods which it had at Detroit.

The other clause which is in the same article of the said letter lays down that M. de La Mothe shall reimburse the said Company for the useful buildings which they have erected at Detroit.

This has reference to the seventh article of the said agreement on which the said M. de La Mothe maintained that he owed nothing for the said buildings, and the parties referred this to the decision of the Comte de Pontchartrain who, having considered the question, would not order M. de La Mothe to pay for the said useful buildings, for two reasons; the first is, that there were none there, the second, that His Majesty had granted a fund for the said post, of fifteen thousand livres, which the Company received. This is proved by the arrangement entered into with the Governor-General and the Intendant dated the 31st of Oct., 1701.

M. de La Mothe maintained this point effectively, and the Company having been sensible of his reasons kept silence because it was not merely paid, but overpaid, by the sum of fifteen thousand livres, since all its useful expenditure was not of the value of three thousand livres; moreover, at the time that M. de La Mothe accepted and was put in possession of Detroit, the houses of the Company had been burnt down.

It is evident that, if the Company had been injured in the said payment, it had a remedy which was to demand the valuation of the houses, buildings, &c., which it did not do for the reasons aforesaid.

M. de La Mothe points out to the Council that, up to this point, this matter has been pursued rightly. The Company reimbursed the King, M. de La Mothe reimbursed the Company. Yet he is dispossessed of his trade and of his property, without having made any surrender of them and without having been reimbursed for them either on the part of His Majesty or of any private individual.

It is true that he had made an agreement with M. de la Forest who was appointed to command in the place of M. de La Mothe, as appears from the letter of the Comte de Pontchartrain dated the 13th of May, 1710, by which said agreement it was arranged that M. de la Foret should give up the command and his claims in favor of M. de La Mothe, in consideration of a gratuity of 600#: but that arrangement has not been in force either altogether or in part, because M. de La Mothe having proposed the Chevalier de Marigny to M. de Vaudreuil to go and take command at Detroit in place of M. de la Foret, who had withdrawn from his command as has been stated, M. de Vaudreuil opposed it and hence this agreement remained null and without effect; so that, while M. de La Mothe was in Louisiana, and since his return, and perhaps for several years more (if the Council waits for explanations from that country), the commandants at Detroit have enjoyed the rights and the property of the said M. de La Mothe without having any other

to say that, M. de La Mothe being commandant at Detroit, & having at the same time the exclusive right of trading, M. de la Foret ought to have it for the same reason, nor his property either, since it is well known that M. de La Mothe was commandant for the King in 1701 and 1702 at Detroit, and that yet the Company carried on the trade; and it was the same thing with the command of the Fort Frontenac.

In the same second article of the said letter of the 14th of June, 1704, it is evident that M. de La Mothe is appointed to the rights of the Company, and that he undertakes the post of Detroit at his own risk.

His enemies have given explanations of great length to these two clauses. But M. de La Mothe has maintained that no interpreter is required for the understanding of the said clause; for, to be appointed to the rights of that Company is to be granted its exclusive right of trading at Detroit, since it possessed no other right.

The other clause is that M. de La Mothe undertook this Post at his own risk; it should not be understood that if this Post had been taken by enemies M. de La Mothe was bound to pay the King for it, since it would have been at the cost of his life if he had betrayed his trust; it must therefore mean that His Majesty transferred to M. de La Mothe the responsibility for any untoward events which might happen to the said Post.

M. de La Mothe maintains that if the Governor-General and the Intendant and the Company had found any difficulty in the term or even any ambiguity, it was for them to clear it up and to tie M. de La Mothe down to it before putting him in possession of Detroit; because after possession has been given, these become new provisions which a contracting party ought not to put up with, moreover the point has been decided by the Court in M. de La Mothe's favor as will be seen hereafter.

The third article of the said letter, which is really the contract of M. de La Mothe, continues to him the command, and leaves him the management of his trading. This arrangement is very just, for at the time when he had command of Detroit for the King, the clerks acting for His Majesty were set by the Intendant to conduct the trade there, the Company afterwards appointed some for its trade, M. de La Mothe did the same.

The Company had permission to prepare at Detroit whatever quantity of castor it wished; M. de La Mothe was restrained from making any more than the quantity of fifteen or twenty thousand livres; and in consideration of that restriction he was released from the offer he had made of the sum of ten thousand livres. All that is just and prudent on the part of the minister who negotiates on behalf of the King with an

zealous for his service; this has reference to the 9th article of the agreement made with the said Company.

In the 4th article of the said letter His Majesty forbids M. de La Mothe to send boats on the lakes or any agents into the interior of the lands, and permits the Company to have an inspector at Detroit at its own expense. This refers again to the 10th and 11th article of the said agreement made with the Company, assisted and well instructed by the Governor and the Intendant.

In the 5th article the Governor General is directed to grant M. de La Mothe the number of soldiers he asks him for, on the understanding that M. de La Mothe shall defray the cost of the conveyance; this has been carried out.

By the 6th article His Majesty permits those who wish to go and settle there to do so.

By the 7th article help & favor is promised to M. de La Mothe; but above all it proceeds to declare that it explains decisively the will of His Majesty to M. de Vaudreuil and to the Intendant and to the Company, in order that the said M. de La Mothe may find no more difficulties in future in that Post. It is indisputable that the rights of M. de La Mothe can never be better asserted than by the force of that expression, for we see that the Governor General, the Intendant and the Company ought to have agreed with M. de La Mothe concerning all the points in question, as they have in effect done, having signed the agreement, and by communicating to him the said letter of the 14th of June, 1704; moreover they were thoroughly informed of the orders of the King; and consequently no one could impose any new condition since such is not receivable after possession has been taken; also the Comte de Pontchartrain thoroughly agreed to this in the letter he wrote to M. de La Mothe, dated the 6th of July, 1709.

In the ninth article of the said letter, His Majesty leaves M. de La Mothe the absolute master in all things at Detroit; he who says "all" excepts nothing. This order was confirmed by the letter written on behalf of His Majesty to M. de La Mothe, dated the 17th of June, 1705, and by that of the 9th of June 1706 on the said article in these terms, speaking of M. de Vaudreuil.

· "I am writing to him also that he ought not to prevent you from

master of it, as is clearly explained in the 6th article of the letter of 1704, and repeated in the two following years in order that there might be no doubt as to the meaning of His Majesty. It is therefore quite indisputable that M. de La Mothe had the power to appropriate to himself lands at Detroit, as in fact he did do. But what lands has he taken? To whom has he done wrong? They were forest lands, which had to be cleared, inhabited by the savages, and not by French people. Was it not natural that he should appropriate them, having made an immense expenditure for the purpose of establishing that Post by having animals, oxen, cows, horses, and all kinds of domestic animals conveyed there; also fruit trees, the materials necessary for making a mill, a barge, houses, and lodging-places; all sorts of grains, and of seeds, all of them in large quantities; a number of workmen, 60 boats of bark, which, all agree, cost him 400# each, the tarpaulins for covering the provisions, and waxed cloths to cover the powder; the conveyance of 150 soldiers, of officers, almoners, missionaries and interpreters; the wages of the workmen, the wages of the Canadians for taking the boats, the wages of those who took the cattle by water and by land, the provisions for all those people; finally, when M. de La Mothe quitted Detroit, he left there forty effective families and he had granted about 140 concessions; moreover he refers to the inventory which was made in 1711 by his wife when she came from Detroit, which inventory is signed by the Almoner of the fort, and by several of the inhabitants.

In the 14th article of the said letter His Majesty permits the said M. de La Mothe to grant lands at Detroit in the manner he finds good and suitable for the interests of the new colony, and that he may allow the soldiers and the Canadians at Detroit to marry.

Here, then, is a complete authority, to be absolute master at Detroit, to do what he pleases without the Governor-General being able to find fault. That authority being constantly in existence, he was able to take lands for himself, for Detroit having 25 leagues on the one side and 25 on the other, that makes 40¹ leagues. The Council will be good enough to observe that he reserved to himself only about 3 leagues fronting the river and as much in the depth of the lands, which estate he assigned to himself as his share.

Again, to be master and to have power to grant lands to the inhabitants is, consequently, to have the power to grant them to his children to whom also he has granted three leagues with the islands which are in the front of their concession. There remain therefore at Detroit 44 leagues frontage besides 200 leagues in depth.

These inhabitants have, however, been defrauded of their concessions

sold their dwellings at Quebec or elsewhere having settled at Detroit in good faith.

M. de La Mothe points out to the Council that there is a declaration of His Majesty which maintains the inhabitants of Canada in the possession of lands they have cleared notwithstanding any grants that may be made in which the said cleared lands may be included. The inhabitants of Detroit would be entitled to their lands under that declaration which however, they do not need since the grants which M. de La Mothe made to them are grounded on the authority given to him by His Majesty; thus it is one title upon another.

For his own part, M. de La Mothe has still better rights. He chose his estate; and partly cleared it or, rather, had it cleared; he sent a copy of the concessions to the Court on which they have all been granted; he took the rank of Seigneur there. This copy was received and confirmed; consequently, the said M. de La Mothe has title on title, and is the possessor in good faith. He adds further, in order to strengthen his claims, that he had the honor of writing to the Comte de Pontchartrain in 1708 that he was prepared to return Detroit to the King in consideration of a certain sum. Here is the paragraph in reply, extracted word for word from the letter of the 6th of July, 1709—"I have given the King an account of the proposal you make to return the land at Detroit when you have put it in the condition you propose. His Majesty will not exact that from you; but, far from desiring that you should study how to draw a large revenue from that place, his will is that you should labor to make its people happy while preserving your interests as far as justice can permit you to do so."

specially prohibited from killing any cattle or arbitrarily seizing them, but only on mutual agreement & payment.

2. To decree that M. de La Mothe shall be paid for the goods belonging to him which have been taken at Detroit for the King's service at their value at the said time at Detroit, such being the custom; also that he shall be paid for those which have been taken from him by the commandants or other officers on their private account, without delay at the price at the said place, in ready money or in saleable furs; and also that M. de Sabrevois may be compelled to pay him the sum of three hundred livres which he has declared that he owes M. de La Mothe for cattle which he had killed at the said Detroit or for having made use of them, having made his declaration in the presence of M. Raudot.

3. That, if the Council thinks it well to re-annex this post to His Majesty's domain, he hopes that it will provide for his being paid for his personal and real property in accordance with the inventory of 1711, with a proportionate compensation for the losses he has sustained since his departure from the said Detroit by not enjoying them, and on the condition that the whole shall be nominated, some by the Intendant of Canada, and others by the attorney of the said M. de La Mothe, who hopes that in the said case His Majesty will consider the enormous expenditure he made without having enjoyed his privilege for more than a very short time.

M. de La Mothe begs the Council to decree that he is also to be paid for the expenditure he made at Detroit for the King's service according to the statements of the said expenditure which were sent to M. Raudot last year, by command of the Council, to be sent on to Canada; which said statements are in the form prescribed to M. de La Mothe by M. Raudot to whom he has sent extracts of articles from the letters of the Comte de Pontchartrain concerning the said expenditures which have been verified by the originals by M. Raudot.

M. de La Mothe cannot send his attorney to Detroit without incurring great expense; for that reason he begs the Council to order the Governor-General to permit the said attorney of M. de La Mothe to go to Detroit with the necessary number of servants in order to have his property valued, and to take in his boat whatever goods he may think neces-

COMMUNICATION TO THE COMTE DE TOULOUZE.

To Monseigneur the Comte de Toulouze.

Your Most Serene Highness is very respectfully begged to take into consideration that what M. de La Mothe asks for is not, by a great deal, all that the King grants to him in the letter of *Mgr. de Pontchartrain of the 6th of July, 1709.* It declares *"His Majesty will permit you to keep Detroit, if it suits you,* after he has withdrawn the troops from it."

There is no doubt—at a time when M. de La Mothe is not to be indemnified for all the money he has expended in order to form that colony; when he is not even repaid the sum which he gave to the Company of the Colony to reimburse it for what it had given to the King—that it suits him to keep all Detroit, and not to be disturbed by anyone whomsoever in that possession. His Majesty in the same letter gives him the socome tolls of the mill, the patronage of the churches which he was to build, and lastly permits him to keep Detroit if it suits him.

In order to prove that the intention of M. de La Mothe was to keep Detroit after His Majesty had withdrawn his troops from it, he produces a copy of the result of the assembly of the inhabitants of that place with the said M. de La Mothe of the 7th of June, 1710, by which all unanimously agree to provide a sum of 500# for the Priest which he asked for in addition to the tithe as it is paid at Quebec, and the said M. de La Mothe undertakes for his part to pay each year to this Priest, one hundred francs out of these 500#. That document proves also that Detroit was well established; but the Register of Concessions which is at Detroit contained a hundred and forty-two grants when the said M. de La Mothe left, making more than two leagues' frontage along the river.

All these facts being certain, he has reason to hope that His Most

CADILLAC OFFERS TO SURRENDER HIS RIGHTS AT DETROIT.

Endorsed—M. de La Mothe Cadillac.

To His Most Serene Highness Monseigneur the Comte de Toulouse, Admiral of France.

La Mothe Cadillac represents very respectfully to His Most Serene Highness that he consents to surrender to His Majesty all the rights and claims, which he has on Detroit consisting of valuable effects, and of lands, mills, buildings, and cattle which are indispensably necessary at that post for the subsistence of the officers and troops which are in garrison there.

Although all the claims and said property of M. de La Mothe are of the value of a hundred and fifty thousand livres, yet he surrenders them to the King for fifty thousand-weights of fine powder which quantity will cost His Majesty only the sum of sixteen or seventeen thousand livres.

Which powder, M. de La Mothe will send, with the approval of the King, to the colonies to trade with it there. By this means M. de La Mothe would be saved from bringing lawsuits (which would not be seemly for him) against the commandants and other officers of Detroit on account of the wrongs and injuries which have been done to him; and also it chances that His Majesty will owe him a part of the sum he asks for, on account of powder, lead and bullets, and other merchandise which have been taken from his warehouses by order of the commandants for the service of the King.

COMPLAINTS AGAINST SIEUR BOUAT.

Endorsed—11th March 1720. Canada

Refer to t.

given him by the Sr. de Ramezay, Governor of Montreal,—who had been informed of his design,—not to do so. It appears certain that this third boat was sent, from the confession of the said Sr. Bouat himself who alleges that it was sent for a hidden store which he said he had at the Cedars. However, although the Sr. de Ramezay gave notice to the Srs. de Vaudreuil and Begon of this act of disobedience no prosecution was instituted, of which His Majesty has disapproved. His will is that a Council should be called together to determine this matter in due form, and that they should report the decision arrived at, with the reasons for it. Moreover, His Majesty wishes the proclamation of the 28th of April, 1716, followed to the letter, and accordingly that all who go up to the upper countries in pursuance of licenses should have them registered, before they go, at the Registry of Montreal. He gives the Sr. de Ramezay orders to stop all boats going without complying with this.

MM. de Vaudreuil and Begon 26th of October 1719 state that, in accordance with His Majesty's orders, a court martial was summoned to try the Sr. Bouat for disobeying the orders of the Sr. de Ramezay by despatching a third boat to Detroit after his prohibition.

The said Sr. Bouat was sentenced to one month's imprisonment and prohibited from carrying on the duties of his office until His Majesty should be pleased to re-instate him.

The ground of his sentence to one month's imprisonment was his disobedience which was sufficiently proved by the terms of his letter which he wrote to the Sr. de Ramezay stating that he took the responsibility on himself, and by the two letters of the said Sr. de Ramezay which the said Sr. Bouat produced, containing the orders given him in the name of the King against despatching the third Boat.

The ground on which he was suspended was that, as this disobedience on the part of one of the chief officers of justice, who ought to have instilled into the people the submission due to His Majesty's orders, was public, it was necessary that he should be deprived of his office, to compensate for this bad example, until it pleased His Majesty to pardon him for this transgression.

Application of M. de Ramezay to M. de Vaudreuil in which he sets Index lett A. 12th Oc 1719. forth that, having received orders from him, M. de Vaudreuil, in his letter of 6th of March, 1718, to grant the Sr. Bouat permission to send two boats to the Sr. de Tonty, Commandant at Detroit, to take things to him which he might need, he had granted it and had taken the names of those who were to go with them. The Sr. Bouat afterwards proceeded to La Chine where, on his own authority, he fitted out a third boat to send to the upper country. Having been informed of this he, the Sr. de Ramezay, wrote him the letter of which a copy is *annexed,* to which he returned the reply, a copy of which is *annexed,* whereupon M. de Marked D. 4 May 1718. Ramezay, on the 5th of May, sent him a letter, copy *annexed,* prohibiting Marked C. Marked D. him from despatching any boats other than the 2 for which he had 5 May 1718. permission under the penalty attaching to disobedience. Bouat replied to the soldier who brought his letter that he had no reply to make to it, and that he would give an account of his conduct in person when he was at Montreal; and he despatched the third boat with the other two.

That when the Sr. Bouat returned to Montreal he came to his house where, without giving him time to ask him what he had done, he told him he had sent off the said boat. He (de Ramezay) pointed out to him that he ought not to have done so contrary to the orders he had given him against it; to which the Sr. Bouat replied in an audacious and disrespectful manner that he ought to have been satisfied with the letter he had written him in which he took the responsibility on himself, and that he was ready to go to law about it if he disapproved of his conduct. This behavior obliged him (de Ramezay) to point out to him how wrongly he was acting; but far from responding to that, he took up an attitude of defiance which went so far as to show contempt for the King's orders, and not content with that he even had the audacity to make it publicly known.

M. de Ramezay makes application that, in accordance with the King's orders, a court should be assembled to examine into and decide on the complaint and condemn him in the penalties set forth in the King's proclamation which not only prohibits going to the upper country without leave, but also prohibits all persons from equipping and supplying goods, to the *coureurs de bois;* that the said Sr. Bouat is guilty both by his disobedience and by his audacity in writing to him that he took the responsibility, by which he has rendered himself liable to the penalties assigned against the *coureurs de bois.*

summoned to be questioned as to the facts set forth in the complaint, the case, and matters connected with it.

Oct. 1719.   Order of M. de Vaudreuil summoning him to appear on the 13th in the morning, before the court-martial assembled, to be questioned.

ex letter
3th of the
(Month).
ex letter
13th idem.

Summons by de Saline, officer of the Court. Writing by the Sr. Bouat, in reply to the facts set forth in the application of M. de Ramezay. States that he is the more surprised to find himself brought before this special court, established only against *coureurs de bois,* deserters, because he has done nothing, either in the discharge of his duties, or in the transaction of the affairs of Detroit on behalf of the Sr. de Tonty, contrary to the King's orders. That, in the month of March 1718, he asked M. de Vaudreuil for permission to send two boats to the Sr. de Tonty at Detroit for the most urgent needs of the fort, and this was granted him.

He remarks that the number of boats for Detroit is not fixed; that the Sr. de Tonty, who commands there, and has the monopoly of the trade of this post, is at liberty to send as many boats there as he thinks fit, whether for himself or for the *voyageurs* who go to trade at his fort and within the limits laid down for him by His Majesty; and that it cannot be doubted that the deponent would equally have been given permission for 4, 6, or 10 boats, if he had asked M. de Vaudreuil for them, as for two. He did not reflect that Madame de Tonty, when going up to Detroit, in the autumn of 1717, had found herself over-burdened & had left at La Chine with Mme. Lorimier 8 barrels of powder, and had made a hidden store of 8 sacks of bullets in the rapids of Fort Frontenac. That, as these stores were necessary for the fort of Detroit and for distribution to the savages which it was advisable to make in the spring, he was obliged to ask M. de Ramezay for permission to send a third boat to convey these stores, to which that Governor replied that M. de Vaudreuil had only told him two boats; but, on pointing out to him that he would have granted more if he had asked for more, M. de Ramezay permitted him to send up the third boat on condition that he sent him the number and names of the men who were to take the third boat. On the petitioner replying that he could not then do so

Some hours after the petitioner left, the Sr. Reaume went to complain to M. de Ramezay, that Adjutant, the Sr. de la Tour had carried off a boat belonging to him into the King's shed, and this in the execution of M. de Ramezay's orders, who replied that he had given no orders on the point. The same day, the wife of the said Sr. Reaume, unknown to her husband, went to M. de Ramezay's house on the same matter: and, unmindful of the respect due to her Governor, she said many impertinent things which angered M. de Ramezay. He thought that it was Reaume who was to take charge of the third boat for Detroit; and, as he was a skilful *voyageur* and had much influence with the savages, which might have made M. de Ramezay think he would go beyond Detroit, this idea and the misbehavior of Reaume's wife, induced him to write the Petitioner the letter above referred to regarding the third boat, forgetting—no doubt—that a few days before he had given him permission for it in the presence of witnesses.

On the 5th of May 1718, at six o'clock in the evening, the Petitioner received a second letter from M. de Ramezay containing a prohibition against despatching the third boat. He immediately made known to the man Blondin and the other three *voyageurs* who were to work the said boat that M. de Ramezay, in the King's name, forbade them to set out until M. de Vaudreuil arrived; to which they replied that they would set out with the others. The Petitioner again repeated to them that he forbade them to embark on behalf of M. de Ramezay, and this in the presence of Madame de Lorimier and of her daughter, of the Srs. de Lusignan, Baby and several others whose names he does not remember. The said Blondin and the others replied that they would not expose themselves to being robbed by the savages at the Niagara portage by going in one boat alone; to which the Petitioner said that he was going to inform M. de Ramezay of it. That was, indeed, all he could do as he had not force with him to arrest them. They added that it had already cost them a good deal, living for a week on the provisions for their voyage. The petitioner mounted his horse to go and make his report to M. de Ramezay; he did not reach Montreal until 10 o'clock in the evening; and next morning he went to M. de Ramezay's who told him that he had considered the matter of this third boat and that he was afraid that M. de Vaudreuil would not approve of it. The Petitioner replied that he had made every effort to stop the men belonging to this boat, in accordance with his orders; but that they had still persisted in their determination to go. To this M. de Ramezay replied that he would

He points out that these boats only took to the Sr. de Tonty a certain number of pounds' weight both in provisions and in warlike stores, and if it had been necessary to fit them out [with goods for sale] it would have cost the Sr. de Tonty more than eight thousand livres.

He also points out that since the Sr. de Tonty has been in command at Detroit, M. de Vaudreuil has never refused the petitioner, acting for the said Sr. de Tonty, such number of boats as he has wished to send up, merely ordering that the number of those who were to work them should be given him exactly.

That M. de Vaudreuil, on his arrival at Montreal on the 15th May 1718, upon the complaint made to him by M. de Ramezay as to the departure of the third boat, inquired into what had taken place and did not consider that he had disobeyed the King's orders but simply instructed him to go to M. de Ramezay and assure him that he had taken no part whatever in the departure of this boat contrary to his orders, and to ask for his favor. He complied with this; and M. de Ramezay answered him that since M. de Vaudreuil consented to forget everything, that it was also at an end on his side, and that he would assist him when occasion offered; and that he has since done him the honor to go to see him at his house three or four times.

That, moreover, it is an actual proof that M. de Ramezay never considered the four men who worked the said boat to be disobedient to the King's orders, or deserters; that when they came back at the end of two or three months they returned to Montreal, and M. de Ramezay did not have them arrested; nor did he even lay any complaint about it to M. de Vaudreuil who was then at Montreal. Yet if there is anyone to blame it is they, after the efforts made by the Petitioner to stop them by informing them of M. de Ramezay's orders.

There are therefore no grounds for his application against him that he should be punished as a deserter and as having fitted boats out with merchandise since he by no means fitted out either this boat or the other two, with goods, but only charged them to take warlike stores and provisions to the Sr. de Tonty up to 600 livres' weight only, and is only concerned in this matter as agent for the affairs of the Sr. de Tonty.

sible for all the consequences until M. de Vaudreuil arrived, he made
this reply to him being convinced that M. de Vaudreuil would not disapprove of it, seeing that it was for taking stores to the post of Detroit;
that he did not intend by that to disobey M. de Ramezay who, in his
letter, only held him responsible for the consequences until M. de Vaudreuil arrived.

That it was not he who consigned the cargo of the three boats; that
they were fitted out with goods by private individuals on condition of
conveying six or seven hundred-weight to the Sr. de Tonty on his giving
them permission to trade with the savages at the fort of Detroit, and
that he had embarked all that belonged to the said Sr. de Tonty before
M. de Ramezay's prohibition.

He further denies all that M. de Ramezay charges him with, as to
having failed in proper respect towards him at his house.

Decree that this should be communicated to the Procureur-Général to 13th Oct.
the Commission.

Request of the Procureur-Général that the written statement of the Index lett
Sr. Bouat should be exhibited to M. de Ramezay, to reply thereto if he I. 13th Ide
thinks fit, and that the brothers Blondin and the others who took up the
third boat should be arrested and taken to prison that the charge against
them may be heard and determined.

Judgment of the Court Martial setting forth that, disregarding the Index lett
request of the Proceureur-Général the case shall be definitely decided L. 16th Oc
1719.
upon in its present form; and that, to this end, the whole of the proceedings be exhibited afresh to the Procureur-Général that he may state
precisely what decision he asks for.

Demand of the Procureur-Général that the Sr. Bouat be sentenced to Index lett
two months' imprisonment, and suspended from the duties of his office M. of the
same dat
until it may please His Majesty to reinstate him, and to the other penalties set forth in the decrees.

and it is easy to see his ill-feeling in that, as he is acquainted with many facts which would tend to the acquittal of the petitioner.

It was necessary therefore to move that a trial should be prepared and brought against the petitioner as having disobeyed the orders of the King, the Sr. de Ramezay wishing to accuse him of sending goods to the upper country and as a *coureur de bois*, a crime of which he is incapable. But it was ordered, on the application, that it should be exhibited to the Sr. de l'Epinay who was acting as Procureur-Général, on whose motion it was decided that he should be questioned before the whole Court Martial. This was done, and he replied to everything he was asked in accordance with his written statement or with the statement of the facts naturally set forth.

His statement in writing was read, and it is easy to observe, according to the examination of the prisoner, that he insisted on all points that the witnesses named by him should be questioned, which they would never grant him.

The Court Martial having ordered that his examination and his memorandum should be exhibited to the Procureur-Général, the latter moved that the said written statement should be exhibited to M. de Ramezay for him to reply to it.

It will be apparent to the Council that this affair was no longer dealt with as a matter concerning a Court Martial: in exhibiting his memorandum to his adversary, that became a case between private persons, whereas the intention of the King was only that the petitioner should be tried on the complaints of the Sr. de Ramezay, and not that he should be delivered up to his ill-feeling.

There was then a final decision in favor of the Procureur-Général. He will not insist on the defects in the proceedings. He is accused of resistance and disobedience to the King's orders, of which he is incapable; and yet, so well did he carry out M. de Ramezay's orders, that he reported them to those who were to make the journey and immediately returned to Montreal to report the matter to M. de Ramezay. Why did not this Governor order the boat to be stopped, as he had asserted he would? And why has he not had the *voyageurs* arrested since their return? It is upon the Petitioner, then, that he has heaped all his vengeance, although he had from him verbal permission to fit out the third boat.

to bring the case under the decree against the *courcurs de bois;* but even supposing that, it was necessary to have the *voyageurs* of the said boat arrested and punished on their return, and not lay the blame on the Petitioner who had communicated to them the orders he had received, and who asked—in accordance with the request of the Procureur Général—to have witnesses heard, which would have served to clear him. He hopes the Council will have regard to this, as it is a formal refusal of justice; begs them to observe that he cannot be brought under the decree against the *coureurs de bois;* that there is a permission to send whatever number of boats he may think fit for the subsistence of Detroit; that he had had permission verbally from M. de Ramezay in the presence of witnesses. And he is so incapable of imposing on the Council that he sends them a *certificate* of the man Blondin signed be- This certii cate is an fore a Notary, declaring that the Petitioner notified him of the order ed hereto. not to set out for Detroit; it is easy to see, from this certificate, that it was not the Petitioner who fitted out the third boat, but the Sr. Reaume in accordance with the verbal permission of the Sr. de Ramezay.

The Council will therefore be surprised that, after the strongest proofs of his good conduct, he should have been suspended from his duties by a Court Martial, and kept in prison for a month; and he hopes that the Council will recognize that he has only adhered to the strict truth, and has stated nothing but what would have been proved by witnesses, if they would have consented to hear them. He has every hope in the justice of the Council.

Madame Pascaud
Rochelle, 28th December, 1719.

Represents that she is the innocent cause of the complaints which M. de Ramezay made against the Sr. Bouat, her brother; for this Governor owed her from nine to ten thousand livres which she had asked for through the captain of one of her ships which she sent to Canada in 1718: that, thinking that she ought not to have asked him for payment of the sum which she had generously lent him, he thought he could not re-

PUNISHMENT OF BOUAT.

Endorsed—To be laid before Monseigneur le Duc d'Orleans. 19th March 1720. Canada.

Approved the opinion of the Council, to remove the suspension.

Council of the Navy
March, 1720.

Complaints having been preferred last year that the Sr. Bouat Lieutenant General of the provostship at Montreal, who had obtained permission to send two boats to Detroit, had despatched a third notwithstanding the prohibitions of M. de Ramezay, Governor of Montreal who had been informed of his intention, orders were given to summon a Court to decide this matter according to rule, and to report the decision and reasons.

MM. de Vaudreuil and Begon write that the Sr. Bouat was sentenced to one month's imprisonment, and suspended from the duties of his office until it should please His Majesty to reinstate him.

The ground on which he was sentenced to a month's imprisonment was his disobedience which was sufficiently proved by the letter which he wrote to M. de Ramezay stating that he took responsibility on himself.

That of his suspension was that this disobedience was open, and it was necessary—in order to make up for this bad example—that he should be deprived of the duties of his office.

The Sr. Bouat represents that the proceedings were not carried out in due form.

The Council, after having looked into this matter considers that the Sr. Bouat has been punished enough and that it is advisable to terminate his suspension, ordering him not to carry on any trade in future directly or indirectly, on commission or otherwise.

INVENTORY OF CADILLAC'S POSSESSIONS AT DETROIT.

Endorsed—April 1720. Memorandum of the sums to which M. de La Mothe makes his claims amount.

Index letter E.

Observations to which Monsieur Raudot is very humbly begged to give his consideration.

To prove that M. de La Mothe is not liable for the charges to which the Company of the Colony was subjected; that is, that he is not bound thereto because he has not been appointed to its rights.

First point,

for example

The Company had the right of transacting all the beaver trade which might present itself at Detroit, without any restriction.

2nd point.

M. de La Mothe, on the contrary, was bound down by being unable to transact it beyond the sum of twenty thousand livres a year at most.

3rd point.

That makes as much difference between the Company and him as, from everything to almost nothing.

4th point.

M. de La Mothe, not having been appointed to the essential rights of the Company, is consequently not liable for its burdens. This is evident, and so much more so that he is not subjected thereto by his contract, which is the letter of Mgr. the Comte de Pontchartrain of the 14th of June, 1704.

The payments made by M. de La Mothe for all his charges amount to 7600#. If M. Raudot thinks fit that half of the loss should fall on M. de La Mothe; which is 3800#, he is content; therefore he leaves this item out of the calculation.

According to the statement drawn up by M. Begon, intendant of Canada, of what is due to M. de La Mothe for expenditure for the service of the King and re-

Cleared lands

400 arpents of land, cleared, at a hundred francs per
    arpent, total ....40,000#— —

Buildings or houses

one warehouse .... 3000#
house of M. de La Mothe............................ 2500#
2 other houses...................................... 1500#
a barn with its [baterie] of joists..................... 1200#
a stable .... 500#
a dove cot .... 400#
                                                     ———
                    Total....................53431# " 7 " 3

an ice house.. 300#
a chapel and the house of the almoner................. 3000#
for the mill .... 8000#

Cattle

29 horned cattle, a horse valued at 400#, for which M. de
    La Mothe found a purchaser at 9000# before his de-
    parture, which the commandant opposed and forbade
    their purchase; total .... 9,000#
goods fit for furniture, and merchandise flour and grains,
    at seven thousand livres.......................... 7000#
for the premium on the said goods at the same rate as was
    settled by the Minister and which M. de La Mothe paid to
    the Company at 4 p.c.—total...................... 2800#
for the loss of the use of 400 arpents of land for ten years,
    it being fit to bear crops every year because it was new

RAMEZAY PREVENTS SABREVOIS FROM GOING TO DETROIT.

Endorsed—Canada 14th May 1720.

Council
as to the Sr. de Sabrevois
Captain in Canada.

Upon the representation in 1718 that the command of the fort of De- troit, with the privilege of carrying on trade there, was granted to him in 1712, and that he.set out in 1715 to go there, in accordance with the orders which M. de Ramezay gave him about it.

That the war planned against the Fox Indians was the cause, or the pretext, which M. de Ramezay made use of in order to prevent him from exercising his privilege of trading there, by prohibiting him from grant- ing permissions to the inhabitants of the country, according to custom, to take goods there.

He would not even permit him to take more than two boats with him, which were not capable of conveying what he needed, and, finally, that he was not able to take advantage of his privilege of carrying on the trade during the two years that he was there. Yet he was obliged to maintain at his own expense an interpreter at 800 livres a year, an almoner at 600, and a surgeon at 150, and to keep the fort in repair.

At the end of that time he was superseded without being told why, by a man who had been in command of this fort before and had been recalled because of the complaints made against him.

That, as he had been unable to obtain repayment in Canada of the expenses he incurred at Detroit, where he was obliged to make presents of the value of more than four thousand livres to the savages in the in- terests of the service, according to the certified statement. He begged the Council to cause payment to be made to him of the expenses which

the Sr. de Sabrevois, regarding the time when he was in command at
Detroit, but finds no reason therein why the Sr. de Tonty should be
bound to give him any indemnification. The fact that he did not enjoy
the privilege of the monopoly of trade at Detroit during the years 1715
and 1716, alleged by the said Sr. de Sabrevois, is one of which he could
have no knowledge as he was in France at that time, and a thing for
which he could have no claim against the Sr. de Tonty, even if it be as
he states, since the latter had no hand in the trouble of which the said
Sr. de Sabrevois complains, as he did not go to Detroit until 1717; and
since he has enjoyed this privilege he has borne all the expenses with
which the said Sr. de Sabrevois was saddled; that, moreover, he induced the said Sr. de Tonty, when he was about to set out for Detroit
in the month of May 1717, to grant two permissions for two boats which
the agent of the said Sr. de Sabrevois sent there, which were allowed
to transact their trade there, although it injured that of the said Sr.
de Tonty, to the extent of 1800 French livres in paper money which the
men who took the boats paid to the said Sr. de Sabrevois, to whom the
said Sr. de Tonty was very glad to show this consideration at his
request.

As regards the repairs to the inclosure of the fort, it is certain that
the said Sr. de Sabrevois made none; for according to the report of M.
de Louvigny the fort was in a very bad condition when he passed there
when proceeding against the Fox Indians in 1716, and the Sr. de Tonty
found it so dilapidated when he arrived there in 1717 that he was
obliged to rebuild it entirely. Proof of the bad condition of the fort,
and that the Sr. de Sabrevois never incurred any expense for it, is
found in a paragraph of the letter which the said Sr. de Sabrevois wrote
to him from Detroit on the 8th of April 1717, from which he forwards
an extract, by which it appears that it was only then that he set himself to the duty of having this enclosure repaired, & that it was the
Voyageurs who supplied the stakes required for this repair, of which
there were only 150 prepared according to his own confession, & that he
never considered that it should be done at his expense.

Note. According to this extract, which is annexed, the Sr. de Sabrevois writes to M. de Vaudreuil that there is one of the curtains of the

Vaudreuil would give orders to the Sr. de Tonty to make these 3 men pay as well as the others who, following their example, would do nothing in the matter.

As regards the presents which the Sr. de Sabrevois claims to have made to the savages of Detroit to induce them to go to war against the Fox Indians, since the two officers whom M. de Ramezay sent, in 1715, laden with presents, to invite all the tribes of the south to that war, went to Detroit that same year and gave presents to the tribes settled there; and M. de Louvigny assured him that he also gave them some in 1716 when he went there on the way to his expedition, of which presents he holds a statement certified by the said Sr. de Sabrevois; he does not see that the latter was right in giving presents himself on the occasion of that war. That, moreover, if it be necessary to go by what was said to him in public by the Outavois chiefs from Saguinan and those of the Poutouatamis from Detroit who came to Montreal in 1717, whose words he forwards, the said Sr. de Sabrevois was far from being as liberal towards the savages as he would have the Council understand.

It will be easy to learn from the complaints then made to him by these savages, (of which, in order to spare the said Sr. de Sabrevois, he did not think it his duty to inform the Council), and from a second extract from this officer's letter of the 8th of April 1717, how little capacity he had for governing them with the tact desirable so as not to alienate them and what credence should be given to the certificates which he touted for and annexed to the memorial which he presented to the Council; what is certain is that the greater part of the settlers who signed them were men against whom the Sr. de Sabrevois had brought serious complaints to him on many occasions, who complained loudly, on their side, of him in writing to their relations and friends to whom they sent word that their only offence consisted in their having refused to submit to the oppressions of the said Sr. de Sabrevois, who made friends with them when he was about to leave Detroit, in order to induce them to sign this certificate.

Note. As regards the words of the chiefs of the savages, which are annexed, they complain greatly of the harshness of the Sr. de Sabrevois and of his greed, which had decided them to go to Orange, to the number of 17 boats, when they met the Sr. de Tonty who induced them to change their minds.

In the second extract from the Sr. de Sabrevois' letter, he states that

however no part in his nomination to the command of that post. M. de Pontchartrain who had appointed him forwarded to him [Vaudreuil] the King's order to send him [Sabrevois] there; he complied with that, but he would have taken great care not to propose to him, as he knew him to be a very selfish man. He does not think he made large profits at Detroit; but it is certain that he did not lose there, for after paying all the sums which had been advanced to him by the merchants, and what he owed to those who were employed by him, he found he had more than 80 bundles of furs left.

The fort of Detroit was completed and entirely finished in 1718, and according to reports of the *voyageurs* and officers who have returned from there, it is the best palisade fort there is in this country. As the Sr. de Tonty has spared no expense to make it substantial and to make himself secure from all attacks there; and as it has cost him more than 2000 livres French money; he thinks it would be just that the Council should grant a gratuity to the said Sr. de Tonty.

Upon all that the Council decided, on 5th March 1720, to grant nothing either to the Sr. de Sabrevois or Sr. de Tonty.

Since that decision the Sr. de Sabrevois has presented two petitions.

In the first he agrees that when the Sr. de Tonty set out from Montreal to go and relieve him at Detroit, he made him a present of the two permissions of which M. de Vaudreuil speaks, which his agent sold for 1800 livres, paper money, which yielded him only 900 livres.

If he did not mention this present when making his requests, it was because he thought that this ought not to serve as a reimbursement to him.

MEMORIAL OF DE LA MOTHE CADILLAC.

Memorial which M. de La Mothe takes the liberty of presenting to His Most Serene Highness, Monseigneur, the Comte de Toulouze, Admiral of France, Head of the Council of the Navy, in order to attain to the execution of the Decision of this Council of the .... of June 1720.

Since the first paragraph of this decision states that M. de La Mothe must be put into possession again of the lands he had cleared, as well as of the rights over the lands he had granted by virtue of the letters of M. de Pontchartrain, of which a concession in due form will be sent to him—

M. de La Mothe thinks that the intention of the Council will be in conformity with that of the Comte de Pontchartrain, which was to grant him the whole of Detroit on account of the heavy expense which he was to incur there in establishing it and which he actually did incur, in taking a number of settlers there, in attracting a number of different savage tribes which compelled the Irokois to make peace, which kept them, and still keeps them to their duty, and which has prevented the English from coming and establishing themselves there as they wished to do.

If the King put M. de La Mothe back on the cleared lands only, according to the terms of the Council's decision, the result would be that he would find himself unable to protect himself against the severity of the seasons, which [severity] is constant in that country, that he would be without woods which are indispensable for building and for all kinds of works; and, lastly, that he would not be able to reach other lands to clear them, and to make new settlements.

His Most Serene Highness is very humbly begged to observe that all Detroit, beginning from Lake Erié up to Lake Huron, was as a whole settled, either by Frenchmen or by the savage tribes that M. de La Mothe attracted there; and that he placed both so as to preserve that new colony and to be protected by it, *so that all Detroit is granted except what M. de La Mothe had reserved for his domain, and except the land round the Lake St. Claire, which is perhaps 30 leagues in circumference.*

For example at the entrance to Lake Erie in the Western part of the

which was approved by the Comte de Pontchartrain; and consequently the children of the said M. de La Mothe have made settlements there. .

From the River Rouge to Lake St. Claire is all granted to French inhabitants, or reserved to M. de La Mothe as his domain, or granted to the Hurons, or reserved to the inhabitants as a common land for cattle.

The inhabitants have different concessions. Those who had families have concessions of four and six arpents' frontage along the river, with 25 arpents in the depth of the woods; the smaller families had two arpents frontage and the same depth, that is to say 25 arpents.

To the south of the river were the Oütavois, the Kiskakoüns, the Nassavüé Kouctons, the Negnoüandechessinis, the Sinagoles, Poutouatamis.

Above Lake St. Claire there were the Anukouék, the Mississisaguez, Outchipouek, and a number of the Nepissing.

When M. de La Mothe distributed the lands to the savage tribes, he explained to them that he gave them to them as their property for so long as they might wish to possess them; but that if they changed their dwelling place, the lands they abandoned would revert to his domain. That is what they agreed to, and what is customary also in Canada, round about Quebec and Montreal; but the savages make no payment while they remain on their lands.

It is evident therefore that, from the entrance to Lake Erié, the islands and adjacent islets, with the mainland along the river up to the entrance to Lake St. Claire, are owned by M. de La Mothe, by his children, by the French [settlers], by the Hurons, and that towards the south it is the savages who hold the lands from Lake Erie up to Lake Huron on the agreement that, if they abandon their villages and dwelling places, the whole would revert to M. de La Mothe. What [could be] more just?

Since it was necessary to send for these tribes to [a distance of] 300 and 400 leagues from Detroit, to make them large presents in order to get them to leave their dwellings, to have forts built for them, to provide houses for Missionaries there, and to pay to each of them 500# a year, to furnish chapels, to pay Interpreters; all this was done at the expense and cost of M. de La Mothe, while the King would not reimburse him.

That M. de la Móthe, in asking for the concession of all Detroit, is asking a small thing considering the 1000 leagues of forests which will remain to be granted to those who wish for them; and he has well paid for these lands by the expenditure he incurred there. With that money he could have bought a fine estate in France.

If he does not obtain what he has the honor to propose to the Coun-

with powers of higher, middle and lower jurisdiction with fishing, hunt-ing and trading rights; and besides this a fief at Port Royal. The whole is now in the hands of the English, and consequently lost to him; so would Detroit be in the same manner:

From all that has just been very respectfully represented To His Most Serene Highness it appears *that M. de La Mothe has every reason to hope that he will move His Majesty to grant him the concession of the whole of Detroit in due form, and with powers of higher, middle and lower jurisdiction with fishing, hunting and trading rights, as well as his rights in the lands already granted.*

[That] it will also please His Most Serene Highness to cause it to be ordained *in the intermediate decree which will be issued that M. de La Mothe shall be put back in possession of the buildings, personal property, and cattle which are found of the same kind as those which he left when he quitted that post,* and that in doing this the buildings which are found built on his ground by the demolition of those he had built there or other-wise, shall belong to him, *and that he may take back his cattle although they may have been sold,* except for the remedy of the buyer against the seller, seeing that the owner of an article takes it back whenever he finds it; also to name the person before whom M. de La Mothe is to sue for the claims he may have against those who have taken and disposed of his goods.

M. de La Mothe *thinks that this should be before the Intendant of Canada* because that will shorten all quibbling, and because he cannot be suspected [of partiality] by any party; and to this end it is necessary that the Council should be good enough to assign the cognizance of this [matter] to him, and to forbid it to every other court and jurisdiction, with prohibitions to the parties against suing elsewhere under a penalty of 2000#, half of which shall belong to the prosecutor.

And as to the merchandise and other property which have been taken for the service of His Majesty or other persons, that M. de La Mothe shall be paid for them *at the price then current at the said place of De-troit* according as they were traded with the savages, as other similar effects were paid for by him by the order of M. de Pontchartrain.

82

THE KING INTENDED TO PLANT A COLONY AT DETROIT.

To His Most Serene Highness Monseigneur the Comte de Toulouse Admiral of France, Head of the Council of the Navy.

Monseigneur,

M. de La Mothe very respectfully represents that he purposes herein to prove the points which he has taken the liberty to put forward which are not thought to be sufficiently demonstrated. The first is with reference to the ownership óf Detroit which M. de La Mothe claims to possess. The second, that it was only by superior authority that all the property he had at that post was seized upon, which property would be lost to him if justice is not done him.

The King had so little desire to remain the owner of Detroit that his Ministers took care that the expenditure His Majesty had incurred on behalf of this post should be repaid. 1st, By the Company; 2nd, By M. de La Mothe. Consequently, if M. de Vaudreuil by his superior authority prevented those who followed from doing the same, M. de La Mothe can apply to His Majesty only, in order to obtain reparation for it.

The first intention of the King was to make a Colony of that Post, and he chose M. de La Mothe to conduct that enterprise. His Majesty defrayed the whole cost of it.

The Company of Canada afterwards asked for the exclusive right of trading because, having taken over that of the Beaver, it thought that this post was necessary to it for limiting the quantities with which people had been able to burden it. That is proved, by the letter from M. de Pontchartrain of the 14th of June, 1704, paragraph 3.

ex letter

This Company not having kept up, the King took up again the design he had had, that a Colony should be established there and charged M. de La Mothe with it at his own cost and expense, and without wishing to draw any direct advantage from that Colony.

His Most Serene Highness is begged to take into consideration that

out loss of time, and that M. de La Mothe should do it all at his own expense as he has done.

It will not be imagined that M. de La Mothe would have been willing to advance so large a sum and that he would have been willing to employ means which were so burdensome to him and so perilous to his family, such as to convey his wife, his children, a number of families, and troops to the number of 200 men, as well as cattle, &c:, the whole at his own expense in order to establish a Colony for the King, and that His Majesty would have wished it.

Moreover this was never his intention nor that of his Minister; as anyone will be convinced who does not object to interpreting favorably to M. de La Mothe the letters which he [the Minister] wrote to him, taking into account moreover the distance of the places and the difficulty of conveyance which often delayed the answers for two years and longer.

The letter of the 14th of June, 1704, paragraph 9, expressly says— Index lett your post of Detroit. A.

It is after this para., and in the same sense that the post belonged to M. de La Mothe, that M. de Pontchartrain says to him in the same letter at the 14th para. that His Majesty permits him to grant concessions as Index lett he may find it good and suitable. D.

In the letter of the 9th of June 1706, para. 6, it is again explained in the same terms, the post of Detroit being called only the post of M. de La Mothe.

In paragraph 12 of the same letter, not only does he again recognize this colony as being the post of M. de La Mothe, but he agrees moreover that he may transfer it to such other part of Detroit as he may judge to be fitting, if that where he began it does not suit him, reserving the interests of the Company.

By para. 17 of the same letter M. de Pontchartrain makes it so well understood that he regards M. de La Mothe as the owner of Detroit, that he compares him with M. de La Salle who, incontestably, held the ownership and the trade of the places which he had discovered or established; that is proved by his concession.

Finally, in para. 18 of the same letter he reassures M. de La Mothe

he looked upon it as belonging to M. de La Mothe and not to His Majesty who had incurred no expense for it.

In the 2nd para. of the letter of the *30th* of June, 1707, the departure of M. de La Mothe is proved and that of all *those whom he took with him.* The Minister recognizes that it is his post and that M. de Vaudreuil likewise recognizes it, that consequently nothing could prevent him from working at it with success. Could M. de Pontchartrain in urging M. de La Mothe on to set to work, have meant that it was for the King? Assuredly not, for His Majesty had borne no expense for it. Therefore it was only because he *looked upon that Colony* as belonging to M. de La Mothe that he called it his post.

And by para. 4 of the same letter, in three different and essential passages, this Minister only refers to that *Colony* [*speaking to M. de La Mothe*] as his post, *as well as in the 9th and 10th paragraphs.* Finally he repeats in para. 12 what he said in para. 18 of the former letter of the year *1706, on which M. de La Mothe has made his remarks.*

In the letter of the 6th of June, 1708, in the 2nd para., wishing to tranquillize M. de La Mothe as to the opposition and hindrances which had been put in his way, he tells me that it appears to him that *MM. de Vaudreuil and Raudot* have no other intention than to assist *his post.*

In the 4th paragraph he again calls it *his post.*

In the letter of the 6th of July, 1709, para. 8, M. de Pontchartrain so clearly recognizes this Colony as belonging to M. de La Mothe that he declares to him that it is not to be expected that His Majesty should undertake any expense on a place which was to yield him nothing.

In para. 9, it is stated that the building of the fort and *that of the church belong to the same category, and that it can only be the one who has the right of drawing profit from the country who ought to be made to build them; and that that was to serve as a rule for M. de La Mothe in future in everything concerning Detroit,* and that he has the

there was a revenue arising from the land, and it is this revenue as well as every óther, that His Majesty does not wish for, and consequently that he allows these contracts to hold good, as will be said directly.

Lastly *he tells him that he has the patronage of the church, without hindrance.*

On the one hand His Majesty desires nothing from the revenues that this Colony may produce, which he leaves to M. de La Mothe; on the other, he gives up to him the patronage. Is not this a sufficient proof of the will of the King concerning a subject who is 1500 leagues away; who cannot beg for a title of concession in due form; and who, being convinced that these letters were more than sufficient, was so very much in earnest that he devoted his person, his family, and all that he possessed to the enterprise.

In the eleventh paragraph of the same letter he again recognizes the ownership by M. de La Mothe of that Colony by approving of his drawing from it a toll for grinding [corn] similar to that which the *lords of the seignories of Canada retain from their manorial mills, namely the 14th minot.*

In the 18th para. M. de Pontchartrain, replying to the offer which M. de La Mothe had made the preceding year, to give back to the King the lands of Detroit, answers him *that he had reported the matter to His Majesty and that he did not wish to require that of him, but that his will is only that he should make this post serviceable to the general good, and the inhabitants happy, while preserving his own interests so far as justice would allow.*

Hence it cannot be said that this Colony belongs to the King, since his Minister declares that His Majesty will not accept the return of it from M. de La Mothe, but on the contrary that he wishes him to preserve his own interests there which *consists in the ownership*, of which the quit-rents and rents, the socome toll and the patronage are really only the fruits and the consequences.

M. de La Mothe very humbly begs that it may be taken into consideration that the title of concession is not, in reality, that which gives the absolute ownership of the seignory; for, without the Settlement [itself], the concession becomes void. It was with the intention of preventing the nullity for want of the settlement that the Company of the Indies began to grant concessions of the lands which it distributed at Louisiana after the applicants had taken possession and had settled [on them].

But if once this settlement [was made] the place could not be taken away again and the concession, in the form in which the King grants them in the Colony in question, becomes a necessary consequence of taking possession and settling [there].

Of this kind is M. de La Mothe's case; he has worked in consequence

He had founded one of the finest colonies which could be made entirely at his own expense, in a place as it were unapproachable both on account of its remoteness and the difficulty of [navigating] the river; and even at a time when there was war at that place he brought it to perfection. His concession and ownership cannot therefore be contested, since he had done all that is necessary to acquire it.

x letter   There now remains only the letter of the 13th of May, 1710, to speak of, which M. de La Mothe did not receive until the month of Decr. following.

By this letter the King grants him the governorship of *Louisiana; and in the 6th para. tells him that His Majesty has selected M. de la Forest to be commandant at Detroit in his place, and directs him to make him acquainted with everything which concerns that post.*

It must be observed here that the King gives M. de la Forest the command only, because His Majesty possessed nothing of the revenues nor of the property; that, therefore, every attempt to extend it beyond that was a molestation. That is what M. de La Mothe is going to speak of directly, which will prove what he has promised regarding the second point.

x letter J.   M. de la Forest, having been appointed to the command of this post did not go there, but obtained an order from M. de Vaudreuil to send M. Dubuisson, Lieutenant of the Company. This is proved by the letter of the 13th September, 1710, written by M. de Vaudreuil to M. de La Mothe.

We must not let ourselves be deceived by the gracious terms of this letter. M. de Vaudreuil was known to be the enemy of M. de La Mothe; and his designs, concealed by this letter but afterwards discovered, were an indisputable proof of it.

There are two things to be noticed in this letter.

1st, That M. de Vaudreuil there states that His Majesty has selected M. de la Forest to command at Detroit *on the same footing as [that on which]* M. de La Mothe *had held it up to that time.*

2nd, He requests him to cause M. Dubuisson to be recognized *on his arrival,* so that no one might be able to pretend that he had reason for

that belonged to the said M. de La Mothe by [the exercise of his] authority.

Yet that was the object of the understanding between these three persons, as is about to be proved not only by the action of M. Dubuisson, but also by the instruction which M. de la Forest had given him and finally also by the conduct of M. de Vaudreuil. M. de Vaudreuil knew that M. de La Mothe had to proceed to Louisiana by land and was not to return to Quebec: his letter of the 13th of September, 1710, proves it. Former Index lett J.

M. de la Forest knew it likewise as is proved by the letter he wrote to M. de La Mothe on the first of October 1710. Index lett K.

It is under these circumstances, and with this knowledge that they press M. de La Mothe to divest himself of the command of the place, without M. de la Forest having given a valid power of attorney to M. Dubuisson to negotiate with him concerning all the property M. de La Mothe had at this place, and [without his having] provided a sum to pay for them. Note.—M. la Mothe it in writɪɪ to M. Dubuissoɪ after it w received the time the difficu

M. Dubuisson had no sooner been recognized as commandant of the post than he began to appropriate everything that M. de La Mothe had at the post.

1st, He forbade the inhabitants to go on paying M. de La Mothe the quit-rents and rents which they owed him under their contracts.

2nd, He opposed M. de La Mothe's granting contracts of concession, of settlements in the country and of sites within the fort.

3rd, He likewise opposed M. de La Mothe's distributing arable lands to the inhabitants for them to sow for their profit on paying him a certain yearly sum, M. Dubuisson pretending that these lands belonged to the domain of the place, as if that fort [ever] had a domain of any use and had any lands in cultivation other than those paid or cleared by M. de La Mothe.

4th, He appropriated to himself M. de La Mothe's cattle on the pretext that he had a verbal order from M. Raudot, the Intendant, to warn him not to dispose of the cattle he had, and, in case M. de la Mothe wished to act otherwise, to oppose his doing so.

5th, He made himself master of the mill.

6th, Likewise of the houses in M. de La Mothe's occupation and others, the rents of which were paid to him.

7th, And lastly, as soon as Mme. de La Mothe departed, M. Dubuisson seized on all the furniture and all the goods of which she had had an inventory made, and he disposed of them at his pleasure.

These important facts are proved both by the orders given by M. de Index lett L.

M. de La Mothe begs that it may be observed here that these remonstrances which M. Dubuisson addressed to him had no other ground
than this, that the said M. de La Mothe found an opportunity of selling
the cleared lands and those [let for] farming, his mill, his houses, all
his cattle, all his household furniture, and all his goods, and that he
had secured a person who would have distributed all his lands to the
inhabitants who might apply for them.

Also that, as the said M. Dubuisson notified verbally all the inhabitants the prohibition against buying or renting anything from M. de
La Mothe, he thereby had his hands tied regarding all that belonged to
him, which remained in the possession of. M. Dubuisson without any
title except that of [brute] force and the authority which the command
confers.

letter   M. de La Mothe, having afterwards proceeded to Montreal, applied
to M. de Vaudreuil, to whom he presented his remonstrance in writing
on all these grievances, pressing him to give decision concerning them,
seeing that he knew the intentions of the Court.

This remonstrance deserves to be read to show, on one hand, the complaints of M. de La Mothe against the force that was used against him,
and, on the other, that he neglected nothing to put an end to it and to
obtain payment for his property.

M. de Vaudreuil would give him no answer to it in writing, and told
him to go to Quebec to M. Raudot to settle this matter, to whom he
wrote that it was for him to adjust that.

M. de La Mothe repaired there, as well as M. de la Forest and M.
Raudot after hearing them refused to give judgment, which obliged M.
de La Mothe to make his private protest to deposit with a Notary, and
to assent to the compromise which was arranged, the agreement for
which was signed in duplicate by MM. de La Mothe and de la Forest by
the assent and good pleasure of the Governor-General.

letter   M. Raudot gave his certificate at the foot of this document, in which
he declares that he has found it in accordance with his opinion. This
certificate is [dated] the 3rd of July, 1712.

Who could have thought,—when the parties interested had signed an
agreement; when they had come to the arrangement by the advice of
an Intendant to whom they had been sent; when this arrangement could
in no way be prejudicial to the King's service; and when on the con-

as Governor General, he had all the King's power in a country 1200 leagues distant from France—to prevent the carrying out of a contract which put an end to so many difficulties and returned to M. de La Mothe what M. de la Forest recognized belonged to him.

Yet that was the procedure of M. de Vaudreuil who, preferring the pleasure of satisfying the enmity he cherished against M. de La Mothe to the interests of the King's service, to justice, and to peace, thereby demonstrated the arrangement there had been between him, M. de la Forest and M. Dubuisson when he sent the latter to take command of the fort of Detroit; and it is that which the petitioner promised to prove.

This unjust and violent proceeding on the part of M. de Vaudreuil obliged M. de La Mothe to present his remonstrance to him in the form of a petition on the 18th of July, *1711*, which contains his explanations, offers and demands, and the surrender he made to him of all the property he had at Detroit, being unable to act otherwise, and being compelled to yield to authority, in the confidence he felt that His Majesty would have regard to the serious loss he sustained and would provide for his indemnification. Index lett P. the readir this docur shows wh took plac that matt

These documents are not served in Canada because there is neither bailiff nor notary there who dare serve them.

M. de La Mothe has thus been the victim of [arbitrary] authority everywhere and always. It was that authority which despoiled him of his property; it was that authority which maintained the usurpation, [even] against the apparent wish of the usurper, and which perpetuated it with those whom M. de Vaudreuil has caused to succeed to the [post] up to the present [ones] who are insolvent.

That if it is objected that the petitioner, when he came to France afterwards, ought to have obtained redress through M. De Pontchartrain, he replies that this Minister was so biased against him by secret intrigues which he cannot explain (unless he is ordered to do so) that he indulged in fits of anger which, at the time, caused some sensation at Versailles. But that in no way affects his right when it is proved incontestable, as it is.

For all these reasons the petitioner persists in his conclusions and asks, conformably to the opinion of MM. de Vaudreuil and Begon in the last paragraph of their answer to the Council, that the King may have the goodness to give him a grant to take the place of all indemnification for all the property, personal and real of which he has been dispossessed, according to the Memorandum of it which he gave to the Council, by which means the whole will belong to the King.

M. de La Mothe has the originals in his possession.

[The following is written on the back of the last page:—]

To be laid before Mgr. the Regent.

séssion again of the lands he had cleared, as well as of the rights over
the lands he granted in virtue of the letters of M. de Pontchartrain of
which a concession in due form will be sent to him. That he ought also
to be put in possession of the buildings, furniture and cattle which there
may be, of the kind he had left when he quitted that post. That with
regard to the other claims he may have, he may sue before whom he
thinks good. That he shall be paid for what he shall prove to have
been taken from his magazines for the service of H. M. That, moreover, it appears that he has suffered heavy losses, and that it is just
to indemnify him by a gratuity.

Discussed the 14th of June, 1720.

La Chapelle

CLAIMS OF CADILLAC.

Endorsed—Colonies 14th of June, 1720. To lay before Mgr. le Regent.
Council

Claims of M. de La Mothe.

The Council thinks it necessary to restore to M. de la Mothe Cadillac the
ownership of the lands he has cleared,
together with his rights over the
lands he granted, in pursuance of M.
de Ponchartrain's letters, a concession of which in due form should be
sent to him. That he ought also to be
given possession of any buildings, furniture and cattle there may be there, such
as he left when he quitted the post.
That, as regards any other claims he
may have, he should bring action before
whatever court he may think fit. That
he should be paid for what he proves to
have been taken from his warehouse for
His Majesty's service. That moreover
it appears that he has lost heavily, and
that it is fair to indemnify him by a
gratuity.

M. de la Mothe has presented a memorial to the Council in which he asks that
Sr. de Tonty and all other persons may
be prohibited from interfering with him
in the proprietorship and lands of Detroit, the personal and real property;
and that he may be granted a concession of Detroit in due form, in order to
avoid contests in future; that it may be
ordered that he shall be paid for the
goods which officers,—commandants or
others—have taken, at the price they
were worth at Detroit; and also for the
cattle, the milk, the use of the lands,
the houses, the fees for grinding at the
mill, the house-rents, quit-rent, rents
and revenues; and that the powder,
lead, bullets, and arms which the commandants have taken for the king's service, may likewise be paid for at the

If His Majesty adds Detroit to his domain, he begs that his claims may be adjusted in accordance with the Inventory which was made at Detroit in 1711 in the presence of the Almoner and some settlers, which Inventory is in the hands of the Sr. Grandmesnil who is entrusted with his affairs; and this according to a valuation to be made of them on the spot by upright men, to be paid in France in cash, with an indemnification for his not having had possession of them, commencing from the first of January 1712, the day on which it was taken back by the King.

If this proposal is not listened to, he begs that orders may be given that the person who has possession of Detroit, and the exclusive right of trading, may be obliged to remiburse him for all his buildings, goods, cattle, personal and real property in accordance with the said Inventory of 1711, to be calculated at the then value of the said goods, and personal and real property, and that they should be valued by upright men who know the condition in which he left the said property when he was recalled from Detroit to go to Louisiana, the said experts to be chosen by the holder of his power of attorney, and a like number by the person who is to possess them who shall be bound to make the said payment as may be agreed; and in case he cannot pay the whole, he shall give reliable security to the agent of the said Sr. de La Mothe before a notary.

The requests of the Sr. de La Mothe may be reduced to 4 heads.

1st Head.

That he may possess Detroit with full proprietorship and lordship, and that the quit-rents and revenues may be paid to him.

2nd Head.

That, if Detroit be taken back to the Domain, he should be repaid for the sites, the houses, the mills, and the lands he had cleared, as well as for having been kept out of possession of them.

3rd Head.

That he should also be repaid the value of the cattle and milk, and for having been kept out of possession of them, and that the value of the goods he left at Detroit should be paid to him at the prices they were worth there at the time he left them.

4th Head.

That, likewise, the powder, lead, bullets, arms, &c., which the said
K. ' e i shoul h

conveyance and the risks to the vehicles.

First Head.

That he may possess Detroit with full proprietorship and lordship, and that the quit-rents, rents & revenues may be paid to
him.

M. de La Mothe represents that the Company of the Colony, which
held the post of Detroit, wrote to M. de Pontchartrain that it was going
to give it up: and the Sr. de La Mothe, knowing how necessary it was
to preserve it, gave M. de Pontchartrain notice of this, and he induced
His Majesty to order the said Sr. de La Mothe to reside at the said
post during the war, and to put into writing the intentions of His
Majesty and the conditions under which this post was granted him, according to the *letter of M. de Pontchartrain of the 14th of June, 1704,*
confirmed by another of 1705; that these conditions are:—

1st, His Majesty appoints the said Sr. de La Mothe to the rights of
the Company, and to have charge of the post at his own risk:

2nd, binds him to pay the said Company for the goods which were at
the post, and to repay it for the serviceable buildings:

3rd, gives the Sr. de La Mothe the command of the post:

4th, grants him the exclusive right of trading there, with the restriction that he shall not trade for more than 20000 livres' worth of beaver
skin a year but shall be at liberty to trade for every other kind of fur;
he shall not be allowed to trade outside Detroit; and the Company shall
be permitted to keep an inspector there at his own expense:

5th, orders the Governor-General to give the said Sr. de La Mothe as
many soldiers as he may ask for, on condition that he shall bear the
cost of their conveyance:

6th, permits all who may wish to go and settle at Detroit, to do so:

7th, orders the Governor General and Intendant to give the said Sr.
de La Mothe the missionaries—necessary for this settlement:

8th, His Majesty leaves the said Sr. de La Mothe absolute master in
all things at Detroit:

9th, permits him to grant the lands at Detroit in such manner as he
may find advisable for the interests of the new Colony.

That, orders having been given in accordance with the above to MM.

That so far this affair was proceeded with in due form. The Company did not give up its rights until after it had taken security from the said Sr. de La Mothe: and he was only put in possession of Detroit after he had satisfied the said Company. For the same reason, no one could have been appointed to succeed to the privileges of the Sr. de La Mothe except by observing the same rule with him. Yet M. de Vaudreuil put.the Sr. de la Forest in possession of that post without observing the same practice,, and this is the authority on which he acted.

In 1710, the said Sr. de La Mothe having been appointed Governor of Louisiana, M. de Pontchartrain wrote to him in these words. *His Majesty having selected the. Sr. de la Forest to command at Detroit in your place, I am sending him orders thereon. It will be necessary for you to make him thoroughly acquainted with everything that concerns the post.*

It appears to him that this is merely a notice from the Minister, giving the Sr. de la Forest no right except to take command; and that it does not confer upon him either the monopoly of the trade, or the lands, or the cattle, nor any property or merchandise belonging to the said Sr. de La Mothe, who thinks that M. de Vaudreuil was not within his rights in putting the said Sr. de la Forest in possession by the exercise of his authority; that M. de Vaudreuil only had the right to put the said Sr. de la Forest in possession of the command, and not of the monopoly of the trade and of the other possessions of the said Sr. de La Mothe who has never surrendered them and claims that his possession still stands and is equivalent to a title.

M. de Vaudreuil has always claimed that the monopoly of trade is inseparable from the command; but nevertheless, the contrary is continually proved in practice.

He sets forth that, after having served His Majesty as long as he has, he will not take away from him a settlement of which he was the projector, which he formed at his own expense—for there was nothing established.there when it was granted to him—and to which he took settlers, cattle, all sorts of grains & tools.

He remained only 4 years at this post when just as he was about to be repaid the heavy expenses he had borne, he was sent to Louisiana.

He has learned that M. de Vaudreuil claims that, as he had no formal concession from the King, the proprietorship of the post does not belong to him.

He replies that the letter of the 14th of June, 1704 would alone be sufficient to overrule this objection; but that, as it was decreed in a proclamation .by His Majesty that all persons who cleared lands in Canada which had not been granted should have the proprietorship of them, and that it could not be taken from them, his right is still further

savages or by any nation, a land absolutely uncultivated—which the
English wanted to seize upon, out of which he granted several concessions
in his capacity as seignior, under the 8th clause of the said letter *which
leaves him absolute master in all things at Detroit;* that he was therefore
bound to believe that he was the seignior and had seignioral rights, for
there was no restriction in his authority as to what concerned him personally, nor as to the concessions he granted, a specimen of which he
sent to the Court; that, in taking the lands of Detroit—uncultivated and
uninhabited—he did no wrong to anyone, and they cannot take from him,
without injustice, about 400 arpents of lands that were cleared by dint of
labor, fatigue, expense, and by endless risks.

ter of 14th
. 1719,
:ked C.
MM. de Vaudreuil and Begon write that there are no documents to
prove the Sr. de La Mothe's proprietorship of the fort of Detroit; that
he bases his claim on the letter of the 14th of June 1704, on the deed
which he executed accordingly with the Company of the Colony, under
which he was appointed to succeed to its rights, and on the provisions
of this deed having been carried out. All these documents simply prove
that he succeeded to the privilege the Company possessed as to the trade,
and not to the proprietorship—since the Company did not possess it, and
it could only have been granted him by a patent of concession or by a
decree of the Council of State.

rked D.
The Sr. de La Mothe, to whom this answer was communicated, writes
that, if the King's object had not been to make a trade depôt of Detroit,
he would not have urged him by the letters of his minister to apply
himself vigorously to the establishment of this post in order to make a
fine colony of it, with the promise of raising it to a governorship and
making a Staff for it; that this is proved by all the letters written to
him from the Court from 1704 up to 1710. He adds that, if His Majesty
had not regarded him as the proprietor of Detroit, he would not have
approved the contracts of the lands which he granted in his own name
to settlers, under which they were bound to pay him quit-rent and rent
and fees for grinding corn; that, still further, he offered the King, in
1708, to give him back the land of Detroit for a considerable sum, but
reserving for himself his garden, merchandise and cattle; and on this,
M. de Pontchartrain replied to him in 1709 that he had reported to the
King the proposal he had made to give him back the land of Detroit,
and that His Majesty would not require that of him, but only that he
should devote himself to the general welfare of the colony, by making
the settlers happy and exacting from them only such payments as justice
would permit; and that this response from the King is quite equivalent

Remark.

It is apparently a question of considering what title the Sr. de La Mothe has to the proprietorship of Detroit. He refers to a letter from M. de Pontchartrain of the 14th of June, 1704, on which he bases his whole claim. It is stated, in the paragraph concerning religion, and about attracting the savages to the post, that the Sr. de La Mothe is left absolute master of everything in that place; and in another paragraph, that His Majesty permits him to grant lands at Detroit as he may think fit and advisable for the welfare of the new colony.

It appears that this letter proves the very contrary of what the Sr. de La Mothe claims; for, if the proprietorship of Detroit had been granted him, as he says, he would not have been given permission to grant lands there to settlers, he would simply have been urged, or perhaps compelled, to put some settlers there, and he would have been told that in default of his doing so His Majesty would take the proprietorship from him.

This permission must therefore be regarded as an authority which M. de La Mothe had to grant lands in the King's name, as the Governors & Intendants in the colonies do; he has imagined the very reverse, and has tried to make people believe it. He granted lands in his name which belonged to the King; he assigned the quit-rents and rents to himself under the contracts; and, although he knows that the Council has cancelled all his concessions, with good reason, he still demands from it, now, that it will have the quit-rents and rents paid to him.

As regards the 400 arpents of land which he has had cleared, it seems right to leave the possession to him, or to pay for them if they are taken for the King. It will be explained hereafter in what manner the value of these lands might be ascertained.

2nd Head.

That in case Detroit be taken back into the Domain he should be repaid for the sites, houses, mills & the lands he had cleared, as well as having been kept out of the possession of them.

The Sr. de La Mothe alleges the same reasons for receiving possession or for being paid for the sites, houses, and mills, as for the cleared lands.

MM. de Vaudreuil and Begon write that the Sr. de Grandmesnil, the agent of the Sr. de La Mothe, has told them that, of all these buildings, none but the mill is left; and that those who have been

That it appears just that he should be paid the cost of the
buildings by those who have profited by them; but, as there have
been various Commandants at this post since he left, they think
it would be advisable that, in order to avoid the law suits he
would have to bring, His Majesty should bestow some favor on
him as full compensation, and allow him no legal remedy against
any one.

M. de La Mothe, to whom this reply was communicated, writes that
the course which has been followed since he was obliged to go and do
duty in Louisiana proves that these people have not thought of forming a rich and large colony at Detroit, though it would be a very great
service to Canada, but only of getting all they possibly could out of it,
by hook or by crook.

That, since MM. de Vaudreuil and Begon think it would be advisable
to hear the Commandants of the post in their defence, they do not question that the facts are as he states, and it is only as to the reasons the
Commandants may have had. But whatever these may have been, they
could not give them the right to take the Sr. de La Mothe's property
and apply it to their profit. He has made a memorandum of his claims
on this head.

ked E.

Cost of the buildings and houses which M. de La Mothe had built at
Detroit.

A warehouse	3000#	
House of the Sr. de La Mothe	2500	
Two other houses	1500	
A barn with its *roof* of beams	1200	
A Stable	500	20400
A dove-cot	400	
An ice-house	300	
A chapel and the Almoner's house	3000	
For the mill	8000	
	20400	20,400

400 arpents of cleared lands at 100 livres per arpent — 40,000

For having been kept out of possession of the said
400 arpents of land for 10 years, it being in a condition to bear crops every year, because it was
new land—at 6 livres per arpent 24,000

For having been kept out of possession of the mill — 34,000

Remark.

It appears that repayment is due to M. de La Mothe for the buildings and houses which he had built at Detroit, and for the lands he had cleared there, and that this payment may justly be made by the King provided that these houses and buildings have served for the officers and troops, and that the cleared lands are also of use to them for obtaining any food from; but it does not seem possible to make a valuation of them here.

We might commission, in Canada, MM. de Vaudreuil and Begon, and M. D'Aigremont, Commissioner of the Navy, who has been on the spot, to give their opinion as to the said valuation, and appoint the Sr. Collet, Procureur-Général to the said Commission.

3rd Head.

That he should also be repaid the cost of the cattle, and for the milk, and for having been kept out of the possession of them, and that the value of the goods he left at Detroit should also be paid him, at the price they were worth at the time he left them there.

M. de La Mothe represents that, but for M. de Vaudreuil, he would have been paid for everything; for the late M. de la Forest, finding that he was unable either to pay him or to give him security, had consented to the Sr. de Marigny taking his place in the command of Detroit in consideration of a gratuity. He had agreed with the said Sr. de Marigny for the monopoly of the trade, for all his goods and effects, and for his buildings at Detroit, but M. de Vaudreuil opposed this arrangement, and a decree was made by M. Raudot, then the Intendant on the 22nd of July, 1711, forbidding further proceedings, against which decision the said Sr. de La Mothe protested that he would appeal at a suitable place and opportunity.

From all the accounts he has given, it appears that he was only put in possession of Detroit by the Company of the Colony having surrendered it to the King in his favor, after he had paid and satisfied the said Company; that as he, for his part, has not surrendered, nor received any payment, his right still stands.

MM. de Vaudreuil and Begon say that the Inventory which Index lett was made when the Sr. de La Mothe left Detroit to go to Louisiana,—of which they forward a copy, given to them by the Sr. Grandmesnil, his agent,—proves that he left at this post a quantity of goods, useful articles, effects, cattle and buildings. That it would be necessary to hear the Commandants on this matter.

Note. This Inventory appears to have been made on the 25th of August, 1711, signed by two settlers of Detroit and the missionary.

should be paid or reimbursed the cost of his goods, property, implements and buildings by those who have profited by them; but
as there have been various Commandants at this post since he
left, they think it would be advisable, in order to avoid the litiga-
tion he would have to resort to, that His Majesty should not permit him any legal remedy against anyone but should bestow some
favor on him to take the place of all indemnification whether for
the repayment he made to the Company of the Colony, or the
money he advanced for the settlement of the post, or the goods
and property, real and personal, which he left there; in this way
all he may possess at Detroit would belong to His Majesty.

M. de La Mothe, to whom this reply was communicated, says that the
truth of this Inventory cannot be denied, nor the justice of paying him
the cost, since he himself was obliged to pay the Company of the Colony
for everything that could be of any use to him.

That it is all the more just that he should be paid for all he spent on
the said place Detroit and on account of the said post, and for all the
property he left there, of whatever kind; because he only left the place
to go and serve the King in Louisiana, and it was during such service
that so great a loss was inflicted on him.

He begs that it may be observed that he has been deprived of these
sums for nearly ten years from which he would have made large profits.

x letter He states in a private memorandum that the animals he had at Detroit
consisted of 29 horned cattle and a horse valued at 400 livres; that he .
found [a purchaser] for these animals at 9000 livres before he left, but
the Commandant opposed it and forbade their being bought.

He values them at..........................	9000#	
Compensation for 29 horned cattle which would have produced, in 10 years, at least 400 additional: for this..........................	9000#	18,000#
	18000	

Remark.

It appears just that M. de La Mothe should be paid for the animals and goods belonging to him at Detroit, by those who have profited by them. He must demand payment from them and a commission might be appointed to decide any contests there may be on this matter.

4th Head.

That the powder, lead, bullets, arms, &c. which the Commandants have taken for the King's service should likewise be paid for, at the price they were then worth at Detroit, as it would not be just to pay him as for similar things at Quebec seeing that it costs a great deal for conveyance, & the risk of the vehicles.

MM. de Vaudreuil and Begon write that it seems just that His Majesty should repay the said Sr. de La Mothe for the powder and lead which were taken from the warehouse of the said Sr. de La Mothe for His Majesty's service, on his producing the orders of the Commandants, without which this expense should not be repaid by His Majesty. Nothing can be decided as to these certificates until it has been ascertained whether repayment has not been made in kind from the King's magazine.

M. de La Mothe, to whom this reply has been communicated, says that the conditions which MM. de Vaudreuil and Begon lay down as to his being paid are strictly right, provided always it is in a country where justice has free play; but at Detroit, where his successors have had no aim but to take everything by force, and no law but their own will, it is certain that they have taken care not to give receipts and that they can only be convicted of what they have done by persons who were present. Moreover it is not for him to know whether these goods have been replaced. M. Begon ought to know, himself, what he did as regards such replacement, which could not have been made to the Sr. de La Mothe; and it is for him to obtain payment for them from the Commandants of Detroit.

Remark.

It appears that the payment demanded on this head can be made to M. de La Mothe on the certificate of the Commandants, which should be countersigned by the Missionary and afterwards by the Governor General.

It is first necessary to consider carefully whether the goods used under these certificates were devoted to the King's service, for others might have been used, which may have been turned to the profit of the Commandants.

The Council might order M. Begon to look carefully into what took

should send to France on the return of the ships, or by those of next year, with the vouchers in support of it, on which the said Sr. de La Mothe might be paid.

Given and decreed, the 14th of June, 1720.

By the Council.

EXPENSES INCURRED BY CADILLAC FOR THE KING.

Endorsed—Canada. 14th June 1720. Follow the advice of M. de Vaudreuil in everything.

Memorandum of part of the claim of M. de La Mothe concerning Detroit Pontchartrain.

He has requested the Council that he may be reimbursed by the King the following sums which he paid while he was at Detroit for which he claims that His Majesty was responsible.

To wit:—

To the expense incurred in order to make peace with the Outavois, the sum of	1086#		
To other expenses incurred for the Iroquois chiefs	51	7s	6d
To those incurred for six Iroquois envoys	439	15	
To ditto for 8 Iroquois	129		
To those incurred for the conclusion of peace with the Outavois	275	8	6
To ditto for various tribes	154	2	6
To expenses incurred for the Miamis, Pepikokias and Onyatanous who defended the fort of Detroit when it was besieged by the Outavois in 1706	905	19	
To expenses incurred to prevent these three tribes from going to war against the Outavois	1931	2	6
To expenses incurred for sick soldiers	455	9	9
To supplies given to the Sr. de St. Pierre by the order of M. de Vaudreuil	209		
To ditto to the Sr. d' Argenteuil to go to Michilimakina.	52	8	
To ditto to La Tour, sergeant & 7 soldiers	85	10	

The statement of these expenses with the documents supporting it, forwarded by M. de La Mothe, was sent by the Council on the 6th of July 1718 to MM. de Vaudreuil and Begon with orders to check them and send their advice thereon.

They reply in their letter of the 14th of November 1719.

That, from the examination they have made of these documents, they think that the King should repay M. de La Mothe the first 12 items above, amounting to 5775# 2s 9d local money, making 4331#, 7s; 1d French money, for the expenses he incurred for presents to the savages and refreshments to sick soldiers, because His Majesty was responsible for these, as appears from the letter of M. Raudot, then the Intendant, of the 18th of March, 1707, and that M. de Pontchartrain of the 6th of June, 1708. But, as regards the 2906# 5 which he asks for, for the pay of the almoner, interpreter and surgeon, they ought to remain chargeable to the said Sr. de La Mothe, for the Company of the Colony, which he succeeded at this post, was liable for them.

The Sr. de La Mothe, to whom the reply of MM. de Vaudreuil and Begon was communicated, claims that, as His Majesty is chargeable with the expenses he incurred for presents to the savages, and on behalf of sick soldiers, he is so likewise with the pay of the almoner, interpreter and surgeon; and accordingly, he says, it was M. de Pontchartrain who, in fact, agreed to this in his letter of the 6th of July, 1709, couched in these terms:—"I have seen what you write as to the conditions which it is sought to impose upon you beyond what was contained in the engagement you entered into. M. Raudot was wrong not to have them included in it, as he had been informed that the intention of the King was that you should enter into the same engagements as the Company which you succeeded. If, however, that was not done, I am writing to him that you ought not to be bound by them."

He adds that he made no agreement but that contained in the letter of the 14th of June, 1704, and entered into no bond with the Company which could oblige him to do so; consequently, under the terms of this letter he was not bound to pay these expenses, and what he paid simply in compliance with M. Raudot's order ought to be restored to him, both as regards the pay of the Almoner and that of the Interpreter and surgeon, since it is a matter already decided by the said letter of the 6th of July, 1709.

Remark.

been done, he was not to be bound by it. No different reply could have been sent him: but this letter does not appear to exempt him from paying the salaries of the almoner, interpreter and surgeon since he himself agrees that he entered into no other engagement but that contained in the letter of the 14th of June, 1704.

It becomes a question of considering the terms of this first letter constituting M. de La Mothe's title to Detroit.

In it is written:—"I have received the complaints of the Directors of the Company of the Colony as to the alleged losses it is making at Detroit; and, as you anticipate them by the offer you make to undertake this post at your own risk, if the Company will give up its rights to you, I have proposed that to the King, and His Majesty has approved of it."

M. de La Mothe having, in consequence of this letter, agreed with the Directors of the Company as to the goods which were at Detroit, and appointed to succeed the Company; and, as it always paid the salaries of the surgeon, interpreter and almoner, it appears that M. de La Mothe should pay them also, as it is nowhere stated that His Majesty should be charged with them.

Given and decreed the 14th June, 1720.
L. A. Bourbon
Le maréchal d'Esteés.

By the Council
La Chapelle

GRANT OF LANDS AT DETROIT, TO CADILLAC.

Brevet of Concession to M. de La Mothe Cadillac of the lands on which he has had buildings erected at Detroit and of the lands which

set and to send in a report of the boundaries within 2 years counting from this day, in order to possess them himself, with his children, heirs or assigns in perpetuity as their own property, and by reason of the present concession they shall not be required to pay to His Majesty nor to the King, his successor any moneys or indemnity, of which, to whatever sums they may amount, His Majesty makes him a gift and surrender on condition of turning the said lands and pieces of ground to account; of giving notice to His Majesty or to the Governor General and Intendant of New France, of the mines, grounds containing metals, and minerals if any are found within the limits of the said concession which His Majesty has reserved to himself; on condition likewise of leaving the roads necessary for public use; His Majesty permits the said M. de La Mothe to have mills built, as he may think fit, whether water—or windmills; His Majesty orders that, in default of the execution of the conditions contained in the foregoing Brevet; which shall be registered at the Superior Council of Quebec, the said ground and lands hereby granted are taken back to his domain; and as evidence of his will His Majesty has commanded me to draw up the present Brevet which he wished to be signed by his hand, countersigned by me Secretary of State of his Council, and of his commands and finances.

.

LANDS AT DETROIT.

Endorsed—Colonies. Canada. Raudot. M. de La Mothe Cadillac 1720.

To be laid before Mgr. the Regent.

The Council thinks that, at present, no change can be made in the decision of the Council, but it thinks that it would be well to write to MM. de Vaudreuil and Begon to learn by whom the lands of Detroit are held, at what time and by whom they were granted, to learn what remains to be granted, in order to see on the whole what favors could be accorded to M. de La Mothe, and, if there are no difficulties, to grant to him the lands not [already] granted and not cleared.

CADILLAC'S POWER OF HIGHER, MIDDLE & LOWER JURISDICTION.

Endorsed—Colonies M. de La Mothe Cadillac 1720. Canada. M. de La Mothe Cadillac & Council. Nothing to be changed in the decisions of the Council which can resolve on nothing until it has received the answers called for from Canada.

Consider on the 20th May, 1721.

To His Most Serene Highness, Monseigneur the Comte de Toulouse, Admiral of France. The Council wrote on the 3rd of June, 1719, and the 6th of July 1718, to MM. de Vaudreuil and Begon concerning the claims of M. de La Mothe Cadillac to Detroit of the Lake Erie.

Their answer of the 14th Novr. 1719 states that their opinion is that His Majesty should indemnify M. de La Mothe for all that he left at the said Detroit, and likewise for what he repaid to the Company of the Colony.

The letters which the Council wrote on the 24th of July, 1720, were sent back to the office of the Navy because the ship in which they were, put back into port.

The Council, in its letter, asked to be informed if Detroit was granted as a whole or in part in consequence of the letters patent of the King of the month of April 1716; to whom; and on what conditions.

The letter annexed proves that there were no concessions granted since M. de Tonty sent back to Montreal all the inhabitants of Detroit, where they had been settled for 15 years. Besides this letter M. de La Mothe can supply the evidence of several other private individuals from

The Council is begged to observe that the letters which are to go this year to Canada cannot get a decision on the answer which will be made until the year 1722, and that those same decisions cannot reach Detroit until 1723, on account of the great distance; so that this delay would not only cause M. de La Mothe to lose all the considerable property which he left at Detroit and other advances, but would make him unable to re-establish that place; since it is certain that M. de Tonty, who knows that he is insolvent, is laying waste and destroying everything in that place that belongs to the said M. de La Mothe.

CADILLAC ASKS THAT ALL DETROIT BE GIVEN HIM, WITH CIVIL RIGHTS.

Endorsed—Canada 20th of May 1721.

No change to be made in the decisions of the Council, which cannot settle anything until it has received the replies asked for from Canada.

Council
M. de La Mothe Cadillac.

The Council having written to MM. de Vaudreuil and Begon on the 6th July, 1718, and the 3rd June 1719, regarding his claims to Detroit on Lake Erie.

Upon the reply they made on the 14th Novr. 1719 it was decided that he should be given back possession of the lands which he had cleared at Detroit, together with his rights over those he granted in pursuance of the letters of M. de Pontchartrain, and that—to this end—a concession of them in due form should be sent to him: that he should also be put in possession of any buildings, movable property and cattle there might be of like kind. A patent of concession was sent to him, of the lands on which buildings had been erected at the said Detroit and of the lands which he cleared there; and, as regards the rights over the lands which he granted, the Council asked MM. de Vaudreuil and Begon, before giving him the title to them, to send word what had taken place, following on the letters patent of the month of April, 1716, regarding the concessions at Detroit, whether they had granted new concessions under them, to whom, and on what conditions.

. After this decision, the Sr. de La Mothe presented new memorials, in which he asked, among other things, that the whole of Detroit should

hunting, fishing and trading rights, together with his rights over the conceded lands. But, as it was not deemed advisable to make any change in the first decision, the Council wrote to MM. de Vaudreuil and Begon —in its letter of the 24th of July, 1720, to send a memorandum explaining by whom the lands at Detroit are held, at what time and by whom they were granted, and what lands remain to be granted; to add to these explanations their opinion as to the said Sr. de La Mothe's request, and if there is no difficulty in the way to grant him the lands not yet granted and not cleared.

The vessel by which this despatch was sent having put back, it was sent back to the Council.

The Sr de La Mothe forwards a *copy of a* letter written to him by the Sr. de Sabrevois, in which he says that he argues, that no concessions have been granted there since the Sr. de Tonty has sent back to Montreal all the settlers of Detroit, who had been settled there for 15 years: and he says that, besides this letter, he can send the testimony of several other private individuals in Canada.

On this ground, which he says is certain, he thinks he has good ground for asking for the concession of the whole of Detroit, as he has already requested, since His Majesty refuses to compensate him; and if there is any difficulty as regards the title, it can be granted him as an hereditary noble exempt from feudal payments, with the same rights as he has asked for, and also an honorable title; and, in order to remove all objections, he will leave the grantees, if there are any, and will not remove any of them, and they shall hold their lands in accordance with the terms of the grants made to them since the proclamation of the month of April 1716, except the lands cleared by him.

He begs the Council to observe that as its despatches have only gone this year, no decision can be given on the replies until 1722, and that its decisions will not be able to get to Detroit until 1723; that this delay

THERESE CATIN COMMENCES A SUIT AGAINST ALPHONSE DE TONTY JR.

To Monseigneur the Comte de Morville, Minister and Secretary of State.

Monseigneur,

Thereze Catin, the wife and agent of the Sr. Simon Reaume, merchant of the town of Montreal in Canāda.

Represents most humbly to your Highness that the Sr. Alphonse de Tonty, junior, an officer of the troops of the Navy, when he was in garrison in the town of Montreal, was often in need of money and of several articles of clothing, and the Petitioner had supplied him with everything he needed during his stay at Montreal; and because the Sr. de Tonty was about to leave for Quebec thence to proceed to Isle Royal, the Petitioner, after having tried all gentle means to induce him to pay her what he owed her, was reduced to the necessity of sending him a notification of her bill together with a summons to appear before the royal judge of Montreal. In order to avoid payment, this officer was false enough to dispute most of the items; but, by a judgment of the 20th of April, 1720, he was ordered to pay the Petitioner the sum of 50 livres under one head, and two livres for two pairs of gloves, both in French money, and the sum of 30 livres in paper money, merely for a set of buttons making 11 livres 5 sols: also to return to her, or to pay her for the ounce of silver which he had from her, and to pay the costs. And, inasmuch as the Petitioner still has in her possession an agreement drawn by the Sr. de Tonty in her favor, she summoned him to acknowledge his signature and his writing set at the foot of the note of hand of the 5th of October, 1719. Upon the summons served on him for this purpose on the 21st of April, 1720, a peremptory judgment was given by which a certificate was granted to the Sr. de Tonty of the declaration that he intended to plead that this agreement was a forgery: and this has been followed by various void and irregular proceedings as to the plea of forgery and finally, by a judgment of the 27th of May in the same year, the document was pronounced a forgery. The Petitioner lodged an appeal before the Superior Council of Quebec, and although these judgments were unwarrantable, especially that given upon the plea of forgery, a decision was given on the 27th Octr. 1721, dismissing the appeals against the judgments of the 20th of April and 27th of May 1720; and ordering that they should be executed according to their form and substance; and, with a view to the fuller investigation allowed by the judgment of the said 27th day of May, 1720, that the note of hand and the document compared with it shall be sent back to the Registry of the royal jurisdiction of Montreal; and ordering the appellant to pay the costs of the appeals.

Although the Petitioner has done her best to obtain a copy of this decision, she has not been able to succeed in doing so because they suspected that she wished to sue before the Council to quash the decision.

And as the Petitioner cannot ascertain on what documents nor on what grounds this decision has been given, and cannot formulate the objections to the decree without knowing what the documents and proceedings examined in the case are—without having a full copy of the judgment—for at present she has only been able to obtain a copy of the order merely.

The Petitioner hopes that Your Highness will grant her protection against the Sr de Tonty; and, that, in order to enable her to obtain the justice due to her, you will be good enough, Monseigneur, to give the necessary orders to the said Intendant of Quebec, president of the Council, to send her immediately a full copy of this decision of the 27th of Oct. 1721, in due form. The Petitioner will pray to God, Monseigneur, for Your Highness' health and prosperity.

gaining his property. In 1718 the Petitioner finding himself deprived of the rights conferred by his contracts, resolved to buy a permit to go to the said Detroit and other places; and being compelled to obtain refreshments at the said Detroit to enable him to continue his towing, he was not allowed to obtain them from the French settlers nor the savages dwelling there without running the risk of confiscation; it was necessary for the Petitioner to buy them from the said M. de Tonty a hundred per cent dearer than they would have cost him from the said Frenchmen and savages, which constitutes a notable wrong to all travellers. But he hopes, by the kindness of Your Highness, that he will regain possession of his property according to his contracts, and that you will extend your favors and your charity to a faithful, though far off people, which cannot exist without the succor of His Highness. They will continue their prayers to God for his preservation.

At Quebec this 30th [day of] Octr., 1721.
Alexis Lemoyne.

CADILLAC AGAIN PETITIONS TO BE PUT IN POSSESSION OF DETROIT.

Answer of MM. de Vaudreuil and Begon:

Extract from a memorial presented to the Council of the Navy by M. de La Mothe Cadillac.

1st.

1st.

Some of the facts on which M. de La Motte Cadillac has been granted a brevet of concession of the ground on which he had buildings erected at Detroit and of the lands he cleared there, are not as he has represented them, since the construction of the buildings and the clearing of the lands have not been done at his expense.

The first paragraph of the decision of the Council laying down that M. de La Mothe must be put in possession again of the lands he had cleared together with the rights over the lands which he had granted in virtue of the letters of M. de Pontchartrain, of which a concession in due form will be sent to him.

2nd.

2nd.

M. de La Motte did not contribute to the peace with the Iroquois for, from the year 1700, the late M. de Callieres had had word from them that they would make it; and in order to settle it,

M. de La Motte thinks that the intention of the Council will be conformable with that of M. de Pontchartrain which was to grant him all Detroit because of the great expense he was to incur

notice to all the savages allied to us to go down to Montreal in 1701 for the purpose of concluding it. It was only in the month of June of the same year, 1701, that the said M. de La Mothe set out from Montreal with M. de Tonty, 50 soldiers and 50 settlers, to form the first establishment at Detroit, the whole expense of which the king paid. Peace having been made with the Iroquois, the designs of the English on the upper countries would have been ineffectual since it was absolutely impossible for them to undertake anything without the aid of the savages. Moreover, these posts having been established at His Majesty's expense, M. de La Mothe has no rights to ask for anything on this account.

of settlers there, in attracting to it a number of different savage tribes, which compelled the Iroquois to make peace, which held them, and still holds them, to their duty, and which prevented the English from coming to settle there as they wished to do.

3rd.

The greater part of the lands forming the Domain of Detroit were cleared at the expense of the King and of the the Company; and those which have been cleared since the time of M. de La Motte and have enlarged the Domain have cost him nothing, having been cleared by soldiers to whom he granted only the use of them for three years on that condition. If the King grants these lands to the said M. de La Mothe, it would be necessary to grant him them with a depth of forty arpents so that he could obtain from them the wood which he would need.

The fort of stakes at Detroit is no longer of the size it was in the time of M. de La Motte having been made smaller on account of the war with the Renards. Thus the place where the old warehouse of the company used to be,

3rd.

If the King put M. de La Mothe back on the cleared lands only according to the terms and decisions of the Council, it would follow that he would be unable to protect himself against the severity of the seasons which is constant in that country, that he would be without the wood necessary for building and for all kinds of works; and lastly that he would be unable to reach other lands to clear them and make new settlements.

up to Lake Huron by Frenchmen and the savages; but there are no other lands occupied [even] now towards the north, where the fort is situated, but those which there are from the River Rouge which discharges itself into the River of Detroit up to the old village of the 8ta8ois, and they measure only about two leagues' frontage by a quarter of a league deep along the said River of Detroit.

In this stretch of land to the northeast of the fort is included the Domain of 40 arpents frontage by a quarter of a league deep, four concessions granted by M. de La Mothe to the [persons] named Delorme, Desrochers, M. Aubin and the widow Beausseron, all four containing two arpents frontage each by twenty in depth, on each of which there are about twenty arpents of land cleared, which makes only forty-eight arpents frontage for the Domain and all the French settled at Detroit together.

The other Frenchmen who are residents there sow the corn necessary for their subsistance either on the Domain lands or on those of the Savages. There is no building on these cleared lands, whether for use as dwelling, stable or barn.

All the houses are within the fort, and the barns and stables are outside under the protection of this fort.

M. de La Motte had granted several other concessions which are now abandoned and [they] formed part of these two leagues' frontage.

The fort of Detroit is situated about in the middle of this stretch [of country.] To the South-west of the fort, inclining towards Lake Erié, are the Hurons and the Pout8atamis who occupy a league of the above stretch, to the south, on the other side of the River, are the 8ta8ois who, together with

Erié up to Lake Huron was, as a whole, settled by Frenchmen or by the savage tribes which M. de La Motte attracted there, and that he placed both so as to preserve that New Colony and to be protected by it also, so that all Detroit is granted except what M. de La Motte had reserved for his domain, and except the [land] bordering the Lake St. Claire which is perhaps thirty leagues in circumference.

Mississagués and Sauteurs whose waste lands contain about three-quarters of a league frontage by fifteen arpents deep; so that, in all Detroit the only cleared lands are the four leagues and three-quarters above explained, including the Domain.

5th.

Neither the eldest son of M. de La Motte nor his other children can claim any benefit under the concession which he made to them of six leagues frontage along the River of Detroit by five in depth together with the large island and the adjacent islands because no settlement has been made there, nor any clearing, and one of the chief conditions of concessions is to have house and home there within a year and a day on penalty of forfeiting them.

6th

No concessions have been granted except as stated above from the River Rouge to Lake St. Claire, distant from each other about four leagues.

7th.

There are no Frenchmen except the four named above, each of whom has two arpents frontage.

5th.

For instance, at the entrance to Lake Erié in the western end of the River up to the River aux Ecorces [and] up to the River Rouge, which makes six leagues' frontage along the River by five leagues deep in the forests, the whole is granted to M. de La Motte junior, an officer, and to his other children, as a fief, and with rights of middle and lower jurisdiction, which was approved by the Comte de Pontchartrain, and accordingly the children of the said M. de La Motte have made settlements there.

6th.

From the River Rouge up to Lake St. Claire is all granted to French settlers, or reserved to M. de La Motte as his Domain, or granted to the Hurons or set apart as common land for the inhabitants for cattle.

7th.

The inhabitants hold different concessions, those who had families have concessions with four and six arpents frontage along the River with 25 arpents in the depth of the woods, the

the Hurons, of 120; and that of the Sauteurs and Mississagués of 100.

9th.

All the savages who are now at Detroit were attracted there by M. de La Motte while he was in command there on behalf of the King and afterwards for the company who defrayed the cost of the presents which were distributed to them to induce them to come there; and, while M. de La Motte was in possession of his exclusive privilege, only the Pout8atamis and the Renards came.

As these savages, except the above two tribes, settled on the lands which were given to them only on a verbal invitation which was made to them on the subject on behalf of His Majesty before M. de La Motte had the trade of Detroit, it follows that when these savages abandon these lands they will revert to His Majesty in the same way as those granted to the savages residing at the different missions of Canada.

10th.

It is not to be supposed that M. de La Motte agreed with the savages dwelling at Detroit that when they should abandon the lands on which they settled, the ownership of them should belong to him since they came there before he had had the exclusive privilege of the place.

The letters of M. de Pontchartrain on which he relied in asking for the ownership of this post give him no right to the lands cleared by the savages, being subsequent to their settlements.

9th.

Above the Lake St. Claire were the Anükouck, the Mississagués, Outchipouck and numbers [of] N' Epissingues.

10th.

When M. de La Motte distributed the lands to the savage tribes he explained to them that [he] gave them to them as their property for so long as they wished to have them, but that, if they changed their dwelling place, the lands they abandoned would revert to his Domain. That is what they agreed to and what is the custom also in Canada in the neighborhood of Quebec and Montreal; but the savages pay nothing for their lands as long as they remain on them.

It is evident therefore that from the entrance to Lake Erié, the islands and islets adjacent and the mainland along the River up to the entrance to Lake St. Claire belong to M. de La Motte, to his children, to the French [settlers], to the

The savages living furthést from Detroit who have been brought there are
the 8ta8ois and the Hurons who were
at Michilimakina, 130 leagues distant
from Detroit. It was in 1701, by the
order of M. de Callieres, that M. de
La Motte invited them to come and
live there; and all the expenses of the
Frenchmen who were sent there with
this invitation and of the presents
which were made to the savages were
paid for by the King, as well as those
for giving notice to the savages of
the Baye and of Chagouamignon of the
settlement of Detroit; so that it has cost
M. de La Motte nothing to attract the
savages there, as explained above.

Neither has M. de La Motte incurred
any expense for building forts for the
savages; they had been built at their
own expense, before he had the exclusive privilege, and they gave the
Frenchmen who worked there with them
a male roebuck skin a day, worth three
livres, besides the food they supplied
to them. The doors of these forts were
made by a [man] called Guay, a carpenter paid by the King; and no houses
have been·built within these forts for
the missionaries as there have not been
any in this village from the first settlement until now. From 1701, at the
time of the first settlement, until 1706,
when M. de La Mothe went up to Detroit again in consequence of his privilege, there was one Almoner, a recollet,
for the fort only, and the instruction
of the Frenchmen, who, not understanding the language of the savages, could
not take charge of them.

Since it was necessary to send 3 and
400 leagues from Detroit for these tribes,
to give them large presents in order to
make them leave their dwellings, to have
forts built for them, provide houses
for missionaries there, and to pay 500 #
a year to each of them, to furnish
chapels, to pay for interpreters; all that
was done at the cost and expense of·
M. de La Motte, and the King would
not reimburse him.

Huron language, and passed the winter hunting with them. He returned to Quebec at the end of three years, and from that time there has only been an Almoner at Detroit.

They had 500 ⚏ a year each and they were paid at this rate by the King from 1706 up to 1709. The Surgeon and the Master Armourer were also paid at the expense of His Majesty during that period; but in 1709, M. de Pontchartrain having explained that His Majesty no longer intended to defray this expense, and that M. de La Motte should be responsible for it, the Almoner has been paid partly by the Commandant, and partly by the inhabitants; the same [arrangement] has been employed by the Commandants who have served at that post since the departure of M. de La Motte; and M. de Tonty, who is there now, has entered into an agreement with the inhabitants under which they have bound themselves to pay half the costs of the Almoner.

Since he paid the company for the ornaments of the Chapel, those that he left belonged to him and he ought to be repaid for them by M. de Tonty according to the valuation which shall be made of them. The expense M. de La Motte incurred for the payment of an interpreter was necessary to him for making the most of that post and for governing the savages. He has been recompensed sufficiently for it by the trade he transacted with them for which he could not do without an interpreter. The Company of Canada paid the sum of 6,000 ⚏ a year to be distributed among the poor families of this colony. It also bound itself by an agreement which it had made with M. de La Motte to pay him every year the sum of 2,000 ⚏ gratuity in his capacity of Commandant, and to supply · him with his

self, his wife, two children and two servants.

M. de La Motte has not been saddled
with the payment of these 6,000 #,
nor of these gratuities and food; he
has neither fed nor paid any of the
officers who served under him, having
only granted them annually certain
permissions, namely, to M. de La Forest
to have brought up there two canoes
laden with merchandise, and to the
other officers one canoe each, from
which it must be concluded that he
enjoyed his exclusive privilege on more
advantageous conditions than the Company.

12th.

The above answers show what the
expenses are which M. de La Motte has
incurred. He has only once, about
thirty years ago, been to the island of
Mondesert, when going to France with
M. de Vaudreuil and M. de Ramezay,
who saw for themselves that there
had been no settlement there then.
Hence the favor which the King did

jurisdiction, with fishing, hunting and trading rights, as well as these rights over the lands already granted.

14th.

It is just that right should be done to M. de La Mothe as to what he may have left at Detroit. When he went away he left certain effects in the hands of a [man] called Pierre Roy, who ought to render him an account of them according to the inventory which was sent to him. The cattle which remain in kind shall also be returned to M. de La Motte's agent when he appears. The buildings which he says belong to him consist of one house of stakes covered with straw, and a warehouse which was [made] of pieces of timber, one upon another, and which was pulled down in the war with the Renards to make a redoubt. They are no longer in existence, and there are no other buildings on these two sites which are now outside the fort.

14th.

[That] it will also please the Council to cause it to be ordained by the intermediate decree which will be issued that M. de La Motte shall be re-put in possession of the buildings, personal property and cattle which are found of the same kind as those he left when he went away from that Post, and that in doing this, the buildings found built on his ground by the demolition of those which he had built, or otherwise, shall belong to him; and that he may take back his cattle although they may have been sold, reserving the remedy of the buyer against the seller, seeing that the owner of an article takes it back wherever he finds it; also to name the person before whom M. de La Motte is to sue for any claims he may have against those who have taken and disposed of his goods.

15th.

His Royal Highness having sent M. de La Motte to sue before whom he shall think good as to all his claims against those who have taken and disposed of his goods, and there being judges in the three towns of this Colony where the persons against whom he has demands to make are residing, it would appear that these suits can be brought before the ordinary judges, and with appeal to the Council.

15th.

M. de La Motte thinks this should be before the Intendant of Canada, because that will shorten all quibbling, and because he cannot be suspected [of partiality] by any party; and to this end it is necessary that the Council should be good enough to assign to him the cognizance of this [matter] and to refuse it to every other court and jurisdiction, with prohibitions to the parties against suing elsewhere under a penalty of 200 ₶, half of which shall belong to the prosecutor.

at the said place of Detroit according
as they were traded in with the savages,
as other like efforts were paid for by
him, by the order of M. de Pontchartrain.

Clauses and Conditions expressed in the concessions granted by M.
de La Mothe Cadillac at the fort of Detroit on Lake Erié to several inhabitants of that colony. Namely.

To Michel Campos, a site of fifty-three feet in length on St. Antoine
Street and seventeen feet on St. Anne Street, at a charge, Namely,
of five livres six sols quit-rent and rent, this......... 5# 6s . . .
and moreover for other rights which M. de La Mothe

has given up which consist of permission for all

trading .... 10 . . . . . .
_____

15# 6 . . .

The whole payable on the Twentieth of March in each year in good,
valuable and saleable skins and at first in coined money which there may
be at the said place.

To take their corn to the mill to grind and to pay out of it, as the fee
for grinding, eight livres, full weight, per minot.

The preference in case of sale.

Not to be able to sell in mortmain without the consent of the said M.
de La Mothe.

Liable for the public taxes and services, and to the fines of alienation.

Not to be able to carry on any trade as a black-smith, an edge-tool
maker, a locksmith, armorer or a brewer of beer directly or indirectly
for [the next] ten years without holding a permit for it from M. de La
Mothe.

Of sending to Montreal or [any] other place in the Lower Colony all
the effects he may have, or of taking them there himself, and bringing
back any merchandise he pleases, and also as large a quantity as he likes,
on the condition that he shall sell his said effects or merchandise at Detroit with his own hands, and himself only, or by other inhabitants of the

In the other concessions, besides the conditions above, the inhabitants are to set up the Maypole before the door of the manor house on the first day of May, and in default of carrying it out, [are] to pay three livres in money or skins.

Given at Quebec, the 4th of November, 1721.

Begon.

LIST OF EFFECTS FROM THE MAGAZINE OF CADILLAC.

Endorsed—Annexed to the letter of M. de Vaudreuil and Begon of the 4th Novr. 1721.

Statement of the effects taken from the magazine of M. de La Mothe Cadillac for the service of the King by M. Dubuisson, the Commandant, for the defence of the fort of Detroit Erié, which statement was drawn up by M. de La Mothe.

Three barrels of powder of sixty-six livres each, weighing
in all one hundred and ninety eight livres at 5# a livre   990# . . .
Eleven bags of lead or bullets making, with eight livres
besides the bags, eleven hundred and eight livres at 3#
the L. 3324   . . .
Ten swords with handles @ 25#.   25
One pair of iron @ 20.   20
4359

As a copy
Begon.

DETAILED DESCRIPTION OF DETROIT.

Endorsed—annexed to the letter of MM. de Vaudreuil and Begon of the 4th Novr. 1721.

Statement of the Sites occupied by the inhabitants of the fort of De-

feet frontage by eighty feet deep on one side, and thirty-nine feet on the other by thirty-seven feet frontage, bought from M. de Sabrevois for the sum of eleven hundred and ninety livres including the corn and other useful things.

in

a
se.

Site of M. Laurent Trudeau bordering on that of M. de Tonty containing twenty-five feet frontage by eighteen deep, on which there is only a very poor house which, on the said M. Trudeau relinquishing it, was valued for making a guard-house.

c-
i

2. Site of M. René Hamelin called la Gausire bordering on M. Trudeau, containing 25 feet frontage by 20 feet deep abutting on Montreal Street.

3. Site of M. Simon Gilbert, sergeant of the garrison bordering on Montreal Street on one side, with 18 feet frontage by 20 deep; granted by M. de Tonty.

4. Site of M. Paul Guillet, bordering on that of M. Gilbert, containing 18 feet frontage by 28 deep.

has
his

5. Site of M. Jacques la Croix, bordering on that of M. Guillet, containing 20 feet frontage by 27 feet deep.

6. Site of M. Louis Roy, bordering on that of M. la Croix at the Curtain of the Hurons, containing 20 feet frontage by 24 deep.

7. Site of M. Francois Barrois the elder, containing 23 feet 8 inches frontage by 25 deep.

by
e

8. Site of M. Jacques Cardinal, bordering on that of M. Barrois, containing 22½ feet frontage by 25 deep.

9. Site of M. Jean Bapt'e Forestier, containing 16½ feet frontage by 29 deep.

10. Site of the late M. Pierre Rocbert belonging to Angelique Tholomée Boucher formerly his wife and to her heirs, bordering on that of M. Forestier, containing 30 feet frontage by 32 deep.

11. Site on which the church, and the house of the R. P. recollet, and its outhouse are situated, abutting on the road of the Curtain of the Poutouatamis, containing 30 feet frontage by 100 feet deep.

St. Jacques Street.

16. Site of M. Michel Campau, bordering on that of M. Neven and contiguous to the road of the Curtain of the Hurons, containing 26 feet frontage by 19 feet deep granted by M. de Tonty *M. de Linetot acquired it from the said Campau*

17. Site of M. Pierre le Breton, contiguous to the road of the Curtain of the Hurons, containing 28 feet frontage by 30 deep;

18. Site of M. Joseph Parent, bordering on that of M. le Breton, containing 32½ feet frontage by 31 feet deep;

19. { Site of M. Pierre Perthuis bordering on that of M. Parent, containing 25 feet frontage by 36 deep; Site of M. Pierre Maillet, bordering on that of M. Perthuis containing 48 feet frontage by 36 deep. *M. Perthuis now has these two sites as the son-in-law of the said Maillet*

20. Site of M. Jacques Philis, bordering on that of M. Mallett, containing 30 feet frontage by 36 deep;

21. Site of M. Pierre Buteau, bordering on that of M. Philis and contiguous to that of the R. P. recollet, containing 30 feet frontage by 36 deep.

St. Anne Street.

22. Site of M. Joseph Vaudry bordering on the back of that of M. de Tonty, containing 16½ feet frontage by 19 deep;

23. Site of M. Louis Hamelin bordering on that of M. Vaudry, containing 38 feet frontage by 19 deep; *Thiery Noland acquired it*

24. Site of M. Nicolas Millet contiguous to Montreal Street, containing 25½ feet frontage by 18 feet deep. *Made over to M. Rocbert in payment.*

25. Site of M. Jean St. Aubin, bordering on that of M. Millet containing 33 feet frontage by 18 deep;

26. { Site of M. Bernard Demouchelles, contiguous to the road of the Curtain of the Hurons, containing 21 feet frontage by 22 feet deep; Site of M. francois de l'Isle bordering on that of M. Desmouchelles, containing 31 feet frontage by 22 deep. *Delisle has also the site of Der'or'chelles.*

27. Site of M. Jacob Desrochers, bordering on that of M. de l'Isle, containing 27 feet frontage by 23 deep.

28. Site of M. francois fasard Delorme contiguous to Montreal Street, containing 23 feet frontage by 24 deep.

29. Site of M. Pierre la Jeunesse, bordering on that of M. de Lorme, containing 26 feet frontage by 24 deep;

30. Site of M. de Tonty bordering on that of M. la Jeunesse and contiguous to St. Anne gate, containing 42 feet frontage by 23 deep. *Chapoteau, Surgeon of the fort, possesses it by transfer which M. de Tonty made o him.*

As a copy

Begon.

THE KING DECIDES NOT TO REINSTATE CADILLAC AT DETROIT.

Endorsed—Canada. Refer the whole to M. de la Grandville.

     Council.
     MM. de Vaudreuil and Begon.

                        4th November, 1721.

Extract from the letter which the Council wrote to them on the 24th of July, 1720.

The Council having reported to the Regent the explanations you gave last year as to the claims of M. de La Mothe Cadillac to the lands and buildings at Detroit, His Royal Highness decided that he *should be put in possession again of the lands he had cleared at Detroit, together with the rights over the lands he granted* under the letters of M. de Pontchartrain, and that to this end a concession of them in due form should be sent to him; *that he should also be put in possession of any buildings, movable property, and animals there may be of such kind as he left* when he quitted that post; that, *as regards his other claims,* he should bring his action before what court he thought fit, and that he should be paid for whatever might be found to have been taken *from his warehouses* for His Majesty's service.

In order to enable the Sr. de La Mothe to reap the benefit of this first decision a warrant has been sent to him containing grants of the lands on which he had buildings erected at Detroit, and the lands he cleared there.

As regards the rights over the lands he granted in pursuance of the letters of M. de Pontchartrain, no title can be given him until the Council knows what took place under the letters patent in the form of a proclamation of the month of April, 1716, as to the Detroit concessions, which were sent to you. You will inform the Council as to what was done in this matter; and, if you granted fresh concessions, to whom, and on what terms.

In compliance with the orders of the Council, they reply that no

There are also difficulties as to these concessions to be made in the King's name; which are—to know whether His Majesty's intention is that they should be made on the same tenure as provided in the grants made throughout the Colony or whether they are to be bound in the same rents, charges and conditions as those set forth in the contracts of M. de La Mothe, from which they send an extract.

Clauses and conditions set forth in the concessions of M. de La Mothe at the fort of Detroit on Lake Erie to several settlers.

Specimen.

To Michel Campos a site 53 feet long in the Rue St. Antoine and 17 feet in the Rue St. Anne at 5 livres 6 sols quit rent and rent.

Note. This is at the rate of 2 sols per lineal foot, and moreover for other rights which the said Sr. de La Mothe has given up, consisting of full permission to trade, 10 livres.

Note. Those who have several sites are not obliged to pay more than the 10 livres for full permission to trade.

The whole payable on the 20th of March in each year in furs, and in coined money when there is any at the said place.

To take their grain to be ground at the Mill, and to pay for its grinding 8 livres weight per minot.

The preference in case of sale.

Not to be allowed to sell in mortmain without the consent of the Sr. de La Mothe.

Bound in public charges and services, and fines on alienation.

Not to be allowed to work, directly or indirectly at any trade as Blacksmith, axe-cutter, locksmith, armorer, or brewer of beer for 10 years, without permission.

To send to Montreal or other places in the lower Colony all the effects he may have to sell, and to bring back any goods he may think fit, on condition of selling them at Detroit himself or by other inhabitants of the place, and not by aliens or strangers, nor by hired men or people not settled there, on pain of confiscation of the property and goods.

In case part of the site is sold to an alien, the purchaser shall pay quit rent in proportion to his purchase, and the 10 livres in addition for the right of trading.

Note. In the other concessions, besides the above charges, the in-

Whether the settlers who have received grants from the Sieurs de la Forest, de Sabrevois, and de Tonty, whether for sites within the fort or for the lands of Detroit, are to have new ones in His Majesty's name, as it is only ordered by the letters patent that they are to be granted to those who had concessions from the Sr. de la Mothe.

There remain only four settlers now at Detroit out of those who had grants from him.

The others, to the number of 30, according to the *list* which they send, have only sites within the fort which have been granted to them by the other Commandants.

These settlers, having no lands, sow corn on the domain for their subsistence under permits from the Commandant.

The permission to trade is fixed by M. de La Mothe's contracts at 10 livres a year. The Commandants who have succeeded him have taken this permission away from them, claiming that these settlers have no right to trade, any more than anyone else who goes there, without buying permission to do so from them, and that they have the exclusive right to it.

The man Alexis Le Moine, a merchant at Montreal, presented a petition to the Council in which he complained that, having bought two sites in 1708 from the Sr. Mallette, situated at Fort Pontchartrain at Detroit on Lake Erie, and granted by M. de La Mothe, he has been harassed by the Sr. de Tonty, the Commandant of the Fort, who for his own

have yet been granted under them, the Council is enabled to grant
him any rights it may think fit over the lands granted by him,
of which the Sr. de Grandmesnil, formerly his agent, has given
them the *list* which they send.   it is annex

MM. de Vaudreuil and Begon think these rights might be reduced to the terms of the dues which are paid in the Colony by
which means the settlers will have the same hunting, fishing and
trading right as the said Sr. de La Mothe.

Continuation of the letter from the Council to MM. de Vaudreuil &
Begon.

You are to give the necessary orders for the said Sr. de La Mothe
being reinstated in possession of the said sites and lands in accordance
with the writ of concession granted to him, and, moreover, of the movable
property and animals which may be found of like kind with those he
left there when he quitted Detroit. You will draw up a statement
of what has been taken from the warehouses of the said Sr. de La Mothe,
and the prices, which you will send to the Council; and, as to the other
claims of the said Sr. de La Mothe, he may sue before whatever court
he may think fit.

The said Sr. de Grandmesnil told them that he wrote to the said
Sr. de La Mothe last year that he could not attend to his business, and that the said Sr. de La Mothe had notified him that he
was sending his power of attorney to someone else but had not
named the person to whom he had forwarded it; when the new
agent comes forward they will give the necessary orders for putting him in possession of the sites and lands spoken of in his writ
of concession, and of the movable property and cattle that may
be found of like kind.

The said Sr. de Grandmesnil has shown M. Begon 2 *certificates* a copy is
of the Sr. du Buisson, Commandant at Fort Pontchartrain in   annexed.
place of the Sr. de la Forest, of what was taken by his orders
from the warehouses of M. de La Mothe in 1712 for the defence of
the fort of Detroit.

The first, of the 9th of June, 1712, sets forth that 3 barrels of powder
and 11 bags of lead, and 8 livres of lead and 10 sword blades have
been supplied from the effects of the Sr. de La Mothe for the defence
of the said fort.

In the second, of the 3rd of July, 1712, the said Sr. du Buisson
acknowledges having received the swords belonging to the said Sr. de

It appears from this certificate that the store-keeper of the King's warehouses delivered to the said Sr. du Buisson, by order of M. Begon, to replace the warlike stores and other goods used up in the defence of the said fort—To wit.

400 livres of fine powder

600 livres of lead in bullets

200 livres of lead in the form of shot.

and 3 minots of salt.

As it is for the Sr. du Buisson who received them to account for them to the said Sr. de La Mothe, no prices have been put to the goods referred to in these certificates.

The said Sr. de Grandmesnil has also shown M. Begon a statement of these same stores, of which he sends a copy, which the said Sr. de La. Mothe made from these certificates.

According to this statement the said Sr. de La Mothe values the 3 barrels of powder, each weighing 66 livres at the sum of 990 livres at the rate of 5 livres per livre weight,—this...... 990#

The 11 bags of lead, each weighing 100 livres, making with the 8 livres overplus, 1108# at the rate of 3# per livre.................... 3324

10 swords with handles for.................... 25

and iron for 20

4359#

M.. Begon remarks that this estimate is not just; that the barrels of powder usually taken to Detroit only weigh about 50 livres instead of 66 livres, and that the bags of leads are usually only 25 and 50 livres' weight instead of the 100 livres at which he puts them. That will be a matter to be cleared up between the said Srs. de La Mothe and du Buisson.

They have examined, together with the Sr. de Tonty, the Sr. de La Mothe's memorial and have made the reply which they send.

EXTRACTS FROM THE MEMORIAL AND REPLY.

Extract from the Reply.	Extract from the Memorial.
1st.	**1st.**
The facts on which M. de La Mothe has been granted a writ of concession of the sites on which he had buildings erected at Detroit, and of the lands he cleared there, are not as he has stated them, since the erection of the buildings and the clearing of the land was not carried out at his expense.	The first paragraph of the Council's decision states that the Sr. de La Mothe must be reinstated in possession of the lands which he had cleared, and of the rights over the lands he granted in pursuance of the letters of M. de Pontchartrain, a concession of which in due form will be sent to him.
2.	**2.**
He did not contribute to the peace with the Iroquois since, in the year 1700, the late M. de Callieres had had word from them that they would make peace; and in order to settle it, he sent the Sr. de Courtemanche the same year into the upper country to notify all the friendly savages to come down to Montreal in 1701 to conclude peace.	The Sr. de La Mothe thinks that the intention of the Council will be in accordance with that of M. de Pontchartrain, which was to grant him the whole of Detroit on account of the great expense which he was to incur in establishing it, which he actually did incur in taking a number of settlers there and various tribes of savages, which compelled the Iroquois to make peace, has kept them, since, to their duty, and has prevented the English from going to settle there.
It was only in the month of June of the same year, 1701, that the said Sr. de La Mothe made the first settlement there with 50 soldiers and 50 settlers, and the King paid the whole cost.	

Peace having been made with the Iroquois, the designs of the English on the upper country would have resulted in nothing because they could not make any attack without the aid of the savages; moreover these posts were established at the King's expense, and therefore Sr. de la Mothe can demand nothing.

3.	**3.**

Mothe, cost him nothing, the work having been done by soldiers, to whom he granted the use of them, for three years on this condition.

If the King grants these lands to the M. de La Mothe, it would be necessary to grant them to him with a depth of 40 arpents, so that he may be able to obtain from them the necessary quantity of wood.

to protect himself from the inclemency of the seasons, which are regular in that country; he would have no woods, which are indispensable for building and for works of all kinds; lastly he would not be able to extend and clear other lands and make new dwelling-places.

The fort of stakes at Detroit has not the same extent now that it had in the time of M. de la Mothe, having been reduced in size on account of the war with the Fox Indians; so that the place where the old storehouse of 'the Company stood, which was also the Sr. de la Mothe's, and his house, is now outside the old fort, and is more than a hundred paces away from it.

4.

4.

At present, there are no lands occupied on the northern side, where the fort is situated except those from the Rouge River—which empties itself into the River Detroit—to the old village of the Outaouois; and they contain only about two leagues' frontage by a quarter of a league in depth, along the said River Detroit.

M. de La Mothe remarks that the whole of Detroit, from Lake Erie to Lake Huron was settled generally, either by the French or by the savage tribes that he attracted there, and that he placed them both in such a manner as to preserve this New Colony; so that the whole of Detroit is granted except what the Sr. de La Mothe reserved

of Missisagues and Sauteurs whose clearings contain about three quarters of a league frontage by 15 arpents deep. Hence, in all Detroit, there are only the 4 leagues and three-quarters of cleared lands above explained including the Domain.

5.

Neither the elder son of M. de La Mothe nor his other children can obtain any advantage from the grant made to them of these six leagues' frontage by five in depth; for neither settlement nor clearing has been made there, and one of the chief conditions of concessions is to keep a hearth and home there within a year and a day on pain of forfeiting them.

5.

From the entrance to Lake Erie to the western extremity of the Ecorces River, with Grosse Isle and the adjacent islands, and from the Ecorces River up to the Rouge River, which make six leagues' frontage along the River by 5 leagues in depth, in the forests, the whole is granted to the Sr. de La Mothe, junior, who is an officer, and and to his other children as a fief, and with the authority of the middle and lower jurisdiction; and this was approved by M. de Pontchartrain; and the children of the said Sr. de La Mothe have accordingly made settlements there.

6.

Nothing has been conceded but what is stated above, from the River Rouge to Lake St. Clair, which are about four leagues apart.

6.

From the Rouge River to Lake St. Clair, the whole is granted to French settlers, or reserved for the Sr. de La Mothe as his Domain, or granted to the Hurons, or set aside for the settlers as a common land for cattle.

7.

There are no Frenchmen who have concessions but the 4 named above who have 2 arpents frontage each.

7.

The settlers have various concessions. Those who had families have concessions of 4 and 6 arpents frontage along the River with 25 arpents in depth in the woods, the smaller families had 2 arpents frontage by the same depth of 25 arpents.

8.

The savages with these different names only make up the Outaouois tribe, except the Poutouatamis, settled on the north, as explained above.
The Outaouois tribe consists of 130 men, the Poutouatamis of 150 men,

8.

To the south of the River were the Outaouois, the Kikakouins, the Massouckouctons, the Neguoüans des Chermis, the Sinagos and the Poutouatamis.

9.   9

All the savages now at Detroit were   Above Lake St. Clair were the Anu-
attracted there by M. de la Mothe while   kouck, the Missisagués, Outchipouck,
he was in command there for the King   and a number of Nepissingues.
and afterwards for the Company, which
defrayed the cost of the presents for making them come there, and while the said
Sr. de la Mothe enjoyed his exclusive right, none but the Poutouatamis and the Fox
Indians came there.

As these savages, except the above two tribes, only settled on the lands which
were given out to them because of a verbal invitation from His Majesty before
the Sr. de la Mothe had the trade of Detroit, it follows from this that when these
savages abandon the lands, they will revert to His Majesty in the same way as
those which are granted to the savages living at the various mission stations
of Canada.

10.   10.

It is not to be supposed that the said   When the Sr. de La Mothe distributed
Sr. de La Mothe made such agreements   the lands to the savage tribes, he
with the savages since they came there   agreed with them that when they aban-
before he had the exclusive right there.   doned them they should revert to his
The letters from M. de Pontchartrain,   domain, and this is the practice in the
on which he takes his stand in asking   neighborhood of Quebec and Montreal;
for the proprietorship of this post, give   but, as long as the savages remain on
him no right over the lands cleared   their lands, they make no payment.
by the savages, as they are subsequent   It is evident, therefore, that from
to their settlement.   the entrance to Lake Erie, the islands
                                          and adjacent islets and the mainland
                                          along the River to the entrance to Lake
                                          St. Clair are held by the Sr. de La
                                          Mothe, his children, the French and the
                                          Hurons, and that, on the south side,
                                          it is the savages who possess the
                                          lands, from Lake Erie to Lake Huron,
                                          with an agreement that, if they aban-

gouamigou of the establishment of Detroit, so that it cost the said Sr. de
La Mothe nothing.

In like manner he was put to no expense in constructing forts for the savages;
they had them built at their own expense before he had the exclusive privilege,
and gave the Frenchmen who worked at the forts with them a fine roebuck skin,
worth 3 livres, per day besides the food with which they supplied them.

The gates of these forts were made at the King's expense, and no houses were
built there for the missionaries as there have been no missionaries in this village
from its first foundation to the present time.

From 1701, the time of the first settlement, up to 1706 there was an almoner for
the fort only; the same year, 1706, M. de la Mothe took two Recolets there, one
of whom remained there three years; and since that time there has been only one
Almoner at Detroit.

. They each received 500 livres a year, and have been paid at that rate by the King
from 1706 to 1709.

The surgeon and the master armorer were also paid at His Majesty's expense
during that period; but in 1709, M. de Pontchartrain having explained that His
Majesty did not mean to bear that expense any longer, and that it must be chargeable to the said Sr. de la Mothe, the Almoner was paid partly by the Commandant
and partly by the settlers. The same custom was observed by the Commandants
who have served at this post since the Sr. de la Mothe left, and the Sr. de Tonty
who is now there has executed an agreement with the inhabitants by which they
have bound themselves to pay half the expense of the almoner.

As the said Sr. de la Mothe paid the Company for the ornaments of the Chapel,
those that he left there belong to him, and he ought to be reimbursed by the Sr.
de Tonty according to a valuation to be made of them.

The expense he bore for the payment of an interpreter was a necessary expense
to him, and he could not have done without one because of the trade he transacted with the savages by which he was sufficiently compensated.

The Company of Canada paid 6000 livres a year for distribution to the poor
families of this Colony; it also bound itself to M. de la Mothe to pay him 2000
livres gratuity every year as Commandant, and to supply him with his own food
and that of his wife, two children and two servants; also, to the Sr. de Tonty,
the captain under him, a gratuity of 1333 ₶ 6s 8d besides his food and his family's.
M. de la Mothe was not burdened with the payment of his 6000 livres or these
gratuities and food. He neither fed nor paid any of the officers who served under
him and only granted them permits every year, namely, to the Sr. de la Forest
to send up two boats loaded with goods, and each of the other officers one boat,
which shows that he enjoyed his exclusive right on more favorable conditions
than the Company did.

12.   12.

The above replies show the expense | The Sr. de La Mothe, in asking for
incurred by the Sr. de La Mothe. | the grant of the whole of Detroit, is

He was once only, about thirty years | asking but a small thing compared with
ago, at the island of Montdesert, when | the 1,000 leagues of forests which will
on his way to France with the Sr. de | remain to be granted; and he has paid

King showed him in granting him this seigniory did not cause him any expense.

If he does not obtain what he asks for, the same thing will happen to him as happened in Acadia, where he held the island of Montdesert, which is 14 leagues in circumference, with 2 leagues on the mainland, by 2 leagues in depth, with the right of higher, middle and lower jurisdiction, and fishing, hunting, and trading rights; and besides that a fief at Port Royal, which he lost through the English taking possession of them.

13.

His Majesty is not bound to have any regard to the demands of the Sr. de La Mothe, for it is notorious that he made large profits by the trade he did with the savages, and these are sufficient compensation to him for the money he spent.

13.

He hopes, for the above reasons that His Majesty will grant him the concession of the whole of Detroit, with the right of the higher, middle and lower judisdiction, with the fishing, hunting and trading rights, together with his rights over the lands already granted.

14.

It is right to do justice to the Sr. de La Mothe as to what he may have left

14.

He asks that it may be ordered by the intermediate decree that he shall be

whom he has a grievance, it appears
that these actions can be tried before
the ordinary judges, with an appeal to
the Council.

MM. de Vaudreuil and Begon think that the request made by the Sr. de la Mothe,
that the whole of Detroit should be granted to him with the higher, middle and
lower jurisdiction, ought not to be complied with, and that it would be treating him
well to grant him this right over the lands cleared by him and those which he
granted.

From his Domain there should be taken away the lands which were cleared on
it at the time of the first settlement by the King and afterwards by the Company,
the ownership in which belongs to His Majesty as it does not appear that the Sr.
de la Mothe paid the Company anything for them.

As the Sr. de Grandmesnil has told them that a measurement was made of the
number of arpents of land which had been brought into cultivation when the Sr.
de la Mothe entered upon the rights of the Company, there is no difficulty in
settling what lands are to be reckoned in the domain of the Sr. de la Mothe.

There is no reason to think that it is in consideration of his labors that a
warrant of concession has been granted him in respect to the lands he built upon
and those he cleared; and that H. R. H. has decided that he shall have the rights
from the lands he granted looking to the fact that he had placed settlers there.
But he seems to have no ground for asking for the proprietorship of lands which
he did not bring into cultivation, nor of rights from those he did not grant.

There are only four settlers who have remained on the lands he granted them;
the others have abandoned those they held only because they have not had the
right of trading which was granted to them by the Sr. de la Mothe in their contracts. It seems right to put those who wish to return there, in possession of
their concessions with permission to trade, and for the Sr. de la Mothe, who
granted them to them, to have the payments from these concessions.

These payments should be reduced to the rent and quit-rent merely, since the
Sr. de la Mothe has now no right to exact 10 livres a year from each of the
families settled at Detroit for permission to trade, for this sum was paid to him
in consideration of the expenses of the post, for which he is no longer responsible;
and it would be desirable that these 10 livres should in future be paid to the
Commandant who is charged with them.

The right of hunting, fishing and trading ought only to be granted him within
the limits of his domain; for, since the King grants lands to the seigniors only in
order that they may establish settlers on them, they retain the hunting, fishing &
trading rights only on the domain which they keep for themselves; and by the
grants they make to their settlers, they surrender those rights at the same time,
in consideration of the quit-rents, rents, and seignioral payments which they fix

of 4 arpents, all twenty arpents in depth, making together 61 arpents frontage without including the concession of 3 leagues frontage by 5 deep granted to Madlle de la Mothe, which is not dated. The remainder of the lands of Detroit have not been conceded, those occupied by the savages not being considered as being so.

M. de Vaudreuil considers that the payment of 10 livres which the settlers will be obliged to make to the Commandant in order to exercise the right of trading is not sufficient to enable him to bear the expenses of the post, with which he is chargeable, and that it would be advisable that the settlers should only be per-mitted to trade in the provisions which their lands produce, as the custom is in the Colony of Canada.

In a Petition presented to the Council a short time ago, the men Langlois, Parent, Trudau, Magnau, de Rivieres, de Ruisseau, Campant, Mallet, du Fresne, Hubert, La Croix and Monier, both in their own names and in the names of the other settlers of Detroit who took grants from the Sr. de la Mothe, complain of the oppression and ill treatment of the Sr. de Tonty.

The ground of these complaints is that he seizes on their lands and forces them to pay 5 livres per square arpent every year.

That he exacts excessive contributions from the outside merchants for staying at the fort.

That he compels the settlers to contribute towards presents for the savages.

That he sells them permissions to go down to Montreal for 500 ⚏ in furs, or 300 ⚏ in corn.

That he is both judge and suitor in all the disputes that arise as to trading; and when anyone tries to maintain his rights, he ill-treats him, having beaten the man de Ruisseau with a walking-stick, and trampled the man Philis under foot, so that he left his room all covered with blood. Those who carry their complaints of this bad treatment to M. de Vaudreuil obtain no justice, and only draw down on themselves his displeasure.

That he prohibits the outside merchants from buying anything from the set-tlers, reserving to himself the power to sell them what they need, making them buy a hundred per cent dearer.

He forbids the settlers to keep any liquor at their houses for their own use,

EXPENSES OF THE WAR AGAINST THE FOX INDIANS.

Endorsed—Canada. Annexed to the letter of M. Begon, of the 10th of November, 1721. Statement of the expense incurred on the occasion of the war against the Fox Indians.

⁂ ⁂

	Livres
Paid to the Sr. de Louvigny on account of the expenses of his journey	1125
To six boatmen who took the said Sr. de Louvigny to Michili-makina & brought him back to this town at 375 livres each for their journey	2250
To the Sr. Pachot	450
To Nicholas Perrot ..:....................................	60
To Joannis for food supplied by him.......................	126
To Corbin for making 2 canoes & fittings...................	1656.11
To Maurice Mesnard	300

To Morant Guillet for the following provisions which he supplied to the said Sr. de Louvigny when he was at Detroit. To wit.

	Livres	
10 minots of Indian corn at 20 livres............	200	
15 minots ditto at 24 livres....................	360	
60 livres of fat at 20 sols.....................	60	
9¾ ells of cloth at 24 livres....................	234	·854

6821.11

* *

Given at Quebec the 10th of November 1721.

[Signed] Begon. `

Endorsed—19th Decr. 1721 Canada.
                    Council
                    MM. de Vaudreuil & Begon.
            *   *   *

MEMORANDUM BY THE KING.

His Majesty is satisfied with the assurances they have given that they will obey his prohibitions against granting any license or permission for going to trade in the backwoods; his will is that this should be strictly carried out.

He also wishes that the prohibition against selling brandy to the savages, under any pretext whatsoever, shall be vigorously enforced, so that he may receive no more complaints of this; and that they will scrupulously carry out the precautionary measures he has prescribed, in order to make sure that there shall be no abuse of the permission he has been pleased to give for sending some for the requirements of the officers and soldiers at the upper posts.

He has again been informed this year that a quantity was taken to Missilimakinac and this caused great disorder among the savages; yet there is a Commandant at this place. But, either he is there without any authority, or else he thinks he is not to use it. Neither alternative is suitable for His Majesty's service; and if they continue to trade in

strict examinations in the houses of all the French people who were at that post, and had had all the casks broken and all the flagons emptied which were found filled with brandy there, without excepting anyone.

The Sr. de Tonty, Commandant at Detroit, who is also at Quebec has assured them that there had been none sold this year, and that even at a council he held with the savages settled there, he informed them that none would be sold to them in future; on which they told him that they should go to Orange for some.

M. Begon will continue to pay all the attention he is ordered to do, in order to see that all those who have acted contrary to these prohibitions are severely punished, in accordance with the information he may receive; and in accordance with the edict of the 24th of May 1679, will condemn those who convey brandy or cause it to be conveyed into the villages of the savages.

*

Memorandum by the King.

His Majesty has approved of the reply which the Srs. de Vaudreuil and Begon made to the orders he had given them last year with regard to carrying out the decrees of the 6th of July 1711, as to taking back lands and seignories in Canada which have not been cleared. But His Majesty's will is that they should warn those who have concessions that, if they do not labor to bring them into cultivation, it will be necessary to take them back in accordance with the said Decrees of the 6th of July 1711. They are to report, each year, the success of this warning.

They reply that they sent notice, by the Sr. Collet on the journey he made last winter, to those who have concessions which have not been turned to account, to work without delay to bring them into cultivation, in default whereof they will be taken back to the Domain in accordance with the said decrees. These settlements can only be made gradually; and, as the families increase, there is also no reason to doubt that those who have concessions will turn them to account as far as they can, as those which are not so improved yield them no income.

approved.

Let them continue to carry out the o which hav been given them in th matter.

REPORT OF CHARLEVOIX ON THE WESTERN POSTS.

Endorsed.—26th Decr. 1721.   To be laid before Monseigneur le Duc d'Orleans.   3.

       Council of the Navy
         December 1721.
           Canada.

f the 27th   Father Charlevoix, a Jesuit, who was sent to discover the Western
uly, 1721.
sea, writes that he has visited all the posts of the upper country except those of Lake Superior where he hopes to find more certain information than elsewhere.

He contemplates returning there next spring. He has no doubt that
many memorandums will be received by the Council as to the discovery
which he is commissioned to make; for he observed, in the course of the
journey which he made, that some persons who wished to appear well
informed told him but little, and that others were making inquiries as
to which they gave him no information.

This lack of common action may do great harm to the public interests;
for a piece of knowledge standing alone, is often of small importance in
itself and remains unfruitful for want of being imparted on occasions
where it might serve to lead to the acquisition of others of more importance.

He asks that an extract from the memoranda which may be sent to

CITIZENS OF DETROIT ACCUSE TONTY OF CRUELTY.

Endorsed.—Canada. M. Raudot.

The inhabitants of Detroit 1721. Council. ·
Complaints against M. de Tonty.
To our Lords of the Council of the Navy.

Langlois, Parent, Joseph Trudot, Baptiste Trudot, Joseph Langlois, Magnan, de Rivierres, Paul Dervisseau, Michel Campault, Mallet, Dufresne, Jacques Hubert de la Croix, Moiniere, also in the names of all the other inhabitants, represent to you that they had taken contracts of concession from M. La Mothe, Seignior, under which they exhausted themselves in order to take their families [there], and have risked their lives numbers of times against the enemies of the State and for the preservation of that post. Now, our Lords, they are defrauded by M. de Tonty of all their rights; he takes away their lands and makes them pay five livres per square arpent for them every year, the price on the domain of M. de La Mothe, and has exacted from the hawkers a payment for residing in the said fort making M. Neven give one bundle of otter-skins, Paul Dervisseau three bundles, Franquelin, two bundles, and several others in the same manner which ought never to be expected from the hawkers and the said inhabitants since they built the fort of my said M. de Tonty at their own cost and expense, and the enlisted soldiers who were obliged to work at it for the good of their said master were condemned to pay a fine of 50# which Jacques Campault, Antaya, Michel Campault, Godefroy, Baby and numbers of others have been forced to pay. If any unfortunate affair with the savages occurs, or if presents are made to them to prevent them from going over to England, it is the petitioners who defray that kind of expense, and this they have always done out of obedience although there is no decree on this subject nor any opportunity to indemnify themselves; on the contrary the inhabitants who wish to go down to Montreal in order to look for what they require, according to their contracts, are compelled to obtain permits from M. de Tonty who sells them 500#'s

Paul Dervisseau, pursuing him out of the Fort, striking him with a stick, in the sight of all the tribes, a thing which has a very bad effect on their uncivilized minds; and the man named Philis, whom he trampled under foot in his room, came out covered with blood. Of this the Marquis de Vaudreuil was very well informed, but to no purpose since all the complaints which we have the honor to make to him against my said M. de Tonty serve only to bring down his wrath on the petitioners. The men Trudot paid my said M. de Tonty their quit-rent and rent according to their contract and afterwards he seized upon their ground and had houses built on it, without any repayment, which is contrary to the intention of His Majesty.

All the boats which are obliged to winter in all the other posts or settlements draw their provisions from Detroit which is no longer an advantage to the poor inhabitants since my said M. de Tonty in the King's name, has forbidden all the inhabitants to sell their corn and has also enjoined the hawkers not to buy from the said inhabitants and resident savages under penalty of confiscation, which is tyranny, since he over-charges for provisions a hundred per cent, being the only one who is granted this permission. He also forbids all the said inhabitants to have any liquor in their houses whether for their own use or to sell to the Frenchmen; it is a right he reserves to himself as he does that of selling it to the savages.

In the present year of the command of my said M. de Tonty, he compelled all the said inhabitants to bring him their contracts of concession, which they submissively did, and afterwards he would not return them

of the Miamis on penalty of a fine of 1100# on [anyone] infringing
[this]. My said M. de Tonty sent a sergeant and soldiers there [and]
afterwards his interpreter who passed all the winter of 1720; and on
the delivery of the goods he took from M. Paul Dervisseaux one roll
of tobacco in which the tobacco was worth 10#a#; from M. Dezonier,
Junior, a barrel of brandy; from St. Reaume a barrel of red wine. which
he would neither pay for nor return. It would be' too great an undertaking, our Lords, to try to detail all the acts of injustice and annoyance which M. de Tonty inflicted on the inhabitants who have abandoned
the said Detroit with regret, and on those who have the ill-fortune to
live there still; there would be enough to weary you. And it cannot
accord with [your] intention, that the subjects of so great a monarch
and so good a King should be enslaved in the midst of the Nation. It
is, however, true, our Lords, that the post of Detroit is most necessary
and most useful to the Colony and the best to live in as well as for
trade. The lands there are very good, the hunting abundant, the climate
temperate.- All the tribes would resort there, if there were a Commandant there more gentle and more judicious. The petitioners will
ever be ready to shed their blood and resume their labors for that post
when it shall please His Majesty to order them [to do so].

Endoine dufrene	Batiste Trudau
Desriviers :	ioseph Trudau
Parant	Michl Campo

CADILLAC'S RIGHT CONCEDED.

Endorsed.—Colonies MM. de Vaudreuil and Begon. No. 7 Council
MM. de Vaudreuil and Begon 17th Oct. 1722.

Quebec, the 17th Octr. 1722.
We have received, with the letter which the Council did us the honor
to write to us on the 15th of June last, the purview of the decree of the

them as a poultry-yard, because it is necessary to learn from M. De Tonty who is now at Detroit the position and extent of the piece of ground which it will be suitable to grant for it. We will send that order next year.

We think that the exclusive [right of] trading belongs to the commandant of that post; he ought to profit by the confiscations.

Vaudreuil   Begon.

THE INDIANS AT DETROIT INTEND TO MAKE WAR ON THE FOX INDIANS.

Endorsed—10th January 1723.

Concerning the intention of the savages of Detroit to make war against the Fox Indians.

Sir,

I have received the letter which you did me the honor to write to me on the 28th of August last.

The Marquis de Vaudreuil has written to me as to his will concerning the intention of the savages here to make war on the Fox Indians when they return from their winter quarters. It will not be difficult for me to make them give up the idea of going to them in a body, because of the information we have that, since they besieged the Illinois at Le Rocher, they have retired towards Les Sejours, so that it would not be possible to go so far after them as an army corps. This reason

seizure made by Mons. de l'Yoetot so that it might not be suspected from whence she had obtained it at Montreal.

It is true, Sir, that you notified me (after the information that the brandy of Antaya and La Janurie had been seized) that I ought not to have allowed brandy to be sold after the prohibition of the King against selling any to the savages. I had the honor of informing you in reply that I had reported it to the Marquis de Vaudreuil and M. Begon, who had not disapproved of it. This prohibition is only as regards the savages, and not the French, who, at this post number more than twenty settlers, nearly twenty men in the garrison, and often more than twenty-five volunteers or hired men to whom we cannot refuse to give something to drink from time to time any more than in the towns, as long as the King's orders are carried out. What could I do better than to put all the brandy under one charge, so that the person who had charge of it should alone be responsible for any illegalities which might occur? The precautions which I had taken in this respect, so that the King should be obeyed, were sufficient to secure me against what might happen. Condemn those who undertook the sale of brandy to the French, as you will see, Sir, from the annexed permit granted to Peletier Antaya and La Janurie; but the former did not state [the matter] to you properly when he told you that I had sold him brandy and had made him take it back when it had been brought up to the house. All these false statements were only to screen themselves, as to the brandy they traded in; of this there should be no doubt as both their wives confessed it to me, giving me reasons which I will state at the proper time and place. And I will acquaint you, Sir, with this matter so as to give you a full explanation of it.

When the [brandy] shop was established, to prevent the savages from going to the English, it was La Mallet who carried on the business, receiving not only the brandy which my clerk gave her but also that of private individuals and travellers. In this she committed several frauds, having done so unknown to me, besides some which she could not prevent me from finding out; these I did not discover until the year she went down, and they were to the extent of nearly two thousand pots, for if there had only been my brandy it would only have been sufficient—at most—for the French people. So, seeing that the brandy

wives and children. This the Governor General did, and wrote me that it was only just to allow the brandy which there was in the shop to be sold, and after that I had nothing to do but to abolish it. ·

The following winter La Mallet, having formed the intention of going down with her family, begged me with many importunities to allow her to give the brandy she had left to her children, wishing—as she said— for the profits. I opposed it strictly, doing my best to induce her to remain, and went so far as to tell her·as well as her husband that whoever gave up his hand lost it. But as they had arranged their affairs and made up their minds, she begged me so many times that I granted her request. As she owed me some money from the previous year, she had payment made to me by her children in the spring in consideration of her handing over her brandy to them, and she got back her note of hand. Hence it was not I who sold Antaya the brandy, as he had the effrontery to tell you, Sir, but really his mother, whose debt he discharged. Yet this deceitful man—and she also—had the impudence to impose on you. Moreover, this brandy was not mine; it belonged to private individuals, according to the annexed certificate of M. de l'Yoetot who seized it.

Peletier and La Janurie had already been some time in possession of the brandy shop when the orders for the suppression of the trade in brandy arrived. In order to let the savages know it was abolished, it was advisable to withdraw it until the King's orders had been intimated in the council which was held on this matter. It is true that they made some difficulty about taking it back, saying that, as they could not sell any more to the savages, it would remain on their hands for

by imposing on you they would gain your assistance, Sir? For La Janurie stated continually, on the way up, that you had assured them that you would have the brandy given back to them, and promised that you would make every effort to do so; that when he was leaving La Chine, you had sent for him and Marsac, and said to them—"Go, my friends, and be assured that I will protect you in all your affairs": that you told Antaya that if he could go up within a fortnight, he had only to go down to Quebec, that you would give him the means to do so. It was Forestier, who was present during all this talk, who told me of it, and M. de l'Yoetot, whom I asked about it, told me that he did not mean to say it to him but rather to the *voyageurs* to whom he told it.

La Janurie's wife, who had confessed to me that her brother had sold brandy to the savages, as I have stated before, in telling me the reason he had for doing so, which she has made public although I am convinced that it is untrue, told me—after her husband's return—that when Antaya, weeping, expressed to you the pain he felt at not going up again, you could not restrain yourself from shedding tears, from promising that you would send him up again, and telling him that you were much surprised that I, who would very soon be near the end of my life, like you, should seek to cause so much annoyance to all the settlers of this place. If they had so much reason to complain of me, why did they not do so when I went down to Montreal, where most of them were? And as they have been absent since that time, what can they say? The falsehoods with which they filled the petition which they presented to the Marquis de Vaudreuil and Monsr. Begon against me ought to lead to the conclusion that they are arrant impostors. But I am unfortunate, Sir, for you condemn me unheard, and I hear that the

pay you the respect I owe you and no one has heard me make any complaint about it. I have always acted in the same manner, Sir, when anything concerning you was in question; for although I was fully acquainted with the matter which Campant was bribed to bring against me, I have never said anything to you about it. Far from that, seeing you at odds with the Marquis de Vaudreuil, I used my interest to set you right with him with such effect that you were so pleased with my negotiation that you sent Monsr. de la Chassaigne to me to assure me from you that you were so obliged to me that there was nothing you would not do to serve me, and that I might count on you as on the best of friends; and this you afterwards confirmed, Sir, the first time I had the honor of seeing you.

What did I not do, Sir, in the matter of your nephew, who killed mine mercilessly? My daughter wished to take her mother to throw herself at the feet of the Regent and demand justice from him; I prevented her from doing so, and forbade her even so far as to quarrel with her. Monsieur de Clerambaut wished two thousand crowns to be given to Madame de la Moillerie for her withdrawing from the affair, without which he would have no arrangement made if she were not given legal compensation; and although I pointed out to him that the mother was not in a position to do so, having only one house which belonged to her children as well as to her, he replied that it must be sold, or that you Sir should contribute with the family to give that sum.

I am stating nothing which is not true; for, having induced a lady of high rank to see him in order to disarm him, she found he was still

position of this wicked man, which he imbibed at his mother's breast, for she is worth no more than he is. This woman, Sir, boasts of being favorably listened to by you, as well as Derochés, who is indisputably one of the most factious and most dangerous spirits here.

Monsieur de l'Ivetot, who is informed of all these matters, will be well able to make known to you—if he is willing to do so—how loudly all this family, and Derochés, publish abroad the patronage which you have given them.

You will allow me, Sir, to represent to you that private persons abuse the permission you give them to bring brandy for their own use, selling it retail to the French people, as La Janurie and de L'isle did. The latter sold a barrel containing three pots to Chauvet; and when it was being drunk at his house at night, a great disturbance took place and I was obliged to go there with the major to put a stop to it. Moreover, I cannot be answerable for what is given to the savages as long as private persons have what they think fit; more especially as I am informed that some of them got intoxicated this winter in the woods. But I do not know who may have given them brandy, any more than what use La Janurie made of the twenty-one pots you permitted him to bring, not having been informed even of how much of it he sold to French people.

If what I have done for you, Sir, cannot induce you to have some consideration as to my affairs, I ask you at least, as a favor, not to condemn me before I have been heard; and this I expect from your justice, Being with great respect, Sir,

I take the liberty of assuring Madame de Ramezay of my most humble respect.

From the post of Detroit on Lake Erie.

The 10th of March, 1723.

THE WORK OF DR. ROBERT CLARK KEDZIE AS A PIONEER.

BY PROF. FRANK KEDZIE.

In a paper presented before this society three years ago and printed in Vol. 29 of your Report, my father gave you some glimpses of his early life as a pioneer boy in the forests of Lenawee county. He spoke of his delight as a small boy in watching his father felling those mighty giants of the forest and letting the light into the space where the log cabin was soon to be surrounded by the growing garden and fields of grain which were to sustain the Kedzie family. The work of the pioneer fathers was to prepare the way—to break new ground. As I look back on my father's life and works I cannot but regard him in the light of a pioneer in many and various directions and one whose efforts throughout his long and active career partook of the self-denying character which the true pioneer must be willing and ready to put forth.

My earliest recollections of him are as Doctor Kedzie—a country doctor at Vermontville, Eaton county, with "a ride" of thirty miles in every direction over roads which were not much more than forest trails. Here for ten years he lived the life of the pioneer physician,—fought death at the bedside of the sick, strengthened the weak-hearted, and *never gave up a patient* until Death had proved his claim.

My mother's kitchen stove was generally partially occupied with kettles smelling of various simmering drugs,—the table in the front room decked

birthday,—January 28, 1863,—to the chair of chemistry in the State Agricultural College at Lansing,—an institution located somewhere in the woods near the capital city—none of our friends knew exactly where. At this newly established school for science applied to agriculture another phase of pioneer work opened before him—chemistry applied to farming. Six years before this institution had opened with most promising prospects. Much good oratory, some poor poetry and a good deal of patronizing interest shone forth on the day of the inauguration of the College. It was followed by strong efforts by earnest men to apply to agriculture the truths of science, give the young men a good, sound English and scientific education, and at the same time pay the running expenses of the institution from the profits derived from the farm.

The problem was too great a one to be immediately and easily worked out. The war of the rebellion was in progress. Numbers of the students had enlisted and were at the front, while others were kept at home because their brothers and fathers were in the army. You will not be surprised then that the total attendance during the entire first year of my father's coming was but 62, of which 19 students were in the regular college course, 43 special and preparatory students.

Nothing daunted by the small numbers, Dr. Kedzie went at his work with pioneer enthusiasm,—wrote his lectures, prepared the accompanying experiments, and delivered them before a class of two young men. Next year there were four in the class,—and so the College slowly grew in numbers during these first struggling years. Industrial education in the early 60's was at its very beginning. In the well-established college of that period instruction in the sciences of chemistry and physics was restricted to one of two methods—either recitations from poorly illustrated textbooks giving long, detailed descriptions of apparatus which the author had used in his experiments and perhaps had illustrated in the book, or, on the other hand, there were lectures illustrated by experiments performed by the lecturer before the class three or four times during the term,—the student being simply a witness of what was performed. Dr. Kedzie as a student at college had suffered from this lack of association of things and ideas in scientific study,—hence one of the primal methods to which he gave his attention in instructing his students is embodied in a sentence which first appeared in the College catalogue for 1866 and has been reprinted yearly since: "Each student applies for himself the tests required to determine the composition and properties of bodies, thus securing a practical knowledge of the methods employed in these investi-

Dr. Kedzie entered into this new field of applied chemistry as a pioneer teacher in a pioneer college; he taught the principles of chemistry in lecture room and laboratory during the forenoon and conducted experiments, assisted by his students, in the field in the afternoon. One of the first subjects for investigation was the chemical nature and physical properties of muck and its value as fertilizer alone or when mixed with plaster or salt and applied to corn and potatoes. A class of five young men did the entire work of the experiment,—applying the fertilizing materials to the crop, assisted in analyzing the muck, recording and reporting the results individually. The outcome of this investigation formed the basis for a lecture delivered before the State Agricultural Society that year which was printed in full in the Michigan Farmer and was, so far as I have found, the first result of an experiment performed at the College which was so reported and recorded. The close association of teacher and student necessitated by such methods of work and study brought them into so intimate relations and left such an impression that the 40 years which have elapsed since this kind of work was begun seem but yesterday in the minds of those students.

Conditions of climate being so intimately connected with the production of crops and the studies of the causes modifying the climate being so important to the farmer, a system of meteorological observations was established in April, 1863, and has been kept continuously since that date. This system of observations, made three times daily, is now the oldest continuous record existent in the north central portion of the United States.

Besides his work in the teaching of chemistry, Dr. Kedzie wrote and delivered a course of lectures in meteorology, which was ever a popular

child. One year when the extra class work was apportioned a class in arithmetic in the preparatory course fell to my father's care. Rather than devote the time to teaching this class he exchanged work with Prof. Fairchild, agreeing to preach for him each alternate Sunday if the professor would take charge of the arithmetic class. This bargain agreed upon, Dr. Kedzie then engaged and paid for, as his substitute, the Rev. S. O. Allen, a Yale graduate, pastor of the Congregational church in this city, a man of fine attainments. Since that time the Lansing clergy have regularly each Sunday preached to the students. (You might consider Dr. Kedzie, therefore, in the light of a missionary preacher by proxy.)

Elected to the legislature from this district, he served in the session of 1867, and was the chairman of a special committee consisting of Messrs. J. J. Woodman and O. H. Fellows, who recommended to the legislature the remission of taxes up to a certain amount for the planting of trees along the highway, and also that in each county the board of supervisors should determine whether cattle should be allowed to run at large on the highway. Acts embodying these recommendations were passed by that legislature and are now in force.

The world's crop of timber begins to show signs of being nearly harvested and no subject at the present is attracting the attention of thinking men more than that of forestry. As early as 1865 and in the succeeding session of 1867, Dr. Kedzie urged before the legislature the necessity for forest preservation for climatic and industrial reasons. He recommended that strips of timber of certain area on each farm, running in a north and south direction, thus serving as wind breaks, be exempt from

a method for preparation of Calcium arsenite, called the Kedzie formula. Yesterday I received a letter from one of his students in South Australia. I quote a paragraph: "It may be interesting to know that Dr. Kedzie's work is appreciated in this part of the world, for on the tongue of every orchardist here is the praise of the Kedzie formula for destroying Codlin moths. It is the remedy universally used and it gives universal satisfaction."

The ten years from 1870 to 1880 were perhaps, all things considered, the most fruitful and active of my father's life. Aside from his college class work he engaged in a large number of investigations. Many will remember, perhaps, the numerous wells put down at Eaton Rapids, St. Louis, Lansing and elsewhere which yielded "magnetic mineral water"—known to be magnetic because a steel needle held in the water as it flowed from the well became strongly magnetized. Dr. Kedzie proved this to be caused by the magnetism of the earth acting upon the iron pipe of the well casing, converting it by induction into a strong magnet and thus magnetizing the needle likewise, the water itself having no power of being magnetized.

The legislature of 1871 passed a bill appropriating $12,000 for the erection and equipment of a new chemical laboratory at the M. A. C. At this time the needs of the College for money were very great, both for buildings and current expenses. The Board of Agriculture, after carefully considering the question, decided *not to include* an estimate for a new chemical laboratory in the sum asked to be granted by the legislature, but allowed Dr. Kedzie as an individual to ask the legislature for an appropriation for a laboratory, which he did, and by dint of hard work during his winter's vacation secured its passage by a majority of one vote in the house of representatives. I was by his side when the roll was called. I shall never

been accomplished by them and the resulting benefits is too extensive a topic to be discussed here, but one can judge of their present extent and value when we compare the past with the present. Starting in 1876 with four institutes carried on at four different points in the State, the work of the present institute year just closing comprised 300 institutes held in as many different localities. At one of the first of these institutes, held in Coldwater, Dr. Kedzie advocated a home-made lightning rod of cheap construction, claiming that they were equally as good protection as the more ornate, galvanized, twisted, insulated and gilded pointed rods put forth by the talk-talented lightning rod agent at an extravagant price.

Coldwater at that time was the distributing point for a large lightning rod interest and the business manager of the concern was present when the home-made affair was advocated. Certain questions were asked the Doctor by the lightning rod man. Did lightning go through the mass of the rod or was it conveyed merely on the surface? His reply was that he was quite sure it was conducted through the mass of the rod. The lightning rod man then said: "Well, Doctor, Professor Joseph Henry, secretary of the Smithsonian Institution at Washington, says not. He says it is conveyed only on the surface. Do you *presume* to differ with such an authority?" Dr. Kedzie *presumed* that he did. How well I remember that succeeding summer. I was busy turning the big glass wheel of the electrical machine while my father experimented with gun barrels, iron and glass tubes coated with tin foil—drawing sparks from the inside and outside. Correspondence was opened with Prof. Henry and the outcome of the controversy was an acknowledgment by the Professor that Dr. Kedzie's experiments seemed to disprove the statement that lightning was conveyed only at the surface of a conductor and that he (Prof. Henry) would experiment further himself and write again. The incident closed there. Since that time many farmers have found the simple, home-made round iron rod advocated by Dr. Kedzie efficient and ample protection against lightning and lightning rod agents.

Dr. Kedzie's methods for arriving at and demonstrating the truth were

slaught on the Clawson wheat was a serious matter to the wheat growers
of Michigan. The variety had been but recently introduced, and was a vigorous kind that resisted hard winters and yielded more grain per acre than
almost any other known wheat. Establishing for himself by careful
chemical analysis the fact that the Clawson *did not* yield an inferior
wheat flour, Dr. Kedzie's next step was to establish conclusively that
Clawson flour would make good bread. Representative breadmakers were
given several different kinds of flour unmarked as to kind with the request
that they make it into bread and return again bearing their loaves with
them. This jury of ladies then together judged the loaves. Clawson flour
stood the test; bread made from it ranked as being among the best and the
verdict against Clawson flour was reversed. The findings of this jury
were published throughout Michigan and by means of it thousands of
dollars saved to the wheat growers of our State. This was my father's
first formal introduction to the milling interests of Michigan, and lest
a wrong impression be left with you by what I have said, let me state
that the Clawson incident led to a better acquaintance and co-operation
between the Millers' Association and the Doctor, both seeking together to
introduce new, hardy and better varieties of wheat from year to year.
Several years later the State Millers' Association at one of their meetings
passed this resolution:

"Resolved, That this Association recommend the farmers of Michigan to
raise Hungarian wheat, from Budapest, . . . and especially Dawson's Golden Chaff for a white wheat, these varieties being the most valuable according to Dr. Kedzie's analysis."

My father's work as one of the pioneers in the beet sugar industry is
too recent and too well known to require mention here. It is sufficient to
say that the experimental work carried out by the College under his

ALLEGAN COUNTY.

BY HON. JAMES W. HUMPHREY.

SPROAT.—Robert Sproat was born near Mansfield, Ohio, April 3, 1821, and died in Dorr township, Mich., August 6, 1902. His grandfather came from Ireland just before the Revolutionary war with four sons, David, William, John and James, and settled on the Pennsylvanian frontier. The name of Sproat is of Scotch origin, and in 1902 there were several of this name in Scotland, including William Sproat, who is the custodian of Castle Douglas, Laurieston, Dumfrieshire. Robert married Sarah Jane Miller in Orange, Ohio, in 1847, and she died near Wayland, Mich., April 28, 1889. Her father, Thomas Miller, an Irishman, served in a company of Pennsylvania riflemen in the war of 1812, participating in the battle of North Point, where the British general, Ross, was killed early in the day after having boasted that he would "eat his dinner in Baltimore, or in a hotter place." Robert's mother was Jennie Johnson, of Irish ancestry. His family emigrated to Dorr, Mich., in 1851. In 1870 the family went to Missouri, but returned two years later, and until the mother's death lived at Wayland. Robert was one of the earliest settlers in Dorr, which in 1851 included Hopkins township also. He took an active part in the development of the new country, and was frequently honored by offices, serving as clerk, justice and supervisor. They had twelve children, eight sons and four daughters. Two sons died before their mother, the other children have homes in western Michigan. Robert Sproat left forty-one grandchildren and eight great-grandchildren.

BAY COUNTY.

BY GEORGE P. COBB.

of his death. He was never especially active in politics and never a candidate for office, but took considerable interest in municipal affairs. Some 25 or 30 years ago he married Miss Lilian Keith, of Bay City, who survives him. Three children, two sons and a daughter, also survive. He was a loyal member of the Catholic church and his funeral was held at St. James' church.

GUSTIN.—During the year 1903 no death occurred in Bay county that attracted more attention or caused more general regret than that of Henry A. Gustin, which occurred in the month of September. Mr. Gustin had resided in Bay City since 1864. Born and reared in Canada, he, like so many natives of that country, became an exemplary American citizen. His first place of business in Bay City was in the Wolverton House, where he opened a grocery. Four or five years afterwards he was located in the Griswold block. Afterwards he took a responsible position in connection with the extensive Ballou lumbering plant located at Kawkawlin, where he remained for three years. Returning to Bay City, he was appointed deputy city treasurer in 1887, continuing in this office for twelve years. He was elected treasurer, from which office he retired April, 1893, with the good will and good opinion of everybody. Born January 3, 1824, his earthly life came to its close in September, 1903. Mr. Gustin was married in 1846, at Hamilton, Ont., to Eliza Keayes, who survives him. Their children are Charles C., Herbert H., Wilbert H., all residents of Bay City; Frederick K., of Chicago; Mrs. D. J. Thayer and Mrs. Stewart Church. Few men have lived so long and been so well known in one locality and left so few enemies and so many friends.

In the spring of 1863 he enlisted as a private in Battery L, First Regiment Light Artillery, Col. C. O. Loomis commanding. The regiment formed a part of the army of the Ohio and participated in many sharp engagements. Later Mr. Brooks accepted a lieutenancy in the Thirtieth Michigan Volunteers and served in that capacity until June 30, 1865, when he was honorably discharged.

After the war he returned to Orangeville, until 1872, when he moved to Hastings and went into the grocery business. Later he became associated with George M. Dewey in the management of the Hastings Banner, and when the firm dissolved Mr. Brooks entered the employ of the government in the capacity of railroad mail clerk. He again entered the grocery business with A. D. Cook, with whom he remained until a severe stroke of apoplexy about five years ago made his retirement from active life imperative.

Mr. Brooks was the father of four children, three of whom, C. F. Brooks, F. C. Brooks and Mrs. Bert Walker, are still living. He was preeminently a man who mingled in the activities of daily life and in his career as pioneer, soldier and merchant he made many sincere friends.

BURTON.—Dr. Charles S. Burton died at Hastings, December 11, 1902, aged 78 years. He was born at Waterloo, N. Y., and was of English ancestry. He was a pioneer homeopathic physician in Michigan. He spent several years, with his wife and oldest son, Charles, in California, and Clarence M. was born at Whiskey Diggings, that State. Returning to Michigan, he edited one of the first newspapers in the State, and was prominent in political work according to his beliefs. He was a strong advocate of education, giving his children many advantages along these lines. He leaves four living children, Charles F. and Clarence M., of Detroit; Edward A., of Hastings, and Mrs. Ellen B. Judson, of Lansing, Mich.

CHANDLER.—Dr. J. I. Chandler died at Banfield, Mich., March 23, 1903, aged 79 years 8 months and 23 days. He was born in Ohio June, 1823, moving to this State in 1854, and settling upon the old Morford place, now owned by Halsey Tungate, where he practiced medicine, entering into the work with earnestness of heart and soul. Many recall the famil-

served three years, receiving his discharge in 1866. The same year he was married to Elsie Haven, of Sylvan, Washtenaw county, and resided there until 1871, when he with his wife moved to Hope, Barry county.

HENDERSHOTT.—Mrs. B. J. Hendershott died at Hastings, Mich., March 12, 1903. Mercy Jane Walker was born in Richmond, N. Y., October 3, 1828, and married B. J. Hendershott April 13, 1848, who for four years had made his home in Michigan. Mr. Hendershott's family came to the State by canal boat, and taking the Michigan Central Railroad at Detroit at 7 o'clock in the morning, reached Marshall at sunset. The young couple began housekeeping at Irving, where they were practically alone in the wilderness, the nearest neighbor on the south being twelve miles away. In 1873 they sold their farm and moved to Hastings. Two sons and two daughters survive them. Mrs. Hendershott was one of the oldest pioneers of the county, and was universally respected and loved.

HINCKLEY.—February 18, 1903, in Carlton, Nelson Morgan Hinckley died at the age of 86. He was born in New York State, August 7, 1816.

In 1834 his parents moved to Ohio. October 28, 1840, he was married to Miss Eveline Sisson. To them was born one son, Lewis S. Hinckley, who died May 14, 1885, leaving three children, Dwight B., of Lansing; Corinne M., wife of J. M. Gould, of Grand Rapids, and Clayton G. Hinckley, of Albion.

In 1853, Mr. Hinckley was infected with the gold fever and joined the great crowds who were flocking to California. After twelve years he returned to Michigan and lived in Carlton until the time of his death.

His first wife died March 16, 1881, and in 1885 he was again married,

KELLICK.—Mrs. Elizabeth Edwards Kellick, aged 72 years, died at Orangeville, Mich., January 27, 1903.

Elizabeth Edwards was born at Worcestershire, Eng., February 18, 1831, and at the age of twenty she took service in the home of Lord Cunningham as cook. Four years later, in 1855, she was married to the butler, Edward Killick.

During their employment with Lord Cunningham, they were with him in London during the sessions of parliament and at other times at his county seat and during the hunting season among the highlands of Scotland, on which occasions the rendezvous of Lord Cunningham was at the castle where Sir Walter Scott wrote "The Lady of the Lake."

The position and circumstances surrounding the then young people afforded them advantages that many of our English residents did not enjoy and after their marriage in England Mr. Killick and his young wife emigrated to America and located at first in Canada near Toronto, and in the fall of '57 moved to Orangeville, where they lived at the time of her death.

IDEN.—Seneca Iden, a pioneer of Barry county, died in Bedford, April 5, 1903, aged 73 years.

He had lived in Bedford for the last thirteen years and in Johnstown township for over forty years.

His wife and one son, C. E. Iden, of Battle Creek, survive. Mr. Iden was well known and most thoroughly respected.

McBAIN.—Mrs. Alexander McBain passed away Thursday, September 18, 1903, at the residence of her daughter, Mrs. William Evans, in Barry township, at the age of 88 years and 20 days. Mrs. McBain was born in the State of Vermont, August 28, 1814. At the age of 25 years she was married to James Farlinger, who died about four years after their marriage. To this union was born one daughter, Sarah. In the year 1850 she was married to Alexander McBain, moving to Battle Creek, Mich., and afterward to Barry county. She was left a widow again February 14, 1898, and since then she has made her home with her children. She was the mother of four children, Sarah, John, Herbert and George.

McELWAIN.—Died September 10, 1902, Mrs. D. R. McElwain, aged 66 years.

Emily J. Evans was born in Cattaragus county, New York, June 2, 1836, and in the same year was brought to Pennfield, Mich., the entire distance being made overland behind a yoke of oxen.

She attended school at Olivet and in 1856 taught in Hastings. Febru-

Mrs. McElwain was well known in the State through her work in I. O. G. T. and social purity circle. In the former she held high offices. She was a member of the Eastern Star and M. E. church.

MATTHEWS.—James Matthews died at the age of 64 years, 11 months and 5 days at his home in Baltimore, March 10, 1903, after an illness of four weeks.

MILLS.—James Betty Mills was born in Washington county, Maryland, February 8, 1836, his parents being Levi Mills and Miss Esther Blair, from whose family the village of Blairs Valley, Md., received its name. The father was a clergyman of the Methodist Protestant church and in 1846 moved to Monroe county, Michigan. In 1854 Mr. Mills started for Kansas to take up a government claim. He returned in 1859, going to Schoolcraft, Kalamazoo county, where on October 2 he married Miss Louisa M. Smith, who survives him.

Shortly afterwards they set out for Kansas and were compelled to make their way over the western plains by means of what were known as "prairie schooners." During this trip the couple met with many interesting adventures, the recital of which was always a source of pleasure to Mr. Mills. The claim which Mr. Mills had taken up lay perilously near to an Indian reservation and as the civil war drew near the Indians began to grow exceedingly troublesome, until finally, in 1861, the settlers were compelled to leave the vicinity without even time enough to sell their claims or to take with them anything but the most necessary household utensils.

They returned to Michigan and during the civil war he tried to enlist but was twice rejected for physical disability.

In 1896 Mr. Mills was elected judge of probate and in 1900 was re-elected and served until his death, April 25, 1903.

Morgan in 1869, whose death preceded his in 1902. One son survives his parents. Mr. Parker was a member of the city council at one time, and one of the Knights of Pythias of the famous Uniform Rank, No. 19, that won three world's prizes.and made Hastings well known throughout the country.

PETERMAN.—Mrs. Magdalena Peterman died September 24, 1903, of old age, at the home of her daughter, Mrs. Sarah Kohler, at Hastings. Deceased was born in Pennsylvania, May 16, 1814, and was married at the age of 19. She was the mother of nine children, eight of whom are living.

PITTINGER.—Joseph A. Pittinger died June 7, 1902, at the home of his daughter, Mrs. Adell Lord, in Hastings.

Deceased was born in New York City, March 3, 1835. He came to Michigan in 1858. He married Charlotte Robinson in 1860; eight children were born to them. He was a sailor a number of years, and served in the Fifteenth Michigan Infantry, Company E.

They came to Barry county in 1869, and have since resided here.

TANNER.—John W. Tanner, aged 82 years, died November 27, 1902, at his home in Hastings. He is survived by a wife and four children.

VAN SYCKLE.—Died at his home in Rutland, August 27, 1902' George I. Van Syckle, aged nearly 73 years. He was born in the State of New York, November 13, 1829, and came to Wayne county, Michigan, when four years of age.

He married Ammorietta Phillips, July 4, 1858, and two children were born to them, Mrs. James Laubaugh, of Rutland, and Mrs. Otis Lawrence, of Hickory Corners, who survive him.

Deceased was possessed of a strong physique, was a hard worker, a kind husband, father and neighbor, and many will regret that "Uncle George," as they remembered him, is gone.

WARRENT.—Mrs. William J. Warrent died at the home of her mother near Kalamazoo, March 4, 1903, aged 53 years.

Susie Calkins was born in Prairieville in 1850 and at the age of 20 was united in marriage to William J. Warrent. To them were born two daughters, Marcia and Elsie. The deceased was a member of the Baptist church and was a noble Christian woman, greatly interested in Sunday school and church work.

became Albion College. In 1861 he married Sarah J. Haight, who with their two children died while he was serving in the civil war in Company K, Sixth Michigan Cavalry. He was married to Mary Ellis in 1866, and became a pioneer merchant in Nashville, Mich. In 1874 his second wife died, and in 1876 he married Mrs. Maria I. McNabb, who survives him. For fifteen years they followed farming in Dakota, but for the last ten years he has been engaged in fruit culture in Plainwell, Mich. He served one term in the Legislature of the State, and was inspector for the State Horticultural Society at the time of his death. For him life suddenly ended, but the fruits of his work remain to prove their value.

WINKLEMAN.—Mrs. Jeannette Winkleman died at Grand Rapids, March 29, 1903, aged 77 years.

Jeannette Dawson was born in Pittsfield, Mass., February 15, 1826, and came to Michigan when seven years old. In 1865 she was married to John Winkleman, who died but a few months ago.

BENZIE COUNTY.

BY WILLIAM A. BETTS.

Four pioneers have died in this county during the last year.

WATERS.—Rev. O. B. Waters, a prominent Congregational clergyman, the second teacher in the Grand Traverse College, who preached at many places throughout the State. He died in Detroit.

BANCROFT.—Robert Bancroft took up the first homestead in Lake town-

rian Sunday school and active in church work. She attended Beloit College and later studied law and was admitted to the bar.

For some time she made her home in Chicago, but returned to Niles and died at her brother's. She resumed work in all the educational and Christian departments of her city, and left memorials and friends to testify to her kindness, intellect and faithful life.

GEORGE.—Died at Benton Harbor, May 16, 1903, Woodbridge, Langdon George, aged 74 years. He was the son of Woodbridge George, a soldier of the war of 1812, and was born in Jefferson county, New York. In 1841 he came to Michigan and served as cook on one of the lake vessels. He became captain of the steamer Mariner. In 1851 he started for California, spending two years in the search for gold. In 1867 he purchased a farm near Benton Harbor and became an expert fruit grower. He held many township offices, and stood high in Masonic and Pythian ranks. August, 1851, he married Ravina Pitcher, of Watervliet, who died in 1887, leaving three daughters.

VAN RIPER.—Mrs. Leah Van Riper, mother of Judge J. J. Van Riper, of Niles, died at the home of her daughter, Mrs. Edwards, of Dowagiac, aged 88.

BRANCH COUNTY.

BY MAJOR GEORGE A. TURNER.

GEORGE.—Died at Coldwater, July 1, 1902, at 80 years of age, Leander George. He married Mary Vanderhill, January 1, 1845, and of the four

county in the Legislature—first in the fall of 1865 and again in 1870, was supervisor of Coldwater township for thirteen years, was county and township drain commissioner for five years, and during the civil war was deputy United States marshal, which position he resigned to take his seat in the Legislature in 1870.

He was public sprited and gave as liberally as his means permitted for the establishment and maintenance of public institutions, civil and religious, usually attending and supporting the Baptist church. From their organization he was an earnest member of the pioneer societies, both State and local, and those who have in years past attended the meetings in this city and vicinity will remember with pleasure his genial and happy way of telling of early times, and "many a tale could tell of accident by flood and fell." Varied as were the scenes of his active life, he was able to reproduce them in an interesting manner; the bits and pieces, kaleidoscope like, ever- changing, yet always forming one bright and pleasing whole.

PEARCE.—Mr. James B. Pearce was born December 18, 1830, at Star Cross, Devonshire, England, and came to this country in 1853, and to Jonesville in 1854, where he remained until 1855. In 1854 he married Miss Eliza Hall, in New York City, and a year later made Coldwater their home.

A brick mason by trade, he helped to lay the brick on Hillsdale College, and after locating in Coldwater helped to build the Southern Michigan Hotel, beside many other brick buildings.

In his death Coldwater loses a good citizen and the Episcopal church an upright, consistent member. His death was due to heart disease.

Seven children were born to Mr. and Mrs. Pearce, three still living—

CLINTON COUNTY.

MRS. RACHEL BRINK, NECROLOGIST.

Name.	Date of death.	Age.
Estes, Mrs. G. W..	November 26, 1902..........	77
Hildreth, Chester C.......................................	September 3, 1902..........	78
Lott, Mrs. C...	December 27, 1902..........	68
Merrihew, John W..................................:...	October 16, 1902..........	100 years 9 months.
Moss, Mrs. C. A..	September 12, 1902..........	66
Moss, Mrs. Edgar..	February 1, 1903......:..	68
Norris, Mrs. Sarah......................................	September 22, 1902..........	85
Perkins, Joseph Y.......................................	February 14, 1903..........	79
Perrin, Porter K..	March 20, 1903..........	70
Reynolds, Sirnion S.......................................	March 4, 1903..........	63
Robinson, Oscar W.......................................	February 21, 1902..........	71
Sowle, Horace A..	November 30, 1902..........	69
Weller, Andrew..	July 5, 1902..........	81
Weller, Mrs. Andrew	January 19, 1903..........	80

CRAWFORD COUNTY.

BY DR. OSCAR PALMER.

BABBITT.—Died at Grayling, Mich., Wednesday, December 24, 1902,

self a more than Spartan mother, keeping and caring for her little ones
and ever ready, as she has been always through life, to extend a helping
hand to those less fortunate than she.

EATON COUNTY.

BY HON. ESEK PRAY.

Name.	Residence.	Date of birth.	Date of death.	Resided here.	Age.
Ashley, Jabez....................	Windsor.............	Jan. 30, 1824	....	50 years..	89
Bunker, John.....................	Eaton Rapids	Nov. 28, 1822	Apr. 18, 1903	67 "	81
Dean, Silas M....................	Kalamo	Nov. 1, 1822	Mar., 1903	66 "	81
Chappell, Mrs. Olive M.........	Walton.............	....	Feb. 22, 1903	....	78
French, Silas....................	Windsor	....	May 22, 1903	47 "	81
Gridley, Reuben.................	Kalamo	Feb. 8, 1823	Nov. 25, 1902	50 "	79
Hale, Mrs. Sarah C. (D. B.)......	Hamlin.............	Apr. 25, 1820	Mar. 31, 1903	51 "	83
Hart, Mrs. Rachel...............	Brookfield.........	Jan., 1814	Mar. 28, 1903	66 "	89

DAY.—Samuel S. Day, of Bellevue, was born March 18, 1824, in Orleans
county, N. Y., and came to Michigan with his father, Sylvester Day, in
October, 1836, traveling the entire distance with an ox team. Died July
5, 1902, aged 78 years.

HAWKINS.—Horace Hawkins, the last living member of the Vermont-

GENESEE COUNTY.

BY MRS. MARY R. FAIRBANKS, OF FLINT.

ADAIR.—Michael Adair. He was a pioneer of Thetford township.

ANDREWS.—Mrs. Nancy Mason Andrews died July 7. 1902, aged 90. She came to Flint in 1836.

BEEBE.—Eli T. Beebe died at West Forest, aged 83.

BLACK.—Henry A. Black died February 26, 1903. He came to Michigan in 1835, the trip from Detroit to Atlas occupying four days. He assisted in making one of the first roads in the county. In 1857 he married Caroline Center. He filled several township offices.

BUTTS.—William H. Butts died at South Grand Blanc, aged 77.

DODDER.—Jacob S. Dodder died at Linden, aged 72. Born of German parents, in New Jersey, he began farming in Genesee county in 1855 and acquired one of the largest farms in the county.

ELDRIDGE.—Abram C. Eldridge died at Flint, April 20, 1903, aged 83. He was twice married, his wives being the sisters Rhoda and Fannie Benham. He was prominent in town and church affairs.

GRIFFIN.—George W. Griffin died at Davison, aged 44.

HIRST.—Edward Smith Hirst died at Fenton, February 13, 1903. He was born in England in 1829. For thirty-three years he has been a resident of Fenton, being actively engaged in business most of this time.

HUBBARD.—Mrs. Charles Hubbard died at Fenton.

LEE.—Silas S. Lee died at his son's home in Detroit, aged 83. He built the first log house in Arbela township, when there were only six families in the county. He was engaged in lumber and business interests, and leaves a widow, two sons and three daughters.

NEWCOMBE.—Thomas Newcombe and his wife died at Flint within two days of each other and were buried in one grave. He was born in Devonshire, England, May 29, 1821, married in Barnstable in 1849, and that year came to Flint. He was sexton of Glenwood Cemetery and five of his children were buried there; four living, D. E. Newcombe and Mrs. C. E. Baldwin, Flint; Prof. Frederick C., of the University of Michigan, and H. G. of Shawnee, Okla.

RUSSELL.—Nicholas Russell, aged 90 years, was found dead in bed at Flint. He served in the civil war and had been pensioned for many years.

GRAND TRAVERSE COUNTY.

CAMPBELL.—Hon. H. D. Campbell died at Traverse City, aged 72 years. He was born in Franklin county, N. Y., and reached Traverse City November 29, 1852. The nearest railroad then was at Kalamazoo, with stage coaches to Grand Rapids and post boys 100 miles south. He worked in the lumber woods first, but finally engaged in mercantile pursuits. He served on the first grand jury and was the first postmaster. In 1860 he attended the State Fair at Detroit on horseback, swimming all streams north of the Muskegon. In 1862 he married Miss C. Carmichael, and leaves four sons and one daughter. He accepted and used different offices of trust to advance the interests of his city.

HILLSDALE COUNTY.

MURRAY.—Elisha Murray, the oldest resident of Litchfield township, died May 13, aged 85. Reaching the State in 1836, he bought his farm from the government office, then located at Monroe. His wife was Jane Roberts, a daughter of Litchfield pioneers. Two sons now remain of the family. He was called the father of the Congregational church and was foremost in its work.

SMITH.—David Lewis Smith died at Litchfield. Born in New York, he settled in Litchfield in 1836. He married Mary M. Murdock, who with

Name.	Residence.	Date of death.	Age.
Ammons, William	Sherman	February 5, 1903	65
Beardsley, Dewitt	Wise	August 29, 1902	73
Best, Jacob	Coe	February 16, 1903	77
Bradt, Amelia	Mt. Pleasant	November 10, 1902	92
Bradt, Symon	Union	October 4, 1902	67
Broachey, Margaret A	Vernon	March 10, 1903	69
Calkins, Lucinda	Isabella	September 15, 1902	79
Campbell, William	Denver	January 3, 1903	76
Collier, Alba	Broomfield	July 30, 1902	72
Cook, Harriet	Gilmore	March 27, 1903	70
Crawford, James	Isabella	November 27, 1902	95
Darnell, William A	Sherman	November 28, 1902	78
Dart, Acostus	Union	January 30, 1903	77
De Forest, Jacob	Rolland	August 17, 1902	69
Deremer, George	Vernon	March 10, 1903	75
Dixon, William Coates	Wise	September 10, 1902	88
Ford, John	Wise	January 25, 1903	71
Gibbs, William K.	Sherman	April 1, 1903	69
Gingrick, Catherine	Sherman	August 13, 1902	61
Grass, William A	Broomfield	September 5, 1902	82
Gruett, Peter	Nottawa	January 26, 1903	93
Hall, Abagail	Chippewa	October 31, 1902	75
Hilton, John M	Mt. Pleasant	July 31, 1902	71
Jensen, Frank	Vernon	October 14, 1902	76
Lansing, Minerva	Mt. Pleasant	October 10, 1902	62
Lestrange, Susan	Coe	February 1, 1903	82
Lewis, Catherine	Coe	July 13, 1902	67
Loomis, Mary	Gilmore	February 7, 1902	63
McDonald, Patrick	Union	December 5, 1902	79
Mathews, Helena	Isabella	October 31, 1902	62
Mayhew, Peter	Nottawa	March 12, 1903	92
Menery, Anna K	Wise	March 2, 1903	62
Miller, Jacob R.	Rolland	December 30, 1902	66
Morrison, Neil	Isabella	August 11, 1902	73
Myers, Joseph	Coe	March 4, 1903	73
Nolan, Martin	Chippewa	March 18, 1903	83
Phillips, Lydia	Union	December 4, 1902	83
Riker, Madison	Deerfield	August 8, 1902	67

Name.	Residence.	Date of death.	Age.
Sands, Elijah	Wise.,	June 2, 1903	70
Schumaker, John	Nottawa	March 23, 1903	
Shaw, James	Union	July 8, 1902	80
Smith, Harriett A	Mt. Pleasant	October 13, 1902	78
Smith, Julia A	Vernon	August 1, 1902	84
Spicer, Louisa	Fremont	August 8, 1902	78
Standish, Charles	Chippewa	February 5, 1903	76
Taylor, Esther	Sherman	September 24, 1902	79
Thompson, Elizabeth A	Sherman	November 28, 1902	78
Thorne, Joseph	Wise	April 13, 1903	72
Truman, Elizabeth	Coe	January 14, 1903	83
Wardwell, Mary J	Lincoln	July 17, 1902	76
Wilson, Mary A	Rolland	July 18, 1902	63
Wreport, Katherine	Nottawa	November 9, 1902	62

KALAMAZOO COUNTY.

BY HON. EDWARD W. DE YOE.

CURTENIUS.—One of the best-known citizens of Kalamazoo, Charles C. Curtenius, died July 15, 1902. His father was Col. F. W. Curtenius, of Glenn Falls, N. Y., where Charles was born, November 23, 1835, coming to Grand Prairie the next year. He held many offices in his town and city, including those of supervisor and alderman, always performing honest and efficient service. In 1862 he married Miss Phoebe Smith, and leaves two children, Elizabeth E. and Edward F., the present supervisor of Kalamazoo township.

KENT COUNTY.

BY W. N. COOK.

Name.	Date of death.	
Allen, Wright C	July	5, 1902
Belknap, Mrs. Charles E	December	18, 1902
Berry, Sidney S	March	9, 1903
Chesbro, Mary O	December	16, 1902
Cowell, Mrs. Leonard	June	18, 1902
Davis, Reuben E	November	4, 1902
Fletcher, E. A	June	2, 1902
Hanshett, Benjamin S	April	14, 1903
Hunt, Deforest	March	10, 1903
Lyman, Mrs. James	January	29, 1903
Patterson, Chancy	February	26, 1903
Randall, Milo H	March	27, 1903
Sears, William	May	13, 1903
Tracey, B. C	November	4, 1902
Weatherly, Warren W	March	8, 1903

BUCHANAN.—In 1843 John C. Buchanan first came to Grand Rapids. He was one of the foremost citizens, prominent in all public enterprises. He served in the war of the rebellion and was wounded in the left arm. He was an influential member of the Baptist church. He died September 3, 1902.

RINGNETTE.—Maxime Ringnette died at Grand Rapids, June 28, 1902. He came to that city in 1835 when it contained only a few log shanties and numerous Indian wigwams, surrounded by dense forests. He was born in Louisville, province of Quebec, and in 1834 walked from there to Detroit. Purchasing a pony, he rode to Ionia. Hearing of the trading post at Grand Rapids, he traded his pony for a canoe and landed here in 1835. He was a shoemaker, and had a small shop which was burned in 1870, but resumed his business on Monroe street. He was very active in the Catholic church work, and when St. Andrew's church burned he gave

nette was nearly 88 years old and was the very last of the old French
traders who once lived in the Grand River valley.

MACKINAC COUNTY.

BY DR. J. R. BAILEY.

Name.	Date of death.	Age.
Burdette, Joseph M.	August 25, 1902.	77
Chamberlain, Eli B.	August 1, 1902	68
English, Daniel W.	December 1, 1902	41
Fair, Alexander.	June 16, 1902	52
Gennell, Mary L.	January 29, 1902	23
Grondin, Theresa.	August 25, 1902	100
Leveille, Elizabeth.	July 29, 1902	69
Meterier, Louis J.	April 12, 1902	57
Moloney, Helen E.	March 7, 1902	66
Murray, Emma	July 26, 1902	32
Newton, Mary J..	January 29, 1902	53
Ryrose, Catherine.	August 11, 1902	64
St. Ouge, Tuffield..	March 5, 1902	67

MURRAY.—Dominick Murray, of Mackinac Island, died on Thursday,
October 16, 1902, aged 84 years.

He was a native of Newport, Ireland, born in 1820, and first came to

was in reality a rescue of the man from the vengeance of the Mormon leaders' infuriated followers. He enjoyed the public trust of his fellow citizens in various official capacities, but his principal public services were seventeen years as sheriff of Mackinac county, when its territory extended from the most eastern point of the upper peninsula to the Menominee river. During all this time as sheriff the late Hon. Daniel C. Goodwin, of Detroit, was circuit judge of this district, holding court on the island once every year (this then being the county seat). The latter · always held Mr. Murray in the highest esteem, especially in upholding the law in those trying and troublesome times. The esteem in which Mr. Murray was held by all denominations on the island is strikingly exemplified by the fact that he was president of the school board for twenty years.

He was extensively engaged in business pursuits as keeper of a store for over half a century, owning a store in St. Ignace, Mich., managed by his son, P. W. Murray, since 1878, and as proprietor of the popular New Murray Hotel, built in 1889. His business integrity was recognized everywhere and he maintained a high standard for honesty.

The funeral took place from St. Anne's church and was attended not only by the entire island population, but by a large number from neighboring points, the ferry boat being specially chartered to take parties from St. Ignace, which included our most prominent people. The sacred edifice was crowded to its fullest capacity, all other churches on the island holding no services that morning.

MACOMB COUNTY.

BY GEORGE H. CANNON.

ANDREWS.—Hon. Charles Andrews was born in Putney, Vt., August 28, 1820, and died at Armada, Macomb county, November 14, 1902. He settled with his parents in Armada township in 1841, where he began the life of active usefulness which became a distinguishing characteristic as long as he lived. Always a farmer, he spent most of his winters teaching music. In 1866 he was elected State senator, and served with distinction two terms. He was supervisor of his township twenty years, and very prominent in agricultural and other societies, as well as a faithful supporter and attendant of the Congregational church.

He was a charter member of the Union church of Washington, continuing faithful and influential to the last. He died October 28, 1902.

CANNON.—Sarah J. Twaddill was born in Scarboro, England, October 22, 1833. In 1834 her parents decided to remove to America, where the mother had a brother, Thomas Littlewood, living in the vicinity of Mt. Vernon. They sailed from England some time in August with their little three-year-old son John and the baby girl. On the journey over cholera broke out on board and the ship was quarantined off Montreal, where Mr. Twaddill died, leaving the young wife to make her own way to the new, strange land. In 1837 Mrs. Twaddill was married to Jeremiah Lockwood, who proved a kind and indulgent father to the little one, who, October 13, 1853, was married to S. B. Cannon. To them were born five children, only two of whom are now living. Mrs. Cannon was a thoroughly domestic woman, her home being her kingdom, which is left desolate by her death. She was a faithful member of the Washington Union society and Sunday school. Her death occurred October 14, 1902, the day following the forty-ninth anniversary of her marriage, and within a week of her sixty-ninth birthday.

GIBBS.—William W. Gibbs was born in Livonia, Livingston county, N. Y., December 21, 1824, and died December, 1902. Mr. Gibbs came to Macomb county in 1852, and at once gave his attention to portrait and landscape painting, in which he acquired considerable notoriety. He was a man of genial good nature, and respected by all who knew him.

GIDDINGS.—Mrs. Sylvia D. (Norton) Giddings was born at Covington, Genesee county, N. Y., April 13, 1822, and died at her home in Davis, Macomb county, September 18, 1902, aged 81 years. She came to Michigan with her parents when very young, and was a veritable pioneer, enduring as well as enjoying the hardships and victories incident to such a life. Her home was the same through life, and in it she won the respect of all who knew her.

LAWSON.—James S. Lawson was born September 1. 1829, in the township of Shelby, Macomb county, and died May 23, 1903, on the same farm on which he was born. He was the youngest son of a family of eleven children. His father, James S., and mother, Rachel Willis, a cousin of the poet, N. P. Willis, were of Scotch descent, and came to Michigan in 1826.

MIERS.—Alva Miers was born in 1812, and died August 14, 1902. He settled in Ray, Macomb county, in 1833, and spent his life as a pioneer, clearing away the forests and making way for the advance of civilization. ·

MARQUETTE COUNTY.

BY HON. PETER WHITE.

HOPKINS.—Henry James Hopkins died May 2, 1902. He was born October 4, 1830, and came to Marquette in 1852. For many years he was a hardware merchant, and occupied many places of public trust, being a prominent and good citizen. He left a wife and two daughters.

KAW-BAW-GAM.—Charles Kaw-baw-gam, aged 104 years. I came to Marquette on the 18th of May, 1849, and found him here. He was a noble specimen of his race, a full-blooded Chippewa, and stepson of the great chief Shan-wa-non, and would have been a chief but for the fact that his tribe were so widely dispersed that they needed none. Kaw-baw-gam was a good man, a good citizen, a good hunter and a good fisherman. He always took good care of his family, and was never idle or lazy. Did not drink, never was arrested, and never fought his own race or any other. He was generous and helpful to all about him. He walked so erect, and looked so vigorous and strong up to the time of his fatal illness, only a few weeks before his death, that many people expressed doubts about his being a hundred years old. All the proof that I have to offer that he did reach this age is that on the 18th of May, 1849, the first time I ever saw him, I asked him how old he was. He replied in his own language, "Just fifty," and he explained just where he had lived in those fifty years. He *looked* to be fifty and I believed him implicitly, and since that day fifty-four long years have rolled around. I feel sure that he was 104 when he died. The citizens are just now making a contract for a bronze statue of heroic size of him, to be erected over his grave on Presque Isle, to be unveiled in July, 1904.

KLEIN.—Andrew Watson Klein died September 24, 1902. He was 37 years old. He was born in Detroit and lived in Marquette about eighteen years. He was cashier with Peter White & Co. for twelve years, and was

by everybody. He is survived by only one daughter, Mrs. F. N. Bronson, of Lake Maitland, Florida.

MUSKEGON COUNTY.

BY MRS. MARY A. CHAMBERLAIN.

AKINES.—Thomas Akines died July 29, 1902, aged 58.

DRENT.—Mrs. Catherine Drent, Cedar Springs, died July 10, 1903, aged 86. She was born in the Netherlands and came to Muskegon in 1866.

FARR.—Mrs. Sophia Farr died at Muskegon, aged 43.

LE TART.—John Le Tart died July 12, 1902, at Muskegon. He was one of the most prominent and oldest French settlers, coming to the city in 1868. He was born in Quebec 85 years ago, and was a shipbuilder for many years.

RESIDE.—John Wiley Reside died at Dalton, January 24, 1903. He was born in Scotland in 1829 and came to New York when very young by the way of the West Indies. In 1865 he moved to Dalton.

RICE.—Mrs. R. B. Rice died at Ravenna, aged 79. Phoebe Young was born in England, 1823. At 17 she married R. B. Rice and they came to Muskegon in the early days, where he worked at lumbering.

TIBBITTS.—Mrs. James-F. Tibbitts died at Ravenna October 30, 1903, aged 70. She was the first bride married in Ravenna, in 1852. Her husband worked at lumbering, but at last was interested, with his son, in the undertaking business.

WILSON.—Ward Wilson died in Muskegon of old age. He had lived there for twenty-three years.

HAMILTON.—Carleton J. Hamilton was born at Bridport, Vt., January 6, 1835. In 1856 he went to Chicago and worked with several lumber firms. In 1860 he went to Muskegon, pursuing the same business; in 1865 becoming a partner in trade.

He held several important city positions and was prominent in Masonic circles. Mr. Hamilton was twice married; his first wife was Eliza Rohrer, by whom he had three children. His second wife was Ella E. Moulton,

81 years. His birthplace was Vermont, coming to Grand Rapids in May, 1838. After suffering the hardships of pioneer life at Alpine, his father died, leaving him to care for the family. He and his brother came to Muskegon and manufactured shingles. He worked his way up and became one of Muskegon's leading lumbermen. He started several enterprises to take the place of the disappearing lumber. He reached the highest degree of Masonry, and erected and gave to the order a fine Masonic temple, costing over $50,000. His first wife was Jane M. Wheeler, of Waukegan, Ill., who bore him six children, only two of whom are living. In 1878 he married Margaret McIntyre, of Kewaunee, Ill., who survives him.

SAGINAW COUNTY.

BY MRS. ANNA A. PALMER.

ANDRE.—Peter C. Andre died at Saginaw in December, 1903, aged 85 years. He served as mayor of his city at one time, and was a sturdy and prominent county pioneer.

KUHN.—Richard Kuhn died in March, 1903, aged 73. A German-American citizen, greatly respected.

LITTLE.—Charles D. Little, about 80 years of age, and one of the most prominent early settlers.

PENOYER.—Mrs. Emeline Penoyer, widow of Lewis Penoyer, died in February, 1903, aged 69. She belonged to the Wisner family, who hold high rank among Saginaw pioneers.

SMITH.—Mrs. Susan W. Smith, widow of the late Jay Smith, died in December, 1903. For nearly half a century Mr. and Mrs. Smith were highly appreciated in social and business circles.

SHIAWASSEE COUNTY.

BY HON. A. H. OWENS.

Name.	Birth place.	Came to county.	Died.		Age.
Conover, Charles...........................	New York, 1830..........	1853.........	April,	1903....:.	73
Fish, Samuel.........................	New York, 1841..........	1857.........	April,	1903.....	2
Miller, Tunis	New York, 1820..........	1864.........	January,	1903.....	83
Pulver, Mrs. Mary E..................	New York, 1850..........	1853.........	February,	1903.....	53
Reynolds, Franklin P...............	New York, 1854..........	1866.......:.	January,	1903.....	49
Sages, Charles H....................	New York, 1835..........	1840.........	August,	1903.....	67
Sloan, James E.....................	New York, 1820..........	1860.........	April,	1903.....	83
Weidman, William.................	Pennsylvania	1866.........	August,	1903.....	81

VAN BUREN COUNTY.

MONROE.—Suddenly at South Haven, June 29, 1902, Mrs. C. J. Monroe died, aged 65 years. Hattie Moorehouse was born at Albion, Michigan, moving to South Haven in 1852, and was its oldest resident. December 18, 1866, she married C. J. Monroe and they had four children, all of whom are now living. She was deeply interested in schools and clubs, holding many offices in the latter and in the Women's Christian Temperance Union. She was a devoted and valued member of the Congregational church. Rev. Caroline Bartlett Crane, of Kalamazoo, paid a glowing tribute to her memory in the funeral address she delivered. South Haven is the richer for her life and services, and by her death experiences a vacancy never again, perhaps, to be filled.

J Willard Bobbitt

flower. On his mother's side his ancestors came from Wethersfield, Connecticut, and knew the man who hid the famous charter of the colony in the trunk of the old tree at Hartford. His grandfather emigrated from Taunton to Danville, Vermont, where the father of Judge Babbitt was born. Danville, at that time very prosperous, is one of the old hill towns of northern Vermont, and the county seat of Caledonia county. Here was published, one hundred years ago, one of the most influential papers of northern New England, the famous "North Star." It was the influence of this old paper, more than any other single cause, which secured the election of a citizen of Danville governor of Vermont for several successive terms on the anti-Masonic ticket, and which induced the state to cast its electoral vote for William Wirt, the anti-Masonic candidate for president. From its foundation in the administration of John Adams to its suspension, not many years ago, the "North Star" was successively an anti-federalist, anti-Masonic and radical Democratic paper. The father of Judge Babbitt came to Ypsilanti with a copy of the Bible and the "North Star" in his pocket. This famous paper bore upon its front page the motto from Thomas Paine, "Where Liberty dwells, there is my country." Grounded in the principles of the Bible, with which all New Englanders of those days were familiar, and inspired by the "North Star" and its noble motto, the father of young Babbitt was, of course, a thorough-going Democrat to the day of his death, in 1891, at 90 years of age. The son early imbibed the political principles of the father and lived and died a stalwart Democrat—a Democrat of the old Jefferson and Jackson school, believing in sound money, in a tariff for revenue only, believing also in the grand old Democrat doctrine, that expansion is the "manifest destiny" of the republic. He was an enthusiastic union man, and soon after the opening of the war of the rebellion he joined the army. Owing to defective eyesight he was not permitted to serve in the ranks, as he desired, but acted as clerk of the commissary department in Kentucky until the close of the war. Previous to the war he had studied law with an uncle, a prominent lawyer at Geneva, New York, and eventually graduated from the law department of the University of Michigan. After the close of the war he visited St. Louis, Omaha and other prominent places in the west with a view of making a permanent settlement for the practice of his profession. But the influence of father and mother, and another influence stronger still, drew him back to his old home.

So, in 1866, he returned to Ypsilanti and the same year married Miss Florence Lewis Smalley, a native of Alleghany county, New York, and thereafter continued to reside at Ypsilanti until his death, November 8, 1901. Mr. Babbitt was an influential man in the politics of his county. He was elected successively circuit court commissioner, prosecuting attor-

with exceptional ability. Business men who entrusted to him their affairs found him a sound and safe adviser. He was a good lawyer. He possessed a natural legal mind. He studied his cases with great care and always considered, first and foremost, the interest of his client. Mr. Babbitt was physically a fine specimen of a man. He always enjoyed robust health, with the exception of a lameness, the result of rheumatism caused by exposure in the army. Mr. Babbitt was not a mere politician or lawyer. He was a man of large general reading and broad intelligence. He had a fine literary taste. He loved poetry and often tried his "prentice hand" in writing it. Mr. Babbitt died in the full vigor of his powers. He had lived in Michigan fifty-three years. During that period he had witnessed wonderful changes in his state and nation. He came to Ypsilanti in a car running upon a strip of iron, spiked upon wooden rails, its terminus in the wilderness of Kalamazoo. He had seen twenty-five states expand to forty-five. He had seen his country, broken and disunited, pass through the most tremendous conflict of all history and come forth more free, more united and more prosperous than ever before—commanding the respect of all governments and all peoples—taking its place by common consent at the very head of that front rank of the most powerful nations of the world. If Mr. Babbitt had faults common to human nature they have been forgiven and forgotten. It could not be otherwise, for he possessed in large degree those virtues of the ancient Roman soldier described by the poet—virtues which have always and everywhere conquered the human heart:

"He was generous, brave and kind."

WAYNE COUNTY.

HICKEY.—Rev. Manasseh Hickey died in Detroit January 2, 1903. He was one of the oldest Methodist ministers in the State, and the last of the circuit riders, his work extending over a period of sixty years. His important service was as a missionary among the Indians, and he was the means of many giving up their pagan gods and idols, becoming converts to Christianity. Rev. F. A. Blades, a colleague for many years, speaks in the highest terms of Elder Hickey and his work. In his intercourse with the Indians he gained their confidence to such an extent that he was always honored by them. During a trial for murder he was given the rare honor of a seat at the right hand of the chief. His voice was very strong and the Indians respect strength. For several years he was presiding elder of the M. E. church. Mr. Hickey took great interest in pio-

APPENDIX.

BY C. M. BURTON.

These explanatory notes were received too late for insertion as foot notes. The remaining Cadillac papers and documents relating to Early Detroit will be included in Vol. 34.

Vol. 33, Page 459. Algremont, François Clairambault, Sieur D', born 1653, buried Dec. 4, 1728, at Quebec. Was sub-delegate and intendant in navy—at Montreal, 1704—Detroit, 1708.

309. Allogny, Charles Henri D', Marquis la Grois, major of the troops, was the son of Louis and Marie Casteigner. He was married Nov. 5, 1703, at Quebec.

707. Antaya (Antayat), was the surname given to a Pelletier family because of the alliance of one member with an Indian woman.

566. Artigny, Louis Rouer, consellor, son of Louis. Was born 1667, and buried July 5, 1744, at Quebec.

688. Barrois, M. François, son of Antoine Barrois, born March 2, 1676, at Laprairie. Married at Montreal, to Marie Anne Sauvage, May 31, 1717. Established at Detroit and called Lothman dit Barrois.

145. Beauharnois, François de, Chevalier, Siegneur de La Chaussay and Beaumort. King's consellor, seventh Intendant of New France; in 1704 at Montreal.

482. Beaujeu, Louis Lienard, Sieur de, chevalier de St. Louis, King's lieutenant and governor of Three Rivers. Was in Three Rivers in 1745.

607. Beletre (Bellestre), François Picoté de, ensign, born Feb. 5, 1677, at Montreal, son of Pierre and Marie Pars; buried Oct. 9, 1729, at Detroit. He married 1st Marie Anne Bouthier and 2d Marie Catherine Trotier.

492. Bienvenue, François de l'Isle, dit Delisle. Married 1st Genevieve Laferriére, 2d Marie Lemoyne. He was father of twelve children, all born at Detroit.

473. Boishebert, Louis Henri Deschamps, Sieur de, born at Quebec. Feb. 8, 1679; married Genevieve de Ramezay. Entered the army in 1699. In 1705, Boishebert was sent to guard harbors of Newfoundland and assisted in capture of three vessels laden with powder, near Boston. Assistant engineer at Quebec in 1711 and 1712. Appointed commandant of Detroit sometime in 1730. (See "Detroit Rulers," by C. M. Burton.)

631. Bouat, François Marie, born 1676. Married 1st Madeleine Lambert and 2d Agathe Legardeur. He was the father of fourteen children, the last one of whom was born Nov. 18, 1726, six months after his death. He was familiar with the entire west in 1702; acted as a guide in accompanying Jacques dit le Castor, a Jesuit lay brother, to Mobile. At the time of his death he was lieutenant general of Montreal. (Tanguay and Jesuit Rel. and Allied Doc.)

688. Boucher, Angelique Tholomée (Ptolomé), wife of Guilleaume Boucher; was married at

493. Campau, Michel, farmer, came to Detroit, August 3, 1707. His wife was Jean Masse. He died before 1740.

373. Cardinal, Jacques, son of Simon Jean and Michelle Garnier. Born 1659. Married Nov. 23, 1682, to Louise Arrivé, at Montreal. Buried at Detroit. May 18, 1724. Father of eight children.

492. Casse, Jean dit St. Aubin. Born 1659. Sailor. Buried at Detroit, Feb. 27, 1759. He married at Quebec, Feb. 7, 1707, Marie Louise Gautier and had one child, Pierre. St. Aubin, Jean, corporal in the garrison, came to Detroit with Pierre Duroy, April 11, 1707. (See "Cadillac's Village," by C. M. Burton.)

636. Cedars. The rapids in Lower Fox River.

107. Chacornac, François Augustin, Baron de Joannes, chevalier and captain on half-pay. Born 1684. Buried Dec. 30, 1754, at Quebec. (Tanguay.)

375. Chantelon, Pierre. Detroit under Cadillac gives both names. (Pierre Chantelor, p. 10, and Chanteloup, p. 22.)

482. Chalus (Chalut), François Chevalier de, dit Lagrange. Born 1651. Buried at Quebec, June 15, 1731.

248. Chambalon, Louis, royal notary, physician. Born 1663. Son of Louis and Marie Prieur. Buried June 15, 1716, in church at Quebec. He married 1st Marie Anne Pinguet and 2d Genevieve Russel.

47. Champigny, Jean Bochart de. Intendant in New France, July, 1686, to August, 1702. Was close friend of Frontenac and like him antagonistic toward the Jesuits. Married Marie Madeleine Chaspoux and had three children.

34. Chardon, Jean Baptiste, Jesuit, born at Bordeaux, April 27, 1672. Entered order at Bordeaux, 1687; arrived in Canada, 1699; died at Quebec, April 11, 1743. (Jesuit Relations, Vol. 71, p. 160.)
Chardon, Pierre Jean, Jesuit, born in Rouen, France, came to Canada, August 27, 1693, and went among the Illinois; died April 21, 1743. (Tanguay.)

34. Charlevoix, Pierre François Xavier, Jesuit, born at St. Quentin, in 1682, arrived in Canada, July 28, 1705, and returned to France, 1722. He is immortalized in Canada by the publication of his "General History of New France," published in Paris in 1744. He died in 1761. (Tanguay "Clergé Canadien.")

596. Chaussegros, Gaspard de Léry, marine engineer, chevalier de St. Louis. Born 1682, buried March 23, 1756, at Quebec. Married at Quebec, Oct. 13, 1717, to Marie Renée Le Gardeur.

534. Chauvignerie, Louis Maray, Sieur de la, officer. Born 1671, married Jan. 24, 1701, at Montreal, to Catherine Joly.

705. Collet, Mathieu Benoit, Sieur, procureur general of the King in upper court of New France.

376. Delorme. (See Fafard in 'Cadillac's Village," by C. M. Burton.)

36. Denonville, Jacques René De Brisay, Marquis de Courtin, governor arrived in New France in 1685 with his wife and part of his family. (Tanguay, Vol. 1.)

492. D'Ervillier. The only person in Tanguay of that name is Benjamin Dervilliers, son of Jean and Marie Audry of Paris. He married Claire Godfroy, at Three Rivers, Nov. 26, 1706. He was Seigneur de la Boissiere, lieutenant of irregular troops.

550. Desliettes, Sieur. The elder Alphonse de Tonty, Baron de Paludy.

689. Desmoulins, Jasques dit Philis, married Marie Charlotte Savarias. Their nine children were born in Detroit.

572. Deville, Louis Marie, Jesuit, arrived in Canada June 28, 1702; died July 8, 1738. (Tanguay.)

480. Dubuisson, Charles Regnault, Sieur, was sent to Detroit to hold that post for La Forest, who was appointed to succeed Cadillac. During his term the post was besieged by Fox Indians and the place came near being exterminated. Dubuisson wrote a history of this siege. After the arrival of La Forest he was second in command. From

1644, married at Quebec, Sept. 14, 1670, Françoise Duquet and became the father of ten children.

565. Du Sablé, widow, Françoise Jobin, wife of Pierre Dandonneau called Lajeunesse, Sieur Du Sablé who died in 1702. The son here spoken of must be Jacques, who died in 1754.

469. Du Tisné, Claude Charles, Sieur, ensign of a free company of marines.

44. Frontenac, Louis de Buade, Comte de, was appointed Governor of New France in 1672. He died Nov. 28, 1698, at Quebec, and was buried Dec. 1, 1698, in the Church of the Recollets. (Jesuit Relations, Vol. 55, p. 321.)

49. Gallifet, François de, lieutenant of the King at Montreal in 1700. Born 1666, married at Quebec, Jan. 14, 1697.

611. Grandmenil, (Grandmesnil), Etienne Veron, Sieur De, merchant, receiver for his highness, the comte de Toulouse, admiral of France. Born 1679, buried April 23, 1743, at Quebec. Married 1st Madeleine Hertel, and 2d Marie Catherine Picard, and was father of six children. (Tanguay.)

377. Guillet, Paul, son of Mathurin. Born at Montreal, Jan. 28, 1690. Married Jan. 31, 1717, to Catherine Pinguet, at Quebec.

591. Guillet, Loranger and Mallet. There were men of these names at Detroit. (See "Cadillac's Village" by C. M. Burton.)

638. Hamelin, Louis, son of Louis Seigneur des Grondines. Was married Feb. 24, 1718, to Catherine Nepveu, at Detroit.

555. Haren, Louis, Jesuit, Province of France. Born 1670, entered order in 1692, arrived in Canada, 1699; died at Quebec, March 26, 1646. This is evidently intended for 1742. (Jesuit Relations, Vol. 71, p. 160.)

36. Hubert, René, door-keeper of the court; chief clerk of the Court of the Prevost of Quebec, 1712; son of René Hubert and Anne Horry. Was born 1648. Married Françoise de la Croix, and became father of eight children. His wife died in 1711 and he married twice. Was buried Sept. 1, 1725. (Tanguay.)

286. Joncaire, Thomas, Sieur de, King's interpreter. Married Madeleine Le Guay.

240. Lacorne, De Lacorne, Jean Louis, Sieur de Chapt., chevalier. Born 1666. Major of Three Rivers. Married twice, and was father of seven children.

41. La Forest, François de, second commandant at Detroit. Born in Paris, 1648. Died Quebec, Oct. 16, 1714. He married Françoise Juchereau, Nov. 11, 1702, and had one child, who died in infancy. ("Detroit Rulers," C. M. B.)

410. La Fresniere, Antoine Foisy, Sieur de, dit Lafresniere, born 1681, married in Repentigny, Oct. 23, 1707, buried May 26, 1760, at Vercheres.

422. La Gauchetiere. There was a Daniel Migeon, Sieur de la Gauchetiére born at Montreal Aug. 6, 1671, son of Jean Baptiste Migeon.

370. La Morandiere, Roebert (should be Rocbert), Sieur de la. There was a Sr. Rocbert, Etienne; lieutenant and engineer, captain of troops, born 1701, buried at Montreal, Nov. 25, 1760. He married Marguerite Puygibault, at Montreal, Jan. 15, 1730.

566. La Nouilliere, Sieur. There was a Jean Eustache La Noullier, who married at Quebec, Dec. 21, 1719, Marie Marguerite Duroy.

567. La Pipardiere, Joseph Antoine de Frenel, Sieur de, ensign, born 1662, married at Champlain, Nov. 25, 1694.

86. La Valterie, Sieur de, surnames Margane and Cottu.

676. Lemoine, Alexis; Malette; Gastinau; Gouin. (See "Cadillac's Village," by C. M. Burton.)

47. Lougvigny, Louis de la Porte, Sieur de, governor of Three Rivers, aide, major of the Royal troops, chevalier of St. Louis. Born 1652. Was married Oct. 26, 1684, at Quebec, to Marie Nolan. Buried June 12, 1730, at Quebec. (Tanguay.)

538. Maillet (Mallet or Malet), Pierre, born 1670, married Jan. 9, 1698, at Montreal, Madeleine Dufresne; they had one child, born in Detroit in 1706.

374. Marsac, Jacob Sieur Desroches, de Cobtrion, sergeant in a company in the detachment of Marines. His wife was Therese David. He was buried at Detroit April 27, 1747, aged 80 years.

528. Marigny, Claude, Sieur de, lieutenant, was in Montreal, June 11, 1707.

611. Marin, Paul, Chevalier, or Marin Cheval; born 1692, buried Oct. 29, 1753, at Fort Duquesne; married at Montreal, March 21, 1718, Marie Joseph Guyon. (Baptismal Register of Fort Duquesne trans. by Rev. A. A. Lambing, p. 41, and Tanguay.)

597. Martiniere, Claude Berman (de), Sieur de la, judge, consellor, lieutenant-general, born 1638, son of Louis and Françoise Juchereau, buried at Quebec, April 15, 1719. Married 1st Anne Despres, 2d Marie Anne Cailleteau, 3d Marie Molin.

609. Monnoir, (see Sieur de Ramezay).

529. Nicholson, Francis, Sieur de, Lieut. Gov. of New England and New York.

195. Nolan, Louis, Noland *dit* Thierry, born 1696, buried Oct. 16, 1738, at Montreal.

376. Parent, Joseph, farmer, master toolmaker and brewer. Wife was Magdeleine Marette, whom he married at Beauport, Jan. 31, 1690, came to Detroit to work for Cadillac.

597. Peire, Sieur. There was a Philippe Peiré born 1692, son of Jacques and Clemence Parage, of St. Vincent. He was married in Quebec, Dec. 2, 1724, to Marie Anne Langlois and had one child born at Quebec.

707. Pelletier, François, son of François and Madeleine Thunés, born Aug. 15, 1691 at Sorel. Married March 25, 1718, at Detroit to Marie Robert. His descendants are at Detroit and Monroe and on Lake Erie.

689. Perthuis, Pierre. There was a Pierre Perthuis who married Catherine Malet; a number of their children were born in Detroit.

86. Ramezay, Mannoir; Louis de, son of Claude and Marie Charlotte Denis, born July 1, 1694, at Three Rivers; Sieur de Monoir. (I think Mannoir is a mistake for Monoir.)

399. Raudot, Jacques, Intendant of justice, police and finances. Was in Montreal, July 1, 1706.

589. Reaume, Pierre, son of Robert Reaume. Born at Lachine, Oct. 6, 1709.. Married 1st Marie Stèbre, 2d Suzanne Hubert at Detroit.

350. Repentigny, Jean Bte., Sieur de, Le Gardeur, son of Pierre Le Gardeur and Marie Favery. Born 1632. Married at Quebec, July 11, 1656, to Marguerite Nicolet.

561. Rouville, Hertel, Jean Baptiste, chevalier de St. Louis, lieutenant of a detachment of marine, captain and commandant of Port de Toulouse, Isle Royale, until 1720, where there is a baptism of one of his children, Sept. 19, 1720.

605. Roy, Louis, came to Detroit as bargeman, May 30, 1705. Born in 1659 and died before 1713.

377. Roy, Pierre, said to be the first man at Detroit. He lived in Indian village before Cadillac came. Married a Miami Indian on March 10, 1707. Owned land at Detroit under Cadillac. (See Cadillac's Village, by C. M. Burton.)

36. Sabrevois, Jacques Charles, Sieur de Bleury, son of Henry Sabrevois and Gabrielle Martin. Born 1667. As a lieutenant he was engaged in several encounters with English and Indians in New York. Was appointed commandant of Detroit in 1712, but was not allowed to go to the post until 1715. Was created chevalier of military order of St. Louis 1718. Commandant at Fort Chambly 1721-1724. He returned to Montreal and was made major of that city. Died while holding office, June 19, 1727. Married Nov. 16, 1695, Jean Boucher, and had six children. (Detroit Rulers, by C. M. Burton.)

562. St. Castin, Anselme, Baron de, ensign of troops.

634. Saline de. officer of the court.

194. Vaudry, Joseph, born 1687. Married Marie Lepage, 1719. Their five children were born in Detroit.

456. Veschere, de, and wife. Jean Jarret or Jaret de Verchères, chevalier and seigneur; born in 1687 and buried at Montreal, Aug. 3, 1752 ; married Nov. 24, 1721, Madeleine Daillebout, whose sister, Louise Catherine, married Monsieur de Noyan.

587. Villers, Jean de, Jesuit, arrived June 24, 1700 ; died Nov. 22, 1732.

193˙ Vincennes, Jean Bte. Bissot, Sieur de. French officer ; born, 1668 ; married, Sept. 19, 1696, at Montreal, to Marguerite Fortier. (Tanguay.)

NOTE* ON THE MEASURES OF CAPACITY.

The chief measures spoken of are the roquille, demi-ard, chopine, setier, pinte, pot and barrique.

The difficulty in assigning any definite value to these is that the same terms were used for different quantities in different localities. The least variable, apparently, were the "chopine," "pinte" and "pot," which might be tabulated thus :

	litres.
1 chopine = (at Paris)	.465
2 chopines = 1 pinte = (at Paris)	.93
2 pintes = 1 pot = (at Paris)	1.861

The metric equivalents are those given in the great encyclopaedic dictionary of Pierre Larousse. It will be observed that the "pinte" = 1⅔ pints English.

Setier. This is the most difficult of all to which to assign a definite value. Fleming and Tibbins' Dictionary give it as "8 pintes of Paris," which is obviously too high, at any rate as a wine and spirit measure. Larousse gives no definite value under "setier." but under "chopine" states that the "chopine" "se divisait en 2 demi setiers * * * et 16 roquilles." The first equivalent supposes the "setier" and "chopine" as identical ; the latter does not agree with the explanation of roquille quoted above.

Roquille. Larousse says this is the fourth part of the setier, or .027 litres (this would make the setier rather larger than the "pinte"). In this letter the roquille is said to be the 16th part of a pot. If both statements are taken as correct the "setier" and "chopine" would appear to have been the same in Canada at this time.

Demi-ard. I have been unable to trace this measure elsewhere, but in this letter we have (page 7) the demi-ard stated to be the 24th part of a "pot." This would make 6 demi-ards, or 3 ards = 1 chopine.

Barrique. At page 3 of this letter we have 800 demi-ards, said to be approximately equal to 1 barrique. This would make the barrel of brandy equal to about 32 pots or about 6 litres.

*This note follows a letter written 15th Sept., 1707, endorsed Colonies, Canada, MM. de Vaudreuil and Raudot.

95

INDEX.

Names of bays, forts, islands, lakes, rivers, ships, societies and straits will be found under these general titles instead of individual names.

plans, 580; poor cared for, 574; posts to be inspected, 346; reports of colony, 44-53; society of, 130; toll of lords of, 653; trade regulations of, 42, 156, 449, 702; western tribes of Indians live in, 552; woods of, 136.

Canadians, allowed to marry at Detroit, 99, 189, 255, 298, 615, 616, 627; asked houses at Detroit, 170; Cadillac asked for, 339; hired by French officers, 95; licentious conduct of, 175; new Frenchmen, 81, 98, 238, 351; replaced old soldiers, 398; settled in Detroit, 202, 494; trade in beavers, 455.

Candlesticks, 254.

Canibas, hired to harass English, 48.

Cannon, George H., vice president Macomb county, 741; elected member committee of historians, 2.

Cannon, S. B., married Sarah J. Twaddill, 742.

Cannon, Mrs. S. B., sketch of, 742.

Canoes, at Detroit siege, 549; made of bark, 33.

Cape Breton, town of, 456.

Capillaire, syrup sent to France, 70, 71.

Capons (fowl), given for rent, 471.

Cardinal, —, Canadians—habitants of Detroit, 494.

Cardinal, Jacques, land grant at Detroit, 373, 379, 688; price for conveying brandy, 428; settler at Detroit, 479. See appendix.

Cardinal, Pierre, Canadian habitant at Detroit, 493, 494.

Cardinal, Marie, married Jacques Hubert, 493.

Carheil (Carheill), Estienne (Etienne), de, Jesuit missionary to Hurons at Mackinac, 102, 114, 115, 118, 121, 183, 235, 237; criticized, 126; good opinion of Detroit, 128; letter from, 124-126; obstinacy of, 159, 162; Quarante Sous complained against, 127; refused charge of plots, 125; sermon quoted, 183; tried to ruin Detroit, 120; visit to

Castor, 598, 625. See Beaver.

Catalagne (Catalorgne, Catalogne), Gideon de, dit Lailberté, French officer, sub-engineer in Montreal, drew maps of Montreal, 458.

Catalaouibois (Kataoulibois, Kataouliboué, Koutaoulibois, Catalibona, Catalaonibois), allowed to trade at Detroit, 360; conferred with Vaudreuil, 366; killed and scalped, 292.

Cataracoui, 113. See Katarakoui.

Catin, Therese (Thereze), wife and agent of Simon Reaume, suit against Tonty, 675, 676.

Cattle, at Detroit, 316, 539; none sent to France, 136; number and value of at Detroit, 415, 595, 642, 666; taken to Detroit by Cadillac, 345; value at Detroit, 642, 666.

Caterpillars, destroyed grain, 44.

Cayuga, N. Y., Father Menard wounded in, 24.

Cedars, 632. See appendix.

Cendret, Madame, widow with two children, 566.

Census, of Detroit 1710, 492; regulation of, 473.

Center, Caroline, married Henry A. Black, 735.

Chabert, Louis Thomas Joncaire, Sieur de, 370. See Joncaire.

Chachagouache (Chachagonesse), Illinois chief, messenger to Vaudreuil, 550, 560.

Chacornacle (Chacornac), François Augustin, Baron de Joannes, Chevalier de, French officer, 151; accompanied Cadillac to Detroit, 202; at Quebec, 110; quarrel with Hauteville, 150; sent to start Detroit post, 107, 109. See appendix.

Chagnais, Madame de —, 456.

Chagnon, Angelique, married François Benoit, 493.

Chagouamigon (Chagoumigour) Point, Indian settlement on Lake Superior, 89, 500, 588, 682, 698, 699; attack of Menomonees, 559.

Morel de la, diligence commended, 47; letter cited, 40; signed deed, 42; took possession of New France, 41. See appendix.
Durham, Mrs. Helen L. Lacey, 728.
Durivage, —, sister captured by Menomonees, 559.
Du Roy, 377, 378, 479. See Pierre Roy.
Dusablé (Du Sable), French officer commissioned, 565; complaints against, 584; reproach of, 583. See appendix.
Dussault, Marie —, married Jacques Langlois, 492.
Dussy, Sieur, —, promotion of, 399.
Dutast, M. —, prevented from visiting Fort Nelson, 48.
Dutch, behavior of merchants, 179.
Du Tisné (Tisnet), Claude Charles, French officer, at Montreal, 469, 566. See appendix.
Dutremble, John Baptist, came to Detroit in 1706, 271.
Dutremble, Joseph, came to Detroit in 1706, 271.
Duval. See Renaud.
Du Vestin, Solomon Joseph, granted Detroit land, 373.

Eagles, 112; divinity of Indians, 239.
Eaton County, memorial report of, 734.
Eaton Rapids, put down mineral wells, 720.
Eau, Chevalier, Pierre D', Sieur de Joliet, escaped from Boston prison, 53.
Edwards, Mrs. —, Dowagiac, 731.
Edwards, Elizabeth, married Edward Killick, 727.
Edinger, Joseph H., read paper at meeting, 2; gifts to museum, 9; loan of Indian relics, 5.
Eight, figure 8 represents obsolete French letter, 113. See 8ta8ois (Ottawas), Sabache (Wabash), P8t8atatins (Potoatatins).
Eldridge, Abram C., death recorded, 735.
Eliot, —, Massachusetts Indian missionary, 23.
Elliott, Richard R., cited, 241; paper by, 22.
Ellis, Mary, wife of L. Wheeler, 730.
Eloüaousse (Eloüaoussez, Eleouaoucssé) chief of Mackinac Ottawas, 234, 235; confers with Vaudreuil, 504.
Enjalran (Enjelran, Angeliran, Angeleran, Angelleran, Anjalran), Jean, Jesuit, missionary, 34, 41, 42; at ville Marie, 40n; certified bill, 47; good opinion of Detroit, 128; letter from, 106-107, 129-130; letter to Duluth, 40, 41; praise of, 105, 106; sent to Detroit, 106; signed deed for Detroit, 42; superior of Ottawas at Mackinac, 41.
England, 120, 152; council of Queen, 561; lost New France, 171.
English, 76, 113, 119, 169, 238, 274, 286, 426; acquire Detroit, 594; allies of Indians, 81, 415, 538, 561; ambush of, 418; at war with French, 174, 216, 309, 405,

tempted to gain Ottawas, 572; attempted seizure of Detroit, 43, 614; beguiled Indians to leave the French, 569, 582, 586; behavior of merchants, 179-180; bribed Indians to destroy Detroit, 537, 549, 568; captured French boat, 565-566; cheap goods of, 43, 199, 424; concluded peace with Abenakis, 69; danger from in upper country, 532, 695; defence against, 341; designs against French allies, 503; desire Louisiana, 575; detained Miamis, 280; Detroit savages near to, 395; differences with western tribes, 542, 543, 545, 546, 550; enemies of French, 48, 97, 397, 399, 400, 402, 413, 490, 564; expedition against, 414, 422; expelled from Detroit, 98; extended posts toward Lake Erie, 97; fleet destroyed, 562; French sent against, 417; Hamburghers and Flemings to be naturalized, 423; hoped to start a post at Detroit, 107; ill treated settlers, 563; incited Iroquois against French, 396, 405, 454, 529, 570; incited Iroquois against other tribes, 591; induce savage trade, 711; intrigues against colony, 158; Iroquois opposed, 415; kept from Detroit, 647; killed de Verehive, 399; make peace with Indians, 533; monopolize trade, 535; necessity of savage allies, 678; presents to savages, 118; prisoners became Catholics, 311; prisoners sent to France, 53; ransom prisoners, 564; repulsed at St. John River, 308; retreated, 554; returned French prisoners, 310; rumor of besieging Quebec, 79, 330, 554; seized Cadillac's property, 601, 619, 649, 684, 700; soldiers deserted to, 284; supply brandy to Indians, 592; threaten Chambly, 596; trade forbidden, 460-461; trade prevented by Detroit post, 132; trade with Indians, 157, 171, 199, 200, 215, 240, 420, 431, 441, 442, 445, 447-450, 461, 579; war with French and Indians, 312; wished lands of Detroit, 445, 614, 662, 678, 701.
English, Daniel W., death recorded, 740;
Episcopal church choir, music by, 2.
Ervillier, D' (Ervilliers d', Dervilliers), Benjamin. French officer, 564; asked leave, 492; not go to France, 535.
Epinay L', (Espinay), 423, 633. See L'Epinay.
Eschaillons. See Deschaillons.
Esgly (Esglis, Desgly), François Mariauchau, Sieur d', captain Governor's Guard, chevalier of St. Louis and lieutenant at Three Rivers, 449, 564, 565.
Estrees (Estrades, Estees, Etrées), Louis Alexandre, Count de Toulouse Le Maréchal d', 86, 639, 646, 670, 674, 705; gave discharges, 608; letter from, 574-576.
Estes, Mrs. G. W., death recorded, 733.
Esteve, Pierre, 379; granted Detroit lands, 375, 377, 380-381; granted garden 382; Detroit settler, 479.
Evans, Emily J., married D. R. McElwain, 727.

Millet, M. Nicholas, land grant at Detroit, 689.

Mills, Albert E., Nashville, 728.

Mills, James Betty, sketch, 728.

Mills, John L., Tacoma, Wash., 728.

Mills, Levi, Maryland, 728.

Mines, copper, 531; description of Ouabache, 481; search for, 164, 189; silver, 531.

Mines (place), stores sent to inhabitants, 48; value of lead mines, 413-414.

Minor, Mrs. E. B., regrets, 8.

Minot, French measure of capacity (1 11-100 English bushels), 495.

Minville, Jacques, came to Detroit in 1706, 272.

Miranbeau (Merambeau), Estienne, merchant of Quebec, witness to agreement concerning Detroit, 248.

Miscouaky, Ottawa chief, brother of Jean Le Blanc, 273, 288, 307; conferred with Vaudreuil, 282, 294, 295, 299, 301, 306, 323; messenger to French, 313, 320, 329; received presents from Vaudreuil, 300; report Detroit war, 319.

Missionaries, abuses at Missilimackinac, 82; accused by Cadillac, 144; by whom paid, 392; Cadillac's treatment of, 344, 372; complaints against trade, 142-143; controlled Indians, 333; cost of, 630, 698; granted to Detroit, 615, 660; ill-treated by Indians, 450; influence on Indians, 239; money and supplies from company, 162; necessity for Indians. 48. 76, 98, 99; one killed by Indians at Detroit, 261; pay of, 461, 648; received goods from fugitives, 146; supplies obtained, 451.

Missions, Arbe Croche, 34; Chequamegon, 31; Huron (Detroit), 34; Illinois, 41; Iroquolan, 24; Mackinac, 33; Mackinac, reëstablished, 454; Miamis, 41; Ottawa, 25; Puans of the Bay, 41; St. Ignatius, 34; Sault Ste Marie, 24, 27; Sioux, 41.

Mississagues (Mississaquez, Missisaguez, Missisaghez, Missisaguets, Missisaquets, Missisaques, Missiague, Missisagues, Missaguez), Algonquin tribe, 272, 274, 431, 572; aid French at Detroit, 538, 549; aided Ottawas, 273, 291; at Detroit, 574, 648, 697, 698; attacked Miamis, 272, 503-504; brought to Montreal, 498; escorted Huron prisoners, 280; feared safety at Detroit, 558; killed Miamis, 532; location, 552; message from French, 501; number at Detroit, 681; Ottawa prisoners sent to, 293; secured powder, 279; threatened Miamis, 563; trouble with settled, 261; village of, 162, 680; went to Topicanich, 551; withdrew from action, 275.

Mississippi (Mississipy), trade with Detroit, 147, 316.

Missouri, Siouan tribe, aid French at Detroit seige, 540.

Mitasse (mittasse), cloth used for shirts, 296;

Moloney, Helen E., death recorded, 740.

Moncour, Sieur Hertel de, 422. See Hertel.

Monet, Pierre. See La Montagne.

Money, bills, 412; difference of exchange, 610; exchange of paper, 646; loss of, 402; paper must be supported, 535; price of exchange, 470.

Monic, Sieur de —, granted gratuity, 49.

Monique, Abenaki convert, 124.

Monnoir. See Ramezay. See appendix.

Monroe, C. J., South Haven, 746.

Monroe, Mrs. Hattie, sketch, 746.

Monseignat (Monseignac), comptroller of the navy, 239; brother-in-law of M. Armaud, 213; examined English vessel, 311; signed receipt, 623.

Montandre, 594. See Bragecongue.

Montigny, Sieur de —, commandant at Green Bay, letter referred to, 301; given de Grandville's company, 416; succeeded Grandville as captain, 410.

Montom, brother-in-law of Latishenotte, 278.

Montour, —, French-Indian parentage, 454.

Monts Dezerts, 77.

Montreal, 24, 32-34, 36, 42, 43, 47, 64, 68, 75, 80, 87, 102, 107, 123, 127-131, 137, 139, 147, 149, 152-155, 157, 160, 166, 169, 170, 171, 177, 178, 193, 196, 199, 202, 204, 205, 211, 220, 223-225, 227, 230, 231, 236, 237, 250, 258, 265, 274-278, 281-284, 288, 296, 298, 300, 302, 304, 305, 308, 312, 317, 319, 328-331, 335, 337, 340-342, 344, 345, 347, 350, 352, 353, 359, 360, 362, 363, 366-369, 370, 390, 396-398, 410, 413, 420, 423, 424, 431, 433, 448, 449, 451, 459, 482, 485, 488, 491-494, 500, 501, 509, 515, 529-533, 538, 540, 543, 547, 552, 558-560, 562, 570, 571, 573, 575, 578, 582, 584, 585, 589-592, 597-600, 602, 605, 606, 609, 632, 633, 635, 636, 638, 640, 645, 646, 656, 672, 674-676, 678, 681, 686, 688, 689, 691, 698, 702, 707, 711, 713; arsenal, 407; assembly at, 106; attitude toward Detroit, 171-172; beaver trade ruined, 311; beer supplied to Indians, 565; brandy at, 451; Cadillac's arrival at, 201; complaints against trade, 468; controlled funds, 393; council at, 588; Detroit troops moved to, 478; fortifications to be kept up, 46, 406; French move to, 708; garrison to be strengthened, 534; history by Dollier, 120; hospital, 318; hospital rebuilt, 88; hospitallers Religieuses, 47, 99; Indians allowed to trade, 323; Indians attracted to, 532; Indians visited, 402; Iroquois envoys at, 490, 569; land grant customs, 648; low prices at, 76, 422, 426, 511, 557; maps of government, 458; neighborhood wasted by Indians, 571; notarial offices, 271; opposition to Detroit, 142; paths open to, 386; palisade repaired, 45; poor-house established, at, 50; Ramezay, governor of, 194; registry and registrar referred to, 243, 244; restrictions Indians

Lightning Source UK Ltd.
Milton Keynes UK
UKHW010003080119

334854UK00010BA/1777/P